I0896363

OSTRAVA AND ITS JEWS

'Now No-one Sings You Lullabies'

Escaping from the Fire with a Torah Scroll. Yehuda Bacon, charcoal on paper, 41.8 x 32.5 cm

Ostrava and its Jews

'Now No-one Sings You Lullabies'

David Lawson,
Libuše Salomonovičová
Hana Šústková

VALLENTINE MITCHELL
LONDON • CHICAGO, IL

First published in 2018 by Vallentine Mitchell

Catalyst House,
720 Centennial Court,
Centennial Park, Elstree WD6 3SY, UK

814 N Franklin Street
Chicago, Illinois
IL 60610, USA

www.vmbooks.com

British Library Cataloguing in Publication Data:
An entry can be found on request

ISBN 978 1 910383 74 2 (Cloth)
ISBN 978 1 910383 75 9 (Paper)
ISBN 978 1 910383 76 6 (Ebook)

Library of Congress Cataloging in Publication Data:
An entry can be found on request

Printed by IPG, Chicago, IL, USA

Contents

PART IV: OSTRAVA POST-WAR

Acknowledgements

This book could not have been written without the involvement and support of very many people. If we were to mention all of them individually, we would add quite unreasonably to the book's length, but some acknowledgements are essential.

The first must be for all the Ostravaks[1] and their families who have been willing to share with us their knowledge, family histories, photographs and information. Their enthusiasm for the project has been as great as ours and their encouragement during the years of gestation of the book has been greatly appreciated. The great warmth with which they have welcomed us, answered our questions and told us about themselves and their families has meant that they have become friends and, in some cases, almost family. Even those whom we can only contact electronically have somehow become close.

The representatives of the City of Ostrava have, likewise, been enormously helpful. Dr Blažena Przybylová, the City Archivist, has provided materials, references, answers to obscure questions and some of her husband's delightful cakes. She also passed on her enthusiasm for Smetana operas, especially Čertova stěna (The Devil's Wall) performed at the Dvořák Theatre, a gem of an opera house, to David. Dr Zdeněk Sladovník of the Lord Mayor's Office, replies to any request for help or information with: 'That's no problem'. Without his help, many of our activities would not have been possible.

RNDr. Jiřina Kábrtová, Director of the Ostrava Museum, was very helpful with information about early Ostrava and provided practical as well as intellectual sustenance with some of her own wonderful baking!

Dr Jiří Jung entered much of our information into the data base of the Jewish Museum in Prague and also provided the basic draft of the section on Ostrava Architects and Architecture, while Dr Jiří Hrdina provided a similar section on Jewish Ostravak photographers. Dr Ludmila Nesládková, Ostrava University, provided much needed guidance on population statistics and Prof. Aleš Zářický, Ostrava University, supplied information on the industrialisation of Ostrava.

All the material and information we have collected has been passed on to the Jewish Museum in Prague where it is preserved and made available to future researchers. Information has been entered into their data base and much is now available on their website. We are greatly indebted to Dr Leo

Pavlát, the Director, for his support and encouragement, and that of his staff, over many years. In particular, we have worked very closely with Dr Michal Frankl (until recently Deputy Director of the Museum), Pavla Neuner and her team all of whom have been unfailingly kind, helpful and welcoming.

Jonathan and Sara Goldstone have been most energetic in following up difficult references and contacts.

H.E. Mr Michael Žantovský, formerly Czech Ambassador in London, extended the hospitality of the Embassy on a number of occasions for our Ostravak meetings and his predecessor, the late Jan Winkler, joined the earlier Ostravak meetings in Kingston Synagogue. Their presence was very much appreciated by all of us who were at the meetings.

Much of the archive material was, of course, in Czech and we are enormously grateful to Jan Bettelheim, Anna Bryson, Victoria Bursa, Anna Pilatová and Lydia Tischler for putting it into English for us.

Of course, translating and similar activities must be paid for and we are greatly indebted to those who have contributed:

- The Czech Embassy, London
- The City of Ostrava
- Vítkovice Machinery Group, Ostrava and its CEO, Mr Jan Světlík
- Tom Auber
- Kurt Berger
- Dr Jan Bettelheim
- Victoria Bursa
- Susie and Cliff Ellis
- Barbara Gilford
- The Goldberg Family
- Anna and Wieslaw Jurkowski
- Michael Karen
- Sandra Renton
- Gita Rind
- The Rix Memorial Trust Fund
- Josef and Elizabeth Salomonovič
- George Tyrell
- Eva White

Libuše Salomonovičová is an author of this book. Her husband, Michal, has been a continuous support and an excellent guide to the many Ostravak visitors returning to their roots. Their son, Radan, has been the unsung hero of the whole enterprise, acting as chauffeur, guide, advisor, and interpreter between English and Czech and has done so with unfailing good humour and a permanent smile. How he manages all this activity with a full time job, a wife and son is an unsolved mystery.

Lisa Hyde, of Vallentine Mitchell, has edited the text with exemplary patience and good humour. The book is much improved as a result of her efforts.

It only remains to say that, despite all this help, the views expressed in this book and all the errors that remain are those of the authors alone.

NOTE

1. Ostravak is a neologism. Someone born, living or who lived in Greater Ostrava and their family members.

Preface

In the Beginning was the Word. Or rather, 79,976 words, as in the beginning there was a *sefer torah*, a Scroll of the Law – the Five Books of Moses written in Hebrew on parchment – which came to the synagogue in Kingston on Thames, England on permanent loan from the Czech Memorial Scrolls Trust.

With the scroll was a certificate stating that it had come from Moravská Ostrava (Mährisch Ostrau).

In 2005, many years after its arrival, David and a few other members of Kingston Synagogue – the 'Kingston Group' – were moved to research the origins of their scroll. The certificate raised some obvious questions: where is or was Moravská Ostrava and what sort of place was it? Who lived there, and how did a *sefer* come from there to Kingston, in South West London? And after these came much deeper questions. What happened to Jewish life

Scroll, open at Exodus XIV verse 33, 'The Song at the Sea'.

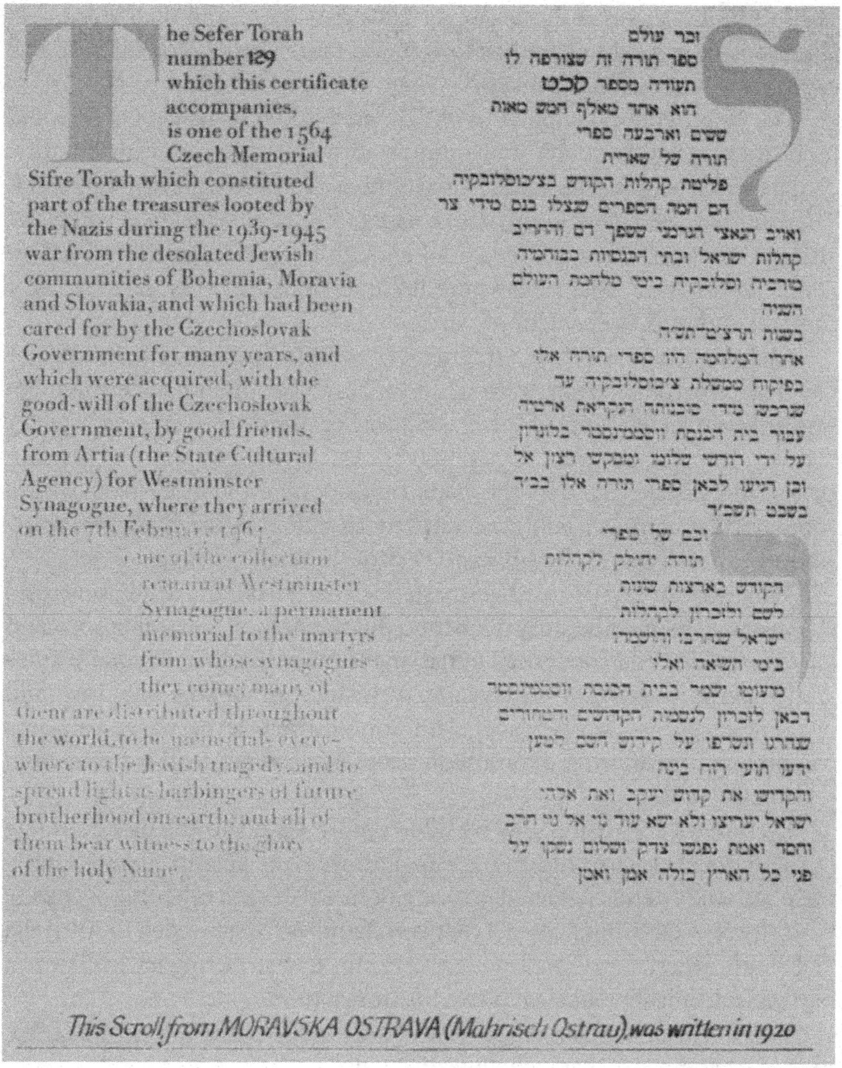

The Sefer Torah number 129 which this certificate accompanies, is one of the 1564 Czech Memorial Sifre Torah which constituted part of the treasures looted by the Nazis during the 1939-1945 war from the desolated Jewish communities of Bohemia, Moravia and Slovakia, and which had been cared for by the Czechoslovak Government for many years, and which were acquired, with the good-will of the Czechoslovak Government, by good friends, from Artia (the State Cultural Agency) for Westminster Synagogue, where they arrived on the 7th February 1964; one of the collection remains at Westminster Synagogue, a permanent memorial to the martyrs from whose synagogues they come; many of them are distributed throughout the world, to be memorials every-where to the Jewish tragedy, and to spread light as harbingers of future brotherhood on earth; and all of them bear witness to the glory of the holy Name.

זכר עולם
ספר תורה זה שצורפה לו
תעודה מספר קכט
הוא אחד מאלף חמש מאות
ששים וארבעה ספרי
תורה של שארית
פליטת קהלות הקודש בצ׳כוסלובקיה
הם המה הספרים שנצלו גם מידי צר
ואויב הנאצי הגרמני ששפך דם והחריב
קהלות ישראל ובתי הכנסיות בבוהמיה
מורביה וסלובקיה בימי מלחמת העולם
השניה
בשנות תרצ״ט־תש״ה
אחרי המלחמה הזו ספרי תורה אלו
בפיקוח ממשלת צ׳כוסלובקיה עד
שרכשו מידי סוכנותה הנקראת ארטיה
עבור בית הכנסת ווסטמינסטר בלונדון
על ידי רודפי שלומו ומבקשי רצון אל
וכן הגיעו לכאן ספרי תורה אלו בכ״ד
בשבט תשכ״ד
יכם של ספרי
תורה יחולק לקהלות
הקודש בארצות שונות
לשם ולזכרון לקהלות
ישראל שחרבו והושמדו
בימי השואה ואלו
מיעוטו ישמר בבית הכנסת ווסטמינסטר
דכאן לזכרון לנשמות הקדושים והטהורים
שנהרגו ונשרפו על קדוש השם למען
ידעו תועי רוח בינה
והקדישו את קדוש יעקב ואת אלהי
ישראל יעריצו ולא ישא עוד גוי אל גוי חרב
וחסד ואמת נפגשו צדק ושלום נשקו על
פני כל הארץ כולה אמן ואמן

This Scroll from MORAVSKA OSTRAVA (Mährisch Ostrau), was written in 1920

Certificate with Scroll #129.

in what we discovered to be an important city, even if one not well known outside the Czech Republic? What can we learn by studying in detail this microcosm of Jewish history in East-central Europe?

The first questions were easy to answer. The internet, which became an invaluable partner in our whole enterprise, informed us that Ostrava is a town in the far north-east of what is now the Czech Republic. It had been part of the Austro-Hungarian Empire, partly German-speaking, and known in German as Mährisch Ostrau.

To find the answers to the deeper questions we set out on a journey of research that proved to be much longer and more challenging than we had expected. This book is the result.

The Internet also supplied us with some basic facts about Ostrava and its history and also, much more importantly, provided us with our first contacts with people who came from Ostrava and were willing to talk to us. They in turn, were able to introduce us to some of their friends whom we also interviewed. Quite soon we had enough basic information to talk to people about 'our' *sefer* and where it came from and this gave us more contacts and more information.

Each interview was like a fragment of old film showing life in pre-war Ostrava. Short, flickering, blurred and incomplete though each fragment was, as we collected more of them a picture began slowly to emerge. Further research into the geography, geology, bricks, stones and rivers of Ostrava gave us more background for the picture and, as more and more people heard about us (the Internet, again!) we added more and more family stories: heart-warming, horrifying, incredible and very occasionally ordinary.

What we started to see, when we stepped back from the detail, surprised us. This was not just the story of Ostrava but the story of Central Europe and its Jews distilled and condensed into a small area of less than 85 square miles and a period of about 150 years. A history otherwise too vast and overwhelming to grasp, except on an abstract level (how can you comprehend the murder of 6 million people?) becomes real and human in scale in Ostrava.

Even more surprisingly, as we added more details to the picture, some of these details turned out to overlap, and we were able to reunite family members and friends who had not seen or heard of each other for over sixty years. By re-establishing contacts between families from Sweden to Australia and South America to Canada we were, in effect, resurrecting Jewish Ostrava partly electronically but also in real life in real time.

The words of the Sabbath service about a *sefer torah*, 'It is a Tree of Life to them that grasp it', had actually come true.

If, in Neville Chamberlain's infamous words, Czechoslovakia was 'a far away country ... of whom we know nothing', Ostrava is truly a place about which almost nothing is known outside the Czech Republic.

Ostrava has never been a beautiful city. It has few buildings of more than local historical or architectural interest. It has not been the site of any epoch-making battles or peace treaties. It was not the home of any great historical figures nor does it house any major art collections or priceless manuscripts. The local countryside is pleasant enough, but a Michelin guide book would not suggest that it was in the category of *vaut le voyage!*

Its Jewish Community was likewise undistinguished, at least by the measures of long history, tradition and historical sites. Unlike many places in Czechoslovakia or nearby in Poland, the Jewish presence in Ostrava is only of recent origin. Its graveyard holds the remains of no wonder-working Rabbis nor did any famous sages live there. No dynasties of famous Chassidim established themselves in Ostrava, nor was there a *yeshiva*[1] whose renown still resonates in our days. Rather, Ostrava was known for its embrace of modernity, economic, social and technological changes and its tolerance.

Until the later eighteenth century, Jews were not allowed to live or even spend the night in the Moravian part of Ostrava, Mährisch Ostrau or Moravská Ostrava. Then in 1781 came the first of a series of Edicts of Tolerance, allowing Jews and other non-Catholics greater freedom to practice trades, to move and to settle in areas of the Austro-Hungarian Empire previously forbidden to them. Jews began to move to Ostrava but they were hardly the only newcomers. The age of industrialisation and urbanisation was coming. Black coal deposits were fuelling the rapid development of iron and steel production in the Ostrava area. Accordingly, in the nineteenth and twentieth century, the population of Ostrava, both Jewish and non-Jewish, grew dramatically by immigration from perhaps less than 3,000 to over 200,000.

The story of Ostrava Jewry spans less than 150 years, from about 1800 to 1939. In that brief period, a group of immigrants developed a fully functioning community with all the social, cultural and commercial institutions that we would nowadays expect. They prospered and integrated into the life of the wider Ostrava community. Ostrava itself prospered and, from almost nothing, became an economic and cultural powerhouse which could call itself the Pittsburgh of the East with hardly any exaggeration. The Jews played a very significant role in this transformation.

In the eighteenth and early nineteenth century, Jews were discouraged or even prevented from becoming part of the Austro-Hungarian civil service, which was still very hierarchical and reactionary, and in which Jews were definitely not welcome and did not fit. They were barred from many trades and professions. This meant that Jews were forced to seek other means of earning a living, whether they wished to or not. On the other hand, most of the restrictions imposed by the Catholic Church did not affect the Jews and, being immigrants away from their elder family and original communities, they were less constrained by traditional orthodox Jewish practices. They therefore found themselves suddenly freed from the stultifying conventions of a very traditional society and most of the constraints of organised religion. The result was a tremendous flowering of creative energy.

To what extent this set free some latent Jewish genius, if such a thing really exists, or whether this was the natural response of an immigrant population suddenly able to pursue life, liberty and happiness, is not clear and hardly matters. And the genius, if that was the driving force, was not directed solely at retail trade as might popularly be supposed. Jews became prominent in brewing and distilling, law, medicine, arts, culture, politics and philanthropy as well. Nor was the presence of coal the only key to this upsurge in economic activity. Coal provided one set of opportunities but brewing, distilling and textiles, among many other areas, also offered opportunities to those who looked for them.

Just like the rest of the population of Ostrava, the Jewish community had its lawyers and bankers, doctors and teachers, shopkeepers, innkeepers and brewers, sausage-makers and jewellers, musicians and writers, politicians, insurance salesmen and farmers. It, too, had its share of divorcees, orphans, widows, children, rich and poor people, and, no doubt, crooks and wastrels. It certainly had politicians and members of parliament.

Together all these ordinary people, busy making a living, achieved something quite extra-ordinary. In just over 100 years, they turned Ostrava from a place of no great importance into an economic powerhouse. By the 1930s it had become a multi-ethnic, tolerant, dynamic and cultured modern city, the third largest and economically probably the most important place in Czechoslovakia, and home to the country's third largest Jewish community.

Ostrava became a bustling, growing industrial town, dirty and smelly, with bars and concert halls, coffee shops and coal mines, trams and tobacconists. It was full of people going about their everyday lives, and the Jews were an integral, and integrated, part of that. The Jews too were busy making a living, bringing up their children, looking after the old people, saving for the future, taking an interest in local and national politics and doing all the everyday ordinary things that we still do today.

Probably because almost everyone in Ostrava was a new immigrant, the Jews became integrated into, and played their part in, the general life of the town. Of course, inter-war Ostrava was no Utopia, but it certainly was a reasonable approximation to the good city life to which we nowadays aspire.

Sadly it was extinguished in a day, on 14 March 1939, when the Germans occupied Ostrava – the day before they occupied Prague – by hatred, racism, greed and envy. It was Sir Edward Grey who is reputed to have said, about the First World War, 'The lamps are going out all over Europe and we shall not see them lit again in our life-time.' It is certain that with the destruction of the Jewish community, the cultural and economic lamps in Ostrava went out and it has taken many, many years for some, and only some, of them to be lit again. In a conference in 2009, the Dean of Ostrava University observed that something was missing in the commercial and cultural dynamism of Ostrava and that was the contribution of the Jews.

We, living our comfortable middle-class lives, can empathise with those living a comfortable middle-class Jewish life in Ostrava. We can try and imagine what they lived through. We can even ask ourselves, as we pray in our synagogue, if they, praying in their beautiful synagogues, thought (any more than we now think, perhaps) about the meaning of the great prayer at the heart of the New Year and *Yom Kippur* (Day of Atonement) Service:

> On the first day of the year it is inscribed, and on the Day of Atonement the decree is sealed, how many shall pass away and how many shall be born, who shall live and who shall die, who at the measure of man's days and who before it, who shall perish by fire and who by water, who by the sword,... who by hunger and who by thirst; who by strangling and who by stoning, ...who shall be brought low and who shall be upraised.

The first transport of deported Jews from Ostrava arrived in the ghetto of Theresienstadt (Terezín, in Czech) on Tuesday, 22 September 1942. It was the day after *Yom Kippur*, the holiest day in the Jewish year. By *Simchat Torah*, less than three weeks later, most of the Jewish deportees from Ostrava had already been transported on to Auschwitz and the gas chambers.

Seventy years or more after that fateful day in 1939, there is little that remains of the Jewish community. The synagogues were destroyed and the cemetery has been flattened. But some of the Scrolls of the Law and other artefacts from the Jewish community were saved and one of them is now treasured in the synagogue in Kingston upon Thames. It is still used today.

Ostrava is situated in the valley of the River Odra where the Ostravice flows into it. The Prophet Ezekiel had a vision of a valley, full of death and destruction. The prophet was set down '...in the midst of the valley, which was full of bones... and, behold, there were very many in the open valley; and, lo, they were very dry'. Ezekiel continues, 'Then He said unto me, Son of man, these bones are the whole house of Israel: behold, they say, Our bones are dried, and our hope is lost.' Ezekiel then describes how these dry bones came together, flesh grew on them, skin covered them, and the Almighty breathed life into them so that they lived.

We cannot bring back to life the vanished Jews of Ostrava but, inspired by the survival of the Scroll, we can try to bring back their memory and so preserve something of a way of life now lost forever. Perhaps even more importantly, we can show that the Ostrava Jewish community, like many others, was not totally destroyed. It has survived and thrived elsewhere and its fascinating history continues.

We cannot, of course, draw a general rule from only one example, but the story of Ostrava and its Jewish life does offer a striking illustration of what can be achieved by freedom and tolerance and how rapidly and completely it can be destroyed by hatred and bigotry. It encapsulates in a compact geographical area and a short timeframe the brilliant and appalling history of Central Europe and its Jews. What happened in Ostrava on a scale that we can comprehend and relate to, was replicated on an inconceivably greater scale throughout Europe.

Yet the story of Jewish Ostrava has not ended. It has entered a new chapter, as a worldwide virtual community of Ostravaks has been connecting to their roots, their history and each other, both electronically and face to face.

David, who leads the Kingston Group, provides the English narrative voice in this project, while Libuše provides the enormous amount of genealogical data and Hana contributes the necessary historical rigour. But the real main contributors are the Ostravaks themselves.

David Lawson
Libuše Salomonovičová
Hana Šústková

NOTE

1. A Jewish theological seminary

Nomenclature and Caveat

In 1976, the political entity 'Greater Ostrava' was established by merging different and previously mainly independent districts, villages, and administrations:

- Antošovice
- Bělský Les
- Dubina
- Heřmanice
- Hošťálkovice
- Hrabová
- Hrabůvka
- Hrušov
- Koblov
- Krásné Pole
- Kunčice
- Kunčičky
- Lhotka
- Mariánské Hory and Hulváky
- Martinov
- Michálkovice
- Moravská Ostrava a Přívoz
- Muglinov
- Nová Bělá
- Nová Ves
- Petřkovice
- Plesná
- Polanka nad Odrou
- Poruba
- Proskovice
- Pustkovec
- Radvanice a Bartovice
- Slezská Ostrava
- Stará Bělá
- Svinov
- Třebovice
- Vítkovice
- Výškovice
- Zábřeh

In this book we use the term 'Ostrava' loosely to refer collectively to all or most of these districts. Where we wish to refer to an area specifically, we use the more definite geographical/political terms given above, e.g. Moravská Ostrava.

For geographical locations we use the modern name in the local language, so, for places in the Czech Republic we use the Czech name, in Poland we use the Polish name and so on. However, where the English name is much more commonly used by Anglophone readers (e.g. Prague, Vienna) we use the English name. The names of concentration and extermination camps are always given in German so we would refer to the town of Oświęcim but the Auschwitz camp.

Personal names are quoted as normally used by the person involved and their family, including diminutives. The full name or the name in the alternative language will be given in parentheses, if that would be helpful to an English-speaking reader.

The picture of the Ostrava Jewish community between the wars that emerges from all this material is an idyllic one. It appears to have been wealthy, well-educated and cultured, integrated and accepted into a dynamic multi-cultural vibrant city society. It is a too optimistic view, although based on the available evidence.

The information we have is based on personal recollections and on documents. The recollection are from Ostravaks who either survived the horrors of the war and the camps or who escaped from Ostrava before the war; and on stories which they told their children and which they have passed on to us. So the recollections we have come, one way or another, from those who survived the war. It is probable that they are not truly representative of the Jewish population of Ostrava.

For those who did know about the misery of some aspects of life in pre-war Ostrava and who did survive, the unpleasant memories may have been drowned by the horrors of what came later and life seemed much better in retrospect than it really was. So personal recollections must be treated with some circumspection.

Documentary records should not be subject to this emotional distortion, but they are subject to their own bias. Clearly we can refer only to surviving records and many records have been lost either by accident or deliberately to eliminate apparently unimportant records. So luck plays a part once again. But, more importantly, in order to survive, there must be original records! And a practising lawyer or doctor who owns an apartment or a building will have more records than an itinerant pedlar or unemployed grave-digger. So as historians search the archives today, they will find more information about wealthy educated people than about the uneducated poor.

So, as the well-known saying has it, there are things we know we do not know and there are things we do not know that we do not know about the Ostrava Jewish community. There are also some slightly known unknowns! Jiří Holuber was born on 16 July 1940 exactly two years before one of our authors. He appears in the deportation lists from Ostrava to Theresienstadt with his father, older sister and his even younger brother. Nothing further is known about them. They all disappear from the historical record and in all probability were murdered before Jiří reached his fourth birthday. But we do not know.

We do know that the information we have about the Ostrava community is almost certainly skewed to present a more positive and rosy picture than was the reality.

Introduction

Scroll #129 and the Creation of the Worldwide Ostrava Community

The inspiration for our researches into the Jews of Ostrava is the *sefer torah* #129. In 1963, Eric Estorik, a Jewish art dealer and collector, was in discussion with the authorities in Prague about works of art. He was asked if he wished to purchase a collection of scrolls that was stored in the Jewish Museum warehouse in Prague and had been there since the war. With the support of Ralph Yablon, a philanthropist who was a member of Westminster Synagogue, Estorik effected the purchase of 1564 scrolls. They arrived in Westminster in 1964, where they were checked, catalogued and cared for. Many of them had been torn, burnt or otherwise damaged.[1]

All the synagogues in Ostrava were set alight on the orders of the Germans in May or June 1939, with the fires later extinguished by the local fire brigades. Yet the Kingston scroll shows no sign of fire or water damage. Lily Reiser's father rescued a *chanukiah,* the eight- branched candlestick used at the festival of *Chanukah,* from the burned-out main synagogue, but the candlestick was brass which might reasonably have survived the conflagration. Scrolls, books and textiles would not have survived so they must have been taken from the synagogues before the fire. Either the local community was warned of the fires in advance or they were sufficiently prescient to take action. It seems most likely that they were warned but who warned whom is not known.

After the German invasion, the Jewish Community in Prague was made the authority for all the Jewish communities in the *Protektorat* of Bohemia and Moravia. It was confirmed that the Jewish Museum would continue to function and its holdings were increased by the addition of the entire collections of the Jewish Museums in Mikulov and Mladá Boleslav, which had been closed down. The German authorities almost certainly wanted to collect the artefacts for their value, either intrinsic for the silver items or resale for the other items, whereas the Jewish Community in Prague wanted to have the material for safe keeping and ultimate return or at least as a memorial for the lost communities. Their interests were thus totally compatible at least until the question of disposing of the collected material arose.

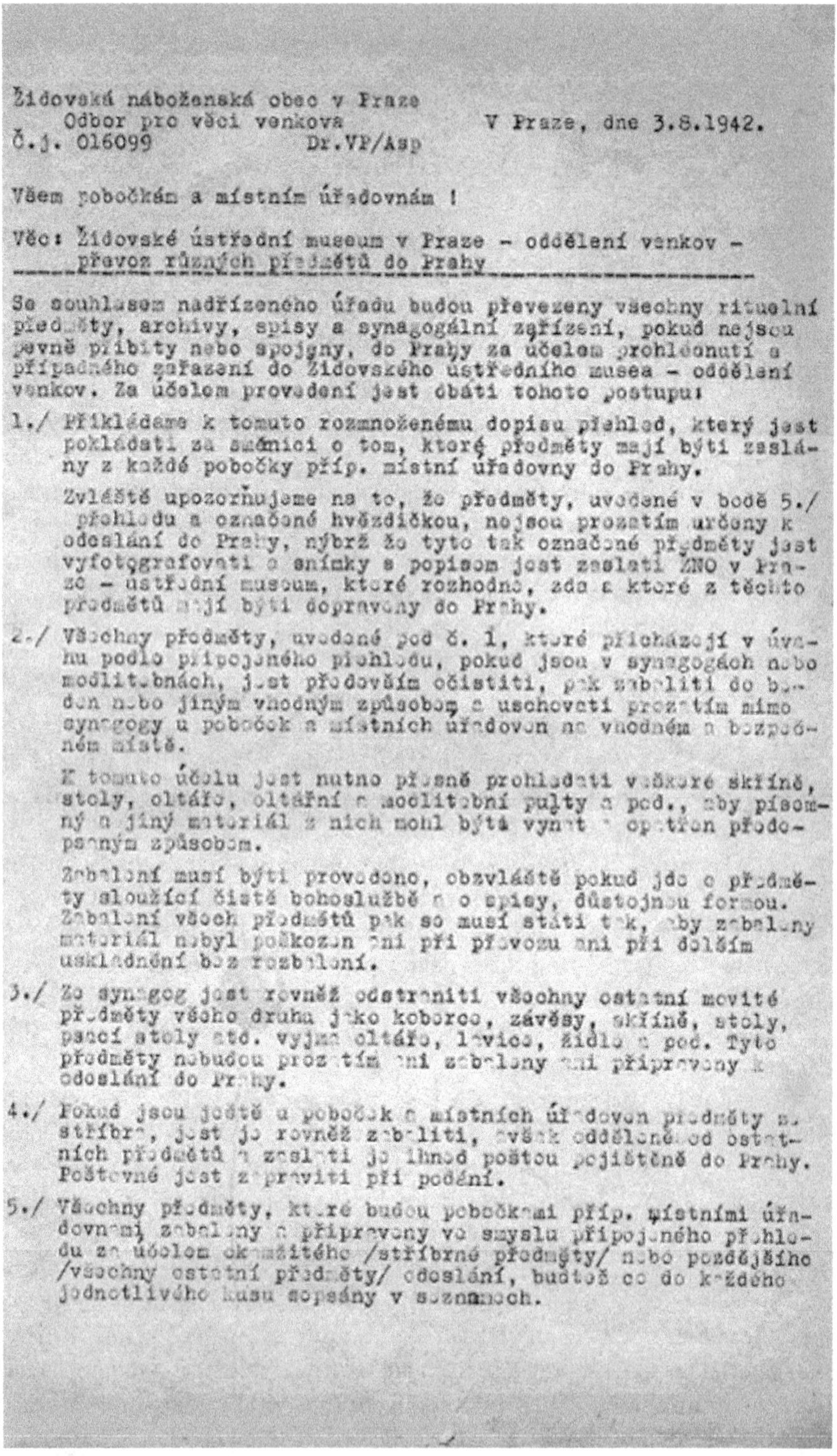

Židovská náboženská obec v Praze
Odbor pro věci venkova
Č.j. 016099 Dr.VP/Asp

V Praze, dne 3.8.1942.

Všem pobočkám a místním úřadovnám !

Věc: Židovské ústřední museum v Praze - oddělení venkov - převoz různých předmětů do Prahy

Se souhlasem nadřízeného úřadu budou převezeny všechny rituelní předměty, archivy, spisy a synagogální zařízení, pokud nejsou pevně přibity nebo spojeny, do Prahy za účelem prohlédnutí a případného zařazení do Židovského ústředního musea - oddělení venkov. Za účelem provedení jest dbáti tohoto postupu:

1./ Přikládáme k tomuto rozmnoženému dopisu přehled, který jest pokládati za směrnici o tom, které předměty mají býti zaslány z každé pobočky příp. místní úřadovny do Prahy.

Zvláště upozorňujeme na to, že předměty, uvedené v bodě 5./ přehledu a označené hvězdičkou, nejsou prozatím určeny k odeslání do Prahy, nýbrž že tyto tak označené předměty jest vyfotografovati a snímky s popisem jest zaslati ŽNO v Praze - ústřední museum, které rozhodne, zda a které z těchto předmětů mají býti dopraveny do Prahy.

2./ Všechny předměty, uvedené pod č. 1, které přicházejí v úvahu podle připojeného přehledu, pokud jsou v synagogách nebo modlitebnách, jest především očistiti, pak zabaliti do beden nebo jiným vhodným způsobem a uschovati prozatím mimo synagogy u poboček a místních úřadoven na vhodném a bezpečném místě.

K tomuto účelu jest nutno přesně prohledati veškeré skříně, stoly, oltáře, oltářní a modlitební pulty a pod., aby písemný a jiný materiál z nich mohl býti vyňat a opatřen předepsaným způsobem.

Zabalení musí býti provedeno, obzvláště pokud jde o předměty sloužící čisté bohoslužbě a o spisy, důstojnou formou. Zabalení všech předmětů pak se musí státi tak, aby zabalený materiál nebyl poškozen ani při převozu ani při dalším uskladnění bez rozbalení.

3./ Ze synagog jest rovněž odstraniti všechny ostatní movité předměty všeho druhu jako koberce, závěsy, skříně, stoly, psací stoly atd. vyjma oltáře, lavice, židle a pod. Tyto předměty nebudou prozatím ani zabaleny ani připraveny k odeslání do Prahy.

4./ Pokud jsou ještě u poboček a místních úřadoven předměty ze stříbra, jest je rovněž zabaliti, avšak odděleně od ostatních předmětů a zaslati je ihned poštou pojištěně do Prahy. Poštovné jest zapraviti při podání.

5./ Všechny předměty, které budou pobočkami příp. místními úřadovnami zabaleny a připraveny ve smyslu připojeného přehledu za účelem okamžitého /stříbrné předměty/ nebo pozdějšího /všechny ostatní předměty/ odeslání, buďtež co do každého jednotlivého kusu popsány v seznamech.

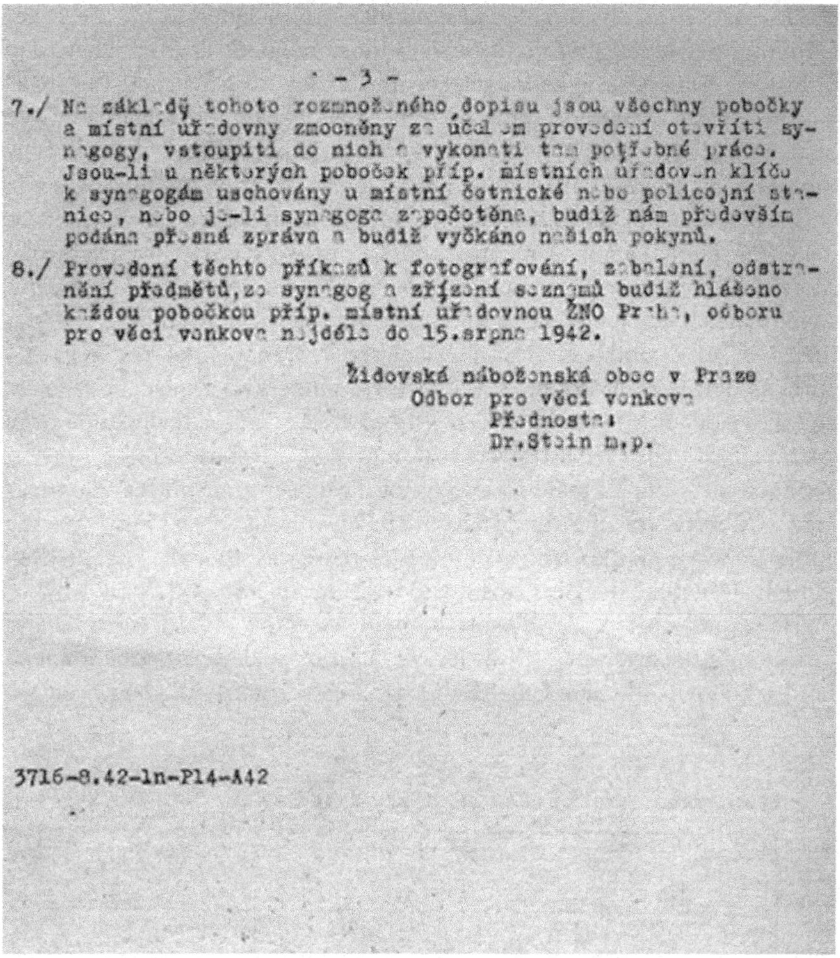

- 3 -

7./ Na základě tohoto rozmnoženého dopisu jsou všechny pobočky a místní úřadovny zmocněny za účelem provedení otevříti synagogy, vstoupiti do nich a vykonati tam potřebné práce. Jsou-li u některých poboček příp. místních úřadoven klíče k synagogám uschovány u místní četnické nebo policejní stanice, nebo je-li synagoga zapečetěna, budiž nám především podána přesná zpráva a budiž vyčkáno našich pokynů.

8./ Provedení těchto příkazů k fotografování, zabalení, odstranění předmětů ze synagog a zřízení seznamů budiž hlášeno každou pobočkou příp. místní úřadovnou ŽNO Prahy, odboru pro věci venkova nejdéle do 15. srpna 1942.

Židovská náboženská obec v Praze
Odbor pro věci venkova
Přednosta:
Dr. Stein m.p.

3716-8.42-1n-P14-A42

Letter from the Jewish Community in Prague instructing communities to send the artefacts to Prague, pages 1 and 3. Summary translation: *Following the orders of the Supervisory Authority, all historic and historically valuable objects in the branches and local offices of the JKGP are to be sent to Prague. We, therefore, request all branches and local offices to follow the instructions immediately. The materials to be sent should be carefully packed to be sent to the JKGP. At the same time, 4 copies of a list of the articles must be prepared, in German. The first 2 copies are to be sent to the JKGP Department of Provincial Affairs. The third copy is to accompany the packed goods and the fourth copy remains with the local office. On the list, each item must be exactly described. Individual items on the list are to be given consecutive numbers. Further, it should be shown where each item came from. In so far as historical data is known on individual items, they should be recorded as notes. The JKGP must be advised in advance of the type, number etc of the packages of the delivery.*
JKGP
Department for Provincial Affairs
The Board
Dr Stein m.p.

In May 1942, the Prague Community sent a letter to all the other Communities requesting them to send those religious artefacts that were of historic value to Prague for safekeeping. They were instructed to make 4 copies of the list of items sent: one to be included with the material, two to be sent in advance to the Jewish Community in Prague and one to be kept by the local Community. On 3 August 1942, a four-page letter, in Czech, was sent with even more detailed instructions for the conveyance of all artefacts, including books, archival records and so on to Prague. It appears that Moravská Ostrava was to be a collection point for communities in its vicinity, so the material sent to Prague from Ostrava included 9 Torah crowns, 15 Torah finials, 21 Torah pointers, 21 Torah shields, 63 Torah mantles, 16 synagogue curtains, 30 covers, 35 Torah scrolls, 38 Torah binders, 23 synagogue valances and many other individual objects. Of those, 14 scrolls actually came from Ostrava itself. The total list covered 10 sides of typed quarto paper.

Such a volume of material could not have been transported 250 miles across Czechoslovakia in August 1942 without clear and specific authorisation from the German authorities: there was, after all, a war on even though at the time the Germans were victorious on all fronts.

The museum recruited staff to help with the task of sorting and cataloguing the artefacts. It was led by Dr Tobias Jakobovits (the uncle of Lord Jakobovits, the late Chief Rabbi of Great Britain) who had been the

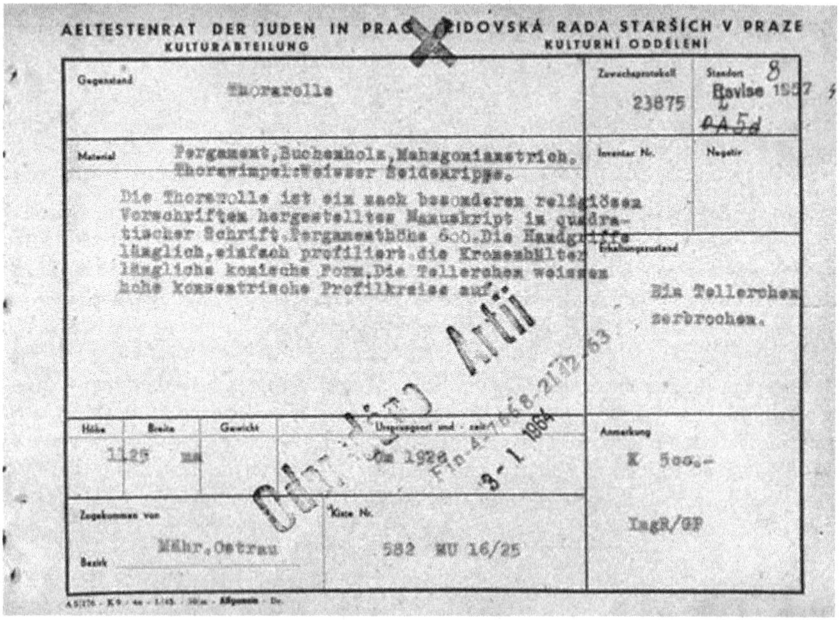

AELTESTENRAT DER JUDEN IN PRAG – ŽIDOVSKÁ RADA STARŠÍCH V PRAZE
KULTURABTEILUNG – KULTURNÍ ODDĚLENÍ

Gegenstand: Thorarolle
Zuwachsprotokoll: 23875
Standort: 8 Revise 1957 AA 5d

Material: Pergament, Buchenholz, Mahagonianstrich. Thorawimpel: Weisser Seidenkrippe.
Inventar Nr.:
Negativ:

Die Thorarolle ist ein nach besonderen religiösen Vorschriften hergestelltes Manuskript in quadratischer Schrift. Pergamenthöhe 600. Die Handgriffe länglich, einfach profiliert, die Kronenhälter längliche konische Form. Die Tellerchen weisen hohe konzentrische Profilkreise auf.

Erhaltungszustand: Ein Tellerchen zerbrochen.

Höhe: 1125 mm
Breite:
Gewicht:
Ursprungsort und · zeit: Um 1920
Anmerkung: K 500.- ImgR/GP

Zugekommen von: Mähr. Ostrau
Bezirk:
Kiste Nr.: 582 MU 16/25

Jewish Museum in Prague Accession Card for the scroll later lent to Kingston Synagogue and numbered 129. Reproduced by kind permission of the Jewish Museum in Prague.

librarian of the Jewish Community in Prague before the war. He was joined, among others, by Dr Josef Polák, an experienced Jewish Museum archivist who developed a system of recording the vast amount of material that arrived in Prague, including a new and specific Accession Card. We have a copy of the Accession Card for our scroll.

While the museum staff was busy cataloguing and organising the vast amount of material that arrived they were safe from deportation but as soon as the work was completed, they were deported to Theresienstadt and thence to Auschwitz and death. The artefacts, now catalogued, were all stored in Prague but nothing further was done with them. They were ignored and then effectively forgotten for almost 20 years, until 1963.

In the early 1960s, the story that the Nazis wished to set up a `Museum of an Extinct Race (of the Jews)' in Prague gained currency, although it is almost certainly untrue. There are three main grounds for doubting it.

First, there is no documentary evidence that the Nazis wanted any such thing. Absence of such evidence is not definitive evidence that they did not

Photograph from the *Jewish Chronicle*, 15 May 1964, l. to r: Mr A. Lourie, the Israeli Ambassador; Dr Isreal Brodie, The Chief Rabbi; the Rev. I. Livingstone inspecting the Czech Scrolls in Westminster Synagogue.

want it, but one would have expected at least some record, somewhere. Further, there is no evidence that the Jewish Museum in Prague took any steps to plan for or implement such a museum. The phrase 'Museum of an Extinct Race' only appeared after the war.

Second, Hitler was known to want the ethnographic collection in Berlin to be destroyed as being of no value so it would seem unlikely that he would want a Jewish museum. Third, in the unlikely event that the Nazis wanted to create such a museum, they had the whole of continental Europe from which to collect material, not just Bohemia and Moravia.

Whatever the motivation, the material was collected and kept in Prague and Estorick was able to purchase 1564 scrolls to be brought to Westminster Synagogue in London, where the Memorial Scrolls Trust was set up to look after them. The scrolls arrived in London in early 1964.[1] Almost immediately, in May, the Chief Rabbi, the Israeli Ambassador and other dignitaries were invited to a very emotional 'At Home' at Westminster Synagogue to view them.

The scrolls were then inspected, sorted, catalogued, numbered and carefully stored. Those scrolls that were still usable were sent on loan to communities throughout the world. One of the scrolls from Moravská Ostrava, which had been given the number 129 by the Scrolls Trust, was lent to Kingston, Surbiton and District Synagogue and started this whole project.

The Prague Jewish Community had wanted the material at least to serve as a memorial to the destroyed communities and in that it was successful. The scrolls have carried the memory of the Czech communities throughout the Jewish world.

In November 2006, Kingston Synagogue arranged a Service of Rededication of its Ostrava Scroll in the presence of the Czech Ambassador, the Mayor of the Royal Borough of Kingston upon Thames and of Rabbi Ginsbury, representing the Chief Rabbi. Bertie Goldberg was invited to recite *Kaddish*,[2] in memory of all those Ostravaks murdered by the Nazis. There was hardly a dry eye in the congregation.

Nowadays, Scroll # 129 is taken out of the Ark when, four times every year, the *Yizkor* Memorial Service is recited. But the Scroll serves not just to remind us of the dead and of past atrocities. It has been the stimulus for ongoing research into Ostrava and its Jewish community. The Kingston Ostrava Group, a small group of members of the Kingston community, has met and interviewed Ostravak survivors and their families, collected stories, photographs and documents from them and built up a significant archive of Ostrava source material. This has all been done with the close support and collaboration of the Jewish Museum in Prague and the material is now stored in the Museum and much of it is available on their public website. The rest of the material may be studied on site.

H.E. The Czech Ambassador, Jan Winkler and Her Worship the Mayor of the Royal Borough of Kingston upon Thames at the Service of Rededication of Scroll 129, November 2006.

Ultimately, however, the project has resulted in more than an archive. It is the story of families today who strive to learn more about their own histories and about Jewish Ostrava. The members of this worldwide Jewish Ostrava network, about 200 families, are now in touch with each other with the help of the Internet and through personal meetings. Among the striking achievements of the project has been putting family members and friends who had lost track of each other during and after the Second World War back in contact. In this way, after a gap of over 70 years, we have been able to connect Peter in Israel with Alfred in Birmingham UK, the brother of Peter's girlfriend in Ostrava who was murdered by the Nazis; and to introduce Tom, from South East England, to a whole branch of his family who still live in Ostrava. Neither they nor Tom had any idea of the existence of the other until last year, when they found out through contacts with the Ostrava group.

The Group has arranged a series of annual tea parties at which 50 or 60 Ostravaks and their families reminisce, usually about the happy times before the war, and explain to the younger members what life was like, 'back there'. The Group has arranged for some of the Ostravak families to have *Stolpersteine*[3] laid in Ostrava in memory of their murdered relatives and has arranged a trip to Ostrava. Inspired by the activities of the Ostrava Group, several families have also organised their own visits to Ostrava.

So scroll 129 inspired not just memories and an archive, but prompted us to create the Ostrava Jewish community once again in virtual reality and then, indeed, to create some aspects of it in actual reality.

NOTES

1. Philippa Bernard, *Out of the Midst of the Fire,* Westminster Synagogue, 2005. Dana Veselská, *The Second Life of Czech Torah Scrolls,* Jewish Museum in Prague, 2006.
2. A prayer recited in memory of the dead.
3. A small brass plaque set into the pavement outside the home from which Jews were sent to their death. See http://www.stolpersteine.eu/en/

PART I

HISTORY OF OSTRAVA

If you were asked to stick a pin into the middle of a map of continental Europe, your pin would come down in or near the city of Ostrava. Situated close to the point where the borders of the Czech Republic, Slovakia and Poland all meet, Ostrava is almost halfway between Vienna and Warsaw, a third of the way from Berlin to Bucharest and some 250 miles east of Prague.

Central Europe with modern borders showing the location of Ostrava.

1

Setting the Scene

The Lie of the Land

This part of Central Europe has been blessed (or cursed) with being the stage for many major historic events, but for most of history none of them seems to have involved Ostrava. Until the mid-eighteenth century Ostrava was a very small backwater, sheltered from the political and military storms that often raged across the region. This was less a matter of luck than of local geography and geology.

The great arc of the Carpathian Mountain range runs eastward from Ostrava, round Slovakia and then south-east into the Ukraine. The western end of the range is formed by the Beskydy Mountains to the south and east of Ostrava, and the Tatra Mountains in Poland and Slovakia, which rise to over 8,000 feet (2,400 metres), to the north and east of Ostrava. The Sudety Mountain range extends to the west of Ostrava, along the present border between the Czech Republic and Poland. The River Odra, Oder in English, rises to the south of Ostrava near Olomouc and then flows north through the gap between the Sudety and Beskydy ranges.

Ostrava Relief Map

This geology means that Ostrava lies open, to some extent, to access from the north across the Polish plain and along the Odra valley, but access from the south and east is hindered by mountains and from the west by the Odra River and the Sudety range. Furthermore, while the valley of the Odra through the mountains provides some north-south access and was part of an early trade route, it was unsuitable for large groups, including armies.

The Ostravice River rises about 40 miles south-east of Ostrava and flows to the north-west, descending rapidly until it joins the River Odra on its journey north to the Baltic Sea. The name Ostravice is derived from the Slavic word 'ostrá', meaning 'sharp' or 'rapid' – referring to the river's fast-flowing waters. Just south of the confluence of the Ostravice and the Odra, the small river Opava which rises in the Sudety range flows from the west into the Odra. Near the source of the River Opava, the River Morava (March in German), rises and flows south/south-east through Olomouc and on into the Danube. The province of Moravia is named after this river.

A stream, the Lučina, joins the right bank of the Ostravice about three miles upstream of its confluence with the Odra. It was here, on a small elevation on the north bank of the Lučina, about 200 metres from the Ostravice, that a small castle was established in the second half of the thirteenth century. It was around the castle and the Ostravice River that Ostrava eventually developed.

On the left bank of the Odra, almost opposite the confluence with the Ostravice, is Landek Hill. Although it is only about 100 metres high it towers above the neighbouring flat countryside. Its northern slopes are gentle, but on the south and south-east the Odra River has eroded the valley wall steeply, exposing the rock formations and, more particularly, the coal deposits. Here, some 20-25,000 years ago, early *homo sapiens* arrived and hunted the game that abounded in the forested hills and the river valley. Traces of mammoth and other animals have been discovered with human remains.

These early hunters made fires and appear to have built stone hearths. Archaeologists have discovered that at least on one occasion, a hearth was made with the local 'black stones' which were partly burnt in the fire. Stone tools and human remains have been unearthed and suggest a significant and possibly settled population. Landek was a source of high-quality flint and it is probable that its flint was traded. Trade and the use of hard black coal go back over twenty thousand years in the Ostrava region!

Among the finds from 20,000 to 23,000 years ago is a striking female figure, 46mm high, made from haematite, red iron oxide, and known as the Petřkovice or 'Landek Venus'. It is thought that the red colour of haematite had some cult or social significance for the people, since two patches of ground, one roughly oval and 170 by 120 cms in size, have been found covered in powdered haematite.[1]

Petřkovice (or Landek) Venus. By permission of the Institute of Archaeology of the Czech Academy of Sciences, Brno. © Martin Frouz.

This figure is unique for the period. Most other prehistoric Venus figures are much more rounded, with prominent breasts, belly and buttocks but the Landek Venus is slender and remarkably modern-looking, which perhaps demonstrates that the people who lived in the Ostrava area were remarkably advanced and forward-looking, even in prehistoric times.

Haematite is not local to the Ostrava region. It almost certainly came from Scandinavia, probably Sweden, and was brought down by glaciers in the Ice Age. Other pieces of haematite have been found in the area among glacial debris. It is, of course, possible that this particular piece was brought for trade from Scandinavia, as were pieces of amber. If so, the ancient link foreshadowed modern times, when iron ore was brought in huge quantities from Scandinavia to Ostrava to feed the iron and steel plants.

The Odra is navigable even today from the Baltic up as far as Koźle, some 60 miles north of Ostrava. In earlier times, with boats of smaller draughts, the Odra was navigable almost up to Ostrava, so it was in the Ostrava region that goods would have been transferred from boats to pack-horses or carts to be transported further south.

The soil in the area of the confluence of the Ostravice and Opava rivers into the Odra is mainly sand and gravel and not very fertile. It has never been suitable for arable cultivation and as a result the settlements were not in the valley itself but on slightly higher ground in the foothills, where Ostrava later grew up. Even here, however, the soil was quite poor and agriculture did not flourish.

Early History

While its prehistoric flowering is of considerable interest to archaeologists, Ostrava then entirely disappears from historical notice until the thirteenth century CE. We can only assume that in the interim the Ostrava region experienced much the same complex movements of people, changes of culture, language and religion as the rest of Moravia and Bohemia. Its consequences and effects can still be seen in the modern history of the Czech Lands and Ostrava in particular. (See **Appendix 1.1** for more details of the early history of the Czech lands.)

It is towards the end of the period of the Great Migrations in early medieval Europe that the Landek Hill reappears in the archaeological record. There are traces of a stronghold dating from about the second half of the 8th century, and remains of occupation up to the tenth and even eleventh century. On the other hand, there is uncertainty as to who built it and even whether it was built to defend against attack from the North or the South.

Ostrava was not a wealthy place and so had little attraction for invaders or migrants. The surrounding mountains protected it from invading armies and kept it relatively isolated. The lack of easy access also inhibited its growth as a city until the advent of modern roads and railways, but its abundance of fresh river water encouraged the development of textile production in the medieval period. This used wool from sheep in the local mountains and locally grown flax, which does not need particularly fertile soil. The navigability of the Odra from the Baltic and the valley allowed further north-south transport by foot and horse, and meant that Ostrava developed as a small market town. Access from the grasslands in the Polish plain combined with access to the south encouraged the development of a cattle market in Ostrava.

The Ostravice River marked the border between the Polish Kingdom and Moravia in the twelfth and thirteenth century and later the border between the Austrian provinces of Moravia and Silesia. Ostrava was very much in the borderlands where the Germanic, and Slav peoples, pagans, Catholics and later Jews and Protestants all mingled, and a frontier town between Moravia and Silesia. This linguistic, cultural, ethnic and religious mixture with the trade opportunities offered by its location gave Ostrava its distinctive character.

It was during the preparations for a campaign to Christianise the pagan Old Prussians that Ostrava entered the written record for the first time, in the will of Bruno of Schaumburg-Holstein, Bishop of Olomouc, written on 29 November 1267, where it is called 'Ostrauiam'. Just over a decade later, on 5 January 1279 the Bishop of Olomouc received Tobias, the newly elected Bishop of Prague, and his party, '*in civitate episcopali, nomine ostrawa*'. The wording shows that Ostrava was known as an episcopal town, owned and controlled by the Olomouc Bishopric.

In fact, there is an earlier mention of Ostrava with a reference to the Polish village of Ostrava in a document from Pope Gregory IX in 1229. Later, we have written records dating from 1297 of the construction of the Silesian Ostrava Castle on the promontory above the confluence of the rivers Lučina and Ostravice to guard the border between the Polish and Bohemian states. Slezská Ostrava is known from earlier records than is Moravská Ostrava. Confusingly, the place was called simply Ostrava in the early sources and later, in German, called 'polnisch' or 'wendisch' Ostrava and even later 'slesisch' Ostrava. By whatever name, Ostrava was now on the map.[2]

Lies, Damned Lies and Statistics

To understand the history of Ostrava and the place of Jews in that history, we need to have some idea of the town's changing demographic profile. In theory, the existence of official census records since the eighteenth century should make that relatively easy to discover, but in fact the apparent precision of these and other population statistics is misleading.[3] Official census data gives numbers of people present, down to single figures, for clearly defined dates and locations, for example 89 people in Mariánské Hory on a specific day in 1772. Whether or not these overall figures are accurate, the breakdowns by national (ethnic) and religious identity given by the census data is more problematic. This is because each individual could decide for him or herself what to declare and that decision might be affected by many factors and might, indeed, change from census to census.

In 1772, the population of Moravská Ostrava was just over 1,000 and the population of what is now Greater Ostrava was less than 3,000. By 1910 the latter had increased to almost 190,000 and 220,000 by 1930. Today the population of Greater Ostrava is just over 310,000, about the same as Nottingham.

Although the effects of the First World War can be seen in a slower rate of population increase in 1918-20, the losses were more than made up for by increased immigration. The effects of the Second World War are much more striking and it took 20 years for population growth to return to the previous trend line.

The population growth data for Moravská and Slezská Ostrava is quite different. It is tempting to infer that the drop in the numbers of inhabitants in Moravská Ostrava from 1940 to 1947 was due to the deportation and murder of the Jewish population, which was heavily concentrated in Moravská Ostrava before the outbreak of the war. The continuous decline in the population of Slezská Ostrava after the First World War may well have been due to the increasing economic, social and cultural dominance of Moravská Ostrava.

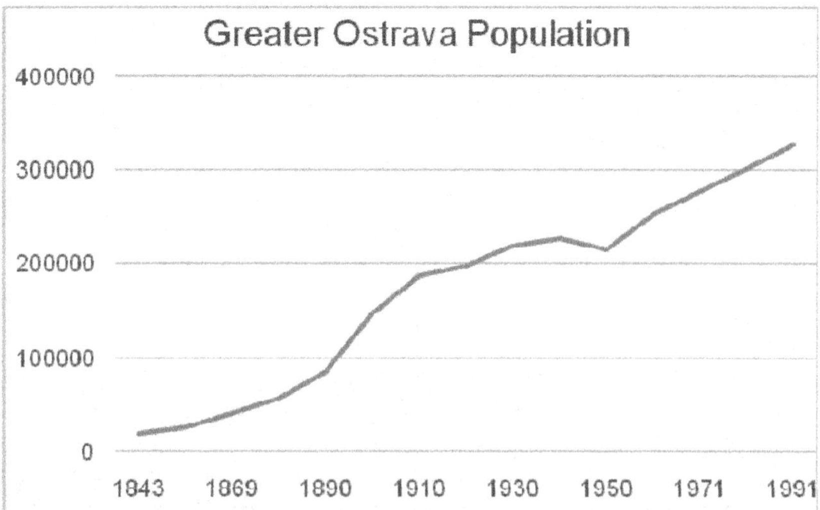

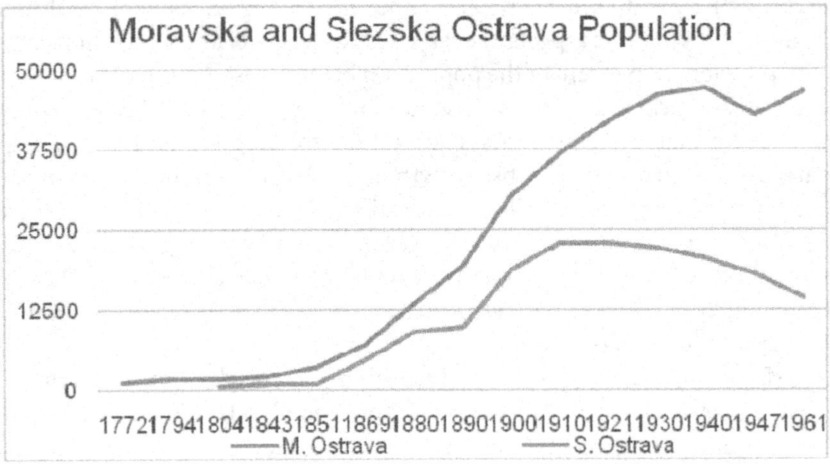

Once we consider the Jewish population, the data becomes quite hard to interpret. Pre-1920 censuses asked respondents to state their nationality which was determined by the language spoken at home, so Czech, German, Polish etc. and religion, as well as recording the total number of people present on the day the census took place. For the 1921 and later censuses, Jewish could be given as a nationality as an alternative to Czech and German, as well as given as a religious alternative to Catholic and Protestant. One could then declare oneself to be Jewish (*židovská*) by nationality although this no more meant being a citizen of some hypothetical Jewish state than declaring oneself to be German meant that one was a citizen of Germany. Religion was still a separate category, so one could still declare oneself to be Jewish *(israelitské)* by religion. Religion and nationality were separate categories, and so each Jew could declare him/herself to be either *židovská* or *israelitské* or both, or neither!

In practice, more people declared themselves to be Jewish by religion than by nationality and we assume that most of those who did in fact declare themselves to be of Jewish nationality would also have said that they were of the Jewish religion. Koeltsch[4] has examined similar census data for Prague in great detail and concludes that the vast majority of people who declared Jewish nationality also declared Jewish religion although 11 out of almost 6,000 who declared Jewish nationality said they were Roman Catholic.

A significant portion of the immigration into Ostrava, both Jewish and non-Jewish, in the late nineteenth and early twentieth century must have come from Galicia, now part of Poland and the Ukraine, which was then also part of the Austro-Hungarian Empire and so there were no major barriers to the movement of population. In the late eighteenth century, Galicia 'was the Empire's most backward province, with its fastest population growth, its most widespread illiteracy, and one displaying a general cultural primitiveness in basic aspects of everyday life (hygiene, healthcare, housing), with probably 10 per cent of the population being Jewish'.[5] Immediately prior to the First World War, there were some 1 million Jews in Galicia. It is hardly surprising that there was mass migration to Moravia and Ostrava in particular, which offered jobs, growth and money. Although most of the immigrants were poor and ill-educated, that was not universally true. There were some Jewish immigrants who were wealthy, educated and integrated into modern western society. One of them was Jakub Freud, a textile merchant, who moved from Tysmenica to Příbor in 1840. His son, Sigmund Freud, was born there.

Most Ostrava Jews would have declared themselves to be German-speakers or of German nationality rather than Czech. This was to some extent a matter of geography, as Ostrava is closer to Vienna than to Prague, which was mainly Czech-speaking. It certainly did not reflect any strong German nationalism but rather a close affinity to and affection for German culture and possibly some patriotism towards the Empire which had treated its Jews relatively well, certainly in comparison with the Jews in Germany or, much more strikingly, Russia.

Slezská Ostrava was almost 90 per cent Czech-speaking and Catholic in the early years of the twentieth century while Moravská Ostrava was almost 50 per cent German-speaking and had significant numbers of Protestants and Jews. There is a correlation between the numbers of Protestants and Jews and the number of German speakers. It appears that most Jews and Protestants called themselves German by language or nationality, at least in the early years of the twentieth century. At the time of the First World War there was an apparent increase in the ratio of German to Czech speakers, almost certainly caused by patriotic fervour for the Austro-Hungarian cause. After the war, the reverse effect occurred as more people declared themselves Czech, to support the new Czechoslovak State.

In 1880, there were 724 Jews recorded as living in Moravská Ostrava and by 1900 the number had increased to 3,272 and 4,716 by 1920. By the early 1920s there were something like 7-8,000 Jews in Greater Ostrava, heavily concentrated in Moravská Ostrava, Vítkovice, Přívoz, and Hrušov. The greatest concentration was undoubtedly in Moravská Ostrava where Jews probably constituted some 15 per cent of the population in the 1930s.

We do not, of course, know how many people of Jewish nationality also said they were Jews by religion but if we make a compromise estimate and assume that half of those who were Jewish (or 'other') by nationality had not said they were Jewish by religion, we could include half of them in the number of 'Jews' for our purposes. That would give us 8,619 as the maximum number of Jews in Ostrava in 1930 and that is probably an over-estimate.

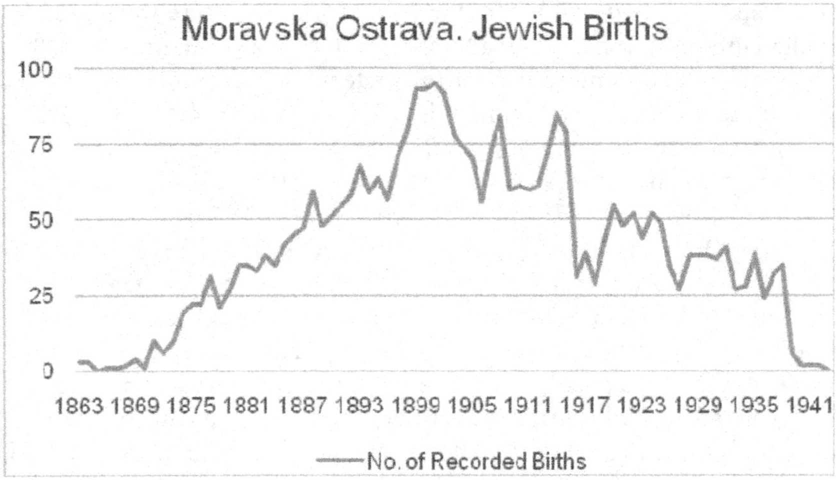

The Register of Jewish Births kept by the Ostrava Community presents a strange and interesting picture. Although the overall population continues to increase after 1900, the number of births recorded falls!

The great increase in births in the early years reflects the increase in immigrant population, probably mostly from Galicia and Silesia. These immigrants were probably relatively young, fecund and had large families. It was not uncommon to have 10 or more children, but within quite a short time, family planning became more readily available and, as observance of traditional religion declined and the immigrants became much more integrated into what was thought of as advanced and modern western society, family planning became more acceptable and probably more widely used. As a result, family size and birth rates declined. After a baby boom following the First World War, the birth rate seemed to settle at about 30 per year, until 1938-9, when no-one wanted to have a baby. Heinz Vogel, as an example, comments that his mother was one of 10 children. She had 5 siblings and 4 step-siblings. Of her siblings, one had no children and two had two each. Heinz himself was an only child.

Richard Drapala[6] was an historian and Ostrava Archivist before the war (and was subsequently dismissed for virulent anti-Semitism). He stated that the Jewish population of Moravská Ostrava 'exceeded 10,000' (in fact he quotes 10,109!) in 1930 but quotes no source for the statement, or for the claim that the 'total number of Jews in Greater Ostrava at the end of 1938 was of the order of 16,000'. He attributes this large and apparently unrecorded number to immigrants finding accommodation with friends and not registering with the police. How he knows how many unrecorded immigrants there are is not made clear, other than quoting 'local estimates'. We doubt the accuracy of his estimates.

Drapala claimed that before the First World War there were 3 Jewish millionaires in Ostrava out of a total of 18, but by 1932 there were 178 of them, but he quotes no source for this statement. Sadly, we have not been able to identify them. He claimed that 'today'(presumably 1938 or 1939), out of 98 Czech-speaking doctors 25 (25.5%) were Jewish and out of 82 German-speaking doctors, 63 (76.8%) were Jewish. Of 112 Ostrava lawyers and 24 articled clerks, 70 and 9 respectively (i.e. 62.5% and 37.5%) were Jewish. Of 360 members of the inn-keepers and hoteliers' co-operative, 100 (27.7%) were Jews. Further 'data' from Drapala is given in **Appendix 1.2**.

Some of his data is highly improbable and should not be taken at face value as they were compiled by a noted anti-Semitic historian, but while inflated by bigotry, the claims have certain grains of truth. Jewish survivors of the Holocaust confirm that Jews held a prominent position, disproportionate to their share of the general population, in the commercial, business and indeed cultural life of Moravská Ostrava.

By the mid to late 1930s, the Jewish population of what is now Greater Ostrava would have been some 7-8,000 people out of a total population of just under 250,000 and they were concentrated in Moravská Ostrava, Přívoz, Vítkovice and Zábřeh. In Moravská Ostrava itself, there were perhaps 6-7,000 out of a total of around 46,000. The Jewish population of Moravská Ostrava increased over fourfold in the fifty years to 1940 whereas the general population increased some two and a half times. In Greater Ostrava the overall population increased by 2.7 times in that period whereas the Jewish population increased some three and a half times. The rate of increase of the Jewish population was certainly greater than that of the overall population in Greater Ostrava and much larger in Moravská Ostrava than the overall population. That is almost certainly due to immigration.

Josef Wechsberg in his book *Homecoming*[7] describes his return to Ostrava immediately at the end of the War:

> The Jewish Community had an office in a nearby house. A man whom I shall call Gerber was in charge. I used to know him well enough, but I wonder whether I would have recognised him if I'd met him outside in a crowd. He couldn't have been over forty years old but looked twice his age. His hair was white, cut very short, prison style, and his mouth was twitching... A deep scar ran across his left cheek from his temple to his mouth. Something was wrong with his eyes, yet I remember his eyes had always been perfect. They seemed sunken and the whites were unnaturally large.
>
> 'Sit down,' he said. 'There's not much to do here. There were eight thousand Jews in this town before the Nazis moved in. Now there are eighty left. Here are the names.' A black notebook was lying on his

desk. He pushed it over to me. 'They're slowly coming back from the various camps. The ones who survived.'

'The lists are incomplete. Miracles do happen. Look at me. I am a miracle I am,' he said, 'the man who survived eight months in Mauthausen.'

He pointed to the scar with his right forefinger. 'It wasn't a holiday.'

The Jewish Community covered more or less the area of present day Greater Ostrava, so we can take that as confirmation that the Jewish population of Ostrava before the war was only about 8,000 strong. Between 200 and 300 people returned.

NOTES

1. Landek, *Witness of a Distant Past*, Pravomil Vokřínek et al. Ostrava: Librex, 1996.
2. Przybylová, Blažena et al., *Ostrava. Historie, kultura, lidé.* Praha: NLN, 2013; Karel Jiřík et al., *Dějiny Ostravy*, Ostrava: Sfinga, 1993; Miroslav Havrlant et al., *Dějiny Ostravy*, Ostrava: Profil, 1967.
3. Census results are held in the National Archive (Národní archiv) in Prague and may be consulted there.
4. *Praha rozdělená i sdílená.* Inez Koeltzsch. Praha: NLN, 2016
5. *Židé v Procesupromĕny poddanského mĕstečka Moravské Ostravy v průmyslové velkomĕsto.* Ludmila Nesládková in Ostrava 20. Šenov u Ostravy:Tilia, 2001.
6. Richard Drapala, *Juden in Ostrau*, Schönbrunn, 1939; *Geschichte der Stadt Mährisch Ostrau* Johann Hoppe, 1933.
7. Josef Wechsberg, *Homecoming*, Alfred A. Knopf, 1946.

2

Market Town

There is no surviving written evidence about the legal and administrative systems in place in fourteenth-century Ostrava but they are likely to have been more or less the same as in other towns founded by the Bishop of Olomouc. Simple legal cases would have been decided locally, but where the matter was more complex it was probably referred to Olomouc for resolution. By the end of the sixteenth century, however, Ostrava had developed to such an extent that episcopal towns in the Bishop of Olomouc's extensive Hukvaldy Estate would send legal appeals there.

The head of the civic administration was a provost or reeve who represented the bishop as suzerain of the town. He also presided over the town court and would be a member of the lower aristocracy. During the fourteenth century the townsfolk began to organize themselves to push for power at the expense of the hereditary reeves and the town council began to have more influence. Latin documents indicate that there were two governing bodies in the town. Apart from the Reeve *(iudex)* there is a mention of councillors *(consules)*, affidavits *(iurati)* and the mayor *(magister civium)*. The town council began to exert some influence as can be seen in the Charter issued by Bishop Nicolas of Riesenburg in 1389,[1] where he waives his rights to inherit the property of intestate burghers. This must have been very welcome to widows and orphans in the town.

In this period, before the Hussite era, the administration seems to have been in the hands of German-speaking townspeople, descendants of German colonists, as can be seen in a German-language charter from 1396 issued by Nicolas Neubeck, the Mayor of Moravská Ostrava and two further charters from 1426. There were also charters written in Czech from 1496, 1512 and 1531[2] so there were clearly Czech speakers living there as well. The largely peaceful co-habitation of the two linguistic groups in Ostrava goes back a long way and ended only in the twentieth century when nationalism became a powerful force.

Although the documentary evidence is sparse, Moravská Ostrava had developed into a significant town by the end of the fourteenth century. In 1362, the Emperor Charles IV granted the town the right to an annual market which meant that Ostrava became one of the most important towns in the area. The grant implies that Ostrava was already an economically significant place with established productive artisans, but the advent of the market gave it even more opportunity for growth. The increased trade, thanks to Ostrava's advantageous geographical position on the border of Moravia and Silesia on the historical North-South route along the valley of the river Odra, led to an increase in money circulation and agricultural production.[3]

Not that life was all roses for Ostrava. Dynastic wars broke out between the Moravian Margraves at the end of the fourteenth and the start of the fifteenth century, with disastrous economic consequences for the Bishopric of Olomouc and hence most of the area. The Hukvaldy Estate and Moravská Ostrava were pawned to the Hungarian King and Holy Roman Emperor Sigismund against a loan. Then the religious Hussite Wars broke out and lasted from 1419 to 1436, which severely affected Ostrava and interrupted its economic development even though there were apparently few Hussite supporters in the town. The Bishop of Olomouc, Jan Železný, was a sworn opponent of Hussitism, as was Sigismund, the Holy Roman Emperor. Prince Bolek of Opole acquired the town, still in pawn, from Sigismund, but then became a Hussite and the town was subsequently conquered by Hussites. There followed a period where the over-lordship of Moravská Ostrava changed hands regularly and frequently. It was a prize to be valued and fought for, as the market town and so the most important town of the Hukvaldy Estate.

The Bishop of Olomouc was determined to regain Moravská Ostrava but as the Bishopric was in a parlous financial position because of the Hussite wars, this was not easy. Bishop Stanislav Thurzo of Bethlenfalva finally managed it, with the financial assistance of his brother György Thurzo, Count of Kremnice and Governor of the Hungarian Royal Chamber, early in the sixteenth century.

Over the course of the sixteenth century, the ethnic and linguistic composition of Moravská Ostrava slowly changed, with the Czechs becoming increasingly important. By the end of the century, the German presence was relatively insignificant because of Czech migration into Ostrava from the local countryside and by the beginning of the seventeenth century Moravská Ostrava was a town where the Czech element clearly prevailed.

In 1556, Ostrava was devastated by a fire which destroyed most of the town. Even the newly-built town hall was consumed, together with the official archives and documents, so there is very little left for today's historians to study. The Church of St Wenceslas (Václav) was also badly damaged and had to be extensively repaired. The repair and rebuilding proceeded rapidly and the town received a prestigious grant from the Bishop, sealed with the red wax otherwise used only for grants to the aristocracy.[4] Ostrava was becoming more important.

It was also becoming more religiously intolerant. The Bishop of Olomouc, Stanislav II Pavlovský, issued a new set of town rules in 1584, regulating various aspects of life for the inhabitants of the town. It dealt with rights to build fishponds and to cultivate and trade in fish but also the influx of hired labour into the town. Anyone not of the Catholic faith and morally blameless was liable to expulsion.

Sadly, the citizens of Ostrava were not to enjoy their newly built town and new prestige for very long before troubles arrived in the form of an outbreak of plague in 1585. At the beginning of the sixteenth century the number of people in Moravská Ostrava was about 1,000, and before the Battle of the White Mountain in 1620, about a century later, the population had increased by only about 1,200.[5] The smallness of the increase was almost certainly due to the plague epidemic. In spite of that, Ostrava, at the beginning of the seventeenth century, could still be considered the largest and most notable town on the Hukvaldy Estate.

The seventeenth century was a period of great turbulence and misery throughout Europe and, indeed, most of the world, with cold wet summers, bad winters and poor harvests exacerbated by volcanic eruptions in Asia which partly blocked the sunlight round the world. Hunger and wars were widespread. Ostrava suffered all that, compounded by the existing religious troubles. It was not a happy time.

The conflicts between Catholics and Protestants in the region deepened. People had been converting from Catholicism even in towns controlled by the bishop. Members of the local gentry supported Protestantism while the Olomouc bishops naturally opposed it. The town thereby lost the goodwill of the bishops, who increasingly favoured the nearby town of Příbor which remained Catholic. Ostrava fell from grace. Mainly it was because of the unwillingness of the Ostravaks to lend money to Bishop Franz of Dietrichstein, so Ostrava was on the wrong side of both God and Mammon! This was demonstrated in 1617 when Ostrava gradually lost suzerain rights over towns in the Hukvaldy Estate and also over towns in the Silesian enclaves. The active disapproval of the bishop weakened the position of Moravská Ostrava, and the town entered the seventeenth century in economic decline.

The beginning of that century was marked by a proliferation of minor armed conflicts, because of the complicated situation prevailing in the lands governed by the Habsburgs and affecting Moravská Ostrava both directly and indirectly. In 1602 the Estates army camped in the Hukvaldy Estate and scavenged supplies in and around Ostrava. In 1604 there was an outbreak of plague and at the beginning of 1605 Hungarian rebels made incursions into Moravia, which naturally provoked a response with the troops of the Bohemian and Silesian estates clashing with the Hungarian raiders. To compound the misery, plague broke out again in town in the autumn of 1606.

In the second decade of the century, events in the Bohemian Lands triggered the Thirty Years' War, which was to engulf much of Central Europe. Ostrava was not to escape the privations and depredations of the war – forced payments for troops, seizure of supplies, looting, hunger and disease. The townspeople were not themselves strongly Protestant and probably just wanted to be left alone but the local ruling families were opposed to the Emperor and to Catholicism. After the First Defenestration of Prague in 1618, the Czech Estates openly rebelled against the Emperor Ferdinand II. In 1619, the Moravian Estates joined the rebellion and the Bishop of Olomouc was expelled from the district in August of that year. His ancestral and episcopal property, including the Hukvaldy Estate, was seized by the Moravian Estates.

Although the town of Ostrava did not declare against the Emperor or for the rebel Estates, Cossacks hired by the Emperor to fight the Protestants attacked the town and looted the church of St Wenceslas as well as much private property. In 1621, the Emperor secured the Hukvaldy Estate but that did not mean that peace returned to Ostrava; there was a continuing to and fro of rival armies and Ostrava lived in constant fear of another invasion. In 1625, plague broke out again and about 500 people, 50 per cent of the population, including the mayor, died of it.

Danish troops occupied Ostrava in 1626, looting and destroying whatever had been left by the Cossacks. When they were replaced by imperial troops, things were no better and then invading Swedish troops took over. They had already had a garrison in Polská Ostrava and had regularly launched pillaging and ransom raids into Moravská Ostrava. The town council had borrowed money to pay off these ransoms and the debt was only paid off in 1741.The Swedes finally left in 1650.

In 1637 there had been 211 houses recorded in Moravská Ostrava but only 121 remained in 1650. What had been a prosperous and growing market town had reverted to something more like an agricultural subsistence economy.[6]

Nonetheless, the town slowly recovered and textile production began to grow again. For the first half of the eighteenth century there is documentary evidence of business contacts with the Jews of Osoblaha (Hotzenplotz in German).[7] They bought textiles, especially linen and lace, from manufacturers in Moravská Ostrava and sold imported goods such as spices to local merchants. The most important of these Jewish merchants was Daniel Šimon, to whom in 1727 ten Ostrava townsmen owed 242 gulden. This debt was only paid in 1735 following the judgement of the bailiff's court. Jonas, also Jewish, had similar problems collecting payments.

According to a census in 1754, Moravská Ostrava had 192 dwellings and 1,152 inhabitants. It was by then the smallest feudal town in the Hukvaldy Estate.

Nine years later, in 1763, something happened that was to be of the utmost importance for the future of Ostrava, even though it had almost no impact at the time. Jan Antonín Alis, a mining expert from Kutná Hora, sent a report to the Royal Office in Opava stating that there was a deposit of hard black coal in the Burňa valley, in the land around Polská Ostrava.[8] The local forests provided sufficient fuel for everyone's needs at the time, and so there was no excitement at the discovery of coal, or rather its rediscovery - since prehistoric man had known of its existence - but the foundation of the industrialisation of Ostrava had been laid.

The population of Moravská Ostrava continued its slow and gradual increase. In the last decade of the eighteenth century the population had risen to over 1,500 but this growth was soon halted by the Napoleonic Wars in the first decades of the nineteenth century. At that time the majority of town dwellers made their living from hand-production and agriculture. As it had been for decades, the main craft was textile production, drapery and the linen industry, based on the abundance of fresh running water from the local rivers. Clothing and food production were secondary economic activities dependent on the primary textile and agricultural output.

Count Wilczek, in Polská Ostrava, encouraged the industrialisation of textile production, possibly associated with the presence in his territory of Jewish merchants. This was competition for the hand-workers of the Moravská Ostrava textile industry and so initially rather threatened its local workforce, but by the fourth decade of the nineteenth century, coal, iron and steel production had developed. The industrial revolution had arrived.

NOTES

1. Codex diplomaticus et epistolaris Moraviae, XII, Nr 346, Brno, 1890.
2. (1396) Codex diplomaticus civitatis Ostraviae - Sbírka listin k dějinám Mor. Ostravy, Nr 7. (1426) Archiv města Ostravy, sign. I A 7.
3. Archiv města Ostravy, sign. I A 1.
4. Blažena Przybylová et al., *Ostrava - historie, kultura, lidé,* Praha: NLN, 2013.
5. Karel Jiřík et al., *Dějiny Ostravy*, Ostrava:Sfinga, 1993.
6. *Ostrava - historie, kultura, lidé.*
7. Židé v procesu proměny poddanského městečka Moravské Ostravy v průmyslové velkoměsto. Ludmila Nesládková in Ostrava 20, Šenov u Ostravy:Tilia, 2001.
8. Ve stínu těžních věží. Aleš Zářický, Ostrava: University of Ostrava, 2004.

3

Into Modern Times

Industrialisation

Industrialisation came relatively late to Ostrava, but when it came, it happened fast. In 1809, a Scottish metallurgist named John Baildon[1] tried to set up a modern ironworks in Ostrava, doubtless inspired by the ongoing industrial revolution in Britain. Alas he failed, and Ostrava fell back into its gentle bucolic torpor for a few more years. There was some coal mining by 1780 in the Hlučín area, about 10 miles west of Ostrava and on the left (i.e. west) bank of the Odra River, but at the time this area belonged to Prussia and the lack of transport links to the rest of Prussia meant that it did not develop. Small local investors started exploitation of seams close to the surface just to satisfy what local demand there was.

This all changed in 1828 when Rudolf Habsburg, Archbishop of Olomouc, decided that he could serve Mammon as well as the Almighty, and issued a deed of foundation for a new blast furnace which was named the Rudolf Foundry in his honour. Then railway mania gripped the Austrian Empire with the *Kaiser Ferdinands-Nordbahn*, the first railway company in the Empire, financed by Salomon Mayer Rothschild. The first part of the track was built in 1837 and then extended bit by bit, reaching Ostrava in 1847. The company needed iron for the tracks, steel for the engines and wagons, and coal to drive the engines. So, for the first time, the Rothschilds appear in our story, taking an interest both in the ironworks and the coal mines.

The Anselm Mine, which is now open to the public as an industrial museum, was the deepest mine in the region. It was probably founded in 1830 by Rudolf the entrepreneurial archbishop, under the name *Ferdinandovo štěstí* (Ferdinand's Luck) and, with other local mines, formed the Consolidated Mines of Hlučín. Rudolf was not the sole owner, since part of the estate belonged to a Herr Stücker and in 1836 Arnošt Czaderský bought the estate and was thereby entitled to half the coal production. This confusing ownership situation was simplified when Salomon Rothschild bought the ironworks in Vítkovice and the Hlučín pits in 1843 and then bought out Stücker in 1844 for 425,000 Thalers. As a result he controlled almost all the coal production in the Prussian part of the Ostrava-Karviná region. There were still two independent mines, with shares owned by Aaron

Landek Mining Museum, underground tunnel.

Jaroslawski (who was Jewish), Bernard Friedländer, Jakob Dresdner, Šimon Löwy and Anton Röhmisch. Alois Miesbach acquired a significant shareholding in these mines to feed the brickworks that he owned near

Vienna, but from about 1850, Rothschild owned all the local pits. In 1855, after Salomon Mayer's death, the mines passed to his son, Anselm Salomon, and the name of the mine was changed in his honour.[2]

In 1868 the Rothschild holdings were consolidated into the *Consolidierte Hultschiner Steinkohlengruben* company and on 1 January 1872 Rothschild entered into a contract with the Gutmann Brothers, by which they leased their mines to the *Witkowitzer Gesellschaft* for 25 years, with the Gutmanns holding 60% of the equity and Rothschild 40%. When Anselm died in 1874 his heirs sold their holding for 2,021,718 Guilders to the *Gesellschaft.* After 1918, the Hlučín region was transferred from Prussia to the new state of Czechoslovakia and the ownership of the mines and the iron and steel works passed to the *Vítkovické horní a hutní Těžířstvo* (VHHT), or *Witkowitzer Berg- und Hüttengewerkschaft* (Vitkovice Mining, Iron and Steel Company) which dominated the economy of Ostrava thereafter.

The original architect of the Gutmann fortune, Wilhelm Isaak Wolf Gutmann, was born in 1826 to Markus Leopold Gutmann, a prosperous wool merchant and his second wife, Bertha, in Lipník nad Bečvou, a town near Olomouc about 50 miles from Ostrava. Eight years later, a second son, David was born. Shortly afterwards Markus died and the family faced serious economic difficulties. Wilhelm's parents had wished him to become a rabbi although that was not really what he wanted. Fate took a hand when his mother developed typhoid fever and was unable to attend to the family business, which closed. Wilhelm had to return from rabbinical studies to get a job and provide for the family. After a number of short-term tutoring and administrative positions he started as a small-scale grain dealer and then had a major stroke of luck when he met a wholesaler of gypsum and Plaster of Paris in Bohumín who wished to expand his business and needed finance. Wilhelm was able to introduce him to three entrepreneurs from Lipník who were in the transport business for gypsum. They formed a joint company and appointed Wilhelm as secretary at an annual salary of 800 Gulden, with a major responsibility for transport. He was able to continue his grain trading as well, and so the family fortunes started to look up.[3]

His employers fired him after about a year as they thought his salary much too high but by that time he was able to pay off his debts and start independently transporting plaster and grain and later expanding his range to include coal. Among his clients for coal transport were the *Kaiser Ferdinands-Nordbahn*, the Danube Steam Shipping Co., and the Austrian State Railway Company. Gutmann not only transported but also traded in coal, particularly on behalf of the Rothschilds' mining business. This growth in Wilhelm's activities meant that he needed help, and so he brought in his 22-year-old brother, David, to run the administrative side of the business, and changed its name to *Gebrüder Gutmann* (Gutmann Brothers) with its headquarters in Vienna.

By the later 1850s the Gutmanns had bought an important stake in mines in the Katowice region. The coal here was particularly high quality and suitable for domestic use. The Gutmanns then became retail distributors of coal in Vienna and soon opened branches in Pest and Brno. By the late 1860s and early 1870s the Gutmann Brothers had control of almost 50 per cent of the coal mining and coke production in the region, with the help and advice of a mining expert called Ignác Vondráček. The collaboration with the Rothschilds grew and culminated in 1873 in the establishment of the Vítkovice Mining, Iron and Steel Works Corporation, under joint ownership.

The Gutmann Brothers were not only dynamic and successful entrepreneurs but were also concerned with social, religious and general charitable works and were major donors, as were the Rothschilds. Both brothers were awarded the Order of the Iron Cross III Class by the Emperor Franz Josef I and in January 1878, Wilhelm was honoured with a knighthood, with David following in December of that year. Wilhelm was obviously not only the elder but also the very dominant brother: the ubiquitous worldwide web has a great deal to report about Wilhelm but almost nothing to say about David, and only one portrait of him. Given the tremendous effects he had on the economic and industrial development of the Ostrava region, we might wonder what impact Wilhelm might have made as a rabbi had he pursued his theological education. On the other hand, perhaps his dominating personality was more suitable to commercial than pastoral activities.

Wilhelm Gutmann.

David Gutmann.

The expanding mining, iron and steel industries required a large labour force and the population of Ostrava grew dramatically. This necessitated a huge building programme to house the increased population, but even as domestic buildings were constructed, yet more mines, coking plants and iron works were opened too, and Ostrava grew with homes cheek by jowl with mines and furnaces. Ostrava had changed from a rather bucolic small country town in 1855 into an industrialised version of an inferno by 1911.

Ostrava, 1855. Lithograph by J. Alt.

Postcard of Ostrava, 1911.

The single-storey wooden cottages and cowsheds were being replaced by steelworks and brick-built workers' accommodation. The Rothschilds and Gutmanns built blocks of accommodation for their manual workers, slightly larger and better equipped buildings for the white collar workers and villas for the senior managers. They also built an impressive works' hotel.

Vítkovice: workmens' barracks.

Vítkovice: Works' Hotel.

Vítkovice: town square.

They built the first school and kindergarten for 2-5 year-olds in 1843 and by 1873 they had to build a much larger one, with fruit and ornamental trees and a grapevine in the garden. Salomon Meyer nominated the teachers and paid for the upkeep of the school and its staff. The Rothschilds continued with this arrangement until 1924, when the school was taken over by the City authorities of Moravská Ostrava, as Vítkovice merged with Moravská Ostrava. The Rothschilds also provided a small hospital, with 6 beds and two nurses, opened in the early 1840s. A new and bigger hospital was built in 1853, with 20 beds in 4 rooms. By 1890, even this facility was too small and a larger and more modern facility was built and this was progressively expanded to 486 beds by 1939.

In the late nineteenth and early twentieth century other public and communal buildings were erected: public laundries, a slaughter house, a poor house and an orphanage, supported both by charitable donations especially from the big enterprises and also from communal funds. Vítkovice, being the centre of this heavy industry, benefitted substantially and the town was debt-free until the First World War! The Vítkovice Town Hall, designed by the Viennese architect Max von Ferstel, was opened in 1902.

In 1847, the Rothschilds built a 'chateau' in the ironworks complex. It was actually a Viennese-style mansion, with a large garden in the French style, but the family rarely stayed there, preferring their nearby county estate of Šilheřovice. The chateau became the headquarters of the company and also the home of the General Manager of the site. It is still the head office of the successor of the VHHT, the Vítkovice Machinery Group.

Vítkovice: The Rothschild Chateau, in 1915 and below in 2016.

After the Second World War, the chateau was abandoned and neglected. By the turn of the millennium it seemed that the only thing to do was to demolish it but in 2003 the site and business were privatised, becoming the Vítkovice Machinery Group, under the control of Jan Světlík. He set about restoring and renovating the chateau and using it as the headquarters of the

The study of the Director of the Vítkovice Ironworks, 1915.

company. By 2010, when we took a group of Ostravaks back to Ostrava, we were able to attend a chamber concert in the restored small concert hall in the Chateau. Mr Světlík has been at pains to restore his office to its former Rothschild glory, as far as possible, and he has been buying period furniture that once belonged to the Rothschild family. He has also been buying original works of art that had once been in the collection of the Company or in the collection of Oskar Federer, the last General Manager of the Vítkovice Mining, Steel and Iron Works Corporation before the war. Federer had one of the best collections of Impressionist art in private hands in Europe but it was seized by the Nazis.

One of the Ostravaks involved in our project, Kurt Berger, was born in Ostrava in 1923. His father was the manager of the *Böhmische Eskomptbank* and they lived above the bank, opposite the Dvořák Theatre, but later moved to Mlýnská Street. Kurt's father, Josef, had met his future wife in Marienbad (Mariánské Lázně), where he had been seconded to the bank to cover the holiday period and she had come on holiday from England. Kurt's English grandfather eventually died, leaving his daughter some money, and so, in 1933, the whole family moved to London. From his early childhood in Ostrava, Kurt remembers that his mother made friends with the Rothschild's gardener, a Scot, as he was probably the only other person in Ostrava who spoke English! Kurt remembers going out to visit the Rothschild's country estate in a horse and carriage and coming back home with his pockets stuffed with 'conkers' (horse chestnuts).

Heinz Vogel with his mother, 1936, opposite their apartment.

It was probably at about this time that the famous Ostrava 'Black Polka Dot Shirt' made its appearance. I was surprised to be told that this was not a new fashion introduced by the Ostrava textile industry but a natural phenomenon. If you went out in Ostrava in the morning in a white shirt, by midday the pollution had spontaneously transformed it into the Black Polka Dot Shirt.

Heinz Vogel, another native of Ostrava, remembers a coking plant immediately opposite their comfortable middle-class apartment, and adds that this was quite usual. Hana Slome, too, remembers the coke and the pollution:

> My brother used to climb the hills of coke that accumulated around the mines. There is a river, the Ostravice, where we used to swim in the summer but only in the Beskydy not in Ostrava. That part used to

> be black I suppose from all the stuff that they threw in from the coal mines.

By a happy coincidence, we discovered that Hana lived at Masarykovo náměstí 21, next door to Dr and Mrs Bernard Grulewski, the grandparents of Jan Buhagiar. Jan remembers his mother describing Ostrava:

> The little I remember about my mother's description of Ostrava was that, being a mining town, there was a lot of soot and coal dust in the air! She said that her father, Dr Bernard Grulewski, had gone to Ostrava because he specialised in lung problems.

Several members of Heinz Vogel's family died of cancer and he is convinced that the polluted environment had a great deal to do with that. The health problems caused by long-term pollution are a problem in parts of Ostrava even today. The town agglomeration of Ostrava-Karviná—Frýdek-Místek, North Moravia, was the area with the heaviest air pollution in the Czech Republic in 2013, according to the annual report released by the Czech Hydrometeorological Institute (ČHMÚ).

It was not just coal, iron and steel that developed in Ostrava. The provision of raw materials and equipment for these industries meant that coke production, heavy engineering, building materials and transport became important industries in their own right. Přívoz, but especially the nearby Bohumín, became one of the most important railway junctions in the monarchy. The availability of coal and steel encouraged primary and secondary metallurgical industries in the region. Probably the most important was *Elbertzhagen und Glassner*, a branch of the Mannesmann concern in Svinov, specializing in the production of seamless pipes. Its beginnings in the year 1892 are connected with a German industrial magnate, Oskar Huldschinsky, who was born in Wrocław but lived most of his life in Berlin and was buried, as a Jew, in the Wannsee cemetery. During his lifetime he amassed a very significant art collection much of which he donated or bequeathed to museums in Berlin, thus joining many distinguished Jewish patrons of the arts[4].

In 1899, the 'Metal Rolling Company' was set up in Přívoz, and this became the monopoly producer of zinc and galvanised steel plate in the Habsburg monarchy. It was part of the Silesian concern, *Tlach und Keil*, based in Opava/Troppau.

Some 50 years earlier, in 1851, the chemical industry had begun its development in the Ostrava region when Karl Christian Hochstetter, a chemist, and the banker and industrialist Josef Maria Miller zu Aichholz set up a sodium carbonate production unit in Hrušov, the *Erste österreichische Sodafabrik*. The sulphuric acid needed in the process was produced on site and the stoneware vessels involved were produced in a factory set up next door. They also produced caustic soda, chlorine and hydrochloric acid and heavy chemical production became centred on Ostrava thanks not only to the local availability of coal and heavy engineering but also the deposits of salt and oil in nearby Galicia[5].

In 1865, a refinery for paraffin and kerosene was set up in Moravská Ostrava by Augustin Dingler and in the 1880s a Viennese entrepreneur, Anton Himmelbauer, established a mineral oil refinery on the boundary of Moravská Ostrava and Přívoz near the railway line. In 1889 Dr Max Böhm, with the financial backing of the Jewish Viennese bankers, M. Thorsch und Söhne, founded the "Ostrava Mineral Oil Refinery" in Přívoz, which continued as a major company, *Česká rafinérská,* until 1997.[6] Naturally, there were many by-products from the refinery and coking operations, and companies were set up to take advantage of them. The first was a tar distillery and roofing felt production unit (the felt making use of the distilled tar) set up by August Luttnar, followed in 1882 by a Berlin company 'Posnansky und Strelitz' opening a similar plant in Vítkovice. The largest chemical plant of this type in the Ostrava area was built in the year 1893 on the edge of Zábřeh nad Odrou by a German entrepreneur, Julius Rüttgers.[7]

The cottage industries of textile production, food and alcohol production and distribution also proliferated and by the turn of the twentieth century Ostrava was the most industrialised centre in the Habsburg monarchy and a major metropolis. In the middle years of the nineteenth century Ostrava had still been a raw rough frontier town with poor roads and civic infrastructure, but large numbers of bars and inns, inadequate housing, education and healthcare provision and little cultural activity. Diseases such as typhoid, cholera and smallpox had still been rife and associated with overcrowding, poverty and lack of clean water and drainage. By the turn of the century, thanks to increasing prosperity and the social care provided by the Rothschilds, Gutmanns and others, the town was gradually losing its rough appearance and becoming recognisably the place we know today.

Civil Development

The ethnic, religious and even social structure of the town was changing. Until the 1830s Ostrava and surrounding villages were almost exclusively Czech-speaking, but in the following decades there was a considerable increase in the German and Polish population, by immigration. As regards religion, the majority continued to be Roman Catholic (up to 90 per cent), but there was an increased number of Protestants and Jews. At this time, the Ostrava area had a very specific social structure, with a very small group of intelligentsia consisting mainly of civil servants, teachers, mining and industrial engineers, lawyers and doctors. A disproportionate number of them were German-speaking and also Jewish and they expected all the amenities of a modern cultural city. Where these were not available, the new immigrants set about providing them.

The influence of an increase in German-speaking immigrants was particularly noticeable in Moravská Ostrava where in the year 1910 almost half the population said that their mother tongue was German (Czech 36 %, Polish 14 %). This reflected the dominance of German social elites in the town and the influence of the financial inflow from the Viennese banking houses.

As the economic influence of Ostrava grew in the Austro-Hungarian Empire, local government politics became more important. Until 1900, only Moravská Ostrava had the legal status of a town but in that year, Přívoz became a town, followed in 1907 by Mariánské Hory and Vítkovice in 1908. Polská Ostrava had been officially made a market town in 1879 and a township in 1919: Michálkovice and Hrušov followed in 1907 and 1908.

Moravská Ostrava itself was always the main centre. In 1894, the police headquarters was established there, although we might wonder why it took so long. In 1900 it became the seat of the District Governor. As a result, Moravská Ostrava became even more the location of civic and professional, especially legal, services. It was the white-collar centre of an essentially blue-collar region. Aspiring lawyers and administrators flocked there closely

Electric Tram.

followed by doctors and then all those who catered for middle-class needs, such as hotels, restaurants and shopkeepers.

By 1901, the tramway from Moravská Ostrava to Vítkovice was electrified and that was probably a couple of years earlier than the appearance of electric trams in London!

In September 1907, the city theatre (today the Antonín Dvořák Theatre) was opened. Ostrava had become, in an incredibly short time, a provincial Viennese capital.

In October 1880, Moravská Ostrava was honoured with a visit from the Emperor Franz Josef I as part of his trip to Silesia, as was Vítkovice. The main part of the journey from Vienna was by the new-fangled and dramatic railway, *the Kaiser Ferdinands Nordbahn*, and the Emperor arrived in Ostrava in a motorcade. His entry into the main square, the Ringplatz, was along what is now the pedestrian 28 October Street, from the direction of the Dvořák Theatre, under a newly-erected triumphal arch.

Had he looked to his right as he entered the square he would have seen the tailor's shop owned by Isaac Reisz. According to Isaac's grandson, Pavel (known as Paul Rice after he came to England), Isaac moved to Ostrava from Slovakia and realised that there was a chance of a good business providing

Main square with Radvanice alehouse (with gables) designed by Felix Neumann, 1891.

Visit of the Emperor to Ostrava, photographed by Otto Brand.

clothing for the coal miners who were very numerous in the town. He prefabricated suits with uncut sleeves and trouser legs and when a miner came into his shop, he only had to shorten them while the customer waited. It proved to be a very good idea and he made a lot of money. He bought two very valuable properties on the main street of the town and for a time his wife also operated a café there, a very profitable innovation. Pavel recalls that both houses were renovated by his grandparents and that his grandmother told him that one of them was the first house in the town with running water, and also that it was from its balcony that the family waved to Emperor Franz Josef when he visited the town.

As the Emperor left the Ringplatz, he would have seen the new synagogue, in Pitlergasse just to the south of the square. The Ringplatz was the location of the Town Hall and of many of the best shops in Moravská Ostrava. It was also the site of the market stalls and pedlars' pitches and was the heart of day-to-day activity in the town. It has the almost obligatory 'Plague Column' dating from 1702 and some splendid Art Nouveau buildings such as the Habsburg Café, now the Academia bookshop. Just off the Ringplatz is Jirásek Square, also with striking buildings. It is known locally as the Chicken Market, in memory of Moravská Ostrava's more agricultural past.

Effects of the First World War and the Creation of Czechoslovakia

This 'golden age' suffered a temporary hiatus with the outbreak of the First World War. The initial success of the Russian offensive in Galicia meant that the Austrian military headquarters had to be evacuated from Kraków and set up in Moravská Ostrava. Local citizens were called up to join the military and we now have a crop of nostalgic photographs of handsome young men in romantic military uniforms. The reality was, of course, bloody and not romantic. Ostrava was never the same again although perhaps the changes were less noticeable on an everyday basis than in other places. Mining and steel production continued during and after the war.

The Russian troops broke through the Austrian defences in Galicia and pushed the front to the south-west. The appearance or even the rumoured appearance of the Russian Army ('The Cossacks') was sufficient to cause many civilians to flee and join the retreating Austrian army. That was particularly so for the large Jewish population of Galicia and many of them abandoned everything and fled to the nearest place of apparent refuge, which was Moravská Ostrava. Moravská Ostrava had an established Jewish community and so the refugees would have assumed that they would find co-religionists, understanding and help, even if not a warm welcome from everyone. They were correct, up to a point, but the City authorities were faced with a massive flood of refugees. Their response and that of the local population was very mixed, much like the current response to the flow of migrants into Europe. In 1914, however, the population of Ostrava was faced not just with migrants but also with the distinct possibility of invasion by the Russian army.

Food became scarce, diseases such as cholera and typhus became rife and the authorities had to institute emergency controls to cope with the problems. By the end of 1914 there were 10,000 refugees from Galicia in Moravská Ostrava, many of them Jewish, but for most of them the town was only a temporary home. They were transported to refugee camps across Moravia and Bohemia. After the war the new Czechoslovak authorities tried more or less successfully to repatriate all refugees living in Ostrava back to their homes in Poland but some 440 Galician refugees, of whom about 400 were Jews, remained there.[8] Many Jews who settled in Ostrava at this point contributed to its life and economy in the 1920s and 1930s.

Ostrava entered the First World War as the centre of a major industrial complex in the Austro-Hungarian Empire and emerged, after the peace, as a border town and one of the most important economic areas in the new Czechoslovakia. The border line between the new countries of Poland and Czechoslovakia in the region of Ostrava was not clear and only finally settled in 1920 by the intervention of the Czechoslovak Army.[9] It was disputed once again and moved in 1938 after the infamous Munich Agreement. At that point a relatively small piece of land which had been Czechoslovak became Polish and this was of vital importance for several Jewish refugees in the period after the invasion of Czechoslovakia in March 1939 but before the invasion of Poland in September of that year.

Following the establishment of the Czechoslovak state, the population of Ostrava was faced with a Czech- rather than a German-language government. Although the new state accepted both Czech and German languages and provided education in both languages, there was an increased tendency to use and promote the Czech language. The bilingual nature of Ostrava society and industry, earlier accepted as normal and not really worthy of comment, increasingly became a source of discord and strife as the 1920s turned into the 1930s. At this point, the rising German nationalist movement, spilling over from the Sudetenland, demanded greater rights and representation for Germans and German, and this produced a strong Czech backlash. In the earlier post-war years, however, all was relatively well and Ostrava relaxed as part of the new nation.

Thanks to its established mining, iron and steel production and heavy industry, Ostrava maintained or even enhanced its economic importance in the new state and its role as an administrative, social and cultural centre became even more important. On 1 January 1924, Greater Ostrava was formed when Přívoz, Mariánské Hory, Vítkovice, Hrabůvka, Zábřeh and Nová Ves were incorporated into Moravská Ostrava. Its new status and wealth was demonstrated with the building of the New Town Hall, opened in 1930. It was and still is the largest town hall complex in the Czech Republic with the highest tower. Its interior decoration is in the art deco style and is most impressive.

In 1919, Slezská Ostrava became part of Czechoslovakia and in 1920 its status was raised to that of a Town. After 1939, it was incorporated into Greater Ostrava.

In the post-war period the French armaments company, Schneider et

Cie. Creusot, took over the Ostrava Mining and Metallurgical Company which also owned mines in the Karviná area, although they did not manufacture arms in Ostrava. Their administrative headquarters was at *Avenue 30 dubna.* Heavy chemical production developed both with the 'Moravská Ostrava Chemical Plant' and, in 1927, *the Czechoslovak Factory for the Manufacture of Nitrogen Compounds.*[10] Local Polish oil and salt sources continued to supply the raw material for these plants.

The first electric tramline was operational in 1901 and electrification continued apace in the immediate post-war years. The first sources of electric power were the power plants of the major industrial units, supplying power through the Moravsko-Slezská Electric Power Company, founded in 1920. The company set up its own generating units first in Moravská Ostrava and later in Třebovice.

The growth and economic power of Ostrava is illustrated by the Vítkovice site whose employee numbers grew from 11,500 in 1900 to 19,250 in 1930. Further data is given in **Appendix 3.1.**

All of this industrial activity naturally involved significant sources of finance and from the 1920s Ostrava became an important financial centre with major banks establishing offices there. Nádražní Avenue was the favoured location for the splendid local headquarters of the banks, with the Czech Union Bank being the first there, in 1921. The *Živnostenská banka,* the Czech Trade Bank, started to build its splendid branch in 1921 and it was opened in 1924. It was the largest building in the town, modesty not being a characteristic of merchant banks, even then. Others rapidly followed: the English-Czechoslovak Bank (*Anglo-československá banka*), the Central Bank of Czechoslovakia Savings Bank and the Moravská-Ostrava Savings Bank (*Moravskoostravsá spořitelna*) and the Czechoslovak National Bank building its branch on the corner of Sokolská and Českobratrská Streets. At the end of the 1920s the businessman Jakub Nesselroth began the building of a complex of department stores and apartments connected by arcades with a dominant seven storey corner tower on today's Avenue 28 Října. The Concordia insurance company rented office space here, as did the Czech Commercial Bank (*Česká komerční banka*). The number and size of the banks testifies to the great economic importance of Ostrava in the new Czechoslovakia.

Bourgeois Life in the Inter-War Years

The increasingly affluent citizens of Ostrava needed places to spend their new-found wealth and to obtain the goods and services appropriate to their new status. Bars and inns there were aplenty and so now came hotels, restaurants, high-quality shops and department stores, and culture in all its aspects.

1921, Czech Trade Bank, 28. října street. (architects: Julius Deininger, Wunibald Deininger).

Czech Union Bank, Nadrážní street. Former Villa of Dr Karl Kraus (architect: Hans Ulrich & Alois Schön, 1910-1911). Rebuilt for Czech Union Bank in 1921-2 to the design of Ernst Korner.

In 1928, the Ostrava branch of the Viennese Department store, Rix, was renovated. It had been managed by Adolf Lüftschitz who subsequently bought it and later changed his own name to Rix to match the store. It was the Ostrava equivalent of Harrods or Bloomingdales. In the same year, the store *Brouk a Babka* opened on Smetana Square. Two years later, the largest store in Czechoslovakia was opened by Igo Wechsler on Avenue *28 Října*, under the name *Textilia,* and designed by the architect Marie Frommer.

Igo had only one child, a daughter Trudy. She went to Czech primary school and Czech grammar school. Her family spoke Czech at home and was very wealthy and Trudy recalls being collected from school in their chauffeur-driven car and being very embarrassed by it. She was sent to finishing school in Switzerland and was there in 1939. Her father was on business in Paris when the Germans invaded Ostrava and her mother was visiting her in Switzerland. They did not return home and their family house became the first Gestapo headquarters in Ostrava.

The Bachner family commissioned Erich Mendelsohn, a well-known Jewish architect, to design a department store in Zámecká Street which was opened in 1933 as *Bachners*. Mendelsohn was a pioneer of the Art Deco and Streamline Moderne styles of architecture and was a friend of Chaim Weizmann, the first President of Israel. He had designed several buildings for Weizmann in Palestine, including the Weizmann House in Tel Aviv, three laboratories at the Weizmann Institute, the Anglo-Palestine Bank in Jerusalem and the Hadassah Hospital on Mount Scopus. Ander and Son, a company from Olomouc with a chain of department stores, built another at the corner of avenue 28 Října and Sokolská Street. The great footwear manufacturer Baťa built a store on the corner of Masaryk Square, which still stands today and a year later, Pešat opened nearby. While it might not have matched the delights of Prague, Vienna or Paris for shopping, Ostrava was an excellent provincial substitute.

Civilised life in Ostrava as well as elsewhere in Central Europe required comfortable locations for ladies to take tea and cream cakes while exchanging the latest gossip, and the gentlemen needed somewhere congenial to read the newspapers, talk business and politics – and gossip – and play cards. So, in 1904, Josef Petzak, a 47-year-old native of Olomouc opened the Imperial Hotel on what is now Dr Beneš Square. The hotel, now called the Mamaison, still stands and provides 4-star accommodation to locals and visitors alike. In 1928, Ferdinand and Jakob Gronner bought the Hotel National on Vojanová, close to the Textilia store and the Dvořák Theatre. They built it into a complex with hotel accommodation, a café and bar, and opened it in 1930, renaming it the Palace. Together with the Europa café, it was a popular location for much of the Jewish community while the bar, the Boccaccio, was a fashionable place for Ostrava's bright young things to meet, drink and flirt.

1922 Advertisement for Mouson cosmetics.

All the socialising and flirting naturally required the application of perfume and cosmetics and these, too, were produced in Ostrava. In 1919, Heinrich Silbermann married Alice Brüllová, the sister of Dr Otto Brüll from Prague, and the two men collaborated in business with the financial backing of the Brüll family. The Mouson company in Berlin made luxury perfumes, soaps and creams and, in 1922, Heinrich and Otto became Mouson's exclusive sales representatives in Czechoslovakia. They also became the exclusive agents for Mühlens, producer of the famous 4711 Eau de Cologne.

4711 Eau de Cologne (Kölnischwasser).

Their joint venture was very successful and they decided to embark on production of their own, setting up in buildings on Church Street that backed onto the Ostravice river front. By 1936, the three-storey building was divided into separate departments, one per floor, for the production of soaps, shampoos, powders and eau de cologne, which they almost certainly produced from concentrate and then poured into their own bottles.[11]

In 1933, they started to produce their own cardboard and wax paper packaging material and at its height the company employed 150 people. Anti-Jewish feeling in German circles, however, meant that the company lost its production licences and was eventually closed down.

The Silbermanns escaped to Paris in 1939 but were arrested there and sent to Drancy and thence to extermination camps. Their son and daughter managed to escape to America as did Otto Brüll. After the war, the company was nationalised and integrated into the company *Milo Olomouc.*

Heinz Vogel's father was an insurance agent in Ostrava before the war and Heinz remembers that his father used to conduct much of his business in the coffee houses of the Palace and Imperial Hotels. These hotels and coffee houses were so well frequented that people, families, or groups had their 'own' tables at them so if, for example, you wished to speak to David Goldberg you could always find him at 'his' table at his favourite café in Masaryk Square.

Commercial and culinary needs having been adequately provided for, cultural pursuits become important. Cultural life reflected the ethnic composition of the population of the town and surrounding area. Each of the main ethnic or national groups – Czech, German and Polish, had its own

Polský dům, the Polish House.

cultural centre. The Deutsches Haus (p.158), opposite the Palace and Imperial Hotels, was built between 1892 and 1895, partly in response to the construction of the Czech National House, which had just begun. This German House was designed by Felix Neumann, a local Jewish architect, and the land for it was bought from Baron Rothschild. The construction budget was 150,000 Guilders and the resulting building, in the Dutch Renaissance style, attracted much interest. It was badly damaged by a bomb in 1945 and demolished after the war by order of the City Council, leaving a very drab open space.

The Polish House (*Polský dům*), an Art Nouveau delight from 1903, is sadly now derelict although there are, and have been for some considerable time, plans to restore it.

The Czech National House was built between 1892 and 1894 on Českých legií Street near the Cathedral of the Holy Saviour. It was designed by Josef Srba in the rather more restrained Neo-Renaissance style compared to either the Polish or German Houses. In 1906, it was taken over as the permanent Czech theatre in Ostrava but after 1920 the Czech Theatre transferred to the City Theatre, now the Dvořák Theatre, and the Czech House reverted to social activities. In 1954 the building was renamed the Jiří Myron Theatre and, after a fire in 1976, it was extensively reconstructed to designs by Ivo Klimeš and Radim Ulmann.

Czech National House.

After the First World War both the Czech and German theatre companies used the town theatre, but by 1921 disputes between the two reached such a pitch that they had to be settled in court. The resolution was that the Czech Theatre remained where it was and the German Theatre received a subsidy to build a stage and theatre in the Deutsches Haus.

The City Archive was begun in 1923 in the City Museum in the old Town Hall building on Masaryk Square (*Masarykovo náměstí*). The museum with its exhibits of Ostrava history is still there but the Archive has moved to the former Town Hall of Přívoz. Fine Arts were displayed in the City Art Gallery, or House of the Arts, founded in 1923, just off Nádražní Avenue behind the imposing new bank buildings; it was designed by the architects Fiala and Wallenfels, pupils of the founder of Czech modern art Jan Kotěra. Today it houses works by old masters such as Dürer, Cranach, Aachen and Hollar. The Viennese Art Nouveau is also represented here (Klimt) as well as important Russian artists (Repin, Shishkin), and Czech modern artists. Cultural life was of importance to the people who built the economic strength of Ostrava.

Ostrava was not just palatial administrative buildings, business blocks and coffee houses; there was also a major problem of basic housing for the population. The major construction companies and also the city itself continued to build residential housing but, even so, supply could never keep up with demand from working families. New building regulations and tax

Ostrava City Art Gallery, 1923.

relief, introduced in 1927, greatly helped and, as a result, 200 blocks with 1,500 apartments were built. Paradoxically, the general economic crisis in the early 1930s actually eased the housing problem as many property entrepreneurs went into domestic rather than industrial or commercial building, considering the former to be financially much less volatile and risky. Thus in 1931 in Ostrava 250 blocks were built with about 1,700 flats, in Zábřeh, Hrabová and Hrabůvka but also in the city centre on the bank of the Ostravice river.

Education

Basic education in Moravská Ostrava was available in both Czech and German language in primary and town secondary schools or in private schools, which included four Polish, two German, and one Jewish primary school and one Polish secondary school. Each of the municipalities that today form Greater Ostrava, had created their own network of primary schools. The Czech classical grammar school was designed for those who intended to go on to study law, philosophy, biology or medicine at university, probably in Prague or Vienna. At this time Ostrava did not have its own university. The Realschule catered for those who wished to become engineers or technicians and such provision was available in Moravská Ostrava and Přívoz. There were mining schools in Moravská Ostrava and also, later, in Mariánské Hory. In Vítkovice there was an apprentice school for iron workers. In Moravská Ostrava there was a Girls' Realschule and a State Grammar school while there was a Teachers' Training College and Realschule for girls in Slezská Ostrava, set up in 1920.

The 1930s brought periods of economic hardship and recovery, but more worryingly political agitation and violence from growing German nationalism in the Sudetenland, which bordered on Ostrava, generated increasing problems in the town. Jews and others began to move from the Sudetenland into Ostrava to avoid the increasingly unpleasant situation. In September 1938, the infamous Munich Agreement which signified anything but 'Peace in our Time' surrendered the Sudetenland to the German Reich and the Těšín area to Poland and brought a flood of refugees. At the same time, transport and economic links were severed and the period of Ostrava's glory came to an end. On 2 October, Moravská Ostrava became part of the short-lived Second Republic but on 14 March 1939 it was occupied by German troops.

The next day, the Germans occupied Prague.

NOTES

1. Myška, Milan, *Rytíři průmyslovárevoluce,,* Ostrava 1997.
2. Zářický, Aleš, *Ve stínu těžních věží,* Ostrava, 2004.

3. Gutmann, Wilhelm von: *Aus meinem Leben*, Gerold, 1911.
4. Zářický, Aleš, *Rothschildové a ti druzí. Dějiny velkopodnikání v Rakouském Slezsku před první světovou válkou*, Ostrava, 2005.
5. *Dějiny Ostravy*, Ostrava, 1993.
6. Przybylová, Blažena (ed.), *Ostrava. Historie, kultura, lidé*, Praha, 2013.
7. Ibid.
8. Ibid.
9. Ibid.
10. Ibid.
11. Ibid.

PART II

JEWISH LIFE

In the second half of the nineteenth century, Ostrava underwent an enormous change, from a small backward town to a major economic powerhouse. There was a large growth in population and almost everything about Ostrava changed. Its built environment, industrial sites and transport infrastructure; its economic and business activities and importance; its social, cultural, educational and welfare activities all grew and developed at a tremendous rate. By the early years of the twentieth century, Ostrava had become a thriving modern metropolis, and immigrants, especially Jews, played a quite disproportionate part in all of these changes, becoming important in all trades and professions as well as highly visible in the arts.

Palace Hotel.

4

The Association, the Cemetery and the Great *Broiges*[1]

Just as Ostrava appears relatively late in the historical record of Moravia, so the Jewish presence in Ostrava appears relatively late in the Ostrava records. Indeed, Jews were forbidden to live in Moravská Ostrava until the nineteenth century, and so the entire modern Jewish population was made up of immigrants or the children of immigrants. By the start of the Second World War, even the oldest established Jewish families in the town could trace their ancestry for only four generations in Ostrava.

Beginnings of the Community

The foundation of the official *Cultusgemeinde* – Religious Community – dates from as late as 1875 (Hugo Gold's[2] suggestion of 1877 is inaccurate) with a membership of only 58 heads of families, fifteen years after a *Cultusverein* or Religious Society had been established under the guidance of the Těšín community. When we refer to the official communal body, the *Cultusgemeinde,* we use the term Community, while the word without a capital refers to the Jewish population in general.

Superficially, the beginnings of the community and Community appear to be well documented. Hugo Gold's *History of Jewish Communities* published in the 1930s seems to provide us with clear and straightforward facts about Ostrava. Gold based his description on a manuscript history of the community entitled *History of the beginning of the Community of Mährisch Ostrau, put together on the occasion of the laying of the foundation stone of the Jewish synagogue on 20th May 1879, 27 days after the 25th Jubilee of the wedding of their Majesties, the all-highest Emperor and his wife,* and signed by 29 leading members of the community. It is now in the archive of the Jewish Museum in Prague.

It describes Mordechai Schönhof as the first Jew to settle in Moravská Ostrava in 1792. Initially we accepted this uncritically. Indeed, several Ostravaks who wrote their own recollections of life in Ostrava repeated it in their memoirs. As we researched further, particularly in the Ostrava City archive, we found that the story was rather more complicated and more interesting than that.

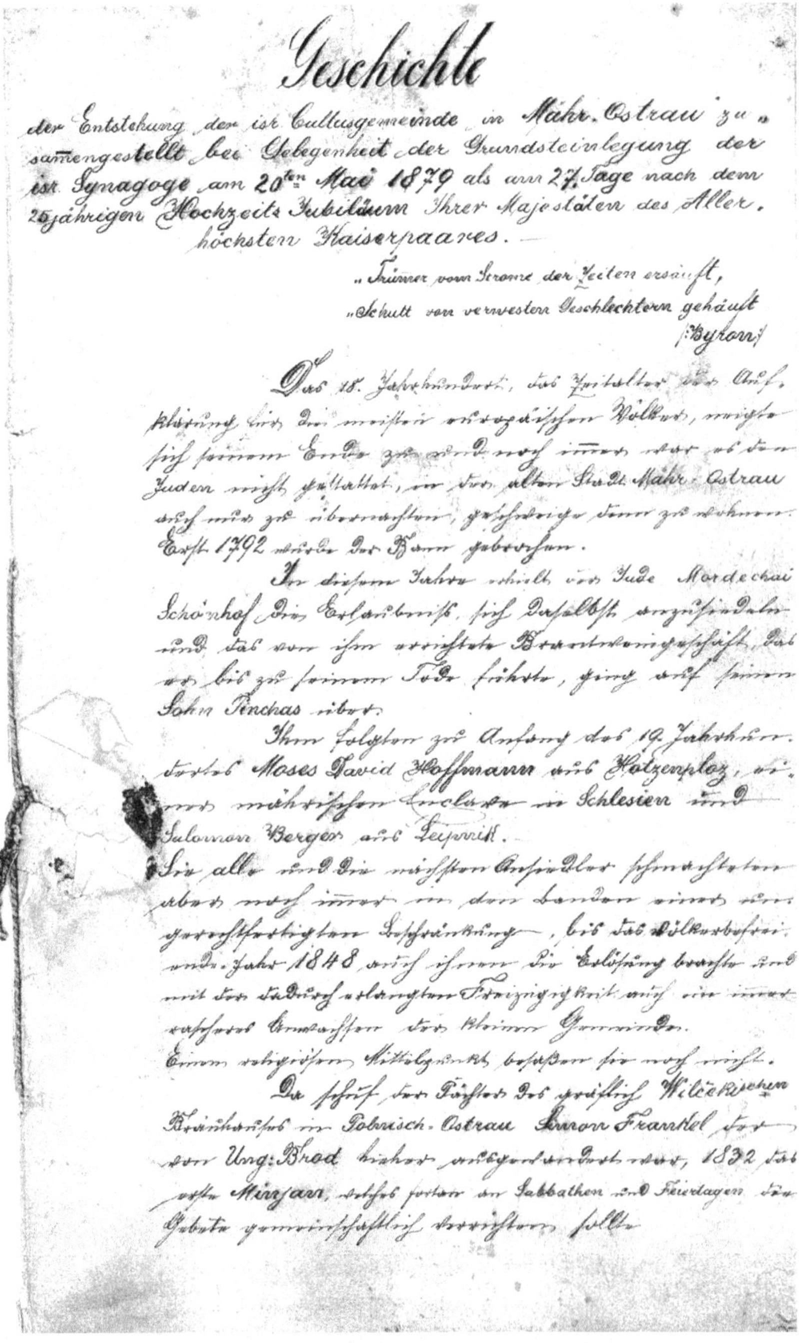

Geschichte

der Entstehung der isr. Cultusgemeinde in Mähr. Ostrau zusammengestellt bei Gelegenheit der Grundsteinlegung der isr. Synagoge am 20ten Mai 1879 als am 27. Tage nach dem 25jährigen Hochzeits Jubiläum Ihrer Majestäten des Allerhöchsten Kaiserpaares.

„Trümmer vom Strome der Zeiten ersäuft,
„Schutt von verwesten Geschlechtern gehäuft
(Byron)

Das 18. Jahrhundert, das Zeitalter der Aufklärung für die meisten europäischen Völker, neigte sich seinem Ende zu und noch immer war es den Juden nicht gestattet, in der alten Stadt Mähr.-Ostrau auch nur zu übernachten, geschweige denn zu wohnen. Erst 1792 wurde der Bann gebrochen.

Manuscript describing the foundation of the Ostrava Community.

Drapala[3] wrote that a Jew, Mohsel Level or Moses Levy, had been present in Moravská Ostrava during the Thirty Years' War, 1618-48. Apparently he was involved in minting coins in Těšín, some 30 kilometres from Ostrava. Drapala describes Levy as a crook, who adulterated the gold and silver in the coins or used short weight in them. Drapala was strongly anti-Semitic, which makes much of his 'history' very suspect, but he can be assumed to have had access to some original sources, now lost, and so Levy was most likely a historical figure even if Drapala's interpretation of him is tendentious.

It is not unknown for the authorities to debase their coinage, especially in times of war or other financial crises, and so Levy may have been acting under instructions from the Těšín authorities; or he may have been the innocent victim of others passing off impure metal, or he may, indeed, have been a crook. Whatever the case, we can be pretty certain that there was a Jew living in Ostrava at that time who was employed as a moneyer, which implies that at least one Jew was accepted by the Těšín authorities as a proper and decent member of society. Drapala records that on 14 June 1652 Levy wrote to Duchess Lukretia, defending his innocence and explaining that he received poor quality metal and it had cost him some of his own wealth to try to maintain standards. The fact that he felt able to write to the Duchess confirms that he had a well-established position in society and that he had a reasonable case to present and to proclaim his innocence.

Ostrava was one of the many towns in Bohemia and Moravia where Jews were forbidden to live or even to spend the night until well into the nineteenth century, although Jews had settled much earlier in Kroměříž and Osoblaha, towns also under the control of the Bishop of Olomouc. The situation started to change, however, in 1782, when the Emperor Josef II issued the first of a series of Edicts of Tolerance, intended to make Jews more useful to the State. This first Edict referred only to Vienna and Lower Austria. It gave freedom of religion to non-Catholics and allowed them to engage in trades, to move and to live more freely and to attend schools and universities. The preamble to the first edict reads:

> As it is our goal to make the Jewish nation useful and serviceable to the State, mainly through better education and enlightenment of its youth as well as by directing them to the sciences, the arts and the crafts, We hereby grant and order…

Subsequent edicts extended the scope to the rest of the Austro-Hungarian Empire and so Jews in and around Ostrava were officially allowed to practise trades, to travel and to settle in places previously barred to them.

The early Jewish immigrants were heavily involved in brewing, distilling and selling alcohol, as this was one trade that Jews had been allowed to carry out before the general emancipation of Jews in the nineteenth century. The involvement of Ostrava Jews with the alcohol trade continued even after emancipation. Why Jews should have been specifically allowed to brew, distil and sell alcohol is not clear. The romantic explanation is that Jews were much more sober than their non-Jewish neighbours and would not drink all the profits, but that seems sociologically improbable and a most unlikely explanation. The intellectual explanation is that Jews were better educated than their neighbours and would therefore understand and control the technical processes better. Yet there is no lack of evidence of non-Jews elsewhere engaged in brewing and distilling and that explanation seems unlikely too. The financial explanation seems the most convincing: Jews, being under the protection of the King or local Lord could probably be relied on to a greater extent than non-Jews to pay all the appropriate taxes for the rights to the alcohol monopoly. Dynner, in his study of Jews and alcohol in Poland,[4] suggests that it was financial reliability and the reputation if not the fact of sobriety that were important.

The first relevant written record relating to Jews and Ostrava is in the archive of the Archbishopric of Olomouc. It dates to 1689, and refers to the cancellation by the city council of Moravská Ostrava of a three-year lease for the distillation and sale of brandy taken out by a Jew, Israel Markus from Lipník. In the mid-eighteenth century a Jewess, Anna, had the lease of an inn in Moravská Ostrava with the monopoly from the town authorities of selling alcohol in the town. Spirits were produced in the town distillery, wine was imported through the Archbishopric of Olomouc, the suzerain of the town, and beer was brewed by individual burghers, members of the Town Brewers' Guild. After the death of her husband, Anna married Markus Mannenberg from Polská Ostrava, who took over the lease of the inn in 1783. He spelt his name randomly as Mannenberg, Manneberger or Meinberg. The inn had been operating at a loss under Christian management presumably before Anna took over and this is probably why the authorities permitted a Jew to take the lease. In fact, the worthy burghers of Ostrava criticised Manenberg and the way he ran the tavern, ostensibly because he allowed drinking during holy days and church services. They also objected to Jews in general being allowed in the town on the grounds that they would interfere with and harm businesses run by Christians.[5] Being the landlord and landlady of an inn would suggest that the Mannenbergs lived at the inn in Moravská Ostrava despite the ban on Jews living in the town, although they may have spent their nights in Polská Ostrava where there was no ban.

On 4 July 1786 the lease was transferred to another Jew, Abraham Hošek, for the remarkable sum of 1,290 Gulden[6] (abbreviated as Fl.) per year, but it was later back in the hands of the Mannenbergs. Abraham signed the lease in Hebrew rather than German script which suggests that he could not write German although he could quite possibly read it. Obviously the town authorities were quite prepared to do business with such a person, and he

Abraham Hoschek signature in Hebrew on the lease of 1786: Abraham b'(son of) H' (Mr) Oshik.

appears to have been integrated into the commercial if not social life of the town.

In 1801, the Mannenbergs agreed on a compensation payment from Vincenc Kramer for his sale of illicit Rosolio, a sweet liqueur made with rose water, not purchased from themselves as the monopoly town source. Alcohol meant money and was seriously protected. Mannenberg signed a 3-year lease with the council, expiring on 16January 1803, for the brewery/distillery. The rent was 707Fl in the first year rising to 907Fl in the second and third years. By 1803, the Mannenbergs have disappeared from the Ostrava story and the lease of the liquor monopoly was taken over by Markus (Mordechai) Schönhof in December of that year. The original manuscript of the history of the Community has it that:

> ...it was still not permitted for Jews to spend the night in the old town of Mährisch Ostrau, so even more difficult to live there. Only in 1792 was the ban lifted. In that year the Jew Mordechai Schoenhof obtained permission to settle and run a spirits business which he established and carried on until his death; it was continued by his son Pinchas.

Whether Mordechai really did move into Ostrava in 1792 with a lease for a distillery or whether this is a slight misunderstanding and refers to the lease which he took over in 1803, he has the accolade of being accepted as the first Jew officially to settle in Ostrava. We will not try to deprive him of the honour, even if it might not be merited. History is not necessarily fair.

Mordechai Schönhof moved into Ostrava from Brušperk in the district of Frýdek-Místek although he was a member of the Lipník community. He was about 50 years old at the time and came with his wife Terezia née Herz, aged 43, and their five children: Josef, born c. 1782; Marianna born c. 1787; Pinkus (Pinchas), c. 1789, Magdalena, c. 1796, and Anna c. 1802. They were certainly among the first Jews to be born in the town. The Schönhof family lived in house number 82, near the Vítkovice gate in the city walls.

Early in the nineteenth century Marianna Schönhof married Josef Žurovec, a member of a prominent Moravian-Silesian family, after her necessary conversion to Catholicism. The Žurovec family held important positions on the Ostrava council and this marriage gave the Schönhofs both social standing and better commercial prospects. The wedding would not have taken place had the Žurovec family not recognised that the Schönhof family had appropriate status and wealth. Intermarriage with Jews was rare, especially for high-ranking Catholic families.

In June 1827, Pinkus Schönhof took over the lease on the death of his father. His sister, Magdalena, married Jachym Mendel, a tavern-keeper in Slezská Ostrava, and through him established firmer connections with the Jews of Těšín and Slovakia. Without suggesting in any way that these marriages were anything other than love matches, it is obvious that the Schönhof family had an eye for opportunities to improve their family fortunes.

An intriguing piece of evidence might suggest that the fame of the Ostrava Jewish community may have reached Palestine by 1814. There is a reference to one Hayyim Baruch of Ostrava being appointed an emissary of Hebron, Palestine, to solicit funds in that year and he apparently succeeded in setting up a network that provided significant sums to the poor of Hebron[7]. Yet given that the Ostrava community was still small and almost certainly not well-known, it is doubtful if Hayyim Baruch did come from Ostrava. In fact, the reference in *Sefer Hevron* is to 'Maistro Rav Chaim Baruch' where Maistro is spelt מ׳איסתרו in Hebrew. It is either an honorific, possibly a surname or job title or, if 'ma' means 'from' in this context, it suggests Hayyim Baruch came from Istro (Istria?). The name was mis-read as Ma'Ostrau (i.e. from Ostrau, the German or Yiddish version of Ostrava). He is described as one of the *chachamim* (scholars) of Zefat (Safad) and the community scribe. In 1800 he travelled to Italy as an emissary of Zefat. This suggests that he was both learned in Jewish Law and probably spoke Italian, both of which make it less likely that he came from Ostrava. There is no extant record of his presence in Ostrava.

Jews seem to have been allowed to settle and establish businesses in Polská Ostrava significantly earlier than in Moravská Ostrava. The settlement of Jews in Polská Ostrava appears to date from early in the sixteenth century when the local Lord, Jan Sedlnický of Choltice, allowed Jews to settle in the area known as Zámostí – 'across the bridge' in 1508 although the town council voted to expel them in 1531. This decision was not fully implemented and some Jews remained there. Jews from Polská Ostrava but mainly from Osoblaha traded with and travelled to Moravská Ostrava as shown in records of bridge tolls across the River Ostravice dating from 1593. Apparently there are documents from 1726 which mention Jews but the source does not indicate whether these are documents from Ostrava or Osoblaha. A document of 1748 reports that there were no Jewish houses in Polská Ostrava although this does not necessarily mean that there were no Jews living or working there.

It was Jan Sedlnický who converted the castle in Polská Ostrava from a fortified place to a much more comfortable renaissance chateau. In 1714 the Sedlnický family sold their estates (including the chateau) to the Habsburg general Jindřich Vilém Vlček of Dobrá Zemice. The family name Vlček was later Germanised, becoming Wilczek. The Silesian Ostrava estates remained in the hands of the Wilczek dynasty until 1945.

In 1832 a Šimon Frankel from Uherský Brod took over Count Wilczek's brewery and the hostelry called 'Harenda' (house) No.38, later No.90 in Polská Ostrava. The inn survived there until the Second World War when all the local buildings disappeared as a consequence of mining activities. Frankel was obviously quite an observant Jew since in1832 he set up a room over the brewery to serve as a prayer hall or *shtiebl* for the community. This location must have made the *minyan,* the minimum of 10 men needed for communal prayer, more lively than is usually the case.

Malka Meir, living in Nahariya, Israel, remembered stories that she heard from her Grandfather:

> ...The first families didn't have a synagogue. In the inn of Frankel they made an *Aron* [An Ark, or cupboard to store the Scrolls of the Law] with Sefer Torah. During the Holidays all the Jews from the area, from the villages came to the inn. They came with wagons and horses, the court was covered with a ceiling and there where the wagons were standing. That was the beginning of the Jewish community.

Gold reports in his book that, 'at the beginning of the next (i.e. nineteenth) century' Salomon Berger moved into Ostrava from Lipník, Šimon Frankel from Uherský Brod and Moses David Hoffman from Osoblaha'. According to the list of town inhabitants from 1848 only one Jew – Moses David Hoffman – lived in Moravská Ostrava and it is possible that the other families we know of were among the seven Jews living in Polská Ostrava from a total of 623 inhabitants in 1843 or the 15 Jews in Zámostí from the total of 373 souls.

In 1834, Max Glasinger, who originally came from Žukov, moved into Moravská Ostrava and in January 1835 acquired house number 34 and applied, together with Pinkus Schönhof, for a licence to sell liquor and to make necessary alterations to the building. The licence seems to have been refused after pressure from the burghers with brewing rights, although Glasinger seems to have sold liquor anyway. Subsequent documents suggest that he ran into financial difficulty and requested time to repay his debts. In 1836, he employed a lawyer to prepare a document officially seeking permission to leave the town but to return at a later date, presumably when he had raised some more money, and referring to precedents of people who have previously done so. Some of the documents are countersigned by Šimon Frankel, and Pinkus Schönhof supported at least some of his appeals.

The town council appeared willing to accede to his request but once again the burghers objected and he and his family were forced to leave the town.

The well-established inhabitants, mainly Catholic and Czech speakers, argued that newcomers might take jobs and trade, but they almost certainly had a deep-rooted antipathy to newcomers, especially Jews. Their objection was officially based on the established right in the town to prevent Jews from living there, except for one who had the alcohol monopoly. Some time after 1844, both Glasinger and Pinkus Schönhof were expelled from Ostrava. The resistance of the Catholic burghers to immigrants and Jews had, for the moment, triumphed. In 1834, an edict from the Emperor banned Jews from acquiring Christian properties but this restriction was removed after 1848. Nevertheless, when houses from the estate of F. Juttner were offered for sale and Jews expressed interest in buying them, the town council objected and the sale was blocked. Only one old Jew, Moses Hoffman from Osoblaha, was living in the town at that time. In 1852, a Mr Alt tried to settle in Moravská Ostrava but was forced to leave after only 8 days.[8]

Moravská Ostrava thus maintained its reactionary Catholic attitude well into the nineteenth century, unlike Polská Ostrava which seems to have been more tolerant, perhaps because of the greater number of Jews over a greater number of years in Polish territory.

In 1831, Rachel Tausk, a Jewish maid from the village of Lúky in Upper Hungary, now Slovakia, came to Ostrava to work and decided to convert to Catholicism. The town authorities required a report from her local priest, Leopold Rada. She was questioned in the presence of two Jewish witnesses before her papers were passed to the regional authority and she was baptised in December 1831 at the Church of St Wenceslas in Ostrava. The presence of the Jewish witnesses implies some delicacy and concern on the part of the Catholic authorities for Jewish sensitivities and possible reaction.

In 1839 Pinkus Schönhof submitted plans with detailed estimates of costs to the town to build a new brewery and distillery, at a total cost of 11674.48Fl. The cost breakdown was:

Material	4656 Fl
Professional Services	5037 Fl
Labour	1987 Fl.

The building would belong to the town, so the town would have to bear the costs. It does not appear as if the proposal was accepted.

In 1841 he obtained the very lucrative contract, presumably through his family connections, to supply beer and spirits to the workers building the railway, the *Kaiser Ferdinands-Nordbahn*, financed by Salomon Mayer Rothschild. This would no doubt have aroused the envy of the other suppliers in the town.

There is evidence of a leather trade in the Ostrava area in December 1853 run by three Jews from Hranice, while in 1854 the town authorities recommended excluding Jews from trading in grain as 'they are known usurers' and in 1855 they even tried to prevent Salomon Mayer Rothschild from building the Karolina coking plant. That dispute was settled by the intervention of the Emperor, Franz Josef I! In that year, Gerson Katz is recorded as having an alcohol licence in the town. In 1856, Wilhelm Gutmann arrived in Ostrava, retained as supplier of coal to the *Kaiser Ferdinands-Nordbahn.* The Gutmann Brothers and the Rothschilds would play a major role in the development of Ostrava.

Members of the Brewers Guild might have complained about the Jewish innkeepers, but the innkeepers also complained about the quality of beer from the town brewery, which, according to them, had gone off in 2 to 3 days. The complaint was treated seriously and inspections carried out both in the inns and in the brewery. The Inspectors reached no firm conclusions but suggested that the problem might be caused by inadequate water purity, the brewers' activities, or watering of the beer by some innkeepers. Watering the workers' beer has a very long history! The report after the inspections recommended that the bars be equipped with smaller barrels to speed up the beer circulation, and that there should be more frequent quality control checks at the brewery. It does not appear that blame was placed solely at the door of the Jews.[9]

Despite the resistance to Jews settling and trading in Ostrava on the part of some of the citizens, in 1855 there are records of 14 Jewish families living in the town. They included the families of Abraham Berger, Salomon Berger, Josef Noé, who is recorded in 1851 as the owner of a horse-drawn cab, Gerson Katz, Jachym Kafka who had taken on the lease of the inn *By the Green Tree* for the large sum of 2601fl/year in 1861, Salomon Spitzkopf, Markus Strassmann, Ezechiel Kulka, Leopold Spitzer, Emanuel Neumann, Leopold Mannenberg, Ignac Schmelz and probably Moses Hoffman and Jakub Tauber, some 50 persons in all.

Moravská Ostrava would change dramatically in only a few years, as mass immigration and tremendous economic development altered the whole nature of the town. The picture of Ostrava in the late eighteenth and early nineteenth centuries that emerges is nonetheless a little surprising. The Jewish presence in Ostrava, although small, seems not to have been poor or totally isolated and ignored by the rest of the citizens. Insofar as there was anti-Jewish agitation, at least some of it was purely economic – a matter of attempting to prevent or reduce competition in the production and sale of alcohol. There was clearly significant commercial contact and some social contact, not to mention inter-marriage, between at least some of the Jews and the rest of the population; and the authorities were aware of Jewish sensibilities in the matter of conversion and ensured that Jewish witnesses were present for the proceedings. There appears to have been a pragmatic 'live and let live' attitude and both Jews and non-Jews seem to have got on with their lives without too much trouble. The fact that many of this first wave of Jewish immigration were relatively wealthy will have helped this spirit of tolerance.

The Shtiebl

Meanwhile, the Jewish population of Polská Ostrava continued to increase and, by 1857, the room in Frankl's brewery/distillery was too small to act as the *shtiebl*, so he took a room in a tavern *Na Závadě* in Polská Ostrava for that purpose. It was located on the left side of Těšínská Street, further up the hill behind the church, now approximately in front of the stairs leading to the new part of the cemetery in Slezská Ostrava and the crematorium. The first floor of the building dates from the middle of the nineteenth century and served as a more roomy prayer hall for the Jews when the older one in the brewery was no longer satisfactory. The last congregation gathered there in 1860 before they moved to the house in Zámostí ('Beyond the Bridge') in the vicinity of the inn *Na schůdkách* ('On the Stairs'). *Na Závadě* was later converted into an apartment house.

Frankel, as well as being a brewer and distiller, and being the dominant character among the Jews of Polská Ostrava acted as the local *mohel*, the man who circumcises Jewish boys when they are eight days old. In May 1856, he is recorded as performing this service in Příbor for the young Sigmund Freud.[10] Confusingly, the name of the *mohel* is given as Samson Frankel, the German version of the Hebrew, *Shimshon*. Frankl would be known in Czech as Šimon with Š being pronounced 'Sh'. The identity of Shimshon and Šimon can be confirmed by the list of Jews in Slezská Ostrava produced by Raab,[11] which includes only one Šimon Frankl who is described as an inn-keeper and *Bestandmann*, one who was permitted to live permanently in Slezská Ostrava but who did not have burgher rights.

Frankel was described as self-opinionated, arrogant and domineering. What effect being circumcised by such a person had on the future development of Sigmund can only be imagined.

The revolutionary years of 1848-9 brought more effective emancipation of Jews throughout the Austro-Hungarian Empire, despite a short period of reactionary laws. After the war with Italy in 1859 Austria was nearly bankrupt and close to an economic crisis. The Ministry of Finance therefore approached Anselm Rothschild for help, but he was reluctant to lend money to the Austrian state when it still limited Jewish rights in many ways. The Emperor Franz Josef I offered his imperial word as a guarantee for the loan but Rothschild requested some even more secure guarantee. In response the Imperial Council (parliament) was recalled and, after the October Edict was published, a more formal constitutional life began in Austria. The Imperial Edict of 10 January 1860 allowed Jews to engage in all trades and to live wherever they thought appropriate. Thus they finally obtained full political and religious freedom and the Rothschild Bank provided the necessary support to the state.

The social climate and environment in Moravská Ostrava became more open and tolerant to Jewish immigrants, possibly because the commercial benefits were already apparent. This was encouraged by Hermann Zwierzina, an industrial entrepreneur and mayor from1861to 1864. His successor from 1864 to1873, Alois Anderka, who was employed from 1848 in the Bielsko shipping firm Schönewald & Frankl as an accountant for the firm's branch at the Moravská Ostrava railway station, was the chairman of the Society of Moravská Ostrava burghers with brewing rights, who were the main opponents of Jewish immigration. Nevertheless, Jewish immigration was increasingly tolerated during his period of office.

From the beginning of the 1860s Jews started coming from the Těšín Region, for example the innkeeper Šimon Berkowitz from Bielsko in 1862 , and, in the same year Natan Spitzer from Grodziec near Skoczów, a producer of 'rosolio' and liqueurs, who founded a branch of his firm in Moravská Ostrava. Bernard Burstein, originally from Hranice, gained a licence to trade in salt on 26 November 1860, and on 3 November 1866, for a grocery as well. Jews are recorded in other trades: cabinet making and manufacture of ready-made clothes for example.

At the same time, a Jewish presence was developing in the surrounding villages, mainly on the basis of hospitality establishments. Abraham Berger, in 1859 became an innkeeper in Přívoz and, in 1862 Filip Forster became a wine vendor and from 1866 ran a Jewish dining room in house no 76, which he had purchased. From 1867 he was the holder of an innkeeper's licence for the same property. The Forster family as innkeepers in Nová Ves was followed in1864 by an innkeeper Bernard Aufricht. In November 1866, Josef Sonnenschein, the tenant of an inn in Svinov, gained a licence for an inn in Nová Ves, house no 31. Economic activity was picking up and the dominance of Jews in the alcohol trade is very clear.

In 1860 the Jews in Polská Ostrava set up the 'Jewish Religious Association for Moravian and Polish Ostrava' and its first chairman was Šimon Frankl (the spelling appears to vary randomly between Frankl and Frankel).

In 1863 the first Jewish school was founded in Polská Ostrava although it was later moved to Moravská Ostrava. Initially it had two classes and was quite unofficial.

Most parents wanted a German education for their children as well as instruction in Hebrew and Judaism and so, in 1871, government permission was sought for a two class elementary school and was granted on 24 November of that year. The school opened with 49 children and two

Jewish School, Class 1, 1898.

Jewish School in Kostelni Street.

teachers. From 1873 it was located in Přívozská Street and was moved to Kostelní Street in 1880.

The school grew quite rapidly. By 1873, there were 3 classes and in 1878 the school added a fourth class with the introduction of technical studies (*Industrialunterricht*) and a kindergarten. In 1881, the school was installed in a specially built house, belonging to Dr Joseph Wechsberg, Vice-President of the Community, in Kostelní Street and had 160 students. The kindergarten had 50-70 children. In 1875, it became the responsibility of the newly-established Community, which then supported it financially.[12]

Cholera and the Cemetery

At this time there was no purpose-built synagogue in Ostrava. Discussions had taken place but no decision could be reached on whether it should be in Slezská or Moravská Ostrava. Most of the communal activities were on the Silesian side of the river, although more of the Jewish population were on the Moravian side, and so nothing was done.

Equally, there was no Jewish cemetery in Ostrava. Bodies had to be transported to Těšín for burial in consecrated ground. Then, in 1872, an epidemic of cholera broke out and claimed the life of Fanny Reicher. The town doctor, Dr Kroczek, reasonably refused to allow the body to be moved, lest it spread the disease, and so poor Mrs Reicher was buried in the local Protestant cemetery. Matters became more serious when, two days later, Bertha Reisz, the daughter of Pinchas Schönhof, died and it was clear that something had to be done. Markus Strassmann, who had taken over the lease of the town's brewery in Moravská Ostrava in 1857, and a timber merchant, Joachim Kafka, took the initiative and bought two parcels of land on Ärarialstrasse, the main road from Moravská Ostrava to Opava. The authorities approved the use of the land as a cemetery and, on 7 December 1872, Mrs Reisz was duly laid to rest in consecrated ground in Ostrava.

The Protestant cemetery, with the body of the unfortunate Mrs Reicher, no longer exists. It was cleared and a Catholic church built on the site.

Shortly after the burial of Bertha Reisz, a meeting of the Jewish Community was arranged at which it was reported that the purchase price of the land was 4000Fl (about £350 at the then exchange rate, equivalent to £26,500 in 2012 using the retail price index). Enough money was raised in 8 days to cover the purchase price of the land, fence it and build a small house for the guardian.

The Great *Broiges*

Having solved the problem of burials, the cemetery then became the catalyst for a classic Jewish unholy row – a *broiges* – involving strong and self-

Cemetery. The Hall is on the right and the stable for the hearse and horse on the left.

opinionated men making mountains of principle out of molehills of no consequence. The cemetery was on the Moravian side of the Ostravice River, whereas Šimon Frankel, the *shtiebl*, and the 'Jewish Religious Association for Moravian and Polish Ostrava' were all on the Silesian side. More to the point, Frankel, an assertive and opinionated character, wanted everything to do with the community to be on the North side of the river while Strassmann and his colleagues not only wanted things to be on the Moravian side, but had also pre-empted the matter by setting up the cemetery in Moravská Ostrava. Frankel refused to allow any funds from the Association to be used for the cemetery, thus exacerbating the row.

The dispute led Berthold Schwartz, a jeweller, and Abraham Berger to propose setting up a separate Jewish Community in Moravská Ostrava. This was agreed, a Charter was prepared which was approved by the authorities on 9 February 1875 and, on 17 March 1875 the Community elected its first Board:

Markus Strassmann (Brewer) – President
Šimon Frankel (Brewer)
Gustav Lichtenstern (Manufacturer)
Dr Joseph Wechsberg (Medical Practitioner) – Deputy President
Franz Gross (Miller)
Philip Förster (Restaurateur)
Hermann Friedländer (Businessman)
Leopold Spitzer (Businessman)

Of course, Frankel refused the position, and so Berthold Schwartz was co-opted in his place. The 'Jewish Religious Association for Moravian and Polish Ostrava' was then dissolved and its property and inventory were taken over by the new *Cultusgemeinde.* The matter was thus resolved to everyone's satisfaction with the exception of Šimon Frankel.

This Jewish political in-fighting took place against a backdrop of tremendous economic activity in Ostrava. In 1828, Rudolf, the Cardinal Archbishop of Olomouc, had built the Rudolf Ironworks in Vítkovice and in 1843, Baron Salomon Mayer von Rothschild, the head of the Viennese family, bought it having previously rented it from the Archbishopric in 1835. Salomon received the permission and approval of the Emperor to set up the *Kaiser Ferdinands-Nordbahn*, the railway that joined Vienna to the Karviná coalfields in 1847 and ultimately to Kraków and Lwów. It probably helped Salomon that he and Chancellor Metternich were sufficiently close friends for Salomon's children to call Metternich 'Uncle Clemens'! In 1873, Anselm Rothschild, Salomon's son, joined forces with the Gutmann Brothers' coal mining concern to set up the Vítkovice Mining and Iron Corporation. This sealed Ostrava's position as one of the leading areas in the industrial revolution in the Austrian Empire.

Despite the resistance of the citizens of Ostrava to small Jewish businessmen coming into the town, the Rothschilds appeared to have had no problems. Presumably being very wealthy and very close to the Emperor and the government worked wonders then, as now.

The development of Ostrava into the economic powerhouse of the Austro-Hungarian Empire and the golden age of its Jewish community in the early decades of the twentieth century were thus based on the enterprise and commercialism of both the Catholic archbishop and a group of Jewish businessmen whose wealth came from coal, brewing and distilling. There is thus a strong stream of alcohol heavily laced with coal-dust that runs through the story of Ostrava Jewry and a clear demonstration that tolerance and co-operation between people of different religions is much facilitated by and produces commercial advantage.

NOTES

1. Yiddish. Pronounced 'broy-guess'. An argument, a falling-out.
2. *Geschichte der Juden in Mährisch Ostrau.* Gold, Hugo. Brünn: Jüdischer Buch- und Kunstverlag, 1929; *Geschichte der Juden in Mährisch Ostrau.*Gold, Hugo. Olamenu, Israel. 1974.
3. *Juden in Ostrau* Richard Drapala, publ. Schönbrunn 1939; *Geschichte der Stadt Mährisch Ostrau*, Richard Drapala, publ Johann Hoppe, 1933.
4. Dynner, Glenn. *Yankel´s Tavern: Jews, Liquor and Life in the Kingdom of Poland.* Oxford: OUP, 2014.
5. *Kořaleční, vetešník, lichvář–bezectní lidé?* Hana Šústková in Člověk v gaú Ostravě v XIX. století.Ostrava: University of Ostrava, 2007.

6. The modern value of payments is difficult to estimate with any precision, compounded by the different currencies used in and around Ostrava over the period in question. In Appendix 4.1 we quote typical costs and wages for the period.
7. http://www.geschichteinchronologie.ch/judentum-aktenlage/il-ps/EncJud_Hebron-ENGL.html quoting O. Avisar (ed.), *Sefer Hevron*, (1970), 89 131, 219).
8. Archiv města Ostravy (City Archive of Ostrava) *Dějiny židovstva ostravského*. Isidor Zehngut. Ostrava 1952, manuscript.
9. *Výčep piva a hostinská živnostna Ostravsku v proměnách 19. století*. Radoslav Daněk in Ostrava 25, Šenov u Ostravy: Tilia, 2011.
10. *Freud. Sein Leben in Bildern und Texten*.Herausgegeben von Ernst Freud, Lucie Freud und Ilse Grubrich-Simitis. Suhrkamp Verlag Frankfurt 1976, pp.46, 324.
11. *Die einstige Macht des Juden in Mähr. Ostrau* Karl Raab. Zeitschrift für Geschichte und Landeskunde Mährens, copy in Ostrava City Archive.
12. *Chronik der Volksschule der israelit. Cultusgemeinde in Mähr. Ostrau*. Hana Adar. Bound MS in the Ostrava archive of the Jewish Museum in Prague.

5

Synagogues, Cossacks and a Holiday Home

The Community having now been established, the Board turned its attention to the creation of a synagogue. In 1876 a building plot in Pittlergasse in the centre of Moravská Ostrava close to the main square was acquired for Fl 4,000 from the heirs of Hermann Zwierzina, and F.G. Böhm was appointed the main contractor. The foundation stone was laid on Tuesday 20 May 1879 and, remarkably, the building was opened, ready for use, on 15 September 1879, 27th Elul in the Hebrew calendar, just 3 days before the Jewish New Year, with seats for 336 men and 252 women. It was subsequently extended to allow some 700 male and a similar number of female worshippers.

Those who are familiar with twenty-first century British building practice will believe this 5-month timescale to be clearly mythological and to be interpreted in the same way as the creation of the world in six days. It is worth remembering, however, that the Provisional National Theatre in

Czech National Theatre, Prague.

Prague was completed in 6 months in 1862, and that was even larger and grander. The initial plan of construction of the theatre was presented during the session of the Regional Committee on the 21 April 1861. A binding decision about its actual construction was taken at the beginning of 1862 and the audience saw the first performance on 18 November of the same year. Nineteenth-century Czech builders operated to a different beat than builders today.

The official opening of the synagogue was carried out by the Royal and Imperial Representative, Herr Franz Richter, and the whole celebration was extensively reported in the newspapers on 18 September, 1879:

> The celebration which opened this festival week was an event of both a solemn and uplifting nature. This occasion demonstrated that it was not a celebration of purely religious character as one might have assumed, for it had a much higher significance as it embraced all inhabitants of our home town, regardless of religious affiliation or nationality. It proved that the people of Mährisch Ostrau have written tolerance on their banner and that any differences of faith have been dropped among the more intelligent elements of our fellow-citizens and that the barriers which had been erected due to mediaeval fanaticism and blind religious zeal between the various faiths have fallen. That was also the subject of the main sermon by Rabbi Dr A. Jellinek from Vienna, which stressed and emphasised this symbol of peace and pure brotherly love
>
> The celebrations started with the assembly and festive procession. Shortly after one o'clock a crowd of many hundreds collected outside the house of the Israelite Community Leader, Herr M. Strassmann, in the Bräuhausgasse. At the head of the procession the mayor, Herr E.U. Grünwald, with members of the town council; the Mährisch Ostrau k. k. District Judge, Herr Carl Simonis, together with k. k. Court Assistant Herr Josef Boubela, many others in gala-uniform, the veterans' society with banner, the voluntary firemen, groups of the male voice choir with their banner and the Israelite school students with banner and a large number of local and other people taking part in the festivities.
>
> At two o'clock, to the sound of the miners' band, the procession got under way through the Rathausgasse (Town Hall Street), the Ringplatz (Market Place), Brückengasse (Bridge Street), arriving slowly in front of the synagogue building in Pittlergasse. Here, with a short address, Herr M. Strassmann handed the keys of the building to Herr Richter, to formally open the synagogue. This was followed with the lighting of the 'everlasting light' while the Rabbi of Troppau (Opava), Herr Dr Blüh gave the blessing. Then, following the Cantor

singing the introductory and vesper prayers, the male voice choir sang Beethoven's 'To the Honour of God', following which Herr Dr A Jellinek, first minister of the Vienna Israelite community, gave the main sermon. There followed more prayers ending with the national anthem, with which the formal part of the celebrations came to an end.

Mähr.-schlesischer
Grenzbote.

76. Mähr.-Ostrau, Donnerstag am 18. September 1879. III. J

Occupation Novi-Bazar's

Zur Tagesgeschichte.

Correspondenzen.

Feuilleton.

Grenzbote, 18 September 1879: Opening of the Main Synagogue.

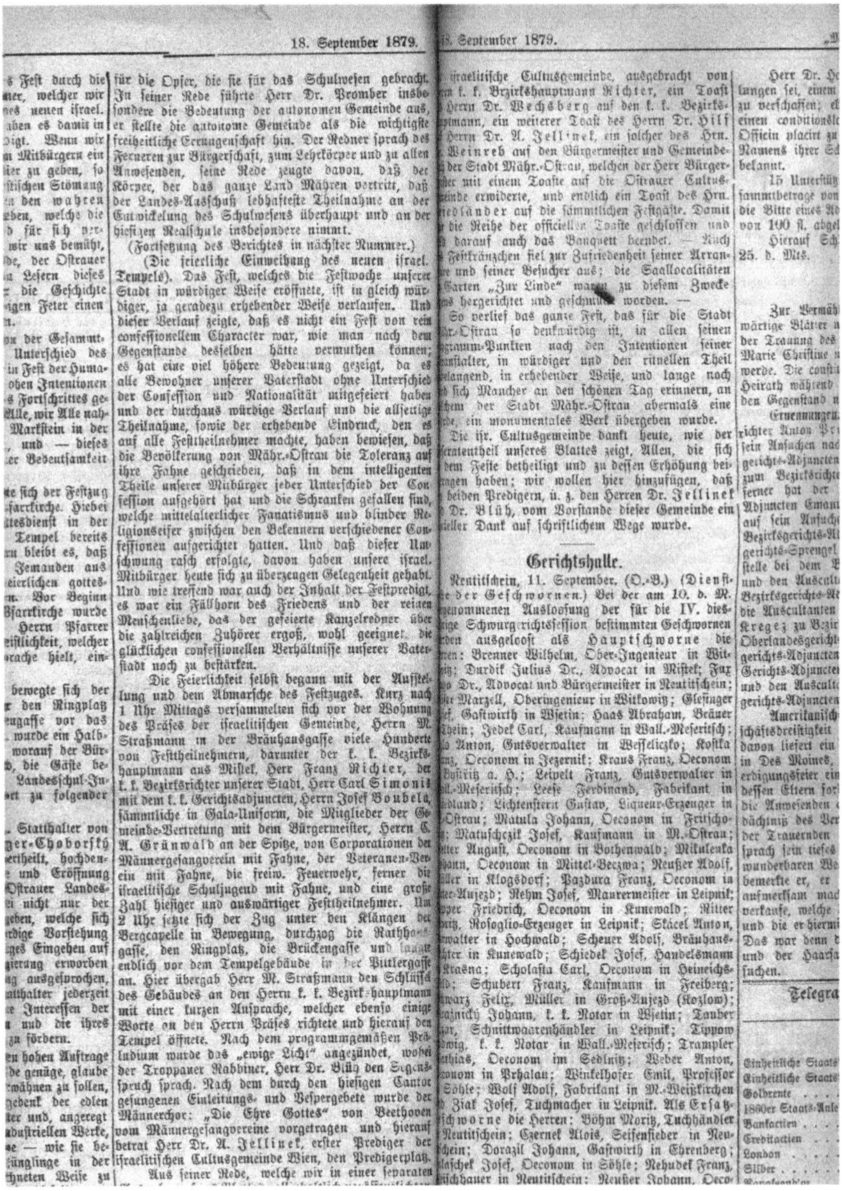

18. September 1879.

für die Opfer, die sie für das Schulwesen gebracht. In seiner Rede führte Herr Dr. Promber insbesondere die Bedeutung der autonomen Gemeinde aus, er stellte die autonome Gemeinde als die wichtigste freiheitliche Errungenschaft hin. Der Redner sprach des Ferneren zur Bürgerschaft, zum Lehrkörper und zu allen Anwesenden, seine Rede zeugte davon, daß der Körper, der das ganze Land Mähren vertritt, daß der Landes-Ausschuß lebhafteste Theilnahme an der Entwickelung des Schulwesens überhaupt und an der hiesigen Realschule insbesondere nimmt.

(Fortsetzung des Berichtes in nächster Nummer.)

(Die feierliche Einweihung des neuen israel. Tempels). Das Fest, welches die Festwoche unserer Stadt in würdiger Weise eröffnete, ist in gleich würdiger, ja geradezu erhebender Weise verlaufen. Und dieser Verlauf zeigte, daß es nicht ein Fest von rein confessionellem Character war, wie man nach dem Gegenstande desselben hätte vermuthen können; es hat eine viel höhere Bedeutung gezeigt, da es alle Bewohner unserer Vaterstadt ohne Unterschied der Confession und Nationalität mitgefeiert haben und der durchaus würdige Verlauf und die allseitige Theilnahme, sowie der erhebende Eindruck, den es auf alle Festtheilnehmer machte, haben bewiesen, daß die Bevölkerung von Mähr.-Ostrau die Toleranz auf ihre Fahne geschrieben, daß in dem intelligenten Theile unserer Mitbürger jeder Unterschied der Confession aufgehört hat und die Schranken gefallen sind, welche mittelalterlicher Fanatismus und blinder Religionseifer zwischen den Bekennern verschiedener Confessionen aufgerichtet hatten. Und daß dieser Umschwung rasch erfolgte, davon haben unsere israel. Mitbürger heute sich zu überzeugen Gelegenheit gehabt. Und wie treffend war auch der Inhalt der Festpredigt, es war ein Füllhorn des Friedens und der reinen Menschenliebe, das der gefeierte Kanzelredner über die zahlreichen Zuhörer ergoß, wohl geeignet, die glücklichen confessionellen Verhältnisse unserer Vaterstadt noch zu bestärken.

Die Feierlichkeit selbst begann mit der Aufstellung und dem Abmarsche des Festzuges. Kurz nach 1 Uhr Mittags versammelten sich vor der Wohnung des Präses der israelitischen Gemeinde, Herrn M. Straßmann in der Bräuhausgasse viele Hunderte von Festtheilnehmern, darunter der k. k. Bezirkshauptmann aus Mistek, Herr Franz Richter, der k. k. Bezirksrichter unserer Stadt, Herr Carl Simonis mit dem k. k. Gerichtsadjuncten, Herrn Josef Boubela, sämmtliche in Gala-Uniform, die Mitglieder der Gemeinde-Vertretung mit dem Bürgermeister, Herrn C. A. Grünwald an der Spitze, von Corporationen der Männergesangverein mit Fahne, der Veteranen-Verein mit Fahne, die freiw. Feuerwehr, ferner die israelitische Schuljugend mit Fahne, und eine große Zahl hiesiger und auswärtiger Festtheilnehmer. Um 2 Uhr setzte sich der Zug unter den Klängen der Bergcapelle in Bewegung, durchzog die Rathhausgasse, den Ringplatz, die Brückengasse und langte endlich vor dem Tempelgebäude in der Pitlergasse an. Hier übergab Herr M. Straßmann den Schlüssel des Gebäudes an den Herrn k. k. Bezirkshauptmann mit einer kurzen Ansprache, welcher ebenso einige Worte an den Herrn Präses richtete und hierauf den Tempel öffnete. Nach dem programmgemäßen Präludium wurde das „ewige Licht" angezündet, wobei der Troppauer Rabbiner, Herr Dr. Blüh den Segensspruch sprach. Nach dem durch den hiesigen Cantor gesungenen Einleitungs- und Vespergebete wurde der Männerchor: „Die Ehre Gottes" von Beethoven vom Männergesangvereine vorgetragen und hierauf betrat Herr Dr. A. Jellinek, erster Prediger der israelitischen Cultusgemeinde Wien, den Predigerplatz.

Aus seiner Rede, welche wir in einer separaten …

18. September 1879.

… israelitische Cultusgemeinde, ausgebracht von … k. k. Bezirkshauptmann Richter, ein Toast … Herrn Dr. Wechsberg auf den k. k. Bezirks-[haup]tmann, ein weiterer Toast des Herrn Dr. Hilf … Herrn Dr. A. Jellinek, ein solcher des Hrn. … Weinreb auf den Bürgermeister und Gemeinde-… der Stadt Mähr.-Ostrau, welchen der Herr Bürger-[mei]ster mit einem Toaste auf die Ostrauer Cultus-[gem]einde erwiderte, und endlich ein Toast des Hrn. … Friedländer auf die sämmtlichen Festgäste. Damit … die Reihe der officiellen Toaste geschlossen und … darauf auch das Banquett beendet. — Auch … Festkränzchen fiel zur Zufriedenheit seiner Arran-[geu]re und seiner Besucher aus; die Saallocalitäten … Garten „Zur Linde" waren zu diesem Zwecke … hergerichtet und geschmückt worden. —

So verlief das ganze Fest, das für die Stadt [Mä]hr.-Ostrau so denkwürdig ist, in allen seinen [Pro]gramm-Punkten nach den Intentionen seiner [Ver]anstalter, in würdiger und den rituellen Theil … langend, in erhebender Weise, und lange noch … sich Mancher an den schönen Tag erinnern, an … dem der Stadt Mähr.-Ostrau abermals eine … ein monumentales Werk übergeben wurde.

Die isr. Cultusgemeinde dankt heute, wie der [In]seratentheil unseres Blattes zeigt, Allen, die sich … dem Feste betheiligt und zu dessen Erhöhung bei-[get]ragen haben; wir wollen hier hinzufügen, daß … beiden Predigern, u. z. den Herren Dr. Jellinek … Dr. Blüh, vom Vorstande dieser Gemeinde ein … [spe]cieller Dank auf schriftlichem Wege wurde.

Gerichtshalle.

Neutitschein, 11. September. (O.-B.) (Dienst-… der Geschwornen.) Bei der am 10. d. M. … genommenen Auslosung der für die IV. dies-[jähr]ige Schwurgerichtssession bestimmten Geschwornen … wurden ausgeloost als Hauptschworne die [Her]ren: Brenner Wilhelm, Ober-Ingenieur in Wit-[kow]itz; Durdik Julius Dr., Advocat in Mistek; Fux … Dr., Advocat und Bürgermeister in Neutitschein; … Marzell, Oberingenieur in Witkowitz; Glesinger … Gastwirth in Wsetin; Haas Abraham, Bräuer … Jedek Carl, Kaufmann in Wall.-Meseritsch; … Anton, Gutsverwalter in Wesseliczko; Kostka … Oeconom in Jezernik; Kraus Franz, Oeconom … Bystritz a. H.; Leipelt Franz, Gutsverwalter in [Wa]ll.-Meseritsch; Leese Ferdinand, Fabrikant in … Lichtenstern Gustav, Liqueur-Erzeuger in … Ostrau; Matula Johann, Oeconom in Fritscho-… Matuschczik Josef, Kaufmann in M.-Ostrau; … August, Oeconom in Bothenwald; Mikulenka … Oeconom in Mittel-Beczwa; Neußer Adolf, [Mü]ller in Klogsdorf; Pazdura Franz, Oeconom in … Aujezd; Rehm Josef, Maurermeister in Leipnik; … Friedrich, Oeconom in Kunewald; Ritter … Rosoglio-Erzeuger in Leipnik; Skácel Anton, … walter in Hochwald; Scheuer Adolf, Bräuhaus-… in Kunewald; Schiedek Josef, Handelsmann … Krasna; Scholasta Carl, Oeconom in Heinrichs-… Schubert Franz, Kaufmann in Freiberg; … Felix, Müller in Groß-Aujezd (Kozlow); … Johann, k. k. Notar in Wsetin; Tauber … Schnittwaarenhändler in Leipnik; Tippow … k. k. Notar in Wall.-Meserisch; Trampler … Oeconom im Sedlnitz; Weber Anton, … Oeconom in Prhalau; Winkelhofer Emil, Professor … Söhle; Wolf Adolf, Fabrikant in M.-Weißkirchen … Ziak Josef, Tuchmacher in Leipnik. Als Ersatzschworne die Herren: Böhm Moritz, Tuchhändler … Neutitschein; Czernek Alois, Seifensieder in Neu-[titsc]hein; Dorazil Johann, Gastwirth in Ehrenberg; … Josef, Oeconom in Söhle; Nehudek Franz, … in Neutitschein; Neußer Johann, Oeco-…

Grenzbote, 18 September 1879: Opening of the Main Synagogue.

In the evening there was a banquet for some 180 guests, where toasts were drank to the Emperor, the town of Mährisch Ostrau and many other deserving worthies. So ended a most memorable day, which will be remembered for a long time.

In the light of the resistance to Jews moving into Ostrava only a few years before, the paean to the town's tolerance in the newspaper report is striking and might, indeed, have been somewhat optimistic. All the same, it is clear that by 1879 there was a well-established and prosperous group of Jews in Ostrava and that the city authorities either wished to integrate them into the civic life of the town or even regarded them as already integrated. The subsequent development of the community in fact demonstrates that the newly promoted tolerance and integration was successful and eye-witness reports from the early years of the twentieth century do speak of a tolerant community. The fact that the great majority of Ostrava inhabitants were, themselves, immigrants of one sort or another almost certainly helped. Ostrava had become a melting pot and, as a result, it was much easier for the Jews to become integrated into local society. In fact, the synagogue became the subject of a local picture postcard, showing that its presence in Ostrava was not only accepted, but had become a source of pride and, at least for postcard vendors, a source of revenue.

The establishment of the synagogue throws more light on the row between Frankl and Strassmann at the Community's inception. Most of the first wave of Jewish immigrants into Moravská Ostrava – the Bergers, Kafkas, Strassmanns, Kulkas, Spitzers, Mannenbergs, and Taubers – came from Lipník and most of the other significant families came from nearby in Moravia, from established Jewish communities. They were already westernised, educated and reasonably integrated into secular society. The new synagogue in

Postcard of the Main Synagogue, published by Julius Kittl.

Main Synagogue

Main Synagogue interior.

Ostrava was to follow the *neolog* style of service, which was considered modern, western, and more suitable for forward-looking cultured people. We would now classify it as conservative or reform as opposed to the traditional orthodox service. From contemporary descriptions of Šimon Frankl we can infer that although he, too, came from Moravia, he was traditional and orthodox. So the argument would not have been just about which ego triumphed or on which side of the river Ostravice the synagogue would be built but about the doctrinal issue of which form of service would be followed. This was an issue that featured in discussions with the rabbis who were subsequently appointed to lead the Community, who wanted a more orthodox service. The matter seems to have been resolved amicably with the rabbis, which had not been the case with Frankl.

In the period 1850-1900, language became an important and divisive issue in Bohemia and especially in Prague. In Prague the general population was increasing rapidly and at a greater rate than the Jewish population so that Jews made up only 4.2% of the population in 1921, down from 6.3% in 1869. This general population increase was predominantly Czech-speaking and in fact an ever larger number of the Jewish population of Prague was also Czech-speaking. In 1876 Czech-speaking Jewish students in Prague set up the Association of Czech Academic Jews to promote Czech nationalism among Jews although at that time Jewish students were well received in German-speaking clubs and associations. By the turn of the century both Czech and especially German nationalism had become increasingly anti-Semitic and so the Jewish population became estranged from both movements.There does not appear to have been a corresponding organisation promoting the Czech language among the Jews of Ostrava, who were predominantly German-speaking and thought of themselves as German.

In 1893 a dead servant girl was discovered in Kolín in Bohemia which led to the accusation of ritual murder by Jews and, in 1899, Leopold Hilsner a Jewish vagabond in Polná, Eastern Bohemia, was accused and found guilty of the ritual murder of the girl although there was no real evidence against him. The future president of Czechoslovakia, Tomáš G. Masaryk, lodged an appeal on his behalf, but it was unsuccessful. Masaryk's enlightened and principled intervention contrasts with the bigotry of the anti-Semitic accusation and the dark thread which runs through Central European history of the period. The murdered girl's brother is reported to have confessed to her murder, on his death-bed.[1]

Happily, Ostrava was relatively free of these tensions and the tolerance described in the *Grenzbote* article seems to have really taken hold. Kieval[2] quotes that German organisations in Prague with many Jewish members had disproportionately few Jewish Directors. Again, that does not seem to have been the case in Ostrava. He goes on to quote the declared nationality of

Jews who, presumably, had declared themselves to be Jewish by religion, in Bohemia and Moravia.

Declaration of Nationality of Czech Jews by % in 1921

	Bohemia	Moravia	All Czechoslovakia
Jewish	13.8	48.7	53.6
Czechoslovak	46.7	15.7	21.8
German	32.7	35.0	14.3
Other	6.8	0.6	10.3

Although it is proper to have doubts about the accuracy of some of these numbers, the overall picture is clear. Moravia is quite different from Bohemia in its degree of Czech and Jewish nationalism. Ostrava Jews appear to be even more 'German' than the average for Moravia. Ostrava was really different!

To ensure that Jewish religious leaders were properly equipped for the modern enlightened Austro-Hungarian world, in 1797 it had become a legal requirement in the monarchy for all rabbis and cantors to have a degree in philosophy from an approved University, a requirement that Jews and others in the UK today might envy. In 1875 the community appointed Dr Samuel Friedmann, who was appropriately qualified, as its first and part-time Rabbi. He came from Těšín and occupied the pulpits in both places between 1875 and 1890. Adolf Mantner taught the children Jewish religion and Berthold Schwartz was responsible for preparing boys for their *Barmitzvah*, when they become adult according to Jewish tradition, at the age of 13. There was originally no *Chazan* or cantor but by 1896 Adolf Türk, calling himself Head Cantor, published a booklet of Songs and Prayers in German, used in the synagogue in Moravská Ostrava. The first of them is of course the prayer for the Imperial Dynasty and is to be heard standing, according to the rubric.

By October 1900, Markus Strassmann had served as President of the Community for 25 years and the community presented him with a magnificent illuminated address.

Strassmann was wealthy, owning and running a brewery in Ostrava and lived next door to it in a large villa that was taken over by the Gestapo after 1939. As well as being the President of the Community, he was a town councillor and served on the committee of several other local and national organisations: he was a person of some importance. He died in September 1903 and Dr Alois Hilf, who had been the Vice-President, took over from him.

After Rabbi Friedmann, Dr Bernhard Zimmels from St Pölten became the community rabbi. Before his appointment was finalised there were extensive discussions over the practice of playing the organ and having a mixed choir of men and women during services for Sabbaths and Festivals.

Sammlung
deutscher
Lieder und Gebete,
welche in der
Synagoge der israelitischen Cultusgemeinde
zu
Mähr.-Ostrau
eingeführt sind.

Zusammengestellt von
Adolf Türk,
Ober-Cantor.

Mähr.-Ostrau 1896.
Selbstverlag von A. Türk, Ober-Cantor.

Collection of Songs and Prayers.

This is contrary to traditional orthodox practice but was regarded by many members as modern and progressive. Herr Kennermann, a non-Jewish opera singer in Ostrava, taught the choir and the organist was also a non-Jew, and so religious sensibilities were cared for, to some extent. Dr Hannah Adar, the daughter of the Head of the Jewish School, Mr Ferdinand Kraus, reported: 'The organ was played by a Christian named Aich. For the main religious festivals the famous opera singer, Mrs Krantz, was invited to sing.' Apparently Mrs Krantz was also not Jewish! Mixed choirs and especially a female singing solo would not be accepted now in an orthodox community, nor would the playing of an organ on Sabbaths and Holy Days even if played by a non-Jew.

Leah Weber, née Ost, was born in 1917. As a child she had a good voice and loved to sing so she joined the choir in the main synagogue, but her family were more traditional/orthodox so they went to the Žerotingasse synagogue. All the same, they were quite happy that Leah was part of the choir. Tolerance was multi-faceted in Ostrava.

Strassmann Address, cover.

Strassmann Address, first page.

Rabbi Zimmels died on 19 August 1893 and a year later Rabbi Dr Jakob Spira became community rabbi, a post he held until his deportation and murder by the Nazis in 1942.

It is traditional for Jewish communities to establish a group of people responsible for ritually preparing the dead for burial, the *Chevra Kaddisha*. In 1881, this numbered 100 people in Ostrava. Together with the numbers of infants and children in the Jewish school this shows a large and involved community with sufficient self-confidence to be visible and to play its part in the life of the town.

On the anniversary of the death of close family members it is the custom to recite a memorial prayer and most synagogues will keep a record of names and dates to remind people. Nowadays, this can be computerised but in the nineteenth century there would be a record book kept by the Cantor's desk so that he could recite the appropriate prayers. This *Haskarah* Book from the main synagogue in Ostrava is now in the Jewish Museum in Prague and records the names of deceased worthies of the community whose relatives had offered a charitable donation to commemorate them.

Haskarah (Memorial) Book, cover.

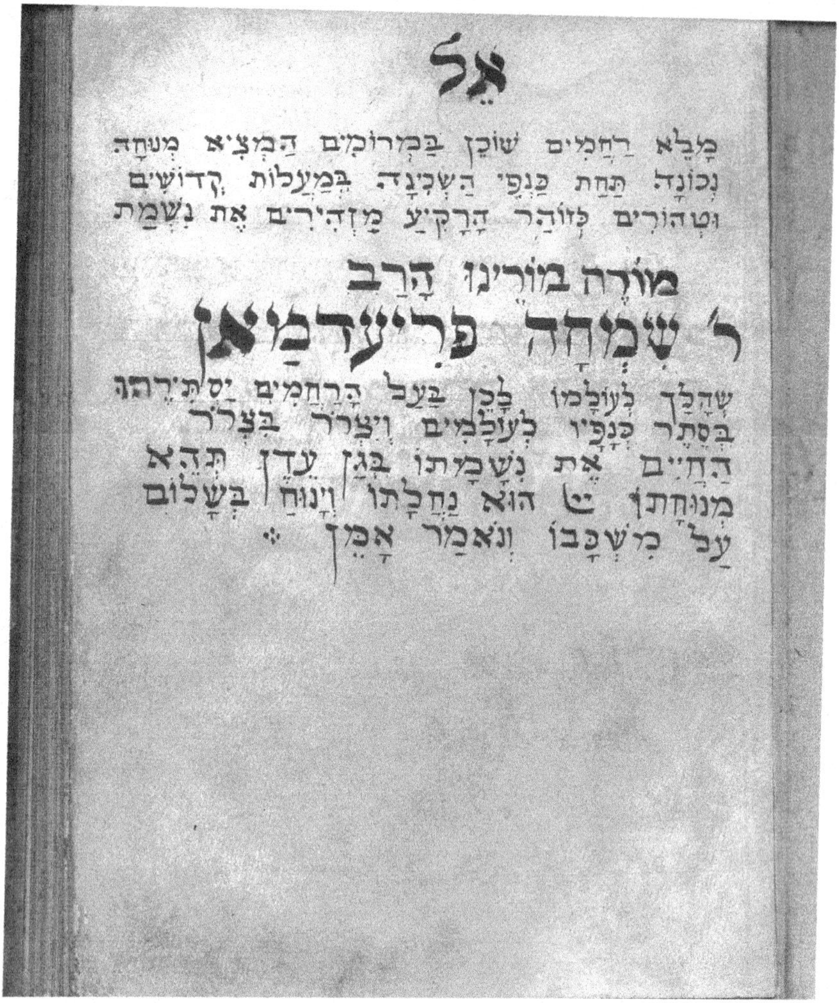

אל
מלא רחמים שוכן במרומים המציא מנוחה
נכונה תחת כנפי השכינה במעלות קדושים
וטהורים כזוהר הרקיע מזהירים את נשמת
מורה במורינו הרב
ר' שמחה פריעדמאן
שהלך לעולמו לכן בעל הרחמים יסתירהו
בסתר כנפיו לעולמים ויצרר בצרר
החיים את נשמתו בגן עדן תהא
מנוחתו ה' הוא נחלתו וינוח בשלום
על משכבו ונאמר אמן

Haskarah Book open at prayer for Simcha Friedmann.

In 1893, the district of Místek had become separate from the Moravská Ostrava Community, which by that time numbered some 3,000 people. Continuing immigration into Ostrava increased the size of the community but meant that there was a need for further synagogues both because of overcrowding and because Jews were settling in the areas round Moravská Ostrava and it was not really possible for people to walk to the synagogue for services on Sabbaths and Holy Days as Jewish law forbids travel by horse or tram on such days. So, in 1900, the Jews of Bohumín established their own synagogue and set up their own Community in 1910, which rapidly became the largest in Silesia.

Ostrava continued to attract economic migrants, both Jewish and non-Jewish, from Slovakia, Galicia, Carpatho-Russia and the area that is now Poland. As a consequence of this increase in population several more synagogues were set up in the late nineteenth and early decades of the twentieth century. The first was in Zábřeh in 1893, then Přívoz in 1904, Vítkovice in 1911 and Hrušov in 1912. Synagogues were established in the area surrounding Ostrava as well. A synagogue had already been established in Hlučín in 1843 and a synagogue and a cemetery were founded in Karviná-Město in the second half of the nineteenth century; a prayer room or *shtiebl* and cemetery were established in Klimkovice, and both an orthodox and a reform synagogue in Orlová in 1900. A *shtiebl* was set up in Petřvald after the First World War and a synagogue established in Karviná-Doly in the 1930s.

Abraham Moses Forscher was born in 1872 in Wischnitz, now in Poland, about 80 miles east of Ostrava. In 1903 he was sent by the Bobover Rebbe, the head of the Chassidic sect from the town of Bobowa, very close to Wischnitz, to the synagogue in Zábřeh to be the rabbi, *shochet* (the ritual slaughterer of animals for food) and *mohel* (who circumcises Jewish boys). He and his wife, Feigl, née Süsskind, had 12 children and lived at Palacký street 210 in a building belonging to the Community of Moravská Ostrava.

At one end was the synagogue and at the other end the living quarters for the family.

Zabřeh Synagogue.

The youngest child, Samuel and his twin brother Solomon were born in 1911. Samuel emigrated to Palestine in 1937, married and had a daughter, Ruth, who had the same name as her mother. Samuel and his family came to London where he was the cantor of the Hammersmith synagogue until his retirement in 1963. His daughter lives in London and she told me that as a boy her father had been taught Jewish cantorial singing, *chazanut,* by Mr Kennermann, the choirmaster of the main synagogue. For the son of a traditional and very orthodox Bobover Chassidic rabbi to be taught *chazanut* by a non-Jewish opera singer speaks volumes for the tolerance of Ostrava society. The two girls in the photograph of the synagogue were two of her aunts Berta, known as Beila, and Anna-Hermina, known as Henne, and they remember the photograph being taken. It must have been quite an event for them.

Ruth joined a group returning to Ostrava in 2010 and visited the site of the synagogue, across the road from the Vítkovice steel works. It is now a petrol station. Not far away was a bar, called *Pivnice u Žida,* 'Pub at the Jew's Place'! Earlier in the day the group had visited Auschwitz-Birkenau and had stood in the watchtower over the main gate, in a temperature of about 35° C, as Ruth's husband Alex recited the Memorial Prayer for those murdered by the Nazis, including several members of the Forscher family. Everyone was looking out of the window at the railway line at the end of which had stood the gas chambers and the crematoria; and wept.

Birkenau, with the tower over the railway line in which we recited *Kaddish.*

In 1894, the main synagogue was enlarged. It was renovated and extended once again in 1928, after a fire.

By the early years of the twentieth century, Přívoz (Oderfurt) had a Jewish population of some 550-600 people out of a total population of 10-12,000. Despite its relatively small size, the Jewish community there built a rather splendid synagogue in 1904, only slightly smaller and less grand than the main synagogue in Moravská Ostrava. It, too, was in the popular Moorish/oriental style.

Leopold Rufeisen set up and became president of the Israelite Temple Association in Vítkovice which led, in 1911, to the building of the synagogue designed by the architect Felix Neumann.

Rabbi Bass served there as did Choir-master Gross, and both were much admired. Leopold Rufeisen was active in the foundation of the synagogues in Zábřeh and, after the First World War, in the building of the synagogue and *mikvah* or ritual bath in Žerotingasse. Leopold was the Vice-President of the Community for many years until his death in 1924 and his son, Dr Josef Rufeisen, was the President of the Czechoslovak Zionist Organisation and, after emigrating to Palestine in 1938, was a Board member of the World Zionist Organisation among many other public positions.

The synagogue in Vítkovice was destroyed in 1939. Recently, some tiles from the synagogue have been found on the site and replicas have been

Přívoz (Oderfurt) Synagogue.

produced. One of them was presented to Tom Auber and his family by the Deputy Mayor when the Auber family held a family reunion in Vítkovice.

In 1912, a year after the synagogue in Vítkovice, the synagogue in Hrušov was opened. It was smaller than that of Moravská Ostrava, Přívoz or Vítkovice, in line with the smaller population.

The Jewish school continued to grow and thrive. Classes were split into parallel boys and girls classes because of over-crowding and by 1899 the school reached its maximum size with 303 children in 7 classes. This

Vítkovice Synagogue.

Vítkovice Synagogue interior.

naturally imposed a significant financial burden on the Community and gave an excuse to the growing assimilation movement within the community to urge that the school be closed. This was encouraged by the national movement to establish German-speaking state schools but the Community voted that the Jewish school should continue, although by a very narrow

Vítkovice Synagogue: copy of an original tile.

margin. After a low point in 1905, when there were only 127 children, the head count grew again to 211 in 1911. By 1924, the school population had once again declined to only 76, in 4 classes. In 1925, the syllabus was adjusted to take account of the establishment of the Czechoslovak state and the ensuing syllabus changes. In the first class there were two hours of Czech teaching per week increasing to 15 periods out of 31 periods in the week in class 4. By the 5th class, all tuition was in Czech.

The First World War caused something of an identity crisis for the inhabitants of Bohemia and Moravia. They were citizens of the Austro-Hungarian Empire which, with its German ally, was at war with Serbia and its allies. Czarist Russia regarded itself as the guardian of all Slavs and was regarded in that light by many Slavs in the Austrian empire, and was allied to Serbia. Great Britain and France were allied to Russia and entered the war

Hrušov Synagogue.

against Austria and Germany. Czechs would have regarded themselves as Slavs and in some cases looked to the Czar and Russia for support but they were now officially enemies. Ostrava Jews would not have had such a dilemma as they did not think of themselves as Slavic. They would face their identity crisis after the defeat of Austria.

At the start of the war the Russian forces advanced into Galicia, driving the Austrian army back into Moravia where the Austrian forces set up a military headquarters in Ostrava. Galician Jews now faced the oncoming Russians with the terrible primeval fear that 'The Cossacks are coming' and many of them fled into Moravia and particularly to Ostrava where they would expect to receive help from the established Jewish community; and did so. It is one of the dreadful ironies of the Ostrava story that, barely 20 years later, between March and September 1939, many Ostrava Jews would flee in the reverse direction, from Moravia into Poland and even Russia, to escape the Germans.

There were two main waves of refugee immigration into Ostrava: in 1914 and 1916. Initially, the Jewish Community provided the necessary financial and practical support but their resources were rapidly depleted, and so the problem became one for the city authorities. Not surprisingly, the presence of a large number of 'foreign' refugees caused political and social unrest, a situation that is now common once again, a century later. Anti-Semitic

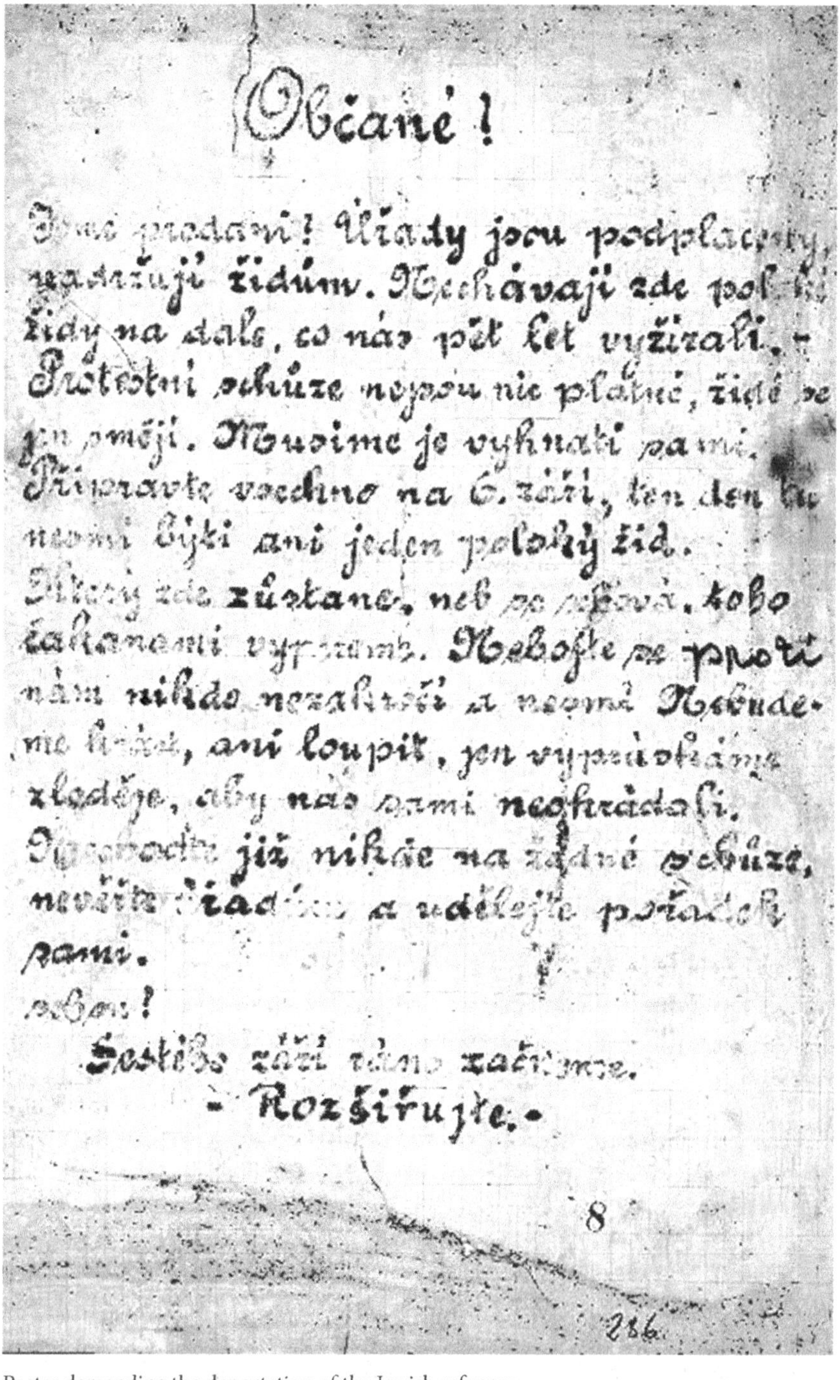

Občané!

Jsme prodáni! Úřady jsou podplaceny, nadržují židům. Nechávají zde polské židy na dále, co nás pět let vyžírali. – Protestní schůze nejsou nic platné, židé se jen smějí. Musíme je vyhnati sami. Připravte všechno na 6. září, ten den tu nesmí býti ani jeden polský žid. Který zde zůstane, neb se schová, toho čakanami vyženeme. Nebojte se proti nám nikdo nezakročí a nesmí. Nebudeme bíjet, ani loupit, jen vypráskáme zloděje, aby nás sami neokrádali. Nechoďte již nikde na žádné schůze, nevěřte úřadům a udělejte pořádek sami.

Zdar!

Šestého září ráno začneme.

– Rozšiřujte. –

8

286

Poster demanding the deportation of the Jewish refugees.

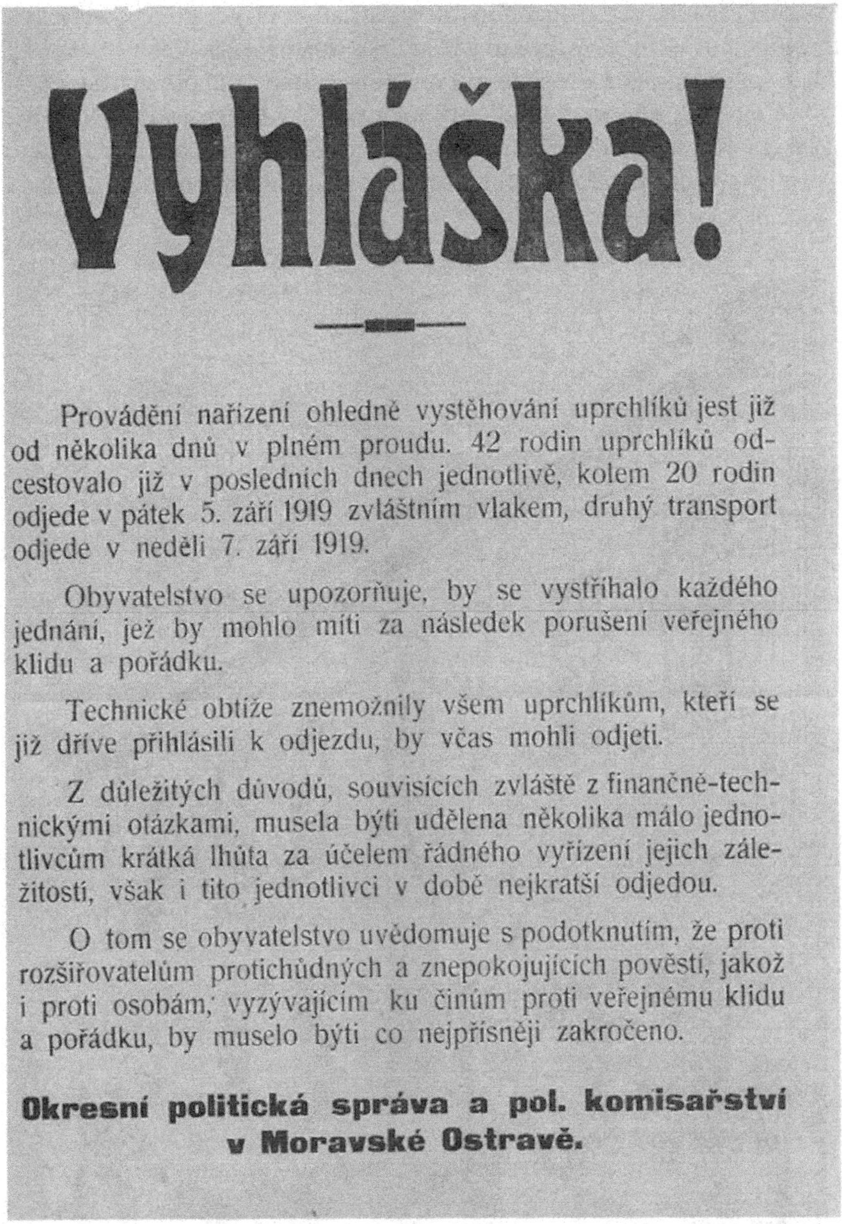

Vyhláška!

Provádění nařízení ohledně vystěhování uprchlíků jest již od několika dnů v plném proudu. 42 rodin uprchlíků odcestovalo již v posledních dnech jednotlivě, kolem 20 rodin odjede v pátek 5. září 1919 zvláštním vlakem, druhý transport odjede v neděli 7. září 1919.

Obyvatelstvo se upozorňuje, by se vystříhalo každého jednání, jež by mohlo míti za následek porušení veřejného klidu a pořádku.

Technické obtíže znemožnily všem uprchlíkům, kteří se již dříve přihlásili k odjezdu, by včas mohli odjeti.

Z důležitých důvodů, souvisících zvláště z finančně-technickými otázkami, musela býti udělena několika málo jednotlivcům krátká lhůta za účelem řádného vyřízení jejich záležitostí, však i tito jednotlivci v době nejkratší odjedou.

O tom se obyvatelstvo uvědomuje s podotknutím, že proti rozšiřovatelům protichůdných a znepokojujících pověstí, jakož i proti osobám, vyzývajícím ku činům proti veřejnému klidu a pořádku, by muselo býti co nejpřísněji zakročeno.

Okresní politická správa a pol. komisařství v Moravské Ostravě.

Decree on the repatriation of Polish Jews. Moravská Ostrava/Mährisch Ostrau, 4. 9. 1919.

attitudes came to the surface, exacerbated by shortages of food, clothing and housing, and there was a general demand that all Galician refugees should be sent back where they came from. This agitation started before the end of the War, but became more strident after 1918.

Leaflets appeared demanding the repatriation of foreign Jews although there did not seem to be the same resistance to non-Jewish refugees and, by 1919, suggesting that the slow or even non-existent rate of repatriation of Polish refugees was because the city authorities had been corrupted by the Jews! In fact, the authorities had laid on transport and encouraged them to leave. Many of the refugees did return but a significant number remained in the new Czechoslovakia.[3]

Žerotinová Synagogue.

Jewish religious practice requires a ritual bath, *Mikvah,* and in 1920 the Community purchased the building housing the Žofia Spa on Žerotín Street. The baths in the basement were converted into a *mikvah* with the upper floors transformed into a synagogue with 500 seats for male worshippers and 300 for women according to the designs of the architect Heinrich Roger. It was opened in 1925 and followed a traditional orthodox form of service.

After the 1914-18 war, the Bleich family, who were orthodox Chasidic Jews, moved into Ostrava and Lea Bleichová set up a *shtiebl,* a small, local, prayer hall, for her husband, who was a rabbi, in Mozart street No. 838. The building was destroyed during the Second War by bombs and the site is now a car park. The Bleich *shtiebl* was not associated with the Community and had few members. After the Second World War, the de-Germanification process meant that the name of the street was changed and Mozart Street became Musorgský Street.

This surge in synagogue building might suggest a community that was religious and observant, but that would not be correct. The Community was a statutory body, with powers granted by the government, as were local Protestant and Catholic parish churches. Everyone had to pay a tax, by law, to their chosen religious Community. This tax income would have made the construction of synagogues much more economically reasonable than it might appear to English-speaking readers today. The Community had the power to summon members who had not paid their dues, a power which modern communal chairmen will envy. The Community acted as registrar of births, marriages and deaths for people within its area of jurisdiction although some of the records have now been lost or destroyed.

The community (with a small 'c') was, in general, socially and culturally rather than religiously Jewish, certainly by the mid-1920s. It reflected the differences in the wider Jewish community in Europe and beyond, between traditional orthodox observance, modern reform practice and even complete assimilation; between any religious observance at all and complete rejection of any religion; between Zionists, non-Zionists and those against Zionism entirely. In this way Ostrava was similar to the communities in Vienna, Berlin and London although probably more inclined to Zionism than the others. Several present-day Ostravaks who were children in Ostrava before the Second World War and remember life then, comment that their parents attended synagogue only on the High Holidays, the three holiest days in the Jewish calendar, and that their parents did not observe *kashrut,* Jewish dietary regulations, at home. This appears to have been quite a common state of affairs and several written autobiographies tell the same story. Almost all of them also comment that their grandparents were much more observant than their parents.

We should remember, however, that our sources of information are not a representative sample. They consist of those who survived and whom we have interviewed or who survived and wrote and published their autobiographies. It is possible, indeed likely, that the poorer, less well educated Jews, who are less well represented among the survivors, were more traditionally observant. It is also likely that the original immigrants, the grandparents of 'our' Ostravaks were more observant and more concerned with establishing synagogues than their children. It is certain that the main synagogue in Pitlergasse followed the 'modern German' form of service that we would nowadays call Reform Judaism. Conversely, the Forscher synagogue in Zábřeh would have followed a very traditional Polish Chassidic form of service.

Despite, or perhaps because of, its modern non-traditional approach, the Community in Moravská Ostrava was regarded as the local religious authority and surrounding communities would seek rulings, advice and guidance from it. The community in Teplitz-Schönau enquired if the Ostrava community had a higher fee for inhumations rather than burial of ashes after cremation. They did. The Community was asked if it was acceptable at all for a married couple to be buried in one grave, in a single plot not a double plot. The answer was that it was possible although highly unusual and only possible in the case of cremations. Modern orthodox Jewish practice does not allow cremations.

As well as being a centre for (liberal) advice, Ostrava was apparently known as being a wealthy Community, as the Community in Stupava (Petržalka) appealed to it for a contribution to enable them to purchase a plot of land for the cemetery from the local council in December 1936. This was a round-robin letter, appealing for Kr.10,000. We do not know if the appeal was successful.

By the early twentieth century the Community was well established and its members turned their attention to the provision of physical rather than purely spiritual care. By 1908, the Community – or rather the Association responsible for the Jewish School in Ostrava – had established a holiday home for Jewish schoolchildren, held in rented property in Frýdlant in the foothills of the Beskydy Mountains, near the Ostravice river. It was not a particularly satisfactory building and was described as 'uncomfortable' and so in the winter of 1911 a plot of land in Ostravice was purchased with the intention of erecting a purpose-built holiday home supposed to be completed by the summer of 1912. Unfortunately but unsurprisingly, delays in planning and ground clearing meant that the children's summer holidays in 1912 were spent in rented accommodation for the last time, with the building ready only in 1913.

The project was entrusted to a committee with Dr Alois Hilf, President of the Community, as honorary president and Dr Ernst Strassmann, the youngest son of Markus Strassmann, as chairman. Ferdinand Krauss, the Head Teacher of the Jewish school was secretary and Josef Spitzer was treasurer. The accounts in 1912 show that the cost of the building plot was Kr 4565.50 and the total income for the year was Kr 12,217.55. Among the items listed in the inventory are 31 iron beds and straw-filled mattresses, 65 large and 35 small enamel plates, 1 wash basket and 1 iron, and 7 shoe brushes. It was not a very luxurious establishment. Bertie Goldberg recalls spending 2 weeks at the home each summer in the early 1920s and enjoying it very much. He commented that his father could afford to pay the costs but there was a fund to cover the costs of children whose parents could not afford it.

The accounts[4] for 1912 list over 500 individual contributions to the running costs of the home, totalling Kr 6838.87. The City, the Community, the Jewish School Association and the Ostrava Savings Bank each contributed Kr 500, the Gutmann Brothers and the Vítkovice Coalmining Company (Rothschilds) each Kr100 and Eugenie Bachrach and many others gave Kr 1.00 each.

The Home could accommodate 40 children at a time in 1913 so 80 could spend 4 weeks there over the summer holidays in two groups of 40 each. The Home survived the two World Wars and was used as an orphanage in 1946 for Jewish children who survived the Holocaust. Bertie Goldberg recalled:

> I remember going to the Jewish children's holiday home, or convalescent home (*Židovská zotavovna*) in Ostravice. It was in

Ostravice Jewish Childrens' Holiday Home.

> operation only during July and August, for two terms and boys and girls alternated there – one month there were fifty boys, next month fifty girls. The less well-off did not pay for the stay but my father could afford it, so he paid. It set him back 150 Crowns, an equivalent of one Pound. The holiday home was directed by the head teacher (*Oberlehrer*) Ferdinand Kraus. There were two huge sleeping dormitories and we had to keep to a military discipline, we had to make our beds and Oberlehrer Kraus used to come to inspect them. If something was not right, he used to turn the bed upside down and we had to start again.

In the years immediately after the First World War, the economy in Ostrava and in most of the newly-established Czechoslovakia went into decline and this exacerbated the perennial problem of unemployment, especially among the young and the recent immigrants from the East. To counter this, the Jewish burghers of Ostrava set up a technical school to train young apprentices in useful trades and crafts. In 1927, Heinrich Süsser, the Chairman of the Association, bought a plot of land in Mariánské Hory and built a home for the students. Later, the *Hechalutz* organisation, the Zionist body that prepared potential immigrants who planned on emigrating to Palestine, moved into the building and used it for their administrative offices.

In the 1920s to 30s, the Community had a budget of 1m crowns and was the third largest and most important in Bohemia and Moravia, after Prague and Brno. The Community employees had similar conditions to civil servants with respect to pay, pensions and promotion. The Community – and the community – must have been very substantial. It was one of the first communities to make a donation of 100,000 Crowns to the *Keren Hayesod* Fund for the purchase and development of land in Palestine. That was ten times more than the average worker's annual income.

In the inter-war years, by no means all the Jews were comfortably middle class, although the records which have survived naturally present that picture. Among the few records detailing the hardship that existed is the story of Herbert Friedlich, who was born in Wrocław, now Poland (then Germany), in December 1923. His mother died and his father, Osias, who had come to Ostrava, paid for Herbert's board and lodging with a Jewish family in Ostrava but otherwise ignored him. The money stopped after a while and Herbert was destitute and effectively orphaned. He describes how he survived: [5]

> ...In my despair, I turned to the principal of my school who came to replace Mr Kraus, Mrs Stefanie Ziffer.
>
> After I described to her my situation, I understood in her face that she is not able to understand to what she is hearing. With it she

> understood that in this situation she must take immediate action. First need is to take care of the food. She gave me a few sandwiches and asked me to come to her office the next day, in my first break. The next day I appeared, as we agreed, and I received from Mrs Ziffer a list of families, times of meals for all the days of the week including festive meals on Friday Nights. She also hinted that in every place I could always ask for extra sandwiches for that evening or morning the next day. Because we are talking about well-known families who had a status in the community, I would like to mention their names: Frischer, Mertz, Artlow, Rosauer, Kresta, Levinger, Krasny, and sometimes during the religious holidays – also Painer. For a boy of 11 years old, this arrangement had even some positive educational aspects. I had to be very careful about the times of the meals, about the way I sat next to the table, about the proper usage of the cutlery, a proper behaviour etc.
>
> So, what this story has to say? It comes to emphasize the generosity and the nobility of the members of the community of Ostrava. Even though I wasn't born in Ostrava, I spent there a number years of my youth and teenage years there.
>
> I would like to put a small layer of justified and well-deserved praise for this community, about their many and diverse wonders in the field of mutual aid.

Nor was he alone in his economic distress. In November 1935, F. Feingold submitted a type-written application, in good German, to the Moravská Ostrava Community for the post of sexton of the Burial Society. He was 40 years old, married and with three school-age children and had been without work 'for a long time'. The post offered a salary of 400 CZK month with a house worth 300/month. He was not accepted.[6]

The community finally turned its attention to the elderly poor and to provision for poor Jewish orphans. The 'Zion Association for an Old People's Home' had been set up in 1920 and by the early 1930s sufficient funds had been collected to begin construction. The building, in *Na Bělidle* Street, was designed by Felix Neumann and built by the contractors Ernst Frischer and Julius Winkelsberg.

It was only 200m from Komenský Park, which would provide fresh air and the possibility of convenient exercise for the 33 potential residents. It was equipped with all modern conveniences, including central heating. The two-storey building was opened on 30 October 1932. After the invasion, in March 1939, the building was confiscated by the German authorities and all the residents transferred to what had been the Atlantik Hotel on Hornopolní Street and later moved again to Hotel Süss in Žofinská Street. In the end, they were all deported to Theresienstadt and on to Auschwitz to be

„Ostrauer Zeitung“

Jüdisches Altersheim in Mähr.-Ostrau

Vor zwölf Jahren wurde in Mähr.-Ostrau der Verein „Union, jüdisches Altersheim“ gegründet, der es sich zur Aufgabe machte, ein Heim für Personen, die das 60. Lebensjahr überschritten haben, zu schaffen und zu erhalten. Der Vereinsausschuß hat durch all die Jahre eine unermüdliche Tätigkeit entfaltet, um das Interesse der jüdischen Bevölkerung für diese in hohem Maße soziale Aufgabe wach zu erhalten und hat durch sparsame Gebahrung aus kleinen und kleinsten Spenden Kapital gesammelt, das schließlich zur Erbauung eines jüdischen Altersheimes hinreichte.

Das Altersheim wird in der Nähe der Křižikgasse, etwa 200 Meter vom zukünftigen Haupteingang in den Komensky-Park (neue Schießstätte) errichtet, so daß seine Inwohner

nicht nur den Vorteil des großen Luftreservoirs des Parkes genießen werden, sondern auch in demselben ihre Spaziergänge ohne körperliche Mühe unternehmen können, wenn sie es nicht vorziehen sollten, im kleinen Hausgarten der Ruhe zu pflegen. Dabei ist das Heim vom Zentrum der Stadt nicht allzuweit entfernt und kann überdies leicht mit Hilfe der bestehenden Autobuslinie erreicht werden.

Das zweistöckige Gebäude, dessen Rohbau bereits fertig ist, ist vom hiesigen Architekten Ing. Felix Neumann nach den modernsten und zweckmäßigsten Grundsätzen projektiert und seine Ausführung ist den Baumeistern Ing. Ernst Frischer und Julius Winkelsberg anvertraut. Im Souterrain befindet sich außer der Baumeisterwohnung, der Waschküche und Zentralheizungsanlage eine vorzüglich ausgestattete, weiß gekachelte Küche mit einem großen, sowohl für Kohlen-, als auch Gasheizung eingerichteten Herd, Spül- und Waschvorrichtungen sowie ein elektrisch betriebenen Speisenaufzug zur Beförderung des Essens in die Wohnstockwerke. Selbstverständlich wird die Küche nach den Vorschriften der jüdischen Speisegesetze geführt werden. Im Parterre befindet sich ein großer Saal, als Gesellschaftsraum und Speisesaal verwendbar, acht einbettige und ein zweibettiges Zimmer, im 1. Stockwerk sind neun einbettige und zwei zweibettige Zimmer, im 2. Stock, der ein vollständig ausgebautes Dachgeschoß darstellt, sind außer der Verwalterwohnung und Personalzimmer noch drei einbettige und zwei zweibettige Zimmer.

Die Ausstattung der Zimmer ist durchwegs neu und wird in modernem und schönem Stil gehalten. Jedes Zimmer hat fließendes kaltes und warmes Wasser und zur Bequemlichkeit der Insassen außer einem Bett eine Ottomane. In jedem Stockwerk ist ein Badezimmer vorgesehen. Den Bewohnern im Heim wird außerdem ein Radio im Gesellschaftsraum zur Verfügung stehen, sowie die Möglichkeit zur Telephonbenützung gegeben sein.

In das Heim werden Personen mosaischen Glaubens, die über 60 Jahre alt sind und keine dauernde Pflege benötigen, aufgenommen. Würdige, mittellose Personen des hiesigen Kultusgemeindesprengels finden nach Maßgabe der Vereinsmittel unentgeltlich Aufnahme. Personen, die über die notwendigen Mittel verfügen, werden sehr mäßige Preisbedingungen erteilt werden. Die Bewerbung um Aufnahme in das Heim kann bereits jetzt beim Vereinsobmann Karl Eichenbaum, Mähr.-Ostrau, Schles. Ostrauergasse angemeldet werden, wobei eine schriftliche Darstellung der persönlichen Verhältnisse des Bewerbers sehr erwünscht ist.

Die Eröffnung des Altersheimes erfolgt voraussichtlich im August dieses Jahres.

Opening of the Old Peoples' Home, 26 March 1932.

murdered. After the war, in 1951, the Union voted for voluntary liquidation, its assets were transferred to the Community and the building let to the County Hygienic Authority for an annual rent of 400,000 Crown.

Ostrava did not have a specifically Jewish hospital until the period of German occupation. After the Munich Agreement and the annexation by Poland of parts of Czechoslovakia, the Miners' Hospital was taken over by the Polish authorities and the patients had to be moved to the State public hospital in Zábřeh nad Odrou. Even after the German invasion of Poland, the border remained as defined after the Munich Agreement.

The Nazis dismissed all Jewish doctors and also forbade them to practice privately. They put in place aryanisation measures, which limited the freedom of movement and social interaction of Jews with the rest of the population. The care in hospitals and alms houses had to be arranged in such a way that Jews couldn't interact with other patients and inmates. On 1 June 1940 on the orders of the Gestapo and the *Oberlandrat* in Moravská Ostrava a Jewish hospital was established, in the former town sanatorium in Přívoz on Koksárenská Street no 13, today's Křišťanova Street. The sanatorium had ceased operation in 1938 and had been converted into a hostel for students of secondary and special schools but was taken over in 1940 for the Jewish Hospital. Medical services were provided by Dr A. Ryšavý, the senior consultant of the Department of Internal Medicine at the first Vítkovice factory hospital, Dr L. Alt, the senior surgical consultant and Dr A. Heitner, senior gynaecologist all of whom had been dismissed from their previous positions as they were Jews. Nursing services were provided by Jewish women, most of whom were completely unqualified. This temporary hospital served its purpose until the last Jews were transported to concentration camps in 1943.

Founded in 1862, the SOKOL organisation was originally designed to provide gymnastic and sporting activities for Czech boys and young men and later became very much associated with the Czech Nationalist movement. It could be rather militaristic and unwelcoming for Jews, although some Jewish Ostravaks were members. There were similar Jewish clubs and organisations which later merged under the Maccabi name and this became an international organisation recognised, in 1960, by the International Olympic Committee. In 1929, the World Congress of Maccabi was held in Ostrava, with a series of sporting and gymnastic events. These developed subsequently into the World Maccabiah Games. The North Moravian Group – *Hagibor-Hamakabi* – met in June 1932 in Oderberg (Bohumín) and published a *Festschrift* or commemorative brochure which includes an article by Václav Hervert of Sokol.[6] He wrote:

> The world organisation, Maccabi, of which you are a part and under whose flag you are organising this memorable meeting has as its task to develop not only physical but also spiritual ideals in harmony.
>
> No doubt you are justifiably proud that the first Jewish organisation, Maccabi, was established by your group in 1893, of all

places in Moravská Ostrava. And there, in 1929, 6,000 spectators from home and abroad watched 100 gymnasts perform.

On this occasion it is my pleasure also to remember the help given to you by members of the local SOKOL, when needed.

Even in 1932, relations between sporting Jews and Czechs were obviously still good.

Maccabi had strong Zionist connections as had the youth group *T'Helet Lavan* (Hebrew – Blue and White) to which many Ostravak boys and girls belonged. Zionism was strong in Ostrava and many families had the ubiquitous blue and white tin collecting box for the Jewish National Fund (JNF) standing prominently at home and into which small change would be dropped by everyone.

The Headquarters of the Czechoslovak Zionist Organisation was in Ostrava and the *Shaliach* (representative from Palestine) in Ostrava was Teddy Kollek, later better known as the Mayor of Jerusalem. In 1932, he appeared as Mordechai, the hero of the *Purimspiel*, a pantomime, based on the biblical book of Esther, performed at the festival of Purim in the early spring.

In 1992 he was invited to return to Ostrava. He was unable to do so, but sent a letter:

Advertisement for a *Purimspiel* 19 March 1932 with Teddy Kollek as Mordechai.

> Dear Friends,
> Unfortunately I can't be with you today because of my work load here, in Jerusalem, but I'm surely with you in spirit. The years of my work in Ostrava with *Hechalutz*organization (pioneers) and *Tchelet –Lavan* gave me not only beautiful memories, but also a great spiritual connection to the beautiful Moravian city and certainly I would find many of my friends from those days among those taking part in the reunion.
>
> The Ostrava community was a magnificent (Jewish) community, lively and proud, and it's not a coincidence that it was the centre of the Zionist organization and activity in Czechoslovakia. Many that immigrated to the land of Israel, made a very important contribution to establishment of the State and developing and empowering of the State in important fields.
>
> I bless all who came for the reunion, that should enjoy the moving gathering of friends from 'those days' and I support with all my heart this project to commemorate the historic, spiritual and cultural heritage of Jewish and Zionist Ostrava.
> Yours,
> Teddy Kollek.

The building which housed the *Hechalutz* and the Czech Zionist organisations was burnt by the Nazis on 27 June 1939. It was rebuilt after the war and used as a police station. Finally, it was restored to the Community and is now the Community centre, containing offices, meeting rooms and a synagogue.

The Ostrava Jewish community was, in general, supportive of the Zionist cause and several Zionist leaders came from Ostrava, including Dr Joseph Rufeisen (1887-1949), Dr Paul Mertz (1894-1941); Dr Franz Kahn (1895-1944); Ernst Frischer (1887-1954) and Shlomo Rozen (1905-1985) who became a Minister in the Israeli Government. Dr Fischel recalled:

> My parent's house was most Zionist. We always subscribed to different Zionist newspapers, like: 'SELBSTWEHR, JUNG JUDA, ŽIDOVSKÉ ZPRÁVY'. On the wall of our dining room there was a *tzedaka* (charity) box for JNF and we, the children, always put coins into it at every opportunity. For example, when we showed our relatives our end of school year diplomas, and we received a few coins as a token, the coins made their way without a hesitation straight to the white and blue box.

However, this support was not universal. Parents in the Jewish school held heated discussions about the extent to which teaching in the school should or should not reflect the views of the Zionist movement.

This divergence of opinion echoed the wider political scene. After the establishment of the Czechoslovak Republic, Jews were, after quite a lot of political agitation and negotiation, recognised as a minority nationality with the right to form a political party and to have parliamentary representation. This afforded the Jews the opportunity to indulge in their greatest passion – furious internal argument, disagreement and falling-out. As always, the Jewish population of Czechoslovakia was split between orthodox, liberal, and totally non-observant; between Zionists and non-Zionists; and between those who thought that the main focus of any Jewish party should be on civic rights for the Jews in Czechoslovakia and those who were concerned to establish a National Home in Palestine. The Jewish population in the Republic, although quite significant in total, was thinly spread. This geographical distribution and the fissiparous nature of the Jewish parties meant that although Jewish parties received a large number of votes they did not receive a large enough share of the votes in any area to qualify for a seat in parliament until the early 1930's. At that time, the party in Ostrava formed a coalition with Polish minority parties which enabled them to establish parliamentary representation. It was not a happy arrangement.

Rather happier were the social clubs such as *Schlaraffia,* which was a sort of Masonic or Rotary club. Paul Rice (né Pavel Reisz) recalls that his father and uncle were members:

> From my age of 15 I have very vivid memories of this strange organisation, mainly because at the time, and even more soon afterwards, I was ashamed of my family's connection with this club because of its 100% GERMAN orientation, which I, principally a Czech speaker, could not understand. The club was based on the idea of a community (normally men, occasionally also women) inhabiting a medieval castle where all members were 'knights' and at the weekly meetings in there wore funny hats with bells and always called each other only by their assumed names which bore some connection to their personalities. Thus my father, Joseph, was known as Aeneas and his identical twin brother Franz was Andreas [a pun in German on the words *Ein As* – One ace and *Andere As* –The other ace] and my uncle Rudi was always known as 'Risotto' due to his surname Reisz.
>
> It was one of the customs of the group to address each other in verse and if this was not possible, then public speeches which were offered at every meeting had to be delivered *in verse*. I remember that my father was able to dictate off the cuff to his secretary a whole speech in verse. The members greeted each other with the phrase 'lulu' which was particularly odd because in German it also was the childish call for, 'I need to have a pee'.

Once a year there was a children's afternoon session in the 'castle' where my uncle in the role of the Chief Knight stood on a stage and threw vast quantities of sweets to be fought over by the assembled children. Those who misbehaved (or pretended to so) were locked up as punishment in a cell resembling a prison and had to ask for mercy to be released.

Sh'viti donated by 'Issachar Schwarz, in the community of Mährisch Ostrau'.

> The 'knights' occasionally exchanged visits with others in 'castles' in near-by cities and I assume that there must have been some good reason why my father and his two brothers, generally very serious-minded men, were keen members of this charade and made fools of themselves, but perhaps it gave them an excuse to be away from their wives for an evening. The 'knights' were racially mixed, possibly half-half Jews and half others.

B'nai Brith, an international Jewish cultural, educational and charitable organisation, was the most important of such Jewish societies in Czechoslovakia. The first Lodge was set up in Plzeň in 1892. The Ostravia Lodge in Ostrava was established in 1924 and eventually had 71 members. B'nai Brith lodges in Czechoslovakia were exclusive, unlike in the UK and USA, and members had to meet rigid social and cultural requirements before being admitted to membership. Records of the activities of the Ostravia Lodge have not been preserved.

Société, a fraternal order with similar aims to B'nai Brith, was founded in 1910 and drew its support from less elevated social and economic strata than B'nai Brith. The Moravská Ostrava branch was founded in 1922 also and officially organised in March 1923 with 26 members. Dr Sandor Teichner became Chairman in 1927 and remained in that position until 1938. During his chairmanship, the Ostrava branch set up a sub-branch in Olomouc. Société was disbanded in 1938 after the transfer of the Sudetenland to Germany.

Many traditional synagogues have a placard hung on the wall in front of the Cantor or even on the Reader's desk in front of him, with a verse from Psalm 16: 'I have set The Lord before me constantly' and other kabbalistic verses. It is designed to encourage devotion and religious fervour during prayer. They are called *Shiviti* after the Hebrew first word. Issachar Schwarz donated one although we do not know to which synagogue or when. It is now in the Jewish Museum in Prague.

Although the Community did not, in practice, place the Lord before them constantly, collectively its members did take reasonable care of the religious, welfare, social, educational and cultural needs of the whole community. Over the period of about 150 years, they may not have built Jerusalem in Moravia's green and pleasant land, among the dark satanic blast furnaces, to misquote William Blake (Appendix 5.1), but they had gone quite a way towards it.

NOTES

1. *Tajuplná vražda. Případ Leopolda Hilsnera.* Jiří Kovtun. Sefer 1994.
2. *Making of Czech Jewry.* Kieval Hillel J. P., OUP. 1988.
3. *The Orient in Bohemia?* Exhibition in the Jewish Museum in Prague August 2014.
4. Holiday home accounts, Jewish Museum in Prague, Ostrava Archive.
5. Quoted in *Město v nás* Marek Otisk (ed.) publ. Montanex, 2004.
6. Archive of the Jewish Museum in Prague.

6

Trades, Professions and Politics

Bankers

Money is reputed to be the root of all evil, but if it is, it is a necessary evil. It might more accurately be described as the root of and raw material for all economic development and growth. Finance for the major businesses, especially the coal and iron companies, came from the Rothschilds and Gutmanns who invested heavily in Ostrava but controlled their businesses from Vienna. The development of smaller local businesses and manufacturing (alcohol and food production, hotels and restaurants; building material production, textiles, jewellery etc) relied on local provision of relatively small amounts of capital and this was covered by local savings and credit organisations. The major banks were not interested in this type of economic activity at the time and so a number of local financial institutions were set up in Ostrava, frequently defined by their language or by the range of business activity they would support.

The German *Vorschussverein* or Credit/Savings Association had been set up in Ostrava in 1870 'to conduct banking trade for the provision of the necessary financial means for trade and business' and had been used by most of the Jewish businesses in Ostrava. The *Mährisch-Ostrauer Handels und Gewerbe Bank* opened in 1898 but it concentrated on businesses in lime, cement and coal and was thus of limited interest for small traders and manufacturers. The *Spar und Vorschussverein für Witkowitz*, was founded in 1883 and concentrated on the rapidly expanding Vítkovice commercial activities and the *Spar und Creditverein der Genossenschaft für freie und concessionierte Gewerbe des Mähr. Ostrau Gerichtsbezirk*, set up in 1889, dealt specifically with smaller businesses. There was clearly a lot of economic activity in Ostrava at the turn of the nineteenth century. Nonetheless shortage of money, in the form of bank credits, in the early years of the twentieth century caused problems for Jewish businessmen in Ostrava and this led, in 1910, to the establishment of the *Mährisch Ostrauer Volksbank*, with Jakob Salomonowitz elected one of the directors. The founding meeting was held on 15 and 16 May 1910. Max Beer, a lawyer, was elected President and Moritz Wechsler, a timber merchant, the first director. The Bank officially opened on 1 August of that year, once all the administrative matters had been dealt with, with help from the *Jüdische Volksbank* in Brno.

The bank had 200 members by the end of 1910, and the numbers then increased to 454 in 1916 and 767 by the end of 1938, when the bank was liquidated. The bank concentrated on what we would now call small and medium enterprises, with modest loans. All Jewish Associations in and around Ostrava were actively encouraged to deposit their funds in the bank and members of the bank were also requested to deposit funds so that money would be available to lend. (For a list of the first Board of Directors and Supervisory Board see Appendix 6.1). Several of these people had practical experience in other organisations, particularly organisations associated with the Jewish Community, and there is a clear emphasis in the composition of the Board on people typical of the client base rather than on professional banking expertise.

Business hours were limited to 3 hours per day, from 10:00-12:00 and 16:00-17:00hrs during the week, from 09:00 to 10:00hrs on Sunday and the bank closed on Saturdays and Jewish holidays. Later the hours were extended and the bank opened on Saturdays, Sundays and Catholic holidays which were specifically mentioned.[1] In the 1920s, the bank employed three officials.

Initially, the bank operated out of a room in the home of one of its members, Jonas Löwy, at 14 Johanny Street. Then it moved to a more convenient location on the premises of Julius Kittl, a printer and publisher, in Pittlergasse, near the main synagogue. At this point the bank purchased a second-hand safe! It is not clear how it had operated previously without one. The rooms in Kittl's print shop were also used by the committee of the Moravian and Silesian Zionist Organisation. By the late 1920s and early 1930s, the *Volksbank* was considering acquiring their own premises but negotiations were never finalised.

In the early years the bank adopted a very cautious prudent approach to loans. The maximum possible amount was 10,000 Crowns and there were very few that reached that limit. After the First World War a few larger loans were made, in particular a loan of Kr 20,000 to the *Gemillus Chasodim* a Jewish charitable organisation, although this was against collateral of Kr15,500 of Government War Loan. The Bank itself invested in Austrian Government War Loans - a total of over Kr 200,000. As a consequence, Max Beer was awarded the War Cross Second Class in 1917 'for services rendered to the War Loan action'. By the end of the war, the bank owned Kr 340,000 of the War Loan, some of it acquired as collateral for other loans it had made. After the war this became a serious financial burden on the bank as it was almost worthless.

Nonetheless, post-war lending increased, the limit was raised and loans of up to Kr 2 million were approved for the purchase of property. Large loans to the Strassmann Brewery were granted but without the necessary due diligence and this, together with the economic slump in the early 1930s, eventually caused the bank to all but cease lending. Business improved to some extent but the political problems in 1938 with the consequent emigration of several members of the bank led to its transfer to the control of a financial commissioner in January 1939, and the bank was then liquidated in October 1939, after the invasion of Czechoslovakia.

From its foundation, the bank sponsored a number of Jewish charitable organisations. In 1912, Kr 796.40 was allocated for this purpose, with *Gemillus Chasodim* receiving Kr250 and Kr50 being given to the Jewish School. The bank donated Kr 6.40 for the planting of one olive tree in Palestine. The cost was actually Kr 7.0 and the difference was covered by Mr J. M. Laufer, one of the Directors.

By the late 1920s and early 1930s larger donations were made and there was a wider range of beneficiaries, including non-Jewish ones. Medical centres in Karlovy Vary, Teplice, and Františkovy Lázně received donations as did the war veterans from the First World War, the Masaryk League against Tuberculosis and the Red Cross. In 1924-7, donations were made to a training fund for teachers for a planned regional Jewish School. The worsening position of Jews in Ostrava in the 1930s is suggested by donations of Kr 1000 per year from 1934-36 to the Jewish People's Kitchen. The Max Beer Foundation, set up after Beer's death in May 1932, received Kr 2000 annually (although that ceased after the 1933 donation, because of the worsening financial position of the bank) and it is thought that the Foundation funded the furnishing of the Old People's Home on Na Bělidle. In its thirty years of existence, the fortunes of the bank reflected the development, growth, philanthropy and ultimately the destruction of the Jewish business world in Ostrava.

Although the Strassmann Brewery clearly ran into financial difficulties in the 1930s, both the concern and Markus Strassmann himself were very prosperous in the latter decades of the nineteenth century when Strassmann was the President of the Community. In 1912, the Brewery gave Kr 50 to the Children's Home and Markus's sons, Adolf, Ernst and Richard gave Kr 170 between them. Markus was a money-lender as well as a brewer although there is no record of the extent of his money-lending activities.

Albert Wechsberg was also a money-lender. His first business was as an innkeeper or restaurateur in Orlová, maintaining the tradition of Jews in that business, although the records are unclear as to whether he ran the business or merely owned the property. As well as being an inn-keeper, he was a corn merchant and successful in both areas. As the business grew he expanded his activities into milling, setting up a steam-driven rolling mill on Nádražní Street and also starting a money exchange and lending business shown on the company seal.

The combination was a little unusual but both branches of his business depended on his possession of significant financial resources. Initially, the

Wechsberg Company seal.

money-changing/lending must have been relatively informal, taking place on market days only and in the market place itself. Wechsberg continued to do well and ultimately converted his money-changing and lending business into a private bank. He bought a large building near the centre of town and set up the bank on the ground floor, administrative offices on the first floor and residential apartments for his sons on the upper storeys. Evžen was on the second floor, then Alfred and Siegfried, the youngest son and the father of Josef, later well-known as a writer, on the top floor.

Albert and the bank continued to prosper and Wechsberg became probably the richest man in Ostrava, known to the townsfolk as 'Albert der Gutiger' (Benevolent Albert) as he would, if he liked you, lend money without security and at the low rate of only 5% p.a. More politely, and presumably to those who actually sought a loan, he was known as Der Herr Bankier and was referred to, rather proudly, as 'Our Rothschild'. In 1912,

Wechsberg building, 2014.

the Wechsberg Bank is recorded as donating Kr 50 to the Children's Holiday Home.

There is a certain irony in the fact that the Wechsberg Bank was ultimately taken over by the Rothschilds (see Chapter 10 for the full story of the Wechsbergs). The Rothschild fortune had begun with money changing and lending before growing into international banking. Albert, who traded

Albert and Františka Wechsberg.

with the Rothschilds, tried to emulate them – he had three sons in the bank with him, although Mayer Amschel Rothschild had all 5 of his sons in the business – and wished, like them, to be ennobled and become 'von Wechsberg'. But the Wechsberg story was not to be so grand.

Once the Wechsberg Bank was taken over, the Banking Hall on the ground floor of the building was let out to a delicatessen run by S. Bitter, to provide some income for the family. Josef, on the top floor and aged 13, thought that the delicatessen was a great improvement on the bank – much more interesting and useful!

Doctors and Dentists

Up to the middle of the nineteenth century Ostrava was a small provincial town with minimal healthcare and legal needs. It offered few career opportunities for members of what were known as the 'free professions'. Everything changed with the development of the Vítkovice Ironworks after they were acquired by the Rothschilds in 1843. Ostrava gradually emerged as the most important industrial city in the Habsburg Monarchy. Alongside the burgeoning industrial sectors, services and education expanded at an increasing pace, the population grew rapidly and with it the prospects for lawyers, doctors, journalists and other educated professionals.

The growth in the number of doctors in the town was closely related to the developing needs of the ironworks, mines and other industrial concerns, which started to employ their own doctors and open hospitals for their workforce. Ostrava directories from the end of the 19th and beginning of the 20th century contain the names of doctors and lawyers practicing in the town and its environs and allow us to trace the rising number of these highly qualified men over time. In 1897 there were 14 doctors, six of them Jews, working in Moravská Ostrava. At the same time there were 16 lawyers in Moravská Ostrava, 8 of them Jews, and to this we can add 10 junior lawyers (articled clerks or 'lawyers in waiting'), 6 of them Jewish, who already had law degrees but were still preparing for professional examinations. In 1914 there were 59 doctors, of whom at least 27 were Jewish in origin, practising in Moravská Ostrava, Vítkovice, Mariánské Hory, Přívoz and other adjoining communities later to be incorporated into Ostrava. The striking number of Jews in the medical profession is even clearer in the case of dentists; 6 out of 8 were of Jewish origin. The situation in the legal profession was similar. Of the 41 lawyers practicing in the Ostrava region on the eve of the First World War, at least 22 were Jewish. Of course, doctors did not work only in private practices. Many were employed in Ostrava hospitals.

Consultants and heads of department at the hospitals would also in most cases have a private practice alongside their salaried posts.

The biggest and most famous of the health facilities in the Ostrava region was the Vítkovice Mining and Smelting Works Hospital. Its transformation into an advanced and major hospital was associated with the initiative of

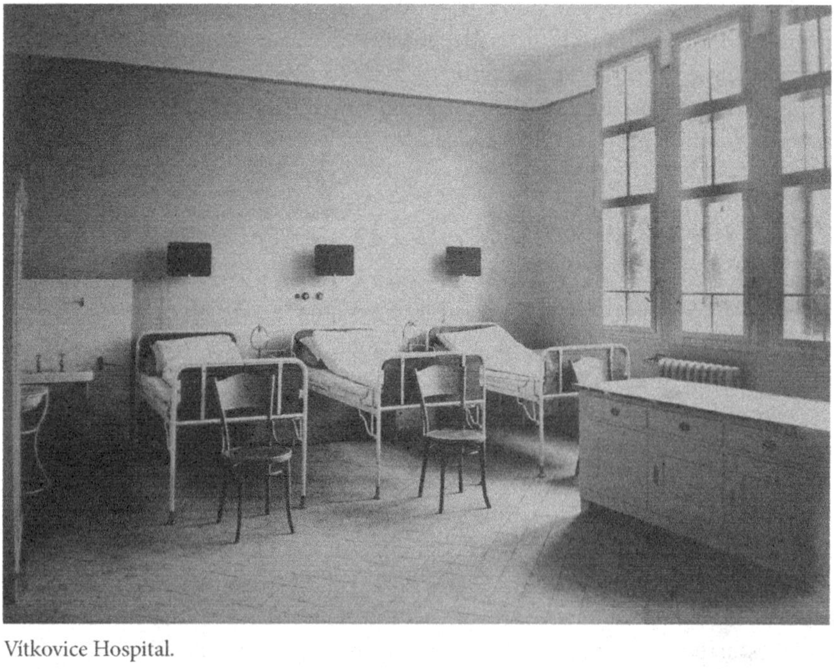

Vítkovice Hospital.

Paul Kupelwieser, who became head of the company in 1876. One of his decisions was to modernise the Vítkovice Ironworks Hospital. He persuaded both families of owners, the Rothschilds and the Gutmanns, to back the plan, and in 1878 managed to persuade MU Dr Maximilian (Miksa) Munk to come from Vienna to take the position of Vítkovice physician. Munk had been born on 5 November 1847 into the Hungarian Jewish family of Gabriel Munk and Szara Zali Munk in Startek, and had two brothers. He studied medicine at the University of Vienna, where he then started his medical career as an assistant at various clinics.

After moving to Vítkovice he assisted Kupelwieser with plans for building a new hospital, but at first he had to make do with the existing facility. It was not ideal, but with the progressive purchases of the most up-to-date medical equipment, and thanks to Munk's talents as a doctor, substantial improvements were made in healthcare for employees of the Vítkovice Mines and Smelting works. Munk also managed to convince the firm's management of the need to employ a second doctor. He concentrated on the battle against TB, which was a scourge of the Ostrava population and one of the most frequent causes of death. Munk went to Berlin to consult Professor Robert Koch, so as to improve his knowledge of the latest advances in treatment of this disease.

When the new Vítkovice hospital was eventually built in 1890 (eight years before the founding of a modern municipal hospital in Moravská Ostrava!) he became its director. He was also responsible for the establishment of a hospital for infectious diseases in Zábřeh nad Odrou. In the ironworks itself he managed to push through installation of expanded and better hygiene facilities such as showers, sinks and toilets for workers, and First Aid centres in the individual Vítkovice plants. He specialised in surgery and was the first doctor to perform many new operations in the Ostrava region. From 1893 he represented the doctors of the Ostrava region in the Moravian Medical Chamber. In 1899 he was awarded the title of Imperial Counsellor for his contributions to the development of healthcare[2].

The Vítkovice Hospital certainly employed a very large number of Jewish doctors. It is worth mentioning that the first woman doctor in the Ostrava region, MU Dr. Stefanie Pollachová, was Jewish. She was born in Hranice in Moravia in 1882 and studied medicine mainly in Vienna. After an internship in Brno she served from mid-August to mid-December 1916 in military field hospitals in Russian Poland and Lithuania. From March to the end of October 1917 she worked in the surgical department of the Vítkovice Hospital. She left Vítkovice to go to Vienna, and then moved from Vienna to the university clinic in Graz.

Munk's successor as head of the Vítkovice concern hospital was MUDr. Rudolf Pressburger. Born in 1869 in Pecs, he too was from a Jewish family. He studied medicine at Vienna University and after graduating in 1895 he joined the Vítkovice Hospital. He specialised in internal medicine. During the First World War he was called up to the front. On his return he became Dr Munk's deputy and later succeeded him as director of the Vítkovice hospital, remaining in the position until his retirement in 1930.[3]

The Vítkovice Hospital employed several other doctors of Jewish origin, such as Leonhard Mandler, Filipp Fuchs and Karl Gütig, who was born on 3 August 1879 in Prague. Gütig had studied medicine at the German University in Prague. After graduating he worked for a short time in Příbram, and then moved on to a surgical internship with Professor Robert Gersuni in Vienna. He joined the Vítkovice Hospital on 15July 1909. In 1919 he became head of the surgical department. He specialised mainly in stomach surgery and was an expert on thyroid gland operations. He published numerous articles in medical journals and was so devoted to his work that he never had a family.[4]

Other Jewish doctors at Vítkovice were more fortunate. They included MU Dr Ernst Nathan Rischawy, born in Brno on 22 May 1897. Rischawy started his medical studies in Vienna, moving in the 1919/20 to the German University in Prague where he graduated in 1923. He started his medical career in the Prague Hospital on Charles Square, and then moved to Vítkovice in 1928. In the same year he married another doctor, Hedvika Holzerová, in the Jerusalem Synagogue in Prague. Like the other Jewish doctors he was dismissed from the mining and ironworks in March 1939. In 1940-43 he headed the Jewish Hospital in Ostrava-Přívoz.[5]

The youngest doctor of Jewish origin employed in the Vítkovice Hospital was MU Dr Jiří Velemínský, born on 19 October 1912 in Mariánské Hory into the family of the local doctor Rudolf Velemínský. The latter was from a Jewish family but identified officially as Czech. Jiří was the eldest of the Velemínský brothers. The younger, Jan (born on 22 June 1914), also studied medicine, and the youngest was Zdeněk (born in March 1918). The boys attended the Czech gymnasium in Moravská Ostrava. After his school-leaving exams Jiří went to Prague to study medicine at Charles University, where he graduated on 29 February 1936. He started work in Prague at the First Internal Clinic under professor Hyner, and then moved to the hospital in Mladá Boleslav where he stayed for just one month before the then director of the Vítkovice Hospital, MU Dr Urbánek, persuaded him to take the position of houseman there from 1 May 1936.

Like his father he identified himself officially as a Czech and was not a religious believer, but when the Nazis arrived he was still fired as a Jew. At the beginning of the war the brothers moved to Prague with their mother, Ida née Kellerová. There they joined the resistance, but in 1943 they were all arrested and sent to Auschwitz.[6]

Lawyers

Not only among doctors but among Ostrava lawyers too, the percentage of Jews was higher than their share in the town population. As we have already mentioned in this chapter, we have precise information on the number of lawyers (advocates) and of junior lawyers (or 'lawyers in waiting'), but the spectrum of people with legal education was much broader. Many of them found employment in state service as judges in various courts, or with the police, while others found posts in the commercial departments of firms, and in banks.

One of them was the lawyer of the Vítkovice Ironworks, Dr Leo Spitzer. He was born in Vítkovice on 25 May 1896, but the family came from Lipník nad Bečvou, a traditional Jewish settlement in Moravia. His father Max settled in Vítkovice in the last years of the nineteenth century and worked in the ironworks. Leo attended gymnasium and then studied law. His first job was in the legal practice of a Dr Königstein in Liberec, but after eight months there he returned to the district of his birth and took up employment at VHHT. In March 1933 he married Suse née Lonnová. Leo at first officially declared himself to be of German nationality and Jewish faith, but from surviving documents we know that he made an official request to the personnel department to change his nationality to Jewish on 27 December 1933.[7]

The most famous of Ostrava's Jewish advocates was Dr Alois Hilf, the second president of the Moravská Ostrava Jewish Religious Community. He came from Prostějov, where he was born on 23 September 1851 into the poor family of Ignatz and Rosa Hilf. His father died when he was only 15 but despite the family's difficult financial circumstances he still managed to study law in Vienna. He gained legal experience as an intern in Opava and in Bohumín, and in August 1876 joined Dr Karel Richter's legal practice in Moravská Ostrava as an articled clerk. In 1881 he moved to Břeclav to take up an opportunity to run his own independent legal practice, but he returned to Ostrava when the departure of Dr J. Schüller opened up a vacancy there. He went on to build up one of the most prestigious advocacy practices in the Ostrava region, its clients drawn mainly from local business elites. He was an outstanding expert on law, with an acute ability to grasp legal issues, and he was an exceptionally good speaker. All of this was also to stand him in good stead in his career as a local politician.

In the years 1885-1918 he was elected representative, for the German Liberals on the local community committee of Moravská Ostrava, and from 1905 a member of the town council. He was responsible for municipal economic and transport agendas. At the beginning of the 1880s he came up with the idea of building a local railway line connecting Moravská Ostrava with the station of the *Kaiser Ferdinands-Nordbahn* in Přívoz. He joined forces with the then mayor of the town, Anton Lux, and the two even managed to obtain a provisional concession for the establishment of a steam tram line, but the whole project was never realised as a result of funding problems.

Alois Hilf was one of the leaders of the German minority in Ostrava. He was involved in the setting up of a German gymnasium in 1896 and a German girls' lyceum in 1902. He was chairman of the *Deutsches Haus* construction association, which secured material and technical support for the building of the German Association House. He was a leading personality in the campaign for a town theatre, which eventually opened in Moravská Ostrava in 1907. As president of the male choir and orchestral society he contributed substantially to musical life in Ostrava (see **Appendix 6.2**).

Dr Hilf also contributed to the industrial and financial development of the region. At the beginning of the twentieth century he won over a number of Ostrava town businessmen and investors to the idea of starting mining in Austrian Eastern Silesia. This initiative led in 1902 to the foundation of the *Dziedzitzer Montangewerkschaft*, which opened the Silesia black-coal mine in Czechowice (Bielsko district, today in Poland). Up to 1917, when the mine was transferred to a Vienna bank, Hilf was president of the company and also executive director. For many years he was a member of the Board of Directors of the Moravská Ostrava Savings Bank. After 1918 he remained at least a member of the board of directors, and in 1929 he became vice-chairman of its audit committee.

Another famous Ostrava lawyer was Albert Herbatschek, born on 10 November 1867 in Šaštín (today in Slovakia). His father, Friedmann, was a wealthy merchant. Albert attended gymnasium in Kroměříž, and in 1885 went on to study law in Vienna, gaining the title of doctor in 1891. In 1896 he joined Dr Karl Richter's practice in Moravská Ostrava. Here he worked as an articled clerk for three years, and then as an advocate, before setting up his own independent practice in 1909. He was the founder and for many years the president of the Society of Advocates in Moravská Ostrava. He specialised in mining law, working on its reform, and he contributed expert articles to the *Bergrechtliche Blätter*, a journal that he co-published. He completed a collection of official regulations relating to mining law which had been started by the Vienna chief mining officer Schardinger. He was active in several German associations. He was adjutant and agent for the volunteer fireman's association, and member of the committee of the Moravian Firemen's Union for the Czechoslovak Republic. He was also the agent for the *Deutsches Haus* Society and the German Tourist Association known as the *Beskidenverein*.

Apart from his works on mining rights, he wrote a two-volume guide to the Beskydy and Tatra Mountains.[8] During the First World War he defended Czech citizens prosecuted for anti-state activities in the courts. He died on

24 August 1926 following an operation in the Ostrava sanatorium of MU Dr Klein.

Many of the children and grandchildren of Ostravaks became successful lawyers in their new home. Among them is Sir Bernard Rix, grandson of the owner of the Rix department store, who became a Lord Justice of Appeal in the UK (**see Appendix 6.3**).

Brewers and Publicans

The first Jews who moved into Ostrava were almost all associated with the production and sale of beer or spirits and this dominance of the alcohol trade continued well into the twentieth century. The trade was always tightly regulated as to who could make or sell alcohol and where they could do so. The rights were owned by the local aristocrat or landowner and sometimes by the town itself, as in the case of Moravská Ostrava (which included some of the local villages such as Přívoz, Lhotka (today Mariánské Hory) and Nová Ves). Frequently the owner of the rights would lease them out so that others did the work while the owner of the legal right collected a fee. And many of the lessees were Jewish.

In the first half of the nineteenth century Ostrava was still a small agricultural and crafts community and this meant that beer was mainly served in tap-rooms on the Main Square and its immediate side-streets, as well as a few coaching inns that provided board and lodging for carriers beyond the town walls. The turning-point came with 1848 and the abolition of serfdom, but above all with the development of industry in and around the town. As Ostrava started to expand it needed new pubs, restaurants, hotels and coffee houses. By 1888 there were 36 pubs and six wine restaurants in Moravská Ostrava, and by 1908 there were 51 restaurants and pubs, six coffee-houses, eight hotels, and 118 shops selling groceries in which alcohol could be purchased in sealed bottles; as well as four special shops offering bottled beer and soda water.

The area with the densest network of pubs and restaurants of varying quality was situated close to the Main Square in what was known as the '*lauby*' ('under the arches') and in Velká, Dlouhá, Kostelní and Pivovarská streets. This quarter was crowded with innumerable shops selling garments, groceries and spirits. The streets tended to fill up towards evening and on Sundays, when they attracted throngs of customers, as well as beggars, tramps, petty criminals and prostitutes looking for business among the workers and market sellers from the surrounding countryside. In the course of the 1870s and 1880s most of the shops and pubs here became the property of Jewish traders and publicans.

Markus, Rudolf and Adolf Haberfeld provide a good example. The brothers came from an old Moravian Jewish family settled in the Slovácko region where their father most probably leased pubs. Markus, the eldest, made a living as a waiter in an inn owned by Sigmund Groag in Vítkovice until he struck out on his own and took on the lease of a pub in Pustá Polom, which he ran from 1885 to 1896. He and his first wife Hermina Herlingerová (1866-1903), had four children. Their first child Gisela died in infancy but they went on to have another three children: Olga (1887-1943) and in 1889 the twins Alfred and Elfriede.

In 1896 Markus got the chance to rent the old Moravská Ostrava tavern from the Kremer family. In the same year the owner died and Markus bought the house from the heirs. The house had several rental apartments as well as the established pub. As soon as Markus acquired the building he embarked on conversion of the tavern interior so that food could be served as well as drink. In the Czech Lands it was already far from easy to comply with the myriad hygiene regulations and so the renovations not only took longer than expected, but were much more expensive - an experience that is still not unusual today.

In his application for permission to serve hot food, Markus stated that his business was intended above all for workers and that the largest numbers of customers came on Sundays and paydays. He was therefore putting in his application for reasons 'of health and hygiene, because drinking cold beer on an empty stomach is damaging and, what is more, hungry customers become drunk faster and drink more, and this leads to various disturbances.'[9] In the end he succeeded and at the end of 1897 he opened the renovated pub restaurant complete with modern kitchen. In 1901 Markus applied for permission to serve hot drinks, tea and coffee and with it rum, brandy and fine liquors, as well as approval for billiards. In 1899 he launched a cabaret show there, with a compere, and to judge by the complaints of the owners of surrounding properties about loud singing spilling out into the streets late at night, it must have been very popular. Another reason why Haberfeld's restaurant was famous was that he employed female waiting staff, which was quite daring at the time.

In 1903 Markus's wife died in Vienna while having medical treatment and in 1905 Markus asked the local district office for permission to lease his restaurant to his younger brother Rudolf on the grounds of his own ill health. This request was granted and the youngest of the three Haberfeld brothers, Rudolf, ran the establishment first as a lease-holder and from 1910 as owner. Rudolf had been helping Markus in the pub-restaurant from an early age. When he became its owner he renamed it the Alhambra, obtained a license to run legally permitted games and also started renting rooms to pub guests. After the outbreak of the First World War Rudolf was called up to the front in 1915. His wife, Hermina née Weissová (*1877), looked after their three small children, and Rudolf entrusted the management of the restaurant to the young German Catholic, Adolfina Friedrich. He came back from the war unscathed and ran his restaurant himself until his death in 1935, when his widow took over the business. None of the three children showed any interest in hospitality as a career. His son Ernst became a doctor and lived in the Liberec region, his daughter Edita married the Ostrava merchant, Jaro Gabriel, and his younger daughter Elisabeth married the owner of a beer warehouse in Olomouc, called Steiner.

The middle Haberfeld brother, Adolf, was born in Kněždub by Strážnice in September 1865. He settled in Vítkovice in the 1880s, when it was already an industrial community with a rapidly increasing population and so hospitality services were in unprecedented demand there. Adolf opened a labourers' pub and became a leading figure in the professionalisation of pub and restaurant staff. He founded and was for many years the president of the Society of Tavern and Coffee-House Owners, and was a co-founder of a vocational school for apprentices in the tavern, hotel and coffee-house trades.

At the turn of the century pubs were springing up like mushrooms in the surrounding communities as well, and many were owned by Jewish families. One example was Roth's tavern in Nová Ves. In 1864 Josef and Kateřina Sonnenschein from nearby Svinov bought house no. 34 in Nová Ves for 5,500 guilders. This was a time when the authorities were still reluctant to grant Jews licenses, and so it was not until 1871 that the Sonnenscheins finally managed to open the tavern, after buying tapster rights from a local citizen called Mácha. They did not actually manage the tavern themselves since they were busy with other shops, and so let it to Leopold Huppert, who ran it up to roughly 1877/78. The pub, on the busy imperial highway linking Opava with Těšín, was not a business success, and in 1878 Josef Sonnenschein's property was subject to bankruptcy proceedings. Josef owed 4,000 guilders to his brother-in-law Ignatz Guttmann, who bought the tavern in 1879 and together with his wife Rozálie and their two daughters became the licensees. Guttmann entrusted the actual management of the tavern to Johanna Franklová.

He took over personal running of the pub in 1884, but died suddenly in August 1886. His widow Rozálie wanted to take over management of the pub, but soon after her husband´s death creditors started to appear on all sides and she found herself in serious financial difficulties, which she partially resolved with a loan from the Ostrava brewer and president of the Jewish Community, Markus Strassmann.

At the end of 1892 their daughter, Hermína, married Sigmund Salomon Roth from Štiavnik in Slovakia and the young couple ran the tavern. Roth came from a family of inn-keepers, and was well prepared for the pitfalls of this kind of business. Roth brought new life into the apparently moribund tavern. He had an entrepreneurial spirit and was determined to clear the debt and launch a more successful era. He expanded the licences to serve meals as well as beer, wine and spirits, but also coffee and other hot drinks, and provide facilities for permitted games. Sigmund Roth eventually bought the tavern from his mother-in-law and had the licence transferred to himself. He immediately started a thorough renovation of the building. He managed to build up a first-class pub-restaurant and his ambitions grew. In 1897 he decided to build a brand new pub designed by the Ostrava architect Šimon Žůrek. It was a grand two-storey building with a spacious bar-room, restaurant salons, billiard room, kitchen, larder, toilets, apartment for the landlord, and extensive cellar divided into dairy, wine and beer sections.

He had managed to turn a village pub into a prestigious establishment where guests were served by liveried waiters and the rooms were stylishly fitted out and decorated. The inn became the centre of social life in Nová Ves; balls and various celebrations were held there, local clubs met there, and the amateur dramatic society used the hall with its stage for rehearsals and performances. The inn and its owner became so famous that when the tramline from Svinov to Moravská Ostrava was completed, the stop close to the inn was named *U Rotha* ('Roth's Place').

Roth's Hotel.

Sigmund Roth managed to rise to become a member of the Nová Ves elite. In March 1905 he stood in the local elections and became the third councillor in the community. Three years later he was second councillor.[10]

His widow Hermína leased out the inn. In September 1913 she married Erich Ralph Freundlich. After the founding of Czechoslovakia in 1919 she and her husband decided to devote themselves to real estate business, building villas and apartment houses, and also to farming. At the beginning of 1924 Hermína Freundlichová was the largest tax-payer in Nová Ves.[11]

In neighbouring Polish (Silesian) Ostrava, the brewery belonged to the Counts of Wilczek. From the 1830s they leased it on a long-term basis to Šimon Frankl who also managed the local distillery and coaching inn. He himself looked after the commercial side of the brewery business, and hired a maltster to oversee the production process. Frankl became very affluent and was among the most important figures in the Jewish minority in the Ostrava region. He held the lease up to 1878, but it was then that the banking house Frankl & Sohn in Moravská Ostrava went bankrupt. It was owned by his son, Sigmund, and he was a silent partner in it, with 80,000 guilders and bonds to the same value tied up in the bank. As a result of the debts arising from the bankruptcy he withdrew from his lease agreement with Count Hans Wilczek and the brewery was leased to Albert Wechsberg who later became the prominent Ostrava banker. The brewery was never modernised; it struggled to recover from a fire in 1872, and ceased to trade a few years later.

In Radvanice by Polish Ostrava there was what was known as an emphyteutic brewery at the local tavern (emphyteutic means that leaseholders had to undertake to improve rather than simply run the property). It was leased from the Counts of Wilczek by Josef Neumann, a member of an old Jewish family from Silesia. Neumann, together with his wife Karolina who came from a well-known Fasal family of Těšín merchants, had leased part of the Radvanice agricultural estate at the beginning of the 1830s. During the revolution of 1848, when there was uncertainty about the future of rights to produce and sell alcohol, Josef Neumann bought the Radvanice tavern from the Wilczeks together with their rights to produce beer and spirits. His younger son Leopold took over the distillery while the elder son, Emanuel, (*1825), took over the brewery which he started to modernise, installing steam power in the 1880s. At the same time he looked for new outlets for the brewery, leasing or buying up tavern concessions in Moravská Ostrava and then stocking them with Radvanice draught beer. In 1874 he purchased a house in central Ostrava and established a tavern in it called the Radwanitzer Bierhalle, later famous as the Hotel Gambrinus.

Advertisements for Hotel Gambrinus.

Emanuel Neumann actively engaged in public life. From the mid-1850s he was a member of the Radvanice community council and several times mayor. Like most Jews in the Ostrava region his politics inclined to the German Liberal Party. At the same time he was a prominent member of the Moravská Ostrava religious community, although he never held any office in it. He contributed abundantly to the poor welfare fund not only of Radvanice but also of Ostrava.

In 1889 Emanuel handed over partial running of the brewery to his eldest son, Arthur, (1856–1931), who after the First World War was to make a name for himself as a brewer in Hamburg. In 1896 Emanuel fell seriously ill and went to Vienna to undergo surgery, but died before the operation could take place. After his father's death Arthur took over the management of the brewery but found it hard to cope with the competition from the Moravská Ostrava brewery of M. Strassmann. He got into serious financial difficulties and was eventually forced to sell the brewery at the beginning of the twentieth century. His younger brother became a lawyer in Vienna and the youngest, Felix (10 September1862-5 June 1942) became an architect.

With increasing industrialisation in the 1850s the brewing sector was set to modernise and expand. In 1857 the Ostrava burghers had leased the town brewery to a young Markus Strassmann, a native of Tlumačov.

Despite being only 26 years old, he had considerable experience with the organisation and management of beer production, since his father Josef

Strassmann's Brewery.

Strassmann was the long-term lessor of the Moravian nobles' breweries in Tlumačov and Lukov. He also had the capital needed to carry out the necessary changes. He was already the owner of a tavern in Slušovice and co-lessor of the Ostrava town distillery. In 1861 Markus started to produce beer exclusively by bottom-fermentation and as part of this strategy he built a modern lager cellar three years later. He was able to increase the volume of production dramatically from 169,000 litres in 1858 to 1 million litres 10 years later, not only because the quality of Ostrava beer had improved.

Strassmann concentrated above all on opening new taverns, in this way accumulating property and making plans to buy the brewery following the abolition of the traditional monopoly rights on production. In 1882 he installed steam power in the brewery but to carry out his planned full-scale modernisation he needed to buy it outright, which he was able to do only in 1889. In 1899 he turned his business into a joint-stock company, the Moravia-Ostrava Brewery and Malthouse Ltd., with a share capital of 2½m Crowns. Strassmann was the largest share-holder and chairman of the board, while his sons Adolf and Ernst became directors.

In 1895-6 Strassmann built a family villa designed by Felix Neumann and named Terezie in honour of his wife. It was taken over by the Gestapo in 1939 and still stands in Ostrava.

Villa Terezie, 2006.

He died soon after, on the 23 September 1903 and was buried in the Jewish cemetery in Ostrava. Today the trade-exhibition centre *Černá louka,* 'Black Meadow', stands on the site of the old brewery.

Adolf, the eldest of Markus's three sons, joined his father's brewery and at twenty-three became its technical director. He substantially diversified the business activities of the firm, for example by buying the steam rolling mill from A. Wechsberg & Company, setting up branches in Tovačov and commercial stores in Slovakia and Sub-Carpathian Ukraine. In the 1920s, however, the firm started to run into economic problems, and with the economic crisis of the 1930s these became too serious to handle. Adolf and his brother Ernest had to resign from their positions on the board of directors and in 1934 hand over the administration of the business to the banks.

Adolf's great passion was the theatre and it is no surprise that he was a member of the committee set up to build a theatre in Moravská Ostrava. He was also on the Moravská Ostrava town council, and was involved in the plan for the New Town Hall building.

One interesting feature of Adolf, eldest son of the first president of the Jewish Religious Community in Moravská Ostrava, was that he married a German protestant, Josefina Glassner, the daughter of a prominent Ostrava entrepreneur in civil engineering and the chemical industry, Karl Glassner. They had two children: Dorothea (*1897) and Josef (*1901).

His younger brother Ernest was director of the brewery from 1926 to 1933. In religious life he took the place of his father and was very active in the Jewish community. He never married, and faced with the awful prospects following the German invasion, he committed suicide on 7 August 1939.

Distillers

Naturally, not only brewers but many producers of distilled spirits lived in the Ostrava region. The great majority of these were of Jewish origin. They included Gustav Lichtenstern, born in 1838 and related to the wealthy family of the Ignatz Lichtenstern. He came to Ostrava at the beginning of the 1860s and embarked on the career of a merchant and tavern-keeper. In 1868 he obtained a license for the production and sale of spirits in Moravská Ostrava. One of his taverns was at the intersection of Velká, Radniční and Pivovarská streets. In the courtyard there was a distillery, converted in 1879 into apartments. In 1877 Lichtenstern purchased an apartment house in what was then Hlavní ulici (today 28. října), where apart from 4 apartments and retail space Lichtenstern had his factory for the production of liquor. Gustav married Eva, the daughter of the Josef Neumann, in 1869. Her brothers, Emanuel and Leopold, were also engaged in the production of beer and spirits.

In the local elections of 1876 Gustav became a member of the Ostrava community council, representing the German liberals, a political position taken by most prosperous Ostravak Jews. He was active in a number of associations, but never took any prominent part in the life of the Jewish community. He died on 14 June 1896 in Ostrava and his business, *Gustav Lichtenstern Fabrik feinster Liquere*, passed to his widow and son.

Hoteliers and Restaurateurs

Much social life centred on hotels and coffee houses. One of the most famous and fashionable hotels of pre-war Ostrava was definitely the Hotel National which was built by the *Kommerz- und Gewerbe Bank* whose director was Siegmund Czuczka, to plans by Wunnibald Deininger. The hotel was opened in February 1913 with 80 rooms, 3 dining rooms, a club and American bar, restaurant, and café for ladies to take coffee and cakes.

Jakob and Ferdinand Gronner took the hotel over in the early 1920s and extended it to 160 rooms but, more importantly, adding the Palace Café and the famous (infamous?) Boccaccio Bar. The café was advertised as a 'Real American café', which appealed to the Ostravaks as they thought of Ostrava as being like an American town. The interior was shiny, functional, full of sharp-edges and staircases with rich lighting and mirrors. It was vivid, noisy and chaotic.

On the semi-circled balcony sat the so called *chachaři*, the 'bad boys', sharp smart young men most of whom later would become directors and

Palace Hotel Café, 1941.

senior managers. Under the balcony was the 'European corner', occupied by decent, honourable citizens. The last part of café was 'Little Asia' full of professional card players and travelling salesmen. It was a place of liberal thinking where Czech and German artists could meet, gossip and discuss the latest trends in art and music. Jazz music was played. The bourgeois ladies would take their coffee and cakes in another part of the hotel! In 1939, the hotel was aryanised and became the 'Palace Hotel', taking on the name of its café.

Politicians and Diplomats

The Ostrava Community, like most Jewish communities in Eastern Europe, was self-governing. Associated with it were various committees, groups and organisations responsible for different aspects of religious, social, educational and welfare activity, and these were also self-governing. The concept of being involved in 'politics' in the widest sense was hence well established among Ostrava Jews and it is not surprising to find some of them becoming active in local and national government and civic organisations. In the late nineteenth and early twentieth century, they were disproportionately represented in liberal or left wing as opposed to conservative or right-wing, parties and this may have been a consequence of the self-help traditions of Jewish groups. It is also probable that the existing conservative groups in Moravia at the time were not very welcoming to Jews or were even antagonistic, whereas liberal and left-wing bodies were more welcoming, at least at that time when right-wing political parties were mostly connected with the landed aristocracy and strongly connected with the Catholic Church.

The Viennese Rothschilds were very heavily involved in Ostrava through the ownership of the Vítkovice Mining and Iron Corporation established by Anselm Rothschild. He was integrated into national and imperial politics at the highest level, his father having had direct contact and a friendship with the Chancellor of the Austrian Empire. Ostravaks could not aspire to such heights but played their part on a more mundane level.

Markus Strassmann was a typical *macher.*[12] He was a well-established member of the town elite. From 1873 he had sat on the Ostrava community council, where he devoted himself mainly to economic and financial matters. He also took a great interest in the life of the local Jewish community, in 1875 becoming the first president of the newly founded Jewish Religious Community in Moravská Ostrava. He contributed regularly to the poor-welfare fund, supported the health-benefits society *Bikur Cholim* and took part in various kinds of charity projects. Politically he inclined to the German liberal camp, sitting on the board of what was the strongest political party in the town at the end of the nineteenth century – the *Deutscher Verein für Mährisch Ostrau und Umgebung.* He was a member of the Board of the local Brewers' Union, elected to the Municipal Committee in 1873 and was a City Councillor in Moravská Ostrava from 1886 until 1903 when he was awarded the title of Imperial Councillor. He was an active supporter of the German-speaking business community in the national linguistic struggles at the turn into the twentieth century. He was sufficiently esteemed by his colleagues on the council that a street was named after him, now Veleslavínova Street, near the City centre.

In between all these activities, he and Terezie managed to produce and bring up 14 children. Markus was described as being energetic and dynamic!

Some of our more elderly Ostravaks claim to remember him fondly as he used to hand out sweets whenever he came on a visit to the Jewish Primary School. This is certainly a mistake since he died in 1903 and they were almost certainly remembering one of his sons, who were also busy philanthropists and businessmen.

Alfred Vogel was hardly as multifariously energetic in public life as Markus Strassmann but he was prominent enough in the German-speaking Social Democratic movement to be advised to flee Czechoslovakia as soon as the Germans invaded. His Jewishness was not as relevant as his political involvement at the time.

Viktor Haas studied law, was awarded the degree of JUDr. from Vienna and practiced in Ostrava. He specialised in labour law and was elected to the Czechoslovak Parliament in 1920 as a member of the *Deutsche sozialdemokratische Arbeiterpartei,* the German Social Democratic Worker's Party, campaigning for the rights of workers and especially miners. In 1925 he left parliament to become head of the Miners' Welfare Insurance scheme in Ostrava, and he held this position until the German invasion in 1939. His wife, Frieda Rippel, was a piano teacher and former concert pianist.

In 1939, like Alfred Vogel, he thought it wise to leave the country before the Nazis arrested him for his political beliefs. He escaped over the border to Poland with Max, his son-in-law, and thence to England where they were able to secure visas for Frieda, Max's wife Olga and their daughter Eva. Max was a medical doctor and Olga a dentist and the family lived in Přívoz before they left for England.

Eva recalls that she and her parents spoke Czech at home and that Viktor was a Czech nationalist. He bought Eva a doll and when she wanted a bride doll insisted that she had a doll in Czech national costume instead. Although Viktor had been brought up, educated and practiced in German he obviously appreciated the fact that after the foundation of the Czechoslovak State, they had all become Czechs.

Another Ostravak, Fred Austin (né Alfred Stiller) was not himself active politically but devoted his career to teaching and his retirement to charitable work with local old people, for which he was awarded an OBE in 2005. His son Ian, however, is very much involved. He was a local councillor between 1991 and 1995 and was then elected a Labour Member of Parliament in 2005, and held his seat in the general elections in 2015 and 2017.

Most of the Ostravak 'politicians' were involved in Jewish organisations rather than local or national secular ones. Thus, Joseph Wechsberg became the secretary of the Jewish Party in Parliament, and was later sent by the Government to America to explain the official Czech position on the Sudetenland question and to influence American public opinion in favour of Czechoslovakia retaining its borders.

Teddy Kollek, future mayor of Jerusalem, came to Ostrava from Palestine to encourage emigration there. He was quite successful and several Ostravaks did move to Palestine. In the 1920s and early 1930s the emigrants were motivated by Zionism and a desire to build the Jewish National Home. Later, of course, it became an escape from Nazism and the Holocaust.

Dr Josef Rufeisen was elected a member of the Zionist Central Committee in 1919 and he presented a paper at the congress on the organisation's statutes. At the second Zionist conference in 1921, it was decided that the seat of the executive would be transferred from Prague to Ostrava. Josef Rufeisen remained president from 1921 to 1938, when he was succeeded by Dr Pavel März. Josef is described as a hard worker, a master of detail but not charismatic, and an uninspiring speaker. In the great split in the world Zionist movement between those who supported Chaim Weizmann and those who did not, Rufeisen was a supporter. Rufeisen was co-opted as a member of the Jewish National Council in 1918. He emigrated to Palestine with his family in 1938.

Pavel März, who succeeded Josef Rufeisen, was born in 1894 and studied law in Vienna but his studies were interrupted by the First World War. After the war, he concluded his studies at Charles University in Prague and joined the law practice of his brother-in-law in Ostrava, specialising in industrial law. He joined the Zionist movement almost as soon as he qualified and later became active in the Jewish political party but his life was not all law and politics. In 1933, the Jewish Winter Sports association was established and Pavel was elected chairman and in 1934 he was elected President of the World Maccabi Congress.

After the German invasion in March 1939, Pavel März, then Chairman of the Czech Zionist organisation, was involved by Eichmann in the 'Emigration Centre' in Prague, which encouraged Jews to leave the country but only after paying the *Reichsfluchtsteuer* or emigration tax and leaving all their property to the government. In 1939, Pavel himself emigrated with his family. In Palestine he was a member of the committee for the development of the constitution for the emerging State of Israel. During the years 1946-1981 he was a member and then vice-president of the High Zionist Court of Justice, which decided cases relating to the Zionist movement and its many factions and disputes. Between 1945 and 1948 he also acted as internal auditor of the *Hagannah*, the underground Jewish defence force. There is something delightfully Jewish in having the accounts of an illegal organisation audited! The experience would have stood Pavel in good stead after the establishment of the State of Israel, when he became head of the finance department at the Ministry of Interior, and carried out this function until his retirement in1965. He had changed his name to David Meretz. In 1961, he was a witness in the Eichmann trial in Jerusalem.

Shlomo Rozen (né Rozenzweig) was born on Ostrava in 1905 and his brother Valtr in 1918. They were both Zionists and held left-wing views. Shlomo made *aliyah* [13] in 1926 and in that year acted as the guide to Tomáš Masaryk who made a historic visit to Palestine, the first Head of State to visit the nascent Jewish State.

Between 1933 and 1935 Shlomo went back to Ostrava to serve as an emissary for *Hashomer Hatzair*, a socialist Zionist youth movement. On his return to Israel, he worked as Secretary of the Kibbutz Artzi movement and became a member of the Knesset in 1965, as a member of Mapam, the United Workers' Party. In 1969, he became Deputy Speaker and Deputy Minister of Absorption in 1972. Although he lost his seat in 1973, Golda Meir appointed him Minister of Absorption, which portfolio he retained until 1977 when he was appointed Minister of Housing, but lost his seat later that year. He died in 1985.

His younger brother Valtr left Ostrava illegally with his two brothers in 1939 and made *aliyah*. He lived in Kibbutz Sarid and later worked as a toolmaker in the armament industry, becoming an official of the Trade Union. Between 1939 and 1948 he was an active member of the *Hagganah*. In 1948, shortly after the foundation of the State of Israel, he and Max Brod, the writer and friend of Franz Kafka, set up the Israel-Czechoslovak Friendship League which is now the Israel Society of Friends of the Czech Republic. He was the initiator of the exhibition of children's paintings and poems from the Theresienstadt Ghetto in the Yad Vashem Memorial Centre. In 1965, he became the first Israeli citizen to be awarded the Gold Medal of the Czechoslovak Society for International Relations.

In 1975 he was elected a city council member in Ramat Gan and was deputy mayor from 1983 to 1989. In December 1991 he was appointed Honorary Consul General of the Czechoslovak Republic and in 1993 the Honorary Consul General of the Czech Republic. He was the initiator of ceremonies to commemorate the first deportation of European Jews from Ostrava to Nisko and in 1994 he was awarded honorary citizenship of Ostrava. On 28 October 1998, the Czech President Václav Havel conferred the Order of the White Lion on him for exceptional services to the Czech Republic.

The Municipality of Ramat Gan set up a gallery of Israeli art in 1987. It was named the Chanan Rozen Museum of Israeli Art in his honour in 2012.

In 2007, he was also honoured with the *Gratias Agit* Award by the Czech Foreign Ministry. He died in 2007. Shlomo and Chanan's sister ran the *T'Helet Lavan* organisation, a Zionist youth group, in Ostrava in the inter-war years.

As we have noted, in the 1920s, the emissary of the Zionist movement sent to Ostrava from Palestine, to encourage emigration, was Teddy Kollek. He later became Mayor of Jerusalem, from 1965-93, and it was during his tenure that Jerusalem was reunited. He was responsible for much of the development of the city and has been described as 'The greatest builder of Jerusalem since Herod'.

According to the Seifter family tradition, there were once two brothers. One was decent, honest and reliable but the other was not. The 'good' brother was concerned that he and his children had the same family name as his 'bad' brother and his children and so he went to the rabbi for help. He was told to add 't', for "*tov* which is Hebrew for good, to his name. And so Seifer became Seifter.

Karel Seifter studied in Leipzig and became a bookseller in Bremen. He and his non-Jewish wife, Anna, were arrested as they were members of a trade union, involved in illegal anti-Nazi resistance and were communists. They were sentenced to 2 years' imprisonment and due to be sent to Dachau afterwards but Karel's sister Grete got them out of the country to Czechoslovakia, as Czech citizens.

When not selling books or engaged in promoting communism, Karel trained the girls' handball team for the *Poale Zion*, a left wing youth group.

In March 1939 the Gestapo moved into the house where Karel and Anna were living with their young son, Pavel, who was born in 1938. Karel tried to flee across the border to Poland but was caught and returned. That happened three times before a friendly border guard (who came from Orlová, like Karel) let him across. Two months later Pavel was pushed across the border in his pram by a friend with an official work permit. Shortly afterwards, Anna came across with false papers and the reunited family went to Sweden and thence to Southend, England.

Pavel went to the Czech schools in Shropshire and later in Wales. At the end of the war, the family returned to Czechoslovakia and Pavel continued his education in school in Ostrava, where he was in the same class as Josef (Pepek) Salomonovič (See Chapter 11, *Such Beautiful Corpses*). He went to university in Prague and to Nancy in France for his postgraduate study. Back home, he lectured for 3 years until he was dismissed by the communist authorities in 1968 for his political views. He became a window-cleaner, although probably not a very good one despite his 20 years of experience of it. During that period, he made friends with a young man who had also fallen foul of the authorities and had a job rolling barrels in a brewery. In his spare time, his friend wrote plays and was interested in politics. After the fall of communism, his friend became a well-known playwright and politician. He was Václav Havel.

Pavel was a key member of the Civic Forum movement during the Velvet Revolution in 1989. He subsequently served as Deputy Director of the Institute of Contemporary History and then as the Deputy Director of the Institute of International relations in Prague. President Václav Havel appointed him Director of Foreign Policy between 1993 and 1997 and to the position of Czech Ambassador to the Court of St James from 1997 until his retirement in 2003. After his retirement Pavel stayed in England as a Visiting Research Fellow at the Centre for the Study of Global Governance at the London School of Economics.

Like Karel Seifter, Artur London (born in1915) was a communist. In his early years he worked in his father's upholstery business but joined the Communist youth league, Komsomol, and later the Czech Communist Party. In 1937 he was a member of the International Brigade in Spain, moving to France in 1939 to work for the International Committee for the assistance of Republican Spain. In France he joined the resistance and was arrested by the Nazis and sent to Mauthausen. He survived, returned to Czechoslovakia and was appointed Deputy Foreign Minister in 1949. He was sentenced to life imprisonment on trumped up charges in a communist show trial in 1951 but the judgement was annulled in 1956.

Paul Schwartz was born in 1882 in Ostrava and studied law in Wrocław, Berlin and Leipzig. He then entered the German diplomatic service, becoming Consul General of the German Reich in India and Consul General in New York in the 1920s.

Werner Reichenbaum was born in Cologne in 1934. His father Artur was born in Ostrava and studied business administration at the University of Cologne. He fell in love with and married his landlord's daughter, Herta Krebs, and worked first for the Oppenheim Bank and then as a sales representative for various food companies. In 1938 he had his work permit revoked as he was a Jew, and so he, Herta and Werner moved to Prague. He was able to obtain only poorly paid work in Prague and Herta became the main bread-winner, as a secretary in German companies. Even this did not last, and she was dismissed as 'politically unreliable' – that is, married to a Jew. Werner's parents decided to divorce so that Herta, at least, could get a job. Werner lived with Artur who kept in as close contact with Herta as he could. Artur did not wear the yellow star despite being Jewish as he did not want Werner to be known as even half Jewish. In January 1944, however, Artur was sent to Theresienstadt (he told Werner he was going to a work camp) and in September to Auschwitz and then to Dachau where he died on 31 December 1944, reportedly of typhoid fever.

After the war, Herta and Werner had to leave their apartment in Prague and lost all their possessions. They were not accepted as Czech citizens so Herta decided to return to Germany.

Main Square with market stalls.

To the Germans in 1934, they had been 'The b****y Jews' and, in 1945 they had been 'The b*****y Germans' to the Czechs. It was not a very auspicious start in life for a young boy. Werner went on to study law at the universities of Bonn, Lausanne and Cologne before taking a doctorate in international law in Luxembourg and Madrid as well as courses at the Academy of International Law at The Hague. He joined the Diplomatic Service of the Federal German Government in 1964. He was Ambassador in charge of North-South Negotiations in international organisations in New York, Paris, Brussels, and elsewhere, and ended his career as Federal German Ambassador to Chile (1993-97) and Mexico from 1997 to 1999.

Shops and Business

By the end of the nineteenth century Ostrava was a wealthy city and its Jewish Community was similarly wealthy. The written records and memories of survivors paint a picture of the Jews of Ostrava as members of the professions, senior managers and self-employed successful businessmen. It appears to have been a golden age, both metaphorically and literally. Yet of course this is only part of the picture. Of the 8-10,000 Jewish inhabitants of Ostrava in the 1930s, we have details of probably fewer than 1,000 and it is they who produce this positive image. Of the remaining 90% of the Jews we know almost nothing but we can be certain that they were not all among the wealthy and successful citizens of the town. They would have included the market traders, pedlars, porters, casual labourers and unemployed beggars

Main Square, before 1911.

who left almost no trace in the archives or even the memory of those who survived.

So, while the picture of Ostrava's Jewish business is accurate as far as it goes, it is definitely incomplete. Many people would have been aware of the prosperity of the few only by looking through shop windows and by being recipients of the support that the wealthy Community could and did provide.

Jews had for many years been brewers and distillers of alcohol and innkeepers and publicans. This involved the provision of food as well as drink and there was a natural progression to becoming hoteliers and restaurateurs. Inn-keeping led naturally to having a small grocery or general store, as a side-line. Many Jewish families would have had the equivalent of 'the corner shop', a general grocery/green-grocery/hardware store serving the immediate local area. Heinz Vogel recalls that his maternal grandfather had such a shop in Frýdek-Místek and managed to feed his large family from it. Many other families did something similar, the commercial equivalent of subsistence farming but with the possibility of developing into something much better for their children if not for themselves.

Salamon Barber was born in 1829 in Halcnow, near Bielsko Biala. He trained as a butcher but became a tavern keeper and toll-keeper, and then in the late 1880s moved to Ostrava and opened a grocery shop. At this point his family began to move up in the world. His great-grandson, Peter, became the Head of the Map Department in the British Library in London.

Bertie Golderberg's maternal uncle, Jakob, had a grocery shop in Bohumín and provided temporary refuge for Bertie and his father when they fled Ostrava in 1939.

Max Pomeranz was the partner of Arnon Smetana's father in a car engine repair shop in Ostrava. Max was married to Millie Schein whose parents also had a grocery shop in Bohumín. The Pomeranz family were living in the same flat as Arnon and his parents when they were all deported to the Kraków ghetto.

Ph Dr Vilém Reinohl has a very interesting family tree, starting with Simon Maier, his great-great-grandfather who was a grocer in Žarošice, near Brno. Simon's fourth child, Viktor, took over the family shop. He, his wife and two of his children were murdered in the Holocaust. His daughter, Lisa, married and continued to live in the family house but the shop had disappeared in the war. Vilém is descended from Simon's first child, Valerie, whose son-in-law Wilhelm Reinöhl was the distributor of Budweiser beer in Moravia. Vilém points out that in the family tree there are a very disproportionate number of degrees and higher degrees, with some members of the family able to speak a remarkable number of languages. A basic food shop can be a stepping stone to academia and linguistic excellence, as many Jewish families can attest.

Henry Heitlinger was born in Třinec in 1921 and lived with his parents on the main street. The house belonged to Mrs Landesberg, who was his godmother and who kept a grocery shop in the house. She was a widow and had three sons, all very intelligent and qualified engineers. Apart from the Heitlingers, there was a veterinary surgeon on the same floor occupying a flat with his family.

Leo Wiener remembers his pre-war family as being wealthy hoteliers but his great-grandmother, Emilie Huppert (née Würzel) owned a small food shop in Mariánské Hory, working very hard by herself while bringing up the younger children of her family.

Ida Salomonowitzová married Julius Hausner in 1898 and from 1909 they lived in Slezská Ostrava where Ida had a small grocery shop while Julius worked as a sales representative. Ida's mother, Henrietta née Hornung, also had a small grocery shop, in Moravská Ostrava. Ida was the great aunt of Miša and Pepek Salomonovič.

Arnošt Rusek's parents had a business (which he described as *Kolonialwaren*, the German name for a grocery) in Bielsko Biala. Eva Krämer came from a family of grocers. Her grandfather, Leopold, owned an inn and grocery shop, while her father Jindřich and her Uncle Salo were partners, owning a dairy, grocers and a wholesaler of coal. Salo later became President of the Jewish Community. Herman Brodavka was a partner in an inn which was very successful and he and his partner, Olsak, planned to open a grocery, butcher and blacksmiths, although family problems caused Herman to abort the plans.

Barbara Wechsberg's Krieger great-grandparents (and the grandparents of Josef Wechsberg) owned an apparently rather up-market store in Ostrava, selling 'the highest quality goods for Passover at good prices!', while Anna Grant's maternal grandfather, Reuben Bergofen, was a wholesale importer of grocery.

Krieger's shop and advertisement.

In 1938/9 there was an organised programme to help Jews from Ostrava to emigrate to San Domingo. The leading figure in this programme was Bruno Kulka who had migrated to Ostrava between 1921 and 1923. In the early 1930's he opened a grocery store close to Masaryk Square in the centre of Ostrava and a year later specialised in importing tea and coffee, trading under the name 'Kolumbia'.

Owning such a shop was not just the ambition of Jewish families of limited means. Eva Erben (née Löwidt) recalls that, as a privileged child,

> To satisfy my desire to be a shopkeeper, my father made me a toy shop, made out of wood and set out as a grocer's, with real drawers with labels, Sugar, Flour, Salt and so on, as well as bags, scoops and a set of scales. I was in seventh heaven!

Children nowadays tend to have more expensive desires!

The preparation of bread and cakes and the killing and butchering of animals for food are activities subject to many special religious regulations which observant Jews will follow, and so Ostrava had a number of kosher butchers and bakers – candlestick makers are not covered by such religious rules. George Tyrell (né Tramer) was born in 1935 in the Vítkovice Maternity Hospital to Otto and Ernestine. His maternal grandparents, Samuel and Toni Ambor, had a kosher butcher's in Vítkovice and the local tram stop was known as 'Ambor's'. Bertie Goldberg remembered Ambor's shop:

Samuel Ambor's Kosher butcher's shop.

> We went to a kosher butcher called Hornung. We had a kosher baker called Mandel (Mandel Bäckerei) and we had another kosher butcher which was frummer (more religiously particular) than Hornung, called Rose. He came from Kežmarok in Slovakia. There were many kosher butchers in Moravská Ostrava: David Hornung on Stodolní street, Bedřich Huppert in Přívoz, Samuel Ambor in Vítkovice, Salomon Efreim Schulsinger in Moravská Ostrava, Abraham Forscher in Ostrava - Zábřeh and others.

Ruth Elias (née Huppert) had a happy and prosperous childhood, living with her grandparents, father and uncles because her parents had divorced. Her father Bedřich and Uncle Zikmund ran a butchery and sausage-making business, both kosher and non-kosher, in Přívoz. Another uncle, Otto, ran a butcher's shop in Mariánské Hory. Henry Heitlinger, Ruth's cousin, recalls visiting the Hupperts in Ostrava and having to eat in a kosher restaurant run by the Webers in Ostrava as the Huppert family did not keep strict *kashrus* at home. The Webers' son married Henry's aunt and she ran a fast food restaurant (almost certainly the first in Ostrava) open 22 hours a day and 7 days a week, near the Rix department store. Ruth wrote her autobiography, with horrifying details of her experience in Auschwitz when she was forced to kill her baby,[14] and it has been published. She recently wrote to us:

> I wanted to pay you a compliment that you are doing such an important work to remember the disappeared big and serious congregation which once had been Ostrava. I wish you plenty of success with your work and am sending you and your collecting-colleagues many regards together with our greeting SHALOM.
>
> Yours Ruth Elias (born Huppert)

It is likely that the Hupperts bought their sausage skins from the Goldbergers who had a butcher's shop and a sausage skin business in Stodolní in Ostrava. The shop is now a bar.

George (né Tramer) Tyrell's maternal grandparents owned a kosher butcher shop, while his paternal grandparents, Julius and Mathilde Tramer, had a retail business called Universum, which dealt in industrial rubber goods, at 26 Tyršova Street. George's father Otto worked in the business but left Czechoslovakia in 1938 via Poland to the UK. George, his mother and grandparents were all deported to Theresienstadt; Julius and Mathilde were shipped off to Auschwitz but George, his mother and her parents all survived. The Germans expropriated the business after the invasion of Ostrava.

The enormous concern Bat'a (pronounced Batya in Czech, not Bata) dominated the shoe business in Ostrava as well as in the rest of Czechoslovakia but there were individual shoe shops and shoemakers although they were the bottom end of the market and not the expensive bespoke shoemakers we know today.

Ernst Frinton (né Frischler) was born in 1917, the son of a shoemaker, and was brought up in poverty together with his younger sister Anni. Ernst was a bright boy and always wanted to study medicine. In 1935 he was accepted as a student at the German university of Prague. In 1938, after the Munich Agreement, the Jewish students were told that they were no longer allowed to study so he worked as a children's tutor for some months before managing to obtain an exit visa. After a frightening train journey through Nazi Germany he arrived in London and was accepted to study medicine in Scotland but had to start the course from scratch and learn enough English to follow the lectures, many given in strong Scottish accents. He duly qualified, married, changed his name from Frischler to Frinton and spent 10 years in the UK before embarking on a successful medical career in Canada. He was never to see his parents or sister again.

Artur Radvansky was 4 years younger than Ernst. He was born in Radvanice where his father owned a shop selling shoemaker's supplies and ironmongery. This suggests that there were quite a number of independent shoemakers or that the poorer members of society made or repaired their own shoes. Henry Heitlinger's parents had a drapery store in Třinec but they also sold shoes. Henry recalls that they also sold coffins, on the top floor of the shop, presumably a 'Pay now, go later' scheme! Rivka Kukuk married Henry Gröbel in 1916 and he had a shoe shop, as did Hugo Eichenbaum.

Pick's leather goods shop.

Emil Pick probably did not supply raw leather to the shoemakers but he had a large leather workshop and an impressive shop in Ostrava.

His grand-daughter, Eva, became a fashion model in the UK and was photographed by Anthony Armstrong-Jones, the husband of the late Princess Margaret. Emil's great grandson, Peter Briess, has written and published the family history.[15] The Briess family lived in Olomouc and dealt in wholesale grain and pulses.

Heinrich Schrötter had a bakery in Svinov but his son, Zikmund, was interested in and trained as a textile engineer although he did help his father in the bakery. Zikmund worked for a shirt manufacturer in Ostrava and ultimately bought the business which he then ran under his own name.

The Goldberg family had a thriving textile business, manufacturing and selling shirts and other items from their shop in the Melcer building just off the main square in Moravská Ostrava. It was not their shop that Zikmund bought.

Edith Rosenbergová's grandfather, Salomon Löwy, died before she was born. He had a textile business in Ostrava. His widow, Johana, married Herman Reiss who ran a substantial business in underwear, bedding etc. on Avenue 28 října in the centre of Ostrava.

The Kasslers were a large wealthy family, connected by marriage to the Hupperts, Heitlingers, Färbers, and Wieners. They had hotels and restaurants in Bohumín. Leo Wiener (b. 1933), who is now the family archivist, remembers Simon Kassler, who ran a large drapery or department store in Nový Bohumín:

Schrötter's shop, 1936.

Simon was a son of my great grandfather Leopold Kassler who as far as I can tell was married 3 times!

The sons of Leopold Kassler were Ferdinand, Jacob, Josef, who was a stamp and coin dealer in Vienna but later moved to Prague after the Anschluss, Isidor who was a chemical engineer or did electric plating and was married to his cousin in Peter Erben's branch of the family - her maiden name was Berta Kassler, Simon, who was married twice, left his second wife and moved to Vienna in 1929 where he got into some serious unknown financial difficulties and was imprisoned for several years.

His only son from his wife was Bedřich, better known as Fritz, who later moved to Prague and produced and made the first film of the Golem legend. A year later he emigrated to New York and changed his name to Frank Kassler, married twice and formed the Kassler Film company.

Ferdinand Kassler also sold clothing, ironmongery and tools in his shops in Nový Bohumín

Kitty Liebreich's grandfather, Izak Borger, opened a new and second-hand clothing shop in Ostrava. His son Markus originally joined his father in the business but later opened his own shop, selling hats and clothing. Markus's business prospered, helped by a dowry from his wife, and they extended into bespoke clothing using English fabrics, which were very up-

Starý Borger shop.

market. Izak's fifth child, Terezie, took over his business with her husband Max Löffler and expanded it to become a well-known department store. To distinguish Izak's business from Max's, Izak's became known as Starý Borger (Old Borger's).

Max's was not the only business producing ready-made clothes. Ignaz Reisz was a tailor who built up a successful business in Ostrava after moving there from Slovakia. He specialised in making jackets and trousers for miners which he kept unfinished in his shop and when a miner came to buy a new suit, it just had to be finished for him and was ready very soon. Ignaz made a lot of money and bought a very valuable plot of land, with two houses, on the corner of the main square and the main street. It was from the balcony of this building that the Reisz family waved to the Emperor on his visit to Ostrava in 1880. Pavel Reisz recalls:

> Grandfather Isaac was married twice but had no children from his first wife. He then married grandmother Katarina and they had 2 daughters and 4 sons, including twin boys of whom my father was one. Both boys looked absolutely identical and only close members of the family could tell them apart. Both were solicitors in Ostrava. One other brother was a bank manager and the fourth also a solicitor elsewhere. Of the 2 daughters one married a dentist and the other the owner of a bank and later of the biggest hotel in the town – he died fairly young, without children, leaving his wife, Aunt Camilla, very rich.
>
> The two houses were rebuilt by grandfather, and grandmother often told me that one of them was the first house in the town with running water. It was on its balcony that the family waved to Emperor Franz Joseph when he visited the town in 1880 or so. My father Joseph was the senior partner in a firm of solicitors and he specialised in commercial law which was very profitable. He spoke Czech reasonably well and had to appear in court occasionally. His twin brother Franz was a nice old boy but not very bright and he had no children but he was a keen philatelist and often gave me lots of interesting stamps. Their office was in the square opposite the new town hall and father walked there every morning at 9.30, then came home for lunch at 1 pm, had a little rest then went to the 'Kaffeehaus' to play a card game called Taroc with his pals, then back to the office at 3 pm and back home again at 6. What a wonderful life!!! On the way home he performed his only domestic duty by calling at a delicatessen shop and brought home every night some sausage, cheese or other delicacy.

Pavel's younger brother was Karel Reisz, the film producer.

In the early years of the twentieth century, Jonáš Löwy had a wholesale and retail business selling porcelain and glassware in the main square in Ostrava. Hugo Strach owned an umbrella shop just behind the Imperial Hotel, and Ferdinand Folkart ran his sign-writing business in the main square.

Advertisement for Hugo Strach's umbrellas, and the Hugo Strach shop in 1906, at the time of the Emperor's visit.

Anyone who has travelled to Ostrava by road or rail will have seen the tremendous forests and timber stores in the neighbourhood and will not be surprised that there were a number of timber and furniture merchants in Ostrava.

Joachim Kafka and Markus Strassmann bought two plots of land for the Jewish cemetery in 1872. Kafka is described as a timber merchant, presumably successful and wealthy. In 1910 the Jewish Bank was set up in Ostrava and Mr. Moritz Wechsler, timber merchant, was elected its first director. Henry Heitlinger recalls having French lessons as a child in Těšín from the daughter of the Fischgrund family who owned a large timber business. John Gould, whose family came from Frýdek-Místek, has traced some of its early members: 'My great-grandmother, Fanny Glesinger (1841-1922), was born near Těšín and was a member of the leading Jewish family, the best known branch of which owned and ran a large timber and wood products business'.

Lindsay Offer's father, Hans Stern, was born in Ostrava in 1912. His father was Arthur Stern and his grandfather was Marcus Stern (born 1848). Markus and Arthur had timber mills and a talcum mine. Erich Mayer owned a wholesale timber business, dealing in treated timber – round timber, joists, plywood etc. – and also leased a saw mill in Slovakia. He was murdered in Auschwitz.

Although Jews were traditionally involved in the timber trade, not all of them were successful at it. Josef Frank was described as a timber merchant but later became partner in the firm Hausner & Co, canning fish in Ostrava, under the trademark HAWE; it was not an obvious career progression!

Barbara Gilford's great-grandfather, Mořic Buchsbaum, was a wealthy and successful timber merchant whose son Ignatz (b. 1877) was destined to join him in the business, although Ignatz would have preferred to study philosophy. In compliance with his father's wishes, Ignatz was apprenticed to his father's timber business partner in Wrocław (Breslau), but he became fascinated by the Marcus brothers' bookshop which he passed every day on his way to work. Finally he was invited to become apprenticed to them as well as to the timber trade. He completed both apprenticeships but decided to devote himself to the world of books. He moved to Prague and worked in a bookshop but soon decided to start his own, so moved back to Přívoz where his married sisters lived. He opened his own shop close to the main square in Přívoz, which is also quite near the main railway station for Ostrava.

His business prospered, diversifying into stationery, toys and publishing and even becoming a sales agent for Biro ball-point pens. His son, JU Dr Hans Buchsbaum, emigrated to the USA in the late 1930s but could not persuade the rest of the family to join him, and so his mother, sister and

Advertisement for Buchsbaum's Bookshop.

Buchsbaum's Bookshop in 2006.

brother-in-law were all murdered by the Nazis. In the USA Hans changed his name to John, married, and had a daughter, Barbara.

Bertie Goldberg's family originally lived in Haydnova Street in a house which was owned by Schreiber, a Jewish furniture entrepreneur. We have not been able to establish a connection to the now well-known UK furniture brand of Schreiber. Julius Laufer owned a famous carpentry business manufacturing various types of furniture, which was located on Pivovarská Street 26. He probably supplied the Kassler furniture store in Bohumín.

Buchsbaum was not the only publisher in Ostrava. Rabbi Dr Ruben Färber, who was born in Oświęcim in 1869, had a shop in Ostrava selling liturgical items. He then founded a publishing house, Ha-Ivri in Ostrava and published such illustrious authors as Max Brod, Vladimir Jabotinski, Dr F Hillel, and Hans Kohn. He and his family made *Aliyah* before the war and lived in Tel Aviv.

Julius Kittl was born in Brno in 1855 but moved to Ostrava where he established a major publishing and printing business and became a town councillor. He was not Jewish although his wife, Ernestina née Liewerová, was. He owned and published the *Ostrauer Zeitung*, the local newspaper.

He also published the *Jüdische Volksblatt* , a Jewish newspaper which had a short life before merging with *Selbstwehr*, the Zionist paper. Kittl published books of Jewish interest although the report in *Jews in Czechoslovakia* [16] that he had published the 12-volume Lazarus Goldschmidt German translation of the Talmud appears not to be true. In 1918 Julius Kittl moved to Austria, where he died in Vienna in 1922. At that time the publishing house was a public business company *Kittl Julius a spol.* (i.e. & comp) and had 4 co-owners. In 1939 all the assets were transferred to Countess Nostitz as part of the Nazi aryanisation programme.

Beautification of the mind being thus provided, ornamentation of the body was offered by a number of jewellers in Ostrava. Berthold Schwartz, a jeweller, was one of the instigators of the foundation of the Moravská Ostrava Jewish Community in 1875. Kitty Liebreich's father, Alfred Borger (born in Ostrava in 1899), was a jeweller and watchmaker, with a shop in the corner of the main square near his father's shop, Starý Borger. Jakub Koppel Melcer married Augusta Weislitzer in 1895 and used his wife's dowry to set up as a watchmaker and jeweller. His son, Leo, studied watchmaking in Switzerland and then joined his father's business. Leo was deported to Nisko and, on his return, the whole family moved to Prague from where they were deported to Theresienstadt and then Auschwitz, where Leo's wife and son were murdered. Leo Melcer was on Schindler's List, probably because of his watchmaking skills, and was liberated from the Brinnlitz camp.

Leo Wiener recalled his early years in Bohumín:

> We occupied one apartment and the other one was let to the Wallner family, who were friends of the family and were in the jewellery business. I don't remember the parents at all but I do remember their son who lived with them in the apartment and he must have been in his early thirties.

One of the Secretaries in the Czech Embassy in London in 2015 recalls:

> I am sure that Mr Wallner is the one who made my grandfather´s watch. I still keep it as I consider it to be part of my family´s history. It is unbelievable how life was exciting in Svinov, when there were local butchers, bakers, hairdressers and jewellers/watchmakers who were part of the community...I enclose an interesting webpage (in Czech) where M. Uhlíř, who is the son and grandchild of the former local hairdresser offers memories. He remembers that his granddad´s closest friend, Isidor Wallner, didn´t want to leave because he was sure that his life was not in danger after the Munich agreement...

Ostrava also came to boast smart, modern department stores. The largest and best-known were Rix and Textilia – the local equivalents of Harrods and Saks Fifth Avenue. The Rix store, just behind the Imperial Hotel on Avenue 28.října was originally a subsidiary of the Rix store in Vienna where Adolf Lüftschitz had been apprenticed. He was sent to Ostrava to manage the store there and he subsequently bought it. Some time later he changed his name to Rix, to match the store. The original building was re-built in 1928 to a very modern design by Ernest Korner. The building was destroyed in August 1944 in a bombing raid on Ostrava.

Adolf's elder son, JUDr Ernst, died in 1935, and so the younger son, Ing. Otto, joined the company. Adolf and his wife were deported to Theresienstadt and on to Auschwitz where they were killed. Otto was warned that he was wanted by the Nazis and escaped to Poland and hence to London with the help of some friends.

Trudy Korda's (née Wechsler) father, Igo, established and built up TEXTILIA and ultimately bought the whole building. Trudy was an only child, and went to a Czech primary school and Czech gymnasium. Her family spoke Czech at home. In the late 1930's she was sent to school in Switzerland. Her father was on business in Paris when the Germans invaded and her mother was visiting her in Switzerland – they did not go back to Ostrava. Their family house became the Gestapo headquarters in Ostrava. They ultimately emigrated to the USA where her son still lives and practices as a lawyer.

Josef Wechsberg in his book *Homecoming* poignantly describes his memories of the main shopping street in Ostrava as he walked down it in the immediate aftermath of the war:

> We were on Street of 28 October. Rubble, emptiness, disorder, chaos. Yet right here had been the most expensive shops – haberdashers, costumiers, hats, jewellers, bookshops, department stores, an antique shop. Moravská-Ostrava was a fast-living, fast-spending town. People liked to buy and show off. This street had been the fashionable promenade, the *corso*. Everybody came here between five-thirty and seven p.m., everybody who 'counted' and wanted to be seen.

What must have been quite a common business activity for women is little mentioned, either out of delicacy or disapproval of such private enterprise, although it certainly flourished.

Ernst Frischler lived with his parents and sisters, maternal grandparents, an uncle and single aunt in a flat, described as 'not much of a flat, it was more like a slum'. His father was a cobbler and had a small workshop in the flat. His mother did bits of dress-making to try and help make ends meet and helped in the workshop as well. At night the workshop became Ernst's bedroom, with the addition of a bit of curtain, four chairs and the board they used as a table making up his bed, with a straw mattress. Despite their poverty, they usually had a maid who came from the countryside nearby and was of course badly paid. Such girls were attracted to Ostrava, whose streets were paved with coal dust rather than gold, but which did offer the possibility of economic progress. They did not stay very long as maids, apparently, as they found that prostitution was better paid and less hard work!

Ernst came to England on a *Kindertransport*, became a qualified doctor and ultimately settled in Canada.

In his memoir, Pavel Reisz remembers:

> Occasionally, when we were 10 or 11 years old, instead of going to the garden we secretly crept into the 'naughty' part of the town, behind the town hall, to observe the local miners going into the well advertised brothels and taverns.

He also had a brooch from his mother from the pre-war period, probably from one of the Ostrava jewellers.

NOTES

1. *Instituce finančního charakteru na Ostravsku do roku 1918.* Blažena Przybylová in Ostrava 19, Šenov u Ostravy: Tilia 1999;*Ostravské finanční ústavy v letech 1918–1953.* Blažena Przybylová in Ostrava 20, Šenov u Ostravy: Tilia, 2001.
2. In 1882 Maxmilian Munk had married Sophie née Mannaberg, born on 15 February 1864 in Budapest. Her parents were Michael (Mihály) Mannaberg and Rosa Rachel Mannaberg née Gutmann from Lipník nad Bečvou, sister of the co-owners of the Vítkovice Mining and Smelting Works, Wilhelm and David Gutmann. Maximilian Munk retired in 1919 and moved to Vienna, where he died on 27 November 1923. Sophie survived her husband for nearly eight years, dying in Vienna in August 1931.
3. In 1906 MU Dr Pressburger had married Lilla Schwarz, born on 15 July 1883. The couple had two sons- Fritz, born on 23 March 1907, and Hans, born in June 1913. After the establishment of the *Protektorat,* Rudolf Pressburger stayed in Prague. He was transported from there to Theresienstadt, where he died on 23 December 1942. Both his sons survived the Holocaust. Hans died in 2001 and Fritz in 1998 in Toronto in Canada.
4. Following the occupation of Czechoslovakia in March 1939 Gütig was sacked as a Jew and went to Poděbrady, where he tried to recover his battered health. He then moved to Prague, from which he was transported in 1941 to the Łodz Ghetto, where he soon died. Two of his Vítkovice pupils and successors from the ranks of surgeons, Dr.Ludvík Alt and Pavel Wurzel, met the same fate.
5. He survived Auschwitz and Buchenwald, and in 1947 officially changed his name to Arnošt Ryšavý. He worked as a doctor in Ostrava until his death on 29 December 1955. His wife Hedvika had been murdered in Auschwitz.
6. Ida Velemínský was transported via Theresienstadt to Ravensbrück, where she was murdered on 30 November 1944. The middle brother Jan was executed in Auschwitz on 30 December 1944. Jiří and Zdeněk were transferred to Gross Rosen and later to

Buchenwald, where they survived until the liberation. Jiří returned to Ostrava where he worked in the Fifejdy Municipal Hospital and became a consultant. He had to leave, however, following the occupation of Czechoslovakia in August 1968 by the armies of the Warsaw Pact. He spent some time in Slovakia but then returned and joined the Regional Hospital in Ostrava. He died on 26 October 1991.

7. Leo was linguistically gifted and apart from his mother tongue, German, he spoke Czech and French and his work primarily involved international trade deals. He was dismissed from his post on racial grounds on 31 March 1939, but had in fact stayed abroad from the beginning of March. He survived the war in Switzerland. His younger brother Hugo Spitzer, who was a chemical engineer and also worked at VHHT as a smelting inspector, was killed with his whole family in Auschwitz.
8. *Die tschechoslowakischen Beskiden und die Fatra. I. Die Beskyden von Friedek bis Bystritz a. H. II. Die Beskiden von Friedek bis Czacza und die Gebirgszüge von Czacza bis Rosenberg (Fatra).* Mährisch-Ostrau, 1922.
9. Archiv města Ostravy, OÚ MO, box Nr 324, sign. Gb 11, inv. Nr 204.
10. Sigmund Roth was a member of many societies including Jewish associations such as the sickness benefit society *Bikur Cholim* in Moravská Ostrava. He was president of the Jewish Community in Svinov and also helped to found the association of volunteer firemen in Nová Ves. In his will he remembered various charitable and religious societies including Christian ones. He died on 23 November 1911 from kidney failure and was buried in the Jewish cemetery in Ostrava in the section reserved for rabbis and distinguished members of the community.
11. Immediately after the German invasion in March 1939 Hermina Freundlichová (Rothová) decided to transfer the licence to Matilda Kučerová, a Czech Catholic, in order to forestall aryanisation of the property. She died shortly afterwards, however, on the 26 June 1939, and was buried three days later in the Jewish cemetery in Ostrava. By the terms of her will, the inn went to youngest son Evžen, who at the time of his mother's death was in the USA, where he was familiarising himself with the management of modern catering businesses and he remained there throughout the Second World War. In November 1942 the whole property was confiscated by the Germans, without compensation, for racial reasons.
12. Yiddish. One who is very busy and involved in committees and organisations.
13. Hebrew, literally 'going up', used to mean emigrating to Israel or, earlier, Palestine.
14. Ruth Elias *Die Hofnung erhielt mich am Leben* Piper 1988. Published in translation as *The Triumph of Hope,* Wiley, 1998.
15. Peter Briess, *The House That Saved Us,* Life Books, 2015.
16. *Jews of Czechoslovakia,* 3 vols., Jewish Publication Society of America, 1968.

7

The Arts

Jewish Architects and Architecture in Ostrava[1]

Ostrava is not rich in historic architecture, although we might expect to find some remains from the city's foundation in the thirteenth century by Bruno von Schauenburg, the Bishop of Olomouc, who was the leading figure in Moravia at the time. He had high hopes for the development of the city as a market town near the river Ostravice on the trade routes east-west from Opava to Těšín and north-south from Silesia to Moravia. Unfortunately these hopes were premature and Ostrava remained a backwater without significant architectural landmarks until the eighteenth century. It was then that Moravská Ostrava slowly began to grow from a small town built around a square with a few low, mostly just one storey, half-timbered houses and short

The Landesrealschule and the Cathedral of The Divine Saviour.

streets. Even this was relatively undistinguished, however, and it was only a 100 years later, in the 70s and 80s of the nineteenth century, that three buildings were put up in Moravská Ostrava that in terms of size, style and impact were quite unprecedented in the town.

These were the Neo-Renaissance palatial building of the *Landesrealschule* (1870); the magnificent cathedral-like Church of The Divine Saviour designed by Gustav Meretta, (1883-89), and the main Ostrava synagogue (1879) in Pittler Street, built in a characteristic Moorish style. The style and form not to mention the cost of these buildings openly reflected the ambitions of their owners: the Town Authority, the Catholic Church and the Jewish Community. All three were determined to demonstrate their wealth, confidence for the future and their determination to transform Ostrava into a modern metropolis.

It is telling that one of this trio of important buildings was a synagogue. There were about 700 Jews (out of a total of 13,500, and so 5% of the population) in Moravská Ostrava, plus a number of others in the neighbouring villages. Their numbers quickly increased by immigration until this community became the third largest in the Czech lands after Prague and Brno. There were many Jewish physicians, lawyers, clerks and businessmen and the Jewish community was relatively wealthy and formed an important part of the bourgeoisie of Ostrava. Not surprisingly, a major part of the most valuable architectural heritage of Ostrava in the first half of the twentieth century is connected with Jewish clients or Jewish architects.

It is quite symbolic that a synagogue stands at the beginning and also at the end of our story of Ostrava's Jewish architecture. A plot of land was bought for the Ostrava Synagogue in Pittler Street, not far from the main square, and the whole building was completed in just four months in 1879 (see p. 78). The facade was dominated by a central trio of portals and high arched windows. Two low towers were built into the frontage. Doors in the towers gave direct access to the staircases to the gallery from the main entrance steps and the onion-shaped domes were topped with Stars of David. Two tablets representing the Ten Commandments were on the pediment. The interior was designed as a three aisled hall with galleries on three sides.

Franz G. Böhm is usually identified as the architect as well as the main contractor but how far this Ostrava builder actually designed the building and decoration is uncertain. The Moorish style and the Arabic motifs of the facade and interior appeared on the facade in a clean mature form and the frontage gave a feeling of balance. The whole building was masterly in monumental impact. It is unlikely that a provincial builder would have been able to achieve this result, but there is no information about Böhm collaborating with anyone else even though we think that the architect was probably Wilhelm Stiassny. Other synagogues in the area (Frýdek 1864, Krnov 1871-72, Cieszyn 1878-80) are by no means its equal, and in later years, when palatial synagogues were built in Přívoz and Vítkovice, the main synagogue in Moravská Ostrava remained unsurpassed.

The Moorish-Byzantine style of architecture became the dominant style for European synagogues of the nineteenth and first half of the twentieth century, clearly differentiating them from Christian churches. The first significant building fully in this style was a synagogue in Berlin on Oranienburgerstrasse by Eduard Knoblauch from the years 1859-66. It is significant that the frontage design in the Berlin and Ostrava buildings is almost identical even in the use of detail. The building in Moravská Ostrava lacked the monumental cupola of the Berlin building and the corner spires were lower. In spite of that, it showed a clear inspiration by this admired building and reflected the ambitions of the new Moravská Ostrava Jewish community.

The oriental style was adopted and modified for the synagogues in Přívoz and Vítkovice. In the Přívoz building, of 1904, there was an eclectic combination of various styles with a predominance of Neo-Romanesque, and in the case of the Vítkovice synagogue, of 1911, it was a modernist Art Nouveau variation on the Byzantine theme. Its author was Ostrava architect Felix Neumann, one of the really remarkable personalities in the history of architecture in Ostrava.

Felix Neumann (1860-1942) was the son of the owner of the Radvanice brewery, Emanuel Neumann, and his wife Karolina, née Loew. After attending Opava grammar school he decided to take up architecture, which he studied with Karl König and Heinrich von Ferstel at the technical college in Vienna. He then joined the large studios of Wilhelm Stiassny in Vienna and later the Kayser & Grossheim studio in Berlin.

In 1889 he set up as an architect and builder in Moravská Ostrava. He was the first Ostrava architect with such a high level of qualification and experience, and it was undoubtedly this fact, as well as his skill and ability to make a good personal impression, that led to his winning the competition for the design of the Ostrava Deutsches Haus, the cultural and social centre for the Germans of Ostrava. This remarkable building in the Nordic Neo-Renaissance style brought him immediate local acclaim and a lot of commissions, mainly from Ostrava's German-speaking upper class, both Jewish and non-Jewish. The style was very popular in Germany at the time but the German House was the first building in Ostrava in that style.

Neumann's architectural work is extensive and demonstrates a wide variety of styles, although almost every project was unique, major and helped to transform the face of Moravská Ostrava before the First World War. These were houses that were completely novel and brought a totally new look to the main square and streets of Ostrava. For his father he built a two-storey palatial house in the Nordic Neo-Renaissance style on the main square in

Deutsches Haus by Felix Neumann.

1891 with the popular Radvanice ale-house on the ground floor. On the opposite side of the square he designed a Neo-Baroque house, built 1898-99, with a luxury coffee house known as 'Union' which was run by Charlotte Schönhof.

In 1907 he built the first ever four-storey house in town for Albert Wechsberg (1831-1913), the important merchant and banker, on Mostní Street. It was in the spirit of late Art Nouveau, with characteristic grinning gargoyle faces under the cornice. He also designed a department store for Sigmund Roth (1909-10) on the main square in the spirit of post Art

Nouveau Neo-Baroque, and a hotel with a coffee-house, the Royal, for Moritz Reicher in 1911-12 on Reální Street.

Royal Hotel and Coffee House, Felix Neumann, 1911-12.

Adolf Lüftschitz commissioned him to design the Rix department store in 1909-11, at the time the largest in Ostrava, to replace the original smaller, Neo-Renaissance building. It was a Neo-Baroque building with a rounded corner, wavy oriel and gables and a huge mansard roof. At the time it was created, it must have attracted attention not only by its size and a huge picturesque silhouette, but above all by the fully glazed shop windows on the ground and first floor. Compared to the other buildings, it must have been quite startling.

There were a number of other Jewish builders and construction companies in Ostrava but none of them achieved such fame and as many commissions as Neumann. The most important others were Eugen Noë & Ferdinand Storch, Vincenc Heinz & Gustav Kulka, Adolf Löwy, Viktor Sonnenschein and Hugo Hermann. It was Hermann who built the Hotel Bellevue for Wilhelm Löwenberg in 1909, close to the Říšský most – the Empire Bridge.

Before the First World War, the image of Moravská Ostrava was significantly enriched by Wunibald Deininger (1879-1963) from Vienna, a highly talented pupil of the Austrian architect Otto Wagner, who at the turn of the nineteenth to the twentierh century trained tens of excellent designers, promoters of Art Nouveau and Modernism in Europe. Deininger, together with his father Johann, also an architect, submitted the winning design for the competition to design the building of the Merchant and Trade bank in Moravská Ostrava in 1904. It was built the following year and blended late

Original Rix Store, Třída 28 října (28 Oktoberstrasse).

historicism and Art Nouveau. The whole effect was rather romantic, which is somewhat unexpected for a bank!

Deininger was not Jewish, but Jews were among his important clients in Ostrava. His engagement in the town continued, due to Rudolf Reisz (1882-1944), the young assistant bank manager. A few years later, in 1910-1911, Reisz commissioned Deininger to design his house on Přívozská Street. Rudolf's father, Ignatz (1839-1906), was a tailor and a successful textile trader, who could afford to buy a house on the main square. His wife, Rudolf's mother, Katarina, née Liebermann (1855-1944), ran the popular coffee house, Central, on the ground floor. This unostentatious Neo-Renaissance house was pulled down in 1912 and replaced with Deininger's newly-built, so-called 'House of the Heirs of Ignatz Reisz' built in 1912-13. The building demonstrates Deininger's interest in Neo-Classical and Neo-Biedermeier styles, including the rather bizarre cornucopias on the façade.

In 1911-13, he designed and built a whole block consisting of the Ferdinand Aufricht house with a fashionable coffee house, Café de L'Europe, and bar called *Bílý havran* (The White Raven) next to the theatre, now the Dvořák Theatre. He also produced designs for buildings erected by the contractor, Vinzenz Heinz and Gustav Kulka, and for the National Hotel in the post Art Nouveau Neo-Baroque style. The National Hotel was run in the 1920s by brothers Ferdinand and Jakob Gronner and later well-known as the Palace Hotel, frequented by the Jewish business and professional men and their wives. Unfortunately the only Deiniger building that today retains its original form is the House of the Reisz Heirs on what is now Masaryk Square.

Ferdinand Aufricht House and Café de l'Europe Coffee House, by Wunibald Deininger.

Sanitorium of Dr Heinrich Klein by František Fiala, 1909-11.

Wagner's architectural special training was passed on by the Ostrava architect František Fiala (1878-1927). Although he was not a Jew, and a large part of his output was connected with contracts for the Catholic Church, one of his most mature buildings was a private sanatorium for Dr Heirich Klein (1858-?).The clean, unornamented design and façades of the sanatorium were an excellent example of geometric Art Nouveau. The composer Leoš Janáček died in this sanatorium in August 1928.

The growth of the Jewish population meant that during the high religious holidays the existing synagogues could not accommodate all the worshippers, and so the leaders of the Community discussed the building of a new synagogue. Remarkably for Jewish committees, this produced a concrete result in the 1913 design by Richard Strassmann, third son of the owner of Ostrava brewery Markus Strassmann, who had his practice in Vienna although he had been born in Ostrava. He produced the design in co-operation with the almost unknown Berthold Marmorstein. It was of a magnificent square building in a style based on ancient Assyrian architecture. The main frontage with three portals lined with tall columns made an austere but monumental impression. Low corner towers magnified the impression of strength and resilience. The pediment above the portico was kept deliberately low so as not to obstruct view of the oriental flattened dome

Jewish Cemetery by Richard Strassmann, 1913.

which spanned the central space. Unfortunately the ambitious design was never translated into reality, because of the high budget of 300,000 crowns and the outbreak of the First World War.

In 1913, a rich complex of ceremonial hall and operational buildings linked by a colonnade for the Jewish cemetery on the road to Opava was built to Strassmann's design. The U-shaped composition was in a style inspired by Byzantine and late Classical architecture (See **Appendix 7.1**).

The year 1918 and the subsequent formation of Czechoslovakia marked a fundamental milestone in Ostrava's cultural as well as its political history. For the first time a Czech, the Social Democrat Jan Prokeš, was Mayor of Moravská Ostrava and under his leadership Ostrava experienced a massive transformation.

In 1924, Greater Ostrava was created from previously separate neighbouring villages and there was a surge in construction. New buildings included the crematorium, Art Gallery, many banks and financial institutions, the Palace of Justice and, above all, the New Town Hall – a dramatic symbol of the new Ostrava. The architects of these buildings were not imported from Vienna, but came mainly from Prague, the capital of the new state. Prominent architects in Prague (J. Gočár, P. Janák, K. Hilbert, V. Hofmann, F. Fiala etc.) were employed to add a particularly Czech character to the city.

Ernst Korner (1888-1966) was an outstanding architect whose artistic importance and range of work paralleled that of Felix Neumann in the previous period, even though he has yet to be fully appreciated. He came from the large family of the distiller Johann Kohn from Uherský Brod. Like his siblings, he studied in Vienna, in his case building construction and architecture. Like Neumann, he was also taught by König and Ferstel. Ernst and his siblings, during a stay in Vienna, changed their name from traditional Kohn to Korner. It is interesting that a large part of the family, after studying, settled in Ostrava even before the First World War. Beno had a construction engineering office, Emil worked in a senior post at the Vítkovice ironworks and metallurgical plant (VHHT), Robert was a lawyer and Henry ran the distillery.

Ernst came to Ostrava in 1920 and immediately won several lucrative contracts, particularly the offices and residential building for the firm of Julius Rüttgers (1921-1922), which is stylistically close to the late works of Felix Neumann and Wunibald Deininger, and the conversion of the villa of Dr Karl Kraus on Nádražní Avenue into the Union Bank (1921-22), involving the addition of a massive classicist portico with a pair of Doric columns to the Neo-Baroque villa, and decoration of the upper storey with stone vases and statues by Augustin Handzel. Undoubtedly through the nepotism of his brother Emil Korner, one of the directors of VHHT, Ernst was charged with designing several residential complexes for workers of the Vítkovice Ironworks. VHHT was very hierarchical, with basic accommodation for manual workers, and better and larger housing for the middle and senior managers, so Ernst designed a set of villas, including a villa for his brother Emil, near the Vítkovice Hospital in1924-1925. He also designed housing complexes on the Ruská (Russian) Avenue (1929-1930) and Štramberská Street (1930) and a large, elegant complex of houses with passageways on the border between Vítkovice and Zábřeh (1930-1938) in a style untypical of Czech cities.

Jubilejní Kolonie, Hrabůvka, by Ernst Korner.

Korner's most important project for VHHT was the Jubilee Colony (1927-1929), a large residential complex built for the 100th anniversary of the ironworks in1928. All these buildings were based on the current architecture of Vienna, particularly the expressionist style known as Red Vienna. This is distinguished by numerous curves, and sharp angled shapes. Korner designed his residential complexes to include a residential courtyard, the so-called Hof, characteristic for German lands but unlike the terraces popular in Bohemia at the time. German or Jewish investors were still attached to Viennese culture. Korner was very popular and much sought after among Jewish clients and had the clear ambition to transform Ostrava into a modern and fashionable city through new architecture.

One example is the complex of commercial and residential buildings that Korner designed for Jakob Nesselroth, a Jewish Ostravak textile trader. The magnificent ensemble that grew up along 28 October Street and Nádražní Avenue in 1927-1935, is only a fragment of the original grandiose project, which included several blocks interconnected by internal commercial passages. Passages, as entrances to the arcades, were one of Korner's characteristic elements, as were angled bay windows and balconies, recalling the Art Deco style. The inspiration was again the architecture of Vienna.

Unquestionably Ernst Korner's most progressive building was the reconstruction of the Rix department store in 1928 replacing the baroque-style building designed by Felix Neumann with a brand new modern and elegant building in the style of Streamline Modern. The dominant element

Jacob Nesselroth commercial and residential buildings by Ernst Korner 1927-35.

New Rix store by Ernst Korner 1928.

was rounded corners with the maximum amount of glazing. The second and third floors extended further out from the building line, overhanging the street, while the upper floors, which were residential, concluded at the top with a neon banner with the inscription RIX. Unfortunately, this gem of Ostrava inter-war architecture fell victim to the Allied bombing of Ostrava in August 1944.

Korner built a department store for Josef Reisz on 28 October Street (1929-1930) and for Isaac Borger, what was known as the Starý Borger (Old Borger) shop on Velká Street (1930-1933) also in the style of Streamline Modern although less bold in form than the Rix. He also built an extension to the Hotel National with a spectacular vestibule (1929-1930), while it was run by the Gronner brothers. In 1938 Ernst Korner and his brothers succeeded in moving from Czechoslovakia to England.

The Rix store's major competitor was Igo Wechsler who had a successful business in textiles and carpets under the name Textilia. His first store was in Herben Street with a number of branches in nearby towns. In 1928 he bought the building formerly belonging to Jakob Goldstein between Deininger's bank and the commercial and residential building of Albert Schmelz designed by Felix Neumann. Wechsler's ambitions to build a truly metropolitan store in Ostrava is best illustrated by the fact that he did not commission the design of the building from any of the locals, but from the Jewish architect Maria Frommer (1890-1976). She came from Warsaw, studied architecture at the Technical University in Berlin-Charlottenburg and in Dresden. From the mid-1920s she had worked as an architect with her own design office and studio in Berlin and tended to the modern style of Streamline Modern.

In this spirit, her design for Textilia was a five-storey building, strictly modern to the point of avant-garde, but soon enlivened with decorative details and elements of Art Deco style at the request of the investor. Instead of full glazing, bright ceramic tiles were applied, the parts above the entrances were filled in, and on each floor there were balconies with the letter T in the parapet grid. The most interesting aspect of the department store is its interior, since Frommer imported into Ostrava the type of commercial building popular in Germany, with a monumental staircase, a vestibule and galleries. Their elegant, perhaps even baroque, curves contrasted with the rigorous regular grid facade.

The last of the big department stores is that of Bachner on Zámecká Street. Moritz Bachner (1871-1935) started out in hardware, kitchen utensils and groceries in the late nineteenth century. Business success, growing demand and the favourable financial position of the family then motivated Moritz to build a new department store in the centre of Moravská Ostrava. He commissioned Erich Mendelsohn (1887-1953), a fairly well-known Berlin architect who had already completed many remarkable modern department stores. Mendelssohn produced a design for Bachner's Ostrava store in 1933, partly from exile because in March 1933 he left Germany for good.

The building was completed and formally inaugurated in the same year. It is a modern six-storey building with a reinforced concrete skeleton structure and outer ceramic panels – a very modern concept. In contrast to his earlier work, Mendelsohn's characteristic dynamism is merely suggested

Textilia department store by Maria Frommer, 1928-9.

by horizontal indentation of the building with compressed windows and distinctive overhanging cornices. The emphasis on the façade was on the advertising sign Bachner above the shop windows executed in forward sloping italics, and then the dynamically extended circular logo of the department store on the level with the cornice. The engagement of an eminent architect undoubtedly contributed to the popularity of the company.

The last of the remarkable series of Jewish Ostrava architects is Elly Oehler or Olár (1905-1953), daughter of Ostrava builder Viktor Sonnenschein. She studied architecture at the German Technical University in Brno, where she met her future husband and working partner Oskar Oehler (1904-1973), originally from Přerov. A female architect was quite a rare creature before the Second World War, especially a Jewish one, but Elly came from a builder's family and so had a ready entrée into that world.

Although the couple opened a joint studio in Prague, they also made a mark on the face of Ostrava. Elly's father Viktor Sonnenschein became the chairman of the Jewish Community in 1934 and remained in office until 1940. One of his first steps was to radically alter the façade of the main synagogue in Pittler Street (1934), where he replaced the original oriental ornaments with simple smooth surfaces, designed by the Oehler couple. It was the last architectural intervention in the synagogue building before it was burned down by the Nazis, on 13 June 1939. The Oehlers were deported to concentration camps only in 1944 and survived, as well as their daughter, who managed to hide in Prague, until the end of the war.

The Oehlers returned to Ostrava and changed their German last name to Olár. Elly was severely affected by the hardships of war. Perhaps as a gesture of gratitude in 1947 she produced a design for a new building for the Jewish community in Ostrava with living quarters, offices and prayer rooms as compensation for all the destroyed synagogues. The plan was characterized by a strict functionalist style and the temple interior was designed as a flat barrel vault with ribbing. The impressive grandeur of space would also have been enhanced by rhythmically spaced pillars along the walls and at the sides of the Ark. Undoubtedly remarkable, this project was never realised as 1948 brought a communist takeover and a wave of migration to the State of Israel. Some further information is given in the Appendix.

It was not just on Ostrava that the Ostravak Jewish architects left their mark. Places as diverse as Prague, Edinburgh and Jerusalem also benefitted from their activities. Berthold Hornung was born in Ostrava in 1925 and his formal education ended abruptly in 1939 with the German invasion. His parents sent him to Prague in the vain hope of his being able to secure a place on a *Kindertransport* train. Instead he learnt carpentry in the training school set up by the Jewish community before he was shipped off to Theresienstadt where he survived the war. Post-war, he graduated from the Technical University in Architecture and Engineering but his initial activities were in designing pig-pens, as he had fallen foul of the communist authorities. Later, however, he was a senior member of the design team working on the Prague metro. In that position, he returned 20 train-loads of substandard Russian rolling stock intended for the metro, which certainly did not endear him to the authorities. In 1968 he and his wife Hana fled to the UK and settled in Edinburgh. There he became Director of the team set up by Professor Colin Buchanan to consider the transport strategy for Edinburgh. In 1972 he was invited by the British Council to head a team working on the re-planning of Jerusalem. In later years he acted as consultant to the Royal Fine Arts

Berthold Hornung, Edinburgh City Art Gallery brochure.

Commission. In 1996 he was awarded the honorary degree of D.Litt., from Herriot-Watt University in Edinburgh. He died in March 1997.

Photographers[2]

In 1839 change was in the air, industrialisation was beginning in Ostrava and the town was open to new people, new ideas and new methods. Photography would be one such. 800 miles south, Louis-Jaques-Mandé Daguerre demonstrated his new method of making a picture using light to the French Academy of Science, and launched what we now know as photography. Within a few months, the technique had appeared in Ostrava, 800 miles away and, as with much else in Ostrava, Jews would be at the forefront of this new activity. Indeed, Jews would be prominent worldwide in this field.

'If you want to be a good photographer you have to be a Jew.' Or so said American photographer Garry Winogrand (1928-1984) who was of course himself Jewish! According to Winogrand Jewish photographers are proud outsiders, irritable, full of irony, breaking and denying all artistic norms and rules. Eugenè Atget (a famous French photographer who documented everyday Paris life at the turn of the nineteenth to the twentieth century) just must have been a Jew, in Winogrand's opinion. This apparently unlikely claim about the overall Jewish role in photography in fact finds quite a lot of support in the history of the field in the hundred years after its invention. We find surprisingly many Jews in all branches of photography, in reportage, fashion portraits but mainly in the photography of daily life. A few names illustrate the point; Alfred Stieglitz, Paul Strand, Man Ray, El Lisickij, László Moholy-Nagy, André Kertész, Brasaïe, Dr Erich Salomon, Martin Munkasci, Robert Capa, Alfred Eisenstaedt, Lisette Model, Helen Levitt, Weegee, Aaron Siskind, Margaret Bourke-White, Irving Penn, Richard Avedon, Arnold Newman, Robert Frank, William Klein, Elliott Erwitt, Garry Winogrand, Diane Arbus, Lee Friedlander, Annie Liebovitz, Mary Ellen Mark, Joel Meyerowitz and Nan Goldin. Ostrava Jews did not figure prominently in this list of illustrious names, but a surprising number of working photographers emerged from their ranks.

Berkowitz[3] in his book on Jews and photography in Britain comments that 'Jews were not only contributors but catalytic agents, advancing studio photography and its business practices from the time of photography's inception…Jews were also court photographers. They advanced film and optical technologies…and played roles immensely out of proportion to their numbers in photo-journalism, advertising, fashion and sports photography.'

Daguerreotypes were initially considered primarily as a valuable new tool of scientific research and the first mention of the technique to reach Ostrava appeared on 25 September 1839 in the *Gazeta Krakowska*. Commercial applications followed rapidly, however, and the first advertisement for a professional daguerreotypist in the region appeared in the same journal on 23 February 1843, less than 4 years after the first announcement of the technique in Paris. It informs the reader that 'Wojciech Hugo Wilczek on his way through Kraków will, with the use of the newest inventions, produce in a few seconds and without regard to the weather, portraits of different kinds with the use of daguerreotypes for a price of 25 zloty.'

The first definite mention of modern photography in Moravská Ostrava can be found in 1863 in the advertisement section of the newspaper *Silesia*, where 'Karl' offered for sale a camera, lens, six cassettes, accessories and literature; all this of course exceptionally cheaply. In a similar advertisement in 1866, the Ostrava goldsmith, B. Schwarz, includes the required chemicals with the camera.

In 1863, Anton Rosner (Rösner) from Komorowic, today part of Bielsko-Biala (Poland), applied for authorisation to operate a photo-studio in Ostrava, most probably in Pittler Street. Bielsko-Biala, a town on the border of Austria-Hungary and Prussia, has much in common with Ostrava which is only about 35 miles distant. Bielsko was a textile town with its Jewish Community founded in 1870. In 1910, 15% of the population was Jewish.

Jakob Borger (born 1855) was also originally from Bielsko. He established photographic studios in many of the local towns before setting up studios in Ostrava-Přívoz and Bohumín. A short article in the 'Opava Weekly' from 21 November 1891 describes a big fire on 18 November in Příbor and the interest of its inhabitants in viewing the debris; 'In the background of the burnt out debris, the local photographer Borger took his photos.'

His peregrinations and business success are to some extent reflected in the variety of places where his eight children were born: Heinrich (1880, Bílovec), Rosalie (1882, Příbor), Rosa (1887, Fryštát), Gustav (1885 Moravská Ostrava), Malvine (1891, Příbor), Hermine (1889, Moravská Ostrava), Regina (1898, Vítkovice), and Leo (1896, Skorotín). His son Heinrich worked with his father in the studio on Nádražní Street 448 in Přívoz in the Bohumil Chvátal building. Heinrich's photos were awarded a silver medal in 1903 at the International Exhibition held in Crystal Palace in London. Jakob's youngest son, Leo, ran the studio in Bohumín. Heinrich Borger died in 1935 and his wife and two sons were murdered in Auschwitz. Later, the controversial photographer František Šidlík, who had been a fascist before the war but became a communist post-war so escaped official censure, operated at the same address, and the photo studio *Fotographia* finally closed in 2012. Today, the premises are used as a casino, one of many in the Přívoz district.

Proof that Jakob Borger was good at investing his money can be found in the 1903 register of houses in Moravská Ostrava, where he is listed as inn-keeper and the owner of a house on Franz Joseph Square. In 1913 he sold his parcel of land in Karviná Fryštát to the local photographer, Leo Beer, who used the land to build a photographic studio.

In1905 Jakob Borger left Ostrava and settled in Bohumín. He combined the profession of photographer with that of inn-keeper in nearby Šunychl. On the postcards of that period we find his name on the signboard of the restaurant '*Na Špici*'. He also worked as a photographer at the Franz Joseph railway station in Bohumín in 1918.

Bielsko was not only the birthplace of Jakob Borger but also the home of the Pateiski family. Jozef Pateiski was one of the more well-known photographers who worked in Ostrava. He was the first photographer there to manipulate images. Of course he had no computer: he made costumes for his models, photographed them, and then cut the photographs out and stuck them onto card or paper with a painted background, sometimes even using multiple images of the same person. He was also an inventor, inventing an air purifier, which was invaluable in Ostrava!

Jozef's mother was a sister of an earlier Jewish photographer from Bielsko-Biała, Albert Ferdinand Thiel. In 1907, After Jozef's death, his widow Josephine opened a delicatessen in the same building where Jakob and Heinrich Borger had their studio, (Nadražní Street 448 in Přívoz). Food for the body as well as the eyes was thus available in the same location.

Although it is most unlikely that there is a Jewish gene or genius for photography, we can see that there was a great and growing demand, both from Jews and non-Jews alike, for photographic records of themselves, their family, their town and places that they visited. Photographs were the Facebook of the late nineteenth century. This spawned a whole new line of business in the form of the picture postcard, where photographs were mass-produced by lithography. The first postcards were so called 'long address' postcards because one side was meant for indicating the address only, while the text was usually written directly into the picture on the other side. The 'short address' as we know it today – address on the right, personal message on the left – came into use around 1904. Even before the spread of printed postcards, photographers were making pictures of cities and landscapes, sticking them on pieces of cardboard and selling them as souvenirs.

Having set up a postcard business in the Altmarkt in Těšín in 1866, three years later the brothers Josef and Edmund Goldmann moved it to Ostrava. Their photographs are tagged with the legend *Goldmann Brüder* on the reverse. Postcards serving as advertisements for their business include views of the castle in Slezská Ostrava, the Chain Bridge (Kettenbrücke, collapsed in 1886), today's Masaryk square and also a panorama of Ostrava from the Jaklovec hill. In all probability these are the first ever photographs of Ostrava. Previously all there had been were lithographs of Jakob Alt or E.W. Knippel.

Bielsko was the birthplace of another Ostrava photographer with the surname Goldmann. This was Hermann Goldmann, who had a studio at Main Street (Hauptstrasse) 23 in Ostrava, in close proximity to the Grand Hotel where he worked at the beginning of the twentieth century.

Postcards could be mass produced, but photographers would also publish their own postcards based on their own photographic originals. These were usually depictions of scenes from everyday family or public life, some were used as advertisements for the photographer's own services, and a few were rather bizarre. Samuel Hahn photographed the arrest of mass murderer Ludwig Wresky and published the photo as a postcard. A person who sent it added a description: 'Let me send you a photo of Ludwig Wresky, four

Samuel Hahn: Photo postcard of mass murderer Ludwig Wresky.

times mass murderer from Moravská Ostrava. He killed two policemen in a brothel, one policeman on the street and even a man and his horse in a forest.' Sex and murder sold, even in those days...

Samuel is one of two photographers recorded in the 1910 census:

- Samuel Hahn, who claimed not to be Jewish, born 27. 10. 1857, of Jewish parents, belonging to the town of Nagyatád (in Hungary)
- Hermina Fleischhammer born 1866, Jewish, belonging to the town of Sabás (Hungary), both of them temporarily residing in Ostrava.

Samuel Hahn settled in Ostrava and bought his first studio from another photographer, Antonín Havránek, and ran another studio at 25 Nádražní Street.

The first permanent photographic studio in Ostrava had been set up in the same street as the main synagogue - Pittler Street, at number 116. Ottmar Rebaglio, Rudolf V. Schigutt and Anton Brand were all connected with the studio. Schigutt was the first known owner (c. 1870) of the studio, but the studio was much older. Probably the Goldmann Brothers and Anton Rösner worked there.

Despite photography becoming 'respectable' and the establishment of permanent studios, the occupation of travelling photographer did not disappear. No fair or festival would have been complete without a travelling photographer. In the Market Rules of Lhotka (Ostrava-Mariánské Hory), photography was classified with the circus and menageries.

Daguerrotype was the very first but not the only early photographic method. Another technology, well suited for use outside brick and mortar studios, was the so-called Ferrotype (better known as Tintype). In the Czech regions it used to be called 'American' photography. This technology was indeed widely used in USA, where it also saw its biggest boom of popularity during the Civil War (1861-1865). Tintype was related to the wet collodion process and was also used in the first coin-operated machines for instant photography. The BOSCO machine was named after the stage magician Bartolomeo Bosco and patented by the German inventor Conrad Bernitt in Hamburg in 1884.

Instant photography was also available in Ostrava, where Rudolf Kulka established his 'Photomaton' in Nádražní Street 14 in Moravská Ostrava, today's LIBREX store.

The inventor of this machine was Anatol Josepho, who may be a classic example of immigrant's success in the USA. His Photobooth was more sophisticated than the BOSCO machine, working with photo-paper and with everything enclosed within the booth.

Although Ostrava was relatively uninvolved in the Czech-German nationalistic struggles of the late nineteenth century, problems arose from time to time, and photographers were not immune. On 6 October 1897, the newspaper *Opavský týdeník* (*Opava Weekly*) carried an anti-Semitic anti-German (the two aspects were frequently conflated. Jews were generally German-speaking) article about Sigmund Teichner:

> News from and around Ostrava. Attention! In the villages around Moravská Ostrava, a certain Israelite Teichner from Moravská Ostrava is hanging around with the photographic machine and offering his "excellent" services. Many people were conned by this Jew and only later discovered that this Teichner is just a bungler, his pictures will get washed out after a few days, that it is just botched Jewish work, but quite expensive. Someone should find out if this kike is paying his taxes, so let this be a warning for both our readers and the authorities.

Looking at the photograph we print here, you can assess how good his work actually is, after more than a hundred years.

Sigmund Teichner started his business in 1882 and worked in his studio in Vítkovice until 1891 when he sold it to Josef Pateisky, and then in the Střelniční Street 14 until 1903. He was born on 5 May 1841, and 21August, 1903 the newspaper *Ostrauer Tagblatt* published his obituary, commissioned by his children. They left Ostrava even before the declaration of Czechoslovak independence in 1918.

Bertha Beckman was probably the first ever Jewish professional photographer. In 1843 following the death of her husband she took over his photographic studio in Leipzig. Later she opened photographic shops in Vienna and New York and may have paved the way for Dory Kallmus, 'Madame d' Ora', the prominent fashion photographer. She earned her place in history not only as a photographer but also as the first woman teacher of photography. She lectured at the school and research institute of graphics in Vienna, where Ostrava photographer, Ortwin Wenzel, was one of her pupils. His father Wenzel Wenzel was born in Bohemia and was a nationalist German. Ortwin served in the Wehrmacht as a photographer. In his recollections he wrote: 'When I saw how he – Wenzel senior – treated the Jews, I was ashamed'. It has to be said, however, that he wrote this in 1980 when anti-Semitism was less publicly acceptable.

His recollections of the photographic scene in Vienna post 1918 are worthy of note:

> ...The school tried to compensate us for the necessary hardship with interesting courses: portrait photography was taught by 'Madame D'Ora' – Dora Kallmus. She later left for Paris. We learnt a lot about composition and photographic design, but had little opportunity for

Portrait photograph by Sigmund Teichner.

> making photos ourselves...I decided, without my parents' knowledge to leave the school and look for work as an assistant with a photographer. At the end of the term I started in the studio of M. Schein in Nussdorfer-Strasse as a dogsbody. Schein was a Ukrainian Jew with the large rough figure of a peasant. One would never have expected the exquisite and delicate portrait photos he created.

In 1938 Schein emigrated to Argentina and his assistant, Mitzi Kasparik, took over his studio. In his new home Schein opened a photographic studio in Buenos Aires, where he spent the rest of his life. He focused not only on studio work but also on artistic portraits and nudes. He was particularly skilful in working with the Bromoil process, a complex printing process which produces rather more painting-like prints than conventional photographic printing.

Ostrava, through one of its natives, František Löwy, is linked not only with this technique but also with the European photographers who had contacts in high society. Löwy was born on 1 January 1883 in Ostrava to Joseph and Helen Löwy and died in Rio de Janiero in May 1949. He was one of the outstanding Viennese high society portrait and fashion photographers. By the first years of the twentieth century Löwy was providing images to all the leading fashion magazines. In addition to his studio in Vienna he had branches in Krnov and Karlovy Vary. In the late 1920s he opened a branch in Paris. One of those whose portrait he took was André de Fouquières, who was brought to Löwy's studio by his wife Rosa née Gutmann whose brother, Max was a co-owner of the Vítkovice Ironworks. When he finally left for Paris before the *Anschluss,* he applied for a passport to the Czechoslovak embassy in Vienna in 1934. In his application he used his Czech name, František, and registered his residence as Moravská Ostrava.

Anton Brand, a native of Vienna, was the most important Ostrava photographer of the late nineteenth century. Even though he worked for less than twenty years in Ostrava he created the most extensive topographic documentation of Ostrava real estate. To this day his work is reproduced in publications about Ostrava, although few writers acknowledge him as the photographer.

His origins and his religion are unclear as he was the illegitimate son of Anna Maria Brand, a Viennese chambermaid. He settled in Ostrava in 1874 with his wife Klementina, in house number 106. On 18 October of that year his son, Otto Josef, was born. Another son, Anton Josef, was born in Ostrava on 31 January 1876, but died in the same year. The family moved to house number 606 but that did not bring much luck as a further son, Albert, born in 1879, did not live to see his first birthday. He died at Zámecká (Schlossgasse) 167, which is the address shown on the back of Brand´s photographs. All these records are listed in the Roman Catholic registry even though Brand's wife is buried in the Jewish cemetery in Vienna and a record of her death is entered into the Registry of Deaths of the Jewish community of Vienna on 20 August 1912.

The first of Brand's photographs date from 1873 and are of local railway stations including Ostrava Přívoz station. The photographs are glued on cardboard with lithography made for Brand by the Ostrava printer E. Hebling and bear the inscription 'Anton Brand, photographer, M. Ostrau'. Hebling also made some cards for Brand for his portrait photographs.

Brand had his first independent studio in Moravská Ostrava in Pittler Street116, at the same address where Rudolf V. Schigutt and Ottmar Rebaglio had worked. When Schigutt moved to Bosnia Herzegovina, he left his studio to Brand, who advertised in the first issue of the local newspaper:

> I have the honour to inform the esteemed public of Moravská Ostrava and its surroundings that I have taken over the photographic workshop of Rudolf V. Schigutt in Moravská Ostrava on Pittler Street 116. I will henceforth make every effort to retain the trust which this workshop has, by first of all producing faultless work. We produce pictures from the smallest up to life size. Yours respectfully Anton Brand.

Brand's name can be found in the trade directory of 1881. There he is listed under 'Photographers' together with an Amálie Kojetínská. He made use of the newspaper, *Local-Anzeiger* in 1877 when he moved his workshop from Pittler Street to Zámecká Street 167, where he '...takes photographs in all weather conditions from 10 o'clock in the morning until 5 o'clock at night.'

In 1884 he extended his activities to Vítkovice, where he opened a branch of his studio in June of that year:

> This is to announce to my honoured public most humbly that on Sunday June 22 1884 I will be opening my new photographic studio in Nové Vítkovice. I will accept commissions every Sunday, Tuesday and Thursday from 9.00am -6.00 pm for all sizes and in all weathers, at lowest prices and of exemplary quality. I humbly solicit your custom Anton Brand, photographer.

In 1880 Emperor Franz Joseph I made a tour of Silesia, making his base in Těšín from 5-19 September 1880. It included the first Imperial visit to Ostrava. The visit is described in the book *Beiträge zur Geschichte der Stadt M.-Ostrau* by Franz Wattolik, who writes:

> ...Following his departure ... photographer Brand showed his Imperial Majesty the album containing the photos of Moravská Ostrava and the surroundings. His imperial majesty accepted the album.

Two further moments in Brand's professional life are linked to the year 1886. He took photographs when a new church in Vítkovice, blessed in honour of Paul Kupelwieser, the director of the Vítkovice Ironworks, was dedicated to St. Paul on Saturday 10 October 1886. Two-day long celebrations included, in addition to the first church services, a ceremonial procession of citizens and workers from the ironworks and evening concerts. Information about this event was printed in the special edition no 21 of the 'Workers Friend' on Friday 15 October 1886. The photo of the new church is stored in the Ostrava museum.

Brand's second 'coup' of the year concerned a more tragic and sensational event:

> ...Just published and obtainable from me are Photographs of the collapsed iron bridge in Moravská Ostrava, taken 10 minutes following the catastrophe by the local photographer A. Brand (size 20 x 24) can be obtained for 1 gulden.

Thus Franz Wattolik enticed the readers of the *Mährisch Schlesischer Grenzbote* into his book shop.

On Wednesday 15 September 1886 just after 8 o'clock (on one of Brand's photos the time given is 8 hours. O5 mins) Uhlans from the 2nd squadron of the 13th regiment of Ludwig, Count Tranin, were crossing the bridge on the way to Orlová, at the same time as some civilians were crossing the bridge. Suddenly the bridge started to swing vigorously and one of the chains on the Moravian side broke away and its 66-metre long middle section was hurled into the Ostravice River. Among the dead were the 10 and 11 year-old Hermina and Johanna, daughters of business man H. Stein from Moravská Ostrava, his servant Barbora Korbašová, the labourer Magdalena Isikova and 18 year-old Jan Orel. Three Uhlans were badly injured. Accounts from that time speak of the whole length of the river as red with blood.

Brand's studio was close by, which no doubt enabled him to act fast. On a further, almost identical photo, taken by another photographer August Rotter, Brand's studio can be seen, with the name A. Brand, Photographer. Rotter eventually bought Brand's studio from him. After August Rotter the studio on the bank of the Ostravice river changed hands and became the Pietzner photographic emporium and later the studio of Adolf Orlich.

Anton Brand was active in the public and social life in MoravskáOstrava. He regularly took part in the Christmas bazaar, together with August Rotter, and in 1897 and subsequent years he was joint commander with Dr Johann Fiedler on the 2nd division of volunteer fireman. He was a founder member of the Association of Artisans in Ostrava, and its chairman in the years 1882-1885.

Anton Brand's return to Vienna and the opening of his studio in Josefstädterstraße 23 is recorded in the Lehman's trade directory for 1890. The studio was known as 'Atelier Clementine' and later as Atelier Brand in Wien IX., Währingerstraße 5 & 7. Following his death the studio was taken over by his wife, but closed after her death in 1912.

In 1903 Brand announced the invention of a new lighting system (*Beleuchtungsart*), which was to be more advantageous for photographic purposes than the existing incandescent or magnesium flash. Also, together with Karl Stumpf and Rudolf Leitner he organised the first exhibition of apprentice works, *Erste Wiener Lehrlingsarbeiten-Ausstellung,* in 1904

Ostrava could not avoid the arrival of two of the Austro-Hungarian photographic chains. In 1902 a branch of the C. Pietzner empire moved into Brand and Rotter's earlier photographic studio on the bank of the Ostravice, and the department store of I. Schmelz became host to a branch of Joachim Wasservogel's business.

> ...Adolf Wasservogel, court, commercial and archducal photographer. As a result of the continuous expansion of my business I am obliged to equip my studio with the most modern equipment and for this reason I was forced to move my studio into the new building of I. Schmeltz, opposite the local railway station. In order to meet a long felt need as a professional I have arranged an outlet with photographic equipment in my studio where amateur photographers will find in addition to professional instruction and advice the widest selection of photographic aids at reasonable prices and prompt attention. Customers can use hoists and as amateurs can make use of the dark room. I graciously request that the confidence placed in me so far will be continued also in my new enterprise. I sign myself with greatest respect Adolf Wasservogel, court, commercial and archducal photographer.

This advertisement of 1912 announces the opening of a new enterprise by Adolf Wasservogel, son of Sigmund and grandson of Joachim. Karel Hůlek worked there as foreman until 1914 when Frank Gabriel took over.

The photographer Joachim Wasservogel was born in Úsov in 1817 and died in 1905. In 1867 he moved with his family to Olomouc. Initially he and his son, Sigmund Salomon, worked as assistant photographers in the studio of Hermann Seeburger but in October 1870 Sigmund Salomon Wasservogel obtained permission to trade as a photographer himself. He acquired the studio of the firm A. Píchler-Čurda in *Horní náměstí* [The Upper Square]. At the turn of the century the Wasservogel photographic studio was one of the foremost studios in Moravia and opened branches in Prostějov, Vienna, Bielsko-Biala, Opava, Krnov and Ostrava. Sigmund

Wasservogel's son Adolf also worked in the studio and eventually took over after the death of his father in 1909.

Adolf Wasservogel was baptised and converted to the Roman-Catholic faith in 1907. He married Hilde Heigel a fellow photographer (born 1888 in Zábřeh). In 1946 she was deported to Germany when Germans were expelled from Czechoslovakia after the war even though she had always been anti-Nazi.

In 1918 Adolf received permission to replace the name Wasservogel with the surname Waldek. The change of name also extended to his wife Hilda and two daughters, Margaret and Joan. In 1918 Hilda Waldek became the company secretary. In August 1918 the firm's name changed from A. Wasservogel to Adolf Waldek. He ceased to trade as a photographer in 1939 and later committed suicide.

His daughter Margaret married Robert Goldberg. In 1942 the couple was deported to Theresienstadt in 1942 with their son, Peter. Margaret and Peter were then transported to Auschwitz and murdered there, and Robert was later killed in Dachau on 8 February 1945.

During the war Hilda and her daughter Joan worked as photographers in the family studio. Both continued to work in the studio after it was nationalised until 1946 when they were expelled to Germany on 5 October.

Adolf Wasservogel is linked to another photographer, Karel Hůlek. They are connected not only by their common profession as employer and employee, but also by their tragic fate during the Second World War.

Karel Hůlek was born in 1872 the son of Karel Hůlek, baker and barley merchant in Libčany. Karel learnt his trade in the Langhans photographic studio in Prague, and then met his future wife Mary while working in the Pfitzner studio in Brno. Karel Hůlek moved to Ostrava around 1898 shortly after his marriage and began working in the studio of Adolf Wasservogel. In the years before and during the First World War he shared his customers with the studios Wenzel and Pfitzner. Most of his customers sought him out mainly as the 'Czech' rather than 'German' photographer.

He was a member of the Ostrava *Matice slezská,* the Czech National Association and regularly took part in its activities. In the archives there are some of his photographs of the Czech national infant school on Harantova Street.

The couple's son Karel was born in Moravská Ostrava in1898. He managed the studio on Nádražní Street during the first Republic, the occupation and thereafter. He married Julie Lauferová (born 1900) in 1921. She was the daughter of Jacob Laufer, who was born in Ostrava Michálkovice and Ernestine Dicker, born in 1864 in Lipník. Julie was working in the Hůlek studio at the end of the First World War.

Karel and Julie had a son, Mirek, born in 1924, and the marriage was dissolved, supposedly on the 13 November 1926, although it is possible that this date is incorrect. Julie was deported to Theresienstadt in September 1942 and there is no further record of her fate.

Jan Hůlek, son of Mirek and grandson of Karel, commented:

> My grandfather was a photographer, my father was a photographer but I haven't followed in his footsteps even if my profession is quite close, I am a radiographer. Even if today most of the work is done electronically I still know the basics of photochemistry.

The photographic firm of Herman Oppenheim was founded in the period of the First Czechoslovak Republic. It was the first to have a photographic laboratory. Herman graduated from the German Gymnasium in Ostrava and studied law in Vienna. The family owned a shop selling sewing machines and bicycles in Mostní (Těšínská). In 1934 Herman married Elsa Mainhart in Ostrava and opened his business in 28. Října Street which he ran from November 1934 until June 1939. The company was then taken over by Viktor Kolář, under the name of Jarmila Podbierová. The name of Viktor Kolář still appears in the register in 1941 (under the name FOTO-KINO-HAUS). Jarmila Podbierová also owned the independent studio at Hrabengasse 1. In 1943 only she was listed at the address in 28. Října.

The firm offered its customers

> ...an extensive assortment of photographic techniques, materials and chemicals including postal services, the processing of all amateur works, developing, retouching, duplicating, and preparation for Bromoil printing –**in short everything** for the amateur photographer. Surviving photos bear the stamp 'Oppenheim Ostrava' and a number, while postcards show the logo '*foto Oppenheim*'.

On one of the main streets in Ostrava, at Nádražní 22, you could find the photographic studio of Joseph Thieberger owned jointly with Irma Karpel and Ruth Wotitz. Gita Rind, née Thieberger, wrote about her father:

> My father was born on 9 October 1905 in Ostrava, where he also got married on 29 October 1933. I remember the studio on Nádražní. My mother told me about my father's work. Tibus, as he was called, worked for one of the Ostrava newspapers. Besides his routine work as reporter he also took photos of theatre first nights, operas and cinemas where he took pictures of important personages visiting Ostrava. Among the most important was President Masaryk. My father photographed the whole visit and even before he left my father had the whole leather album with the photos ready and presented it

> to the president as a memento of his visit. Perhaps this album still exists today. Father also photographed and filmed his funeral.
>
> Shortly after the occupation he was arrested by the Germans who released him and he went with the first transport to Nisko. From there he escaped to Russia. Mother and I followed him in March 1941. When war was declared in 1941 father joined the Red Army. He was accepted into the air force as a photographer. His last letter dated October 1941 arrived from Poltava or Charkov, I don't remember precisely. We heard nothing more about him. When my mother searched for him after the war she received a reply form the Russians *propol bez vesti*, 'Missing'.

While Joseph Thieberger served on the eastern front, another Jewish Ostravak soldier, Sigmund Kohn, served on the western front. He had the misfortune to be forced to emigrate twice from his homeland and he told his story in a newspaper article: 'Twice-expelled Czech finds asylum':

> ...A man who was twice forced to leave his native Czechoslovakia – first by the Nazis and the second time by the communists – arrived in Gravesend on Friday together with his 33 year old wife and three children. The man from behind the Iron Curtain is 44 year old Sigmund Kohn. He recounted the story of his country which, during two years found itself twice 'in chains'.
>
> In 1938 before the Munich Agreement, Mr Kohn was a corn merchant. Shortly before the Germans marched in he moved to Prague. When the Czech army mobilised he also donned a uniform. In March 1939 he emigrated to England for the first time and immediately following the declaration of war he reported for the British army. After the fall of France he became a member of the Czechoslovak army unit in England. During military service he met a teacher, Miss Marion McCombey, whom he married. With the advent of peace Sigmund Kohn returned home to face family tragedy.
>
> His 83 year-old mother died in a Nazi concentration camp, his sister and brother-in-law disappeared. Painfully he tried to put together the shattered parts of his life. For a time it went fairly well. The Soviet army withdrew from Czechoslovakia and life gradually returned to its old grooves. However storm clouds were gathering. In 1948 the communists seized power. At the time when the Russians were in Czechoslovakia, they had time to organise the civil administration on the Soviet model. They placed their people in key positions in industry. Those who did not agree with their policies were quietly removed. 'The atmosphere in my country was awful. People didn't dare to talk to each other, you couldn't trust anyone. As

> someone who served in the western army I was constantly under surveillance and the situation constantly deteriorated. Travel to the west is impossible which meant that my wife could not visit England. In the end I decided to search out the British consul in Prague. After seven months of waiting we finally got permission to emigrate. Before leaving Czechoslovakia I had to sign a document leaving all my possessions to the State.'

And so Ondřej Markus Kohn, a boy born on 28 April 1948 in the factory hospital in Ostrava, became Andrew Kohn. Andrew spent his childhood in England and in 1955 his family moved to Dublin.

Andrew's whole professional life has been linked to photography. In 1969 -1972 he studied at the School of Photography, University of West London where he gained a diploma and qualified as a commercial photographer. In Dublin he worked with Paddy Monaghan, in London with James Wedge, photographer for Vogue and also with Robert Taft. In the late 1960s he founded the firm Grain Limited in Dublin and in 1997 he began to travel and went to the USA working in the photographic studios in Dallas Phoenix and San Francisco. Following his return to Ireland he taught photography at St Peter's College Dublin. And in the end the profession of photography brought him back to Ostrava in 2014 – the longing to see his birthplace again, to visit Bruntál where almost five generations of his family lived, as well as Theresienstadt and Auschwitz where the life of his relatives so tragically ended.

Ziporah Nir was born in April 1926 into a German-speaking orthodox Jewish family. Her father, Leopold Löwinger, taught religion and Hebrew in the elementary Jewish school. After the annexation of the Sudetenland, the Löwingers had some Jewish refugees staying with them temporarily as they made their way out of Czechoslovakia. The Löwingers did not follow their example, unfortunately, and so were in Ostrava when the Germans invaded. Leopold was arrested but released after a few days. He was later among the group of men deported to Nisko and returned to Ostrava when the camp was dismantled.

As Jewish children could not attend the local schools after March 1939, Ziporah studied mainly at home as an external student of the Jewish High School in Brno. German regulations were that all Jews should have an occupation and Ziporah decided on photography and took a job in a photographic laboratory as well as studying the subject. After about 6 months she had to travel to Brno to take a photography examination. She had to get official permission for the train journey and the trip was unpleasant as her carriage was full of Germans while Ziporah had the yellow star with *Jude* on her coat. She continued working as a photographer from 1941 to 1942, mainly for the community, producing ID cards with a big letter

'J' on them. In September 1942, the whole family were deported to Theresienstadt where Leopold was killed. Ziporah survived Auschwitz and emigrated to Palestine after the war, where she married.

So Jewish photographers have recorded almost the complete cycle of life and industrialisation in Ostrava, from the beginning, 150 years ago, to today, reflecting the development of photography itself as they did so.

Artists, Writers and Musicians

Given the rather apocalyptic landscape of industrialised Ostrava it is quite surprising that the arts feature at all in its story. Where there's muck there may be money, and in the case of Ostrava that was certainly true, but the presence of the fine arts is unexpected. While Ostrava produced no Rembrandt or Michelangelo, a remarkable number of significant artists were associated with it, and many were Jewish. The biblical prohibition of making graven images had inhibited the emergence of Jewish painters and sculptors for many years and it was only in the nineteenth century, with the emancipation of the Jews and their greater involvement in secular culture, that they began to practice fine arts. In this aspect of cultural change, as in so much else, Ostrava was a prime example.

Emil Spiegel was born in 1882. Sadly we know little about him except that he was a professional painter and taught art at Ostrava High School. He was a member of the Ostrava *Kunstring* (Artists Circle) and clearly a fine draughtsman. He drew a portrait of Eva Hornungová, the grandmother of Uriel Meretz (nephew of Dr Pavel März,) before Uriel left Ostrava for Palestine in 1939.

Ferdinand Folkart was born in 1864 in Wadowice, Poland, about 100 km east of Ostrava and later more well-known as the birthplace of Pope John Paul II. He moved to Ostrava with his wife, Cecilie, and set up a successful business as a sign-writer which was later taken over by his son, Zikmund, who according to his daughter Lydia was a much better sign-writer than businessman! He and his two daughters survived the Holocaust and came to England. Ferdinand took on the 15 year-old David Friedmann as an apprentice in 1908.

David had been born in December 1893, the fourth child to Sophie and Heinrich Friedmann who had moved to Ostrava from Bielsko-Biala. Heinrich was a tinsmith, the son of a tinsmith, so there was presumably a lot of inherited manual flair and skill in the family and sign-writing would have seemed like a most suitable trade for the young David to follow. In 1911 he received his official certificate on completion of his apprenticeship. He was now a qualified sign-writer and moved to Berlin where he started to practice his trade, but his real ambition was more oriented to painting and drawing and the life of an artist. Initially, he joined a theatre company as a

Eva Hornungová by Emil Spiegel, 1939.

painter of scenery while studying art with Leo Kober and at the school of Lewin-Funcke. By 1914 he had become known as an artist and now joined the master class taught by Lovis Corinth as well as studying etching with Hermann Struck. David was also a fine violinist and seriously considered becoming a professional musician before deciding that his future was in drawing and painting.

He served briefly as an artist in the Austro-Hungarian Army on the Russian front in the First World War, drawing troops in action and being himself decorated for bravery. In 1923, he returned to Ostrava for the Chess Championships and drew a series of portraits of the chess masters, including Lasker who won the competition. 50 sets of 14 lithographs were produced and sold at 500 Crowns per copy. Jakob Salomonowitz, with his glass eye (see Chapter 10 'The One-eyed Chess Gambit, an Unknown Woman and a Lady with Family Trees'), was not among the 14.

The Chess Master portfolio was part of an exhibition in Ostrava in the Slatner Gallery in 1923. This 'gallery' (actually more like a shop) was owned by Heinrich, one of Heinz Vogel's maternal uncles. Sadly, Heinz remembers neither the uncle, who died when Heinz was only one year old, nor the shop. Heinrich dealt not only in paintings but also Persian carpets, furniture and antiques and presumably had quite a wealthy clientele.

Friedmann's work was exhibited in major public galleries in Berlin, Munich, Dresden and many other cities. His career flourished and all was well until the Nazis came to power in Germany and Jews were forbidden to work as artists and all Jewish art was removed from public galleries. Jews were allowed to work as builders and David built up a successful business renovating and developing Berlin buildings and was sufficiently prosperous and settled in 1937 to marry Mathilde Fuchs, the daughter of Professor Maximilian Fuchs. In September 1938 they had a daughter, Mirjam Helene.

Their joy was short-lived and in December 1938 they fled from Berlin to Prague, leaving most of their belongings and especially David's art collection behind. Three months later the Germans invaded Czechoslovakia. David was able to continue painting and drawing, producing portraits of leading members of the Jewish community in Prague. In October 1941, however, the family were deported to the Łodz ghetto where he worked in the *Metal II* section, designing jewellery, badges and other small items as well as painting scenes of life in the ghetto. In 1944, the family were transported to Auschwitz, where David's wife and child were murdered. David survived and ultimately returned to Prague where he produced a series of harrowing drawings and paintings of his experiences in the ghetto and camps. He married Hildegard Taussig, another camp survivor, in 1948 and fled to Israel after the communist takeover of the Czechoslovak government. From Israel he moved to the USA in 1954, where he began a new phase of his career, in advertising. He and Hildegard had a daughter, Miriam, born in Israel, and today the vigilant guardian of David's oeuvre and reputation.

While in wartime Prague, David drew the Krafft Quartet, an interesting but apparently not very remarkable group portrait. A whole 73 years later, in 2014, we published a short article in the Newsletter about an Ostravak family in Israel and mentioned a connection with Erich Brauner. Miriam Friedman (the family dropped the second 'n' from their name in America) asked if he could be the violinist (actually, the viola player) in her father's portrait of the Krafft Quartet. Incredibly, it was the same Erich and we were able to provide the Brauner family in Israel with a drawing of their uncle, whom none of them had ever seen!

'A few Seconds before Execution' by David Friedmann.

Leo Haas was born in Opava, in the Sudetenland, to parents of Slovakian origin. He was the oldest of four children. He studied piano and voice in addition to painting, a talent he inherited from his grandfather, who painted murals in churches. His art teacher recommended that he continue to study art and to do so he moved to Karlsruhe in Germany, attending the art academy there. His first year of studies was financed by a rich relative from the United States, but when the relative died Haas had to support himself as a musician in bars or restaurants. Haas produced paintings and lithographs depicting these scenes – artistic subjects that were common at that time.

Krafft Quartet by David Friedmann.

In 1921 Haas moved to Berlin and studied with Emil Orlik, who made him his assistant. In 1922 he became assistant in a graphic design studio and from then on his main source of income was from painting. In 1923 he travelled to France – first to Paris and then Albi, Toulouse-Lautrec's birthplace, where he studied the artist's works in the local museum. From there he moved to Arles, in the steps of Van Gogh. His last stop before returning home to Opava was Marseilles.

In 1924 Haas tried his luck as a journal caricaturist in Vienna and in 1926 he returned to Opava, working in advertising and as a set designer for a theatre troupe. In 1929 he married Sophie Hermann, whose family came from Ostrava and so provided the link between Leo and our story of Ostrava. He became quite well-known as a portrait painter in Opava, earning enough money to support his family and even help out his parents. In 1935, when with the pro-Nazi German movement made sweeping electoral gains in the Sudetenland, Haas abandoned his art activity and became the director of a small printing house.

The first pogrom in Opava took place in 1937. Haas's works were branded 'degenerate art' and, after *Kristallnacht* in November 1938, he and his wife went to live with her parents in Ostrava. Four months later, on 14 March 1939, the Germans occupied Ostrava and in October, Leo with 2,000 other Jewish men between the ages of 16-60 was sent to Nisko nad Sanem in Poland. There he was employed as a wagon driver bringing food and construction materials from Lublin, and also as a tailor's and shoemaker's apprentice.

While in Nisko, Haas painted portraits of SS soldiers, for which he received better food and art materials. He was also able to move freely around the camp, which enabled him to draw the building sites, portraits of his comrades, transports arriving and leaving, and the general life of the camp. More than a hundred works from that period have survived and they provide important documentation for this concentration camp for Jews. Among the 'portraits' of the internees is one of Oskar Liebreich, and Pepek Salomonovic gave me a copy. When I showed it some years ago in a talk I gave, it caused great excitement. Lydia Tischler was in the audience and revealed that Oskar was her uncle. She had never seen the picture before! Oskar had been a railwayman before the war. He returned to Ostrava from Nisko but was subsequently sent to Theresienstadt and thence to Treblinka where he was killed in 1942.

Oskar Liebreich, drawn in 1940 in Nisko Camp by Leo Haas.

When the Nisko camp was dismantled Haas returned to Ostrava, where he separated from his wife Sophie. Painting was at that time an unpromising way of earning a living and so he worked at cleaning and renovating sewers – work organized by the Jewish Community. While there he met Erna Davidovits, the woman who would become his second wife. Her family helped with the illegal smuggling of residents to Poland, an activity which Haas himself took part in after the death of his father in 1941. Haas was arrested by the Gestapo in August 1942 but was released from the Ostrava prison through the help of the Jewish Community. Of course, this merely postponed the inevitable for a few weeks and he was included in the next transport to Theresienstadt which left at the end of September 1942.

On 1 October 1942 Haas and his new wife, her parents, and his sister, Elvina arrived at Theresienstadt where they were forced to separate, men to one barrack while the women were sent to another. At first Haas was put with the group of prisoners that transported building materials for the railway tracks. Thanks to Yakov Edelstein, of whom Haas had made a portrait, Haas was transferred to the *Zeichenstube* (Drawing Office). The department's job, among others, was to organize the construction of the railway line that ran through the camp. Several other famous artists worked in the *Zeichenstube*, among them Otto Ungar, Ferdinand Bloch and Bedřich Fritta. Fritta headed the team and became a close friend of Haas.

Haas drew portraits of his colleagues. He also gave painting courses for the children of the ghetto, for which he received a little food. He used this to prepare original meals that became famous among his circle. Work in the Drawing Office enabled its employees to visit other parts of the ghetto and to make drawings of ghetto life. He had to do these in secret in an attic or while surrounded by large groups of prisoners in case the SS discovered this forbidden activity. His drawings included: searching for food, people waiting to be transported, the transfer of internees from one barracks to another, the buildings, portraits of inmates, sketches of the elderly, the sick, the dying, and the dead. Haas, Fritta and Ungar would often meet in the evening to work on their drawings. Collectively they created a large body of work, now dispersed among several museums, illustrating all aspects of life in the Theresienstadt ghetto.

On 25 October 1944 Haas and Fritta were sent to Auschwitz. Haas arrived on 28 October and was classified as a political prisoner with the number 199885. Fritta fell seriously ill with dysentery as soon as he arrived in Auschwitz and despite treatment by Dr Wrocław, who was also a prisoner in the camp, he died of blood poisoning eight days later.

In November 1944, Haas, other artists and a number of chemists from Belgium were transferred to Sachsenhausen camp where they were set to work counterfeiting British and American currency and documents. This remarkable story was portrayed in the film, 'The Counterfeiters'. On 5 May

1945 the prisoners were transferred to Ebensee camp, where they were liberated the next day by the Allied forces.

After his liberation Haas returned to Theresienstadt and there, in the Magdeburg Barracks, he found his entire art collection as well as many works produced by Fritta. Fritta's wife Johanna had died in Theresienstadt in February 1945, leaving a small son, Tommy, who was born on 22 January 1941. Haas's wife Erna had also survived but was in very poor health. The couple adopted Tomáš Fritta and settled in Prague. Erna died in 1955 and Haas moved to East Berlin, where he married for a third time. After the war Haas published a book, through the Jewish Museum in Berlin, of drawings that Bedřich Fritta had made for Tommy, for his third birthday in 1944. Haas died in 1983.

Salomon Salomonowitz was the second son of Jakob Salomonowitz, the one-eyed chess player. Born in May 1902, he was a year younger than Leo Haas. He studied at the *Kunstgewerbeschule* (Arts and Crafts College) in Vienna from 1917 to 1922. Oskar Kokoschka had studied there some twenty years previously. Salomon went on to complete his art studies in Germany and France before returning to Ostrava where he was a founding member of the *Kunstverein* (Art Association). The City Art Gallery hosted exhibitions of his work between 1925 and 1938 when he emigrated to Palestine. He had first visited Palestine in 1928 and made a return visit in 1932. He was made a member of the Association of Israeli Painters and Sculptors in 1940.

Before he emigrated Salomon had drawn a wonderful portrait of his nephew, Michal. He had also painted a portrait in 1935, which was reported in the Ostrava newspaper, *Ostrauer Zeitung* of 7 November 1935. The title of the painting was *Damenporträt* and was sold for 900 Czechoslovak

Bedřich Fritta, 'To Tommy, for His Third Birthday in Terezin, 22 January 1944'.

Crowns. The subject of the portrait was not known until we met Roy Seger, in London in 2008. His mother, Edith Bettina Gottlieberová, was born in 1914 and came from Ostrava. Roy had a fine oil painting of her by an unknown artist so it was a great surprise to both of us to find the signature 'Salomonowitz' on the back! Salomon's works are exhibited in the Ostrava City Art Gallery and the Jewish Museum in Prague, among other locations.

Erich Lichtblau was born in Hrušov, now part of Ostrava, in 1911, some nine years later than Salomon. His early career was as a designer of shop-window displays but he entered the Hamburg Decoration and Design Technical College in the early 1930s before returning to continue his career

Portrait of Edith Gottlieberová, signed Salomonowitz.

in design and window-setting in Ostrava. In later life he said of himself, 'I was not a famous painter: I was just a little man' but while that might do justice to his reputation and modesty it definitely underplays his skills.

He married Elsa Silbigerová in 1937. After the German invasion they moved to Prague where Erich became a construction worker and in 1942 they were deported to Theresienstadt where Erich was assigned to work as a builder. After a time, however, the Jewish authorities in the camp allocated him to the *Graphik und Reproduktion* section, which was much more in keeping with his skills. Here he worked on scenery design and production for the theatre.

His new role gave him the means and opportunity to draw and paint what is effectively a diary of daily ghetto life in Theresienstadt. He produced a series of sardonic sketches with ironic or bitter captions, but later on he removed most of these captions and, indeed, tore up many of the pictures. Fortunately, Elsa managed to save and hide the pieces which were recovered when Erich and Elsa were liberated at the end of the war. In October 1949, Erich and Elsa, with their two children, changed their name to Leskly and emigrated to Israel. Erich later reproduced many of his ghetto drawings and added others. They are now on display in the Los Angeles Museum of the Holocaust.

Edith Löwy was five years older than Erich, born in 1906. She qualified as a linguist, taking a PhD degree in philology at Charles University in

'Prague is Free of Jews', Erich Lichtblau ©Los Angeles Holocaust Museum.

Prague, and it was only much later in her life that her practical artistic talents became apparent. She described her young self as 'strange', being much more interested in antiques and beautiful things rather than the fashions and parties that a young girl a might be expected to be interested in. Her linguistic skill and love of beautiful things was inherited from her father, Arnold.

She married Otto Rosenberg just before the war. He was a military judge and, when the Germans invaded Czechoslovakia, he fled to England. Edith decided to remain to stay with her mother, although a major reason was her fear of the foggy weather in London! She survived Theresienstadt, Öderan and Auschwitz and came to England after the end of the war.[4] She suffered from depression and was advised to take up art as therapy. She demonstrated great talent as a sculptress, with an exhibition at the Camden School of Art, in London. Edith wrote her life story with her memories of life in the camps and published it as 'I did survive' with the nom de plume ELRO. The front cover was illustrated with a photograph of the bronze head that she had sculpted (see p.333).[5]

Yehuda Bacon was born in 1929 to an observant Chassidic family living near the small Blech *shtiebl*, the first son after two daughters. He remembers his first ten years as being very happy, surrounded by a loving family and going to the Jewish primary school. Indeed, quite remarkably, he can recognise the faces from the class photograph and remember the names of well over half his class-mates after almost 70 years! He was obviously a close observer of life and was keen on drawing and painting, even as a child.

The donations book for the Old People's Home in Ostrava records modest donations of 20 crowns from Baruch Bakon (spelt with a 'k') and 5 crowns from Israel, Yehuda's father, in October 1934. The gift suggests a family of limited means but one involved with the local community.

Yehuda was deported with his family to Theresienstadt in September 1942, when he was just 13 years old. He was fortunate to be one of the few children to be housed in the children's barracks rather than packed into general barrack with the rest of the prisoners. While there he worked in the Technical Department and had the chance to get drawing and painting lessons from Leo Haas, Karl Fleischmann and Otto Ungar, although this was strictly against the rules as Jewish children were barred from all education. Yehuda remembers seeing the headmistress of his Jewish primary school in Theresienstadt and seeing her again later, shortly before the Red Cross inspection of the camp. It was being 'beautified' in preparation for the Red Cross and many of the old people were being shipped off 'to the East' and Yehuda saw her, by then a shrivelled old woman with a card round her neck with her transport number, sitting on her bag, waiting. How does a young boy cope with that sort of experience?

By 1943 it was the turn of Yehuda and his family to be transported to Auschwitz. He was 'lucky' in that he was sent to the 'Family Camp' where the inmates were marked as '*6 Monate SB*' which meant that they were to receive *Sonderbehandlung*, a German euphemism for being gassed, but only after 6 months. Again, Yehuda was 'lucky' because shortly before the allotted time, the plan was changed and he was sent to the work camp with his father. He never saw his mother and sisters again. His father was murdered at 10.00

In Memory of the Czech Transport to the Gas-Chambers, 1945. Yehuda Bacon. © Yad Vashem, Israel.

in the evening on 10 July 1944. After the war Yehuda drew a portrait of his father appearing, as a ghost, in the smoke from the crematorium chimney, with the time and date of his death to the side. It is entitled 'In Memory of the Czech Transports to the Gas Chambers'.

Yehuda was assigned to the 'Carthorse Commando', a group of young men and boys who dragged carts round the camp collecting and delivering goods, wood for the crematoria and bodies from the gas chambers to the crematoria. Occasionally, when they had brought a load of wood and there was a rare pause in the use of the crematoria, the Kapo said to them, 'Kids, you have finished with the wood, you can go and get warm in the gas chamber'! One of their jobs was to spread the ashes from the crematorium over the icy roads.

On 18 January 1945 he left Auschwitz on the Death March, walking non-stop for 30 days and nights. He was liberated by the Americans at Gunskirchen camp, near Mauthausen, on 5 May 1945 and hospitalised because he had typhus and was at death's door. After his recovery he emigrated to Israel and with the help of some extraordinary friends secured a place to study at the Bezalel School of Art in Jerusalem. Times were very tough in Israel at that time, especially for art students, but again fortune smiled on him. A relative from South Africa found him and took him to South Africa where he was able both to study and paint. After a short time he had a successful exhibition of his work. On the strength of that success he came to London to study. There he became involved with orphans rescued and living in Lingfield House, looked after by Anna Freud, Sigmund's daughter. She had the idea of encouraging the orphans to forget all about their past, including even their names, and had their camp numbers removed. Yehuda spent some time giving them drawing lessons. Later he became involved in helping some of them retrace their families.

Yehuda went on to study in Paris before returning to Israel where he became a professor at the Bezalel School at which he had earlier studied. He continues to paint and exhibit now that he has retired from teaching. In an interview after the war, Yehuda commented:

> Do you know when I first saw a funeral after liberation, I burst out laughing! 'People are crazy; for one person they make a casket and play solemn music? A few weeks ago, I saw thousands of bodies piled up to be burnt like so much junk.'
>
> And I remember when I went to a theatre, I found myself calculating how long it would take to gas the audience, and which of their clothes would be salvageable, and how much gold their teeth would yield, how many sackfuls of hair they were worth. These thoughts came automatically. They even seemed funny, for if you weren't able to laugh, you just didn't stay alive for a moment.

Over his career Yehuda's style has evolved and he has produced some delightful paintings. It is hard to believe they are by the same person who said that and drew the portrait of his father and 'Escaping from the Fire with a Torah Scroll'. I asked Yehuda many years after he had made that drawing what lay behind it. He explained that, after the war, he had nothing. There were no physical things remaining from his past life; all there was, was the teaching of and love for Judaism which he had absorbed as a child. So the drawing was a sort of self-portrait of himself escaping from the hell of the past years, carrying his Jewishness with him. We have made it the frontispiece of this book.

Dr Glenn Sujo produced a three-volume Catalogue Raisonée of Yehuda Bakon's works for his PhD thesis at the Courtauld Institute in London and a copy is in the Jewish Museum in Prague. Some of Yehuda's works are in the Drawing Collection of the British Museum.

As a child, Yehuda was both inquisitive and had an artist's eye for accuracy and detail coupled with an excellent memory. This was put to very sombre use in the trial of Adolf Eichmann in Jerusalem. Yehuda was able to draw detailed plans of the gas chambers and crematoria in Auschwitz, which had been destroyed by the Nazis before they evacuated the camp. This was invaluable in the trial and in the conviction of Eichmann. Yehuda also recalled an occasion when an SS man was kind to him and some others:

> ...Suddenly an SS man summoned 10 men to the gate, which was very dangerous. He could have shot them or done who knows what to them. I was one of the 10. He took a stick of salami and cut a piece for each of us and said 'Clear off!' That was such a sudden gleam of humanity. By the way, this Baretzki (that was his name) was the only one in the whole Auschwitz trial who accepted his guilt.

Mihal Efrat, née Evelina Schlachet, was born in Ostrava in 1926. Her grandparents ran a chocolate shop in the centre of Ostrava, and Evelina remembers a prosperous and happy childhood. As a girl she was a very keen dancer and attended classes at the Czech National Theatre. She may have inherited this love from her grandfather who was also very keen on and very good at dancing. She also loved painting and took lessons with Leo Haas until she and her family were deported to Theresienstadt. Evelina took drawing materials with her to Theresienstadt as part of the food and clothing she was allowed to take. The family thought that they would return to Ostrava in 3 or 4 months, and their main concern was the fate of their piano!

Her grandfather was sent away the day after the family arrived in Theresienstadt and before he left he told Evelina prophetically, 'only you will survive'. Her father died shortly afterwards and Evelina had to look after her mother and so had no opportunity for painting or drawing. She was deported to Auschwitz, then to Hamburg and finally Bergen-Belsen where she was liberated. She returned to Prague entirely alone in the world and passed an examination in Graphic Art for the High School in Prague. She lived almost without any money and describes how she ate mainly bread and mustard and goulash soup at a cost of only one crown. The poverty and hunger were bad but, compared to the previous 3 years, life was idyllic. In 1949, she made *Aliyah* to Israel and joined a Kibbutz where she still lives. By 1952 she had started her career illustrating children's books and has just completed her 52nd of them.

Although these artists are fine enough and a few of them are exhibited in major galleries, we have not yet spoken of anyone among the first rank. But Ostrava can boast of an association with one truly great artist whose work was condemned as degenerate by the Nazis and who painted a self-portrait 'As a degenerate artist' in Ostrava. Oskar Kokoschka was born in Austria in 1886 of Czech parents. He studied at the Arts and Crafts School in Vienna. In 1934 he fled Austria for Prague having been condemned as a degenerate by the Nazis. There he met Olda Palkovská who became his partner and subsequently his wife. In 1937 they moved to Ostrava to stay with her grand-parents and it was during this stay that Oskar painted his self-portrait and the park, which looks much more bucolic than most of Ostrava! In 1938 they fled to England.

With all these Ostrava artists there must have been a significant number of people buying and collecting their works. Of these patrons the best known was Oskar Federer, the General Manager of the *Vítkovické horní a hutní těžířstvo* or VHHT, the Vítkovice Mining and Iron Works owned by the Rothschilds, before the Second World War. He is reputed to have had the best and largest private collection of Impressionist works in Europe. Naturally, it was seized by the Nazis. His successor, Jan Světlík, today the Chairman and Chief Executive of the Vítkovice Machinery Group (VMG), shares his passion for art collecting. He has already built up a significant collection in the Rothschild Chateau, the Headquarters of the VMG and is trying to recreate the glory days of the Chateau by buying up items from Federer's collection whenever they come onto the market and also by acquiring Rothschild furniture of the type that would have been in the Chateau before the war. This is not just nostalgia for a vanished Golden Age which was almost certainly not as golden as memory would suggest, but a genuine attempt to bring back something which contemporary Ostrava had lost, a more cosmopolitan culture and entrepreneurialism.

The Vítkovice Machinery Group is one of the sponsors of this book and Mr Světlík has donated a woodcut, 'Children in the Ghetto', by Helena Salichová, an almost contemporary Ostrava artist, to the Ostrava Scroll Group.

'Children in the Ghetto', Woodcut, Helena Salichová (1895-1975).

While Michal Efrat illustrated children's books, Gita Rind (née Thieberger) wrote one, 'The Magic Doll'.[6] Gita is not the only Jewish Ostravak to write and publish their stories. There are several of them, all of which are a wonderful record of usually terrible events but few of them are of much literary merit. They all, of course, have a (relatively) happy ending as they are all written by those who survived the Holocaust or their children. This means that the depression caused by reading of man's inhumanity to man and realising that it has not changed, however many times we say 'Never again', is ameliorated by the hope that the children and grandchildren of the survivors might have learned something.

Ruth Elias (née Huppert) wrote her story, which was published[7] as she said, to explain to her children why they had no grandparents or cousins, aunts or uncles. She had a happy childhood and youth. She met, fell in love with and conceived a baby with a boy while they were incarcerated in Theresienstadt. They were sent separately to Auschwitz and she never saw him again. Later, she gave birth to a baby boy in the camp, under the 'tender care' of Dr Mengele. She was ordered to bind her breasts and forbidden to feed the baby as Mengele wanted to see how long he would survive. One of the Jewish women dentist prisoners managed to get some morphine which she gave to Ruth with which to inject and kill her baby. Ruth then returned to the work details in the camp, survived and subsequently married in Prague before making *Aliyah*. In Israel she had two happy healthy children for whom the book was written.

Peter Erben (né Eisenberg) was born in 1921 into a wealthy family who ran a hotel and brewery in Přívoz. As a boy and young man, Peter was very athletic and keen on sports, especially football. It was this early fitness that probably enabled him to survive Theresienstadt and Auschwitz when most of his family perished. In Theresienstadt everyone had to work, including the children who tended the vegetable garden in the moat. Peter, being older than most of the children, was the leader of a group of working children that included a young girl, Eva Löwidtová. She, too, survived and they met after the war in Prague, fell in love and subsequently married and emigrated to Israel. Peter wrote his story and it was published in German as *Auf eigenen Spuren*.[8]

Ilse Herlingerová was born in 1903, the daughter of Moric Herlinger and his second wife, Terezie. They ran an inn, *Na Fojtsví*, in Vítkovice and Ilse had a happy and comfortable childhood. Her parents donated a torah mantle in 1907, to commemorate the consecration of their house. In 1930 she married Vilém Weber, the son of Samuel Weber and Jetta Stiebel. Jetta also donated a torah mantle in 1935, to commemorate her husband's 70th birthday. They ran a kosher restaurant in Ostrava. Both the Herlinger and the Weber family were quite observant Jews but Vilem and Ilse were much less so. Ilse (see **Appendix 7.2**) was a strong willed girl. When she told her mother that she was going to marry Vilém, her mother asked if he knew about it. 'Not yet, but I will tell him' was the reply.

As one of the children of a restaurateur, Vilém became an accomplished cook, unlike Ilse. We do not know if that was part of the attraction for her! As a young man, Vilem had become a staunch Zionist. He therefore did not take up his father's suggestion of studying law or of taking over the restaurant but concentrated on studying agriculture, prior to going to Palestine, where he remained for almost 9 years before contracting malaria and deciding to go back to Ostrava. On his return, he started a debt collection agency which prospered until the partition of Czechoslovakia after the Munich Agreement when things became very difficult, not just for the Webers.

When Ilse got married she could proudly call herself 'authoress' as three of her children's books had already been published. After the wedding she became what is so beautifully called 'a normal housewife'. Hanuš was born in 1931, and Tommy, named after Tomáš Masaryk, in 1934. In spite of the fact that Ilse was fully occupied looking after her family, she managed to write for different newspapers and make programmes for radio in Ostrava. Her correspondence was extensive. Ilse became a well-known writer and poet and published, among many other volumes, a book of children's stories under the title '*Mendel Rosenbusch*', illustrated by Salomon Salomonowitz. [9] Although she was planning on writing a great novel there was, apparently no opportunity for any more books until it was too late. Ilse, Vilém and Tommy were deported to Theresienstadt and thence to Auschwitz where Ilse and Tommy were murdered. Vilém survived.

Hanuš had been sent on the last *Kindertransport* out of Prague to England, where he stayed with a Swedish diplomat, a close friend of Ilse's. He subsequently moved to Stockholm and now lives in Sweden. He has a son whom he named Tommy after his murdered younger brother.

While in Theresienstadt Ilse wrote some poems, including one to her son in England. Incredibly, it survived and was taken out of Theresienstadt towards the end of the war by some Jewish prisoners who had been freed to go to Sweden. The poem, 'Letter to my Son' was translated into Swedish and published in *Dagens Nyheder*, a newspaper in Stockholm. Some of Hanuš's friends saw it and immediately identified it as relating to Hanuš and Tommy, so it now takes its rightful place in Ilse's works. When I talk about Ostrava, I frequently refer to the poem and I used to try to read it but I always broke down after a few lines. As a father and grandfather, I found the whole idea too distressing to be able to read. So now I hand out printed copies (See **Appendix 7.3**).

Visitors to the old Jewish Cemetery in Prague usually go to the grave of Franz Kafka, stand in silence for a moment, then turn and walk back towards the main entrance. Many of them notice a modest plaque hanging on the wall near the grave. On it are the names of six Czech-Jewish authors who were murdered during the Holocaust. One of the names is Ilse Weber.

Two days after Yom Kippur in 2009, Anne-Sofie von Otter presented a programme of songs and music from Theresienstadt at the Queen Elizabeth Hall on the South Bank, London. Among the songs were three by Ilse Weber and Anne-Sofie sang another of Ilse's poems about her son.[10]

Joseph Wechsberg's life and writing are much less full of pathos and much more fun, despite the death of his father on the Russian front at the start of the First World War when Joseph was only seven years old, and the family losing most of their money after the war. His grandfather was Albert Wechsberg the banker, and so Joseph's early years were very comfortable.

He was something of a polymath, taking up the violin at the age of eight and at first aiming for a career as a concert violinist, entering the Vienna State Academy of Music but later studying law at Prague University and practicing in Ostrava. He capitalised on his violin playing to take temporary jobs as an entertainer on a number of French ocean liners, which he later described entertainingly in some of his books:

> ...I later found the same ambience, *L'atmosphere transat*, aboard the unforgettable *Île de France* where I briefly achieved the exalted position of *chef d'orchestre*, being a sort of nautical mini Herbert von Karajan.

He also played in Paris nightclubs and seems to have had a great time. He wrote articles for Viennese and Prague newspapers and so started his journalistic career.

In 1936 Wechsberg was appointed parliamentary secretary for the Jewish Party in the Czechoslovak parliament and was sent to America by the Czech government in 1938 as an expert on the Sudeten problem. He did not return to Europe and became an American citizen and Americanised his name to Joe, although he never lost his heavy German accent. He wrote in German, Czech and French and subsequently in English. Remarkably his English prose is sharp and clear and shows no trace of his German-speaking background. His magazine stories were regularly published in *Esquire* and *The New Yorker* in 1943.

In 1943 Wechsberg was called up to serve in the American army and was sent to Europe and worked there as armed forces correspondent. He was in Prague in the American sector at the end of the war and determined to go back to Ostrava to see his mother and home town. He subsequently wrote *Homecoming*,[11] describing his trip across the Russian sector of Czechoslovakia, exchanging American cigarettes for bottles of vodka and lifts in Russian Army trucks. It reads as great fun and an adventure but when he reached Ostrava he found that his mother and almost all his friends and family had been murdered.

After the war he worked for the US War Crimes Commission and published numerous accounts and contributions for different newspapers and magazines. From 1949 until his death he worked as a European correspondent for *The New Yorker* magazine. In 1967, he published *The Murderers Among Us: The Simon Wiesenthal Memoirs*, in which he fused the research of Simon Wiesenthal with his own direct observations while working for the War Crimes Commission. In that book, he details how much of the Nazi political machine was preserved in Germany, and also through asylum overseas in Argentina, Chile, and Paraguay. He published books on musicians and music which remained a lifelong passion for him, as well as on food, which he loved almost as much. He wrote about Jewish Bankers, having a family interest in the topic, and also a series of books about his own life and experiences, tinged with nostalgia for the lost golden age of *Mitteleuropa* and the life in Ostrava (see **Appendix 7.4**).

Josef was not the only Ostravak lawyer to be an accomplished musician, as Madeleine Isenberg discovered. Her uncle by marriage, Adolf (Dolek) Seifter was a shoe buyer for the well-known department store of I. Magnin, in Oakland, California, who used to play the piano for relaxation in the evening. He was a qualified lawyer from pre-war Czechoslovakia but the qualification was of no value in the USA, hence his career in footwear. He died, childless, in 1987, and when his wife died in 1998, Madeleine and his other nieces and nephews had to sort out their papers. At this point Madeleine was in for a surprise. Among the assorted papers, she found a ragged, dog-eared, yellowed magazine, *Tonfilm Theater Tanz*, (sometimes simply called TTT), stuck together with sticky tape, that had photos of Dolek and his brother Leo with a short write-up about them and the sheet music of a well-known tango of that time, composed by the two of them.

It seems that while still in Czechoslovakia, Dolek and his brother Leo, the violinist, liked to compose music as a sideline. This tango, immediately christened 'Uncle Dolek's Tango', was considered a great hit at the time of its composition. The brothers seemed to have been well-known and popular composers of swing music performed at the German theatre in Ostrava. The newspaper reported that they were composing their own operetta.

After the excitement came a disappointment. The copy of TTT was, in fact, a mixture of 3 editions, stapled together and the tango music was incomplete! Madeleine finally found the correct copy of TTT, with the complete score, on sale on the web and arranged to buy a scan of the missing parts of the music. In November 2012, we held a Reunion of Ostravaks at the Czech Embassy in London and Evelyn McGilloway gave the first public performance of Uncle Dolek's Tango for almost 75 years. Madeleine had

Dr Dolek and Leo Seifter, *TTT*, 1934.

found the words (given in **Appendix 7.5**) and, although we did not sing, we could at least imagine.

Evelyn is no amateur pianist. She enjoyed a career as a professional concert pianist. Her grandfather, Adolf, owned the Rix Department store in Ostrava. His elder son, Ernst, died of leukaemia so the younger son, Otto, joined his father in the business. Otto had been educated in the very modern disciplines of business and economics, but his real love was music. He was an accomplished piano player and his playing is mentioned in *Homecoming* by Joseph Wechsberg. When the Germans invaded Ostrava, Adolf and his wife were arrested by the Gestapo but Otto escaped, being driven to the Polish border by his friends. He came to London and took a job with Marks and Spencer. Family history reports that, during the war, he met a beautiful young lady in the romantic location of the forecourt of Golders Green tube station in London, fell in love with her and they subsequently married.

Evelyn was born in 1942 and her brother, Bernard, who subsequently became quite a successful lawyer (see **Appendix 6.3**), in 1944. Otto wrote a waltz for his wife, to be played on the piano. Evelyn inherited her father's ability at the piano and played with the Ernest Reid Youth Orchestra at the Dukes Hall and also with the Royal Philharmonic Orchestra at the Royal Festival Hall. In June 2010 there was a visit to Ostrava by a group of Ostravaks. The City of Ostrava arranged a small concert for the occasion with the Brno String Quartet in the Rothschild Chateau. As an encore to their performance, Evelyn played the waltz that her father had written for her mother. It was a very emotional as well as musically delightful event.

The City council had also arranged an exhibition in the City Art Gallery (*Důmumění*) of works by Ostravak Jewish artists to coincide with our visit. We admired and remembered.

Edvín Scharf (*1908 Přívoz) studied at the gymnasium and music school in Moravská Ostrava. He played the violin, clarinet and saxophone. He was deported to Nisko with his father but managed to escape. When he arrived in Lwów, he sold his Swiss watch and bought a violin, which he held onto for the whole period of the war. First he played in cafes to make a minimum living, and then in an orchestra which in leisure moments gave concerts in the labour camp for construction of the canal, and from 1942 in Buzuluk, where he became a member of the Czechoslovak battalion. He became the conductor of the army orchestra and composed music for it.

Many Ostravaks described themselves as keen and competent amateur musicians and singers, including Leah Weber who, as a girl, joined the choir in the main synagogue although her parents attended the more traditionally orthodox services in the Zerotingasse synagogue. Bertie Goldberg's voice was not good enough for the synagogue choir but he claimed that as a young man he could sing the whole of Rigoletto. This claim has not recently been put to the test but the idea of an orthodox traditional Jew singing Verdi, as of a policeman humming along to Haydn's imperial anthem and much of the population of Ostrava swinging to Uncle Dolek's Tango conjures up an image of inter-war Ostrava as relaxed, cultured, tolerant and happy. It is an attractive vision and one that survivors from the period definitely confirm.

Theatre

It is unlikely that the Ostravaks agreed with Shakespeare that all the world's a stage, as they were too hard-headed and concerned with the practicalities of day to day living to indulge in such fancies. All the same, they would have regarded the stage as an almost essential component of that living, both to provide entertainment and relaxation and also for moral and spiritual uplift. As always, Jews played a prominent role both on stage and in the audience. Paul Rice (né Pavel Reisz) wrote in his memoir:

> Ostrava had (and still has) a magnificent theatre to which we went most Saturday afternoons to plays and concerts using a 'students' pass for cheap entry. 'The Bartered Bride' by Smetana was performed at least 5 times a year but many other operas were included in a wide international range of music, opera, operettas and stage plays in Czech

> by Shakespeare, Shaw, Goethe, Schiller and others. The most popular English playwright was Oscar Wilde. There was also a German theatre which had a similarly high standard. I and my friends were fanatic admirers of the Threepenny Opera by Brecht and Weil (which I still love) and of the works of two Czech political satirical entertainers Voskovec and Werich. Our favourite author and playwright then was Karel Čapek and my musical needs were covered by New Orleans Jazz. My parents were members of an extensive social circle and entertained a lot. Classical music, theatre and literature were highly rated.

Bertie Goldberg remembers that his parents went to the theatre frequently (the Deutsches Haus or Německý dům). Bertie went to the theatre on cheap student tickets and was brought up on opera. Most of the Ostravaks make similar comments about their parents. Paul Rice and his family were unusual in that they went to the Czech Theatre, whereas most of the Jews would have frequented the German Theatre.

Josef Wechsberg also remembers the social hierarchy associated with the theatre:

> The directors of the Vítkovice Works had always thought of themselves as the aristocrats of local society. They claimed and were given feudal prerogatives that had long ago become an anachronism. Their clan had a *stammtisch* (regular table) at the coffee house, their own dress balls, parties, clubs. They went to the theatre only on Mondays and Fridays – subscription series 'yellow' and 'brown' – when they were sure to be 'among themselves'. The rest of the theatre-going population – professors, doctors, businessmen, journalists, and related 'intellectual' hoi polloi – were supposed to go to the theatre on Tuesdays and Wednesdays, subscription series 'red' and 'green'.

Guido Prager was from Vienna and took a doctorate in economics from Vienna University but after a short career in Vienna, his love of theatre and opera drove him to a job in the German Theatre in Ostrava where Otto Zeisel, also Jewish, was the director.

Guido's immediate boss was for a short time Otto Preminger who went on to make a very successful transition to the cinema and Hollywood, while Guido was persuaded by his family to return to a more 'regular' and reliable career. Dr Josef Ambach worked in the same German Theatre in Ostrava as a writer and literary advisor from 1931 to 1934, before he joined his father-in-law's business which was, presumably, better paid and more regular than the stage.

Mihal Efrat (née Eveline Schlachet) is now an artist and illustrator in Israel, but she recalls her different ambitions in her childhood:

Ostrava Theatre Company. Dr Guido Prager circled.

> I was a very good student and learning was very easy for me. But all my thoughts were focused on dancing. I wanted to be a dancer and my mother let me participate in the dancing department of the National Czech Theatre, it was my whole world.

Artur Radvansky remembers taking part in theatrical performances as a young man, but these were probably amateur dramatics and might have been put on in the inn owned by Gustav Glesinger, which had a spacious ballroom, which was used for balls and amateur theatre performances.

Gertruda Roth married František Zelenka, a famous architect, scenographer and graphic designer connected with the *Osvobozené divadlo* (Liberated theatre) an *avant-garde* theatre group in Prague, founded in 1926. In that year, Leo Haas worked as a set designer for a theatre troupe in Opava

There was a Jewish audience for theatre not just in the cultured language of German, or even Czech. In 1925, there is a record of a Yiddish Theatre visiting Ostrava so there must have been enough Yiddish-speakers who had the time, money and interest to go to the theatre.

The involvement of Jews in the theatre was even noted in the anti-Semitic *Juden in Ostrau*; 'While the Czechs occupied most of the civil service, official and administrative positions by driving out the Germans, the Jews were also driving out the Germans from leading positions in industry and trade, in the liberal professions and also, in part, in the higher teaching posts, in the theatre.'

Cinema

Cinema came early to Ostrava; the first public showing in Ostrava was in October 1896, and preceded the arrival of cinema in Prague. The first permanent cinema facility, named grandiloquently *The Empire Bio Company*, opened in a wooden building in Antonín Square near the city theatre on 6 July 1908. A few weeks later the first permanent cinema opened in Vítkovice. In 1910 Adolf Haberfeld opened a cinema in his famous Vítkovice inn and soon afterwards he opened a purpose built cinema, *The Imperial*. By 1926, Greater Ostrava could boast 28 cinemas and two years later as many as 40. Bertie Goldberg was a frequent cinema-goer as was Paul Rice, who recalls:

> I especially remember Charlie Chaplin in 'The Circus', the first ever sound film, and Fred Astaire in 'Top Hat', which I saw on the night of my last departure to England! As boys we went to the pictures quite often.

Paul's younger brother, Karel was to have a much closer and longer-lasting association with cinema than Paul. He came to England on one of Nicholas Winton's *Kindertransports* and joined Paul at Leighton Park School where he learned English and began to lose his Czech accent. After wartime service in the RAF he read Natural Sciences at Emmanuel College, Cambridge and went on to become a well-known and very successful British film director. Among his many successes were *Saturday Night and Sunday Morning; This Sporting Life; Isadora* and *The French Lieutenant's Woman.*

In 2009, the City of Ostrava unveiled a memorial to Karel above the door to the apartment block in what had been the Reisz building, from which his grandparents had waved at the Emperor in 1880. The memorial is in the form of a movie camera lens. Paul returned to Ostrava for the occasion. Three years later, in 2012, Paul went to a concert in the Bridgewater Hall in Manchester to hear the first performance of 'The Last Train to Tomorrow' written and conducted by Carl Davis:

> The principal item, 50 minutes long, was a composition for a small orchestra and 50 young singers and 6 solo voices and its theme was the 'Kindertransport' from Prague to London in 1939. The composer/conductor explained to the audience the background of this action and the six solo voices described the background to the need to save so many Jewish Children and how they were separated from their parents at Prague station, their travel difficulties across Germany, then Holland and the sea crossing to Harwich and the well prepared arrival in London and welcome by their 'new' parents. The whole thing was most emotional due to the impressive libretto and first-class

Memorial to Karel Reisz.

performance by the orchestra and conductor. At end there was an 8-minutes ovation. Full Marks to the Halle and Manchester!!

Hans Otto Löwenstein was born of Jewish parents in Přívoz in 1881 and became a successful film producer. He was sufficiently successful for him to be claimed as Austrian rather than Jewish or even Czechoslovak, by the Austrians!

Leo Wiener's family is large and complex. His great grandfather Leopold Kassler seems to have married three times, and one of Leopold's grandsons was Bedřich Kassler, known as Fritz, who emigrated to the USA and changed his name to Frank Kassler. In 1936, he produced a film, *Le Golem*, directed by Duvivier. Later, Frank set up his own film production unit in the USA.

The Reisz building featured in the history of Ostrava theatre once again in the 1990s, when a theatre was opened in the building and *The Taming of the Shrew* was performed there.

NOTES

1. This section is based on original material provided by Dr Jiří Jung, University of Ostrava.
2. Adapted from the PhD thesis submitted by Jiří Hrdina by public lecture at FAMU, Prague, translated by Lydia Tischler.
3. *Jews and Photography in Britain* Michael Berkowitz, Austin: University of Texas Press, 2015.
4. Edith Rosenberg (age 79) recorded 7 hours of her memoirs on audio tape for the Imperial War Museum in London, ref: 9169/14/01-14.
5. *I did Survive* ELRO (Edith Rosenberg) Regency Press 1978.
6. *The Magic Doll,* Gita Thieberger-Rind, Enviro Books 2005.
7. *Die Hofnung erhielt mich am Leben,* Ruth Elias, Piper 1988. *The Triumph of Hope*, Wiley, 1998.
8. *Auf eigenen Spuren*, Peter Erben, Hartung-Gorre Verlag, 2001:
   I met Peter at a conference in Ostrava in 2009, when he and his wife attended a ceremony to unveil a memorial to the Jews of Ostrava who had been deported to Nisko. Eva, who was born in 1930 in Děčín, and who had survived Theresienstadt, Auschwitz, Christianstadt and a death march during which her mother died in her arms leaving her entirely alone in the world, had been hidden by a Czech farmer's family at the end of the war. She also wrote and published her story but asked me to write and publish an English version of her story, which I did, as *Escape Story,* now also translated into German and published as '*Fluchten*'. So David can claim to be another author with Ostrava connections!
   Escape Story, Eva Erben, adapted and translated David Lawson. Sharron Publishing Services, 2001.
   Fluchten, Stiftung Denkmal für die ermordeten Juden, Europas, 2014.
9. *Mendel Rosenbusch,* Ilse Weber, illustr. Salo Salomonowitz, Herodias, 2001 trans. from original German version: Mendel Rosenbusch, Mährisch Ostrau, 1929.
10. Poem, by Ilse Weber *Und der Regen rinnt.*

Und der Regen rinnt	**And the rain falls**
Und der Regen rinnt, und der Regen rinnt..	And the rain falls, and the rain falls..
Ich denk im Dunkeln an sich, mein Kind.	In the dark I think of you, my child.
Hoch sind die Berge und tief ist das Meer,	High are the mountains and deep is the sea,
Mein Herz ist müd und sehnsuchts schwer.	My heart is weary and heavy with yearning.
Und der Regen rinnt und der Regen rinnt…	And the rain falls, and the rain falls..
Warum bist du so fern, mein Kind?	Why are you so far away, my child?
Und der Regen rinnt, und der Regen rinnt..	And the rain falls, and the rain falls..
Gott selbst hat uns getrennt, mein Kind.	God Himself has parted us, my child.
Du sollst nicht Leid und Elend sehn	You are not meant to see sorrow and misery
sollst nicht auf steinigen Gassen gehn.	You are not meant to walk in stony alleyways
Und der Regen rinnt, und der Regen rinnt..	And the rain falls, and the rain falls..
Hast du mich nicht vergessen, Kind?	Have you not forgotten me, child?

The final work in the concert was a lullaby by Ilse Weber. She worked as a nursery nurse in Theresienstadt and when the time came in 1944 for 'her' children to be sent to Auschwitz she decided that she could not let then go on such an awful journey alone, so she went with them and was murdered with them. The last lines of the lullaby are:

Wiegala – a Lullaby

Wiegala, wiegala, wille	Wiegala, wiegala, wille
Wie ist die Welt so stille!	How silent is the world!
Es stört kein Laut die süsse Ruh,	No sound disturbs the lovely peace.
Schlaf, mein Kindchen, schlaf auch du.	Sleep, my little child, sleep too.
Wiegala, wiegala, wille	Wiegala, wiegala, wille
Wie ist die Welt so stille!	How silent is the world!

The first mass transport of Jews from Ostrava to Theresienstadt arrived the day after Yom Kippur, 1942.

11. *Homecoming,* Joseph Wechsberg, London, Michael Joseph, 1947.

PART III

OSTRAVA AT WAR

Life in Ostrava in the decade or so that followed the First World War was good. The population increased, technological progress accelerated, health and wealth all improved. Ostravaks felt comfortable and optimistic as part of the newly created Czechoslovakia. But it was not to last in Ostrava, Czechoslovakia or, indeed, much of the rest of the world. The early 1930s saw probably the greatest financial crisis that modern civilisation had yet experienced. The economic problems brought social and then ethnic problems in their wake. States adopted 'beggar your neighbour' protectionist policies, tensions rose across the world and an unhealthy social climate developed.

The inability of states to deal with so far-reaching a depression and the strains on social welfare systems unable to cope with the numbers of unemployed and impoverished citizens opened the way for totalitarian groups to achieve political power. European society experienced a polarisation between radically left-wing and radically right-wing movements and opinions. Deep disillusionment with economic 'liberalism' meant a decline in the popularity of social liberalism, and tolerance was in retreat.

Global trends could not but find a reflection in Ostrava too. The short era of the 'Golden Twenties' ended abruptly with the crash on the New York stock exchange. The ethnic animosities that in the times of prosperity had been at least partially lulled to sleep awoke with new energy and with an even more aggressive and repulsive rhetoric than in the times before and just after the First World War.

The City authorities in Ostrava had tried to stop the spread of nationalism and antisemitism. In 1923, they dismissed Richard Drapala from his post in the City archive for his virulent antisemitism. He worked as a clerk in the Vítkovice works and as a journalist until the German invasion of Ostrava, when he was re-instated as the Director of the City Archive.

Although the troubles were possibly milder in Ostrava than in much of the rest of Europe, the change of atmosphere inside Ostrava society can be seen from the shifting profile of the political parties that gained representation in the city council in the course of the 1930s. Comparing the results of the local elections of 1935 with those of 1929, we can see how the popularity of Czech movements with fascist tendencies (Národní sjednocení – National Unification, Národní obec fašistická – National Fascist Community) and communists had grown at the expense of the Czech Social Democrats. In the same way, the German Social Democrats lost ground to the pro-Nazi parties like the Deutsche Nationalpartei and Deutsche Nationalsozialistische Arbeiterpartei, both of which were banned in the autumn of 1933 for their open relations with the German Nazis in the Reich. In the Sudetenland, Konrad Henlein set up the Sudetendeutsche Heimatfront (The Sudeten German Homeland Front) in 1933, which in 1935 became the Sudetendeutsche Partei or SdP and a general right-wing pro-German party. It was openly and explicitly anti-Semitic, following the example of the German Nazi party propaganda.

Anti-Semitic articles appeared routinely on the pages of the German and Czech daily newspapers. As the economic problems of the middle classes grew it was easiest to blame Jews for the crisis and its deepening effects, but until 1938 direct physical attacks on the Jewish inhabitants of Ostrava were very rare. Jewish children noticed that some of their former friends started to avoid them and a few children started to wear long white socks, a sign of their – or their parents' – support for the far right.

Nationalism developed throughout the 1930s. Oskar Federer, the Managing Director of the Vítkovice works, was heavily criticised by both German and Czech nationalists for favouring the other side, and probably the Jews in particular, in employment and promotion. There is no objective evidence that he did any such thing, but it is a sign of the times and the tensions.

Social life became ever more fragmented, conducted by each ethnic or religious group in mutual isolation. Some coffee-houses were Czech, some German, while Jews tended to meet in others, although there was never any complete segregation. It was only in the course of 1938, after the Anschluss with Austria, and then after the annexation of the Czechoslovak borderlands, that there were demonstrations, above all by Henlein sympathisers in the ranks of the local Germans or Czech fascists, that ended in physical expressions of antisemitism. Jewish Ostravaks who can now recall that period do say that they were aware of increasing, although relatively minor, anti-Semitism in their daily life, especially towards the later 1930s. Almost all of them contrast it with the early 1930s when they were unaware of any anti-Semitism. Ostrava seems to have been a relatively tolerant place even in intolerant times.

The activities of Henlein and the SdP in the Sudetenland were major factors in laying the groundwork for the infamous Munich Agreement and consequent annexation of the Sudetenland by the German Reich. The SdP merged with Hitler's Nazi party on 5 November 1938. Henlein joined the Nazi Party in January 1939 and was appointed to the Reichstag.

In the period of the Second Republic, from October 1938 to March 1939, rising antisemitism became evident even on the official level as civil servants of Jewish background were fired from their posts. This measure, which according to official propaganda was supposed to vacate places for Czech refugees from the borderlands, also affected Jewish doctors in state or municipal hospitals. Even before the occupation Jewish children were excluded from German schools in Ostrava. This was not initially official policy, but Jewish children were effectively intimidated out of their classes and so moved to Czech schools. Following the establishment of the Protektorat the policy became official by a decree of the Reich Ministry of Culture of 12 July 1939, and later Jewish children were entirely deprived of the chance of school education with a ban on their attendance even at Czech schools, issued on 7 August 1940. In Ostrava they were still able to gain an elementary education at the Jewish school, but only until 24 July 1942, when it was officially closed. In May and June 1939 Ostrava's synagogues were burned down at least in some cases on the direct instructions of the German occupying forces.

Throughout the First Republic the Czech Social Democrats had been the dominant political force in the Ostrava town hall, but following the economic crisis they lost their commanding positions quite quickly and had to compromise with their political opponents in the framework of various coalitions. What had been a liberal tolerant civic society quite rapidly became nationalistic and intolerant, with those of minority religions or politics being increasingly marginalised and excluded from employment and society.

Similarities with the situation in Europe and the Middle East in 2016 are chilling.

8

War and the Holocaust

Invasion

After the Munich Agreement of September 1938 Ostrava became once more a frontier town, on the border with two other and unfriendly states – Germany and Poland. Germany occupied the Sudetenland while Poland occupied former Czech land, pushing the border south and west. Both states had a similar hostile attitude to the remnant of Czechoslovakia and both wanted to exploit the industrial potential of Ostrava for their own ends.

The agony of the Second Czechoslovak Republic lasted roughly half a year from September 1938, culminating with the events of March 1939. On Tuesday 14 March the Republic watched proceedings in the Slovak Parliament, which ended in the declaration of an independent Slovak state. At that moment the fate of the remnant of Czechoslovakia was also sealed, and the citizens of Ostrava were among the first to witness the consequences. Shortly after 5 o'clock in the afternoon, when the Czechoslovak president Hácha was already sitting in a train bound for Berlin where he was supposed to meet the Reich Chancellor, Adolf Hitler, German units that had for some days been massing in the German Sudetenland close to Ostrava, started to move. These troops headed into the town in four streams, from Koblov, Petřkovice, Svinov and Polanka. From Ostrava they advanced into Frýdek and Místek.

By half past seven in the evening all the districts of Moravská and Slezská Ostrava, Hrušov and Muglinov were in German hands. The surprised Czech population, including the town leaders and even President Hácha, believed that this was merely a temporary occupation and that the troops would be moving on into Slovakia. The local Germans, however, had been very well informed about the whole action and had made advance preparations to welcome the columns of the German army.

That evening, the National Moravian-Silesian Theatre was performing in the City Theatre (now the Antonín Dvořák Theatre). Jan Pacl, who was playing the hero, wrote about that fateful evening in his memoir:

> We were getting ready for the performance when the news came about the Germans occupying Ostrava. Everyone was upset, of course, and we asked ourselves if we should go ahead with the performance. The

German troops entering Ostrava.

The German House illuminated to celebrate the invasion.

The New Town Hall illuminated with a Swastika.

> theatre director was in Prague that night and I was the only employee of the City Theatre and decided that 'The show must go on'. Some actors went to the main square to see what was happening. There were German soldiers everywhere and there were some scuffles between them and the civilians. The audience that night understood why we felt it necessary to carry on with the performance. It was necessary to show disinterest in the upset to our lives.

Klaudia Eibenová[1] reported:

> ...the actors, who already knew that the fascists were in Ostrava, knelt on the stage and prayed for the Czechs. It was typical early spring weather, rain and snow fell.

That night they were performing the operetta by Josef Stelibský, *Na šťastné planetě*, 'The Happy Planet'! The planet would not be happy again for many years.

The troops were housed in local school buildings that were immediately commandeered, and later in the barracks in Místek. Subsequently new barracks were built in Nová Bělá. With the Wehrmacht came other units of the German repressive apparatus – the Gestapo, the German criminal police, gendarmes and *Sicherheitdienst*.[2] The Gestapo immediately occupied the police directorate building in Ostrava, disarmed Czech policemen and arrested the police chief, Emil Bača, and ten other police officials as a revenge for their alleged ill treatment of the German minority. Unfortunately the Gestapo managed to seize the police archive, almost complete, as it had not been burned in time.

The general staff of the occupation force, headed by Major General Keiner, settled into the New Town Hall. The German units also immediately seized the main post office and occupied the Vítkovice Ironworks. Indeed it was fear that the Polish would get their hands on the giant industrial concern first that was one of the main reasons the Germans took control of Ostrava earlier than had been first planned. Just after nine o'clock that night, the Germans occupied the radio building and imposed their own political management on the headquarters of the so-called Jewish newspapers, the *Ostrauer Zeitung*, *Silesia* and *Morgenzeitung*. A state of emergency was declared in the town, including a ban on assembly and orders for the surrender of arms and ammunition. Overnight, cars and trams had to start driving on the right not left side of the road. Swastika banners draped German private homes and all public buildings, and pictures of Adolf Hitler appeared in shop windows. Postage stamps were overprinted with a swastika and a postmark appeared celebrating the occupation as *Befreiung*, liberation.

Envelope with invasion postmark 'The day of the liberation, 14.3.39'.

Anti-Jewish activities began immediately and on 15 March most Jewish shopkeepers preferred not to open their shops and some left the town. A German sign declaring Jews unwelcome appeared on the entrance to the Palace Hotel which was owned by the Jewish Gronner brothers and had been one of the favourite meeting places for the Jewish bourgeoisie before it had been commandeered by the Germans. It had caught the eye of Major General Keiner and he moved into it with his staff. The Gronner brothers managed to escape to Rumania via Poland, but their wives and daughters were not so lucky and they were deported to the Łodz Ghetto, where they died in 1942.

When the Germans occupied Ostrava, the local department stores belonging to Jewish owners, such as Rix, Textilia, Schön and Bachner were almost immediately taken over. They were placed under the control of supervisory commissioners. The town council of Slezská Ostrava immediately halted payment of any funds from the local treasury to Jewish inhabitants and at the same time ordered them to pay any arrears by 16 March 1939. In the first days of the occupation Jewish property was 'aryanised', taken over and put under the control and ownership of approved Germans or Czechs of German ethnicity.

National and local regulations restricting the rights and freedoms of Jews were imposed. They began with Jews being prevented from practicing in the professions, barring of Jews from further education, and the reallocation of Jewish university graduates to forced manual labour, for example clearing the course of the Lučina and Ostravice rivers and construction of a weir in Kunčice. During March and April 1939 all Jews working in the Vítkovice Ironworks were not only fired from their jobs but stripped of all the benefits relating to work in the ironworks; accommodation, pension entitlements and welfare payments.

Anti-Semitic sentiments had been intensifying in the later 1930s and, in view of the events in neighbouring states to the west and the deteriorating internal political situation, members of the local Jewish community had increasingly been talking of emigration. Something that they had once regarded as only a theoretical possibility now took on more concrete shape. After the Austrian *Anschluss*[3] and the Munich Agreement, some Jewish groups considered emigration in terms of real, practical options.

The expression 'Solution to the Jewish Question' had started to appear on the pages of the press even before the occupation of Czechoslovakia, in the period of the Second Republic. The theme of the Jewish refugees from Germany was much discussed, and there were also reports of efforts to organise the emigration of Czechoslovak Jews. At a meeting at the end of December 1938, representatives of the Palestine Immigration Office in Prague and the Prague Jewish Community tried to persuade representatives of other Jewish organisations and communities to convince Jews of the need to leave Czechoslovakia and go abroad but they had met with limited success.

From January 1939 the Ostrava police directorate had been monitoring the mood among local Jews. The forced deportation from Ostrava of foreigners, that is non-Czechoslovak citizens of Jewish origin, naturally contributed strongly to the Jews' nervousness. It was the better informed and the more affluent that tended to make plans for actual departure. Unfortunately, most were for many reasons unable to act on their decisions to emigrate before the occupation of Czechoslovakia. Apart from administrative and economic obstacles, major factors were sentiment, anxiety about leaving family members behind, psychological reluctance and a lack of contacts abroad.

Traditionally Jewish emigrants had headed for the USA, Britain and Palestine. Now they considered countries far more exotic for Central Europeans – Ecuador, Brazil, Cuba, Uruguay, Paraguay, Columbia, Peru and the Dominican Republic, but also China or the island of Mauritius. Whether legal or illegal, emigration would liberate the Jewish inhabitants from the power of the Nuremberg Laws, and enable them to escape the ever more degrading prohibitions and regulations that initially limited 'merely' their freedoms but would later reduce their human dignity almost to nothing. Emigration represented hope for a better or at least a safer and more dignified life. For most Jews, however, flight to these countries turned out to be a never realised dream, their last dream.

Some people did escape the Germans. Tom Auber's mother worked for a transport company, and one of the lorry drivers telephoned the office to say that the German tanks were approaching the city. His mother went straight home and she and his father, who had relatives in Poland and papers allowing them to cross the border, decided to go to their relatives to await events. They took only their papers, toothbrush, and overnight clothes, but missed the tram so took a taxi. The taxi was thumbed down by a Czech army officer going in the same direction, whom they dropped off shortly before the border. Having dropped him off, the taxi turned a corner, to be stopped by German tanks blocking the road. His parents had to show their papers but as they had nothing else but night things, they were allowed to continue over the border. There they caught up with the tram they had missed, and whose passengers weren't aware that the Germans had reached Ostrava. They spent a short time in Poland and then travelled separately, via Sweden to England.

In the first months of the occupation, a number of the Jewish inhabitants of the town committed suicide.

Deportation to Nisko

The Germans invaded Poland on 1 September 1939 and they lost no time in making use of the newly acquired territory. Less than 6 weeks later, on 6 October, Heinrich Müller the Head of the Gestapo, issued an order for the transfer of 70-80,000 Jews from the Katowice area to the territory east of the River Vistula. The order also mentioned the transfer of part of the Jewish population from Moravská Ostrava and its environs. Later the transfer of Jews from Vienna was included in the plan. The transports were organised by the staff of the central offices for Jewish emigration in Vienna and Prague, but officially it was claimed that this was a voluntary initiative by Jewish religious communities. The coordination of the actions was the responsibility of Müller's subordinate, Adolf Eichmann, Head of the Gestapo's Office of Resettlement and later of the Office of Jewish Affairs.

Hugo Gold in his 1974 History of Ostrava Jews[4] quotes from the official record of the Eichmann trial a statement from a meeting between Eichmann and Müller: 'This activity should primarily serve to get experience which could be used to carry out the deportation of larger numbers.' Eichmann first arrived in Ostrava on 9 October to discuss the compilation of the lists of Jewish men to be transported, and supervise plans for the construction of camp buildings, supply of the materials for running the camp and the logistics of the whole policy. The Jewish Community was told to draw up lists of Jews for deportation immediately. On 11 October, on the orders of the Gestapo, the Community declared that all Jews above 14 years of age were obliged to register. The Community then issued a proclamation requiring all Jewish men to assemble at the Ostrava Riding School on the morning of Tuesday 17 October for departure for 'retraining'. Meanwhile, between 12 and 16 October the front pages of the Ostrava editions of the newspapers *České slovo* and the *Mährisch-Schlesische Landeszeitung* carried front-page warnings to anyone thinking of ignoring the orders.

Merkblatt

zur Zusammenstellung der Ausrüstungsgegenstände.

Wir geben Ihnen tieferstehend Richtlinien für die Zusammenstellung der Ausrüstungsgegenstände. Es bleibt jedem Einzelnen vorbehalten, mehr oder weniger mitzunehmen. Jeder Mann ist verpflichtet RM 300.- d. s. K 3000.- mitzunehmen; für den Fall als ihm dies unmöglich ist, hat er den fehlenden Betrag sofort mit den im Merkblatt angeführten fehlenden Gegenständen der isr. Kultusgemeinde zu melden.

Die Ausrüstungsgegenstände für den notwendigen Tagesgebrauch müssen im Rucksacke, die anderen im Koffer untergebracht werden.

Fehlende Ausrüstungsgegenstände, welche trotz vorhandener finanzieller Mittel nicht erhältlich sind, sind genau zu bezeichnen.

Ausrüstungsgegenstände, die trotz verhandener Mittel nicht angeschafft werden können, werden von der Leitung versucht zu beschaffen. Wir legen jedoch nahe, sich diese Ausrüstungsgegenstände womöglich selbst zu besorgen.

Für die wahrheitsgemäßen Angaben haftet jeder Teilnehmer **persönlich** und machen wir auf die Folgen unrichtiger Angaben nachdrücklich aufmerksam.

Der Vorstand der israel. Kultusgemeinde:

Mähr. Ostrau, den 12. Oktober 1939.

SALO KRÄMER m. p.

Vorschlag für die Ausrüstung eines Mannes.

1. Kupékoffer (bis 80 cm)
2. 1 großer Rucksack und 1 Brotsack
3. 4 warme Hemden
4. 4 warme lange Unterhosen
5. 3 Paar lange warme Wollstrümpfe
6. 3 Paar Wollsocken
7. 3 feste Handtücher
8. 12 Taschentücher
9. 2 Geschirrtücher
10. 2 Putzlappen
11. 6 Paar Flanellfußlappen
12. 1 Paar hohe Gummistiefel od. Stiefel od. Ledergamaschen
13. 1 Paar feste Schuhe ev. Skischuhe
14. 1 Paar warme Hausschuhe
15. 2 feste Arbeitsanzüge (Kniehosen, Skianzug)
16. 1 Wintermantel
17. 1 Pullover oder Weste mit Ärmel
18. 1 Paar Wollhandschuhe
19. 1 Paar Fäustlinge
20. 1 Wollschal
21. 1 Trainingsanzug
22. 1 warme Kopfdeckung
23. 1 Paar Ohrenschützer
24. 1 Flanellbauchbinde
25. 1 Zeltblatt
26. 1 Wolldecke
27. 1 Hosenriemen
28. 3 kleine Riemen (Leder), Schuhriemen
29. 1 zweiteil. Menageschale
30. 1 Essbesteck (rostfrei)
31. 1 Topf mit $^{1}/_{2}$ l
32. 1 Feldflasche mit Überzug und Riemen
33. 1 Trinkbecher (Metall)
34. 1 Flanellpyjama
35. 1 starkes Taschenmesser
36. 1 Petroleum-Sturmlampe, kleines Format
37. 10 Pakete Zünder
38. 6 Wagenkerzen
39. 1 Kleiderbürste
40. 1 Kotbürste stark
41. 1 kompl. Schuhputzzeug
42. 1 Dose Lederfett
43. 1 Nähzeug (Nadeln, Schere, Zwirne, Sicherheitsnadeln Knöpfe, Wolle, Flecke, Spagat, Nagelfeile)
44. 1 Reinigungsbürste
45. Zahnbürste und Zahnputzmittel
46. 1 Waschlappen
47. 1 Rasierzeug mit Seife und Reservemesser
48. $^{1}/_{2}$ kg Seife
49. $^{1}/_{2}$ kg Waschsand
50. 1 kompl. Taschenapotheke
51. Schreibzeug, Verbandpäckchen
52. Rauchmaterial
53. Papier
54. Matratze oder Strohsack oder Schlafsack
55. RM 300.— oder K 3.000.—

List of things to be taken with the deportees to Nisko.

The men received a list of things that they would need to bring with them: suitcase, backpack and knapsack, enough underwear and winter clothing, personal hygiene articles, work tools and so on, including 3000 Crowns. At the same time the Community offered assistance for poorer Jews in obtaining these things.

Moravská Ostrava Jewish engineers were ordered by the Nazis to draw up plans for building the camp, with the necessary building materials to be supplied by local Jewish firms. For example the builder Sachs had to supply

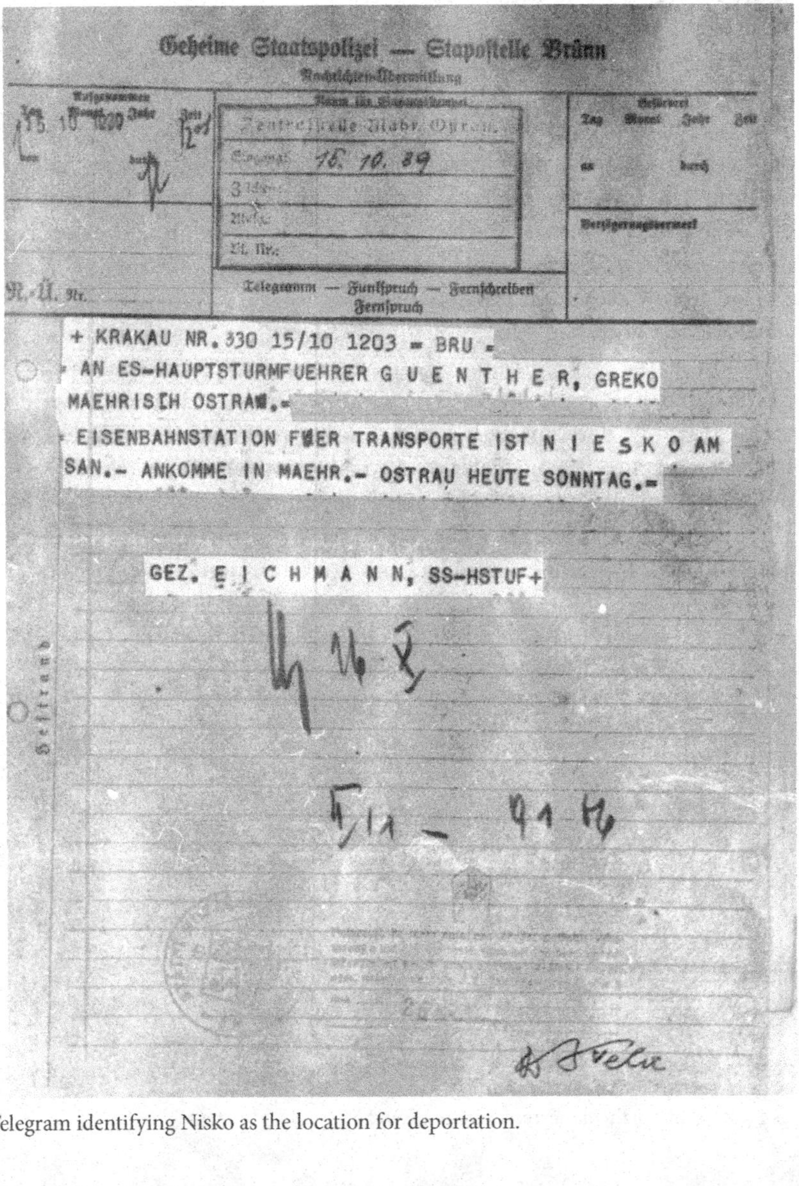

Geheime Staatspolizei — Stapostelle Brünn

Nachrichten-Übermittlung

Telegramm — Funkspruch — Fernschreiben
Fernspruch

+ KRAKAU NR. 330 15/10 1203 = BRU =
AN ES-HAUPTSTURMFUEHRER G U E N T H E R, GREKO
MAEHRISCH OSTRAU.=
EISENBAHNSTATION FUER TRANSPORTE IST N I E S K O AM
SAN.- ANKOMME IN MAEHR.- OSTRAU HEUTE SONNTAG.=

GEZ. E I C H M A N N, SS-HSTUF+

Telegram identifying Nisko as the location for deportation.

part of the timber required. The community had to obtain any materials that the Jewish firms did not have, at its own expense, from other sources.

Eichmann's telegram informing the authorities in Ostrava that the destination of the transport would be Nisko nad Sanem did not arrive until 15 October. There was general confusion around the organisation of this, the first Jewish transport of the European Holocaust. The religious community in Frýdek was not informed that all its male members over 14 years of age were required to assemble in the Ostrava Riding School until just 20 hours before the departure, and so many of its members came to Ostrava in the morning without luggage.

On the morning of 17 October the final selection of Jews from the first of the transports was made in the Riding School.

The selected 901 Jews were taken by bus to the freight station in Přívoz, where a specially prepared train composed of passenger and freight wagons awaited them. Once the people had got onto the train they were not allowed out again. The train was sealed, but remained in the station for the whole night. A surviving report by the Nazi authorities mentions that the departure of the transport was accompanied by 'loud expressions of sympathy for the deported from Czechs and Jewish women'.

Before departure the Jews in the train had to hand over all articles made of precious metals. The train set off on the morning of Wednesday 18 October at half past eight. It passed through Bohumín, Dziedzice, Oświęcim, Kraków, Tarnów, Rzeszów and Przeworsk before arriving in Nisko. Max Burger later recalled that no water was available and when, at Kraków station, those in the train pleaded for water, and Poles on the platform wished to help them, Stormtroopers chased away the Poles 'with rifle blows'. When they reached Nisko, all engineers, builders and doctors among the deported Jews

Riding school where the deportees were to assemble.

were ordered to leave the train. Because the doors of the train were sealed, they had to climb through the windows. Then, surrounded by SS guards, they found themselves among other Jews who had been deported from Prague and Vienna. A German officer addressed them. He was Adolf Eichmann. 'About seven or eight kilometres from here,' Eichmann told them, 'across the river San, the Führer of the Jews has promised a new homeland. There are no apartments and no houses – if you will build your homes you will have a roof over your head.' There was 'no water,' Eichmann added. 'The wells are full of epidemics, there's cholera, dysentery, and typhus. If you dig for water, you'll have water.' The deported Jews were then sent across a pontoon bridge to the 'resettlement' region.[5]

From there the deported Jews had to walk across the heavy marshy terrain, over the river San to the village of Zarzecze, where they started to build the camp. The first death occurred on the march.

The interned Ostravaks were surprised when the very next day, after selection of experts essential for the running of the camp, the others were just set loose and driven away. The Nazi planners had changed their minds; the territory of former eastern Poland was no longer supposed to become a 'Jewish reservation' but instead the base for the Wehrmacht's intended assault on the Soviet Union. Nonetheless, to spare the German police units loss of face, the second and third transport were still dispatched from Ostrava to Nisko. The second transport left in the evening of 26 October 1939 carrying around 400 Jews, most of them men from Brno who had tried to escape the first transport and been arrested by the Gestapo. This train linked up in Katowice with another, containing around 1,000 local Jews, and later the second transport from Vienna arrived with 669 people. None of these deportees actually reached the camp, however, because having been robbed of all their valuables on the way, they arrived in Nisko only to be driven away, on foot, further to the east and the Soviet border and left to their fate. The Germans relied on the hostility to Jews among the local population, hoping that they would 'take care of' the fleeing deportees. In fact the great majority of people from these transports managed to cross the border into the Soviet Union, but most of them were arrested there and after the outbreak of war with Germany were transported to gulags in Siberia, where many of them perished. From 1942 Czechoslovak and Polish Jews were allowed to join army units formed on Soviet territory. 300 Czech Jews from the Nisko transports subsequently served in General Svoboda's army. They fought in the battles on the Eastern Front and about 90 survived to return home. The Austrian Jews from Vienna were not given an opportunity to fight, however, being regarded as enemy aliens rather than Jews, and most of them perished in inhuman conditions in Siberia.

Those Jews from the Nisko transports who managed to avoid the Soviet NKVD and remain in the Ukraine fell victim to the Nazi massacres. The third and last Nisko transport was from Ostrava only. In its ten wagons were 332 prisoners sent by the Gestapo, in most cases from Prague. The train left on the morning of 1 November 1939 but never reached Nisko, because the San was in flood and had swept away the provisional bridge providing the only access to the camp. The train was diverted to Sosnowiec in Upper Silesia, where the first Jewish concentration camp was set up for the deportees. Initially the plan was for them to be transported to Nisko as soon as conditions allowed, but this never happened.

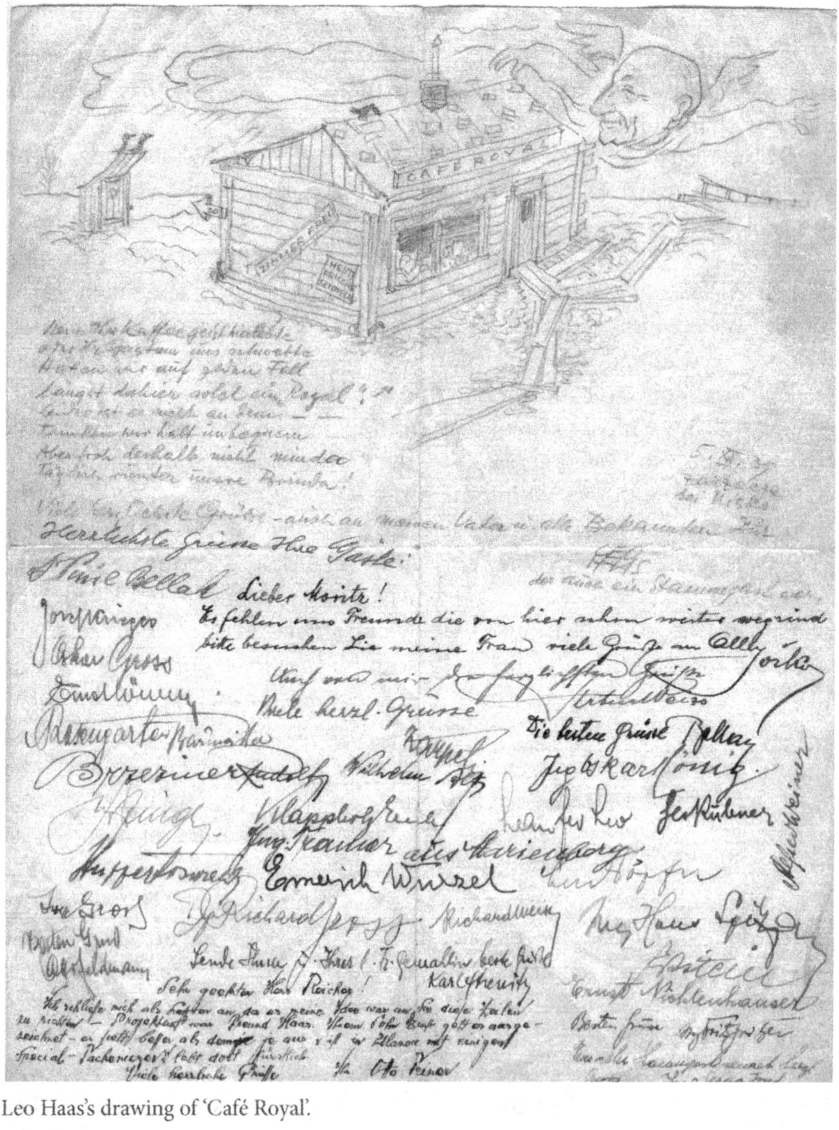

Leo Haas's drawing of 'Café Royal'.

Among the Ostrava prisoners in Nisko, was the artist Leo Haas and he drew 'Café Royal', a favourite meeting place in the Palace Hotel in Ostrava, on a postcard which many Ostravaks signed and sent back home. (see **Appendix 8.1).**

The camp in Nisko was abandoned in the spring of 1940. Those who were freed after their period of forced labour in the camp received a Pass, showing that they had served their time and been freed. After its liquidation

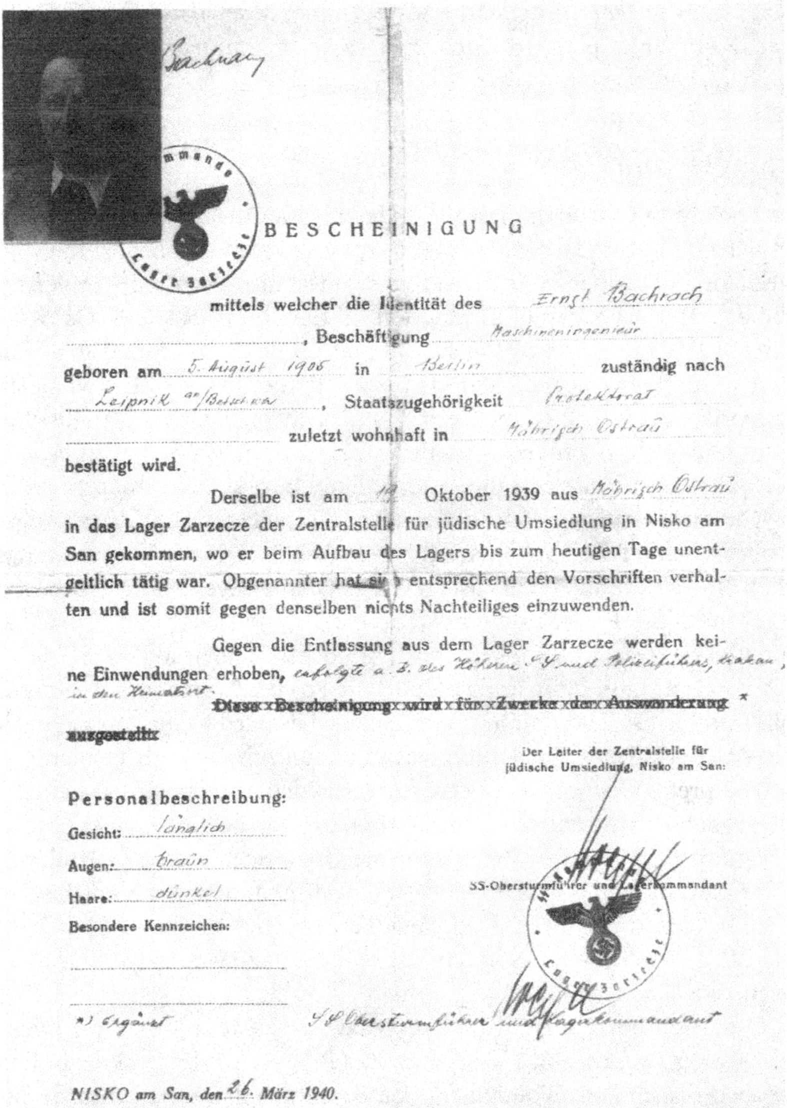

BESCHEINIGUNG

mittels welcher die Identität des Ernst Bachrach, Beschäftigung Maschineningenieur

geboren am 5. August 1905 in Berlin zuständig nach Leipnik a/Betschwa, Staatszugehörigkeit Protektorat

zuletzt wohnhaft in Mährisch Ostrau

bestätigt wird.

Derselbe ist am 19 Oktober 1939 aus Mährisch Ostrau in das Lager Zarzecze der Zentralstelle für jüdische Umsiedlung in Nisko am San gekommen, wo er beim Aufbau des Lagers bis zum heutigen Tage unentgeltlich tätig war. Obgenannter hat sich entsprechend den Vorschriften verhalten und ist somit gegen denselben nichts Nachteiliges einzuwenden.

Gegen die Entlassung aus dem Lager Zarzecze werden keine Einwendungen erhoben, erfolgte a. B. des Höheren SS und Polizeiführers, Krakau, in den Heimatort.

~~Diese Bescheinigung wird für Zwecke der Auswanderung ausgestellt.~~ *

Der Leiter der Zentralstelle für jüdische Umsiedlung, Nisko am San:

Personalbeschreibung:

Gesicht: länglich

Augen: braun

Haare: dunkel

Besondere Kennzeichen:

SS-Obersturmführer und Lagerkommandant

*) Ergänzt

SS Obersturmführer und Lagerkommandant

NISKO am San, den 26. März 1940.

Ernst Bachrach's permit to leave the Nisko camp.

516 men returned to Ostrava on 13 April 1940, of whom 301 were from Ostrava (Haas was among them), 18 from the Těšín region and 197 from Vienna. To these returnees we should add the more than 100 people who found their way back independently after being driven out of the camp. Most of those who returned, however, were eventually transported to Theresienstadt in the course of 1942 and from there to one of the extermination camps.

More than 5,000 people were transported to Nisko. The great majority of them (around 4,000) were driven out of the camp, north towards Lublin and the new eastern border of the Soviet Union, where they were left to their fate. Eichmann's plan, to gain experience for the deportation of larger numbers, had been a success.

Schindler and Ostrava

Even before the occupation of the Sudetenland, Ostrava had been a centre for German intelligence gathering, or spying, about the disposition of the Czech forces and their state of readiness. It was also a centre for undercover sabotage and propaganda production. After the invasion of Ostrava in March 1939, the target of the spying and propaganda shifted to Poland. German black propaganda and sabotage activities had kept the whole area in a febrile state to 'justify' the German attack on Poland. On 22 August 1939, Hitler had told his generals: 'I will provide a propaganda *cassus belli*. Its credibility doesn't matter – the victor will not be asked if he told the truth.'

The most serious provocation was the 'Gleiwitz Incident' on 31 August. It appeared as if Polish soldiers had attacked and taken over a German radio station at Gleiwitz and broadcast anti-German messages before being driven off. Some of the 'Polish' soldiers had been killed. In fact, the attack had been mounted by German troops in Polish uniforms. The dead 'Polish soldiers' were concentration camp inmates, poisoned by the Germans and dressed in Polish uniforms. Their bodies were shot and defaced so that they appeared to have been killed while fighting but could not subsequently be identified.

The pretext for war had been duly provided and one Oskar Schindler was probably involved in its preparation, having already been engaged in spying for several years. This is the same Oskar Schindler who would later be the hero of the book *Schindler's Ark*[6] and the film 'Schindler's List' and would be named as one of the 'Righteous among the Gentiles' by *Yad Vashem* in Israel. In 1939, he was certainly not righteous and was, in fact, a traitor to Czechoslovakia.

Oskar was born in April 1908 in Svitavy in Western Moravia about 100 miles west of Ostrava and 120 miles East of Prague. His father, Johann Hans, was a womanising drunkard and Oskar certainly inherited the first of those characteristics. His mother, Fanny (née Luser) bought the family house in the prosperous *Iglauerstrasse* and so presumably she came from a fairly wealthy family. Hans initially made a reasonable living making and selling farm equipment but after the depression in the late 1920s and early 1930s he turned to selling electrical generators, and was not very successful. Oskar joined him in the business, which meant that Oskar travelled widely and this would later lead him into his espionage career.

In 1924, Oskar had been expelled from his technical school for faking his report, showing the first signs of Oskar the chancer and fantasist, someone who would throw caution to the winds and would always rely on something turning up – or being fabricated – to get him out of trouble. As a travelling salesman, Oskar honed his considerable skills as a silver-tongued charmer, which stood him in good stead both commercially and romantically. On one of his sales trips with his father in 1927, Oskar met Emilie Pelzl, the daughter of a local wealthy farmer. He persuaded her to marry him in 1928 and they moved in with Oskar's parents in Svitavy. Emilie's father gave Oskar a dowry of 100,000 Crowns, a considerable sum, which Oskar spent on a fast car and women, presumably also fast.

Oskar ran through a series of jobs, from running a driving school to owning a chicken farm including working for the Moravian Electrical Company (MEAS), which unfortunately went bankrupt in 1931 leaving Oskar unemployed for a year. During that period Oskar was arrested twice by the police for drunk and disorderly behaviour. In 1931 he joined the Jaroslav Šimek Bank of Prague, selling government property, where his charm would have been a great asset. He left the bank in 1938 but continued in the same line, working for a businessman in Brno.

Oskar and Emilie moved out of Iglauer Street into their own home in Baderova Street and this was a rather grand house. Clearly, by this time Oskar was somehow making quite a lot of money, sufficient both to have the house and to have an ongoing affair with Aurelie Schlegel, his father's former secretary with whom he had two children.[7]

To what extent the money came from Oskar's spying activities is not clear. Like much of Oskar's story, the tales he told of himself do not always agree with each other or with documentary evidence. And documents relating to spying and police security investigations are, themselves, suspect as they could have been written to protect or promote the writers. What is clear is that Schindler joined Henlein's pro-Nazi *Sudetendeutsche Partei (SdP)*, in 1935. The SdP recruited extreme right-wing Sudeten Germans and Oskar thought of himself as a Sudeten German and a strong German nationalist even if not a real Nazi, although in the autumn of 1938 he applied to join the Nazi party itself. At about the same time, he had his first contact with, and probably joined, the *Abwehr*, the German counter-intelligence organisation. He was introduced to them by a girl in Kraków, with whom, typically, he had an affair.[7]

Subsequent stories offer different dates and methods of contact with the *Abwehr*. This might reflect Oskar's ability to fabricate stories to enhance or minimise his role, or merely his ability to romance a good story. Equally, as the *Abwehr* was restructured and had its remit changed, it could reflect Oskar's contact and involvement with different sections of the organisation. What is clear is that Oskar collected and passed on information about military matters and that he also recruited other agents. The Czech police were aware of his activities and he was arrested in the summer of 1938. A report by the Czech police on18 July 1938 described him as a 'high-calibre spy and an especially dangerous type' mainly because his German handler was a certain Kreuziger whom the Czech police report described as 'one of the leading figures of the German espionage service'. Oskar was imprisoned and remained in jail until October 1938 when he was released from Brno after the Munich Agreement and returned to Svitavy. The *Abwehr* promoted him and sent him to Moravská Ostrava as second in command (some report as effectively in command) of 25 agents. He arrived there in January 1939. At that time, what remained of Czechoslovakia was still independent and Ostrava was still Czech.

In Ostrava he was supposedly given or acquired an apartment at 25 Sadová Street very close to the New Town Hall. Other reports suggest that Oskar and Emilie lived at number 27 Sadová Street and that there was an office as well as an apartment so it is possible that two flats were involved. In her autobiography,[8] Emilie says that they lived at 24 Sadová Street, but Emily had a healthy disregard for accuracy and her account cannot be relied on. The Mayor of Ostrava lived next door to them and subsequently the headquarters of the Gestapo and the *Sicherheitsdienst (SD)* – the Security Service, the sister organisation to the Gestapo – were nearby. The Schindlers' flat was in a good and desirable part of town. Oskar had come up in the world.

Oskar and his team of 25 agents were part of *Abwehr II*, under the command of Colonel Erwin Lahousen. *Abwehr I* in Ostrava was under the command of Colonel Hans Piekenbrock. The *Abwehr* in Ostrava, with two colonels each running a section, must have been a large and important organisation and almost certainly known to both the Czech and the Polish authorities and intelligence agencies. At one point, Oskar bought 40 carrier pigeons so that he could more easily communicate with his agents and the *Abwehr*. They could hardly have escaped notice! Emilie comments in her book that Oskar, typically, rapidly lost interest in them and she had to feed them. After a short while, she released them and they flew away although, being well-trained, they later returned.

Early in 1939, their flat was broken into and ransacked although little of value was taken. They assumed, as did the Gestapo investigators, that this was the work of Polish agents looking for espionage material. Oskar assured the Gestapo that he did not keep sensitive *Abwehr* material in his apartment but, as he had nowhere else to keep it, this seems unlikely to be true. Emilie carried out general secretarial and administrative for Oskar and the *Abwehr* as well as looking after the household and, of course, the pigeons.

After the occupation of the rump of Czechoslovakia in 1939, and the creation of the *Protektorat* of Bohemia and Moravia, German attention and planning focused on the invasion of Poland. Admiral Canaris, the overall head of the *Abwehr*, was one of the few officers to receive a copy of Hitler's directive for the invasion of Poland, dated 3 April1939 – *Fall Weiss* (Case White) – and Schindler's activities assumed a much greater importance. Not only were the *Abwehr* to collect information about Polish troop movements and capabilities but they had to infiltrate Poland itself, destroy some key transport locations while occupying others to prevent Polish troops destroying or occupying them.

Planning for the Gleiwitz operation called for some 150 Polish army uniforms. Oskar is reported to have obtained the first of these from a Polish soldier and then sent it on to Berlin to be copied. According to Emilie's possibly unreliable account, the uniforms were stored in Oskar's flat, prior to the actual attack. As with much of Oskar's early spying career, exactly what he did is not clear and recent historians doubt that Oskar was involved to any great extent or even at all, although obtaining a Polish army uniform would have been a typical Oskar activity. Nor is his position certain. The Gestapo investigation of the break-in at his flat describes Oskar not as a member of the *Abwehr* but as a 'confidante' of Major Plathe who was in command of the Gleiwitz incident. Yet whatever his official position, Oskar was clearly important and well-connected.

The Gleiwitz Incident was propaganda but Schindler was also involved in the preparations for real military action. The railway tunnel in the Jablunkov Pass was identified as a key target which had to be secured by the Germans before the Poles could destroy and block it, and so plans were made to infiltrate men and armaments into Poland before the start of the war to take and hold the tunnel. Oskar was involved in collecting intelligence about the Polish military positions in the pass and probably also in smuggling guns into Poland for the attack. In the event, the attack failed and the Poles held the tunnel, but the German invasion was not seriously hindered by it. Poland quickly fell.

Almost immediately after the fall of Kraków in September, Oskar was sent there by his *Abwehr* masters, or went on his own initiative, to pursue his *Abwehr* activities but also his own business plans. He already had an apartment there and as both his business and intelligence work prospered, he moved to bigger and more luxurious apartments while all the time keeping his house in Sadová in Ostrava. Emilie continued to live there initially but when she moved to Krákow, the Ostrava apartment was used by one of Oskar's many mistresses, so presumably Oskar returned to Ostrava frequently. He always quoted Sadová as his home address during the war.

Oskar was not a very secret 'secret agent' during his time in Ostrava. His 40 carrier pigeons must have attracted some attention. Alois Polansky, who was sentenced to 15 years imprisonment by the Czechoslovaks after the war for his collaboration, reports that Oskar used to meet Lt. György, one of the *Abwehr* officers in the Imperial Hotel before the German invasion of Ostrava. The Imperial Hotel was one of the major meeting places for the bourgeoisie in Ostrava before the war and it is unlikely that such meetings would have been unobserved.

There is now scholarly disagreement about exactly what Oskar actually did for the *Abwehr* and what he achieved as an undercover agent.[9] Oskar would have been delighted at the uncertainty and debate that he generated 70 years after the event. Whatever historians or hagiographers write today, the German authorities clearly had a very high opinion of him. Polansky records that Oskar received many awards for his work, including an expensive Horch sports car. One of Oskar's many mistresses, Marta Kisza, has provided some background to this. She and Oskar were in Berlin and saw the car in a showroom window. The car had been made specially for the Shah of Iran but never delivered because of the outbreak of the war. Oskar persuaded the *Abwehr* to give him the money to buy it![10]

Whether or not the Germans' high regard for him was actually justified, it subsequently enabled him not only to live a life of luxury during the war but also to save the lives of some 1,300 Jews and to become, genuinely, one of the Righteous.

Jewish Life under the *Protektorat*

When the Germans invaded Ostrava on 14 March 1939 they did so with well laid plans, not just for the military occupation but for administering the occupied territory. Czechoslovakia had been forced to cede the Sudetenland to Germany in October 1938 and it had been incorporated into the German Reich. On 14 March 1939, not only was Ostrava occupied but the fascist parties in Slovakia declared independence, with German agreement. On 15 March, the rest of what remained of Czechoslovakia was occupied and on 16 March Hitler declared Bohemia and Moravia to be a Protectorate of Germany in a speech in Prague Castle. It had been Hitler's ambition to 'settle the Slav problems in the Czech Lands' for some time and he now began to do so.

Within days of the invasion, German plans for dealing with the Jews were put into operation. Their experience in dealing with the Jews of Germany and Austria after the *Anschluss* could be used with advantage. The Germans had lists of leading Jewish businessmen and political leaders who were to be arrested and of businesses to be expropriated and 'aryanised' – put under the control and ownership of Germans or German-speaking Czechs. For those aryanised businesses, the Germans had already identified and named

German-speaking Czechs who would take over the business, usually senior and trusted existing employees of the company. Large houses owned by Jews were taken over either as offices (the Gestapo headquarters was established in the house of Igo Wechsler) or as lodgings for senior Nazis.

The Vítkovice Works was, at least initially, protected from expropriation, as the Rothschilds had transferred ownership of the company to the Alliance Assurance Company Ltd., an English company connected with the Rothschilds. Before September 1939, when war was declared, British citizens and businesses were protected by international convention and were safe. The Nazis had wanted to buy the company from the Rothschilds, and meetings between them and the Germans were held in Switzerland. An agreement had been already signed but the war began before the Germans had paid for the ironworks, so the deal was not completed.

It was not just wealthy Jews who were affected; new regulations were issued that affected all Jews and almost all aspects of life. By 22 June 1939, only three months after the occupation, more regulations were issued to supplement those already in place.

Jews were ordered to hand over to the German authorities all their jewellery, motor cars, radios, fur coats, skis and savings. Jews were reduced if not to penury, at least to relative poverty unless they had hidden some of their assets and not declared them to the Germans. They were barred from

České Slovo 20 h

ČTVRTEK 22. ČERVNA 1939 LIST NÁRODNÍHO SOURUČENSTVÍ ROČNÍK XI. – ČÍSLO 168

Židovské zákony v Protektorátu již vyhlášeny

Nařízení říšského protektora v Čechách a na Moravě o židovském majetku

Trestní sankce

Změna zákona na ochranu státu

Nařízení o zákonu na obranu státu bývalé Československé republiky ze dne 20. června 1939

22 June 1939: Regulations concerning Jews.

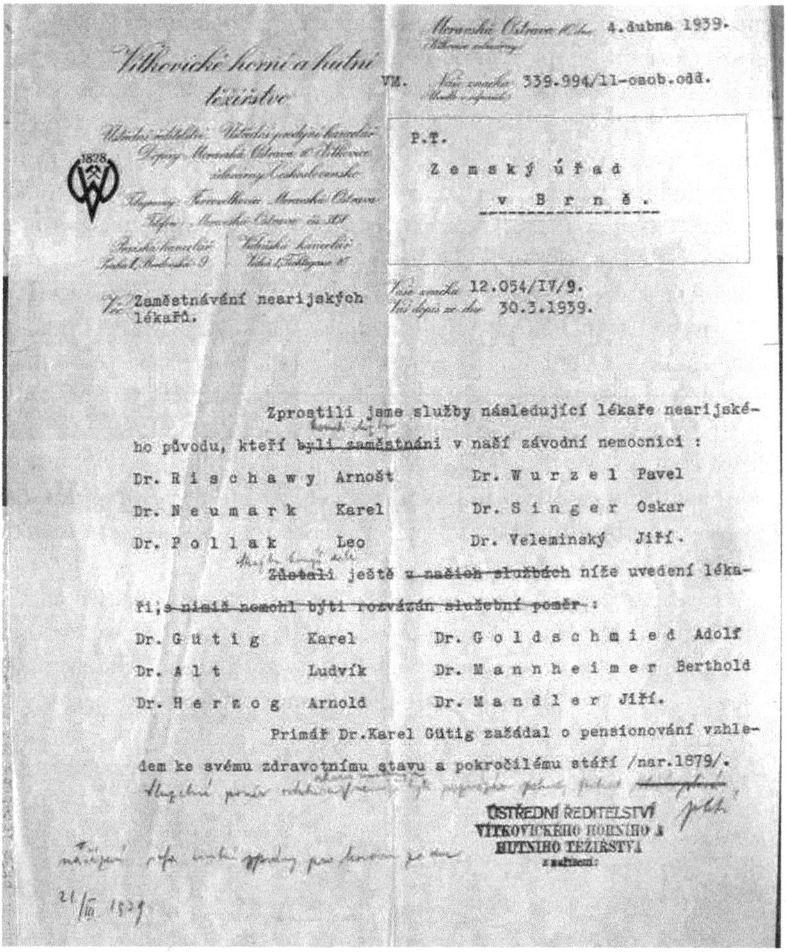

Vítkovické horní a hutní těžířstvo

Moravská Ostrava 10 dne 4.dubna 1939.

VM. Naše značka 339.994/11-osob.odd.

P.T.
Zemský úřad
v Brně.

Věc: Zaměstnávání nearijských lékařů.

Vaše značka 12.054/IV/9.
Váš dopis ze dne 30.3.1939.

Zprostili jsme služby následující lékaře nearijského původu, kteří byli zaměstnáni v naší závodní nemocnici :

Dr. Rischawy Arnošt — Dr. Wurzel Pavel
Dr. Neumark Karel — Dr. Singer Oskar
Dr. Pollak Leo — Dr. Veleminský Jiří.

Zůstali ještě v našich službách níže uvedení lékaři, s nimiž nemohl býti rozvázán služební poměr :

Dr. Gütig Karel — Dr. Goldschmied Adolf
Dr. Alt Ludvík — Dr. Mannheimer Berthold
Dr. Herzog Arnold — Dr. Mandler Jiří.

Primář Dr.Karel Gütig zažádal o pensionování vzhledem ke svému zdravotnímu stavu a pokročilému stáří /nar.1879/.

ÚSTŘEDNÍ ŘEDITELSTVÍ
VÍTKOVICKÉHO HORNÍHO A HUTNÍHO TĚŽÍŘSTVA

Doctors dismissed from the Vitkovice Hospital 4 April 1939.

parks, cinemas, restaurants and other social spaces and had to suffer a series of virulent anti-Semitic articles in newspapers. Jews were also dismissed from civil service posts. Doctors, lawyers and other professionals were barred from practicing and, to make clear that the Germans knew who the Jews involved were, lists of barred doctors and lawyers were published in the papers. The Vítkovice Hospital had, by 4 April – less than 3 weeks after the invasion – already dismissed some of its Jewish medical staff and were in the process of dismissing the rest.

Jewish doctors were able to continue to treat Jewish patients but the economics were not very encouraging. The doctors would have lost the majority of their patients and those who remained, the Jews, were financially under pressure and would not have much spare money for healthcare.

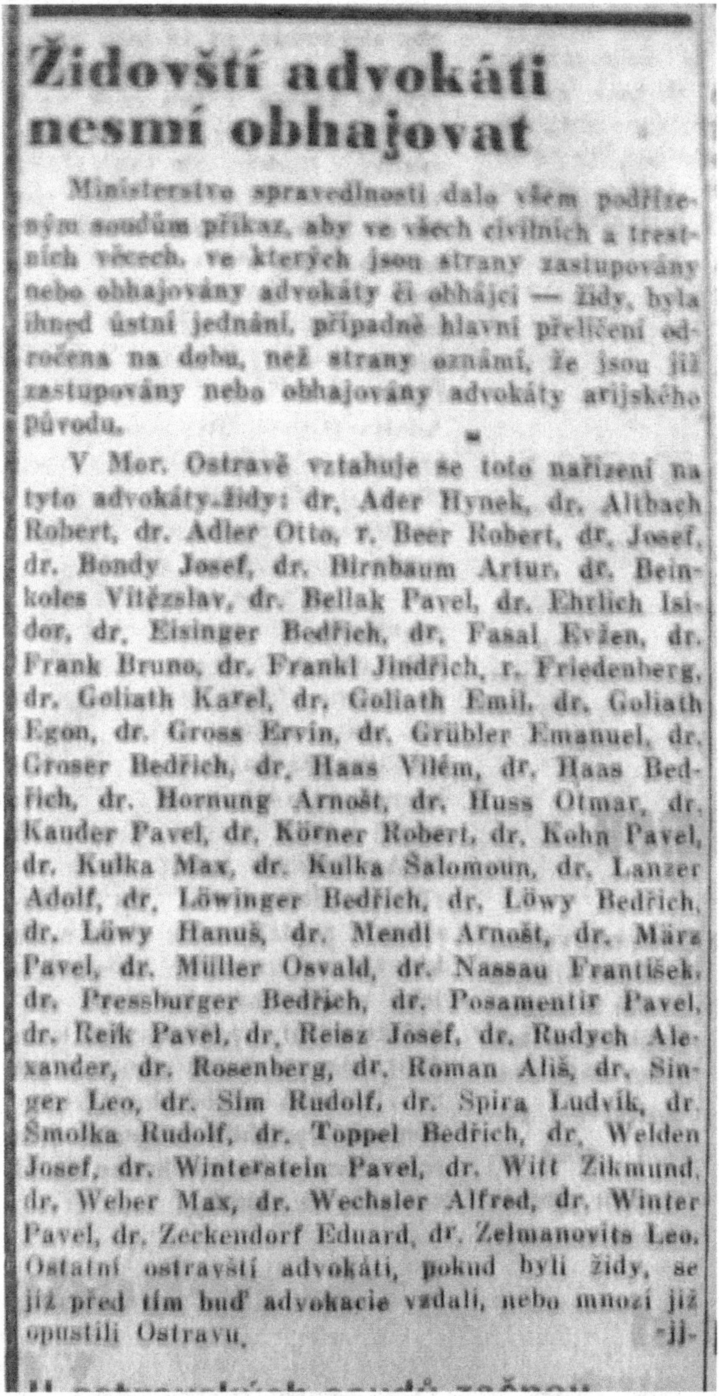

Židovští advokáti nesmí obhajovat

Ministerstvo spravedlnosti dalo všem podřízeným soudům příkaz, aby ve všech civilních a trestních věcech, ve kterých jsou strany zastupovány nebo obhajovány advokáty či obhájci — židy, byla ihned ústní jednání, případně hlavní přelíčení odročena na dobu, než strany oznámí, že jsou již zastupovány nebo obhajovány advokáty arijského původu.

V Mor. Ostravě vztahuje se toto nařízení na tyto advokáty-židy: dr. Ader Hynek, dr. Altbach Robert, dr. Adler Otto, r. Beer Robert, dr. Josef, dr. Bondy Josef, dr. Birnbaum Artur, dr. Beinkoles Vítězslav, dr. Bellak Pavel, dr. Ehrlich Isidor, dr. Eisinger Bedřich, dr. Fasal Evžen, dr. Frank Bruno, dr. Frankl Jindřich, r. Friedenberg, dr. Goliath Karel, dr. Goliath Emil, dr. Goliath Egon, dr. Gross Ervín, dr. Grübler Emanuel, dr. Groser Bedřich, dr. Haas Vilém, dr. Haas Bedřich, dr. Hornung Arnošt, dr. Huss Otmar, dr. Kauder Pavel, dr. Körner Robert, dr. Kohn Pavel, dr. Kulka Max, dr. Kulka Šalomoun, dr. Lanzer Adolf, dr. Löwinger Bedřich, dr. Löwy Bedřich, dr. Löwy Hanuš, dr. Mendl Arnošt, dr. Mära Pavel, dr. Müller Osvald, dr. Nassau František, dr. Pressburger Bedřich, dr. Posamentir Pavel, dr. Reik Pavel, dr. Reisz Josef, dr. Rudych Alexander, dr. Rosenberg, dr. Roman Ališ, dr. Singer Leo, dr. Sim Rudolf, dr. Spira Ludvík, dr. Šmolka Rudolf, dr. Toppel Bedřich, dr. Welden Josef, dr. Winterstein Pavel, dr. Witt Zikmund, dr. Weber Max, dr. Wechsler Alfred, dr. Winter Pavel, dr. Zeckendorf Eduard, dr. Zelmanovits Leo. Ostatní ostravští advokáti, pokud byli židy, se již před tím buď advokacie vzdali, nebo mnozí již opustili Ostravu. -ji-

List of lawyers forbidden to practice.

Jewish children were banned from state schools, both German and Czech-speaking, from early 1939 but they were able to continue their elementary education in the Ostrava Jewish School, which continued to function until September 1942. Some older children were sent to Olomouc or Brno where there were Jewish secondary schools were still functioning.

On 6 June 1939, the Vítkovice synagogue was set on fire and destroyed.

This was followed four days later by the Přívoz synagogue and two days later, 12 June, by the destruction of the synagogue in Hrušov. The following day it was the turn of the Žerotínova synagogue and two days after that, on 15 June, by the Main Synagogue. George Roden remembers the firing of the

Vítkovice synagogue during and after the fire.

main synagogue and how German troops kept away all onlookers or people who might have tried to extinguish the blaze. Four days later, on 19 June, the last synagogue in Ostrava, in Zábřeh, was destroyed. Nor were synagogues the only targets. On 26 June, the *Hechalutz* (organisation to encourage immigration into Palestine) offices were burned. The only physical manifestation of Jewish communal life remaining was the Jewish school, probably because it was in a block with other buildings and could

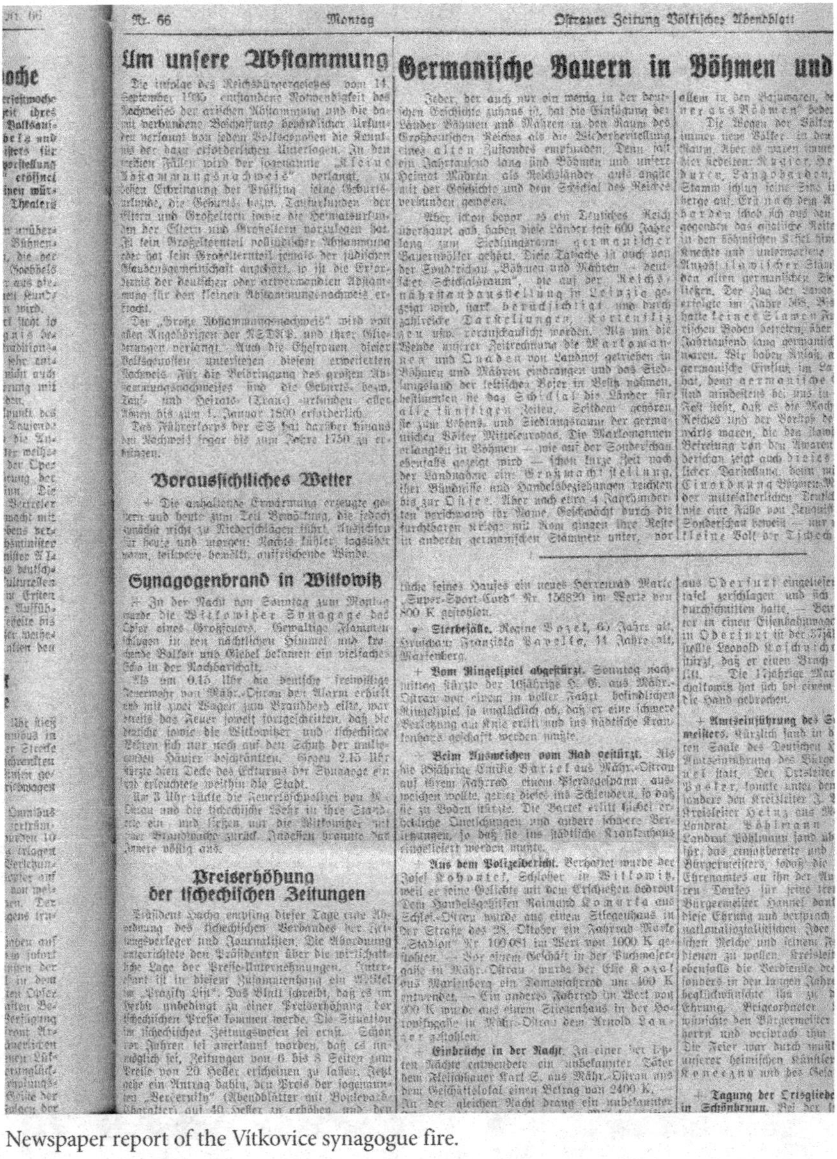

Nr. 66 Montag Ostrauer Zeitung Völkisches Abendblatt

Um unsere Abstammung

Germanische Bauern in Böhmen und

Voraussichtliches Wetter

+ Die anhaltende Erwärmung erzeugte gestern und heute zum Teil Bewölkung, die jedoch zunächst nicht zu Niederschlägen führt. Aussichten für heute und morgen: Nachts kühler, tagsüber warm, teilweise bewölkt, auffrischende Winde.

Synagogenbrand in Witkowitz

+ In der Nacht von Sonntag zum Montag wurde die Witkowitzer Synagoge das Opfer eines Großfeuers. Gewaltige Flammen schlugen in den nächtlichen Himmel und krachende Balken und Giebel bekamen ein vielfaches Echo in der Nachbarschaft.

Als um 0.15 Uhr die deutsche freiwillige Feuerwehr von Mähr.-Ostrau den Alarm erhielt und mit zwei Wagen zum Brandherd eilte, war bereits das Feuer soweit fortgeschritten, daß die deutsche sowie die Witkowitzer und tschechische Wehren sich nur noch auf den Schutz der umliegenden Häuser beschränkten. Gegen 2.15 Uhr stürzte die Decke des Eckturms der Synagoge ein und erleuchtete weithin die Stadt.

Um 3 Uhr rückte die Feuerlöschpolizei von M.-Ostrau und die tschechische Wehr in ihre Standorte ein und ließen nur die Witkowitzer bei der Brandwache zurück. Indessen brannte das Innere völlig aus.

Preiserhöhung der tschechischen Zeitungen

Newspaper report of the Vítkovice synagogue fire.

not have been fired without damaging other buildings and organisations. In fact the shell of the Hechalutz building remained standing and was restored. Today it houses the Jewish Community offices.

The fires were all reported in the local newspapers.

The report of the fire of the Vítkovice synagogue tells how the alarm reached the local German fire brigade at 00.15hrs. They were joined later by other volunteer fire services but the interior of the synagogue was totally destroyed.

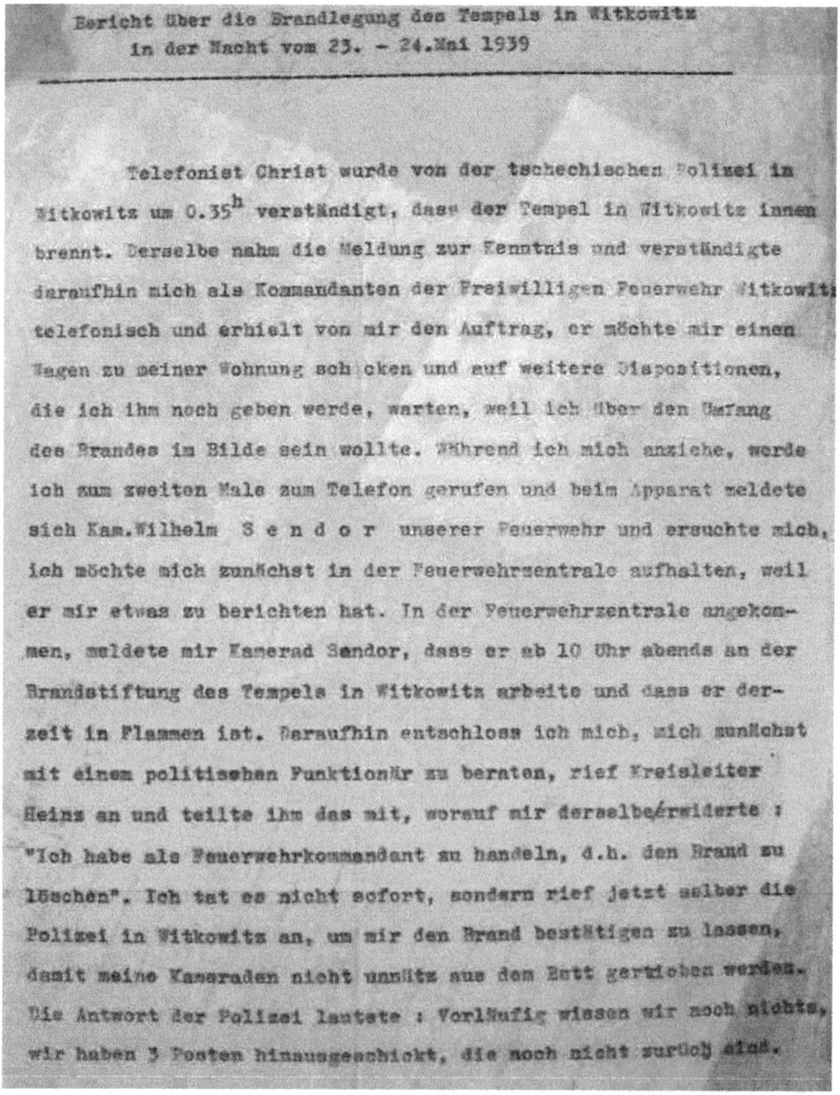

Bericht über die Brandlegung des Tempels in Witkowitz
in der Nacht vom 23. - 24.Mai 1939

Telefonist Christ wurde von der tschechischen Polizei in Witkowitz um 0.35h verständigt, dass der Tempel in Witkowitz innen brennt. Derselbe nahm die Meldung zur Kenntnis und verständigte daraufhin mich als Kommandanten der Freiwilligen Feuerwehr Witkowitz telefonisch und erhielt von mir den Auftrag, er möchte mir einen Wagen zu meiner Wohnung schicken und auf weitere Dispositionen, die ich ihm noch geben werde, warten, weil ich über den Umfang des Brandes im Bilde sein wollte. Während ich mich anziehe, werde ich zum zweiten Male zum Telefon gerufen und beim Apparat meldete sich Kam.Wilhelm S e n d o r unserer Feuerwehr und ersuchte mich, ich möchte mich zunächst in der Feuerwehrzentrale aufhalten, weil er mir etwas zu berichten hat. In der Feuerwehrzentrale angekommen, meldete mir Kamerad Sendor, dass er ab 10 Uhr abends an der Brandstiftung des Tempels in Witkowitz arbeite und dass er derzeit in Flammen ist. Daraufhin entschloss ich mich, mich zunächst mit einem politischen Funktionär zu beraten, rief Kreisleiter Heinz an und teilte ihm das mit, worauf mir derselbe erwiderte : "Ich habe als Feuerwehrkommandant zu handeln, d.h. den Brand zu löschen". Ich tat es nicht sofort, sondern rief jetzt selber die Polizei in Witkowitz an, um mir den Brand bestätigen zu lassen, damit meine Kameraden nicht unnütz aus dem Bett getrieben werden. Die Antwort der Polizei lautete : Vorläufig wissen wir noch nichts, wir haben 3 Posten hinausgeschickt, die noch nicht zurück sind.

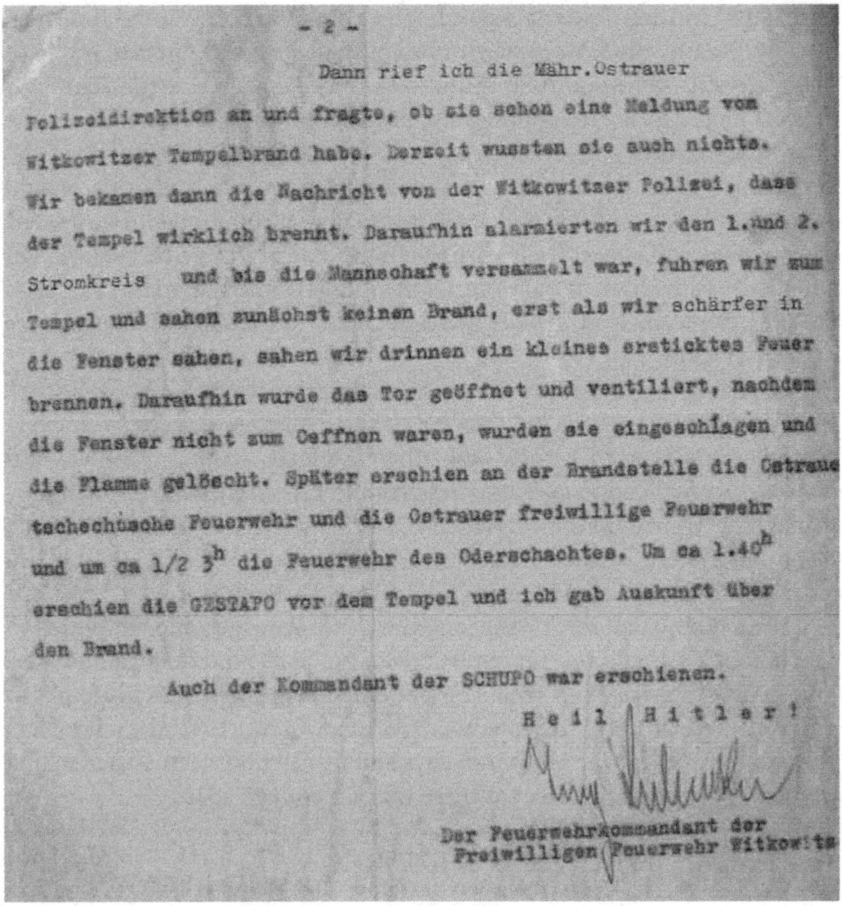

\- 2 -

Dann rief ich die Mähr.Ostrauer Polizeidirektion an und fragte, ob sie schon eine Meldung vom Witkowitzer Tempelbrand habe. Derzeit wussten sie auch nichts. Wir bekamen dann die Nachricht von der Witkowitzer Polizei, dass der Tempel wirklich brennt. Daraufhin alarmierten wir den 1.und 2. Stromkreis und bis die Mannschaft versammelt war, fuhren wir zum Tempel und sahen zunächst keinen Brand, erst als wir schärfer in die Fenster sahen, sahen wir drinnen ein kleines ersticktes Feuer brennen. Daraufhin wurde das Tor geöffnet und ventiliert, nachdem die Fenster nicht zum Oeffnen waren, wurden sie eingeschlagen und die Flamme gelöscht. Später erschien an der Brandstelle die Ostrauer tschechische Feuerwehr und die Ostrauer freiwillige Feuerwehr und um ca 1/2 3^h die Feuerwehr des Oderschachtes. Um ca 1.40^h erschien die GESTAPO vor dem Tempel und ich gab Auskunft über den Brand.

Auch der Kommandant der SCHUPO war erschienen.

Heil Hitler!

Der Feuerwehrkommandant der Freiwilligen Feuerwehr Witkowitz

Internal report by the local fire brigade of the Vítkovice synagogue fire.

The internal typewritten report of the Vítkovice fire brigade throws a clearer light on the events of the night. The Commander of the Volunteer Fire Brigade was told about the fire at 00.35hrs on the morning of 7 June but was told to come to the station before going to the scene of the fire, so that he could be briefed, effectively told that the fire had been started by one of his own men at 22.00hrs the previous evening. The commandant asked the political authorities what he should do, as he had a responsibility to extinguish the fire. There followed some telephoning for more guidance but finally the volunteer brigade went to the scene and saw a small, almost smothered, fire. So they opened the door and smashed the windows to ventilate it and then 'put out the flames'.[11] The Gestapo and the *Schupo* also appeared at the fire.

This destruction of the Ostrava synagogues appears to have been a local initiative, despite the detailed planning that obviously went into the occupation and anti-Jewish actions. In other places in Moravia and Bohemia, notably Prague, the synagogues were not damaged and, indeed, many of them are still standing today. Some have been restored as museums or concert halls. Whoever planned the destruction in Ostrava, in each case the German authorities instructed the Jewish Community to clear the dangerous shell of the building, at its own expense, or the authorities would arrange for the demolition and send the bill to the Community. The lessons of *Kristallnacht* had been well learned. In the case of Vítkovice, the German authorities came back to the Community in 1941, instructing them to clear the site completely from broken tiles and debris, as the site was to be used as a sports ground.

The firing of the synagogues raises a major historical problem. The fires were very extensive and the interior of the synagogues were completely destroyed and yet 14 scrolls and other artefacts, including books and textiles, survived and were sent to Prague in 1942. It seems unlikely that they would have withstood the conflagration. Is it possible that members of the community were warned in advance by members of the volunteer fire brigade and so were able to remove items to a place of safety?

We do know that the Jewish School was not damaged and continued to function as a school until September 1942, but it also did double duty after June 1939 as a synagogue. Peter Erben remembers going with his father to a service there in 1941. In September 1940 and August 1941, the school was used for services for the High Holydays and instructions were issued telling women not to attend services as there was not enough space:

ORDERS
Concerning Services for the High Holydays

The following Orders are made concerning participation in Services for the High Holydays, to take into account the constraints at that time:

1. To enter as well as leave the Jewish Primary School, use the passageway from the riverbank through the schoolyard.
2. As always, any gathering of any sort on the street is to be avoided.
3. Congregating on the street during pauses in the service or for any other reason is forbidden. The schoolyard is available for that purpose.
4. Ladies are requested not to take part in the evening service and also during *Rosh Hashannah* and also *Kol Nidre* in consideration of the limited space available.
5. The regulations concerning the approved persons must be absolutely adhered to.
6. Bringing of children is not allowed and forbidden.
7. You must leave the Prayer Hall immediately after the Service to allow it to be aired and prepared for the next service.

Moravská Ostrava 21st August 1941

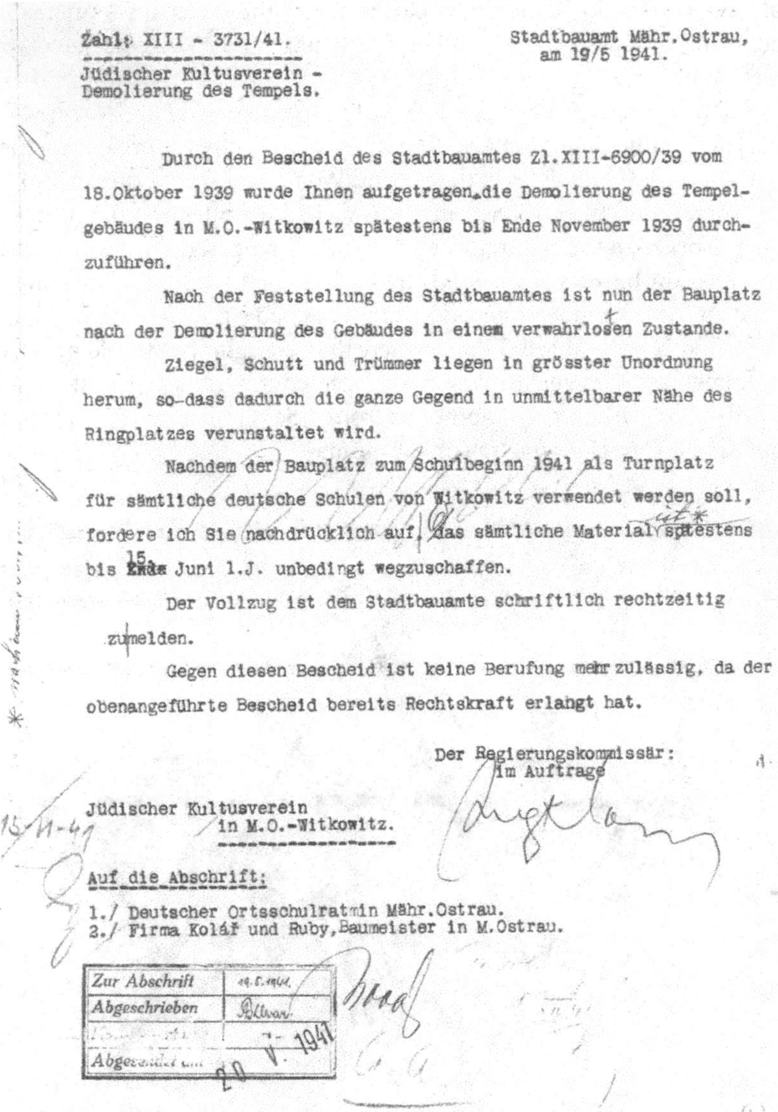

Zahl: XIII - 3731/41.
Jüdischer Kultusverein -
Demolierung des Tempels.

Stadtbauamt Mähr.Ostrau,
am 19/5 1941.

Durch den Bescheid des Stadtbauamtes Zl.XIII-6900/39 vom 18.Oktober 1939 wurde Ihnen aufgetragen,die Demolierung des Tempelgebäudes in M.O.-Witkowitz spätestens bis Ende November 1939 durchzuführen.

Nach der Feststellung des Stadtbauamtes ist nun der Bauplatz nach der Demolierung des Gebäudes in einem verwahrlosten Zustande.

Ziegel, Schutt und Trümmer liegen in grösster Unordnung herum, so-dass dadurch die ganze Gegend in unmittelbarer Nähe des Ringplatzes verunstaltet wird.

Nachdem der Bauplatz zum Schulbeginn 1941 als Turnplatz für sämtliche deutsche Schulen von Witkowitz verwendet werden soll, fordere ich Sie nachdrücklich auf, das sämtliche Material spätestens bis 15. Juni 1.J. unbedingt wegzuschaffen.

Der Vollzug ist dem Stadtbauamte schriftlich rechtzeitig zu melden.

Gegen diesen Bescheid ist keine Berufung mehr zulässig, da der obenangeführte Bescheid bereits Rechtskraft erlangt hat.

Der Regierungskommissär:
Im Auftrage

Jüdischer Kultusverein
in M.O.-Witkowitz.

Auf die Abschrift:

1./ Deutscher Ortsschulrat in Mähr.Ostrau.
2./ Firma Kolář und Ruby,Baumeister in M.Ostrau.

Zur Abschrift
Abgeschrieben

Letter instructing the Jewish community to clear the site of the destroyed Vítkovice synagogue 19 May 1941.

Between March and September 1939, Poland was still free and Europe was nominally at peace. Some people took the opportunity to flee from Ostrava across the border into Poland and, sometimes, on to England, Sweden or other countries. Others managed to obtain visas, legally or otherwise, to allow them to travel across Germany to Holland, France and onward, while others tried to emigrate to Palestine. But this brief window of opportunity for escape was closed when the Germans launched their attack on Poland on 1 September and Britain and France declared war on Germany.

The invasion of Poland was horrifyingly successful and swift; within a month of launching the attack, the Germans were already organising the first mass deportation of Jews in the Second World War from Ostrava into Nisko nad Sanem in Poland. The camp was disbanded after about 6 months and the prisoners were either returned to their town of origin, were driven across the Russian border or escaped themselves, or had died from illness and exposure. Meanwhile, some of their families had either fled, gone into hiding or moved, for example to Prague where they thought they would be relatively unknown and less visible. Jews were ordered to wear a yellow star with the word *Jude* (Jew) on their clothes as from 1 September 1941, to mark them out as being an *Untermensch* or sub-human.

The Yellow Star which Jews were forced to wear.

Jewish School, 1942.

By the summer of 1942, life under these appalling conditions had become 'normal' and somehow the remaining Jews of Ostrava managed to survive and the children were loved, cared for and educated. They appear reasonably nourished, clothed and happy in the school photograph from 1942, each of them with their yellow star.

By the end of the year, almost all of them had been murdered. In September 1942 the first group of Jews was ordered to gather at the Habrmann School in Přívoz for deportation to Theresienstadt. The first transport from Ostrava arrived in Theresienstadt on Tuesday 22 September 1942. It was the day after Yom Kippur. By the end of the festival of Tabernacles, 12 days later, most of the Jewish deportees from Ostrava had already been shipped to Auschwitz and the gas chambers. Other transports followed in swift succession. Jewish life in Ostrava had ceased.

Liberation

By the autumn of 1944, it was clear that the end of the Third Reich was imminent. September saw the start of the battle for Dukla Pass on the Polish-Slovak border, although it was to take a month of heavy fighting before the Red Army and the Czechoslovak Tank Brigade were able to reach the Slovak side of the pass. In fact this key victory, very dearly won, did not immediately presage the liberation of Ostrava. Ostrava's coal and steel production was increasingly vital to the Nazis as they lost other industrial centres to the advancing Allied armies, and so the defences of Ostrava and Opava were heavily built up. Ostrava's geography, surrounded by mountains and the marshy Odra valley, meant that it was very difficult to mount a mass tank attack. Furthermore, Ostrava was not of strategic importance for the Soviet advance which was targeted on Berlin, and so the right flank of the Soviet advance was planned to go north and west of Ostrava while the left flank went south and east.

Meanwhile, Ostrava suffered its largest air raid in August 1944 and began to receive German refugees fleeing the advance of the Red Army. The armed forces of the 4th Ukrainian Front of the Red Army and the 1st Czechoslovak Independent Tank Brigade engaged in heavy and bloody combat during the Ostrava-Opava operations against heavy resistance. By February 1945, however, it was clear to the defenders that they could not hold Ostrava and they began to disassemble and remove industrial plant, railway rolling stock and other vital material. Plant that could not be removed was destroyed *in situ* until *Oberlandrat* Gustav Jonak issued an order on 28 April forbidding such destruction. That did not prevent all further destruction nor the pillaging of private property by the retreating soldiers.

The formal campaign to liberate Ostrava was launched on 10 March 1945 from the Polish cities of Żory and Źywiec along the Slovak border. This 4th Ukrainian Front was commanded by Gen. Andrei Ivanovich Petrov, later

Liberation! A Red Army tank.

Tearing down the Nazi flag from the old Town Hall.

replaced by Andrei Ivanovich Yeremenko, whose forces included the 1st Czechoslovak Army Corps and the 1st Czechoslovak Mixed Air Division. On 30 April at about 4 o'clock in the afternoon, the first troops crossed the Odra River and entered Zábřeh and on into the rest of Ostrava. Over 350 Soviet and Czech troops were killed in the battle to liberate Ostrava and by 2 May1945 the whole of Ostrava was free after more than 6 years of occupation.

As might be imagined, the joy of liberation was enormous and the Czech and Soviet troops were welcomed with great excitement.

Someone climbed up to the tower of the former Town Hall, today the Town Museum, to tear down the Nazi flag. The liberation also unleashed a wave of violence and pillaging against German civilians in Ostrava as well as against the German troops.

After the excitement had settled down a little, the City organised a Liberation Parade, on 13 June, with the Czech and Russian troops, including Kurt Karel Smulovič (see Chapter 9), parading. The local newspaper printed an announcement about it:

Liberation Parade.

> Today at 9 o'clock there will be a parade of the 1st Cz tank brigade from the USSR at the Jiří of Poděbrady Square in Vítkovice. After the parade the troops will march accompanied by tanks through Štefanikova, Revoluční, 28 October Avenue, Nádražní and Božena Němcová to Sokolská Avenue where there will be a reviewing stand.
>
> Teachers and professors of all schools of Greater Ostrava will take pupils to the nearest sections of the stated streets, so that the school children would line the streets where our troops will pass in order to salute them. Authorities, works councils and corporations will send their representatives to the parade, where they will take places on the honour stand at the Jiří of Poděbrady Square.

Bureaucracy had returned with freedom!

NOTES

1. Klaudia was working for the Ostrava City of Culture campaign in 2011 when she made that report. In 2016 when asked for the original source, she wrote: 'I spent several hours looking for the original source of the text from 14.3.1939. Still, I was not successful. I remember that I was so touched by the text that I did not pay attention to the source.' So we do not know if this actually happened or is a romantic fiction of what should have happened.
2. Security forces. Effectively part of the Nazi intelligence apparatus.
3. *Anschluss* – The incorporation of Austria into the German Reich on 12 March 1938.
4. Gold, Hugo, *Geschichte der Juden in Mährisch Ostrau.* Olamenu, Israel. 1974.
5. Martin Gilbert *The Holocaust; The Jewish Tragedy.* Collins, 1986; *Transporty do Nisko nad Sanem.* Conerence Ostrava University 2009; *Nisko nad Sanem 1939-1994.* Conference, Ostrava University, 1995.
6. Thomas Kenneally, *Schindler's Ark.* Hodder and Stoughton, 1982.
7. Crowe, David M., *Oskar Schindler.* Cambridge University Press, 2012.
8. Emilie Schindler with Erika Rosenberg, *Where Light and Shadow Meet : A Memoir.* Translated from the original Spanish by Dolores M. Koch.
9. Tomas Sniegon, *Vanished History.* Berghahn, 2014.
10. Like many of Schindler's dramatic or romantic escapades, documentary evidence for this is lacking. The Horch Museum in Zwickau has no information at all. The Audi Museum replied to our enquiry: '...been forwarded to Audi Tradition for a reply. I'm afraid we cannot be of much help regarding your research on Oskar Schindler's Horch. All we know is that he obviously owned an eight cylinder Horch and that he drove this Horch when he and his wife fled from Brünnlitz (Czech Rep.) westward at the end of the war. It is said that they were stopped by Russian troops at the town of Budweis and that the Horch was eventually confiscated. They continued their journey by train and on foot. As regards the Horch car we have no information whatsoever. Some say it was a two-seater, some say it was a Horch 853 (four-seater convertible). Nor can we confirm that Schindler's Horch was initially built for the Shah of Persia. Unfortunately all Auto Union commission files have been destroyed due to the war.'
11. *Bericht über die Brandlegung in Witkowitz in der Nacht von 23-24 mai 1939.* MS, Ostrava Fire Service.

9

Soldiers

The First World War

The idea of 'Jewish Soldiers', particularly from Central Europe, seems to be a contradiction in terms. In the popular imagination, Jewish soldiers disappeared after the Old Testament period, to reappear only in 1948 with the Israeli War of Independence. Yet this is highly misleading with regard to Jewish history, and does an injustice to the many Jewish soldiers who served their countries in Europe in the nineteenth and twentieth century.

After the Enlightenment, emancipation and the political reforms introduced by Napoleon, Jews became citizens on more or less equal terms with their Christian neighbours. Once they were citizens with a stake in the country, and with the growth of nationalist sentiment encouraging patriotism and even chauvinism, Jews identified with the states in which they lived and were ready to defend them. Jews became soldiers willingly, even if they were conscripted. In this, the Jews of Ostrava were no exception. After the Edicts of Tolerance in the late eighteenth century, Ostravak Jews became integrated into the life of the town and were, apparently, genuinely supportive of the Austro-Hungarian Empire. They played their part in the Austrian Army during the First World War, even if it was a not very distinguished one.

Although the Jews of Ostrava were patriotic and became soldiers, there is little evidence among them of the militarism that we associate with the Germans of the period. On the other hand, there was a definite liking for dashing romantic uniforms which was a fondness they shared with their Austrian compatriots. The difference between this period and that of the Second World War is very striking.

Evžen Wechsberg,[1] the third son of the banker, Albert, was called up as a reserve captain in the cavalry of the Austrian army at the start of the First World War, despite being the head of the bank since Albert's death in 1913. His service was peaceful and unexciting in the Quartermaster's department in Těšín. Evžen, according to his grand-son, loved the uniform and dressing up, a true Viennese operetta soldier! He even polished his boots himself when he first went to join his regiment. Siegfried, the youngest son of Albert and father of the writer Josef, was also called up to the colours at the start of the First World War. Sources give his rank variously as first lieutenant or captain (probably first lieutenant). Whichever it was, he was killed on the

Evžen Wechsberg.

Russian front on 22 November 1914. Alfred, the other Wechsberg son, was excused duty 'because of ill-health' which, according to family gossip, he had carefully arranged.

Viktor Lichtenstern came from a wealthy family of alcohol distillers in Ostrava. He studied law in Vienna and lived and practiced there up to 1939, when he and his family fled to England. He married Olga Löw, the daughter of the manager of the Ostrava gasworks. Before their marriage he wrote to her frequently from Vienna, with the letters addressed to the gasworks, hardly the most romantic of locations. In the First World War he was conscripted and served in Pula in what is now Northern Croatia, in the main Austrian naval base. He was quite a dashing young man with a striking moustache and looked very military sitting with his colleagues in the photograph. In fact his service was purely administrative and unexciting, but he wrote frequently to his wife – lawyers were prolific letter-writers, even in those days! – and this correspondence is preserved in the archive of the Jewish Museum in Prague.

Arnold Löwy was almost two years younger than Viktor but sported a similar dramatic macho moustache. He too was stationed on the Italian front but his war was much more eventful than Viktor's. A telephone operator, he was buried alive in his blockhouse during one attack. He was the only member of his group to survive and was rescued on his 10th wedding anniversary so he had gold rings made, with the date engraved, for each member of the family to commemorate the event. They wore these rings until they were all confiscated by the Nazis in 1939.[2]

Lt. Viktor Lichtenstern (far right, second row from front, sitting) (Marked X); in Pula.

Arnold Löwy.

Alfred Vogel's initial military career passed peacefully. He was conscripted and reached the elevated rank of lance-corporal and spent the First World War guarding a disused railway junction. As perhaps befits a non-commissioned officer, he did not have a moustache.

Alice Anson's father, **Otto Gross**, was born in Ostrava where his father had sold Lotto tickets and was well-known and well respected, receiving a glowing obituary in the *Ostrauer Zeitung* of 19 August 1913. His son Otto sported a splendid moustache when he was 19 years-old but later, when he became a bank manager in Vienna and a reserve officer, it was rather more subdued. He was called up, became a serving First Lieutenant and was decorated by the Emperor Karl in 1917. Alice was born in Vienna where her maternal grandfather had a shop selling Dunhill pipes and, through contacts,

L. Cpl. Alfred Vogel.

Alice and her brother were sent to England before the Second World War. Otto and his wife went to Palestine and then came to England so the family were reunited.

Guido Alis reports that his father served in the Kaiser's army and was awarded three medals for bravery. The photograph that he sent us was taken in 1916 and his father would have been 18 at that time. His arm is in a sling due to war injuries.

David Friedmann served as an artist in the Austro-Hungarian army on the Russian Front in the First World War. He sketched combat scenes and portraits of soldiers distinguishing themselves in battle and was decorated for his bravery. War artists were not invented by the British in the Second War.

Firm conclusions cannot be drawn from such a small number of examples, but we can tentatively identify some patterns. None of the Jewish soldiers reached a rank above reserve captain in the Austrian Army. Siegfried Wechsberg was invited to become a regular officer but declined because, according to his son Josef, he did not relate to the officer class. It seems that despite Ostrava being relatively well integrated and free of anti-Semitism or discrimination, senior officers in the Austrian army were 'gentlemen' and therefore not Jews.

Gross family, 1908: Otto, age 19, standing 3rd from left.

Emperor Karl I awarding the Gallantry Cross to Lt Otto Gross (3rd from left). Arch-Duke Franz Salvator on ext. right.

1916: Guido Alis's father.

Although the people we know about all joined more or less willingly and out of a sense of duty to serve the Emperor, there appears not to have been the idea of fighting to right a wrong or to defend freedom, as there was in Britain. But there was, perhaps, a certain light-heartedness, as there was at the start of the war in Britain as well – a belief that the war would be short and not too serious. Sadly, this was a mistake. Twenty years later, the attitude was quite different. Ostrava Jews were now fighting for the survival of themselves, their families, their people and their State. Very many Jews joined the Soviet forces after the Germans invaded Russia and several units of the Czech army in the USSR had a majority of Jewish members. In the post-war period, this was a source of some embarrassment to the Soviet authorities and the information was suppressed. Others joined the French, British and American armies. They all played a valuable role in the liberation of Europe.

The Second World War

Otto Gross had been decorated by the emperor. His daughter, Alice, was to join the RAF in the photo-reconnaissance section and served for 4 years. Although she was not decorated by the King-Emperor for that service, she did feature in an exhibition in the Imperial War Museum in London. Her husband, Colin Anson, was a German refugee, Claus Ascher, who also joined the British forces and served for 6 years. He was advised to anglicise his name and Colin was an obvious choice from Claus. Claus was not sure what surname to select, but was inspired by a military aircraft landing nearby. It was an Anson. His remarkable story, from German schoolboy to a British commando, has been published.[3]

Alfred Vogel was conscripted into the Czechoslovak army in 1938. After his arrival in England he joined the Czech battalion in the British Army, still with the elevated rank of Lance Corporal. He wryly recalled that he had been in three different armies before he managed to be on the winning side! He had obviously acquired a British sense of humour with his new nationality.

Josef Wechsberg joined the American armed forces and served as a technical sergeant in the psychological warfare division. His brother, Max, who had also reached the USA, became a captain in the US Army during the war and the two of them met in Paris.

Hanuš Buchsbaum, the son of Ignatz, the publisher, left Ostrava before the war and emigrated to the USA where he became an American citizen. He joined the US army and in its ranks participated on the liberation of Western Europe. The family estate was restored to him after the war, but the political situation and the communist takeover in February 1948 made him decide to return to the USA. Hanuš, who called himself John in the US, was

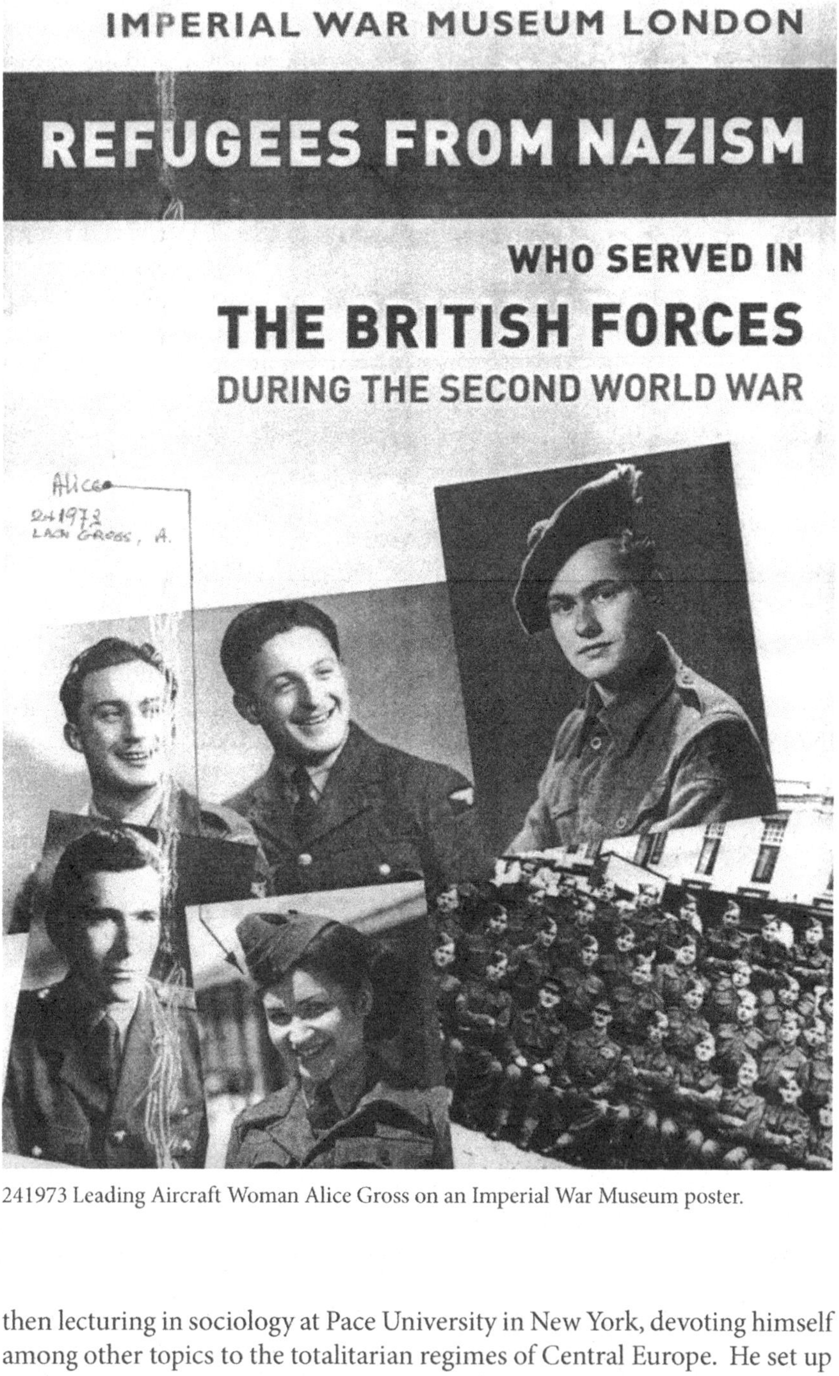

241973 Leading Aircraft Woman Alice Gross on an Imperial War Museum poster.

then lecturing in sociology at Pace University in New York, devoting himself among other topics to the totalitarian regimes of Central Europe. He set up a scholarship in memory of Ignatz and Klara Buchsbaum for the most successful history graduates.

George Roden (Jiří Rosenstein) remembers the destruction of the main synagogue in Ostrava on 2 June 1939, the day of his parent's Silver Wedding He was sent to England on a *Kindertransport* in 1939, sponsored by the Mobbs, a Methodist family in Boston, Lincolnshire who were friends of a friend of George's elder brother. Sponsorship involved placing a guarantee of £50, a significant sum in 1939. George owes his life to the kindness of such people, who were complete strangers to him. In 1941, he joined the Czech squadron of the RAF, became an armourer and a sergeant. He served in Europe and returned to Ostrava at the end of the war and completed his education there before returning to the UK. George wrote:

> My parents and brother did not survive but I was reunited with two brothers of my mother. Uncle Viktor and Uncle Otto escaped from Nisko into the Soviet Union. There they were interned in a Gulag in Siberia but when the Germans invaded they were allowed to join the newly formed Czech Brigade. After severe fighting they succeeded in reaching Czechoslovakia. Uncle Viktor was able to find his wife in Theresienstadt but Uncle Otto lost his wife and son in Auschwitz.

George ended his career as a director of a tailoring company owned by Sir Bernard Wetherill, formerly the Speaker of the House of Commons. One of his clients was HM Queen Elizabeth, the Queen Mother.

The Buchsbaum Hairdressing Salon, 1923. Alfred, age 4, on right.

Josef Buchsbaum had an up-market ladies' hairdressing salon in Ostrava. He sent his wife (Sarah née Sturner) to Vienna to learn how to do perms, and Josef had the first perm machine in Ostrava. As soon as the Nazis occupied Ostrava, Josef, Sarah and their two sons, Alfred (known as Fred) and Leo left across the border to Poland, leaving everything behind. The Czech Trust Fund arranged for them to go via Sweden to England where

Fred and Josef Barton (né Buchsbaum) in France.

Josef set up another hairdressing business. Fred decided to join the Czech Army, then in France, and after a short while, Josef joined him. They had to pay their own fare to get to France.

When the French army disintegrated, they walked to Dunkirk but were too late for the evacuation so they all marched to the south of France (about 5,000 men) where they were picked up by a Royal Navy destroyer and taken to Gibraltar and thence by an Egyptian coal ship to go to UK. Josef started to sell hairdressing for the wives of the officers on board at 9d (old pence, equivalent of about 4p) each. He was told it was too much and he could only charge 6d so he threw his hairdressing kit overboard in disgust. After his return to England, Josef joined the Czech War department in London.

Josef was sent to Prague after the war with the Czech War office and took lots of cigarettes with him. The Czech Government wanted him to stay so he bribed a pilot with the cigarettes to bring him back to the UK. Fred started to work with Josef in his hairdressing business in England, then became a representative for a textile firm and then, with help of his wife's brother, bought a feather hat making business which did very well. Queen Elizabeth the Queen mother wore one of his hats, possibly with one of George Roden's dresses!

Betty Barton, Fred's wife, wearing one of his feather hats, as sold to HM Queen Elizabeth the Queen Mother.

Pavel Vransky was born in 1921 in Lipník nad Bečvou, the son of Philip Wechsberg, distantly related to Albert Wechsberg. He went to school in Bohumín and Gymnasium in Ostrava. He studied cheese-making in Kroměříž but his career was interrupted by the German invasion. He returned home to Ostrava and immediately tried to cross the border into Poland, with the help of friends. After hiding for a short time hanging from the rafters in a chicken coop to escape the Germans, who looked into the coop but only at ground level, he reached Poland where he joined the Czech forces. They were interned for some time by the Russian authorities during the period of the Nazi-Soviet pact but later were sent to the Middle East, where he fought in Tobruk and Eritrea. He recalled that in the Tobruk campaign he had pulled the tripwire of an Italian mine. Fortunately, only the detonator exploded so he was not harmed, although totally shocked. He volunteered for the RAF and served the rest of the war hunting U-Boats with the rank of Flight Sergeant.

After the war he worked for Czech Airlines until the communist takeover and then as a translator and in the civil aviation sector. Latterly, in his own words, his career was 'as driver and dogsbody'. After completing his studies after the war, he was promoted to second lieutenant. It was not until 1999,

Gen. Pavel Vransky (left) with Michal Salomonovič, 2016.

however, when there was finally recognition of the heroism of Czechs who had fought with the Allies, that he was promoted to major and retired in 2009 as a colonel, following a proposal from the Czech Union of Freedom Fighters. He was three times awarded the Czech Medal for Valour and the Military Medal of Merit and Merit Cross III; the British Africa Star and the Aircrew Europe Star, among other decorations. In 2017 he was awarded the rank of Brigadier General in the Czech Army.

Otto Hornung's father, Arnošt, qualified as a lawyer in Vienna. While studying, he joined the IVRIA, the Jewish fraternity, a sort of *Burschenschaft*. Its motto was *Mit Wort und Wehr zu Juda's Ehr* (With Word and Arms for Judah's Honour). He was a keen and skilled fencer and took part in several duels during his time in Vienna. Otto recalled that his father had a scar from such a duel which ran from the forehead to the back of his head. After the German invasion of Ostrava, Arnošt was sent to the Nisko camp but escaped to Poland where he was later shot by the Germans. Otto decided that he should leave Ostrava as soon as possible, go to Poland and then travel to join the British armed forces.

Otto's aunt had a tenant, a postman, who took the letters early every day from Ostrava to Bohumín, which after the border adjustment at the time of the Munich Agreement, was now in Poland. Otto took his place one morning and so arrived in Poland where he approached the British consul in Kraków and asked to join the Royal Navy, but was turned down. He joined the Czech forces and went with them to Rumania, but they were interned by the Russians until the German invasion of Russia. They were then sent to Lebanon and he was later taken by ship to join the defence of Tobruk. He returned to England and then was part of the invasion force that liberated France in 1944. Otto was shot, with the bullet narrowly missing his heart, and requested demobilisation rather than accepting promotion to the rank of captain. He became a journalist and a well-known and highly respected philatelist.

While in the Middle East he met up with an old friend, Liese Tschiassny, who had left Ostrava in 1939 for Palestine. She was a member of the dancing club that Otto had attended in Ostrava. In Palestine, she introduced him to Barbara, who became his first wife.

Otto's mother was Hungarian by birth and after the death of Arnošt managed to get permission to join her sister in Budapest where she received a *Schutzpass* issued by Raoul Wallenberg, the Swedish diplomat in Budapest who was determined to save as many Jews as he possibly could.

Henry Heitlinger also managed to flee Czechoslovakia to Palestine and joined the British army there, but his posting was in the NAAFI and purely administrative! After the war, he stayed in Jerusalem and worked in the King David Hotel and was there when the Jewish underground blew up one of its wings. Henry later became an informant (or, more accurately, a spy) for the

Barbara and Otto Hornung, 1943.

Haganah, the precursor of the Israeli army, before he moved to England and a career as a night club manager.

George Tyrell (né Jiří Hanuš Tramer) was born in the maternity wing of the Vítkovice steelwork's hospital in 1935 to Ernestine, known as Esther, and Otto. He was an only child. Otto Tramer (*1907 +1977) left Czechoslovakia in 1938, because the Czech police were after him. George believed that this was because Otto was Jewish but it was probably because Otto had not obtained Czech citizenship and had a German name. George and his mother spent the war incarcerated in Theresienstadt. Twice they were due to be deported to Auschwitz. On the first occasion George was given an injection that gave him a fever. Bizarrely, it seems that for propaganda purposes the Germans had a policy of not transporting sick Jews to the concentration camps. On the second occasion, George and Esther were taken to the train station, where Esther protested that she was needed in the maternity hospital, which resulted in both her and George being returned to the camp.

Otto went to Poland and Belgium before arriving in England, where he joined the British Army. He was initially in the Pioneer Corp but moved, via the artillery, to intelligence which is where many refugees served, using

SCHUTZ-PASS Nr. 85/20

Name: dr. Aranka Hornung-Krausz
Név:

Wohnort: Budapest
Lakás:

Geburtsdatum: 10.April 1900.
Születési ideje:

Geburtsort: Bustyaháza
Születési helye:

Körperlänge: 165 cm.
Magasság:

Haarfarbe: schwarz Augenfarbe: braun
Hajszín: Szemszín:

Unterschrift: Dr. Aranka Hornung Krausz
Aláírás:

SCHWEDEN SVÉDORSZÁG

Die Kgl. Schwedische Gesandtschaft in Budapest bestätigt, dass der Obengenannte im Rahmen der — von dem Kgl. Schwedischen Aussenministerium autorisierten — Repatriierung nach Schweden reisen wird. Der Betreffende ist auch in einen Kollektivpass eingetragen.

Bis Abreise steht der Obengenannte und seine Wohnung unter dem Schutz der Kgl. Schwedischen Gesandtschaft in Budapest.

Gültigkeit: erlischt 14 Tage nach Einreise nach Schweden.

A budapesti Svéd Kir. Követség igazolja, hogy fentnevezett — a Svéd Kir. Külügyminisztérium által jóváhagyott — repatriálás keretében Svédországba utazik.

Nevezett a kollektiv útlevélben is szerepel.

Elutazásdig fentnevezett és lakása a budapesti Svéd Kir. Követség oltalma alatt áll.

Érvényét veszti a Svédországba való megérkezéstől számított tizennegyedik napon.

* Reiseberechtigung nur gemeinsam mit dem Kollektivpass. Einreisewisum wird nur in dem Kollektivpass eingetragen.

Budapest, den 26.September *1944*

KÖNIGLICH SCHWEDISCHE GESANDTSCHAFT
SVÉD KIRÁLYI KÖVETSÉG

Kgl.Schwedischer Gesandter.

Schutz-Pass for Dr Aranka Hornungová, Otto's mother.

their language skills and knowledge of the countries and customs of the places where they originated.

Pavel Reisz had come to England to school, to learn English well before the war. His uncle had told the family that English would, in future, be the key worldwide commercial language and that Pavel should learn it to secure his future. It was a remarkably far-sighted forecast. After the German invasion, Pavel's parents could not send money for his fees and upkeep, but the school – a Quaker foundation – waived them.

Pavel's younger brother, **Karel**, managed to leave Ostrava on one of Winton's *Kindertransports* and was taken in by the school (Leighton Park School), on the same charitable basis. Later in his life he would be well-known as a film director ('Saturday Night and Sunday Morning', 'The French Lieutenant's Woman' and many others) but after leaving school he joined the RAF and trained as a fighter pilot although the war ended before he saw active service.

Joseph Thieberger was a photographer with a shop in Ostrava and one in Orlová before the war. As soon as the Germans invaded, he left Ostrava with his wife and daughter, Gitta, for Russia. He and his wife were staunch communists and were unlikely to survive in freedom after the invasion. Joseph joined the Red army in aerial reconnaissance and was killed in action. Gitta subsequently wrote and published a fictionalised and simplified version of her life as a children's story.

Eric Auber (né Erich Auerbach) was born in 1914 in Vítkovice and was bilingual in Czech and German. He trained in the accounts department of the Rothschild-owned Iron and Steel Works where he met his future wife, Margaret (Gretl) Wolf, who was Romanian by nationality whom he married in 1938. Early in 1939, a lorry driver who worked for the same transport company as Gretl telephoned to say that German tanks were on their way to Ostrava, and Eric and Gretl, then expecting their first child, collected a bare minimum of personal effects and caught a taxi to relations living in Poland. From there they made their way to England via Sweden, not expecting to stay beyond the end of the war. Their travel documents bears stamps reading 'Leave to land granted at London this day [4 and 9 May 1939] on condition that the holder will emigrate from the United Kingdom and will not take any employment or engage in any business, profession or occupation in the United Kingdom.'

In 1943 he volunteered to join the Czechoslovak Forces but was rejected on health grounds. His father, Josef, had served in the Austrian Army in the First World War with the rank of lieutenant. Josef and Bedřich, his younger son, were both deported to Nisko and after the camp was disbanded, they escaped to the USSR and eventually joined the Czech Army in Buzuluk. Bedřich ran a tank repair shop with the rank of lieutenant while Josef served in an auxiliary unit. After the war, Bedřich advised Eric not to return to Czechoslovakia because of the imminent communist takeover, so that branch of the family remained in England. Eric's son, Tom, has a cache of family letters including one from Gretl's sister Hannah ('Hanni') about the death of their sister, Gertrude ('Trude'). Hanni and Trude served in the Czech forces during the war, and Trude was killed in 1945: 'We buried her in her uniform in a beautiful coffin with a guard of honour at the graveside. We couldn't do anything more for her. She´s buried at a place of honour.'

Isidor Zehngut describes how many other of the deportees to Nisko also crossed into Russian territory when the camp was closed and then joined the nascent Czech army in Buzuluk:

> Now I will deal with those groups of prisoners transported to Nisko, who were driven further East from the camp.
>
> On their way to Russia they had to face not only the difficulties of the march through unknown territory in hostile weather, but they had also to defend themselves against the armed gangs, which attacked and robbed them. After a great effort they all finally crossed the demarcation line into the eastern part of Poland, mostly around Lvov, occupied by the Red Army. In Lvov itself there were about 200,000 refugees from Ostrava, Těšín, Vienna and all parts of Poland. A few lucky refugees found shelter with the local Jewish families, whilst the majority looked for shelter in cellars, on staircases and wherever possible.
>
> The refugees were registered on the 29 June 1940. Those who were allowed to remain rejoiced. It turned out to be their tragedy. They perished when the region was attacked on 22 June 1941 and occupied by the Germans. An escape was not possible. For about 2 weeks they were within the firing line and later the retreating Russian Army blocked all the possible routes.
>
> After the registration on 29 June 1940 the major part of the refugees was moved into the old Russia into a variety of labour camps and so survived the Jewish catastrophe. However, the constitution of some was not strong enough to withstand the unusual climate and changed conditions but the prevailing majority survived till the beginning of 1942 when they were released from the labour camps and enrolled into the Czechoslovak army unit then forming at Buzuluk under the command of the colonel, later general, Ludvík Svoboda.
>
> The Czechoslovak Army unit, with numerous Jewish fighters who all fought bravely, was fighting along the famous Red Army and took part in battles at Sokolovo, Bílá Cerekev, Dukla, Ostrava and others.
>
> In eternal memory of the Jewish heroes from the Ostrava Region who sacrificed their lives for the liberation of our dear homeland and for the better and happy future, he produced a list of Ostravaks who served. The list contains 54 names.[4]

Evžen Lanzer escaped from Ostrava to Poland with his family. In 1942 he and his sons volunteered to join the Czech Army in Buzuluk. Evžen died of exhaustion the day after they arrived in Buzuluk and two of his sons were killed in the battle of Sokolovo.

Col. Emanuel Gramisch, 1980.

Emmanuel Gramisch was deported to Nisko. After escaping he was one of the founding members of the 1st Czechoslovak Field Battalion in the USSR and became a communications officer with the tank battalion and commander of communication of the Czechoslovak Corps in July 1944. He took part in all the important battles from Sokolovo to the liberation of Ostrava. After the war he remained with the army and retired with the rank of colonel.

Herman Brodavka's grandson, Arnošt, son of his eldest daughter Gizela, was deported with the very first Jewish transport from Ostrava to

Nisko. After the camp was closed, he fled to the USSR and was accepted into the Czechoslovak army unit in Buzuluk. He was killed in the battle of Sokolovo on 8 March 1943, and was awarded a post-mortem Order of the Red Banner.

Karel Hahn also joined the Czech army in Buzuluk after Nisko and was assigned to the 1st Infantry Company under First Lieutenant Otakar Jaroš, with whom he fought in the battle at Sokolovo, where he led a mortar team. After Sokolovo he attended a school for reserve officers, tank school and after completion the course, he held various positions in a tank unit.

Viktor Fisch was the brother-in-law of Karel Hahn. He, too joined the Czech Army in Buzuluk and was killed in the battle of Sokolovo. Corporal Viktor Fisch was decorated, 'In Memoria', with the Czechoslovak War Cross 1939, Sokolovo Memorial Medal and a Golden Star For Freedom.

Victoria Bursa's (née Melcer) uncle, Viktor, joined the Czech regiment of the Red Army after escaping from Nisko, but was killed in the battle of Sokolovo. He received two medals which Victoria still has with their citations.

Eduard Graf also reached Buzuluk after the Nisko camp was closed and joined the Reserve Regiment as second lieutenant, but died shortly afterwards. His two nephews, Erich and Egon Traub, were also in the Czech Army; Egon was killed in the battle of Charkov.

George Roden's (né Rosenstein) uncles, Viktor and Otto, escaped from Nisko into the Soviet Union. There they were interned in the Gulag in Siberia but when the Germans invaded they were allowed to join the newly formed Czech Brigade. They survived the war, despite being part of very severe fighting. After the war, Viktor was able to find his wife in Theresienstadt but Otto lost his wife and son in Auschwitz.

Erich Rosenzweig followed a similar path from Ostrava to Nisko and to Buzuluk where he joined the paratroop brigade and was sent to support the Slovak uprising in 1944. He remained with the partisans after the suppression of the uprising until he was posted to the tank battalion in 1945.

Peter Bachrach was also a member of the Slovak partisans. His father had been a high-ranking officer in the Austrian Army in the First World War but that did not prevent him being sent to Nisko and from being shot when he tried to escape. Peter joined the partisans as a 13 year-old. After the war, he returned to Ostrava to complete his education but left in 1948 to emigrate to Israel. Peter then served in the Israeli army finishing his service as a Colonel in the tank brigade. Peter's son, Doron, was killed on active service in the Israeli army. In 1990 Peter returned to Ostrava where he became the President of the Jewish Community. In the end he retired to Israel.

Hanuš Rosenbaum also served for 7 years in the Israeli Army. His father, Eliáš, had fled east from Ostrava with his wife and two children.

Erich Rosický né Rosenzweig.

In 1942 Eliáš died of a heart attack and his widow and children all joined the Czech Army where Hanuš served as a signaller with the artillery. After the war, Eliáš's widow remarried and the whole family emigrated to Israel. After his Israeli army service, Hanuš changed his name to Hanan Ron and joined the Foreign Service and later the *Mossad* or Israeli secret service.

Arnošt Rusek was born in 1921. His parents had a grocery shop. He was sent to Nisko in October 1939 and his father sent there a week later.

Within some 2 weeks, Arnošt escaped and fled to Russia where his father later joined him. They both joined the Czech army in Buzuluk and his father died there. Arnošt went to army school to be trained in ant-tank warfare and in his first engagement he was wounded in the leg and found by people collecting dead bodies! The wound became gangrenous and he lost his leg but fell in love with and married his nurse. He stayed in the army until 1955 and later taught at the Engineering Technical High School in Vítkovice until August 1989.

Kurt Karel Smulovič.

Bedřich Kopold was born in the same year as Arnošt's parents who owned a restaurant/inn. In October 1939, he was deported to Nisko with 960 other men. When the camp was closed the guards took many of them to the Russian border. Gangs of Poles stole everything he had, which was very little, but he managed to get to USSR and went to Lwow where he met many other refugees. He went to Dombass and worked in the mines and later in a car factory, learning Russian and German. In 1941, he left and went to Buzuluk to join the Czech army. He commented that by 1944, his segment of the army was 50% Jewish. He stayed in the army post-war but was arrested in 1950 and sentenced to 18 years as part of infamous Slánskýanti-Semitic political show trials.

Kurt Karel Smulovič, born in 1908, beat Alfred Vogel's record by being in four different armies – in only one war! – before being able to celebrate a victory.

His grandfather was a tailor in Ostrava and his father, Berthold, an engine driver. Kurt Karel, however, went to university and graduated with a doctorate in Metallurgy in Příbram. After two years in the Škoda works in Plzeň he was conscripted as a Lieutenant in the Czechoslovak Army. After the invasion he was arrested by the Gestapo but released (he recalls that this was because he was 'insufficiently Jewish'). Then, with 25 men from his army company he crossed the German-Polish border, 'removing a German frontier guard; we drowned him in the marshes'. The men were allowed to stay in Poland on condition that they left for France, which they did. Kurt joined the French Foreign legion and was sent to Sidi bel Abes in Morocco.

After the German invasion of Poland and the start of the Second World War, he returned to mainland France and fought on the Seine and Loire to defend Paris, but in vain. They retreated to Lyon, Bezier and Montpelier and were evacuated to England. According to his memoirs, he was awarded the Croix de Guerre on board the ship to Liverpool.

He was commissioned as a captain in the British Army and sent to Tobruk and Alexandria but the Czech Government requested his return to England to be sent to join the Red Army, which was short of officers, Stalin having purged them before the war. He fought at Stalingrad and was made liaison officer and commander of a tank company. He later took part in the battle of Dukla Pass which he described in his memoirs:

> ...the position was not easy to recapture. The mountain range was 2,000 feet high with the only pass through the Carpathian Mountains mostly covered in ice. But a very small passage was known to me, because in my younger days as a second lieutenant I had been a frontier guard. But all this was delayed by Marshall Malimorsky[5] after an assault of the 17th Cossack Division and the 1st regiment of the Czech Army which ended in a terrible massacre. I was wounded in

> my right ear. Thanks to my decorations, I was taken to Moscow for an operation. After 3 weeks, I was back on the front. Malimorsky mounted a big assault against the German defence line on the Dukla Pass.
>
> I refused to go. I did not care about Malimorsky's order to go to jail. I went the way I knew around and landed in the rear of the German line. I sent a message to Malimorsky about my position and informed him that at 5 o'clock in the morning I will bombard the Germans with my tanks, and he agreed. On 12th January 1945, my tank brigade with 44 guns bombarded the Germans and Malimorsky succeeded in getting through. The Germans were on the run.

Kurt later took part in the battle to liberate Ostrava. He was demobilised in 1947 with the rank of Major. His Czech army record shows he received

War Memorial in Sleszká Ostrava, with Neil and Tanya Bintcliffe (grand-daughter of K. K. Smulovič).

the Czech Military Cross 39 and the Memory Medal with the label F-GB. His grand-daughter visited Ostrava with her husband in 2010 and were photographed by the war memorial in Slezská Ostrava, to commemorate Kurt Karel.

The war record of Ostrava Jews is a proud one, although full of sorrow. There were no dashing operetta soldiers in the Second World War but only, to borrow a phrase, blood, toil, tears and sweat.

NOTES

1. Information in this chapter is from the Ostravak families involved. Further detail may be found in the archive of the Jewish Museum in Prague where all material collected for this book has been deposited.
2. Edith Rosenberg. Imperial War Museum.
3. Helen Fry. *German Schoolboy, British Commando* (London: History Press, 2010).
4. Isidor Zehngut's manuscript with the full list is in the Ostrava Archive of the Jewish Museum in Prague.
5. This is almost certainly an original transcription or typographical error. The name is Malinovsky.

10

Stranger Than Fiction

Survivors all say that their survival was just a matter of luck and that people who were stronger, cleverer, richer, or better connected than they, all perished. It is, however, not as simple as that. Luck was necessary, to be in the right place at the right time or not to be in the wrong place at the wrong time, otherwise you were killed. But it was not enough for ultimate survival. Organising an escape from pre-war Ostrava involved strength, initiative, contacts and probably money as well as luck. Survival in Theresienstadt and Auschwitz required great strength, physical and psychological, as well as luck. Those who were mentally and physically not so strong, who had little or no money or education, were unlikely to have much chance either of getting out of Ostrava before the Holocaust or of surviving the camps. So they did not live to tell the tale. Those who did survive and were able and willing to tell us of their experiences disproportionally came from the upper echelons of Jewish society and whose life had, indeed, been very comfortable. Possibly they either did not remember or even did not know about the hard and difficult lives that others experienced. Here are some of their stories.

Hysteria in Croydon or Pure *Mazl*[1]

Dovid Chaim Goldberg was officially illegitimate. He was born in 1882 in Oświęcim, and named for his father (Dovid) who had died before he was born. Dovid senior had married Pessel Goldberg but had not registered their marriage with the Austro-Hungarian authorities, most likely because it was conducted by a rabbi not officially recognised by the state, as was not unusual in Galicia at the time. So Dovid Chaim was, in the eyes of the state, illegitimate. For the same reason, Pessel retained her maiden name and Dovid Chaim took it as his family name.

Dovid Chaim lived in Oświęcim with his wife Rosa (née Bronner) and their two children. In the initial phase of the First World War, in 1914, the Russians advanced from the East into the Austro-Hungarian province of Galicia and were approaching Oświęcim. Dovid Chaim with his wife and two children fled, out of the primeval Jewish fear, 'The Cossacks are coming!' and settled in Moravia, in Moravská Ostrava. Their third child, Max, was born there late in 1914. Four of Rosa's brothers, Jakob, Mendel, Heinrich and Leopold Bronner, also left Oświęcim in 1914 to escape the Russians. The

Bronner family had a secular education in German and Polish as well as being religiously observant ('frum') like the Goldbergs. Dovid's youngest son, Bertie, remembers that they had nice handwriting, which he said, in those days was essential for success in business or white-collar employment of any sort.

Mendel settled in Berlin but later moved back to Oświęcim for business. He exported kosher wine from Poland to Germany. He had a full beard as befitted a purveyor of kosher products and a serious Jewish businessman. Heinrich moved to Strasburg while Jakob lived in Oderberg (Bohumín in Czech) which in 1918 became part of Czechoslovakia. He had a general grocery shop there and was quite prosperous. He and his family visited the Goldbergs often and they reciprocated.

Although the family had moved from Galicia to Moravia, they were still within the Austro-Hungarian Empire and Dovid Chaim was called up to the Austro-Hungarian army in 1915 where he served until 1918. Rosa was left to look after the children, of whom there were 4 by the end of the war: Oskar, Tereza-Ráchel, Max and Eleanora, called Lilli, born in 1917. At the end of the war, the Austro-Hungarian Empire was dismantled and new states, among them Czechoslovakia and Poland, were established. Perhaps because of bureaucratic difficulties or perhaps his habit of avoiding all apparently unnecessary contact with the authorities, Dovid did not take out Czech citizenship. Nor Polish. He and the family were therefore technically stateless. There is no evidence that this caused practical problems for them at the time, but it would have fatal consequences twenty years later. Despite the remembered lack of papers, it is clear that they, or Oskar at least, did have some official documentation which allowed him to cross the border into and out of Poland on business.

Dovid worked hard and fairly soon established a successful textile business, making and selling shirts and similar items. He had a shop close to the main square in Ostrava, on Mostní Street, later renamed Třída 28. října– 28 October Boulevard, and the family lived in the centre of Ostrava near the Imperial Hotel, on Haydenova Street 985/3 in a building owned by Mr Schreiber, a furniture entrepreneur. There their fifth child, Norbert (called Bubik by his family and known as Bertie later, in England) was born on 27 July 1919. He was named for Rosa's father, Nechemia Bronner. Bertie remembered that near their house was an Italian ice-cream shop but he was not allowed to have any as it was not kosher! Nevertheless, he remembers a very happy childhood in a warm and loving family. Also near the house was a toyshop into whose windows Bertie would gaze almost daily. It was run by the Deutsch family, whose daughter now lives in Bristol and has reminisced about it with Bertie. The family was completed in 1921 with the birth of Matylda, called Tildy-Matuscha, on 12 December.

Although Dovid was an industrious businessman, once the business was established he used to leave the shop in the care of Rosa and spend his time on the first floor of the local coffee shop with the other Jewish businessmen of Ostrava. If anyone wanted him, Bertie would be sent off to collect him. Rosa was not alone among Jewish women in being left to 'run the shop'. At the time, Jewish women in Ostrava were relatively well educated in secular subjects and were also socially and commercially active but it is possible that this progressive attitude was partly to enable the menfolk to spend their time on more important matters, for example playing cards in the local coffee shop!

As a child, Bertie went to a local Czech-language kindergarten and learnt to sing all the Czech Christmas carols (despite his orthodox Jewish family background). In old age he claimed that he still remembered them. From the age of 6 to 11 he went to the Jewish primary school and then on to a Czech school in Mariánské Hory. This meant that, rather unusually for a Jewish family, he was educated in Czech and he and his brothers spoke Czech to each other although their parents spoke German at home. He later went to a Czech language business school in Mariánské Hory. It was quite usual for educated people, especially those in business, to speak both languages fluently and switch from one to the other as needed.

He was the only Jewish boy in his class and, as the state specified that all children should have appropriate religious education, once a week Rabbi Eibenschütz came to the school to give religious lessons to the Jewish children. He was a chazzan [Jewish cantor] in the Main Synagogue. Bertie says that he never felt that he was not wanted, nor was he at all self-conscious about his religion. There was certainly no official anti-Semitism and he could recall no anti-Semitism throughout his youth in the 1920s and early 1930s. Instead, his attendance at a Czech school won him appreciation, since the majority of Jews spoke German as their first language.

Goldberg family life was very much the archetype of upwardly mobile Jewish migrant families worldwide. Dovid, as *pater familias*, imbued the family with his commercial high moral standards, industry and self-sufficiency. He insisted that his three sons joined him in the business, with the family motto 'Nothing comes from nothing' and a deep appreciation of the value of money. Rosa was the provider of love, comfort and food, a real 'Yiddische Mama'. She, too, set high standards, teaching good table manners, and would sing to her family. The Goldbergs flourished. By the late 1930s, they were one of the wealthiest families in Ostrava, with a telephone and a motor car!

Their life up to then seems to us today like a fairy story, a real 'rags to riches' or at least a 'refugee to prosperity in less than 20 years' story. Unfortunately it was not to last. On 14 March 1939, the Germans occupied Ostrava and the Goldbergs' lives, along with that of Ostrava itself, was shattered. When the Germans marched into Czechoslovakia, Oskar, the eldest of the three brothers, was in Poland on business. He was travelling around the country selling Goldberg shirts. Poland was a very good market at the time because prices there were much higher than in Czechoslovakia and Czech suppliers could more than compete with the Polish manufacturers. As soon as the Germans invaded Ostrava, the Goldberg family contacted Oskar in Poland, which was still free, and told him not to return to Ostrava.

Oskar was not short of money, so he spoke to a few friends and they chartered an aeroplane to fly them from Warsaw to London. In the pre-war days, a visa was not needed to travel to England on a Czechoslovak passport but by the time they arrived in Croydon the situation had changed. Czechoslovakia was now an occupied territory and so the British authorities demanded a visa, which Oskar and his companions did not have. Although they claimed refugee status, this was not accepted, and they were to be sent back to Poland.

Oskar, as the effective leader (At least Bertie's version of the story made Oskar the effective leader!) of the group of ten young men from Czechoslovakia, felt he had to do something to prevent them all being deported. So, as they were about to board the plane heading back to Warsaw, he threw a hysterical fit, kicking and screaming. Not to be deterred, a group

Oskar Goldberg being carried back onto the plane. *Daily Mail* 30 March 1939.

of policemen took hold of his arms and legs and carried him onto the plane. The scene was witnessed by a *Daily Mail* photographer, and Oskar appeared in the papers on Friday 31 March 1939 having been in the country only a few hours.

The plane and pilot were both Danish and the pilot refused to have Oskar back on board, as he was clearly mad and a danger! So all ten were imprisoned, while their future could be decided. The photograph and the story caused quite a stir, made all the more intense because they were still in prison during the Jewish festival of Pesach (Passover). A local Jewish Professor (sadly his name is not now known although he was probably someone connected to one of the Jewish relief organisations) brought them kosher food for Pesach. Finally the ten were released from prison and after a few days received permission to stay in England. So Oskar was in England, living in the Jewish Temporary Shelter in London's East End.

Meanwhile, in Ostrava, Dovid, as one of the wealthiest Jews in town, was told it was best for him to get out of Czechoslovakia altogether before the Germans arrested him. He decided to leave immediately with his two younger sons, Max and Bertie. Rosa and their daughters together with their two grand-daughters, Judyta and Matylda, daughters of Rachel and Simon Rose, remained in Ostrava as it was believed that the Germans would never harm women and girls! So, on Friday morning the three male members of the family set out to walk to Bohumín, by then in Poland, where Rosa's brother, Jakob Bronner, lived. All they took were a *Tallith* (Prayer shawl) and *Tephilin* (Phylacteries), both items essential for the morning prayers of all Jewish men. Bohumín had been part of Czechoslovakia but when the Germans moved into the Sudetenland in early October 1938, the Polish government had occupied part of the territory on the border near Ostrava, and so Bohumín was then in Poland. Bertie recalls the event:

> So we walked across the new German-Polish border, with a guide. The Germans were not watching the border too closely yet and our Czech guide knew exactly where the German guards were stationed. It was not done for free though. Nothing was done for Jews out of love for them. We had to pay a large sum of money and were not guaranteed success. We believed that had the Germans caught us - they would have shot us and let the man go. This is why I always say that getting out was only a matter of luck and G-d's will.

From Bohumín, the three of them went on to Oświęcim where Dovid had been born and had come from twenty years previously. Their Polish family made them very welcome. It was not the return of the Prodigal Son but rather the return of the wealthy and successful son who was facing what they supposed to be just a temporary problem.

Meanwhile, Oskar had found out that it was possible to travel through England on the way to Shanghai, which was an open port and almost anyone would be admitted. Money was available and so he bought tickets on a boat for his two brothers to go to Shanghai. Since they were already in Poland, he sent the tickets to them there. Max and Bertie took the tickets to the British consulate in Katowice for transit visas via the UK to Shanghai, which they obtained. A letter from Max in Poland to Oskar before they had obtained transit visas describes the tortuous process:

> I have just been to the British Consul and was there from 10 o'clock this morning until 3:30 and then from 4:30 to 6:30 but achieved little. I did get to spend half an hour with the consul and went through all the questions in detail and this is what I learnt:
>
> The consul will do whatever he can but it isn't as easy as we imagined, he does not have the power to give a refugee a visa, he must first of all send the form to Warsaw for permission, then it goes to the Home Office in London for permission and the whole palaver ['Maise', Yiddish for a story] can take at least 2 months and even then he is doubtful of the result, then I will have no documents and possibility of getting to Eretz [Hebrew, the Land, here meaning Palestine] because a tourist visa for Palestine is not counted as a legal document here, according the Consul they won't carry out a legalisation in the Land and so I had to go back to England!
>
> The British definitely don't want to keep people permanently, they want to get rid of all those they have got already. And I don't even have a document so that I can get into the Land.
>
> However, the Consul will do everything he can and will try to get a favourable result. He said that, seeing that I have a brother in London, I should ask him to arrange this document for me directly through the German Jewish Aid Committee in Bloomsbury House.
>
> Therefore, please:
>
> Go there immediately, the documents are enclosed, you have to arrange the missing ones yourself, specifically that we have got money (you must find out there how much is needed) and, in case you need it, details of our previous occupation and our special skills, you can also tell them what we know.
>
> I am enclosing the list of documents, which I got from the British Consul. I hope you can sort out which documents are needed.
>
> Please Oskar, arrange that for me, as you are my only hope. I believe that if you take this in hand, it will go faster, much faster. It is, after all, not so difficult but you must work at it. Please do this for me and for Bubik, so that it is sorted out as quickly as possible. I should dearly love to see us all in Eretz.

Bertie's retrospective comment is:

> And that's how we got to England. So my eldest brother in his wisdom and with luck saved our lives. It was all pure *mazl* (Just Luck!). Max and I arrived in England in June 1939.

The once close Goldberg family was now split. The three sons were in London, Dovid was with his mother and family in Oświęcim, and Rosa with the girls were still in Ostrava. And the nightmare began. Dovid appeared to be safe in free Poland and the womenfolk were determined to make every effort to leave occupied Czechoslovakia and emigrate to Palestine or at least to flee to England. But bureaucracy defeated them.

The same administrative jungle faced the girls as had faced Max and Bertie but it was possibly even worse for them. The German/Czech government did not want them. The Poles did not want them. No-one wanted them. The anguish is expressed in another letter to Oskar from Max while he was still in Poland:

> They have expelled[2] the girls. That is the most important thing!!! So you must immediately take care of the permits, and you must immediately send a document from some official in London to Lili and Mathilda saying that the permit is in process and will be ready on such and such a date, in case we cannot get the permits in Ostrava before the 15th June because the girls will be expelled on 15/6. I do not want the girls to come to Poland; they just would go to ruin here. In London, they will be useful right from the beginning, then, if the furniture arrives, they can be our housekeepers, learn English and get to know the local conditions. [...] They need the official document because, in case the permit does not come before the date for deportation, they can ask for an extension. Perhaps the girls will get preference at refugee offices in London because they are stateless? They still do not have passports, so what should we do? I do not think they will get Polish passports! [...] Please, consider everything carefully as it is complicated. And then get on with it right now.

By September 1939, Oskar would probably have secured entry visas for the girls had not war broken out, which meant that they could not leave Czechoslovakia in any case. They decided to go into hiding in the country and moved to a small village, Solopisky, just outside Prague. In Ostrava, being close to the border, they were very exposed to being noticed, arrested, and pushed across the border into Poland or at least into no-man's land, whereas they could escape notice in the country. This was initially quite a success and the girls lived quietly and undisturbed for some time. But in

1942, they were advised by the Prague *Kultusgemeinde* that they would be safer in Prague itself. Sadly, they followed the advice and were rounded up by the Gestapo. A month later, all of them were deported to Theresienstadt. Only four weeks after their arrival in the ghetto, Rosa, Eleonora and Matylda were deported to the extermination camp in Treblinka. Rachel with her children Matylda and Judita were sent, in December 1943, to the Theresienstadt Family Camp in Auschwitz-Birkenau. None of them returned.

We know the whole story because the Czech family were able to send letters to the brothers in England. Initially, post came through free Poland but after September 1939, mail had to be directed through neutral countries, so delay and misadventure were built in. The Goldbergs had contacts in Tangier through their business connections, and this was the circuitous route that they used to send letters. Despite the delays and difficulties, a series of letters got through, from May 1939 until the last letter arrived, dated 11 August 1942, well over a hundred and fifty in total, a heartbreaking archive kept by Bertie.

In their last letter, all of the women wrote a few sentences. Eleonora wrote that Rachel and Matylda had been ill. It was the first time in three years that anybody had been sick, but their parents were healthy. They had not received any letters from the brothers for a very long time. They hoped that they would be permitted to celebrate Rosa's birthday at home. That would be the greatest present for all of them. Matylda wrote about her illness. Rachel wrote that her daughters were her only happiness and were very sweet. Rosa sent greetings to the boys in England.[3]

It was the last time Oskar, Max and Bertie heard from their mother, sisters and nieces, for 18 months later, they had all been murdered. The three brothers now had to earn a living somehow, in wartime London, although first they had to learn enough English to cope with everyday life. Oskar had been living in the Jewish Temporary Shelter for Refugees but when Max and Bertie arrived they moved in together, living in one room in Pattison Street in London's East End with only one bed and an outside toilet. It was quite a contrast with Ostrava! Each of them took jobs in various clothing companies and quite soon their combined income reached £18 per week, or £6 each per week which compared well with an annual salary of £350 for a clerical officer in the Civil Service at the time[4]which was relatively good. Bertie remembered that they felt like millionaires and they moved into a better flat at 222, Whitechapel Road.

Their experience in the manufacture of textiles stood them in good stead and being Jewish provided an introduction to existing Jewish textile businesses. Oskar was working for Ellis and Goldstein, and had been promoted to a cutter, a skilled job. He brought Max and Bertie into the company with him. Max also became a cutter while Bertie was a machinist,

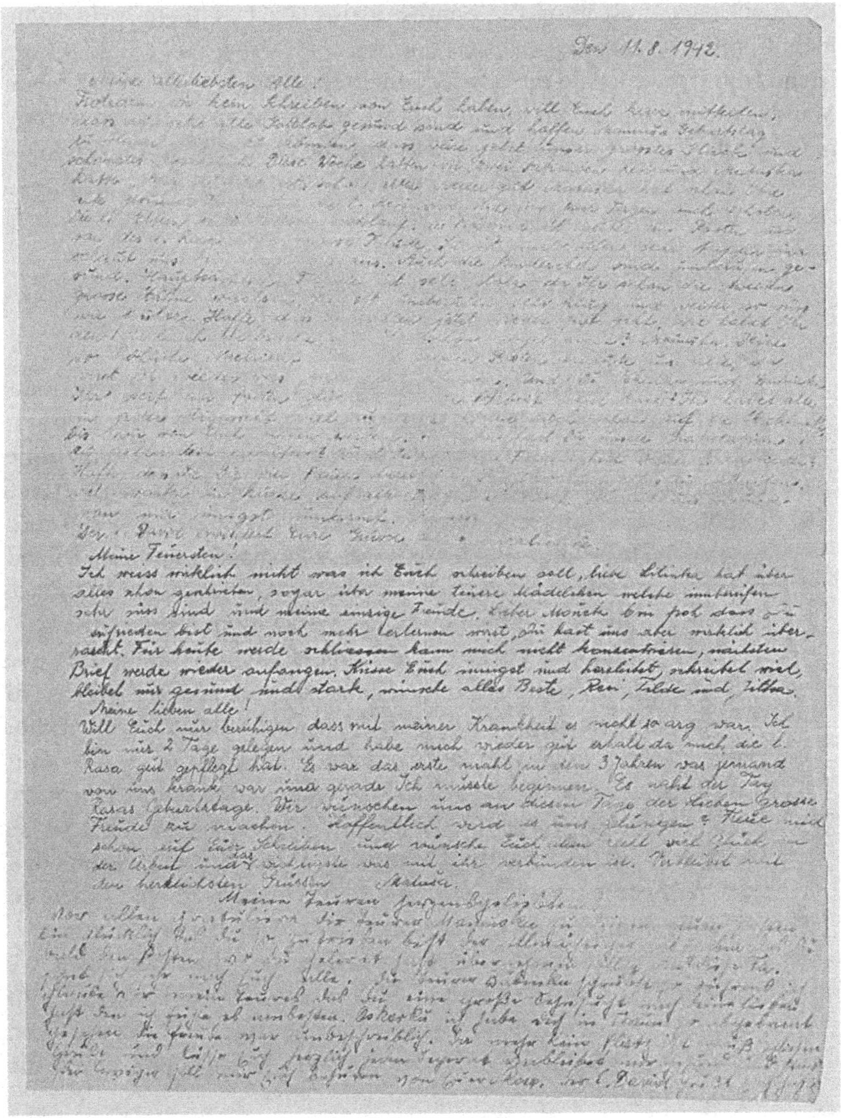

The last letter Oskar, Max and Bertie received from their mother and sisters, dated 11 August 1942.

sewing army uniforms. The factory was destroyed in the blitz, but they were regarded as key workers and asked to move to Luton, to a sister factory. Their first concern was about Jewish life in Luton, but once they had satisfied themselves that there was a synagogue and a rabbi, they happily moved and brought with them a Jewish housekeeper who was also pleased to escape the blitz and nights in an air-raid shelter. Luton became a haven for many people escaping the bombs or displaced by them in London, including Jewish refugees. That is how, in 1943, Oskar met an old school friend from Ostrava who introduced him to the brothers Raphael and Sam Mandel, owners of a small clothing factory above a shop on the main street in Croydon. They had unused capacity and the Goldberg brothers bought a 50% share in the business for the princely sum of £300! It is a tribute to their industry and thrift that they were able to save such a sum over the 4 first years of the war.

The next phase in the story of the Goldberg Brothers is best reported in Bertie's own words (except for some spelling and syntax corrections):

> This gave us the opportunity to use our newly acquired skills and mass manufacturing experience to start a business. I chose skirt making as it did not require any investment into special machinery. Some time earlier I had made a skirt for a girl friend. I borrowed it from her to take to London as a sample to show skirt wholesalers the quality standard we planned to produce. But it was not easy. Competition was severe and nobody was looking for another skirt maker. There was also a shortage of cloth and the government introduced strict rationing of clothing.
>
> I did not know anybody in the business, so I just walked from one firm to another in the London West End's 'rag trade area' and persevered showing my one sample and offering to make skirts for them. But Hashem (the Almighty, in Jewish tradition the name of God is never used; Hashem is Hebrew for 'The Name') was good to me. One man, whom I will never forget, by the name of Jack Saville, from the Saville Sportswear Ltd., took the trouble to say more to me than 'I have enough skirt makers'. He actually asked me some personal questions: 'Where do you come from and why do you want to go into this cut-throat business?' He was indeed G-d sent, the first one to offer me a chair to sit down. We talked and he took an interest in me. He seemed to be fascinated with my story… At the end of our conversation, he said: 'I will give you some cloth length and you design for me skirts that will look new, and of the standard of quality as this sample and we will see…'
>
> I worked as I never had done before, virtually day and night. The following week I went to show him four styles. He liked them and said he would show them to his main buyers and would let me know… So I waited…And prayed. All week, nothing happened. On Friday, just as we were about to go home for Shabbat, the phone rang. It was Mr Saville. My heart stopped for a moment. 'Bertie, about the style no. 123… How many pieces could you produce a week?' That was it, we were in business, in a tough market. We became skirt manufacturers against all odds. This was our lucky day and the beginning of Mangold Ltd. and later SKIRTEX Ltd.

And so in 1943/44 we established our skirt factory Mangold Ltd. Half Mandel and half Goldberg. During the war, clothing was rationed in England. Coupons were issued by the government. Every item of clothing had a different coupon value and these had to be handed over upon purchasing any article in a shop. Saville Sportswear was selling our skirts well and Mangold Ltd. thrived and prospered. We moved to a bigger factory on Midland Road and began producing skirts from our own cloth as well as began supplying stores and mail order companies.

My brother Max did not join the business from the beginning. He wisely wanted to see how we got on before giving up his job. But he joined later and thus made the Goldberg brothers team complete. Our partnership with the Mandel brothers served two purposes. We had a ready production unit to start our business. And as aliens we could not be directors of a business without English directors as partners.

The mayor of Luton, Councillor Hedley Laurence and his wife, played a big role during our residence in Luton. He was a Quaker by religion and the Quakers rented their Prayer Hall to the Jewish community for their 'High Holidays'. He took a particular liking to three young men from Czechoslovakia and later sponsored us to become British citizens. Thanks to his standing the whole process was made much easier. We became British subjects in 1948 with all the advantages the citizenship brought. He also helped us when we wanted to invest money into property by introducing us to the right people, agents and lawyers. In fact, he brought many deals to us and became a partner in some of the deals we did. We became great friends and it was a pleasure to do business with him.

Mangold Ltd was doing well and we became more ambitious than our partners to expand the business, so we decided to acquire complete control of the company and made the Mandels an offer for their share of the business. The terms were that if they didn't want to sell to us, we were prepared to sell to them under the same conditions as was our offer. They bought our shares for an agreed sum of 15,000 pounds. This turned our 300 pound investment in 1943 into 15,000 pounds in five years. We were then offered and bought another clothing factory for 5,000 pounds. We named our new business SKIRTEX. Our slogan: 'Don't say skirt – say SKIRTEX' became well known all over the country. Ten years later we received an offer for Skirtex from Selincourt Ltd., a quoted public company, amounting to over one million pounds. This is how hard work and dedication turned 300 Pounds into over one million in about 15 years.

Life was not all work and worry. Oskar, Max and then Bertie all married, although Bertie's engagement was originally not without its own stress. His fiancée, Hannah, was the daughter of Mrs Hofmann, a widow and the owner of the Sandringham Hotel in Torquay whose brother, Josef Weil, was the President of the Adath Yisroel Synagogue in Stamford Hill, London. The Hoffmann and Weil families were from Germany and German Jews thought themselves superior to all others and especially to Polish Jews and Bertie's Czech statelessness did not add to his social cachet! But love triumphed, aided to some extent by the Goldberg's thriving business. The marriage went ahead and they lived happily ever after.

Bertie, inspired by our research into his family history, took a group of his children and grandchildren back to Ostrava in July 2006 to retrace his roots. They prayed the morning service in the small modern synagogue in the community centre, re-establishing Goldbergs in the religious life of Ostrava after a gap of over 65 years. The visit produced the classic question from one of Bertie's grandsons, the question all of us of a certain age have had to answer: 'Grandpa, how can you remember the details of all the people and places from so long ago and yet you cannot remember our names?'

In November 2006, we, in Kingston Synagogue, held a Service of Rededication for the Ostrava Scroll, and Bertie was invited to recite the

Bertie and family in the Ostrava Jewish Community Centre Synagogue, 2007.

Kaddish, the Memorial Prayer for the Dead. At that time, he was a great-grandfather, prosperous, surrounded by friends and family and recalling events from over 60 years previously, but he still broke down while making the prayer, and many members of the congregation did not have dry eyes either. The following year, Bertie and Hannah took all their children, grand-children and great-grandchildren with their spouses, to Kibbutz Lavi in Israel, to celebrate their 60th Wedding Anniversary and, again inspired by our research into their family, published a book of their family history for their family members. Just before Yom Kippur (The Day of Atonement, the holiest day in the Jewish calendar), Bertie used to carry out a census of all his direct descendants and their husbands and wives. In 2015, the total number was 120!

Bertie had a family business involving children and grand-children and went to the office every day (claiming to be one of the first there!). Hannah still provided him with sandwiches for his lunch. In July 2015, he celebrated his 96th birthday but sadly passed away shortly before his 97th. In the recent heated discussions about migrants and their alleged adverse effects on local societies, it is worth recalling the Goldbergs and their contributions to the Czechoslovak and British economies.

The One-eyed Chess Gambit, an Unknown Woman and a Lady with Family Trees

On 19 April 2005, early in our researches into Ostrava and its Jewish community, we gave a talk to members of our synagogue and visitors to tell them about what we had discovered about Ostrava (which was very little at

Bertie, Hanna and their family, Kibbutz Lavi, November 2007, celebrating their Diamond Wedding Anniversary.

the time) and what we hoped to do in the future. In the audience was someone we had not met before and he introduced himself as Michael Karen. He had come to find out who we were and what we were doing. Heinz Vogel, who was the first Ostravak that we discovered, had told one of his friends about our talk and he, in turn, told his friend in Vienna who told Michael who lived 5 miles away from our synagogue! So, in this rather coincidental and unexpected way, we first met the Salomonovič family who would play a major role in our ongoing story. The Salomonowitz (the original spelling of the name) family story reflects the history of Ostrava Jews.

Salomon Salomonowitz was born in Oświęcim in 1835 and married Henriette Hornung there before moving to Moravská Ostrava. 100 years later, many of his descendants would make the reverse journey in horrifying circumstances. Salomon's 5 children were all born in Ostrava, over the years that the Community was being established. They were:

1. Fany in 1872
2. Jakob in 1874
3. Rosa in 1877
4. Ida in 1878
5. Siegfried in 1885

Salomon's children married into Ostrava families that would become quite well-known in later years. Jakob married Felicitas Altová in April 1900 and had 4 children:

1. Josef Paul (b. 1901)
2. Salomon (b. 1902)
3. Erich (b. 1903)
4. Emilie (b. 1904)

Jakob inherited a general store from his parents, which provided a very comfortable living for the family and a position of some standing in the community. He was a member of the Ostrava Municipal Council and on the Board of the Jewish Community. As the proprietor of a general store he was a member of the Free and Licenced Trade Association and became a committee member. He was also elected to the Board of the *Mährisch Ostrauer Volksbank*. Jakob was a romantic at heart and wrote a love poem to Felicitas in February 1896 when she was obviously going on a trip:

To Friendly Remembrance, M. Ostrava 21/2/1896
It must be very lovely in Heaven above
Only peaceful people in that place
Genuine Heroes, Gods and little Angels

The general store and house that Jakob and his family lived in on 28.října number 652 (second building from the left).

Lovely maiden, you also come from there
Your nature is so charming to the senses
Like Circe, and you are so good
Always filled with gentleness, wise, delightful
Eyes filled with faith/trust; how that makes me feel so good
Oh, you want to leave, You will soon not be here any more
May sweet remembrance remain with me,
Your devoted Friend, Jakob Salomonowitz

He was a very keen chess player, a founder member of the Mährisch Ostrau Chess Club in 1891 and its Life President. He organised a European chess competition in Moravská Ostrava in 1923 and invited the world champion, Emmanuel Lasker from Germany, to join. Not surprisingly, Lasker won, beating Richard Réti of Czechoslovakia.

Lasker also played Jakob and although the result was not recorded, we can assume that Lasker won that game too. As well as being a skilful chess player, Jakob was an expert at Gamesmanship. He had a glass eye, and when he was in a difficult position playing chess he would take his eye out and roll it round the table to distract and confuse his opponent. Presumably this would be known as the Nelson Gambit! In fact one-eyed Jakob is not the only connection between the family and the Battle of Trafalgar. Dora

1923 Chess Championship. Jakob Salomonowitz is 3rd from the left, back row. Emmanuel Lasker is 4th from left, front row.

Kupfermann married Erich, Jakob's third son. Her brother, Michael Karen's father, married a direct descendant of Captain Hardy, who commanded HMS *Victory* in that battle.

Jakob's eldest son, Josef Paul, studied at the Technische Hochschule in Vienna from 1918, although he had originally intended to study agriculture. He was a member of the Zionist Blau-Weiss (*T'helet Lavan*) organisation and emigrated to Palestine in 1925 where he changed his name to Ben-Yaakov, married and had a family. The family inherited his love for agriculture: one

1936: Salomon Salomonowitz with his nephew, Michal.

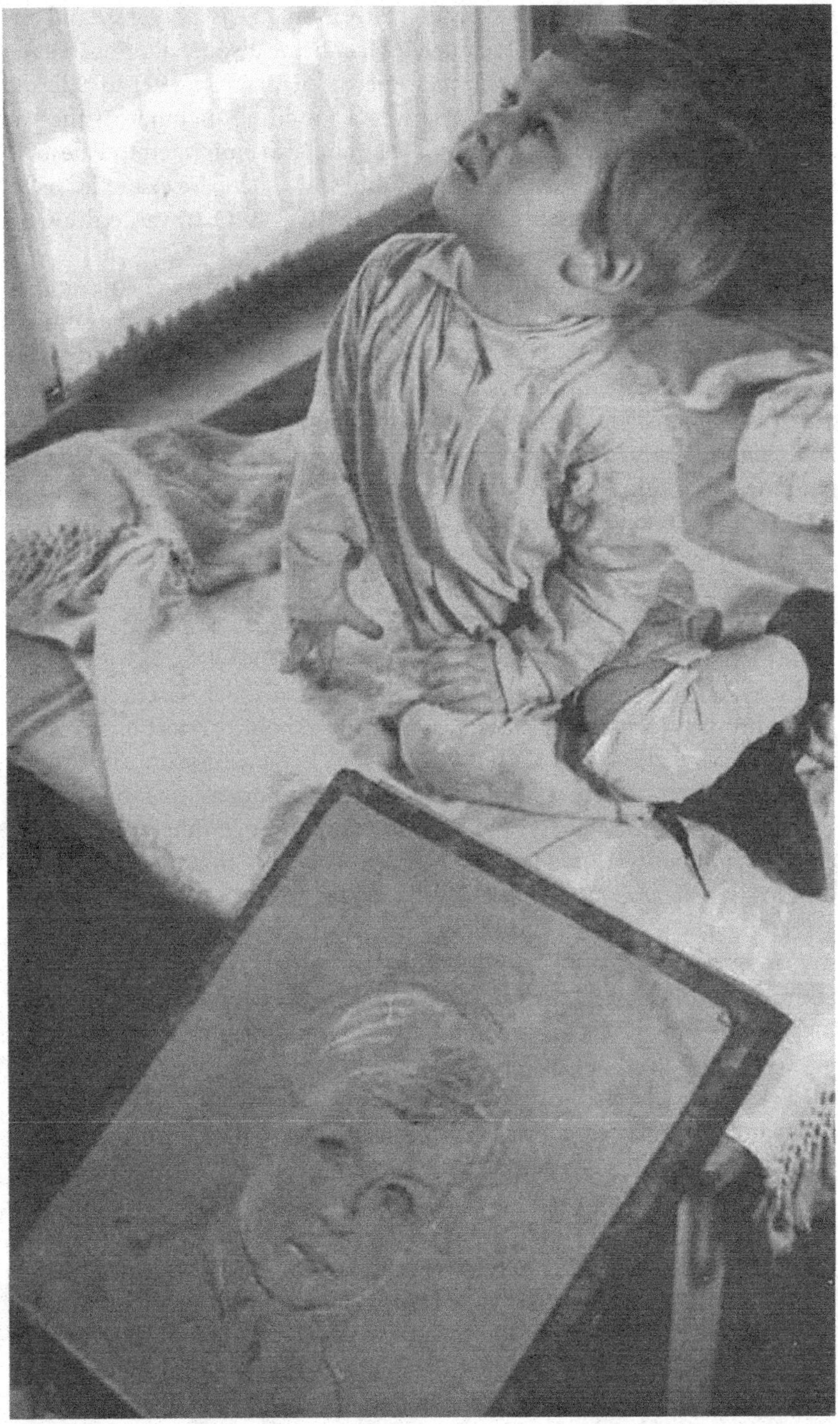

Michal with the drawing by his uncle Salomon.

of his children is an expert in avocado cultivation, one is a botanist and one is an agricultural machinery technician. Jakob's next son, Salomon, was an artist and studied at the *Kunstgewerbeschule* in Vienna from 1917 to1922 and later in Munich and in France. He was a founding member of the Art Association, *Kunstverein,* in Ostrava. Salomon also emigrated to Palestine, in 1938, where he continued to paint prolifically. There are examples of his work in the Jewish Museum in Prague. In 1936 in Ostrava he drew his nephew, Michal, who still has the drawing.

In 2008, Roy Seger- another Ostravak, showed us a portrait of his mother, Edith Gottlieberová by 'an unknown artist'. However, when we examined the painting we found that the unknown artist had actually signed it, on the back: 'Salomonowitz'. In the Ostrauer Zeitung of 7 November 1935 there is an article about the painting by Salomon Salomonowitz, called 'Portrait of an Unknown Lady'. Neither the sitter nor the artist are now unknown. The painting was originally sold for 900 Crowns.

Erich, the next son, completed his technical studies and joined the mineral oil refinery in Přívoz where he worked until the outbreak of the Second World War. He shared his brother's artistic talents, being a skilled photographer and craftsman. Erich married Dora Kupfermannová in Moravská Ostrava in 1929 and had two children, Michal (b. October 1933) and Josef (b. July 1938). It was Josef who told Michael Karen, the son of Dora's brother, to come to our talk, and so started our connection.

After Michal's wife, Libuše, retired from her position in the Human Resources Department of the local mining company she decided to investigate her and Michal's family history and, through diligence, patience and sheer bloody-mindedness, became the expert in the genealogy of Ostrava Jewish families. She has helped many of our Ostravaks uncover their lost family roots. Michal and Libuše have a daughter and son, Radan, who studied nuclear physics at Oxford and the Weizmann Institute in Israel before taking up a commercial career in Prague. He is the proud father of Samuel. In his 'spare' time he acts as translator and guide for the genealogical contacts between Libuše and her many correspondents.

Erich was deported with the first transport of Jews to Nisko nad Sanem camp and, after his return, was deported with the whole family to the Łodz ghetto and from there to Auschwitz, Dresden and finally to Stutthof where he was murdered. Dora was a trained nurse and after the war she worked in the Children's Holiday Home in Ostravice, which had not been damaged in the war and which had been converted into an orphanage and convalescent home for children, supported by the United Nations Relief and Rehabilitation Administration (UNRRA). Dora was known to all the children as Tante (Aunty) UNRRA.

Emilie married Dr Leopold Oppenheim in 1932 and emigrated to Palestine in the same year. Their two sons are also medical doctors.

Ostrauer Zeitung 7 November 1935: Portrait of a Lady.

Through the Mines

Heinz Vogel was the first Ostravak we met as we began our researches. He had written a brief autobiography for his grand-daughter[5] and posted it on-line where we found it when we were searching for Ostrava references. At the time, Heinz was living less than 10 miles away from our synagogue and so we were able to enrol him in our research team. He could remember pre-war Ostrava, could understand Czech and German and was invaluable in providing some context and background to the Ostravaks we interviewed subsequently.

Heinz was born on 18 February 1928 in Přívoz into a nice middle-class secularised Jewish family in the after-glow of the Austro-Hungarian Empire and the dawn of the new democratic Czechoslovak Republic. He was the only child of his parents, Alfred and Ethel née Slatner, and lived in a 3-room first-floor apartment on Nádražní Street (Bahnhofstrasse or Station Road), the road from the centre of Ostrava leading to the main railway station in Přívoz. Alfred was himself an only child, born to Adolf and Henriette née Kürschner on 6 January 1899 in Vítkovice.

Adolf came originally from Opava in Silesia where he had three brothers, one of whom was a partner in *Hermann und Vogel*, Opava's second largest department store. The whole family were fairly secular Jews, and so although they observed the major Jewish festivals and dietary regulations, the observance was fairly nominal. In this they were not untypical. Henriette came from Oświęcim in Poland, from a much more orthodox family and had some family members living in Bielsko-Biala in Poland. She would later teach Heinz some Polish for fun but it would in due course prove to be very useful to him, as would the family in Biala.

Heinz's mother, Ethel, was born on 6 December 1899 in Kunčice pod Ondřejníkem in Moravia. Her father, Leopold, was born in 1850 Nové Mesto in Slovakia, and was a widower with four children when he married Emilie née Altmann, who was born in 1863 in Muglinov, Ostrava. They were married in 1892 and had 6 children of whom the middle one was Ethel, Heinz's mother. The family initially lived in the village of Kunčice pod Ondřejníkem, where Leopold was an innkeeper and where all the children were born. In the early 1900's they moved to the nearby town of Frýdek-Místek, some 12 miles south of Ostrava, where Leopold opened a grocery shop which provided a good living for the large family. One of Ethel's step-brothers, Zigmund, known as Zigo and married to Bertl, had a tobacconist's shop in Ostrava and Heinz knew them well. They had a son, Pauli, who was a year older than Heinz and a very close friend of his, and an older daughter Edith who made a great fuss of Heinz. Their apartment and shop were very close to where Alfred, Ethel and Heinz lived when they moved to central Ostrava when Heinz was about 3 years old.

Alfred was what we would now call a social or cultural Jew rather than an observant or orthodox one. He did not believe in what he called 'organised religion' but he did recite the *Kaddish* or memorial prayer for the dead for a year after his father died. He held left-wing political views, somewhere between Communism and the Social-Democratic movement. He contributed articles and reviews of the latest productions at the German

Theatre in Ostrava to the German Social-Democrat newspaper and was very well versed in German literature and culture, except for music which he called *organised noise,* with the exception of Johann Strauss whose music he liked. During his early years in Vienna he always went to the Silvester or New Year's Eve concert of Strauss music. At home the family spoke German but on the census forms Alfred would always have described himself as 'Czechoslovak', not Czech, German or Jewish.

Thus Heinz was born in Ostrava into a family with roots in German-speaking Moravia and Silesia as well as Slovakia and Poland. He would attend both Czech and German language schools and would be at home in both languages. He received basic Jewish religious education but his family did not take their religion very seriously although his Polish grandparents were more observant.

Alfred had been called up into the Imperial Austrian Army towards the end of the First World War and was awarded the rank of lance corporal on demobilisation. He was posted to guard a railway line and railway crossing in Silesia against the on-coming hordes of Russians. In fact, the line had been closed and no trains ran on it and no Russians appeared to attack it, which did not worry Alfred who was a communist at the time and had pacifist tendencies. After the war, he studied in a commercial college in Vienna and later became a qualified dental technician. Dentistry was not to be his destiny. His father, Adolf, had been a representative of the Anglo-Elementar Insurance Company when he died of a heart attack in 1926, leaving his affairs in some disorder. Alfred had to take over from his father to restore the family finances and to pay off his debts, which he achieved thanks to his commercial training. By the time of Heinz's birth, Alfred was well established and the family finances were secure.

Alfred's business was commercial and industrial, not personal, insurance. He ran a Škoda car to enable him to visit his clients' sites which, in the late 1920's, suggests a significant level of commercial and personal prosperity. The roads round Ostrava were not paved and were thus in a poor state, so that all cars needed frequent servicing. When the family moved to central Moravská Ostrava, on Nádražní Street, in 1931, when Heinz was 3 years old, Alfred gave up the car.

Their new 4-room apartment was opposite the German Theatre and close to the Palace and Imperial Hotels, which were both very convenient for meeting clients and friends. Although Alfred had an office in the town centre, most of his working meetings took place in the cafes in the hotels, which is where much of the commercial life of Ostrava was conducted.

Heinz's two grandmothers both lived nearby as did several aunts and uncles. Equally important was the cinema, approached through an arcade off the road near grandmother Slatner's. This was where Heinz went to watch Mickey Mouse films and, later, westerns on Saturday mornings. Omama

Emilie Slatner with her grandchildren in 1937. Back row, l. to r. Pauli, Kurt, Edith, Heinz Front row: Eva, Vera and Emilie (aged 79). Kurt, Pauli and Edith were all murdered by the Germans.

(grandma) Vogel's flat was filled with antiques and the living room was furnished with Biedermeier furniture. More importantly from Heinz's point of view, there was a state of the art wind-up HMV gramophone with 78 rpm opera records which he was allowed to play.

From the family's own apartment Heinz could look out to the left, at the Palace Hotel across the road and to the right, at the large coking plant and coal mine. The Avenue of 28 Října, which crossed the end of Nádražní Street just outside their building on the left, led past the Imperial Hotel to the main Market Square and on to the bridge to Slezská Ostrava, while in the opposite direction it became the Vítkovice road to the steelworks with its huge blast furnaces, 2 or 3 kilometres away. To a small boy, it was a fascinating place. He did not notice the dirt and pollution until much later when he looked back on his life there. Many of the Slatner siblings died relatively young, from cancer. Whether this was caused by the pollution in Ostrava is not known but it is interesting to reflect that those of the family who moved away did not suffer this fate. Slezská Ostrava, neither then nor now of great interest, featured largely in Heinz's life as the home of the local Slezská Ostrava Football Team and its football ground.

Heinz went to his first school in Ostrava, the *Deutsche Gemeinde Volks und Mädchenbürgerschule*, near the New Town Hall. It was German-speaking as the Vogels spoke German at home. A year later, in 1935, Alfred was transferred to Opava, in the Sudetenland. In 1935, the German Sudeten Party, led by Konrad Henlein, was strong and increasingly strident in Opava and Jews were tending to keep their distance from these Nazi sympathisers whenever they could. Consequently Jews sent their children to the Czech Schools and so in Opava Heinz went to the Czech primary school. The change of language did not bother him, but his teacher did. She and he did not get on well and he received a '2' for behaviour from her. In those days, anything less than 1 was considered a serious matter. Fortunately, in 1937, the family moved back to Ostrava and Heinz went to yet another Czech school. He liked the school and his teacher and his behaviour was rewarded with '1'.

Czechoslovakia provided a welcome for refugees from the Spanish Civil War and the German bombing of Guernica and, later, to refugees from Austria after the *Anschluss* and from Germany after *Kristallnacht.* All these events received widespread coverage in the newspapers and even as a child Heinz was aware of the gathering threats and the general atmosphere of fear and foreboding. After September 1938 and the infamous Munich Agreement, all of this became much more intense. Invasion by the Germans became not merely possible but clearly probable.

On 23 September 1938, there was a national mobilisation of the Czechoslovak forces. Alfred was called to the colours for the second time in his life, this time for the Czechoslovak Army. Ten days later, he was back home, commenting sourly 'That's the second war I've lost – not bad for a convinced pacifist.' It would not be his last!

The Jews in particular were very conscious of the threats and were looking for places where they might find refuge and safety - places like USA, Palestine, England, Scandinavia and even the Dominican Republic although no-one really knew where that was, and Java in the Dutch East Indies. English lessons became very popular and Heinz still has his *Basic English for Czechoslovak Students* book. On 14 March 1939, all fears proved only too well-founded and all doubt vanished as the German troops occupied Ostrava

The Nazis were intolerant of any left-wing criticism, particularly from those who were German speakers. Alfred realised that he met all their criteria – and he was Jewish as well – so would certainly be on the Nazis' Black List. His freedom, at the very least, was under threat. He therefore went to Prague to 'disappear' but after a few days during which life appeared to return to some sort of normality he returned to Ostrava, determined to escape over the border to Poland. This appeared to be quite a simple undertaking because the Poles had occupied parts of the Czech border regions at the time of the Munich agreement, bringing the Polish border to the outskirts of Ostrava. One night, Alfred left with a guide to cross the border. They passed the German guards without being challenged, but the Polish border patrols spotted them and turned them back. This was quite dangerous as they then had to pass the German guards from, as it were, the wrong direction, but they managed it. Some days later, Alfred tried again with a different guide but when he realised that the guide was taking him along exactly the same route, he returned home himself without even attempting the crossing. He was a nervous wreck but he could not stay at home and so in the middle of April he set off again and this time in a much better organised fashion.

He was collected by car and was even permitted to bring a small suitcase with him. He was driven to the gates of one of the many coalmines in Ostrava, checked through and, together with two other escapees, escorted to the train which ran across the whole site. The three of them were then taken, on the footplate of the train, to the other side of the site which was in the area that was now Polish. From there, he was taken rapidly by car away from the mine and the border. Alfred then made his own way to Bielsko-Biała to his mother's family and sent a postcard home, with a coded message that he had arrived safely. The family's anxiety as they waited for the postcard to arrive, to learn if Alfred was safely in Poland, had been arrested or shot can hardly be imagined.

Then it was Ethel's turn to make her escape and leave family and home behind. She packed a couple of cabin trunks with the family's most treasured possessions, including the family photograph album, and sent it to an accommodation address in England, to be collected at some time in the future, hopefully. The next thing was to get across the border with her 11 year-old son without alerting the German authorities that she was about to do so. Emotional leave-taking from the family had to be avoided but at the time no-one realised this would be leave-taking for ever. It was, nevertheless, very stressful and emotional even if the cross-border route was less dramatic than Alfred's. Heinz remembers saying goodbye (*au revoir*, as they thought) to both his Grandmas, his Uncle Zigo, Aunt Bertl and his two cousins, Pauli and Edith. He told his schoolteacher that he was going away for a holiday. The teacher replied with a knowing smile that that was a good idea and wished him well.

In the end they crossed the road from their flat, and walked past the Palace Hotel and the Czech Theatre to the tram terminus where they took a tram to Karviná which was now very close to the moved border. Then a short walk through the woods to the border where the German guard was not very interested in them but 100 metres further on the Polish guard was much more suspicious. Heinz had been told to go and play in the woods while his mother talked to the Polish guard and explained to him that they were returning to Poland having come across the border to see Heinz's

Ethel, Heinz and Alfred, Kraków 1939.

grandmother. He seemed unpersuaded by this story and, after what seemed like an hour, Heinz was totally bored and went to see what was happening. When the guard saw him he asked Ethel if that was her son. When she confirmed it, he accepted the story and let them pass.

The two of them walked or ran about one kilometre up the road to an inn with a small shop that had evidently been identified to Ethel as the place to make for, because they were immediately taken in, given a cup of coffee and told to wait for about half an hour until the delivery lorry arrived which would take them to Bielsko-Biała. After an emotional reunion with Alfred and a good night's sleep, they set off to Kraków where the Social Democrat Party had a reception centre for refugees.

In Kraków, the Vogels were accommodated in one room with a Polish family by the Czechoslovak *Deutsche Sozialdemokratische Arbeiterpartei* (The Czechoslovak German Social Democratic Workers' Party) while their colleagues in Poland covered their immediate living expenses and a little pocket money as well. The family with whom the Vogels lived had two daughters age 11 and 13 and through them, as well as on the basis of Grandma Henriette's earlier Polish lessons, Heinz soon became quite fluent in Polish and had quite a pleasant time, with his pocket money to spend. Life for Alfred and Ethel must have been much more fraught as they waited and waited for the necessary papers to leave for anywhere safe but particularly England which Ethel's brother, Hugo, and his wife Edith, had managed to reach by early June, with the help of the Society of Friends (the Quakers). Their daughter, Eve, had been sent on ahead by her parents on one of Nicholas Winton's *Kindertransports* without her or her parents knowing if they would ever see each other again. After what seemed like an eternity but was actually only a few weeks, the Vogels' names appeared on the approved list for England and so, on 16 June 1939 they took the night train to Gdynia and then on to the *MS Sobiesky* for the crossing to Dover. Although they had awful premonitions they did not know at the time that war would break out in less than 3 months. The ship and the crossing did not make much of an impression on Heinz despite his never having seen the sea before, but he was impressed by the red and white coach of the East Kent Motor Company that took them to London.

After a brief stay in a hostel in West Ham, during which Heinz received his first taste of English school life, the Vogels were sent back to Kent, to live in Montrose College, Cliftonville, which had been converted into a refugee hostel with one family per room and where they were able to receive Red Cross letters from home. Education was not neglected, as one of the refugees was a former German-speaking headmaster who set up a 'school' for the children there with the help of some of the other refugees, including one young 'teacher' who was keen on DIY and who imbued Heinz with his lifelong love of engineering and practical work. Alfred, with his habitual

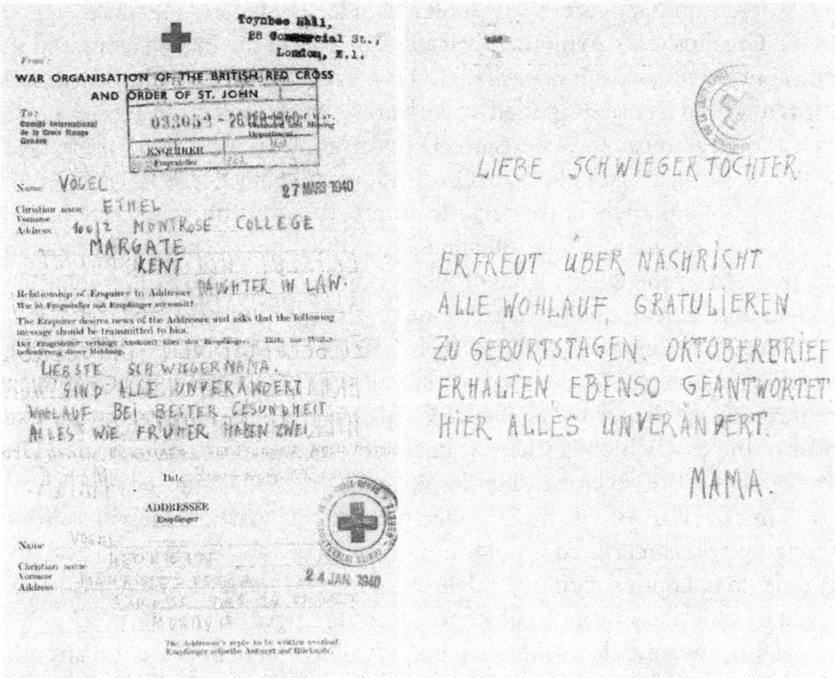
Toynbee Hall,
28 Commercial St.,
London, E.1.

From:
WAR ORGANISATION OF THE BRITISH RED CROSS
AND ORDER OF ST. JOHN

To:
Comité International
de la Croix Rouge
Genève

ENQUIRER
Fragesteller

Name VOGEL
27 MARS 1940
Christian name ETHEL
Vorname
Address 100/2 MONTROSE COLLEGE
MARGATE
KENT

Relationship of Enquirer to Addressee DAUGHTER IN LAW.
Wie ist Fragesteller mit Empfänger verwandt?

The Enquirer desires news of the Addressee and asks that the following message should be transmitted to him.
Der Fragesteller verlangt Auskunft über den Empfänger. Bitte um Weiterbeförderung dieser Meldung.

LIEBSTE SCHWIEGERMAMA.
SIND ALLE UNVERÄNDERT
WOHLAUF BEI BESTER GESUNDHEIT
ALLES WIE FRÜHER HABEN ZWEI

Date

ADDRESSEE
Empfänger

Name
Christian name
Vorname
Address

24 JAN 1940

The Addressee's reply to be written overleaf.
Empfänger schreibe Antwort auf Rückseite.

LIEBE SCHWIEGERTOCHTER

ERFREUT ÜBER NACHRICHT
ALLE WOHLAUF GRATULIEREN
ZU GEBURTSTAGEN. OKTOBERBRIEF
ERHALTEN EBENSO GEANTWORTET
HIER ALLES UNVERÄNDERT.

MAMA.

Red Cross letter to Ethel from Henriette Vogel, 1940.

disdain for any form of authority, did not want Heinz to have such a narrow German education and so took him away and enrolled him at the local English school, despite Heinz having only rudimentary English.

After a few months, the Vogels moved to nearby Birchington on Sea for Alfred to join what was effectively a Czech Home Guard battalion and, later, the Czech Brigade of the French Army at Agde in the south of France in May 1940. From there they were sent north just in time for the German breakthrough in France leading to the evacuation from Dunkirk. This meant that the South Coast of England was declared a 'Protected Area' and all aliens, refugees from the Nazis or not, had to leave. It is why Ethel and Heinz ended up in Marple in Cheshire while Alfred and his colleagues retreated southwards to the Mediterranean coast from which they were evacuated by ship to Liverpool. Back in England in July, Alfred was based at Malpas in Cheshire, which meant that he could return home on leave from time to time. On one occasion, the whole family took a trip to the centre of Manchester and visited Lewis's, one of the biggest department stores in the city. After only a few minutes, Alfred insisted they all rapidly left the building. He confessed that the crowds terrified him as he imagined the carnage if a dive-bomber attacked the store.

Alfred's military career now took a turn for the better. He was assigned to the Czechoslovak Armoured brigade attached to the British army and in due course crossed to France after D-Day. The brigade helped to surround the remaining Germans in the Dunkirk area, which took quite a time. Once that was cleared up, they were attached to Gen. Patton's 2nd US Army and with him headed east to liberate Czechoslovakia. They got as far as Plzeň in western Bohemia where they had to stop because at the Yalta conference, Stalin, Roosevelt and Churchill agreed that most of Czechoslovakia was to be liberated by the USSR. That probably counted as the fifth different army he had joined before he managed to be on the winning side.

Once they joined up with the Russians, Alfred was able to go to Prague and Ostrava, where he discovered that all the remaining family had been murdered. At the same time he realised that the communists would take over in the end, which is when he decided to return, demobilise in the UK and apply for British citizenship despite his earlier left-wing views.

After the war Alfred and Ethel had a variety of jobs managing hostels for foreign workers recruited into the cotton mills in Lancashire, before finally ending up in London, running a delicatessen in Hampstead which was much loved by the local European descendants and refugee community.

Heinz meanwhile completed his education and became an aircraft designer and aerodynamics expert, helping to design and develop aircraft like the Avro Vulcan delta-winged jet bomber, the Saro Pricess 10-engined Brabazon flying boat, the English Electric Canberra RAF bomber, the BAC One-Eleven short-haul airliner, finishing up with the Airbus A-320 airliner and finally becoming Chief Engineer of Future Projects and Research at British Aerospace, involved in the Anglo-American supersonic vertical take-off Harrier replacement.

Today (2016) in Britain there is an argument about whether parents should be allowed to take their children out of school during term, for a holiday. One view is that even the loss of a week will jeopardise their future educational success and career. It is therefore worth noting that Heinz had attended eight different schools by the time he was 13, in 3 different languages one of which he did not speak at all when he arrived. He had missed several months of schooling while suffering the trauma of leaving his home and family, worrying if his father – and indeed all the family – would be killed, and having to settle in a totally foreign environment. He ended his career as Emeritus Professor of Aeronautical Engineering at Kingston University.

Nice Nazis

Ostrava was home to a large German-speaking minority in the inter-war years and it is not surprising that some of them held anti-Semitic and fascist

Heinz Vogel, 2015.

views and that some actually joined the Nazi party. What is surprising is how some of these Nazi sympathisers actually behaved when faced with real Jews who were their neighbours. Nazis, like Jews, are not all the same.

Alfred was not the only person who used the mines as an escape route to Poland in the period between the German invasion of Czechoslovakia in March and the outbreak of war in September 1939. **Artur Radvanský** was born into an orthodox Jewish family in Radvanice near Ostrava in November 1921. His parents ran a shop selling ironmongery and shoemakers' supplies and Artur helped after school. He had two younger brothers, Karel and Max, who were deaf-mutes and Artur regarded it as his duty to protect them so he became - in his own words 'a tough guy'. After the German invasion in 1939, they were taken off to Kroměříž where they reportedly died of TB but Artur knew this was euthanasia. In 1939, Arthur left school and was apprenticed to the firm of Sigmund Roth, a shop with shoemakers' supplies in Jirásek Square in Ostrava. Artur was a member of *Hashomer Hatzair,* a left-wing Zionist movement and was heavily influenced by them. In 1939, he started to take people over the border:

> I took them to the spoil heap of the Ludvík colliery from where they were taken underground across the border to Poland. Because I played there as a child before the war I knew every tree in the area. Those people were mostly Jews. My parents knew nothing, I was afraid to tell my father. But it so happened, that I took across the borders two Germans. They reached Katowice. Between Katowice and Kraków the Poles caught them and the Polish military police forced them back. They shouted and consequently were caught by the German border patrols. They beat them till they revealed who took them across the border and that was that. We were arrested in the night of 27 August 1939 and because I was not yet 18, my father was taken as well.
>
> We were taken to the Gestapo in Ostrava and a small miracle happened there. There was a German soldier, a chauffeur, named Gebauer. He was a shoemaker who used to come to my father to buy supplies and on top of that they were together in the war at the time of the Austrian Empire. When we were taken for an exercise in the prison he said: '*Um Gottes Willen,* Markus what are you doing here?' My father told him what has happened. Gebauer put on his uniform and a rifle as if he was taking us for an interrogation and led us out. He put us into a car and took us home. There we packed a few things and he took us to the Polish border. We spent one night in Karviná-Sovinec at my father's friend who took us further to a Polish-German border. At that time there was not yet a war and hence there was a German-Polish border. We wanted to get to the Polish Army but we

> were late by 12 hours. If we had been 12 hours earlier our fate could have developed quite differently. We were caught by the German military police.

Artur spent the whole of the war in a series of concentration camps but, being the tough guy that he was, he somehow managed to survive and was liberated by the Americans from Mauthausen camp. His parents did not survive.

Heinrich Goldberger (1844-92) had a general store in Hrabyně, near Ostrava. His son Ferdinand was born in 1878 and ran a successful business in Ostrava selling butchers' supplies with sausage skins as his speciality. Ferdinand's own son, born in 1907, was called Heinrich after his grandfather. Heinrich Jr. had a poor non-Jewish German-speaking friend, called Müller, who used to eat lunch a few times each week with the Goldbergers, and was so penurious that these were almost the only lunches he had. In the early 1920s, Müller ran away from home and was not seen again for many years. Meanwhile, Heinrich had completed his studies but was unable to find a job as it was the depth of the depression, so he joined his father's business. This did not last very long as the two of them did not get on well, so Heinrich left and developed a successful career selling imported Chinese sausage casings. He married and had a son, Petr.

Then, in 1939, shortly after the German invasion, Müller appeared again in Ostrava, this time in the uniform of an SS captain. Ferdinand met him one day in the street and was told to send his son, Heinrich Jr., to Müller's office the following day. An instruction like that, from an SS officer, caused great anxiety but had to be obeyed. So Heinrich went to the office, he did not see Müller but had his passport taken away and was left to wait in great trepidation. After some time, his passport was returned with an exit visa stamped in it! With it he was able to get out to London and from there tried to get visas for his wife and son. He obtained the visas, but in the meantime Britain declared war on Germany in September so there was no possibility of them making use of the visas. Heinrich left England for Rio de Janeiro, to be in a neutral country. From there he was able to get visas for his wife and son who undertook the tortuous journey by train from Prague via Berlin to Moscow (the Russian-German pact was still in place) and on to Kobe in Japan. Thence they took a boat to Rio arriving after a journey lasting 41 days! They subsequently emigrated to the USA. The rest of the Goldberger family, who remained in Ostrava, were murdered by the Nazis. Heinrich later heard that Müller had been shot by the SS for helping Jews to escape.

Ann Altmann (née Körner) has a remarkably similar story about her father, Štěpán (born 1913). Štěpán qualified as a lawyer at Charles University, Prague . He had really wanted to be a philosopher but his father persuaded him that he would have a better living as a lawyer, for in the eyes of Jewish parents down the ages a well-stocked larder has been preferable to a well-stocked mind if one has to choose. In the event, Štěpán managed to make a successful career as a philosopher.

Shortly after the German invasion, Štěpán was staying with his parents in Ostrava in their apartment when a young man in Nazi officer's uniform knocked on the door and said 'Štěpán, if you do not leave today, you will not be able to leave tomorrow!' Štěpán left that night with two friends and walked across the border into Poland. From there they travelled via Sweden to England where they joined the Czech Army although it is unlikely (according to Štěpán's daughter) that any of them made much of a contribution to the Allied victory. While serving in the army, Štěpán took a PhD degree in philosophy at the University of Cambridge and he ended his career as head of the Department of Philosophy at Bristol University. His parents were killed by the Nazis, probably in Auschwitz. He never saw them again. Many years later, Štěpán's daughter, Ann Altman, discovered the last letter from her great-aunt and uncle which mentions the deportation and death of Anny and Emil, Štěpán's parents. The translation reads:

> Brno, May 17, 1942
> My beloved best darling boy,
> In two days we are leaving for the unknown. If fate has meant for us never to return and perish nameless, in a foreign land, we at least want to tell you that all our thoughts are with you and even the slightest spark of hope that we might see you again gives us the courage to continue to live because, at the time I am writing this to you, it takes more courage to live than to die...We are praying for you that a friendly fate shall protect you from tragedy and enable you to become a good and happy man.
>
> You have always been a good son. May God repay you for your love.
>
> Aunt Nelly, Uncle Carl and also Aunty Anny, although of the latter I cannot say it with certainty, are at the present time in Poland. Poor Uncle Emil died on November 13th, 1941 in Litzmannstadt (Lódź) of bronchitis due probably to excessive strain.
> ....
> To you, the best imaginable, everything that parents could ask for, for their only, dearly beloved child. I cannot go on. May God protect you.
>
> Countless kisses, your Mother
>
> Hopefully it will be granted us to see you, dearest Leo, again. Heartfelt kisses, Your Father.

The Nazi officer had been at school with Štěpán. It is tempting to think that the two Nazi officers were one and the same, Captain Müller. Perhaps they were, but Heinrich was 5 years older than Štěpán and, presumably, their friends would also be of different ages. If so, there were two Nazi officers in Ostrava for whom decency was more important than fascism.

Sandra Renton's husband, George (né Jiří Reichenbaum) was born and lived in Ostrava. His father was an architect and master builder and used to play chess with the local Chief of Police. One day in 1939, the Chief of Police telephoned him unexpectedly to say 'If I don't see you again, best of luck'. George's parents took this as a serious hint and so told Mitzi (their maid) to put the dinner back in the oven. They took a small case and went into woods on the Polish border and across to George's grandparents in Poland. When they phoned Mitzi she told them the police had arrived 20 minutes after their departure. They later managed to take a boat from Gdansk to Malmö and thence to Tilbury. George's father was not able to take up his old profession and so he worked as a warehouseman in the East end of London. At one point he had to sell his bed and sleep in an armchair so that he could use the money to send his two sons to school. George achieved a doctorate in physics and became a patent attorney while his younger brother, Peter, became a consultant radiologist at University College Hospital in London and published a number of medical textbooks. In his spare time, he wrote and published a book on the lost synagogues of London.[6] The number of lives saved by one simple humanitarian telephone call was considerable.

Not all 'Nice Nazis' were Ostravaks. **Otto Hornung's** father was a lawyer in Ostrava and was sent to Nisko in 1939. After the camp was closed, he tried to escape into Poland where he was subsequently shot by the Nazis. Otto escaped across the Polish border, having taken on the identity of a local postman apparently delivering mail to Bohumín, then in Poland. Otto's mother moved to Prague with her daughter. She was Hungarian and was in contact with her family in Budapest. Her sister, Zuzi, invited her to come back to Hungary 'to buy horses'. At that time conditions for Jews in Hungary were somewhat less dangerous than they were in Czechoslovakia and so Otto's mother dressed in her best clothes and went to the local Gestapo office to appeal for an exit permit. The Gestapo officer said to her, 'I will let you go on one condition only'. She expected the worst but the condition was that she had to promise not to return to Czechoslovakia! Once in Budapest, she received a Swedish *Schutzpass* (safe permit) issued by Raoul Wallenberg and was able to find somewhere to live in a Swedish protected house.

Unfortunately the German Nazis took power in Budapest also and began to send all the Jews to concentration camps, including those in protected houses and including Otto's mother. She had been hiding in the cellar of the house and was found by a young Hungarian Nazi. She appealed to him, in good educated Hungarian, 'You must have a mother and/or a sister and would not treat them like this'. He looked the other way as she made her escape!

The whole project of researching the story of Ostrava and its Jews was initiated by a *sefer torah* saved and catalogued by the Jewish Community of Prague with the agreement and support of the German authorities (see Introduction – Scroll 129). While the Germans would have had their own reasons, possibly financial, for giving their approval to the plan to save the scrolls and keeping alive those involved in the cataloguing, at least some good came from their support. They may not have been disinterestedly decent, but they were not wholly evil. Niceness was not too common and manifestations of it should be remembered.

A Magic Doll - Book cover.

A Magic Doll

Gita Rind (née Thieberger) published a lovely simple story for children, *A Magic Doll.*[7] It tells of a young girl who has to leave her home with her parents and flee to another country to avoid a war. Almost the only thing she can take with her is her doll, which becomes her constant and sole companion in the new country where she does not know the language and so cannot speak to the local children. But the doll, being magic, can speak to her.

After a while, she learns the language and plays with the other children. The doll speaks to them, too. The war has reached their country and food is very scarce when one of her new friends falls dangerously ill and wants the magic doll for herself as she thinks it will help her get well. The sick girl's mother offers a bucket full of potatoes and carrots for the doll and the deal is done. The sick girl recovers, and the heroine of the story, her mother, and the doll all survive. Magic indeed. The father has gone off to war and is never seen again. The story is, of course, essentially true and autobiographical.

Gita's father, Josef, came from a rabbinic family. His father, grandfather and almost certainly earlier generations were rabbis. His father, Chaim, had 6 children of whom 5 were communists and the other child, a daughter, followed her father's religious tradition, but had a communist husband. So Josef had a religious and socialist background and was a Social Democrat in his youth. His wife, Matylda ('Tilda') Lichtblau, came from a much more conservative background. Tilda's grandfather, Samuel Storch, whom Gita called Opa Sami, was an ardent supporter of the emperor but Tilda became a communist and persuaded Josef to join the Party.

Tilda's mother married Josef Lichtblau (an uncle of the artist Eric Lichtblau – Leskley), a well-known tailor in Ostrava. Family tradition is that there was a pogrom in Ostrava in 1920 and his tailor's shop was ransacked and everything of value stolen. Probably it was a general riot against declining living standards with the targets being any shops or stores, examples of prosperity. Many of these shops were Jewish owned so the anti-poverty riot inevitably had anti-Semitic overtones. Josef died of a heart attack on the spot, leaving his wife with 4 children. Shortly afterwards, Gita's grandmother met and married Max Teichner, who became a treasured grandfather to Gita. Maxi (as Gita called him) had fought in the Czech Legion and with the Russians against the Germans in the First World War and had married a Siberian girl with whom he had a child. The whole family returned to Czechoslovakia after the end of the war but sadly the child died and his wife returned to Siberia, so Maxi and she divorced. Gita traces her communism to stories she heard from Maxi:

> Tilda had originally wanted to study art and design in Hamburg but her grandfather had been against it on grounds of propriety. She had

> therefore decided to study languages in Prague but that was no more acceptable. So she stayed at home, looked after her grand-parents and studied languages in her spare time, for which she later earned her degree. After Tilda married Josef Thieberger, she taught English at home while Josef devoted himself to his photographic business. Tilda, Josef and, later, Gita, lived in an apartment in the Storch family house where Gita, the first grandchild to both families and first great-grand child to the Storch's, recalls being terribly spoiled by all the rest of the family members. Gita recalled: '...Scenes like coming in from a walk in the park with mum and before she could open the door grandmother was there with a chicken patty on a lovely little glass plate and mother saying 'don't feed her now she'll have lunch soon'. 'One little patty won't hurt her', except there were three and by the time the argument finished so were the patties.
>
> Behind the house was a largish backyard, which was divided by a short picket fence behind which Great-Grandfather Samuel grew all sorts of berries, gooseberries, cranberries etc. At the back was a gazebo covered in creepers. We used to have Succot[8] in there and on rainy summer days the adults played cards.

Then, in March 1939, this capitalist-socialist paradise came to an end, as the Germans invaded and suddenly Gita could no longer go and play in the park, or even walk to her father's shop on the pavement (she used to ride her tricycle there but that was no longer allowed by the Germans). In October, Josef was deported to Nisko but managed to escape over the border into the Soviet Union from where he was able to send news to his wife through the communist underground, urging her to join him. Through the communist underground, Tilda was able to get false papers showing that she was an expatriate Russian living in Czechoslovakia and so was able to get official permits to join her husband in Moscow. It was 1941, during the period of the Soviet-German pact.

Once the Germans had attacked the USSR, Josef joined the Red Army as an air-force photo reconnaissance officer and then went missing, presumed killed in action. Tilda and Gita were left alone in Siberia for the rest of the war. Tilda scraped a poor living teaching English and German but times were hard and food was very scarce. The story of the sale of Gita's doll for some vegetables is true and the vegetables helped the two of them survive. In 1947, they returned to Czechoslovakia but soon decided to emigrate to Palestine and took a train to Italy as the first part of their journey.

Bert and Leo, two of Tilda's brothers, had already emigrated to the UK and persuaded Tilda to join them rather than going to Palestine. In Italy,

Gita, then 14 years old, fell in love with the man she later married. He emigrated to Australia and in 1952 Tilda and Gita left to join him and lived happily in Kangaroo Valley.

The rest of Gita's family did not fare so well. Her great-grandmother luckily died at the age of 93 just before the transports but Opa Sami went to the gas chambers at the age of 87. Opa Maxi died in the streets of a Polish ghetto (he was a diabetic and starved to death), Grandmother was gassed and the rest vanished, all except one of her mother's cousins who went with the Kindertransport. She was about 13 at the time. She is the Lizzi after whom the doll in the book is named. The house is still there, Janáčkova10. Lizzi lived on the top floor.

Ostrava to Hampstead via Ecuador

By the time **Bernhard Krieger** died in 1925, he was the owner of a large general store on the main street in Ostrava which he ran with his three sons. According to a glowing obituary in the *Ostrauer Zeitung*, he was very well-known and respected both in the commercial world of Ostrava and in the Jewish Community. Two daughters of his elder brother, Adolf, had married two sons of Albert Wechsberg, the banker, much to the dismay of Albert, who did not think the Kriegers were his equals, socially or financially, despite the encomiums lavished on Bernhard.

Bernhard's third daughter, Ida, wanted to become a nurse, which meant remaining unmarried, but her parents did not approve. Of course, nice Jewish girls got married and had babies, so Ida was introduced to and married Eliáš Rothfeld, a lawyer, in 1913. They moved to Kraslice where they had two children, Walter in 1914 and Käthe, four years later. Eliáš had left-wing political views and a social conscience, and worked *pro bono* for people who could not afford his services.

Käthe went to London in the late 1930's to study English and secretarial skills at Pittman's College, while Walter studied law at Charles University in Prague. Their education was cut short by the German invasion of Czechoslovakia. Funds for Käthe's course and living expenses stopped and Walter was excluded from the university. Käthe's friends then used to take her home for meals and she received ten shillings a week from the British government for her support.

Ida and Eliáš made their way to the UK, probably in 1938 or very early in 1939, bringing a suitcase in the bottom of which they hid some of the paintings they had collected and which they removed from their frames, as well as Ida's jewellery. Stella, their grand-daughter, still has two of her grandmother's rings. Walter managed to make his way from Prague to London via Italy, and the whole family was reunited in the unromantic location of the Edgware Road in London. Even this took money and so Ida and Eliáš found jobs, but only as domestic servants, which was quite a contrast with their previous life in Ostrava. Käthe met her future husband Peter Rosza in the Czechoslovak Club in Tottenham Court Road. In his spare time, Peter played chess with Eliáš. Life was grim and the future looked even grimmer, and so Peter and Käthe decided to leave for somewhere more promising. The only countries that would accept Jewish refugees at the time were Ecuador and the Dominican Republic, and they decided on Ecuador.

Peter and Käthe married in Ecuador and shortly afterwards, Ida, Eliáš and Walter joined them. Ida later said that she remembered 'watching the U-Boats go by' on the voyage out, but this was almost certainly before war was declared. Initially, Walter drove a tractor on a farm and Peter became a milkman, as he was the only one of the family able to count up to ten in Spanish! Eliáš opened a store selling bicycle wheels and similar items in Quito. Walter started to make gloves from home while Käthe and Peter opened a coffee house which was frequented especially by immigrants - a small piece of home transplanted to the Southern hemisphere. Cakes baked using recipes from Ida's cookery book must have helped. The establishment provided a reasonable living, if not great comfort. The young couple's daughter, Stella, was born in 1944 and her sister, Vera, in 1947. Walter, meanwhile, had married, divorced, and moved to Los Angeles, where he worked for Sears Roebuck. His second cousin, Eleanor, was in touch with him and they subsequently married and moved to Philadelphia, where his parents visited them and had an entertaining photograph taken of the four of them as rather unlikely-looking Jewish cowboys. Later they moved back to Ecuador, where Walter opened a sock factory, demonstrating great entrepreneurial flexibility.

In 1951, Peter and Stella came to London to visit Peter's uncle and mother. The latter had been widowed and had come to London to see her son just before the war, but had been told by her family in Slovakia not to return. Stella was invited by her great-uncle to stay in London to learn English, which she did, subsequently taking a secretarial course. Peter meanwhile opened a grocery store and had two shops in Quito, with a partner. He later sold it as the family moved to Guayaquil where he started selling jewellery, Swiss watches and fluorescent light tubes. Stella worked for the UN Food and Agriculture Organisation in Ecuador but in 1961 she went to Zurich to start an interpreting course at the university. When the attempted US invasion of Cuba, the Bay of Pigs, started, she feared an imminent outbreak of war and phoned her great-uncle who told her to come immediately to London, which she did. It was there that she met her future husband, Anton, and married him. They live in Hampstead and now have two sons and five grand-daughters.

Ecuadorean cowboys!

A Railway Carriage all to Myself!

According to his younger daughter, **Zikmund Folkart** was a much better sign-writer than businessman but he managed to support his wife and two daughters in modest comfort. Zikmund was a Zionist and not very observant of his religion but Lydia remembers attending the children's service in the main synagogue on Friday evenings Lydia and her older sister, Ruth, went to the Jewish primary school in Ostrava, not out of any great religious devotion but to avoid any possible upset to Zikmund's Czech- or German-speaking clients! All the same, Lydia learnt and spoke fluent and correct German.

They lived in an apartment in a block near the New Town Hall, built by an insurance company. The block was built round a small square with a swimming pool in the centre, which must have been great fun for the children. Lydia describes her childhood as 'comfortable and uneventful' which is probably how most people would have described life in Ostrava in the 1920s and early 30s. Zikmund had been born in Vítkovice but his father, Ferdinand, had not bothered to register their nationality after the foundation of Czechoslovakia in 1919, as it did not seem very important at the time. As a consequence, the family were officially stateless[9]although this was in practice of no importance and their comfortable uneventful life could continue happily until 1939 when, suddenly, nationality became of vital importance.

After the German invasion Zikmund was arrested, actually by the Czechoslovak police, but released after a short time. He then fled to Kraków and on to England via Sweden, leaving his wife and two daughters to follow him. Elisabeta, Lydia's mother, did not want to leave her mother, but Elisabeta's brother managed to get papers for the family to leave for Poland on 21 August 1939. There were some difficulties raised by the Polish border guards but a German soldier helped them to get across and they spent the first night in Těšín, in Poland. From there, they went on to Kraków to stay with Zikmund's sister, engaged to a Mr Feldman who had a glass factory and shop there.

The respite was short before the Germans invaded Poland and war broke out. Mr Feldman fled East and reached England after the war, but the Folkart family were now stuck in Kraków. The Germans commandeered the flat in which they were living and a *Luftwaffe* officer was billeted with them. He was 'very decent' and brought them bread and some other basic necessities unobtainable through normal channels. The Germans wanted the keys of the glass factory and asked Lydia to deliver them, as she spoke German and some Polish, which was sufficiently similar to the Czech dialect spoken in Ostrava. The Luftwaffe officer promised that no harm would come to her.

The mother of Anne Karpf, the writer, had lived in a flat across the landing from the flat where Lydia and her family were staying. She was a well-known concert pianist and had fled from Kraków leaving her maid in charge of the flat, which was subsequently taken over by the Germans and occupied by 5 officers. Lydia, age 10, became their interpreter! When the

Germans demanded that all Jews over the age of 12 should wear a white armband with a blue Star of David, to mark them out from the general population. Lydia felt deprived as she was not obliged to wear it.

Elisabeta's younger sister, Charlotta, had married Šimon Wasserlauf in Ostrava. She had two stillbirths and her husband died in October 1939, leaving her alone, but she was able to send some parcels to the family in Kraków with the help of a non-Jewish lady who acted as courier, since the situation in Ostrava was not as bad as in Poland. The Germans very soon commandeered the whole building and the Folkarts had to move out, returning to Ostrava with Lydia travelling as the daughter of the lady courier. They moved in with Charlotta ('Lotte') who had a flat near the site of the Zerotingasse synagogue, although by then the synagogue itself had been destroyed.

Elisabeta could not cope with the situation either financially or psychologically, and so Lydia and her sister were sent to Jewish orphanages in Prague. In 1939/40 they were still functioning as was the Jewish Gymnasium which Lydia attended. She also now had to wear a Star. But even this refuge did not last and in 1942 Lydia had to return to Ostrava. She cannot now remember why, but it is probable that the orphanage was being closed. So 13 year-old Lydia took the overnight train from Prague to Ostrava, all alone. A German soldier and his 'floozy' got onto the train and demanded Lydia's carriage but the Czech guard refused to allow it, quoting German regulations that a Jew was not allowed to travel in a carriage with other people; Lydia retained her sole occupancy.

In Ostrava Lydia took up her studies at the Jewish school but was deported to Theresienstadt in September 1942 along with almost all the Ostrava Jews. Her mother and older sister were then deported to Auschwitz and Lydia volunteered to go as well rather than be left behind by herself, but she was at first refused as the trucks were full. An extra truck was found so that in the end Lydia, too, was sent to Auschwitz. Fortunately, she and her sister did not stay long there but were transferred to Öderan, a sub-camp of Flossenbürg for women, some 50 miles west of Dresden. Their mother, Elisabeta, was murdered in Auschwitz.

In Öderan they worked outside – an *Aussenkommando* – converting an old textile mill to munition production. This involved carrying and laying lengths of heavy electrical cable but it was a great improvement on conditions in Auschwitz. As they were clearing the mill they found old pieces of linen and one of the girls, who had been a corsetiere in her previous life, made brassieres for them all. The psychological boost was even greater than the physical one and they began to feel almost human once again. Of such things can self-worth be made.

There was a prisoner-of-war camp nearby and they were able to get some news of the progress of the war, and knew of the Allied advance. In April

1945 they were transported back to Theresienstadt in open cattle trucks when the camp was abandoned and Lydia was liberated from there by the Red Army. Lydia went with some small children to a castle in Czechoslovakia to recover after the war and then flew to Scotland with a group of Polish boys, while her sister went to Prague with her boyfriend.

Lydia had made contact with her father in England at the end of the war through a Czech newspaper and he was waiting for her when she came down by bus from Scotland to Windermere. She subsequently married, had children and practiced as a child psychologist, her own experience giving her a great insight into and empathy for the traumas suffered by children.

From Draper's Shop and *Haganah* Spy to *The Talk of the Town*

The Talk of the Town was a famous nightclub in London's West End from 1958 to 1982. Judy Garland, Eartha Kitt, Shirley Bassey, Frank Sinatra, Engelbert Humperdinck, Val Doonican, Dusty Springfield, Tom Jones, Lulu, Matt Monro, Cliff Richard, The Shadows, The Seekers, Stevie Wonder, Sacha Distel and Neil Sedaka all appeared there. The musical, *End of the Rainbow* is set in the club. It is an unlikely place to find a former spy for the *Haganah*[10] as its manager. And he was a most unlikely person to fill either role.

Třinec is almost equidistant from Ostrava and Bielsko-Biala, each about 20 miles away, and it was here that Henry Heitlinger was born in February

Heitlinger's shop in Třinec.

1921. His mother, Regina Huppert, had close family in both Ostrava and Bielsko-Biala who ran butchers' shops, restaurants and an inn. Her husband, Josef, also had family in Bielsko-Biala but they were poor. Regina and her husband ran a business selling clothing, sewing materials and even shrouds and coffins in Třinec.

Henry and his younger brother, Otto, grew up in a comfortable orthodox Jewish household and were looked after by a nanny, Grete. Henry attended the Czech primary school and later the Czech Gymnasium in Český Těšín. As there was school on Saturday morning, Henry would stay over Friday night with the Grün family in Těšín, returning home on Saturday evening after the end of the Jewish Sabbath. The Grüns were the parents of the younger Grüns who rented rooms in the Heittlinger's house.

The business prospered and three assistants were employed, one of them Leo Schlachet, who played a key role in Henry's later life. Leo was the younger brother of Artur Schlachet, who was later the father of Mihal Efrat (see Chapter 7). Henry started to learn French at school, supplemented by twice weekly private lessons, and he also studied the violin with lessons twice a week. In 1934 Henry had his *Barmitzvah* in the synagogue in Třinec, 'attended by many people'. Henry was aware of the growth of anti-Semitism in Germany and Austria from reading the newspapers and knew about the anti-Semitic agitation stirred up by Henlein, the head of the German Nationalist Party (a proto-Nazi party) in Czechoslovakia but Henry did not experience it himself at school or socially.

In 1935, Regina took Henry to stay with Dr Ascher in Aix-les-Bains in Switzerland, to improve his French. When not studying, Henry and the other students went for long walks and played sports. Henry was a keen walker and later joined the Czech Touring Club, an event with crucial consequences for him. In 1936, he went to Besançon University to perfect his French and in 1937 he went to Nancy University to continue his French education.

By 1937, Josef was concerned enough about the political situation to visit Palestine to check on conditions there, with a view of possibly emigrating. Shortly after his return, the infamous Munich Agreement was signed and the Germans occupied the Sudetenland. At the same time, the Poles occupied Třinec and the surrounding area and the Heitlingers woke up to see Polish soldiers patrolling the streets. Henry's school moved to Frýdek, still under Czechoslovak control, and he had to enlist in a new Polish school in Třinec.

Josef was summoned to see the Police Chief and told that he had to leave Třinec. Naturally, he asked for time to sell his house and business and was told that he could take them with him if he wished but must leave as soon as possible. So he left for Palestine, leaving Regina to run the shop and look after the children. Henry received a smuggled message from his schoolmaster that he should come to Frýdek in June to take his final matriculation examination. The family tried, in vain, to obtain visas for England and, in late May, after the German occupation of the remainder of Czechoslovakia, Henry and the girl student who had brought him the teacher's message crossed the border into Czechoslovakia and reached Frýdek. Henry lodged with a Jewish family whose husband had won the Iron Cross in the First World War. He passed his examination and returned to Třinec, taking a train to Ostrava and then a tram to Karviná, at that time in Poland, and on to home. His diploma was posted to him, so that it would not be found on him if he was stopped at the border.

Living conditions became increasingly difficult and Regina contacted a friend of the family, Mr Klotzman, who lived in Warsaw and owned a razor blade factory in Rishon le Zion in Palestine. She sent some suitcases with clothes and other items to the Klotzmans and arranged to stay with them in case of emergency. At the beginning of August, Henry and Leo Schlachet, the shop assistant, decided to flee to Kraków to get away from the border and, hopefully, the danger of war. Henry fell ill there and Regina came to visit him at the end of August. It was the last time they would see each other for a long time; and the last days of peace.

On 1 September, the Germans invaded Poland. Henry, despite being ill and weak, took a rucksack with a few clothes and he and Leo joined the thousands of others fleeing the advancing army. The streams of refugees were easy targets for Luftwaffe pilots who shot at or bombed them. Henry and Leo, like everyone else, begged or stole food and slept in abandoned barns. When they reached a small town, they would immediately head for the synagogue in the hope of being helped by the local Jewish community. Despite the appalling conditions, they usually did get food and shelter, at least for one night, before setting off again.

On one occasion they were sleeping in a barn when a party of Polish soldiers came and demanded to see their papers. The only identity document that Henry had with him was his membership card for the Czech Tourist Club! The Polish soldiers could not read but were finally convinced that it was not German, so left the fugitives alone.

They arrived in Kolky on the eve of Yom Kippur, the holiest day of the Jewish year and a 25-hour total fast. They found some shelter with a Jewish tailor but he had no spare food, and so Henry and Leo found a white beet in a field, usually given to cows to eat, and ate it raw as preparation for the fast! Henry commented in his memoir that it was the most devout service he had ever attended. At the end of Yom Kippur they set off eastwards once again and reached Lwów, then controlled by the Russians. There he fortuitously ran into the family of Dr Grunbaum, who had come from Kaunas in Lithuania where they had met Regina and Otto, who had managed to reach Lithuania safely. Henry immediately wrote to her and Regina replied telling him to join her in Kaunas and asking a friend of hers to help him on

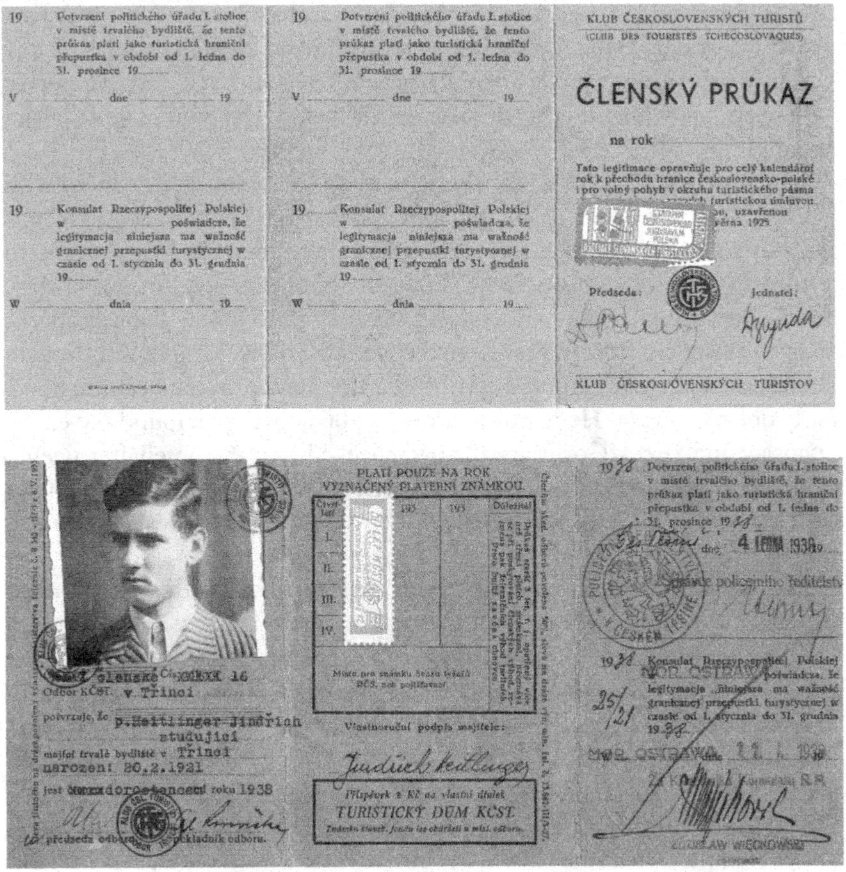
19 Potvrzení politického úřadu I. stolice v místě trvalého bydliště, že tento průkaz platí jako turistická hraniční propustka v období od 1. ledna do 31. prosince 19......

V .... dne .... 19....

19 Konsulat Rzeczypospolitej Polskiej w .... poświadcza, że legitymacja niniejsza ma ważność granicznej przepustki turystycznej w czasie od 1. stycznia do 31. grudnia 19......

W .... dnia .... 19....

KLUB ČESKOSLOVENSKÝCH TURISTŮ
(CLUB DES TOURISTES TCHÉCOSLOVAQUES)

ČLENSKÝ PRŮKAZ

na rok ....

Tato legitimace opravňuje pro celý kalendářní rok k přechodu hranice československo-polské i pro volný pohyb v okruhu turistického pásma ... turistickou úmluvou ..., uzavřenou ... října 1925.

Předseda: Jednatel:

KLUB ČESKOSLOVENSKÝCH TURISTOV

PLATÍ POUZE NA ROK VYZNAČENÝ PLATEBNÍ ZNÁMKOU.

Místo pro známku Svazu tešařů ...

Vlastnoruční podpis majitele: Jindřich Heitlinger

Příspěvek 1 Kč na vlastní útulek TURISTICKÝ DŮM KČST.

členské číslo 16
Odbor KČST. v Třinci
potvrzuje, že p. Heitlinger Jindřich studující
majitel trvalé bydliště v Třinci
narozen: 20.2.1921
jest ... roku 1938
předseda odboru ... pokladník odboru.

1938 Potvrzení politického úřadu I. stolice v místě trvalého bydliště, že tento průkaz platí jako turistická hraniční propustka v období od 1. ledna do 31. prosince 1938.

... dne 4 LEDNA 1938

Správce policejního ředitelství

V ČESKÉM TĚŠÍNĚ

1938 Konsulat Rzeczypospolitej Polskiej MOR. OSTRAVA poświadcza, że legitymacja niniejsza ma ważność granicznej przepustki turystycznej w czasie od 1. stycznia do 31. grudnia 1938.

25/21

MOR. OSTRAVA 11. I. 1938

Henry Heitlinger's Touring Club membership card.

the journey. At the Polish-Lithuanian border, which was controlled by Russians, the peasant guides demanded more money than had originally been agreed, which meant that Henry arrived in Lithuania with almost no money or possessions, but he was able to reach Kaunas and meet up with his mother and brother.

Life in Kaunas was almost normal at that time and they were able to cable Josef in Tel Aviv that they were all safe and trying to obtain entry visas for Palestine. The visas for Regina and Otto arrived but not for Henry or Leo. Regina had their Czech passports which were sufficient to apply for transit visas through Russia. Once again, Henry and Leo could not get transit visas without the entry visas, but they did finally arrive. Josef sent money from Palestine for the trip, from Kaunas to Kiev via Moscow and then on to Piraeus and thence to Haifa. On the train journey, some very drunk Russian soldiers offered a large amount of money for their shoes. Sadly, Henry and

Leo did not have any spare shoes so the deal was declined. In Kiev, they sold a cardigan and used the money to buy food and had enough cash left to buy tickets to see *Aida* at the Kiev opera – 'magnificent and lavish'. There cannot have been many Jewish refugees, fleeing the Nazis, who paused to watch an opera!

Finally they reached Haifa where there was an emotional reunion with Josef. The family lived in a small flat in Tel Aviv and Leo moved to Rishon-le Zion to a job in the Klotzman's razorblade factory. Henry went to Jerusalem to enrol at the Hebrew University but found the lectures boring, mainly because his Hebrew was not good enough to follow them properly. So in 1941Henry wrote in French to the manager of the King David Hotel in Jerusalem, and was appointed controller of customer accounts at the hotel. Early one morning – Henry started work at 06.00hrs. – he found the entire Yugoslav and Greek Governments had checked into the hotel after fleeing from the invading Nazis. They all tried to change their home currencies but Henry, who had experience of suddenly worthless currencies, refused to do so.

Early in 1942, the situation in North Africa and the Middle East looked very dark for the British and Czech forces there and Henry volunteered to join up. He was posted, unheroically, to the NAAFI (Navy, Army and Air Force Institutes – the canteen for the British armed forces) in Cairo. Henry used to send rice in an envelope back to his parents in Tel Aviv, as it was unavailable in Palestine at the time. Henry was demobilised in March 1946 and returned to his old job in the King David Hotel. In June, Regina came to Jerusalem to renew her Czech passport and she and Henry had lunch together in the hotel. After lunch the hotel operator received a telephone call telling her to evacuate the hotel as it was about to be blown up! Henry saw some men in Arab dress carrying guns going into the hotel through the tradesmen's entrance and shortly afterwards there was an enormous explosion – the west wing of the hotel, where the Government and Army offices were – had been blown up. The rest of the hotel was then commandeered to replace the destroyed offices and many of the staff were laid off but Henry was kept on to help with administration and to make an inventory of all the hotel assets that had to go into storage.

Shortly afterwards Henry was approached by the *Haganah*, to provide information about happenings in the hotel and to do so through one of the hotel gardeners. Henry married Grete, a girl he had met in Cairo, in the office of the Chief Rabbi of Tel Aviv. They lived in a small flat in Bakaa, a suburb of Jerusalem.

When the UN observers came to Palestine to try to sort out the Jewish-Arab problems there was a welcoming cocktail party at the King David Hotel and Henry asked Count Bernadotte for his autograph. Henry was the last person to see him alive, except for his killers.

After May 1948, when the State of Israel came into existence, the UN stationed their observers in the hotel and Henry continued his gentle espionage activities with Shlomo the gardener. During the fighting for Jerusalem Henry could not leave the hotel as the Haganah battled with the Arab forces for control of Jerusalem. Even after the cease-fire, life was very difficult, food was short and rationed and things were very tense. Henry applied for hotel school in Lausanne, with a recommendation from the General Manager of the King David Hotel, and was accepted.

Henry's further career as a hotelier in Switzerland and later in the UK is uneventful. Indeed, when he wrote his memoir, it stopped at the point that he arrived in Lausanne. He had had enough excitement for one lifetime. No doubt his experience as a spy, of watching, listening and remembering, stood him in good stead in his last position as manager of the *Talk of the Town* nightclub in London. But this time he did not pass on the secrets he discovered.

The Story of a Handbag Revealed

West Hill Court, a block of 38 apartments, stands in extensive grounds in Highgate, North London. Built in the early 1930s, it is adjacent to Hampstead Heath in a very sought-after residential area which has always been very popular with artists and literary figures. It also became very popular with refugees fleeing Nazi persecution before and after the Second World War.

When Dr Deborah Brown was house-hunting and first saw Apartment number 23 in the early 1990s, it was unoccupied but still furnished. She remembers that her immediate reaction was, 'How curious to find such large pieces of middle-Europe furniture in a small apartment in North London'. The place was being sold by someone in Switzerland who had inherited the apartment from the recently deceased owner. The vendor arranged for the furniture to be removed but when Dr Brown moved in, in September 1992, there were still a few things left.

One was a slim black leather handbag that had slipped down between the structure of a built-in cupboard and the wall in the small room at the far end of the hall. After finding it, Dr Brown put it aside somewhere and forgot about it. Over the years she moved again several times, inadvertently taking it with her, and it was not until 2011 that she rediscovered it. The handle was broken and the lining had been ripped which was why, presumably, the bag had been pushed to the back of the cupboard in the first place. Slipping her hand down the rip in the fine calfskin lining of the bag Dr Brown found four small coins trapped at the bottom between the lining and the outer leather. There was one German coin and three Czech coins, all from before the war. Inside the bag she found two ticket stubs for concerts in the Royal

Coins from the handbag Deborah Brown found.

Albert Hall in 1947. The concerts suggest a person who enjoyed good music, but it was the coins that really interested Deborah and jogged her memory.

Deborah remembered that she had bought the apartment from the heir of Otto Rosenberg, who had died in 1989, and that the porter of the block of apartments had mentioned that Otto's wife, Edith, had been in concentration camps during the war. She had died the year before Otto. In her later years she had been a sculptress and Deborah also remembered that one of Edith's sculptures had stood on a bird bath in the garden of West Hill Court. Inspired by these memories and the possible historical interest of the bag, Deborah started an Internet search and found the Rosenbergs mentioned in a newsletter article by the Kingston Ostrava Group, as Edith and Otto had come originally from Ostrava. Deborah contacted the Group and so started the research into Otto and Edith's life story.

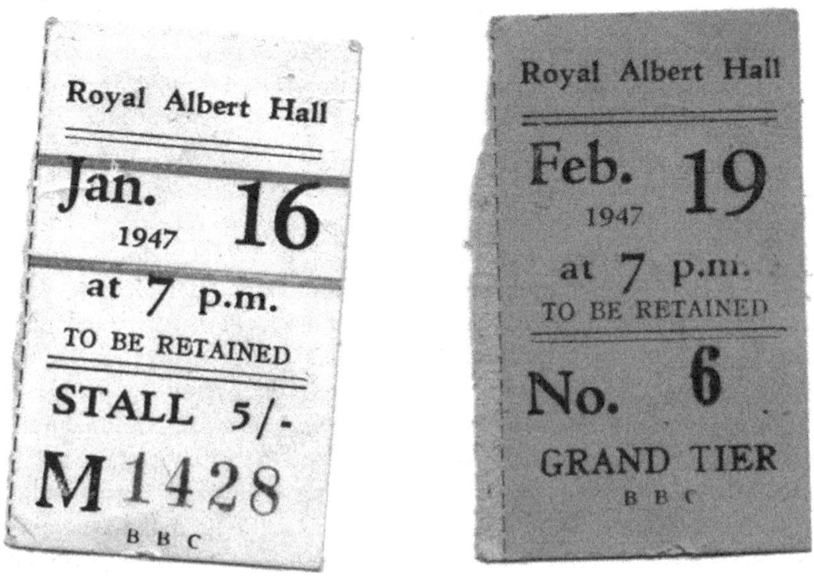

Ticket stubs from the handbag.

Edith (née Löwy) was born on 24 April1906 in Moravská Ostrava. Edith's grandfather, Salomon, ran a bar/restaurant known as *The Grand Automat*, with his wife Johanna (née Steiner). They had six children, four sons and two daughters. After the death of Salomon, the bar/restaurant passed to Arnold, Edith's father and Salomon's second son. Johanna subsequently married Hermann Reiss who had a business making ladies' and gents' wear and trousseaux. After the death of Herman, Johanna ran that business with her children, particularly her son Jean, the eldest. As well as the home market it had an extensive export market particularly in Scandinavia. The trade mark for their shirt business was a lion, on a bolt of cloth.

Arnold married Marie Feinerová (born 23 March 1887) in 1905 and Edith was born in 1906. Twin boys, Hanuš and Bedřich were born in 1910. After Arnold's death in 1926, the businesses were transferred to Marie, Bedřich and Hanuš while Edith worked with her uncle Jean in the Reiss business. They had a new four-storey Reiss building erected in 1929 to replace the previous two-storey building. The shop was beautifully fitted out with plate glass display cases and the shop had central heating! A newspaper report described it as being 'like a jewel-box'.

Edith's brother Bedřich had fathered illegitimate twins with Marie Wenig, a nurse. They were born in 1935 but the younger twin, Emil, died within 2 days although the elder twin, named Bedřich like his father, survived. Bedřich junior lived with his mother in Ostrava as his parents were not allowed to marry because of their religious and class differences. Bedřich Jr. studied mining engineering in the Mining High School in Ostrava and eventually married Marghita Skala with whom he lived in Opava before moving to Winterthur in 1968, probably advised by Edith. They had one child, Elen who married Christopher Gräzer. Elen and Christopher have two daughters. Bedřich Jr. was the heir of Edith and Otto and it is he who sold the apartment in West Hill Court in 1992, following Otto's death.

As a child of a wealthy family, Edith had a series of governesses, including a baroness, allegedly part of the Austrian Imperial Family. Arnold was artistically inclined, a connoisseur and collector of fine and beautiful things. Edith inherited these tendencies and, indeed, artistic skills. He also wrote poetry and his literary proclivities were also shared by his daughter. She studied languages at Vienna University, then at the Sorbonne in Paris and took her PhD in philology at Charles University in Prague.

Arnold had been a soldier in the Austro-Hungarian army in the First World War, and stationed on the Italian front. He was a telephone operator and was buried alive when his blockhouse was destroyed by artillery fire during one attack. He was the only member of his group to survive and was rescued on his 10th wedding anniversary. To commemorate the event he had gold rings made, with the date engraved, for each member of the family. Edith wore this ring until she was forced to give it up, with all her other

Advertisment for H. Reiss.

jewellery, to the German authorities in 1939. After the war, Edith tried to obtain compensation from the German authorities, without success.

According to Edith, her mother, Marie, 'almost became a Jewish Member of the Czechoslovak Parliament', but failed to get elected. Marie did become a strong Zionist, inspired by her brother who died of his wounds in the First World War. She attended one of the World Jewish Congresses and was a friend of Dr Chaim Weizmann, subsequently the first President of Israel. Marie was a strong character who did not easily tolerate disagreement. Edith clearly inherited her strength of character.

Marie's family had a large estate in Moravia. Marie had fair hair and 'a little upturned nose' which Edith thought was because Marie's family must have had a number of Protestant ancestors. This was perfectly possible, since in the 17th century a number of Moravian Protestants had converted to Judaism rather than become Roman Catholic or be executed - the choice offered by the authorities. Edith said that as a young girl, she, too, had platinum blonde hair. She was a very good-looking girl.

On the day she was awarded her PhD in 1929 she married JU Dr Otto Rosenberg in a register office, not in a synagogue, despite her mother's Jewish and Zionist inclinations. Otto and Edith had been in the same class in the Gymnasium in Ostrava and both studied at Charles University. They lived in Prague after their marriage. Otto Rosenberg had been born in Ostrava, in January 1906. His parents, Hugo and Gisela (née Huppert), ran a restaurant in Vítkovice.

Otto studied international commerce in Vienna before studying law and qualifying as a lawyer at Charles University in Prague. From July 1929 until August 1932, Otto was an articled clerk in the offices of JU Dr Paul Posamentir in Ostrava and later practiced on his own in Ostrava. Subsequently he was appointed a military judge. He sat on a number of trials of German-speaking Sudeten agitators before the war. As a consequence, he was on a Nazi black-list and the Czech authorities issued him and Edith with a second passport, in case of trouble. Edith and Otto set up an anti-racist organisation in Prague. Otto was the treasurer and administrator. When the Germans invaded Czechoslovakia, in March 1939, Edith burned all the papers relating to this organisation to stop them falling into the hands of the Nazis. Otto was away on a trial and Edith sent him a message to leave the country immediately and not to return to Prague in case the Nazis caught and arrested him. He fled to Kraków, where he had an aunt, and ultimately made his way to England. He joined the Free Czech Army and was made a lieutenant. Otto was sent to France, was badly wounded in Dunkirk and invalided out of the army.

He was then employed by Grosvenor House Limited as book-keeper and later as Chief Cashier. When the previous Chief Cashier was demobilised and returned to Grosvenor House, Otto worked as a Czech interpreter for a

Edita Rozenbergová née Löwyová.

Restaurant owned by Otto Rosenberg's parents in Vítkovice.

sub-office of the Office for Economic Warfare of the USA. In 1947, he became the London representative of a Czech Import/Export company, probably Centrotex Ltd.

When the Germans invaded Ostrava in 1939 they had seized the family businesses and Edith's twin brothers had been deported to Nisko in Poland. When the Nisko camp was dismantled, they returned to Ostrava. From there they were eventually deported and both were murdered in 1942 in Treblinka.

After Otto had escaped from Czechoslovakia and reached England, he sent Edith a visa for her to join him in England. Edith said that the Gestapo confiscated it. She had suffered a serious attack of tuberculosis, but although she had recovered she feared that the 'foggy weather' in London would cause a resurgence of the disease and so was unwilling to go there! Edith's mother had been arrested in Ostrava by the Gestapo and Edith spent some time persuading the authorities to free her. This also prevented her leaving for England, so she remained and spent time with her mother in Ostrava. Edith remembers seeing the main synagogue in Ostrava burning in June 1939 when she was on the way to the cinema. She made arrangements for some furniture, which had been made especially for her, to be sent over to England but the Germans prevented it. (After the war, however, some of it was in fact shipped and was the furniture seen by Dr Brown in West Hill Court.)

Edith's mother left Ostrava and went to live on the country estate of a Roman-Catholic admirer to avoid the Gestapo, but later she moved to Prague where she married Dr Richard Kohn, who died in 1942. In Prague Edith studied art and fashion at the Rotha School. This was very useful, she said, as after the war in London, she was able to earn money by sewing gloves, making jewellery out of pieces of leather and by making and selling miniature copies of famous paintings on imitation mother-of-pearl.

Edith received a letter from the Prague Jewish Community ordering her to join the assembly for transportation to the Łódź ghetto. Her mother went to the Gestapo to volunteer to join her. They stayed in Łódź working for almost 3 years and were sent to Auschwitz only when the Russian advance neared Łódź. While there, Edith gave English lessons in return for small amounts of food. She also heard rumours there about the Warsaw Ghetto Uprising.

In tapes recorded for the Imperial War Museum in London after the war, Edith describes her time in Łódź and Auschwitz, where her mother was murdered. She describes how, one evening in Auschwitz, the Gestapo guard told her and the other women in her barrack, that 'tomorrow you will all be gassed'. One of the women became quite hysterical as a result, but Edith and another prisoner spent the night, their last as they thought, talking about all the places they had ever visited. In the morning, they were all sent to Öderan, to work and not to be gassed. Finally she was sent to Theresienstadt where she was liberated. Then she finally came to London. Edith comments in her tape that being in Auschwitz, 'You lost all ability to feel pity'. She also said that she lost all ability to feel the cold, which stayed with her even after the liberation.

In her taped memoirs,[11] she says of life in Auschwitz, 'It was so unimaginable that someone had to stay alive to report it'. The tapes run for almost 7 hours and confirm Marie Eichler's comment that Edith could talk and talk! It is clear that Edith, despite the lengthy answers to the questions on the tape, is omitting much detail either because of tact or poor memory.

Edith described how after her release from Theresienstadt she went back to Prague. Some friends found a copy of her pre-war entry visa to England so she took it to the British consul who suggested that rather than go through the official channels to get her to the UK he would send her as an interpreter with a plane-load of orphan children who were being admitted to the UK. Otto was told of this and arranged to have a week's leave from his job immediately Edith arrived. Unfortunately, the flight was delayed by a week and when it finally arrived in Windermere in the Lake District in the North of England people there told her that Otto could not be found. So it was only about 3 days later that Edith herself phoned London and found him. Her first words to him on the telephone, after 6 years of separation and war, were 'You idiot! I have been waiting for you for 3 days now!'

After the war, Otto and Edith lived in a very small apartment in Bayswater, in West London. Some years later they moved to West Hill Court.

It remains to be discovered how the bag came to London. We know from Edith's tapes that the Gestapo confiscated many of her possessions and that her lovely pigskin suitcase was stolen almost immediately she arrived in the labour camp. However, we also know her mother hid possessions with her Catholic boyfriend and that Edith returned after the war to arrange for furniture she had stored with a furniture maker to be shipped to England. This was, of course, the 'Middle-European' furniture that Deborah Brown discovered. Also, in 1945, just before Edith flew to England, the daughter of a Czech journalist, who had been Edith's pupil in Ostrava, returned some clothing that Edith had lent her. The bag may have been included with them. We may never know, but we do know that Edith loved beautiful things. In a slightly fictionalised autobiography[12] she wrote after the war, a character tells how she treasured her father's wallet of 'fine crocodile skin', bought in Venice. The black crocodile handbag may be associated with this memory.

Edith had mental and physical problems after the war and suffered for several years from serious depression. Otto devoted himself to looking after her. Edith describes how, during a serious depression, she went with a friend (an officer friend of Otto who, having been in Auschwitz himself was able to empathise with her better than anyone else) to a concert in the Wigmore Hall in London and expressed surprise at how few musicians there were. Her friend pointed out that it was a concert for string quartet! In the tape, Edith comments that she was very disturbed at the time but also mentions a friend of hers, living in Israel after the war, who said, 'But Edith, you were never normal!'

Otto could not practice as a lawyer in England and so worked as a salesman for a textile company. Edith, when she was well enough, made pieces of jewellery and painted miniatures on imitation mother-of- pearl, which she sold through department stores in London as well as directly to small shops.

As a child in London, Peter Barber knew Otto and Edith well. They were friends of his parents as they had been before the war in Czechoslovakia. He remembers Edith as 'a bit of a misery' but Otto as very lively. Since Otto and Edith had no children of their own, Otto would take Peter and his younger brother to the circus and Peter thought Otto was great fun. Peter has been able to add more detail about Edith's painting business. Peter's aunt, Helga Wolfenstein (1922-2003), was born in Brno. She later changed her name to the non-Germanic Velin. She was a professional artist and had been employed in the artists' section in Theresienstadt. Like Edith, she had been very traumatised by the war. She and Edith became friends and, after the war, used to spend time together and went on holidays together, particularly to St Ives. Helga painted at least some of the miniatures which Edith framed and sold.

Bertold Eichler was a close friend of Otto Rosenberg in Ostrava before the war. Bertold escaped to England just before the war, married and had two children, David and Marie. Marie remembers that Otto made a great impression on her mother's family when he came to see them once in Deepcar UK, near Sheffield in the north of England, where they lived, in full Czech cavalry uniform! After the war, Otto and Edith often visited the Eichlers in Deepcar and when Marie went to college near London she used to visit the Rosenbergs at their house in Porchester Terrace, Bayswater and later in West Hill Court. Marie says that Edith was a 'great talker and a great salesperson. She never stopped talking and if she tried to sell you something, you had to buy it just to get her to go away!'

Marie also remembers Bedřich Jr. coming to Deepcar immediately after the war to stay with the Eichlers for several months.

Marie describes Otto and Edith as being deeply in love with each other, despite continuously arguing and screaming at each other. They were passionate about opera and often used to go to Covent Garden, in full evening dress as was the custom then. Otto was fun and charming, a real ladies man. He was also very fond of greyhound racing and used to watch it regularly at the local Haringey track. Once, when Marie visited and asked where Otto was, Edith told her 'The dog has gone to the Dogs!'

Edith described herself as being 'odd'. She was always much more interested in art, music, literature and beautiful things than the more mundane everyday necessities. She had studied the philosopher Brentano and nursed an ambition to write a book on 'pure beauty'. She said that she did not know where the food shops were in Ostrava, but knew all the antique shops and florists. That changed after the war and she could identify all the food shops in Highgate, but Marie Eichler remembers that whenever she visited Edith in London, she almost always had to go to visit an art gallery with her. As a child, Edith received a book about Greek and Roman heroes from her father after a trip to Vienna. She said that she was so taken with the beauty of the stories that she cried! Later, when she gave English lessons in Łódź in exchange for small bits of food, she always used these stories in her lessons.

Edith was ultimately advised to write about her wartime experiences and to take up her art again, as part of her therapy. She took a course in writing at the City Lit[13] in London and wrote her memoirs, in the form of apparently fictional short stories, published as *I Did Survive* under the *nom de plume* of ELRO (**E**dith **L**öwy**Ro**senbergová). They are clearly based very closely on Edith's actual wartime experiences and the incidents described in the tape that Edith made for the Imperial War Museum are almost identical to the ones in the stories. In the stories, she describes the heroine as having a close friend, a Czech officer in London, who was a friend of her husband and who spent a lot of time with her helping her through the long period of depression. The story is not specific, but the implication is that the heroine and the officer were more than good friends. The implication from Edith's tape was also that the Czech officer and she were more than merely friends, although the tape is not clear on the point. Peter Barber suggests that the Czech officer may have been Bruno Goldman, an Ostravak known to the Barbers and Rosenbergs. He was, apparently a serial womaniser and had

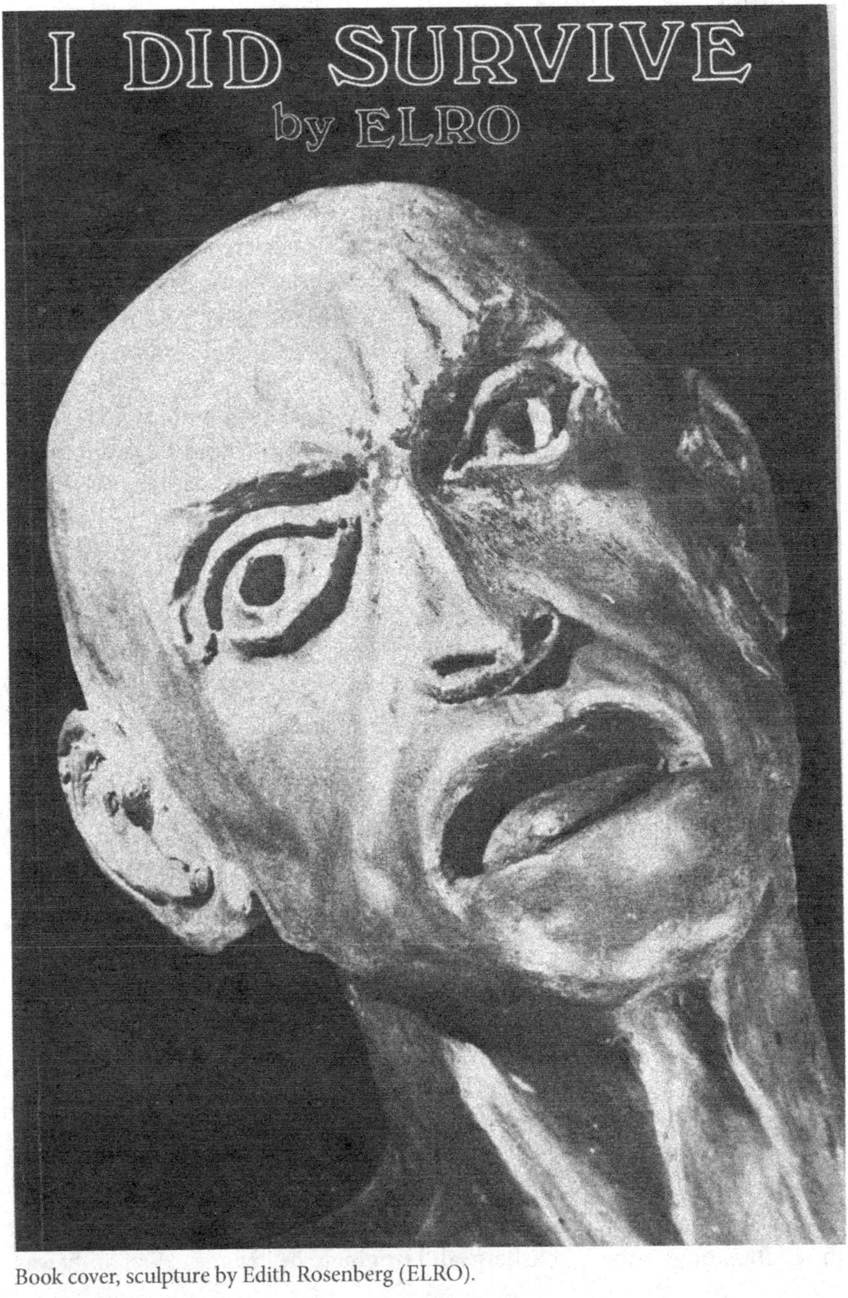

Book cover, sculpture by Edith Rosenberg (ELRO).

been barred from the Barber house as he flirted with the *au pairs*! The therapy was extremely successful and Edith blossomed into the bright person she had once been, while Otto went into a decline and, in turn, became a misery himself!

In fact, Otto had Alzheimer's disease and Edith researched treatments for it (this was before the internet!) and ultimately found some special medications being developed in Hungary and imported them into the UK specially for him.

The head on the cover of her book was sculpted and cast in bronze by Edith herself, who attended art classes in Camden Institute, London. People in West Hill Court recall her sculpting in her small apartment and also, in the summer, in the garden of the block of apartments. She cast a small sculpture of a baby for one of her neighbours to celebrate the birth of her grandson in 1979. The same neighbour also bought a bronze of dancing figures by Edith, 'as it is so joyful'. A copy of the photograph of the Head was deposited in the Imperial War Museum, London. Camden Institute organised a posthumous exhibition of Edith's works.

Edith died in 1988 and Otto in 1989. Marie remembers that Edith contacted her when she became ill and was admitted to hospital at the end of her life and Marie came to London to see her. Marie was with her when she died and had the awful job of telling Otto, who had Alzheimer's disease, of Edith's death. Otto died a few months later and they are both buried in Hoop Lane Jewish Cemetery Golders Green, London in London. The bottom line of the inscription reads '*Deeply mourned by the Wenig-Graezer family.*'

Bedřich Jr and his daughter Elen visited Otto and Edith in West Hill Court. A photograph taken at the time shows clearly the 'middle –European' furniture that Deborah Brown remembers. Other photographs show many of Edith's sculptures and suggest a fairly cluttered apartment. Edith was certainly no "hausfrau".

A Horse and Cart, a Chicken-Coop and the Medal of Merit

Family tradition, as described by Josef Wechsberg, is that his grandfather Albert Wechsberg, the founder of the family fortune, came by himself to Ostrava in 1847 from 'The East' on a hay cart (or rather a cart with corn), as a 16 year-old, to try to make a living. One imagines him lying on the corn sacks on a sunny autumn afternoon, chewing on a straw, dreaming of fame and fortune while the horse plodded slowly into town and violins played gently somewhere in the background. It is definitely the stuff of fairy stories. Sadly, the reality is rather more prosaic.

Albert actually came from Šenov, which is all of 10km from Ostrava, and so he was certainly not venturing into the unknown nor did he arrive from the East, although the Wechsbergs did originate in Poland. His family was reasonably wealthy and able to back him and his business ventures with money. His arrival in Ostrava with a cart full of corn certainly implies as much. Nor was he alone in Ostrava – not that his immediate family were far away – as Dr Josef Wechsberg was in Ostrava and a member of the first Board of the Community. Albert's story was remarkable enough without the family myths.

He combined his corn-trading with being an inn-keeper in Orlová and his first five children were born there. He extended his interests into milling and then into money-lending before opening the Wechsberg Bank in the centre of town. The bank counters occupied the ground floor, the administrative offices the next and then the three sons involved in the business lived on the upper floors with the youngest, Siegfried, on the top floor. Albert became active in the Community, and contributed to the building fund for the synagogue and the Jewish school.

Albert had married his cousin, Františka, daughter of Pinchas Wechsberg, who came from Staré Hamry some 50 kms from Ostrava. They had 9 children, six sons and three daughters:

1. Vilemína (1861)
2. Rudofína (1863)
3. Hugo (1864)
4. Rudolf (1868)
5. Max (1870)
6. Gabriela (1871)
7. Evžen (1873)
8. Alfréd (1875)
9. Siegfried (1878)

Františka's sister, Anna, married Dr Josef Wechsberg who was the Vice-President of the Community. The lack of surviving records means that we cannot be certain of the relationship between Alfred and Josef but they were contemporaries. There cannot have been many Wechsberg families in the close vicinity of Ostrava in the mid-nineteenth century and, as Albert and Josef married two sisters who were also Wechsbergs, we can reasonably assume that Albert and Josef were brothers or, at the very least, cousins. Unusually, the three elder sons did not join Albert in the business but established independent careers. Hugo studied chemistry, moved to Hamburg and later married in Berlin where he subsequently died, childless, in 1922. Rudolf qualified as an engineer and Max became a well-known gynaecologist in Vienna. He did not marry but devoted much of his time to having affairs and gambling. His father had to bail him out on a couple of occasions and he committed suicide in Siegfried's apartment at the age of 40.

The three youngest children joined Albert in the bank. Josef, the son of Siegfried the youngest who lived on the top floor of the bank building, became a well-known writer in the USA and it is to him that we owe much of the information about the family. Josef also had a penchant for the raffish life, and so a soft spot for his uncle Max, although he probably had no personal memories of him but relied on stories his mother told him. She, very obviously had a soft spot for Max, who always brought her presents whenever he visited and was very complimentary about her.

The three families lived above the business but Albert and Františka had a villa out of town and the three sons had to report to him regularly on the bank's activities. Františka died in 1904 and Albert invited his 16 year-old grand-daughter, Martha Gold, Rudolfína's daughter to join him to run his house. This cosy arrangement survived until just before the First World War.

Evžen married Irma Krieger from a family who were prosperous members of the Ostrava community but Albert thought that the Kriegers were not his social or economic equals and did not approve of the match. Nevertheless, Siegfried married her sister, Hermina Krieger, and so once again two brothers married two sisters. In November 1914 Siegfried was sent to the Russian front and was killed on active service, leaving Hermina with two sons, 7 year-old Josef and Max, only 2 years-old, living on the top floor of the bank building.

Several of the books that Josef later wrote in English in the USA describe his early life in Ostrava and there is a gentle sense of loss for a vanished golden age. He describes the confectioner's shop where the youngsters had their first dates. The pastry was not as good as at Rokyta's, which was the town's most fashionable place, but they had privacy there 'with no familiar faces, shocked relatives or snooping teachers. Small boxes, dimly lit and cosy.' Later he describes The Yokohama night club, the most interesting features of which were the three *chambers séparées* in the rear of the room: 'We all went there and drank third-grade champagne with the 'girls...' The Boccaccio Bar was another place of slightly *risqué* entertainment. Josef wrote:

> It was one of the reasons why the people of Ostrava liked to think of their town as an 'American' town. You could order such authentic American inventions as Dry Martinis, Tom Collinses, or Manhattans, none of which the customers were able to pronounce correctly...The jazz-age had reached out from that far-away exotic bewildering continent they called America. Everybody sang 'Yes, we have no bananas' in Czech or German translation...

He also talks about the more cultured aspects of Ostrava life, including the class hierarchy involved in visiting the theatre, with the directors of the Vítkovice Works going to the theatre only on Mondays and Fridays so they did not have to mix with the rest of the population who went on Tuesdays and Wednesdays.

As a child, Josef had a serious lung infection and was sent to Merano in Northern Italy to convalesce and it was a favourite place with him for the rest of his life. He was brought up speaking both Czech and German and never lost his German accent. At the age of eight he started to learn the violin and music remained a lifelong passion of his. He attended the local grammar school in Ostrava and later studied music and business in Vienna. He later moved to Paris where he studied law at the Sorbonne and became a qualified lawyer in 1930. Meanwhile, his skill as a violinist gave him the opportunity to travel and he played in the orchestra on board the liners *Normandie* and *Île de France* and travelled for the first time to the USA. While studying in Paris, he played the violin in a number of night clubs and he appears to have enjoyed his exposure to the seamier side of life. He wrote articles for Prague magazines about his experiences and this started his journalistic career.

Back in Ostrava Josef started to practice law but in 1936 he became the parliamentary secretary of the Jewish Party in the Czechoslovak Parliament and was sent to America in 1938 to explain the Czechoslovak position with regard to the Sudetenland issues. After the Munich Agreement in September 1938 he was advised not to return to Europe so he and his wife remained in America and he became an American citizen in 1944. In 1943 he had been conscripted into the US Army and was sent to Europe towards the end of the war. He was thus able to return to Ostrava after the armistice and he wrote an entertaining but ultimately sad book about his return. He light-heartedly describes his trip from the American lines across Czechoslovakia, swapping American cigarettes for vodka and rides with the Russian troops, and then the mood changes as he reaches Ostrava:

> We were on Street of 28th October. Rubble, emptiness, disorder, chaos. Yet right here had been the most expensive shops – haberdashers, costumiers, hats, jewellers, bookshops, department stores, an antique shop. Moravská Ostrava was a fast-living, fast-spending town. People liked to buy and show off. This street had been the fashionable promenade, the *corso*. Everybody came here between five-thirty and seven p.m.; everybody who 'counted' and wanted to be seen. The large windows of the Baťa Shoe Company building, an ultra-modern steel-and-glass construction was boarded up…The old pillar with the statue of Saint Nepomuk, which had been erected after an epidemic of cholera had miraculously by-passed the town in the 'eighties, still stood in the middle of the square. From Těšínská Avenue I took the first side street to the right. It was called Temple Street. The synagogue stood there. I turned into the street and walked half a block – and stopped.

> For a moment, I thought I had taken the wrong turning. There was no synagogue there. Perhaps it had never been there. The house that I remembered to the right of the synagogue was still there, and the print shop on the left side. In between, where I remembered the synagogue – no, I couldn't be wrong – was a vacant lot, covered with scattered clumps of weeds and bush grass. Scraps of paper and rubbish lying around. The grass and weeds looked as though they had been there for ever. Or at least five years.

In fact, the synagogue had been destroyed five years previously, in June 1939. Josef found a former waiter who remembered the Hotel Royal, where the waiters always wore dinner jackets with green or brown hats, and the Boccacio Bar: 'Sure', he said. 'I used to work at the Palace Café in the old times. Later in the Boccaccio Bar. Those were the days! Until 1939 I made more money on tips in the Boccaccio Bar in one night than working a couple of weeks in any coffee-house in town. The German dogs changed all that. First thing they did when they came into town was to put up a notice: "This place Verboten to Jews." Or maybe it said "Verboten for Dogs and Jews."' He said: 'After that, there wasn't any money in being a waiter. The Jews had been the only ones who gave decent tips.'

Josef's uncle Evžen died in 1940 in Ostrava and Evžen's son, Kurt, and daughter-in-law Ruth were deported to Zamoście where they were murdered. Evžen's son Dr Hans Wechsberg was sent to Nisko in 1939. He survived and returned to his wife, Käthe (née Teichner) but they were both deported to Theresienstadt and thence to Auschwitz in 1942, where Käthe was killed. Hans survived and, in 1946, married Lilly Lea Lewin in Prague in 1946. Hans was refused a post in a Vienna Hospital in 1947, for which he was apparently well qualified. He had a major problem with his C.V. – he was Jewish! In Vienna in 1947 that was an insuperable barrier to professional progress. In 1966 they obtained permission to leave Czechoslovakia and went to Israel with their two children, Ruth and Daniel, who still live there.

In 2008, David met and interviewed Daniel who had researched the history of the Wechsberg and Krieger families. He was able to fill in several gaps in our knowledge and correct some errors of fact. Daniel explained that he wanted the unvarnished truth not some romantic fantasy of the sort that surrounds many family histories, especially those involving Holocaust survivors. That philosophy matches ours in writing this book. As Daniel said, the stories are no less fascinating for being true and, as we believe, more interesting and worth study for not containing demonstrable errors. Daniel worked in publishing and was partly responsible for the Czech and Hebrew versions of the book '*Město v nás*' ('The Town in Us'), memoirs of Ostravaks after the Holocaust.

For a time we had no more information about the Wechsbergs but, by one of the many happy co-incidences in the research on Ostrava, we were contacted by Barbara Wechsberg from near San Francisco. She was able to provide some missing details and in return we were able to put her in touch with Stella Alexander, a long-lost relative through the Krieger family. Barbara is the daughter of Max Wechsberg, the younger brother of Josef the musician, diplomat and writer.

In March 1939, Max left Ostrava. As a Jew and a former officer in the Czechoslovak Army he thought it best to leave before the Germans rounded him up. His mother, Hermina, refused to leave as she thought that the Germans would not harm an old woman like her. Such was the Jewish confidence in German culture and civilisation! It was ill-founded, as we know only too well. Max escaped through the coal mines, going down in Ostrava and emerging on the Polish side of the border. From there, he went through Yugoslavia to Merano. Thence, by a complex route via Morocco and Spain he sailed to Havana and finally his brother Josef, who was already in America, was able to secure a visa for him and he arrived in Florida on 4 November 1940, his birthday. In January 1941, he enlisted in the US army and became a US citizen. After training, he joined General Patton's Army as an interpreter and interrogator of prisoners and landed on D-Day on Omaha Beach. He fought across France and Germany. At the end of the war, he heard that his mother had been deported from Theresienstadt to Auschwitz and died just 14 days before the ceasefire. In England, preparing for D-Day, Max married Renee Lawrence. They were to have two children, Peter and Barbara.

Pavel Vranský was born Josef Wechsberg in 1921 in Lipník nad Bečvou. His grandfather Sigmund Wechsberg was the brother of Františka, who married Albert Wechsberg the banker, and Anna who married Dr Josef Wechsberg. Pavel's parents owned a grocery shop and a small biscuit factory in Frýdlant. Pavel studied cheese-making and looked forward to a quiet life making and selling foodstuffs, but it was not to be. In 1938 and 1939, he had had fights with Henlein supporters and in May 1939 he was warned not to return to the school hostel as the Germans were rounding up some of the students, so he went back to Ostrava where his parents were living, but did not go to his parents' house but to a friend. The friend sent word to Pavel's parents who sent him food and money and he planned to escape to Poland and then on to Russia. He spent the night with a friend but was awakened and told that the Germans were about to search the house. He fled and hid in a chicken coop, hanging from the roof beam by his arms and legs.

Pavel's father also fled to Poland a few days later and the two of them tried to join a Czech army unit there but Pavel's father was rejected as he was thought to be too old at 50. The pair subsequently escaped to Russia, ahead of the invading Germans, and Pavel joined the Czech Army and was shipped to the Middle East where he found his younger brother who had emigrated to Palestine before the outbreak of the war. Meanwhile Pavel's father escaped from Poland through Lithuania to Norway and thence to the UK. After the war he returned to Czechoslovakia.

Pavel served in Beirut, took part in the defence of Tobruk and then volunteered to join the RAF. He was transferred to England with 311 Squadron, in anti-U-boat warfare. In total he flew more than 935 hours. He was demobilised with the rank of sergeant but subsequently awarded the rank of Major in the Czech armed forces. He was twice awarded the Czechoslovak War Cross, three-times awarded the Medal for Valour, the Medal of Merit First Degree and other Czech and British decorations. After the war he flew with Czech Airlines and later worked in the Ministry of Aviation, retiring as Deputy Head of the Civil Aviation Department. In 2013, Pavel was awarded the Medal of Merit by Miloš Zeman, the President of the Czech Republic, as a state veteran and, in 2017, was made a Brigadier General in the Czech Army.

NOTES

1. Hebrew, 'Luck'.
2. The German-Czech Government tried to drive non-citizens, especially Jews, across the border out of Czechoslovakia.
3. Scans of all the letters are now held in the Ostrava Archive in the Jewish Museum in Prague.
4. Hansard.millbanksystems.com/written_answerw/1960/nov/29/national-average-wages.
5. *http://www.vogel.org.uk/memoirs/index.html*
6. Peter Renton, *The Lost Synagogues of London*, Tymsder Publishers, 2000.
7. Gita Thieberger-Rind, *The Magic Doll*, Envirobooks, 2005.
8. Jewish Festival during which observant Jews take all their meals in a temporary shelter, partly open to the sky, for 8 days.
9. As with many memories of childhood recalled in later life, there is a lack of clarity about citizenship and nationality which were different, at that time. Not being Czechoslovak citizens became very important under the *Protektorat* as the German authorities could use lack of citizenship, especially for Jews, as an excuse for denial of some or all civic rights. Before 1939, lack of citizenship did not apparently mean in practice being unable to live, work or travel or, presumably, pay taxes.
10. The paramilitary organisation that became the Israeli Defence Force.
11. Edith Rosenberg (age 79) recorded 7 hours of her memoirs on audio tape for the Imperial War Museum in London, ref: 9169/14/01-14.
12. ELRO (Edith Rosenberg Löwy), *I Did Survive*, Regency Press, 1978.
13. City Lit is an organisation in London providing adult education courses in literature and other arts subjects.

PART IV

OSTRAVA POST-WAR

In the 70 or so years since the end of the Second World War, Ostrava and Czechoslovakia have undergone many and major changes: not only the repair and restoration of war damage, but the Communist takeover of 1948, the Warsaw Pact invasion of 1968 leading ultimately to the Velvet Revolution and the re-establishment of democracy in 1989. Four years later, Czechoslovakia split into two, the Czech and Slovak Republics, both members of the EU.

For the Ostrava Jewish community, the war marked effectively the end of viable Jewish life, although the community was re-established and it continues to function with few members, most of whom are elderly. However, a new 'community' has been created, the worldwide network of Ostravaks connected electronically in virtual reality and also, on occasion, in real life and in real time. In the Yiddish words of the Song of the Warsaw Ghetto, '...mir zaynen do!*' – We Survive!*

11

Ostrava Post-War

Because of its demographic and economic history, after the war Ostrava faced a number of problems that were by no means unique but were more severe than in most Czechoslovak towns. Air raids in 1944 and 1945 caused significant damage, estimated at 9 billion crowns. Nearly 3,500 buildings were damaged or destroyed, especially those associated with Ostrava's heavy industry. About 8,000 of Ostrava's Jews were murdered in the camps, 800 non-Jewish Ostravaks were executed or killed in the concentration camps and 600 people were killed in the bombing. Malnutrition meant that infectious diseases took a heavy toll in the immediate post-war period, especially among the young, old and returnees from concentration or prisoner-of-war camps. In addition, there were 16,500 Germans living in Ostrava at the end of the war whose rights of citizenship and domicile were revoked by presidential decree. Over 10,000 fled and only some 6,000 remained in Ostrava. Some of them were put to work clearing the rubble from the Deutscheshaus which had been damaged in the bombing. There was no intention of rebuilding a German National House in Ostrava. The site is now an open area in front of the Imperial Hotel.

The result of this ethnic cleansing was that Ostrava changed from a multicultural city to a predominantly Czech and Catholic one without Jews and with few Germans. Industries and businesses that had previously relied on Jewish and German experts now had to employ Czechs whose level of education and expertise was not always of the necessary level.

As early as the autumn of 1945, mines, steelworks, banks, insurance companies and other large enterprises were all nationalised. The Vítkovice Mining and Metallurgical Company was split into two, the Vítkovice Ironworks National Corporation and with the mines going to the newly formed Ostrava-Karviná Mines. After the communist takeover in 1948 state control meant that heavy industry was prioritised over consumer products and social concerns, and so industry in Ostrava thrived. This took its toll in terms of pollution and damage to the environment, but workers in these industries were relatively well-paid and nowadays there is a certain amount of nostalgia for 'the good old days'. The increasing need for labour in Ostrava encouraged immigration once again, mainly of Slovaks and Roma, but many of them found the work too demanding. There was a significant rise in alcoholism, absenteeism, robbery and violence.

From the 1960s there were fitful attempts to rebalance the economy towards consumer industries, but excessive ideological attachment to heavy industry and the demands of the USSR meant that Ostrava continued to rely on coal mining and steel even though the plants were becoming increasingly obsolescent, inefficient and uneconomic. Production eventually declined, and more recently plants have been closed or taken over as engineering works rather than for primary iron or steel production. Much of the Vítkovice site has been converted to a concert hall and museum, thanks to the drive and investment of the Vítkovice Machinery Group.

In the post-war years social housing projects proliferated to house those made homeless in the war and those moving into Ostrava, especially in Zábřeh and Poruba. The buildings were of relatively high quality even though the Socialist realism style of architecture was not to everyone's taste. The great need meant that more flats were crowded into a given space than would nowadays be considered acceptable, and 320-380 inhabitants per hectare was usual. In the later years of communism and afterwards existing buildings were not properly maintained; they deteriorated and it is only in very recent years that this trend has been reversed.

Up to the mid-1980s over 50% of the working population in Ostrava were employed in heavy industry – a unique situation in Czechoslovakia. Educational attainment gradually rose, however, and by that time only 43% of the population were without any secondary education, as compared to 79% in 1961, and 6% were university graduates, up from 3% in 1961.

In 1991, the University of Ostrava was established and it now has some 15,000 students.

In 2014, Ostrava had a population of over 300,000. It has an International School providing education from age 4 to 19 in English. In 2014 over 9,500 students attended Ostrava University, 16,500 studied at the Technical University and almost 2,000 attended the Business School. Ostrava attracted more foreign investment than Brno or Plzeň, although its unemployment rate was still high.

In 2015, Ostrava submitted a bid to become one of Europe's Cities of Culture, but the choice fell on Plzeň. Nevertheless, it shows that Ostrava is slowly emerging from the long dark times and beginning to regain its former economic and cultural dynamism

The Jewish Community[1]

Only about 200 Jewish survivors returned to Ostrava from the camps and most of them did not stay, but the Jewish Community was reconstituted in Ostrava after the war. Today it looks after quite a wide geographical area but has fewer than 200 members and no rabbi. It is based in the former Hechalutz offices where there is a small synagogue. The Community has effectively come almost full circle, from a room above the brewery to a room above offices. The Community cares for a small number of Holocaust survivors, helped by a volunteer from Germany doing his/her national social service. Through the efforts of the Kingston Ostrava Group, the Community has been supplemented by a worldwide network of Ostravaks, connected electronically in virtual reality and occasionally in real time and in real life, to Ostrava and its Community. Newsletters, emails and visits bind the generations and locations. The Ostrava Archive in the Jewish Museum in Prague provides both a memorial and also a rich source for future researchers.

What Can the Ostrava Story Teach Us?

The story of Ostrava illustrates many of the themes of the liberal enlightenment; that human spiritual and physical welfare can improve if people are free of the constraints of religious and political dogma and at liberty to pursue their own interests in a tolerant society. When those freedoms and tolerance are destroyed, so too is the well-being. Ostrava could act as a case study for those wrestling with the problems facing Europe in the second decade of the twenty-first century.

Ostrava was situated on the border between Moravia and Silesia or between Austria and Poland, depending on the period of history. Ostrava was also a frontier town, in the borderlands between Germanic Europe to the West and South and the Slav lands to the North and East. That location gave it a distinct cultural and ethnic mix. Until the late 18th century the town was small and insignificant with a population in the whole area of what is now Greater Ostrava of fewer than 2000 people and no Jews or Protestants. Some 150 years later, by 1930, it was a town of 225,000 people and an economic and cultural powerhouse. It had a population of almost 10,000 Jews and in the central part of town, in Moravská Ostrava, Jews made up some 15% of the population.

This dramatic transformation was driven by two events, the discovery of hard black coal and the Edicts of Emancipation. The coal was suitable both for iron and steel manufacture and for burning in steam engines. The industrial revolution had arrived in the Austrian Empire. The Emperor Joseph II had issued edicts allowing non-Catholics to study at University, practice trades and professions, and to move and live where they wished. Suddenly, Ostrava offered huge opportunities as industrialisation developed apace and large numbers of immigrants, including for the first time Jews and Protestants, arrived.

So Ostrava became a town of migrants and their descendants. These migrants, determined to seize the opportunities offered and, freed from constraints of family, religion, or custom, all of which had been left behind, made the town into a dynamic forward-looking and advanced place. It had electric trams before London, and photographers operated there within a year of the development of photography. The Rothschilds and the Gutmanns developed the coal, iron and steel works to rival anything in Sheffield or the Ruhr.

The new migrants built and patronised theatres, opera, and concert halls. They became doctors, lawyers, engineers and musicians. They built hospitals, an old people's home, schools – including a Jewish School – an orphanage and an apprentice training school and hostel. Restaurants, coffee-houses and department stores grew up. The immigrants transformed Ostrava into a cultural centre and an economic powerhouse.

The multi-ethnic nature of the population continued and mutual tolerance was widespread. Until the late 1930's there was almost no serious anti-semitism and Jews were well integrated into the life of the town. The tolerance extended to within the Jewish community itself. The main synagogue followed what we would now call a reform or liberal service, with an organ on Shabbat and Yom Tov (played by a non-Jew!) and a mixed choir. A non-Jewish female opera singer performed on High Holy Days. At the other extreme, Rabbi Forscher was sent to Ostrava by the Bobover Rebbe, who followed a very orthodox traditional form of Chassidic Judaism, to be minister, *shochet*, *mohel*, and *chazan* to the Zabřeh synagogue. Everyone seemed happy with this wide spectrum of religious service and observance.

The Zionist organisation in Czechoslovakia had its headquarters in Ostrava and Teddy Kollek, later mayor of Jerusalem, was the representative of the Palestine immigration body and appeared as Mordechai in the *Purimspiel*. The Maccabi movement held its international games in Ostrava in the 1920s. Social and political Jewish life thrived, as did wider civic society and its myriad activities.

It was not the Garden of Eden or Utopia, but it was a close approximation to a good civil society. And it was all destroyed within three months, in 1939. The Germans invaded Ostrava on 14 March 1939 and by the end of June all the synagogues had been destroyed, Jewish doctors, lawyers and civil servants had been prevented from working and Jewish children barred from school. Civic life and the rule of law disappeared.

So What is Interesting About Ostrava?

Immigration and tolerance lay behind and drove the tremendous economic and cultural flowering of Ostrava. The efforts and successes of 150 years were destroyed by racism, bigotry and totalitarianism within a few days and have barely been recreated now, over 70 years later. And this destruction was carried by what was probably the most cultured, educated and technically advanced nation in Europe.

The main lesson we learn from history is that we do not learn lessons from history! However many times we say, 'Never again'; however many times we decide that now we know what we must or must not do; however many times we study history and vow to learn its lessons, we never seem able to transfer the intentions into real and relevant decisions or actions. While we might, as individuals, learn from our own experience we do not seem able to learn much as a group or as a government. So most probably the case study of Ostrava will remain a theoretical one with, sadly, no practical application.

Bertie Goldberg's view is that who survived and who was murdered in the Holocaust was purely down to luck. Luck was a prerequisite for survival, not being in the way of a bullet or a selection, but it was not enough. Those lucky ones who missed the bullets, selections and other random disasters and who finally survived were both physically and psychologically tough as well.

The following final case studies are remarkable primary sources, which illustrate the spirit and resilience of some of those who came from Ostrava and what their fates were.

Such Beautiful Corpses

Michal (Miša) Salomonovič stands two metres tall, ramrod straight, with clear blue eyes and a shock of thick grey hair despite his 82 years. He looks more like a retired grenadier guardsman than a Holocaust survivor. He is a quiet, softly spoken gentle man, modest to the point of self-effacement. His younger brother Josef (Pepek) is smaller, darker, and gregarious with a twinkle in his eye and a mischievous sense of humour. He was not quite one year old when the Germans invaded Ostrava.

In October 1939, a month after the invasion of Poland, their father Erich was deported with almost 1,200 other men from Ostrava, to Nisko nad Sanem in Eastern Poland about 180 miles from Ostrava, where they were to set up a camp as a trial for future mass deportations of Jews, organised by Adolf Eichmann. When the experiment had, sadly, proved to be a success the camp was dismantled and Erich returned to the family. In his absence, Miša, Pepek and their mother, Dora, had moved or been moved from their family home to a room above the Strach umbrella shop in the centre of Ostrava. They shared this room with Rosa Liebreich with whom, fortunately, they were already friendly. Oskar Liebreich had already been deported to Nisko, with Erich. The Liebreichs had no children and so Pepek was everyone's darling. At least that is the story Pepek tells today!

After the war, the Imperial Hotel built an extension at the back, where Strach's umbrella shop had been. In 1995, Pepek had to return to Ostrava on business and stayed in the Imperial Hotel. His bedroom was in the new extension, in fact on the very spot that the shop and their room had been. He found it remarkable to be sleeping in exactly the same spot once again after 55 years. It is more remarkable that, after his experiences during the Holocaust, he was sleeping anywhere.

After Erich's return from Nisko in mid-1940, the family decided to move to Prague to keep as far away from the borders as possible and to keep out of sight of the Germans by mingling with the larger population of Prague. They were not to be left together in relative peace for very long, however, because soon they were all deported to the Łodz ghetto.

In November 1941 they were told to assemble in the Letná Fair Ground in Prague where they were all given numbers to be used in future instead of their names – Jews were now things, not people. Pepek was quite excited by the whole event. Their mother, Dora, had told him they were all going on a trip and being together with so many people in the fairground was, at least initially, a big adventure. He had been given a rucksack, which contained his potty and toilet paper, and his father had made him a new pair of braces for his trousers. He felt quite grown up as number 815 even though the rucksack was too big for him and it kept banging on the back of his knees!

In Łodz Erich, Dora and even Miša were put to work: Erich, as an engineer, in the metal work shop, Dora in the paper factory and Miša, despite being only 9 years old, as a junior or trainee fitter in the metal workshop. He was a big strong boy and looked much older. Pepek was younger and much smaller and was left in the ghetto while the rest of the family were sent out to work. Their living quarters were next door to the metal works and Pepek remembers Erich putting his (Pepek's) bed on the roof of the works during the hot summer months. Life there as a 4-year-old was initially not too bad. It was still possible to correspond with family members back home and they could send at least some food parcels to people in the ghetto. So, Pepek, aged 4, was conscious of seeing an egg for the first time. Aunt Berta had hidden it in a jar filled with flour, parcelled up with some margarine, sugar and tobacco. Pepek saw his father roll a cigarette for the first time and smelled the 'unusual' smell when Erich kissed him.

Among the goodies sent by Aunt Berta was some ersatz coffee, probably made of chicory and roasted barley. After the family had drunk their 'coffee' they carefully collected the grounds, mixed them with some of the flour and a small amount of margarine, and made small flat cakes which were roasted on a hot plate and later spread with a tiny amount of jam. They were to be saved to eat in the evening. Pepek, left alone, was carefully instructed not to touch them. But when the family returned, exhausted, at the end of their day's work, they found the coffee balls all gone. Pepek had eaten them.

> 'Who ate them?' my mother asked horrified. 'I did'. 'And who gave you permission to do that? You know very well that this was for the whole family for the entire week'. Yet I answered with determination: 'The man told me I can do it'. 'Which man?' 'Well, the man at the window.

> I asked him and he said yes'. I had seen the reflection of my own face in the window and had given myself the answer. This response was accepted by my parents with a smile.

It is possible that the smile is a much later memory. But these 'happy' times soon came to an end when the family were moved to the 3rd floor in Hohensteinerstrasse, 56. Three families lived in the one room and there was no piped water. Water had to be collected from a pump in the courtyard and carried up three flights of stairs. Dora always boiled the water because of the risk of typhoid, which was endemic in the ghetto. She had to do this at four in the morning before she went to work at half past six. The stairs were too steep for Pepek so he was forced to stay there or to remain outside when the family went out to their forced labour. He generally stayed outside and wandered about. His favourite pastime was watching a bridge which was being built above the street. Both pavements were fenced in because they belonged to the ghetto but the street itself was part of the Polish city of Łodz so Pepek was able to look out at something approximating to real life outside the ghetto as he crossed the bridge from one part of the ghetto to the other.

People who were too old, ill, or young to work did not receive a ration card so the family had to exist with only three cards that provided less than starvation rations for three people, although they were four. At one point Erich had to swap his aviator's watch for a large loaf of bread. Pepek had always liked this watch because of the illuminated dial which he could see shining brightly during the night, but food of any sort was now much more valuable than any possessions.

The Germans ran what were effectively search and destroy missions through the ghetto from time to time, gathering up the old, sick, young or anyone without the correct papers or just in the wrong place at the wrong time, and then sending them to Auschwitz and extermination. During one such operation, Pepek was hidden in the attic of their block by a friendly fireman. Pepek was terrified of the ladder as the rungs were too far apart for him easily to climb up and down. When the operation was over and Pepek came down again, he found that all the children that he used to see and play with had disappeared. The only children still there were those of the *Prominenten*, the important ghetto families. The fear of ladders remains with him to this day.

In March or April 1944, Pepek, who was 5 years old, became very ill with a middle-ear infection and pneumonia. There were, of course, no drugs available although there was no shortage of excellent advice from all the doctors incarcerated in the ghetto. Because of, or despite, this advice, he survived, although he remained ill and suffering from serious malnutrition until the end of the war.

At this time, the metal works and paper mill were dismantled and shipped west to escape the advancing Russians, and the plan was that the able-bodied experienced workers would be sent to join them once the plants had been re-erected. Meanwhile all the people from the ghetto were deported to Auschwitz for a *Selektion*, when the sick and infirm would be weeded out and sent straight to the gas chambers. The whole Salomonovič family were piled into a cattle truck and shipped out. Pepek remembers their arrival:

> We were received by prisoners in striped suits with triangles in different colours sewed on. They wore caps and wooden clogs and were accompanied by German shepherd dogs (it was the first time I saw animals that were not horses) and men in white coats. The dogs were not the friendly creatures that we see nowadays and they did not have their names on their collars. Rather they had the SS flash and a black triangle. They were vicious. Men – including my father and my brother – were taken to a camp for men and my mother and I to a camp for women.
>
> The event I will now describe has been – as it were – written in indelible ink in my memory and as such has remained unique in the story of my life. We were all taken to barracks, had to undress, were shaved, checked for gold and other valuables and bathed and deloused. The women prisoners on one side, the guards on the other. Every woman got 'new' clothes (in fact, clothes from previous prisoners who had been murdered and the clothes disinfected and recycled) and wooden clogs. When it was my turn, the woman guard looked at me (in my eyes she was the most beautiful woman because she had a head full of hair and was nicely dressed), took me by my hand and went back the long way to the place where we had had to deposit our clothes. When we arrived there I saw a huge heap of clothes, shoes and a box (probably valuables, I don´t remember). The guard told me to look for my things among these heaps. I was lucky and found my white boots from Prague, my white winter coat and the pants with the leather braces which my father had made for me and which were decorated with a flower on each side; in the middle my name Pepek was written with indelible pencil. Presumably there were no other clothes suitable for a very small boy, so I was able to get my own clothes back. In the pocket of the winter coat I found the only object which endured during the three years and seven months in the concentration camps, a gem which I still possess: A tea spoon with the inscription 'SANDRIK* Anticorro'. This spoon was life-saving for me.
>
> After getting back my clothes, the guard smiled at me, embraced me and put something into my mouth that I had never tasted (it was chocolate). She took me to the other side of the barracks where my

> mother was waiting. The woman´s name was Katja and she promised my mother to get stockings for me. She also went to the fence separating us from the men´s camp so that I was able to see my father.

Pepek remembers that once he had found his clothes and boots he ran back to his mother for her to tie up his laces as usual but could not immediately find her. She had been totally shaved so she was bald and wearing different clothes. Fairly soon, Miša was transferred to the women's camp but after about three weeks, the whole family were sent from Auschwitz to Stutthof. Each adult received a small loaf of bread, some margarine and a piece of extremely salty sausage which prisoners in the know said they should not eat. Some of the prisoners ate it and died in agony and thirst in the cattle trucks on the journey to Stutthof, as there was no water to drink on the train. In Stutthof, Erich became ill and was killed by an injection of phenol.

Every day there was a roll-call at 4:00 a.m. and in October the temperature was often below freezing point. Since then Miša has suffered from frostbitten toes. Pepek had his 'Prague' boots and had not grown during the entire period in camps so was still able to wear them, which protected him. Moreover, they had to muster in rows of five and since as a small child he was not counted he was able to stand between his mother's legs thus helping to keep both of them slightly warmer. Miša had to manage by himself.

The women slept in wooden bunks in dormitories, each bunk holding up to 5 women. Each women had a blanket and three planks width of space. There was so little room that turning from one side to the other reduced the available space and Pepek, being a child who was not counted, had no allocated space at all. So there were nights when he had to sleep on top of Dora. At the entrance to the dormitory there was a room for the guards, with a W.C. which Dora used to take Pepek to, surreptitiously, but not for the intended purpose. They drank the water.

There were some Norwegian prisoners-of-war in the camp. They were allowed to receive Red Cross food parcels and were better treated than the Jews. Some of them were about to be repatriated and two of them gave Pepek a carrot and a tin of Norwegian sardines. Dora gave Miša and Pepek the oil from the sardines to drink as well as the sardines to eat. Pepek comments that nowadays he never feels either cold or hungry but sardines are one of his favourite foods.

In October 1944 the metalworking machines from Łodz had been installed near Dresden, so Dora, Miša and Pepek were sent to Dresden as part of the new workforce.

Food was extremely scarce but with the help of a most unselfish Dutchman, Mr. van der Bosch, they were able to re-establish contact with Berta who was still alive in Ostrava, and still able to send some small food parcels addressed to him. He received some tobacco from the parcel as a token of thanks and the rest was hidden under a staircase where Dora retrieved it later in the day. Berta lived as a 'submarine' in Ostrava, below the Germans' radar, using false papers identifying her as a Roman Catholic.

The extra food could not be eaten openly so Dora gave it to the two boys only at night, in the dormitory while everyone else was asleep. She gave them a piece of bread (in Pepek's case without crust as he had no teeth and could not bite it) with some margarine and a sprinkling of sugar. He immediately wolfed it down, but Miša pushed the margarine and sugar to the edge of the piece of bread and ate it all in the last mouthful and then stuck his tongue out at Pepek, to show that he was the bigger and smarter brother! Sadly, Mr van der Bosch was killed during an air raid and the food parcels ended.

Dora and Miša were sent to work in the 'cigarette' factory (actually a factory making bullets including the internationally banned dum-dum bullets). When Dora and Miša went off to work, they put Pepek in a dustbin so that the guards would not see him wandering about during the day and Dora would know where to find him on her return. This stratagem worked for a while but one day an SS guard found Pepek in the bin and said 'Der Dreck muss weg' ('This filth must be cleared out'), a clear sentence of death. That night was the night of the great allied fire-bombing of Dresden and that saved Pepek's life! German attention was diverted from 'clearing out filth' to more pressing matters of self-preservation.

Everyone was herded into the air-raid shelters and whenever they heard the whistling sound of a falling bomb nearby, the storm-trooper who was guarding the shelter warned them to open their mouths which helped to equalise the pressure caused by the explosion. Some people who failed to do so were killed by the pressure differential.

After the raid they were marched through the still burning city to Pirna. Pepek remembers that the asphalt was hot and partly melted from the fires and it was difficult and tiring for him to walk over the sticky mass. The Jews were put to work clearing up after the firestorm. Dora and Miša had to go into the basements of buildings, which was deemed too dangerous for Germans to do, to pull out the bodies of people who had taken shelter there and been killed in the fire. Pepek remembers the 'beautiful' corpses of the German civilians. They were so different from the emaciated and diseased corpses he saw in the camps and, indeed, from the living Jewish prisoners who looked no different from the corpses, except that they still moved.

Somehow, possibly from the bombed buildings, Dora scavenged a matchbox and three sugar lumps which she gave to Pepek as emergency rations in case she and Miša were killed and Pepek was left quite alone in the world. He was given strict and repeated instructions not to eat them otherwise, and Dora's authority was such that he obeyed, despite his appalling hunger.

They were then sent to Zwodau, part of the Flossenbürg camp, but after a short time that camp was evacuated ahead of the Russian advance and the prisoners sent on one of the many death marches. Those too weak to march or too slow were simply shot by the guards. After some days of this forced march, Dora and the two boys managed to escape from the march and hid in a hedge near a railway line and a level crossing. They found a friendly Czech railway employee who took them to a farmer who hid them in his barn. He was already hiding two American escaped prisoners-of-war in his other barn and one of them, who had probably been working in a metal workshop, gave Pepek a small model aeroplane he had made.

The farmer, Pan Seidenglanz, apparently told his daughter to bake an extra two loaves of bread when doing the baking although he did not explain why. There were German soldiers still in the village and he did not want her to know about the hidden Jewish and American escapees, although she must have guessed. They stayed there until 5 May when the US Army liberated Domažlice (Tauss), where they were hiding. In the late 1990s Pepek and Lisi, his wife, went back and found the barn and the farmer's daughter who had baked the bread.

Miša and Pepek celebrated their liberation in a bizarre fashion. On 6 May a Red Cross helper gave them a jar of stewed cherries which they immediately ate with the predictable results – 'diarrhoea of hitherto unknown dimensions'.

Pepek with the model plane.

Mrs Seidenglanzová, now aged 92. She baked loaves for the hidden prisoners.

When I first met Pepek at his home I was invited to stay for an excellent dinner by Elizabeth (Lisi) whom Pepek accurately if unromantically calls 'My first wife'! He has not lost his mischievous sense of humour, inherited from his one-eyed Grandfather, despite his horrifying early life. As we were eating dessert, Lisi pointed out 'That's Pepek's spoon'. It clearly was a teaspoon-sized spoon and Pepek was clearly using it, so this seemed a piece of fairly redundant information.

Pepek's milk teeth had all fallen out quite early in his life, but because of his extreme malnutrition his permanent teeth had not erupted so he had no teeth at all. He could not eat solid food and had to take whatever nourishment there was in the form of a mush. After the bombing of Dresden, the Salomonovičes found a can of vegetables but of course their only means of opening it was Pepek's spoon. Later, on the march from Zwodau, they found some frozen turnips in a field (their only food at that time). The only way that Pepek could eat them was by scratching at the frozen lump with the spoon to form his usual mush, which he could then swallow. He, and possibly Dora and Miša, probably owe their lives to the qualities of a Czechoslovak stainless steel teaspoon. Sandrik still manufactures cutlery in Slovakia.

When they returned to Ostrava Dora weighed only 34 kg (about 75lb) and Pepek had barely grown. He was also covered in boils – they counted 21 of them! Miša was in scarcely better shape. After the war former slave labourers received some modest compensation from the German Government for their suffering, but Miša was refused as he had been only a child at the time and therefore would not have been used to work in the camps!

In 2015, Miša's grandson received his degree in physics, specialising in optics and the study of lasers. His older grand-daughter, Magdalena, has a Master's degree in Jewish History from Palacky University in Olomouc. Miša's family has clearly been bitten by the history bug – Miša made history, Libuše uncovers history, Magdalena studies it and Miša describes it during his many trips guiding school parties round Auschwitz! Pepek's grand-daughter, Lilly, is still too young for academic distinction. She excels by being gorgeous! Lilly's mother, Katja, is a psychotherapist in Vienna. She is named for the Auschwitz Capo who allowed Pepek to retrieve his clothes and who gave him a piece of chocolate.

So much can depend on such apparently trivial acts of kindness and on the quality of a teaspoon!

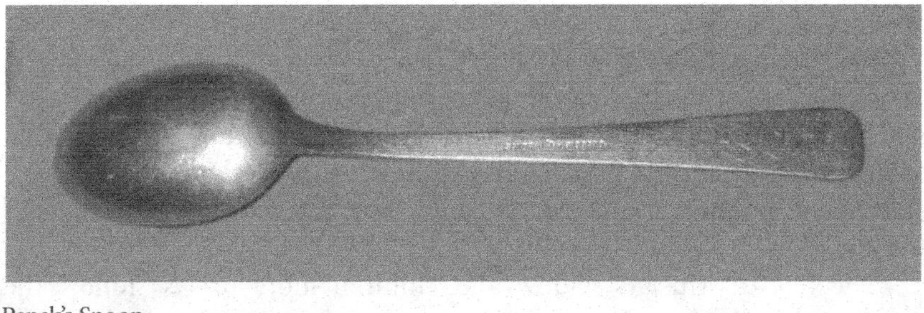

Pepek's Spoon.

The Killer, the Poem, the Crook and the Soldiers

Herman Brodavka is the unlikely 'anti-hero' of a poem well known to almost all Czech children. It was written by the brilliant, mysterious but also unfortunately anti-Semitic Silesian poet Petr Bezruč, and published in the late 1890's. Entitled *Maryčka Magdonová*, it starts with the following lines (in translation):

Went homeward old Magdon,
Homeward from Ostrava,
Stopped by in the Bartovice inn,
Fell into a ditch with a broken skull,
How she cried Maryčka Magdonová.

It describes how Maryčka's father was thrown out of the inn, fell into a ditch and broke his skull. Her mother was later run over and killed by a coal truck, leaving several orphan children. Maryčka herself was caught stealing wood from Archduke Friedrich's forest and she committed suicide. It is not a jolly poem. The real story is much less dramatic but still very sad.[2]

Herman was the owner of an inn in Bártovice. At about 2 a.m. in the morning of 14 August 1887, František Musial, a 46-year-old coal miner and owner of house No 107, approached the inn to get a bottle of spirits. Musial was a known drunk and already under the influence of alcohol when he demanded access to the pub, shouting and banging on the door. The Brodavkas were, of course, safely tucked up in bed and asleep when this din erupted. Herman's wife was frightened and woke her husband up, assuming somebody was trying to burgle or even murder them. Herman jumped up, got hold of a gun, which he kept for personal defence, opened the bedroom window and fired two shots randomly into the street apparently in an attempt to discourage the robbers. He then went back to sleep, thinking nothing of it. It was an unpleasant surprise when he discovered that one shot had killed Musial, who fell into the ditch where he was discovered.

These events were then examined by a judicial committee on 15 August 1887 resulting in a criminal charge being brought in Těšín. Even before the opening of the legal proceedings, Brodavka donated the considerable sum of 200 Gulden to the widow Miriam Musial.

Details of the court proceedings are not known but the judgement took into account Brodavka's behaviour, the donation to the widow and his marital status. It was decided that his deed constituted gross negligence against the safety of life but he was sentenced to only 3 weeks in jail with 2 fasting days weekly.

The fate of Musial's widow and children more or less follow the description in the poem.

Herman Brodavka was born in 1857 in Biala, Poland and completed his military service with the 40th infantry regiment. After leaving the army he started to work as a publican in Staré Město (Old Town) by Fryštát and moved to Bártovice at the beginning of 1885, one of the many immigrants to that town. He would nowadays be described as an economic migrant. He was of medium build, with an oval face and black eyes and hair and a narrow moustache. He spoke German, Czech and Polish.

He was hired by Mr. Antonin Olšák as an assistant publican and he gained the necessary licence from the authorities in Těšín on 31 January 1885. The business prospered and Brodavka and Olšák built a residential house, plot 614/1, and another one on plot 235. Their aim was to expand the business to include a butcher's, a grocery and a blacksmith's shop. Herman's wife, Růžena Friednerová, helped him run the business and the family prospered.

Then came the fatal night of Saturday to Sunday 13/14 August 1887, with consequences that marked the rest of Brodavka's life.

Naomi Finkelstein tells of a family tradition that it was Ernst Lanvok, a senior military officer, who was killed, which confirms the danger of taking personal memories at face value, without checking.

After Herman Brodavka's short stint in jail, he returned to his inn and his partnership with Olšák. Within two years, however, Olšák's health had deteriorated to such an extent that he applied for a formal approval of the transfer of the lease of the pub – at the considerable annual rent of 1,500 Gulden- to Brodavka, and this was approved. The regional authorities confirmed the lease on 30 September 1889. Brodavka was clearly a person of some wealth by this time.

The business prospered until 2 peasants were severely beaten in a pub brawl in 1890. After that there began to be some anti-Brodavka feeling, connected with local political and nationalist agitation. The population of about 1,600 was quite ethnically homogenous. The majority was Czech, with only a few Germans and Poles, while Brodavka was the only Jew. German speakers mostly supported Brodavka while his opponents were Czech. The situation was further complicated by the growing competition among local pubs and the prosecution of a local politician, Mr Urbanec, for tax evasion. The owner of Brodavka's pub building was a witness against Urbanec, who consequently led the anti-Brodavka faction.

To make matters even worse, yet another row happened in the pub on 16 November 1895 and the incident was widely publicised with agitation against Brodavka. Although Herman seems to have attracted violence or at least violent customers, and a photograph of him with some friends has him looking, at least to modern eyes, rather like a real desperado, at least some of the trouble was endemic at the time, caused by political and nationalistic strife.

The trouble gave Urbanec the opportunity to make a formal application for the removal of his pub licence. The investigation that followed resulted in evidence of health and safety transgressions leading to a fine of 15 gulden. An orchestrated anti-Semitic move against Brodavka followed. In response, 85 of his regular clientele met and signed a petition praising Brodavka and his services, cleanliness etc. They were largely German-speakers, and so the agitation seems genuinely to have been inspired by nationalism. The accusation was followed by an appeal to the Ministry of the Interior, which eventually took his side and confirmed Brodavka as a publican.

The nationalist and anti-Semitic agitation against Brodavka continued, with calls for a boycott of his shops. The majority of the locals ignored them. A dance evening by the local 'Czech Readers Group' was organised in his pub with a great success on 19 January 1898 with 68 young couples attending.

Some of the Czech nationalists agitated against the use of Brodavka's pub for such occasions apparently because Brodavka and a number of other Jews supported the Social Democrats who were non-nationalistic. His pub was the venue for a number of Social Democratic gatherings, while many others had refused to host them. In spite of these controversies his pub prospered and Brodavka with Olšák, whose health had presumably greatly improved, decided to build new premises on plot 613 just across the road. The new

Herman Brodavka and friends.

building, No.150, received a licence on 17 January 1899. This date therefore signifies the end of the old 'harenda'.

Brodavka's pub also hosted a very early meeting of the local Communist Party at which the later communist leader Klement Gottwald made his inaugural speech. Presumably Herman's entrepreneurialism could accommodate anti-capitalist meetings provided the attendees drank enough!

Clearly, although there was nationalist agitation, and language and politics were very significant matters at the time, many of the local population did not carry them over into their social or drinking life.

Brodavka's brother-in-law, Gottlieb Brunnwald, appeared in Bártovice in the same year and settled in the house No149 belonging to the miller Golath from whom Brunnwald rented a shop, but as a consequence of a major coal miners' strike of 1900 he suffered great losses and was sued for debts by his creditors, including Brodavka. In a forced sale of Brunnwald's assets Brodavka bought his house and shop and consequently appointed Brunnwald as a manager with a monthly salary of 100 Gulden.

Brodavka further expanded his business interests in the locality of Paseky opening a pub, *U VÁCLAVKA*, and extending it in 1906 with a dance hall, but his further application for a new licence was not granted because of local objections. It was the son of his partner Olšák who wanted to run the pub in No150 himself who probably raised the objections, and so Herman came to the conclusion that he had to move out of Bártovice. He therefore bought another pub in Radvanice – Lipno No. 43, part of Slezská Ostrava which had a more numerous Jewish community.

Herman and Růžena had 9 children of whom the fourth, Karel (born May 1890) caused real trouble to his parents. He was a well-known hooligan who started to steal his father's supplies, selling them to a local shopkeeper in Radvanice, Jan Vicherek, costing his father a great deal of money. When this became general knowledge, Vicherek committed suicide. Prosecution of Karel Brodavka was stopped, but the costs of this were such that Brodavka himself could not repay his own debts to A. Immerglück, one of his suppliers, who sued him for 1,250 crowns.

Brodavka was forced to pass the licences to his daughter Marie but even so the profits were not sufficient to cover the debt repayments. The outbreak of the first war only aggravated his situation, and the inn was sold in a public auction to cover the debt to the Moravská-Ostrava People´s Bank. Finally Brodavka was declared bankrupt in January 1916. He died on 9 December 1917.

Karel was called up to the Austrian army in 1914 and returned in 1918, apparently a totally reformed character. He leased an inn in Radvanice until 1924, and later rented the *Alhambra* bar in Ostrava. In 1921 he married Olga Rosenzweig and after the deaths of Herman and Jindrich (Karel's younger brother), Karel and Olga looked after the rest of the family. Hilda, the daughter of Richard, Herman's 7th child, described Karel as a 'good cheerful soul' and Olga as a 'true lady keeping all the Jewish traditions'. Hilda describes how she used to act as cashier on Saturday night to replace her Aunt Olga. She and Pavla, her younger sister, were allowed in the bar but not in the rest of the premises. Karel became quite prosperous until 1939 when he was forced to give up the *Alhambra*.

Karel was deported to Nisko nad Sanem in 1939 and was subsequently declared missing.

In her memoirs Hilda records that her grandmother, Růžena, gave birth to Richard at 4.00 a.m. and was back serving in Herman's shop at 6.00 a.m. There were at least 4 other children who did not survive more than a few days.

Karel and Olga had two children, Gertrude (who was murdered in Auschwitz, aged 21) and Leo, known as Brandi, born in 1923. Brandi went to the Jewish elementary school, as did his father. At home, Brandi and the family spoke German and the first two classes at the elementary school were taught in German with Czech being taught in the third year.

Brandi studied at the technical college in Vítkovice before the war. He was a very passionate Zionist as a young man and was active in *T'chelet Lavan* (Blue-white) the Czech Zionist organisation and stayed in the Children's Home on a number of occasions. He was deported with his sister and mother to Theresienstadt and volunteered to go with his mother and sister to Auschwitz where they were separated and the women were murdered. Leo was transported to Blechhammer, where he was eventually liberated.

After the war, he returned to Ostrava and studied engineering for a period before being sent by the Czechoslovak Government to accompany a shipment of arms to Israel. He made formal *aliyah*, becoming an Israeli citizen. In Israel, Leo was known as Arie (Hebrew for lion). He married Judit, who came originally from Zakopane. They had twin girls, Nurit and Naomi. Each of them had three children and both are now (2014) grandmothers. Leo did not speak much about his father, possibly because he had been a black sheep and a major disgrace for the family.

Arie (Leo) was a full-time soldier in the Israeli army. After his retirement, he would lead groups of soldiers and young adults on pilgrimages to Auschwitz.

Herman's grandson, Arnošt, son of his eldest daughter Gizela, was deported with the very first Jewish transport from Ostrava to Nisko nad Sanem. As soon as he was released from Nisko, he escaped to the USSR and was accepted into the Czechoslovak army unit in Buzuluk. He was killed in the battle of Sokolovo on 8 March 1943, and was awarded a post-mortem Order of the Red Banner.

His daughter Naomi reports a family tradition that the Brodavkas are descended from a moneyer in thirteenth-century Kraków although we have not been able to find any documentary evidence for this.

Leo Brodavka with Nurit and Naomi, in Israel.

Arie (Leo) Brodavka at Birkenau, 1984.

The 1939 World Fair

By the second half of the 1930s, America was very slowly emerging from the Great Depression. As part of the recovery programme it launched the World Fair, to be held in Flushing Meadows, New York, in 1939. The theme of the fair was to be 'Building the World of Tomorrow' and the slogan was 'Dawn of a New Day'. The idea was to tell the visitors, 'This is what we believe the future will look like'. Naturally, Czechoslovakia planned to have a pavilion there and a note in the New York Public Library gives some idea of the design concept behind it:

> Czechoslovakia's Pavilion at the New York World's Fair is designed on bold modern lines with coloured and stained glass windows used in generous expanses providing a pleasing relief against the cool grey walls. A terrace surrounds three sides of the building, with a walk connecting the Pilsen Restaurant and beer garden which are features of the entire display. Exhibits within include glass and ceramics, steel and steel instruments, agriculture and textiles. The architect is Kamil Rostok of Prague. A second exhibit in the Hall of Nations is devoted to the arts.

The steel work for the pavilion was supplied by the Vítkovice Mining and Iron Corporation and, in 1938, Robert Förster, the son of Fritz and Amalia née Rosenzweig, was sent with three colleagues across to the USA, on the RMS *Queen Mary*, to work on its installation. Robert had studied at the

Design drawing for the Czech Pavilion.

Robert Förster (left) on site at the World Fair in New York.

Grammar School in Ostrava and later at the Technical University in Brno, partly financed by his aunt in Vienna as Fritz was not very reliable as a husband or as a breadwinner for his family.

Robert had a job as a structural engineer at Vítkovice and had been working on plans to strengthen some railway bridges to take the heavier trains that had been introduced when he noticed that the original plans had been prepared and signed off by his grandfather, Filip Förster, who had also been a structural engineer at the Vítkovice works. The engineering tradition continues in the family as Frederic, Robert's son, set up a business maintaining solar panels in the USA.

By the time work on the pavilion was underway, Germany had occupied the Sudetenland, and before the erection was complete Germany had invaded and Czechoslovakia was no more. The Nazi authorities in Prague demanded the return of the money and material that had been sent to the USA for the pavilion, but none was returned as the authorities in the USA and those

In exile Czechs marketed souvenir stamps (left) to raise funds for the completion of the Pavilion. Interior stained glass (right) in the Pavilion.

The Czech Pavilion, completed.

responsible for the Fair did not accept the German's claim to be the legal government. New York City Mayor, Fiorello La Guardia, denounced the 'betrayal' of Czechoslovakia. 'The Czecho-Slovak building,' said the Mayor's executive secretary, 'should remain unfinished as a silent monument to the tragedy of the Czecho-Slovak Republic. That will be a much more stirring message than to complete the building. It was initiated by a republic and not by the present totalitarian rulers.'

In fact, La Guardia set up a committee to raise funds to ensure that the Czechoslovak Pavilion could be opened, as it was on 31 May with a 15-gun

You're invited!
Sunday, May 4, 2014
HMS Queen Mary
Long Beach, California

To Celebrate Fred's 70th Birthday
and

The 75th Anniversary of the Opening of the Czecho-Slovakia Pavilion
At the 1939 World's Fair in New York
and

The 75.5th Anniversary of Robert (Papa) Förster's
Crossing of the Atlantic on the
HMS Queen Mary to come to the US to supervise the construction of the Czech Pavilion at the World's Fair

4:00 PM Private Ship Tour
5:00 Dinner

Invitation to Fred Foster's 70th Birthday Party.

salute. President Edvard Beneš made the dedicatory address, concluding with the words: 'We believe that a nation which knows how to create — as seen in this pavilion — a nation which continues to work and to fight so ardently for the survival of its spirit in its democratic traditions — we believe that such a nation cannot die.' 'Our national life,' he said, is based 'on eternal moral principles, the principle of which is displayed in the coat of arms of the free Czechoslovak Republic. It reads, "Truth prevails!"'

On the wall of the Pavilion was written, 'After the tempest of wrath has passed the rule of thy country will return to thee, O Czech people.'

Robert did not return to Czechoslovakia but remained in the USA, working for engineering companies including Ford and Ferguson. He married his English teacher and they had two children, Joan and Frederic. In 2014, Frederic celebrated his birthday and the 75th Anniversary of Opening the Czechoslovak Pavilion – and the 75½th anniversary of Robert's voyage – with a party on the *Queen Mary*.

NOTES

1. See **Appendix 11.1** for information about Polish-Jewish refugees in Ostrava, postwar.
2. The life story of the Jewish family of Herman Brodavka and the harenda of Bartov, Osudy židovské rodiny Heřmana Brodavky a "bartovská harenda", Václav Štěpán in Ostrava 17, Ostrava: Sfinga 1995.

Appendices

1.1 Early History

The Roman historian Tacitus recorded that the inhabitants of the area we know as Bohemia and Moravia were Celts of the tribe of Boii mainly in Bohemia (hence the name) and the Cotini in Moravia. Strabo reported that the Boii had repelled an attack by the Germanic Teutoni and Cimbri tribes.

In 9 BCE, Roman legions under Nero Claudius Drusus defeated the Germanic tribe of Marcomanni, ('Men of the Morava River', named after the River Morava). After the defeat by Drusus, they retreated eastwards into Bohemia while other Germanic tribes moved in from the East until they in turn were defeated by the Romans under Marcus Aurelius in 166/7 CE. Some 250 years later, the Huns destroyed the Roman rule but were then themselves displaced by the Avars from the East who occupied a large area of what is now Hungary, Slovakia and the Czech Lands, while Slavs also moved into Europe from East of the Carpathians.

The area of Moravia became effectively a Slav buffer zone between the Avars to the East, the Germanic people to the South and the Franks to the West. It is striking that the place names Moravia and Slovakia have Slav roots, while Bohemia is etymologically Celtic/Germanic. There is no Slav equivalent of Bohemia; the area is known to Czechs themselves as 'Čechy'(Č pronounced as 'ch' in cheese and ch as in loch). This linguistic and cultural duality has had formative effects on the history of the Czech, or Bohemian, Lands until far into the twentieth century.

Charlemagne, in alliance with the Slavs, defeated the Avars and this paved the way for the emergence of what is known as the Great Moravian Empire, extending to include present-day Slovakia, Bohemia, parts of Hungary and Poland and even parts of Germany, including Berlin. In the ninth century, its ruler tried to strengthen his position with support from the church. He looked to the Pope in Rome for help, but had little success and so turned east, to Byzantium, and asked the Byzantine Emperor, Michael III, for ecclesiastical support and for missionaries who knew the Slav language. Both were forthcoming. The two brothers, Saints Cyril and Methodius, were sent on a mission. Methodius introduced the Glagolitic alphabet used to transcribe Old Slavonic, which still survives in the liturgy of the Orthodox Church, and both of them converted many Catholics to the Orthodox Church.

By 900 CE the Magyars invaded the territory of what is now Moravia and Slovakia and the Slovaks were thus under the domination of the Magyars, while the Bohemian tribes to the west of the River Morava were not. The ruling Bohemian tribe adopted the name "Czech", which was originally the title of the ruling class, and swore allegiance to the Holy Roman Emperor. The Moravians looked to the Eastern Church while the Czechs, that is the Bohemians, established links with the Western Church. By the later Middle Ages, Moravia too became part of Western, Latin Christendom, but new religious and ethnic tensions were to develop in the territories, especially after the Czech rulers of Bohemia invited many Germans to colonise the borderlands.

In 950 C.E. the Holy Roman Emperor, Otto I, led an expedition against Bohemia. It became subject to the Emperor and the Duke of Bohemia became one of the Electors of the Holy Roman Empire. In 985 or 990, Poland acquired Silesia from Bohemia, which later led to Silesian Ostrava acquiring the alternative name of *Polnisch Ostrau*, and allowed the Polish King to establish a fortified village by the confluence of the Lučina and the Ostravice rivers, now known as Slezská Ostrava.

In 1063 the Prince of Moravia established the Bishopric of Olomouc in thanks for receiving the crown from the Holy Roman Emperor Henry IV. Subsequently, he granted the town and land around Ostrava to the Bishopric of Olomouc.

In 1253, the ambitious and energetic King of Bohemia, Přemysl Otakar II, became Duke of Austria. His territories extended to the Adriatic in the South and included Bohemia, Moravia, Silesia and parts of what are now Poland and Germany. He took part in the expeditions against the Prussians (who were pagan at that time) in 1266 and 1267 and founded the town of Královec, later called Königsberg and presently Kaliningrad. He had planned to make Olomouc into an archbishopric for his close collaborator Bruno of Schauenburg, but this plan failed and it was not until 1777 that Olomouc became an arch-diocese. He put forward a claim to be elected Holy Roman Emperor in 1273, but the Pope preferred a less powerful candidate and Rudolf of Hapsburg was elected. The angry Přemysl Otakar II rejected the result and the matter was only resolved by a battle in 1278, which Rudolf won and where the Czech king perished. The Hapsburg battle-cry was 'Rome', whereas the Czechs' was 'Praha', Prague.

1.2 Lies, Damned Lies and Statistics

Drapala commented, very sourly, on the Jewish influence and ownership (through the Rothschild and Gutmann families) of the mining and steel industry. In the Vítkovice mining and steel group, with Federer as the Director General, there were 5 directors of whom 3 were Jews. 6 of the department heads and 3 of their deputies were Jews in the early 1930s.

In the period 1922-30, 42,000 miners were employed in the Karviná region and their total wages were some 450 million Kr per year. Drapala suggested that most of this money went to the main department stores in Ostrava; Rix, Textilia, Bachner, Schön, and Borger, all of which were Jewish-owned 'so it is not surprising that these Jews could build palaces for themselves'!

Claiming to base his conclusions on the tax returns for Moravská Ostrava, Drapala stated that:

1. Every single pharmacy, motor repair, beer outlet, diamond polishing, dental depot, sales representative company, poultry merchant, crockery business, typewriter sales and repair , cigarette sales and many other sectors was owned by Jews.
2. Every second taxi, featherbed dealer, postage stamp dealer and others was Jewish owned
3. Every third building material business
4. And so on, to every sixteenth building contractor and timber merchant being Jewish owned.

3.1 Vítkovice data

In 1900, the Vítkovice site employed 11,500 workers and produced almost 282,000 tonnes of pig iron and 150,000 tonnes of steel. By 1930, the number of workers had increased to 19,250 and they produced 648,000 tonnes of iron and 713,000 tonnes of steel. The mines in the Ostrava region produced 2.8 million tonnes of coal and 340,000 tonnes of coke in 1892 with 14,400 people but by 1930, there were almost 44,000 people employed in producing 10.7million tonnes of coal and 2.7 million tonnes of coke. In March 1939, Ostrava produced ¾ of the coal and coke and ½ of the iron and steel in the new Protectorate of Bohemia and Moravia imposed by the German invaders.

4.1 Money equivalents

1 Viennese Gulden (VG) is composed of 60 Kreuzer (Kz)
2.5 VG is equivalent to 1 Austrian Gulden (G). G used exclusively after 1852
1 G is composed of 100 Austrian Kreuzer

In 1892, the Austrians adopted the Crown (C) as their currency
1G is equivalent to 2C
1C is composed of 100 Heller (H)

After 1918, the Czechoslovaks introduced Czech Crowns (CzKr) equivalent in value to an Austrian Crown and composed of 100 Heller.

The present day value of money in previous centuries is not easy to estimate. Comparison with income of a typical worker in the relevant years can give an idea of values. The table shows wages of typical workers and costs of everyday items for the period 1830-1930

Item	Daily Wage	Costs
1834		
Miner	35Kz	
Sheet steel roller	1VG 5Kz	
General labourer	18Kz	
Director General - Annual salary	1250VG+5% profit share	
61.5 litres of rye		6VG 18Kz
61.5 litres of wheat		4VG 52Kz
61.5 litres of peas		6VG 10Kz
61.5 litres of lentils		8VG
1lb butter		30Kz
1lb lard		33Kz
1lb beef		20Kz
Short woollen coat		2VG
Woollen trouser		1VG 24Kz
Silver watch		15VG
Straight razor		16Kz
Live sheep		7VG 30Kz
Rent for 1 room near Ironworks		Up to 8VG/month
1853		
Miner	36-40Kz	
Sheet steel roller	2G	
General labourer	Ca 25Kz	
Director General	4000G+1500VG profit share	
61.5 litres of rye		5G 12Kz
61.5 litres of wheat		4G 10Kz
61.5 litres of peas		5G 13Kz
61.5 litres of potatoes		1G 33 Kz
1.4 litres beer		7Kz
1lb beef		10Kz
Cloth cap		55Kz
leather trousers		2G

Rent for 1 room near Ironworks		5-9 G/month
1889		
Miner	1.9G	
Smelter	3.51-3.98G	
General labourer (female)	30-64 Kz	
Director General	14,000G+5% profit share, which was 88,323G	
1kg of rye flour		7.5-14 Kz
1kg of wheat flour		14.5-18 Kz
1 kg of bread		18-20 Kz
100kg of potatoes		1.7G
1kg beef		58 Kz
1 kg sugar		34-39 Kz
Woollen trousers		5G
Men's suit		8-12G
Silver watch		5G
Rent for 1 room near Ironworks		2.5-8 G/month
1911		
Roller	6.13C	
Smith	11.1C	
General labourer (female)	2.13C	
Director General	100,000C+5% profit share	
1kg of bread flour		0.32 C
1 Litre milk		0.22C
1 litre of beer		0.32C
100kg of potatoes		8C
1kg beef		1.9C
1 kg sugar		0.83C
1 pr men's boots		10.5C
Men's suit		20C
Winter coat		80C
Rent for flat – room, kitchen garden - near Ironworks		14C/month
1923		
Roller	40.88 CzKr	
Smith	34.53 CzKr	

General labourer (male)	22.48 CzKr	
Director General	600,000 CzKr	
White shirt		36 CzKr
1 pr men's boots		85 CzKr
Ladies' coat		98 CzKr
Rent for flat – room, kitchen garden - near Ironworks		15-100 CzKr/month

5.1 Jerusalem by William Blake, published 1808:

'…And was.Jerusalem builded here,
Among these dark Satanic Mills?

……

I will not cease from Mental Fight,
Nor shall my Sword sleep in my hand:
Till we have built Jerusalem,
In England's green & pleasant Land'

6.1 Members of the first Board of the *Mährisch Ostrauer Volksbank:*

- Max Beer, Solicitor President
- Jakob Salomonowitz, businessman
- Hermann Fuchs, Solicitor
- Josef Zenker, Property owner and innkeeper
- Karl Eichenbaum, Trader
- Moritz Wolker, Timber merchant
- Sigmund Weiss, Broker
- Emanuel Herz, Trader
- Josef Adler, Railway official
- Leopold Löwy, Trader
- Rosenberg, Trader
- Salomon Schornstein, Landlord
- J Laufer, Wood turner
- Adolf Roth, Innkeeper
- Klein, Trader
- Jakob Kohn, Trader
- Josef Süssmandel, Clerk

Members of the Supervisory Board were:

- Sigmund Huppert, Trader
- Julius Berger, Trader

- Julius Forster, Trader
- Herman Schindler, Trader
- Siegfried Sax, Clerk
- JakobWulkan, Broker
- Julius Knöpfelmacher, Landlord

6.2 Dr Alois Hilf

Another important side of his activities was his dedication to the Moravská Ostrava Jewish religious community. He sat on its committee for many years, became its vice-chairman, and after the death of Markus Strassmann was elected chairman and retained that position for the rest of his life. In 1918 he was a moving force in founding of the Union of Jewish Religious Communities in Moravia and became its president. He was also involved in the establishment of the Supreme Board of Jewish Religious Communities in Bohemia, Moravia and Silesia in 1927, and became its vice-chairman. Under his chairmanship the Moravská Ostrava Jewish religious community became the third largest in Czechoslovakia, with more than 10,000 members and a budget of over a million crowns. In the 1920s Ostrava became a centre of the Zionist movement and leading political and cultural centre for Czechoslovak Jews. On the occasion of the 25th anniversary of Hilf's election as chairman of the community a foundation bearing his name was created for the support of poor people unwilling to admit their poverty.

Alois Hilf married twice. His first wife was Johanna Kessler from Opolí (today Opole, Poland), with whom he had four children – Otto (*1880), Elsa (*1881), Robert (*1883) and Egon (*1886). Johanna died soon after the birth of her youngest son. In 1889 Alois married again in Vratislav (today Wrocław, Poland). His second wife was Elisabeth Ring, and the couple had two daughters: Gertrude (*1892) and Edith (*1895). Alois Hilf died in Ostrava on 26 July 1934.

6.3 Rix department store

Bernard Rix tells what is possibly a romanticised family history. Adolf Lüftschitz was a peasant with several children whom he sent out into the world to make their fortune. Adolf went to Vienna where he was apprenticed in a department store. He did well and was sent to manage their branch in Ostrava, where he married. His wife suggested that he used the dowry from her father to buy the business, which he did. It was very successful but local traders objected that someone called Lüftschitz should be trading as Rix, so Adolf changed his name to match that of the store. He had two sons of whom the elder became a lawyer and was destined to join his father in the business, but he died, so the younger son, Otto, joined his father. After the German invasion,

Otto fled across the border and came to England while his parents were murdered by the Germans. Otto married and had two children, Evelyn who became a concert pianist and Bernard who became a Lord Justice of Appeal.

7.1 Architects

In the period after the communist putsch in 1948, the Jewish heritage of the city was viewed in different ways, but mainly through the lens of practicality. No one showed any interest in the original inhabitants and the people who had built it and lived there. Although the Jewish cemetery with the complex of buildings by Richard Strassmann survived the *Protektorat* without serious damage, it was dilapidated and lost its original purpose, and in the 1980´s was gradually demolished, with virtually no public reaction. Hundreds of tombstones and monuments were destroyed, and with them vanished the last relics of the important Jewish families that had so recently contributed to the transformation of the small Moravian Ostrava into the modern city, and had helped to define its character.

Libuše Salomonovičová made a detailed study of the cemetery before it was razed and a copy of her work is held in the Jewish Museum in Prague, as part of the Ostrava archive. Today, at a time of renewed interest in local history and the stories of individuals and families, it is the architecture that speaks most directly of the Jewish community in Ostrava. It demonstrates its economic potential, entrepreneurship, taste and desire to participate in the transformation of the city, to overcome provincialism and to be indelibly inscribed in its fabric. Jewish architects, builders, building owners and investors made important contributions to the metamorphosis of a neglected small town into a modern city with the character and face of a metropolis.

7.2 Ilse Weber's Early Life

Ilse's mother had been a gifted singer and had received her music education in Vienna where she had an audition with Gustav Mahler. Her career ended before it began as her husband didn't like the famous composer's interest in his wife. Ilse's love of music was perhaps inherited from her mother. From an early age, Ilse was a voracious reader and wanted to be a writer.

Every year a band of gypsies came to Vítkovice and set up camp for the winter in the large garden that belonged to the inn. When spring came the families went away, but one year a wagon was left behind. In it lay a young woman, who was expecting her first child. One night her husband came crying to Ilse and her mother and begged for help. His wife seemed to be very ill. Ilse fetched the family doctor who came immediately, but he was powerless to do anything. The young gypsy woman died but her child survived. Fourteen-year-old Ilse, who had just been through a course to become a children's nurse, promised to look after the baby. The next winter, the gypsies returned and the child's father, who had remarried in the interim period, jubilantly collected his healthy and happy son. As a token of gratitude Ilse received a beautiful balalaika with the inscription I.H. on it.

7.3 Letter to my Son, by Ilse Weber

My dear son, three years have passed today,
alone you left for a world so far away.
I can see you at the station there in Prague,
tearfully, bidding us goodbye.
You lean your brown and curly head to me
and beg: "It is with you I want to be!"
To say farewell was hard for you to take –
you were so little, frail and only eight
and when we had to walk home without you,
I felt my heart would break in two.
I've cried so much and wished that we were near,
still I'm happy that you are not here.

An unknown woman took you as her son.
She will go to heaven for what she has done.
I bless her with every breath I take –
be good and love her for my sake.

Life here is dismal now and full of fear,
they took all we owned and held so dear,
our house and home, everything is gone.
They plundered us and nothing's left alone.
They took your train set and without remorse
even your brother's little rocking- horse...
We couldn't keep our names. They stripped us bare
and gave us numbers round our necks to wear.
Marked like cattle, I'd bear the disgrace
if your father could live with me in this place!
Your brother cannot even stay with me...
I am as lonely as one ever can be.
You're still too little to grasp what it means...
We carry the pain of loneliness in tears,
body against body, in one room,
lying together in sorrow and gloom.

Are you healthy and learning well, my dear?
Now no one sings you lullabies, I fear.

At night you're there before my eyes
and once again I feel you at my side.
Think, when we meet again someday,
you will be wondering what I say.
I suppose you have forgotten all your German
and Swedish is too hard for me to learn!
Wouldn't that be strange? It would be fun,
all at once to have a grown-up son.

Do you still play with tin soldiers today?
A real barracks is the place where I must stay
with cold, dreary rooms and dark, damaged walls,
no sun, no trees, no leaves at all.
I work here as a children's nurse
comforting and helping so they don't feel worse.
I keep guard and watch them through the night.
The room has just one lamp, a feeble light.
I sit in silence and protect their sleep
and every child is "you" who I can't keep.
So many thoughts and dreams that we were near –
still I'm happy that you are not here.

Things precious to me have been taken away,
all joy is gone since you left that day…
the burden, which is often hard to bear.
I'm relieved to know what horrors you are spared.
A thousands torments I can still endure
if a happy childhood is for you ensured.

Now I must get some rest, it's getting late.
I wish that I could see you for one moment!
But dearest son, I can only write to you
letters of longing – that will not get through...

7.4 Joseph Wechsberg

In 'Sweet and Sour ' he describes musical soirées at his Uncle Bruno's flat. Bruno was a paper salesman who hated paper but was addicted and dedicated to music and who could play the violin, viola, cello, piano, clarinet and French horn. He lived alone except for his cook and was the only tenant in the block, which allowed him and his friends to play from late at night until well into the early hours of the morning. One evening, Bruno and Joseph were joined by an eminent lawyer and a surgeon to play string quartets. In the early hours, during a Smetana quartet, the cook erupted from her room screaming at them to stop the noise so that she could get some sleep. She was told to go back to her room and leave the musicians alone!

They decided to end the evening by playing Haydn's beautiful Quartet in C. This had been written for the Emperor Francis II and had been adopted as the national anthem of the Austro-Hungarian Empire. It had therefore been banned in the newly formed Czechoslovakia. When the group were interrupted and challenged by the local police inspector, summoned by the sleepless cook who reported the group for 'sedition and high treason', for playing the Imperial anthem, they invited him inside. To demonstrate their innocence Bruno then invited him to listen himself as they played the piece announced as in C minor, the wrong key. The inspector listened, said that it clearly was not the anthem, offered to arrest the cook for causing a nuisance, and was given a glass of slivovitz and a piece of cake. Then another glass and he sat quietly drinking and enjoying the music!

This sounds like something out of a comic opera set in Ruritania, but also evokes Joseph's post-war nostalgia for the happy tolerant inter-war years which themselves were tinged with nostalgia for Ostrava's golden days under the Empire.

7.5 'Uncle Dolek's Tango'

Nimm deine Fiedel, spiel mir mein Liedel, Jozsikam Du Zigeuner.
Bei Deinem Spielen kannst Du fühlen das sich so überglücklich bin.
In Deinen Tönen liegt so viel Sehnen, Joszikam Du Zigeuner.
Ganz neues Leben kannst Du geben.
Ich geb' mein Alles dafür.
Wer kann mein kleines Lied versteh'n,
Die kleine Melodie sie soll mir nur ihr Herz erfleh'n, den ich liebe nur sie.
Die ganze Welt gehört jetzt mir, das Glück ist bei mir Gast.
Ach, bitte, bitte, sag mir doch dass Du lieb mich auch hast.
Mein Herzes singe, mein Lied erklinge,
In schönsten Harmonien nür für Dich allein.
Jetzt könnt ihr wohl mein Lied versteh'n,
dass es nur für mich gibt die süsse kleine Melodie,
den ich bin so verliebt.

Take your fiddle, play my little song, Jozsikam, you gypsy.
When you play, you can sense how deliriously happy I am.
So much longing can be found in your sounds, Jozsikam, you gypsy.
You can inspire new life
For which I`d give everything.
Whoever can understand my little song,
She whose heart can be moved by the little melody, only she do I love.

The whole world now belongs to me, happiness dwells with me.
Oh, please, please say that you love me, too.
May my heart sing, let my song resound
In the most beautiful harmony for you alone.
Now you can all really understand my song,
and know that this sweet little melody is mine alone,
For I am so in love.

In the spirit of the words, Evelyn played it with a gypsy lilt and a rather plaintive air. It was great experience. Pavel Seifter is a second cousin of 'Uncle Dolek' (Adolph Seifter). After the performance, he wrote: 'It was a very good event indeed and I was pleased to see the Embassy room full. I really enjoyed listening to Dolek's tango and was amused seeing even the Rabbi moving and tapping in rhythm and carried away by the tune. One could imagine the fullness of the social and cultural life in pre-war Ostrava.'

8.1 Postcard from Nisko

The text reads:

Wenn Ihr Kaffeegeist hier lebte,
Oder Ihr Geist um uns schwebte
Hätten wir auf jeden Fall
Längst dahier solch ein 'Royal',

Leider ist es nicht an dem - -
Trinken wir halt unbequem
Aber froh deshalb nicht minder
Täglich runter unsere Brinda!

Which translated freely reads:

If your coffee spirit lived here
In any form – you'd have no fear
For in absolutely no time at all
We'd have built ourselves a Café Royal

But in fact there's no spirit of the kind
And we drink down – though we don't mind –
Discomforted though happy no less
Our daily brew right to the dregs

Brinda is a nonsense word, to rhyme with '*minder*' but it really is the Czech slang word, Brynda which is the equivalent of the German slang, 'Gesoff' and means muck, brew, swill; gnat's piss or poor watery beer. But there is another meaning, hence the pun. Brynda (slang.) means 'in a hole'; in trouble, a nice mess. So the doggerel is meant to reassure the families back home in Ostrava that life is not too bad while the men sit uncomfortably drinking awful stuff and 'in a hole'.

11.1 The Chief Rabbi of Palestine and 500 Polish Orphans in Ostrava

After the end of the war, Jewish refugees from Poland and further east began to move across the border into Czechoslovakia *en route* to what they hoped would be a safe haven in the UK, USA or Palestine. Some of them paused briefly in Moravská Ostrava on their way where the very small Jewish community would have provided sympathy, support, some food and possibly somewhere to stay for the night.[1]

Among them, on 23 August 1947, were 500 Polish orphans accompanied by 100 carers and Rabbi Ithak Eisik Ha Levi Herzog, Chief Rabbi of Mandated Palestine. The original plan had been for Polish orphans and *yeshivah* students, 750 people in total, to be collected in Łodz and Katowice and travel by train to Prague, accompanied by Rabbi Herzog who had come from Palestine to be with them.[2] The Polish government had organised the train to go to Paris to collect wounded Polish soldiers and repatriate them so the empty train could be used on the outward journey for the orphans.

Bureaucratic problems had reduced the total number to 500 and further problems delayed the departure of the train. As a result, it was only in the afternoon of Friday 23 August that the train crossed the border into Czechoslovakia and it was clear that it could not reach Prague before the advent of the Sabbath. That would be a major problem as orthodox Jews are not allowed to travel on the Sabbath, so Rabbi Herzog decided that they should all leave the train in Ostrava and spend the Sabbath there. Frantic telephone calls to and from Prague and lots of rushed arrangements enabled the party to be accommodated in the Moravia Hotel and fed. Even *Challah* (special plaited white loaf for Sabbath) and kosher wine was provided!

At least, that is how the story was reported although we can reasonably doubt that, in August 1947, the very small Jewish community in Ostrava could provide *challah* and kosher wine for 600 people at a couple of hours' notice. We can be sufficiently impressed that they could provide enough food of any sort.

NOTES

1. *The Unlikely Hero of Sobrance* by William Leibner (Larry Price Jewish Gen, Inc., 19 Oct. 2016). https://www.jewishgen.org/yizkor/Sobrance/Sobrance.html
2. Ibid., Chapter 5.

Bibliography

This bibliography is not an exhaustive list of material relevant to the history of Ostrava and its Jewish community but gives the main sources we have used and which would be the starting point for further research. The literature on the Holocaust is vast and not listed here.

There is a great deal of original material held in the Ostrava City Archive, in the Archive of the Vítkovice Holdings a.s. and in the Jewish Museum in Prague archive. All the material collected during our research is deposited in the Jewish Museum in Prague and may be consulted there. Much of it is available online on their website.

Baránek, Daniel: *Židé na Ostravsku: Dynamika a Pluralita židovske společnosti* (Ostrava, 2017).

Boesch, Ina, *GrenzFälle, von Flucht und Hilfe, Fünf Geschichte aus Europa*, Zurich, 2008.

Borák, Mečislav: *The First Deportation of the European Jews.* (Opava: Silesian University, 2010).

Drapala, Richard: *Geschichte der Stadt Mährisch Ostrau.* (Mähr. Ostrau: Johann Hoppe, 1933).

Drapala Richard: *Juden in Ostrau.*(Schönbrunn, 1939).

Gold Hugo: *Geschichte der Juden in Mährisch Ostrau..* In: Hugo Gold, *Die Juden und Judengemeinden Mährens in Vergangenheit und Gegenwart. Ein Sammelwerk.* (Brünn: Jüdischer Buch- und Kunstverlag, 1929).

Gold, Hugo. *Geschichte der Juden in Mährisch Ostrau.* (Olamenu, Israel. 1974).

Jiřík, Karel et al.: *Dějiny Ostravy.* (Ostrava: Sfinga, 1993).

Jiřík, Karel et al.: *Dějiny Ostravy.* (Ostrava: Profil, 1967).

Klenovský, Jaroslav: *Židovské památky Ostravy.* (Moravskoslezské nakladatelství, 1998).

Myška, Milan: *Rytíři průmyslové revoluce.* (Ostrava: Tilia, 1997).

Myška, Milan et al: *Člověk v Ostravě v XIX. století.* (Ostrava: University of Ostrava, 2007).

Ostrava 1.–30. Proceedings on history of Ostrava Region. (Issued by City Archive Ostrava 1963–2016).

Przybylová, Blažena et al: *Ostrava. Historie, kultura, lidé.* (Praha: NLN, 2013).

Przybylová, Blažena (ed.): *Ostrava a vyvoj středověkékeho města, Statuarni město Ostrava* (publ. Ostrava, 2017).

Przybylová, Blažena (ed.): *Ostrava v datech statuarni město Ostrava* (publ. Ostrava, 2017).

Society for the History of Czechoslovakia. *The Jews of Czechoslovakia, 3 vols.* (The Jewish Publication Society of America, 1968).

Vokřínek, Pravomil: *Landek. Witness of a Distant Past.*(Ostrava: Librex, 1996).

Zářický, Aleš: *Ve stínu těžních věží.* (Ostrava: University of Ostrava, 2004).

Zářický, Aleš: *Rothschildové a ti druzí.* (Ostrava: University of Ostrava, 2005).

Zehngut, Isidor: *Dějiny Židovstva ostravského/History of the Jewry of the Ostrava Region.* (Theresienstadt Martyrs Remembrance Association, 1952).

Židé a Morava. Proceedings of Annual Conference on Jewish history in Moravia (hosted by Muzeum Kroměřížska 1994–2016).

Autobiographies and biographies of Ostravaks

Adelsberger, Lucie. *Auschwitz, A Doctor's Story.* (Northeastern University Press, 1997).

Austin, Margaret and Fred. *Czech and Mate.* (HIP, 2009).

ELRO (Edith Rosenberg). *I Did Survive. (*Regency Press, 1978, reprinted by Vallentine Mitchell, 1998).
Erben, Peter. *Auf eigenen Spuren. (*Hartung-Gorre Verlag, 2001).
Erben, Eva and Lawson, David. *Escape Story. (*Sharron Publishing, 2011).
Fischler-Martinho, J. *Have You Seen My Little Sister?*
Frinton, Ernst. *Memories.* (Deskside, 1994).
Fritta, Bedřich and Klima, Ivan. *O chlapci, který se nestal číslem.* (Prague: Jewish Museum, 1998).
Fry, Helen. *German Schoolboy, British Commando.* (History Press, 2010).
Goldberg, Bertie and Hannah. *Goldberg Family.* (Private publication, 2007).
Har-El, Moshe. *Von Mährisch Ostrau in die Berge der Tatra und nach Israel.* (Labhard Verlag, 2001).
Hořak, M. and Voves, P. *The Face of Memory.* (Živá pamět', 2009).
Huppert, Hilde and Shmuel. *Hand in Hand with Tommy.* (Gefen, 2004).
Jirousková H. *Kronika , mého rodu a mého života.* (Schenk Press, 2000).
Končický, M. And Vranský, P. *Bez nároku na slávu.* (Montanex, 2015).
Lánícek, Jan. *Arnošt Frischer and the Jewish Politics of Early 20th Century Europe.* (Bloomsbury Academic, 2016).
London, Artur (translated Alastair Hamilton). *The Confession. (* Morrow, 1970).
Radvanský A. *A přece jsem přežil.* (Goldenbogen, 2008).
Rosenbergová, Edith. *Memories.* 7 hours of tape in the Imperial War Museum, London, 1985.
Ross, Eva. *Come, Make Me Happy. (*M&N, 1998).
Stargardt, Nicholas. *Witnesses of War. (*Pimlico, 2006).
Thieberger-Rind, Gita. *The Magic Doll.* (Envirobooks, 2005).
Thieberger-Rind, Gita. *When Sirens Sounded.* (Dew, 2008).
Weber, Ilse. *Wann wohl das Leid ein Ende hat.* (Hanser, 2010).
Weber, Ilse. *Nedkonočené verše.* (Deutsch-Tschechischen Zukunstfonds).
Wechsberg, Joseph. *Die Manschettenknöpfe meines Vaters.* (Hugendubel, 1979).
Wechsberg, Joseph. *Homecoming.* (Alfred A. Knopf, 1946).
Wechsberg, Joseph. *Sweet and Sour.* (Michael Joseph, 1949).
Wechsberg, Joseph. *The Vienna I knew. (*Doubleday, 1979).

Photographs of Old Ostrava

Ostrava 1880-1939 Irena Korbelářová et al. (Wart, 2000).
Ostrava in Period Postcards. Barteček, Ivo and Tejkal, Jan (Repronis, 1997).
Ostrava. Řesnìček, František (Repronis, 2007).
Ostrava. Polášek, Miloš. (Librex, 1996).
Ostrava. Polášek, Miloš and Sikula, Petr. (Osveta/Profil, 1985).
Vítkovice. Kocierzová, Lenka et al. (Wart, 2002).

There are several websites with photographs of old Ostrava, including:
https://www.facebook.com/plugins/video.php?href=https%3A%2F%2Fwww.facebook.com%2Fkomentovane.prohlidky.ostravy%2Fvideos%2Fvb.181863811876211%2F1152416398154276%2F%3Ftype%3D3&show_text=0&width=560
https://youtu.be/kBFoe-F_XFY
https://www.youtube.com/watch?v=OSoFNx5F158&feature=youtu.be

https://www.youtube.com/watch?v=c0drYglU0Js

Newsletters

The Kingston Ostrava Group publishes a regular Newsletter. A complete set of them can be found on the website:
https://ksds.org.uk/archive/ostrava-archive/

Index

Note: Bold page numbers denote photographs

I0881359

The Heart of Lebanon

Middle East Literature in Translation
Michael Beard *and* Adnan Haydar, *Series Editors*

THE HEART OF LEBANON

Brief Excursions into Our Mountains and History

AMEEN RIHANI

Translated from the Arabic by Roger Allen

Syracuse University Press

Originally published in Arabic as *Qalb Lubnan*. Edited by Ameen Albert Rihani, 5th ed. (Beirut: Dar al-Kitab al-Lubnani, 1975).

Syracuse, New York 13244-5290

First Edition 2021
21 22 23 24 25 26 6 5 4 3 2 1

∞ The paper used in this publication meets the minimum requirements of the American National Standard for Information Sciences—Permanence of Paper for Printed Library Materials, ANSI Z39.48-1992.

For a listing of books published and distributed by Syracuse University Press, visit https://press.syr.edu.

ISBN: 978-0-8156-1129-5 (paperback)
978-0-8156-5514-5 (e-book)

Library of Congress Cataloging-in-Publication Data

Names: Rihani, Ameen Fares, 1876–1940, author. | Allen, Roger, 1942– translator.
Title: The Heart of Lebanon : brief excursions into our mountains and history / Ameen Rihani ; translated from the Arabic by Roger Allen.
Other titles: Qalb Lubnān. English (Allen)
Description: First edition. | Syracuse : Syracuse University Press, [2021] | Series: Middle East Literature in Translation | Includes index. | Summary: ""The Heart of Lebanon" is an English translation of a work by the Lebanese-American writer, Amin al-Rihani. His journeys from his own village of Freike into the mountains of Lebanon allow him to tell the stories of people, villages, and monuments—each journey offering depictions of spectacular scenery and a fascinating cast of characters"— Provided by publisher.
Identifiers: LCCN 2020037348 (print) | LCCN 2020037349 (ebook) | ISBN 9780815611295 (paperback) | ISBN 9780815655145 (ebook)
Subjects: LCSH: Rihani, Ameen Fares, 1876–1940—Travel—Lebanon. | Lebanon—Description and travel.
Classification: LCC DS80.2 .R513 2020 (print) | LCC DS80.2 (ebook) | DDC 956.92—dc23
LC record available at https://lccn.loc.gov/2020037348
LC ebook record available at https://lccn.loc.gov/2020037349

Manufactured in the United States of America

To my friend,
Charles Corm

Ameen

Mahboub, Rihani's travel companion.

Where Rihani left to travel in the heart of Lebanon.

Dear Albert,

How generous you have been to your brother, to Arabic literature, and to your homeland in publishing *The Heart of Lebanon*! Many readers of this precious travelogue will say exactly what I am now going to say: Bravo, bravo! Thank you, thank you!

The hours that I have spent accompanying Ameen on his Lebanese travels have been a source of enjoyment for body and soul alike. He serves as a subtle commentator, inspired poet, precise historian, and sage—someone who can extract a piece of wisdom from seemingly trivial matters and events. He is the ever-alert traveler; nothing escapes his attention. Humorous storyteller, astute critic, and surgeon with a sharp scalpel, he borrows without spreading malicious gossip or indulging in distortion.

Here then is Lebanon, with its lofty heights, its murky depths, its springs, its rivers, its boulders, its forests, and its inhabitants' clothing; their habits, their morals, and their beliefs—Lebanon, whose lengthy history stretches from the dawn of history itself until the present day, this Lebanon that Ameen loved to the point of veneration, all so that he could use the pages of his book to reveal its true face. And there it is to be found, in flesh and blood, with all its fascinating and more pedestrian aspects, its human and divine elements, its frailty and might, its traditions and fairy tales.

As I have accompanied Ameen on his travels, I have never had the feeling that I was still in this world while he was in the next, or that we were separated by a veil called death. To the contrary, his image has ever been before my eyes, and his voice has echoed in my ears. It has been as though he were present in flesh and blood on every single page of his book. By my very life, that is the magic of the pen through which courses the very blood of life; and death has no dominion over it. My salute then to it and its author, and heartfelt thanks to you, Albert.

Mikha'il Nu'aymah

Contents

Foreword to the English Translation

MAY RIHANI

ROGER ALLEN and I stood on the balcony of the Freike home and looked at Sannine. This was in January 2018. We were both totally enchanted by the beauty and majesty of Sannine. Hues of white and light blues covered the noble mountain. After few minutes of silence, Roger said softly, "Ameen Rihani must have been influenced by this ethereal scene."

Roger was right. We were standing exactly where Ameen Rihani stood every day at around 6:00 p.m., on the balcony of his home, looking at Sannine, reciting his prayer, An-Najwa. No doubt, Ameen Rihani was influenced by this ethereal scene.

Just before we stepped out on the balcony, I was taking Roger on a tour of the Ameen Rihani Museum and his home in Freike, Lebanon. This visit to Ameen Rihani's home and museum could be the primary reason why Roger decided to translate *Qalb Lubnan* into English.

I always regarded Roger Allen as a major bridge between the Arab world and the Anglophones of the world—or, perhaps, the ambassador of Arab literature to the Anglophone world. After all, Roger has translated more than forty major Arab literary oeuvres into English. He translated numerous modern Arabic novels, including five by the Nobel Laureate Naguib Mahfouz. Allen started, in 1973, by translating a collection of short stories by Mahfouz, *God's World*, which was cited by the Nobel Literature Committee in 1988. It is important to note that Roger Allen was involved in the Nobel Prize nomination process itself. Roger has also translated works by many important figures of the modern Arab literary scene, including Jabra Ibrahim Jabra,

Yusuf Idris, ʻAbd al-Rahman Munif, May Telmissany, Bensalem Himmich, Ahmad al-Tawfiq, and Hanan al-Shaykh.

Roger has maintained close contacts with litterateurs in the Arab world. He has been a frequent visitor to Cairo and the conferences of Al-Majlis al-Aʻla li-al-Thaqafa. He has also been involved in the activities of the University of Tunis at Manouba, and a number of universities in Morocco, including those of Muhammad V in Rabat, Fez, Oujda, Casablanca, Muhammadiyya, and Kenitra. Lately, Roger presented literary papers at two universities in Lebanon, the American University of Beirut, and the Lebanese American University.

The connection between Roger Allen and Ameen Rihani was inevitable.

They both used Arabic and English as two pillars in their lives.

They both fell in love with two languages and have spent precious time mining the origins of words.

They both acknowledge that language has the ability to sharpen minds and caress hearts.

They both recognized that languages are vehicles of cultures and conduits of a deeper connection among different civilizations.

They both value the fact that main literary figures are the voice that clarifies the struggles and triumphs of their people.

And they both believe that through the oeuvres that are the peak of literature, the different faces of humanity become better understood.

Dear reader, enjoy traveling with Ameen Rihani through Lebanon's magnificent mountains and clusters of villages on the wings of Roger Allen's English.

August 2019

On the Names of Persons and Places

ROGER ALLEN

AS RIHANI NOTES in the opening retrospective segment of his first excursion in *The Heart of Lebanon*, he had returned to his native country after spending several decades in New York City. He was indeed a pioneer figure in the modern Arabic literary movement established by Lebanese émigrés in the Americas, north and south, known as the Mahjar. While living and working in these new environments, the writers usually adapted their Arabic names to the languages and spelling conventions of their new residences. Thus, Rihani used Ameen as his first name, and often dropped the *al-* from the family name, emerging as Ameen Rihani. Similarly, in English-language works we encounter names such as Kahlil Gibran, Mikhail Naimy, Charles Corm, and Elia Madey. With that intercultural context in mind, I have adopted the version of their names that they themselves chose for this English translation.

In rendering Lebanese place-names into English, my first resort has been the website List of Cities, Towns, and Villages in Lebanon, at libandata.org. I have then checked the names and locations on Google Maps Lebanon, an extremely useful resource as I have followed Rihani on his excursions into Lebanon's mountains and valleys. On those rare occasions when further questions have arisen as to the current transliteration of the name (that being heavily influenced by French spelling), my colleague Henri Zghaib has provided me with the latest information on the subject.

I should also point out that this English translation is based on the text of the fifth edition of *Qalb Lubnan*, edited by Albert Rihani and published in Lebanon in 1975 by Dar al-Kitab al-Lubnani.

The Heart of Lebanon

Introduction to the 1975 Arabic Edition

AMEEN ALBERT RIHANI

ON APRIL 25, 1939, Ameen Rihani sent a letter to his brother, Yusuf, in which he said that he was busy working on a book about Lebanon. He notes that

> this book is part of the debt that I owe to our mountains and ancestors there . . . a book of short excursions to some unknown locations in the mountains, places where the old life is still intact and unsullied, with all its attractive customs and traditions. This is going to be one of my best books in Arabic since I am pouring my whole heart into it. I may call it *The Heart of Lebanon.*

These words give the reader some idea about what *The Heart of Lebanon* meant to Rihani—emotionally, intellectually, and literarily—the radiant mental state in which he lived for almost three years while busy writing something that he himself considered to be "part of the debt that I owe to our mountains and ancestors." However, we do not know exactly when he started working on the book. On June 29, 1937, Rihani wrote the following to the editor of *National Geographic*:

> You have asked me for some pictures of Lebanon. Here they are. If you would like me to write an article on the subject, I would be delighted. I am thinking of some descriptive pieces of the kind that

From Rihani, Ameen Fares, *Al-A'māl al-'Arabiyyah al-Kamilah* [Complete Works] (Beirut: Al-Mu'assasah al-'Arabiyyah li-al-dirasat wa-al-nashr, 1980), 3483–85.

> I am currently working on for a book about Lebanon. (*Rihani's English Correspondence*, Rihani Museum)

Based on the text, I believe that Rihani begin writing *The Heart of Lebanon* early in 1937, if not slightly earlier. The book was not published until 1948 (posthumously).

When the first edition of *The Heart of Lebanon* was published, some thought it was a piece of travel literature. What they did not realize was that it is a return to the ancient land, to the beloved terrain, to Mother Nature; a return to the secret of that emotional tie that binds humanity to the geographical location where they belong, to the sweet fragrance that they inhale, to the waterwheels and springs where they wash, and to the trees beneath which they sit and contemplate. On the pages of this book Rihani is summoning those who inhabit their ancient land, calling them, consorting and conversing with them, recrafting with them both past and present, and designing the outline of the future.

It is a private conversation with rocks and oak trees, a landscape that gets its colors from village peasants, the faces of women, children, and grandees; a work grounded in a land where the author is familiar with its valleys, its plains, its flatlands, its depths and its peaks, with the bends in its villages and the squares in its cities, the extent of its gardens, and the turns in its rivers. It is an ode to the land that Rihani has loved to distraction; neither exile, nor his travels in different countries, nor the interweaving of cultures have managed to distance him from it. It is a Lebanese anthem of anthems par excellence, a literary epistle, realistic, spiritual (spiritualistic), an existential, sentimental text, symbolic, transcendental, one in which Rihani reveals the import of his love for Lebanon, the extent of his affection for the land that gave him birth, and for the nature that he replicated, as it did him. From it he learned how to penetrate those luminous tracts leading toward Mother Nature and the ancient land, a night journey with the very essence of Lebanon, a stairway through him and from him to the ultimate goal.

It is the book of Oriental transcendentalism, literature of realistic exceptionalism, the itinerary of the spiritual, spiritualist word, which at a certain moment in time in Lebanon rose to the luminous heights—people, soil, and rocks; present, past, and future. So here it is, a continuous confession, both frank and direct, showing quite how far Rihani was attached to the soil of his country and the traits of his family, his people, and his kin. The philosopher of Freike collected them all—one moment, one breath, one scene at a time—in order to use the assembled materials to build a pulsating heart, a strong, solid heart that is *The Heart of Lebanon.* It may have been this that led the itinerant journalist Alexander al-Riyashi to write with a golden pen:

> *The Heart of Lebanon* is a Lebanese gospel, perfect in every detail for this era . . . It is an eternal gift to Lebanon and the Lebanese.

The Heart of Lebanon consists of seventeen excursions, visits, trips, or pictures, of which Rihani completed only nine stops. The rest are still in the initial compositional stage in design, context, and textual format. That is because fate caught Rihani by surprise before he could finish *The Heart of Lebanon.* The book has thus been published as the author left it, including the unfinished parts and individual texts, all so as to give readers a clear and complete idea about the book as its author originally planned it.

The Heart of Lebanon is Rihani's final book, the only one that is incomplete. It is as though fate wanted the book to remain open-ended—with a beginning but no ending. *The Heart of Lebanon* thus remains the work of Rihani that is open to all meanings, all possibilities, and all the intellectual and spiritual potential that Lebanon knows and controls. It is no accident that in this incomplete book we find Rihani saying, "We have a rendezvous in a thousand years' time" (Sixth Journey: Afqa).

"A rendezvous in a thousand years' time"—that is, a rendezvous with history, with human thought, with every literary creation that constitutes a fresh addition to culture. With his enlightened legacy Rihani manages to fix this possible, impossible rendezvous, his rendezvous in a thousand years' time, a rendezvous to celebrate the victory of humanity's values and progressive liberal principles, a rendezvous to celebrate the literary, intellectual, and scientific revival—East and West, North and South, and all because it is a rendezvous in celebration of humanity's victory over itself in every corner of the globe.

Ameen Albert Rihani, Editor

Revision

IN THE SECOND EDITION, we had decided not to include the outlines of those excursions where fate intervened between Rihani and their realization, something that we had previously done with the first edition. However, as a result of the insistence on the part of readers that those outlines should be restored and printed, as was the case in the first edition, we have acceded to their wishes and restored those extracts to the third edition, and also to this and all subsequent editions to come, all in response to their expressed wishes.[1] We have added some colored pictures, some unnumbered pages, and the names of prominent figures, minerals, animals, and plants to those incomplete accounts of excursions that were previously omitted from the index for a number of reasons.

In this fourth edition, the notion of an index has been expanded so that the items are enhanced by dictionary definitions, giving readers additional information about the entire contents of *The Heart of Lebanon*, all with the goal of the best possible integration.

Ameen Albert Rihani
Beirut, August 1971

1. Translator's note: Because of the fragmentary nature of the textual materials devoted to the later journeys, this translation is limited to the first nine journeys—all of which are complete.

In collecting this information and other facts that Rihani was unable to assemble, he had in mind to write a kind of introduction to The Heart of Lebanon. *However, fate intervened to prevent that. We have therefore decided to include these pages of information so that readers can imagine for themselves what that introduction might have been.*

Dimensions of Lebanon

One hundred and eighty kilometers long, and twenty-nine kilometers wide in the south.

The mountains are wider and higher from the southwest to the northeast. Between Sidon and Mashghara the width is no more than twenty-nine kilometers, and between Tripoli and Hermel forty-six kilometers.

Some scholars say that in former times the mountains were about three hundred meters taller than they are today; with every passing era, natural factors lopped off a few meters from the mountaintops. If that is true, then so is the statement made by the ancients—namely, that Lebanon was crowned in eternal ice, and so was called Lebanon, meaning "white mountain."

The Languages of the Lebanese

Babylonian (Tel al-Amarna correspondence) was written in this language blended with ancient Egyptian (cuneiform and hieroglyphic). There followed in succession Aramaic, Babylonian, Canaanite, and Arabic. It was the Itureans who introduced the Arabic language to Lebanon.

Names for Lebanon

Assyrian: *Labnanu*
Hebrew: *Labnun*
Aramaic: *Libnun*

From these sources the Greeks and Romans derived the name *Libnanos.* Over the ages the name did not change very much—its basic meaning being "white mountain" because of the white snow that covered its mountaintops. In earlier languages, as later in Arabic, Lebanon has another meaning: *luban* (frankincense). It was so called because of the perfumed scents exuded by its aromatic trees and plants.

Oaks, sunflowers, olives, cedars. Responding to people who say that cedars are a kind of pine, Prince Mustafa al-Shihabi states: "Cedars belong to the pine genus, but they are not pines. They are different from cypress, although they are also called 'cypress.'" Professor Mahmud Mustafa al-Dumyati responds to his statement in *al-Muqtataf*, citing Arabic dictionaries to the effect that cedars are indeed pines; they are the male of the genus. In the dictionary *Taj al-'Arus*: "*Al-Arz* (cedar) with an *a* vowel: "A kind of pine tree." Under the heading *sharbin* (cypress), the Dutch Orientalist Dozy notes: "A word coined from Aramaic equivalent to the French 'le cedre ordinaire.'"

The cypress tree called *sharbin* in Lebanon is called *sarw* in Egypt and Algeria. The juniper (*'ar'ar*) in Greater Syria is called *sharbin* in Algeria.

Electric lights get confused with the stars. So you are confused: do you say, "That's a star in the heavens," or, "That's light in a Lebanese house"?

First Journey

To the Cedars

Contents

A Glimpse into the Past

FOR THE HUMAN SOUL, a return to the past is both soothing and troubling. When we recall events from the past, we feel refreshed and pensive; we smile, then feel depressed. That said, we thank God because we can invoke memories of the past, and yet that same past can never return.

Which of these memories are entirely cloudless? Which of them restore for us whiffs of life's perfume without any trace of pain or shadow of error? Which memories can revive a happy feeling and renew some previous sense of delight without at the same time provoking nostalgia and a wistful sadness that inevitably accompanies it?

Are any of life's truths more plain and obvious than the one that has occurred just the day before, in memory or imagination? In both its outer shell and core, is the past anything but a shadow cast over the totality of shadows? Even so, it is still worthy of some reflection and thought. To be sure, it comes in a variety of aspects and different colors, and there exists a large gap between images of what is now and what has been. And yet, provided we can ignore the fiery heat of the imagination and the siren calls of nostalgia, a look back into the past is not entirely lacking in things that can gladden the heart, even though they may only consist of an author's words, a poet's ode, or an artist's painting or image.

In adopting this approach, I am not intending to burden memory with moral advice. To the contrary, my only wish is to use memory to revive certain aspects of the past and to offer them to you as a picture without commentary or explanation.

I begin by expressing my reliance on both God and my own memory. Then I go back some thirty years. It is 1907, and I am standing on the shoulders of the Freike Valley in order to present to the reader a young man from Lebanon who had emigrated to America and come back home loaded down with works of literature rather than banknotes. He adopted the valley as a retreat and built a temple there—in fact, he came to regard every single vista in the valley as a temple—or rather, every single location where his heart was content, his mind was inspired, and his spirit felt both humble and reassured.

That young man was passionate about books and writing; all his manic efforts were devoted to them both. He avoided social contacts except with peasants, and he did not communicate with the jinn unless one of them happened to be related to a poet or was twin brother of a jester. He thus maintained a kind of friendly familiarity, sometimes claimed to be prophecy but never holiness.

But he decided to worship God in the much larger temple: in the open, in fields, in the valley, in the shade of pines and olive trees. People said he was an unbeliever who denied the existence of God. Others heard him say, "Nature is my mother," and he would then repeat it. They also claimed that he cursed Almighty God.

They would spot him standing rapt by a birds' nest where the fledglings were cheeping, by a flower blossoming amid the rocks, by a candle sharing its scented smoke with the bushes, or on a grassy hill atop a bare, speechless mountain. They would see him wandering through fields and glades. They used to say that he emulated the jinn, met up with them in the valley cave, and was himself possessed. That is why they would all meet, and he would make them laugh, as they did him. The swallow flying overhead would shake its head, perplexed. "I wonder," it would ask, "who's sane here and who's the madman?"

That young man had already spent half his life in the great city of New York, and he returned to his birthplace chanting the realities of the wider universe. He discovered them in isolation, or in that isolation he discovered a way to connect him to them. He discovered them in nature—or rather, in nature he discovered evidence that made them all that much clearer. He discovered them in simplicity, or in simplicity he discovered one of their most charming aspects. He discovered them in beauty, or in beauty he discovered their most enlightened symbol. He discovered them in meekness—or rather, in meekness he discovered their most magical images, as they sat beside their sister the sun and their brother the moon.

In that particular year where we have paused, 1907, that young man was sitting on a rock in the valley. With every lofty pine tree he had the sense that a hand was brushing his forehead and rubbing between his eyes. He realized that he was in the valley of holiness. Its sons were still building churches. Wherever he turned, he could see a trace of the Creator in the beauty of the valleys and the splendor of the mountains above. He also realized that worship never wears dark clothes, holiness never puts on a gloomy face, and that a radiant smile and laughter are both God-given favors.

These truths all revealed themselves to that young man one day while he was sitting on a rock. He was looking out over a deep chasm, which ended up by the banks of a river decorated with poplar and oleander trees, which shaded the water as it flowed serenely to irrigate the orchards in the plain below. God bless the dry soil beneath your feet, the beauty between your two hands, and the growth and fruits before your very eyes! Yes indeed, by the Lord of the Cedars, the sun dances on the rocks, it rests beneath the poplars and oleanders, and in the orchards it works with the soil in pious devotion.

The holy mountain—Mount Lebanon.

Another truth now revealed itself clearly to the young man: the holiest things on the holy mountain were the Cedars. How could the worshipper build his temple in the valley and stay there as a son of nature for three years without visiting the holiest site in Lebanon? Not make a pilgrimage to the Cedars? That was the essence of unbelief. That young man promised himself not to be an unbeliever.

Preparing for Travel

I DECIDED TO TRAVEL NORTH to visit the Cedars. I started planning things and making preparations. In those days travel was not the way it is today, easier than composing poetry and safer than sitting in a cinema. To the contrary, and truth be told, it was both significant and dangerous. The two rhyming synonyms tell the truth: travel and travail.

When it comes to the obstacles that you face and the difficulties that take away all strength and resolve, leaving behind nothing but spirit, then you need to talk about them frankly. How many there are, in those numerous valleys, so remote and high level, each one lurking behind the other, the first connected to the Dog River and the last to the Kadisha River.

The only modes of travel in those days were carriages in a limited number of locations, mostly on the plains, and riding animals in mountains and their tracks.

The carriages were a living symbol of Eastern ingenuity. Anyone who chose to ride in one could only rely on patience and faith. The carriage tracks and sultan's highways were no less fine and ingenious than the carriages themselves.

For those who did not wish to rely on patience and faith there remained riding animals. These consisted of four types: donkeys, mules, nags, and horses. Camels were not used for travel in Lebanon because their humps were of no use in the mountains. There were no horses for hire in the mountains.

Like the camel, nags had no place in the mountainous terrain; they were used on the plains, for ploughing, and to pull carriages in the city. When a nag's working life came to an end—in other words, when it could no longer do the work—it would be put up for sale. A Moroccan would buy it; he used to tour the country selling medicine for people in pain—"Me . . . dic . . . ine," he would yell, "I've me . . . dic . . . ine"! This Moroccan with his herbs and potions and the nag were seldom apart in reality, and indeed seldom apart in the more intimate portrait of that reality.

There were various types of donkey in the mountains, but not the one that is by far the best and most beautiful—namely, the Cypriot. I have never set eyes on one in Lebanon. I have seen its like in the Hijaz and Bahrain and have ridden a few of them on some of my trips there. I was very impressed by them, the way they move, and their general behavior. Even its bray is different from that of other types of donkey. The linguist scholar has described it as "a ringing sound"; in other words, a "pure bray." In Lebanon there are no Egyptian donkeys descended from the Cypriot ones. Even though Lebanon is so close to Cyprus, there are no heavenly donkeys in Lebanon, just animals with defects and diseases.

All of which leaves mules. Here I make a distinction between the male and female of an animal that is renowned far and wide for its stubborn streak, its attributes being virtually reduceable to species and blood. However, when it comes to details and particulars, the distinguishing criteria are both visible and hidden. The hidden ones are known only to muleteers, while the most important visible ones include neck, eyes, ears, and hooves. With male mules the neck is sharply pointed, unbending to the tip of the halter that the rider uses like a whip, even when blocked by the muleteer's hand. The eyes are inflamed and become even redder when the mule is exposed to even the slightest external incident. The ears are clustered at the front of the head and prick up whenever there is a risk of danger or disaster. The hooves can respond rapidly to dictates from eyes and ears; mules will repeatedly kick their back legs into thin air, if that is all that is available. Turning stubborn, they will first stop and spin round and round. Then they will panic and go charging off until they go really crazy and smash into the very first mulberry tree or rock ahead of them. If their load consists of packages of goods, then it will be transferred from its back to its underbelly. But if it is a human being, even an expert rider, he will wish that he was on the ground—good for those on the ground! He will soon be in need of medical attention.

The female mule is exactly the opposite of all that has just been noted. Her neck is soft and delicate, her eyes are sleepy, her ears are smooth and floppy, and her hooves are rarely raised into the air.

Female mules differ from males in their relationship with human beings and the fine qualities that they inherit as a result of that linkage. How can it be otherwise when the only human beings they have known have been virtuous people and others both pious and intelligent? The animals have been honored by the names of such people and have gained fame through their intellectual and spiritual qualities. "The judge's mule, how wonderful!" "The president's mule, the bishop's mule, the sharif's mule!" Among mules in history we can mention Ibn Khaldun's, which Timur Lang came to love before he even saw it. Sometimes the ear loves something before the eye, even when talking about animal qualities. The renowned historian gave Timur Lang his mule on the day when the former accompanied the Damascus delegation, which went to negotiate a peace treaty. Then there is the swaying of the grey mule that the Muqawqis, the ruler of Alexandria, offered the Prophet Muhammad. There are many other distinguished mules, but God did not favor them with a poet to sing of their beauty, nor a historian to ennoble his pages with mention of their exploits.

So it is by mule to the Cedars. But where is the female mule that I need? The village priest heard me asking that question. "Mahboub has one," he replied. "No muleteer is more reliable than him, and no one knows the mountain tracks better than him. No female mule is more intelligent than his; she is obedient, gentle, blessed, and graceful."

With that the priest clasped his thumb with his other four fingers to demonstrate the veracity of what he had just said.

Having heard this from the priest, I went in search of Mahboub. We reached an agreement: one government Majidi coin for every day that I hired both him and his mule, along with a guarantee to pay the cost of the mule should we be attacked by brigands who liked the mule and preferred to take it rather than our money or ourselves, and a nice tip once we made it back safely from the Cedars. We both signed the agreement, duly witnessed by the village mayor and priest.

That day everyone in the household rolled up their sleeves—mother, sister, male and female servants, all helped by their neighbors—and all started collecting provisions. "Ameen, may his life be long!—he's traveling to the Cedars." The kibbe was pounded, grilled, and fried into kebabs and patties. A large chicken and rooster were slaughtered. Potatoes and eggs were boiled and cooked, spinach was fried in oil, stuffed grape leaves were prepared, and Saj bread was baked . . . all so that we would have a supply of fresh bread. Ameen's mother, Umm Ameen, dedicated candles, oil, and incense to the two churches in Freike and Qornat al-Hamra in prayers for the great traveler, asking God to protect him on his journey and bring him home safely.

Thus went the preparations for the journey, or at least some of them. The next morning at dawn Mahboub arrived, the bars of his moustache looking just like bird perches. He was leading his beloved female mule, Mahbouba. Her neck was weighed down with all kinds of necklets and collars with tassels, bells, shells, and bags, and blinkers over her eyes with layers of wool, red, blue, and green, all twisted together and intertwined. In the middle was a collar inlaid with shells and decorated with a row of curved yellow cowbells—twenty of them. The mule was a mobile orchestra; whenever she shook her neck or got rid of a fly, the bells would start clanging, startling other animals and disturbing birds.

I told Mahboub that we could keep the necklet with the amulets, the red and green tassels, and the beads to ward off the evil eye. But the cowbells—cowbells, Mahboub!—those are children's toys. Your mule is grown-up, noble, and respected; things for younger mules are not suitable for her.

Nodding in agreement, Mahboub removed the necklet from his mule. "She likes the sound of bells," he said, as though talking to the air.

As though to disprove what he had just said, Mahbouba looked at me with her sleepy eyes, shaking her head as though to express her gratitude for being relieved of this decoration.

Now the servant arrived with a rug and two pillows. Mahboub put the rug on the mule's back and placed the two pillows underneath it, one in front and the other behind. After they had been tied down with ropes, the assemblage became a sturdy, comfortable saddle. The servant came back, along with the mayor's wife, bringing the heavy saddlebag; in one side was the food and in the other various other travel items. It was fastened to the back of the saddle.

"Here's a pistol, Mahboub. You carry it, and use it sensibly."

The pistol, with its leather strap, was a dangerous military weapon with a long bore. I had bought it in New York before coming back to Lebanon because I had been hearing rumors about so-called fliers, bandits operating in the Lebanese mountains. But I never carried it myself and never used it.

Even so, I got used to having it in my desk drawer, and had no qualms about letting people know I had it. So I became famous. People would talk about Rihani's pistol, the same way they would mention the British fleet. Then they would fall silent.

The Dog River

WE SAID FAREWELL to relatives and neighbors amid floods of kisses and tears. The mother's kiss for her son was the warmest of all, followed by the sign of the cross that she drew on his face and chest.

Mahboub pulled the mule, and I walked behind them as far as the edge of the village; that was because the priest had given me instructions as to the customary principles when it came to riding mules. He recited the advice the same way he would recite the Ten Commandments: "Don't shake your legs," "Don't gesture with your hand," "Don't bend your back," "Don't pull the halter tight going uphill, and don't slacken it going downhill," "Don't ride inside the village," "Always honor the muleteer," and "Don't gallop as soon as you start riding."

We left the village on foot and passed by the ancient church on the edge of the next village. Mahboub stopped by the door, brushed the threshold with his hand, and kissed it. He then made the sign of the cross on his face. "Okay, sir," he said, "you can ride now."

With God's help I mounted the mule; with the muleteer's help as well because he was holding the halter.

"I'll lead her for this downhill stretch," he said to reassure me, but I was not reassured. He took the saddle ring out from under the blanket. "Here," he said, "grab this and don't be afraid."

I felt crushed. "Don't be afraid!" This was the first time I had ridden on a mule since my return from America. I made an effort to suppress my worries. Truth be told, it worked because I was forced to overcome my fears, and I did so.

Even so, the descent became steeper and more uneven. This descent to the Dog River was one that I already knew, but on foot. I was aware that the bravest muleteers and most skillful horsemen would not ride down it. So I dismounted and walked behind Mahboub and his mule, Mahbouba.

In the Lebanese mountains there are defiles that are longer and steeper than the one down to the Dog River, but in terms of rough terrain, slippery rocks, and winding paths, that particular descent is unusual and almost unique.

It is still called the river track. Oh no, sir, if that were so, its waters would be similarly uneven and winding.

Is it really the path toward the river? No, dear sir, it's a series of ridges, outcrops, and holes—broken rocks all the way down the mountain to the river. But the mountain folk and their mules have managed to dig ridges, and they have changed the color. It is now a darker red. If you look at it from a distance, from the opposite mountain, it looks like a track between green undergrowth and dust-colored rocks.

I was talking about "mountain folk and their mules," but I was exaggerating—or rather, I was not being precise. Both of them have helpers whose hands cannot be seen and whose actions cannot be measured according to human criteria. Here, for example, is one high, rugged level followed by another one that is low, smooth, and easy, both of them made by feet over the generations—humans and animals, long ago and more recently. Here is a rocky outcrop destroyed by rain and wind, turned by the passage of days and nights into levels and gaps, each one fused with the next. Then here is a rock moved by an earthquake from the heights of eagles' wings to be trodden underfoot by mules. It made animals feel uneasy, so they made a circle round it and cut an easier path for human beings as an inheritance. Is the fall of one hoof after another any stranger than seeing riding animals stop when they smell something acid, or when droppings fall on top of each other? These rocks strewn one on top of the other in some kind of pattern looked just like the rows of stone on the Giza pyramid.

Here now is a heap of white stone, which connects the way down to an open pathway with a tarred surface. Humans and animals alike heave a deep sigh as they stop to listen to the sound of the river as it plunges from a cleft between the two mountains. We approached the cavern even though it was still hidden behind a veil of pines. The sound of the river was still reaching us; it sounded just like the muted distant lowing of animals carried to us and magnified by the morning breezes so that it sounded like roaring lions.

"This cave," Mahboub told me. "Stand where I am and look between those two pines over there. You can see the water in front of the entrance."

His mule stopped beside me, with her hoof right on the edge of the track overlooking the mountain cleft. She then turned to look at the place that Mahboub was indicating. An obedient mule that understood things!

We now proceeded happily with the mule on this gently sloping path, with wide slopes and no debris to cause alarm. The river was clearly visible now, and I admired the way it looked like a sword gleaming in its scabbard. I also made out the pool where the village children would go for a swim whenever they felt that the valley was safe enough, a pool in the middle of the stream surrounded by dark rocks.

The elements and time had turned one of those rocks into a kind of chair with a hollow seat and rests for back and hands. The river water would flow over it; when you sat in it, a silver waterfall would cascade over your shoulders and chest and between your hands. This was the blessing from the river, from the valley, from nature—the mother of the valley, the river, and of you and me.

This then was the throne of the god Neptune; I think I was the first person to sit in it and call it a throne. Afterward, it became well-known by that new name. When I pointed it out to Mahboub the muleteer, he told me that now he understood why his son Hanna used to tell him that he and his friends were going down to the river to sit in the throne and turn into sultans.

"Good God, sir," he said, "there are still a number of sultans and kings in Freike!"[1]

"Mahboub," I replied, "you're a sultan too!"

"All thanks be to God, sir," he said. "In this world anyone with a clean sheet is a sultan! By the very lives of Hanna and his mother, I've a clean sheet—no debts or do others owe me anything. I own this mule, and I wouldn't sell her for all the sultan's money. In hemp season I get a good load, from my vines I can get three casks of wine, and my olives give me enough oil for an entire year. I pay taxes to the government, an exact tithe to the bishop on demand."

"The sultan doesn't pay taxes or tithes. You're better than he is!"

"All thanks be to God!" he said again, kissing his fingernails and then raising them to his forehead. Then he stopped, and so did the mule, and so did I.

"I've a question for you, sir," he said. "Please answer it. You read books and know everything. Who named this river Dog River and why?"

"I'll answer as we walk," I replied. "It's true that I do read books, but it's certainly not the case that I know everything. Mahboub, one of the things I don't know is how this river got that name. Books don't have anything specific to tell us. They say that the Greeks called it Wolf River. How wolf turned into dog I don't know . . ."

"Maybe the astrologer would know?"

"He might, but scholars don't have the answer."

I might just as well finish writing down what I told Mahboub. Maybe others would want to know the answer, even though in this case it's useless.

The answer to his questions is to be found in the legends of the ancients. The river course used to be guarded by a huge, dangerous dog; it was eloquent and loved riddles. He used to pose riddles to passersby to

1. In Freike there used to be a man called Sultan and another called Malik (king). We will be telling you about them later.

solve. Those who did so were given a pass and allowed to proceed. Those who failed the dog swallowed whole without breaking a single bone.

Legends also say that at the mouth of the river people constructed a dog statue, which they used to worship because it would always spot enemies in the distance and bark loudly to let them know and warn them. They also claimed that some of the rocks close to the river look like that statue.

"Look like dogs?!"

"Yes, some of the rocks look like pigs and bulls. I've been told that near Faytroun there are lots of them. You'll see them today."

I'll tell you, Mahboub. If the first person to name this river Dog River were a writer like me and realized, as I do, how curious people can be, he would certainly have recorded the name in books and explained why it was called that. I'm going to record all the events of this trip in writing, including you and the mule, and I won't forget the rock in the middle of the river that I have named the throne. No one will need to wonder or make a guess about it all, especially in the future. No one will need to ask the kind of questions that scholars answer, even with fairy stories that make no sense.

By now we had reached the mills. The river water cascaded from their outlets like a gigantic white dahlia flower or a large Catherine wheel.

We stopped by the stores so that Mahboub could buy a box of candies and ask how the owner of one of them and his wife were doing. We then walked to the bridge with one high arch and crossed to the north side of the river. We were now in Kesrouan, at the foot of the mountains garbed in silky green pine forests. The path ahead was inviting us to climb.

"Come on, sir," Mahboub said, "get on the mule."

After a struggle I was safely installed in the saddle.

"Don't pull on it," he said as he handed me the halter, "and don't let it go slack either. That way . . . don't be scared."

Once again I had to bottle up that "don't be scared." I decided that, before we reached the final stage of our journey that day, I would provide Mahboub with the proof he needed. I know no more about fear than I do about the true origin of the name Dog River.

I started using the edge of the halter to drive the mule, using it to touch her neck. The mule now started speeding up in the incline.

"Slow down, sir," Mahboub yelled, "slow down!"

It was at this point that I remembered one of the basic principles that the village priest had told me: do not go too fast when you have only just mounted.

The track wound its way, quietly and expansively, around the pine-tree roots, with their refreshing perfumed shade. Mahboub kept using shortcuts to keep up with us.

When we had almost reached the top, he gestured that we should stop, so I did so. He came over, panting.

"A nice cigarette under this pine," he suggested.

I lit my pipe. We decided to eat lunch before we reached Rayfoun; we would not stop there but carry on as far as Mayrouba and spend the night there.

We started riding again. Mahboub was walking beside the mule, not behind it. If I gave her a prod so that she speeded up, he would hurry over and walk slowly with his head on her neck. She would then go at his speed, even though her rider and his halter had indicated otherwise.

We passed the edge of Jeita, looking down on an olive orchard with aged trees, some of them over a thousand years old. An hour later we stopped on the mountainside by a store and tent amid some pine trees that offered plentiful shade. Mahboub tied the mule and took down the saddlebag, then took his red handkerchief out of his pocket and mopped his brow.

Of all the views in this mountainous area around Ajaltoun, none is lovelier than the other side of the valley from which he had just come. Bikfaya was there beneath the brow of the lofty mountain, Beit Chabab in the middle right under it, and, moving west from there, a whole chain of villages: Achaouya, Freike, Qornat al-Hamra, Mazraat Yashouaa, Deek El Mehdi, and Bayt El Chaar, each of them connected to the next. Then there was the Rihani house, situated just a little back from the slope down to the edge of the valley, so that anyone looking out of the house would get the impression that it actually stood right on the edge of the big drop into the valley.

Mahboub emerged from the store, followed by the owner, with a water jar, two chairs, and a small table. As Mahboub was taking the food out of the saddlebag, he pointed to his mouth with his thumb. I ordered him a glass of arak, and he downed it at one go.

"Today's your birthday, sir," he said as he ate some kibbe. So I ordered him another glass of arak.

Once we had finished lunch, I looked at him and at the empty pipe in my hand. He understood immediately.

"Bring a nargileh for the gentleman," he told the store owner. "We've time, and the nargileh will be nice under these pine trees.

Mahboub had divided the trip into three stages, so as not to tire me out (as he told me). Even so, I realized that this graded division was also intended to allow both him and his Egyptian mule, Mahbouba, to rest as well. I had also come to the conclusion that he was one of those people who, while they never say it, firmly believe that haste is the work of the Devil.

So we did not make haste in the tent in Ajaltoun, nor did we hurry on the way from Ajaltoun to Rayfoun. But, as we were on our way up to Faytroun on stark, rocky terrain with no shade, I felt hot. So I prodded the mule, and she responded willingly; she trotted, the sound of her hooves on the rocks echoed around. Mahboub ran behind us to catch up as we passed through the village.

"Falling off amid these rocks is really bad!" he said in a disapproving and slightly fearful tone. "Slow down, sir, slow down!"

"Don't be scared, Mahboub," I responded in a tone that blended success and reminder, "don't be scared!"

"By God, sir," he replied with a laugh, "you've become a real cavalier!"

Just at that moment Mahbouba came to a sudden halt and gave a violent kick as she whipped her thighs with her tail to get rid of a fly that was bothering her. It all happened so quickly, I was caught off guard. This redoubtable "cavalier" panicked and collapsed on her back. But for God's good grace and Mahboub's as well, I would have landed on the rocks. How humiliating for the cavalier!

After that we proceeded without problems and arrived at the Museum of Rocks near Faytroun in the late afternoon. The region is renowned for the volcanic rock formations that are unique in Lebanon; they are not known merely for their number of structures but also for the shapes that they take. It is almost as though the hand of the Great Creator, the hand of an artist, has decided to sit down here and work on these rocks. From them he has managed to create everything that the most fertile poetic imaginations could conceive. Among the images and shapes are things that are beautiful, amazing, nasty, ugly, weird, and funny. It is no exaggeration to state that this is a museum of rocks.

It is impossible to get an eyeful of it all in a quarter of an hour. I emerged from this museum to nature filled with desire to go back, one that was to be realized some years later.

The museum is not far from the village. It is a recreation spot for the villagers, especially the young boys and girls. At sunset you could see them all amid the rock exhibits, looking like a flock of sandgrouse or a herd of gazelles.

Once we had passed by the monastery, we were greeted by a man who seemed to know us and welcomed us. Somewhat perplexed, I dismounted to return his greeting.

I did not know anyone in Faytroun, but later I learned that word of our trip to the Cedars had reached some friends in Beirut, and they had a friend in Faytroun. They had written to him to say that we were coming and had entrusted him with our care.

That was how a friendship grew with our host there, Doctor Hanna Diryan, one that was to last like wine and time. He was to become a close friend of long standing.

The Iron Spring

SO WE STOPPED IN FAYTROUN. A single night in the Diryan household was something to be remembered and indeed repeated. Afterward there were many other such visits, and each time we had the same feeling that we had had on the very first visit: amazement and delight.

Hospitality in Kesrouan has some features that are difficult to define and describe. There is generosity, kindness, and gentility, and along with those qualities other things that tradition and custom does not regulate. Those customs may change, but often they do not change, as is the case at this moment in time. Hospitality in Kesrouan is essentially Lebanese, but Lebanese hospitality is not always like that of Kesrouan.

With this Kesrouani hospitality there comes a particular problem, one that makes the guest feel a certain concern along with the joy. There is no denying the fact that the host will always be delighted by the efforts he expends on his guests. Yet the guest—particularly if he comes from the Matn or Shouf regions, where there are a number of new houses, and the more traditional brand of hospitality is fairly rare—will often feel worried in case he might be unable to cope, as he inevitably would be, should the tables be turned and his host became the guest in his own house.

The host is never afraid of anything negative being said about his generosity, kindness, and gentility, but he does worry in case it is suggested that, when a guest is leaving, he does not insist that he should stay as his guest for another day, week, or month and tear his clothes to prevent his guests from leaving.

Next morning as we were leaving, Dr. Hanna Diryan did indeed tear my clothing. He would only let us leave after we had sworn a solemn binding oath—on my honor, by my own mother's life—to turn off and pay them a visit on our way back from the Cedars and stay with them for at least a week.

"The saddlebag's full, chock-full, by God! Thanks to your charity and God's, we have enough for the journey to Aleppo!"

This is what I heard Mahboub saying as I left the house.

"This isn't enough for you," I heard the servants saying as they were packing piles of food and bottles of wine into the saddlebag. "We're sorry, it's not what you deserve."

At this point Dr. Hanna arrived with a letter he had written to a friend of his in Mghayreh.

"Spend the night in Mghayreh," he said as he handed it to the muleteer. "Don't go any further today even if you get there by noon." So what risk is there? "There's no risk, but we want the gentleman to feel relaxed."

However, the muleteers to whom Mahboub had spoken the night before had told him that the upper track—up in the clouds—had its risks. They advised him to stick to the lower track to Lassa: first forests, then Mghayreh.

Faytroun is located at the same elevation as the heights of Dhour Choueir (1,150 meters), although it may be a bit higher. But the land goes uphill to Mayrouba, whereas below it the terrain is coarser and more uneven than that in the Choueir heights, for example, or Ayntoura in the Matn region. But that is not surprising since Matn's destiny has seen more prosperity than Kesrouan's.

The route from Faytroun to Mayrouba may be rideable, and at certain points may pass through vineyards, but the terrain is freezing cold and rough as well; in fact, it is a Kesrouani track, with sparks and pebbles flying from underneath the animal's hooves, the noise that they make clearly audible as it bounces off the rocks and bends in the track.

After two hours we passed the high outskirts of Mayrouba and made our way from there up through the vineyards to the genuine uplands, where all verdure disappears and shadows fade. You find yourself in an arid, stony wilderness. It is extremely hot, the sunshine is abundant, and any notion of tranquility is remote. Even so, it is not lacking in varieties of natural beauty; indeed, it has two tremendous boons: a cool, refreshing breeze, and cold, invigorating springs.

Lebanese people who cling to their mountain rocks are just like those mountain heights in their roughness, their breezes, and their springs. They are that perfumed breeze in all its gentle softness, that limpid, clear spring flowing so liberally. Beyond that you can say what you like; they are still the hand of charity in exquisite balance.

These are the names of the springs up there: Barn Spring, Arrow Spring, "Bust Your Bag" Spring, and Iron Spring!

What brought us to Iron Spring? Mahboub was supposed to take the lower route to Lassa, far away from eagles' nests and robbers, but he lost his way amid all the rocks without telling me. Instead, he took us on the route that worried him, the high route to the Afqa Cave.

I had asked him to take us by Afqa, but he had started mumbling. "What is there in the Afqa Cave?" he asked. "What is the Afqa Cave? Just a hole in the mountain. Tomorrow I'll buy you a picture of it in Beirut. You'll see that it's not worth visiting. The picture's nicer than the actual thing."

So here we are at the Iron Spring. It is only an hour from the cave, and the track goes downhill. To get here we have crossed the highest point in the mountains: the Iron Spring is at 1,590 meters; it is an oven-shaped pool—or rather, a rock-pool—with water cascading down on to the bubbling surface, as though it were all boiling. If you put your hand in the water, you would not keep it there for more than a quarter of a second, so freezing cold is it.

We tried it. I put my hand in fifteen times, and quickly pulled it out again in pain. Mahboub made it up to twenty. But the goatherd who was there when we arrived did it thirty times and proudly withdrew his hand without any fuss.

It is quite normal to see goatherds by the Iron Spring. I can still recall that young goatherd whose outstanding mountain beauty is riveted in my mind: his huge shiny black eyes and his wide, crimson mouth, as though he were the god Tammuz.

He had opened his knapsack and taken out some dry bread. He proceeded to moisten it with the water, bend it over, and make two bites out of it. Once in a while he would pick up a stone and throw it at a straying goat to bring it back to the herd.

We shaded ourselves beneath one of the rocks. Mahboub took down the saddlebag and opened it. The aroma of roast chicken and grilled kibbe wafted into the air. The young goatherd was still moistening his bread and making it into bite-sized pieces. I called him over, but he said, "Thanks very much. God bless you, but . . ." When I insisted, he came over, hesitant and bashful. With apologies, he sat on a rock. We shared our food with him.

"Please wait just a minute," he said. Leaping over the rocks like one of his goats, he soon came back with a milk pail, the milk still warm from the udder. We put the pail into the spring to get cold. Within seconds, it was like frozen milk.

All the while I watched as the muleteer chatted to the goatherd.

"That way leads to Afqa," I heard the latter say, and, as he tossed a stone underarm that made a lofty arc, "that way leads to Lassa."

Mahboub was taking a route that scared him to a place where I wanted to go but he did not because he was worried about bandits. When we reached the spot where the goatherd's stone had disappeared, we could make out the path that first curved to the northwest and then went straight west, crossing a waterway called the River Boundy. We would pass by the village of Chouata, whose inhabitants, some three hundred in number, were all Shiʿa. From there we would make our way to Lassa.

When Mahboub had earlier refused to take me to Afqa, wanting instead to buy me a picture of it, which would be more beautiful, I assumed that he was being lazy and wanted to make the trip shorter. But when I now realized that he was really scared, was taking a long detour and avoiding Afqa, I changed my mind and told myself he was a coward.

Then something else happened, which told me even more about him and made me change my mind again. We were heading downward toward Lassa and passed through a forest of flowering Judas trees.

"Take this knife," I told him, "and bring me a branch."

"There's plenty of your so-called Judas trees ahead of us," he replied.

All he had to do was to climb over a wall no more than a meter high and walk a few meters to the tree. He refused to do it. With that, I wrote him down as both lazy and a coward.

"Afqa's just a hole in the mountain; pictures of it are more beautiful than the place itself"—a fine example of "philosophical cowardice." "There's plenty of your so-called Judas trees"—noble, mendacious sloth.

There is nothing quite like travel to reveal hidden traits of your companion as well as God's kindness toward us and the concealment of our faults.

The Sacred Valleys

AMONG THE WONDERFUL ASPECTS of this trip to the Cedars is that it goes through mountains. You cross three historic rivers: the Dog, the Ibrahim, and the Kadisha. There are also three remarkable historic caves: Jeita, Afqa, and Bsharre (Kadisha).

Among the attributes of these rivers and caves is one of sanctity, its seeds long since sown by shamans, developed by devout people of faith, and magnified by the censers of time. People of both the East and West have planted along the banks of these rivers seeds of legend and folktale and have given it a national religious tinge. For a while it was all Phoenician, then Greco-Roman, and then Aramean (Syriac), or Arabic.

We passed some Greek and Roman ruins by the Dog River, and now we are overlooking some Phoenician ones embodied in this river, which today has a Semitic name, one that is not Phoenician.

The name given to the cave is actually closer to the source of its sanctity than that of the river. If it were not for the muleteer's cowardly attitude, we would have taken the high road to it; the difference in distance is no more than ten kilometers.

Even so, Mahboub's cowardice was not without its benefits. If it were not for him, we would have been deprived of the view of a town in this sacred Phoenician valley, one whose situation was very peculiar.

It is a tiny village nestling quietly in the bend of the valley from whose summit the Iron Spring emerges and at the valley's floor flows into the River Adonis. This village has three contradictions to life in general: its name, its people, and its episcopal seat—its Tibetan name, its Shi'a Muslim population, and its Maronite seat. Where are Adonis,

Ashtarut (Venus), and all their devotees amid all this diversity and separate sects?

I do not think that John Murad, the bishop of the Diocese of Baalbek, can tell us the source for the village's name, it being the bishop's summer residence. Lassa, from where did that name make its way to Lebanon?

Lhasa, the capital city of Tibet, is renowned for its monasteries, monks, and Buddhism, with its multiple rituals and legends. *Lhasa*, meaning "the throne of the gods" in the ancient Indian tongue, the holy city from the Lama and his followers. What, I wonder, can be the connection between it and the Lebanese *Lassa*, a village that has a few Maronite families connected with the Maronite seat and a number of Shi'a families?

This time I was the one asking a question, and it was directed at Mahboub rather than Mahbouba the mule. We were making our way downhill toward Lassa. The mule stopped before Mahboub did; we were alongside a house.

"Last time I stopped here," Mahboub said, "it was to buy some beans. She still recognizes the house. With that in mind, can we deny any longer that she's an intelligent mule?!"

"Why didn't she continue on the upper track to Afqa, then?" I asked. "You told me that you've taken it many times."

"Because she's clever, sir. Does an intelligent person erect his own gallows? No, and an intelligent mule doesn't either. Don't forget, sir, that I'm responsible for you. I've told you that pictures of Afqa are nicer than it is. You'll be seeing it tomorrow, and then you'll say that Mahboub was right!"

"You haven't answered my first question."

"About Lassa, you mean? By God, sir, its people are human beings. When it comes to bartering with them, they are all known to be honest. But when times get tough, they turn into ravenous eagles. They go up to the top of the hill and set up roadblocks."

"Do you think they're braver than other people?"

"I think they have better weapons."

"Better than the weapon you're carrying, Mahboub?"

"Oh please stop asking so many questions, sir. I've told you that I'm responsible for you. Even so, if you're so eager to go to Afqa, then so be it!"

With that, Mahboub banged the mule on its neck, and she spun round like a wheel. As Mahboub led her uphill, he kept yelling, "Dih, dih" at it, and cursing both Afqa and the Cedars.

"Don't get mad, Mahboub, don't get mad!" I told him. "We're almost at Mghayreh. Once you've had a rest, you'll feel better."

"I'm fine, sir. It's just that your questions are enough to roil even the Iron Spring."

"This time, Mahboub, I'm asking about Lassa . . ."

"All I know about Lassa is that we transport pottery from Beit Chabab and sell it to the villagers at inflated prices. From them we purchase beans, humus, lentils very cheap."

After passing by the village with the Tibetan name, we entered Forests Village, whose name reflects reality, in that the place is full of trees, forests that were there long before humans came. The village was built on the banks of the river to the south, the Ibrahim River. We crossed the bridge to the north side and after a quarter of an hour reached a watercourse where the Aqoura River was flowing, joining up after Forests with the waters of the historic Ibrahim River. We crossed the other bridge and entered Mghayreh, the village where we had a letter to deliver.

In olden times, Mghayreh had a Phoenician name: Yanouh. In the Phoenician period it had a temple to Adonis, the same time as the temple in Afqa. In the Christian era it became a monastery, which later became the seat of the Maronite Patriarchate. Eighteen patriarchs lived and died there, all mentioned by Patriarch Al-Duwayhi in his *Lebanese Community*. There are still some Phoenician remains in Mghayreh, parts of a palace and legal texts; from the heads of the Maronite community there remain lands of whose bounty we will partake tonight.

We went up to the house of Daoud Malkoun, who at the time was an associate of Bishop Yusuf Diryan with a piece of property he owned in Mghayreh.

I can still remember Daoud—modest, always smiling, and good company. He was as good at telling jokes as he was as a host to his guests. Along with his innocent smile, I can also recall his peppery conversation. That night, Mahboub was its victim. We had sat down to eat on a carpet on the ground spread over a mat. The food was served on a copper tray. The conversation turned to bandits.

"Poor devils!" Daoud proclaimed as he poured some arak into Mahboub's glass. "They're scared to death of their own shadows. But their voices carry a long way, and their moustaches have long sidebars like yours, Mahboub! They've started calling them *fliers* because one day they'll be here, the next day by the spring, then the cave—just like birds although the comparison is not very accurate. The government, over and over again, is scared of these fliers, and they themselves are scared of their own shadows."

"Is the government the only one scared of them?" I asked. "Here's Mahboub!"

Mahboub was furious even before I got to his name. Cursing and swearing at fliers and Afqa, he threw his glass of arak away.

Now I had to recall the advice I had received from the priest in Freike, the principles to be applied in riding animals. The last one was: "Respect your muleteers. Above all, don't get Mahboub angry. He's very irascible!"

Even so, the word that escaped my lips gave me some more information, and there's always some benefit in everything that you learn. All of which led me to keep things to myself during our trip, if only to maintain the peace. In fact, I started being extra polite with him. For example, "If you please, Mahboub, bring me the water jug," or "Please open the saddlebag," or "Please spread the rug."

This mode of talking impressed Mahboub, and he borrowed it for himself. After that particular night, he started using it randomly. "Please, I'd like to sleep on the roof," he would say to Daoud when the servant girl was laying out the bedding for sleep.

During those days our host, the bishop's associate, was clearly well-off, whether he received a half, a third, or a quarter; a man of great dignity, especially since he was a partner of the bishop or of a major influential landowner. Daoud was in fact the sheikh of the village, with assistants to help him keep things profitable and a village woman to serve him in the household.

The house was like all peasants' and associates' homes, with one or two roofed sections open on one of their two sides to a vaulted terrace beneath. This terrace was shaded by a bower made of either wormwood or a vine trellis. The house faced east, and winds toyed with it—except, that is, for its dark, scary roof—which was supported by a single rock pillar with a wooden beam and girders. Smoke from the oven had turned it black, and insects and snakes hid up there. Once in a while one of them might fall into your food while you were eating or on your bed while you were sleeping.

But on the day when we were Daoud's guests, nothing of that sort happened. We ate his roasted chicken and drank his matured wine, then went to sleep feeling secure and comfortable in his capacious, clean beds.

This was hospitality delightful for its modesty and wonderful for its spirit. The next morning, we were hardly ready to leave before Daoud was getting his donkey ready, and the servant woman and Mahboub were exchanging compliments and apologies. She was adding yet more provisions to what we already had. Our saddlebag now became like the magic knapsack of the famous Kurd. How much fruit and vegetables do you need? How about other things to eat? What about drinks—wine, arak, fizzy drinks?

Daoud rode with us to the Pearl Spring, a distance that took an hour and a half. We stopped by a house made of animal hair in a district there in which Daoud—God have mercy on him!—knew the beautiful owner. He greeted her with great affection, and she returned his greeting in the same fashion. They joked and laughed for a while, then Daoud pointed with his cane at the dome shape under her bosom.

"Whose son is that?" he asked her.

"God knows!" the beautiful lady responded with a laugh.

Daoud showed Mahboub where to go next, then we all said farewell by the Pearl Spring. We traveled northeast, passed above Tannourine, and climbed up to the mountain covered in cedars known as Hadath cedars or Patriarch's cedars. That is because the forest with cedars and cypress were assigned to the people of Hadath; they were allowed to exploit the proceeds jointly according to a system arranged by the Maronite Patriarchate and were in charge of the trees' preservation.

From this forest, which is close in height to the famous Cedars of Lebanon, we went downhill to Hadath; we left the rocky mountain track for a carriage road, which went all the way from the middle of the mountain range via the rim of the Kadisha Valley, from Hadath to Hasroun, then Bazaoun and Bsharre. The height above sea level varied from 1,200 to 1,400 meters.

Mahboub the muleteer was still in a bad mood and sulking over what had been said the previous night. Throughout this third trip of ours, the situation only grew worse. He started losing his temper with his own shadow whenever it loomed beside him or in front of him. He was cursing everything in sight, and only because he was tired and aggravated.

He even started cursing his own mule Mahbouba as she was climbing up the Hadath mountain like a thoroughbred horse. He threw a stone, which hit her behind the ear. That made her rear up and swish her tail. If her rider had not by now become a skilled horseman, she would have thrown him to the ground.

Once we reached the cart track, he went over to the mule and told me not to use the halter to goad her. We slowly made our way from Hadath to Bsharre without stopping to rest. Mahboub wanted us to stop for lunch in Hasroun, Bazaoun, or Bsharre.

"We're not eating or stopping," I told him firmly, "till we get to the Cedars."

That only made him even more bad-tempered.

"Dih, dih!"

We were over halfway between Bsharre and the Cedars. We were going up a narrow, twisting track, its surface in pieces and its outer edge totally dilapidated. It kept on spiraling as we found ourselves hemmed in between a high wall that glowered down at travelers, and on the other side a deep abyss that was always ready to welcome them.

By now I was totally fed up with this route; Mahbouba's slow pace and hesitancy were boring me. Mahboub had told me not to use the halter or touch her neck with it. I decided to try and get her to move faster by using flattery and compliments:

"Respectable lady," I said, "jewel among mules, lovely bride of the mountain vales, Mahboub's pride and joy, blessed one, Mahbouba, and finish what you've begun. On this sacred mountain track do not now sacrifice all the glory that you have earned during this entire journey!"

I then addressed her in muleteer's talk: "Dih, dih!"

"Forget the 'dih, dih,' sir," Mahboub yelled. "Forget it! The mule doesn't understand your dialect. Leave her to me. I'll talk to her."

"Dih, by your masters' religion," he now told the mule, "dih!"

Mahbouba now took a few disjointed steps, then stopped. Mahboub kept treating her patiently as he walked, then stopped alongside her. When he saw that she was in the middle of the track, he leaned down to the ground. Hurling the first rock, he scraped her thigh; with the second he straightened the bend in her neck. That done, he ran behind her, put her back on the track, and, holding on tightly, walked beside her. I was feeling furious by now and tugged the halter. The mule swung round hard, and her haunches hit Mahboub hard on the chest. He fell to the ground right on the edge of the abyss and almost fell off. I could imagine him rolling like a rock down that appalling slope to the very bottom of the valley. I was in a complete panic.

"I'm so sorry, Mahboub!" I said, "I apologize!"

Mahboub got up, brushed the dirt off his trousers, and adjusted the cap on his head.

"Let's go, sir!" he said. "Let's go. If we hang around everywhere blaming each other, we'll never get there today!"

However, praise be to God, just a short while later we were overlooking the Cedars. To be precise, it was at 2:00 p.m. on August 10, 1907, that we entered the sacred enclosure safe and sound.

The Cedars

YOU CEDARS OF LEBANON, we have reached you safe and sound!

However, when we looked down on your majesty heaped beneath the mountain's rim, hope came crashing down from above, imagination veered from its firmament, and heart swerved in its faith and affection.

I had envisioned you as being spread across mountain heights, camped on top of plains and hills, and rising high like a rainbow over valleys and flatlands. Your sweet scent would waft the perfume of blossoms and sweet basil, and every kind of verdant plant would cluster in your shade, extending your splendor over the water's surface, among the rocky streams, and at the concourse of ravines and mountain trails. I had imagined the Cedars in this all-inclusive guise of glory. But what I saw instead was a secluded spot huddled in a bend by the edge of a drainage ditch.

I had imagined the mountains as being in the shadow of the Cedars, but instead the Cedars were in the mountains' shadow.

I had imagined that time itself would be embodied in the cedar forest, whereas I saw the Cedars belittled by the hand of time.

I had imagined a green landscape, one where the human gaze would balk at its own inadequacy and eagles' wings would crack as they soared toward its widespread roots. Instead, I saw a blackened patch of ground on a gloomy bend, with eagles' wings outspread arrogantly overhead.

I had imagined a splendor engulfing the mountains far and wide, high and low; from its heights it would emit a scent to perfume the meadows, an essence to anoint the plains.

I had imagined a splendor with the sun's gleam at its door and moonlight in its sanctum. It would be sending them sacred sounds, to be repeated over generations and times.

I had imagined silken splendors on golden thrones in divine precincts.

I had imagined all of this before I stood by the gate, feeling a sense of shock and burning despair.

Are the Cedars a page from history?

Are the Cedars a poetic ode or prophetic canticle?

Are the Cedars lines in a much-beloved book?

Are the Cedars frankincense in the censer of time?

Are the Cedars a sign from a pen or a drawing on a flag?

It has been said that every great work of nature and art is small in the eyes of those close to it. We have to move away from it a little in order to see its eminence and beauty clearly and appreciate the genuine glory and sublimity that it possesses.

That statement is true for some things, but not for others. For example, it is true for high mountains: you cannot appreciate how high they are when you are standing on their slopes. Standing on the slope of the Cedar Mountain you can imagine yourself climbing for another hour to the very top. If you look at the moon as it rises from behind a treetop, you can imagine that, if you had wings, you could easily reach it by making a single leap from a cedar branch. It is all trompe l'oeil, making you think that distances are foreshortened.

But with palaces, major temples, and lofty trees, the opposite is the case. You can only gauge how amazing tall buildings, such as skyscrapers in New York City, actually are if you are close to them.

You can only sense how amazingly high the six pillars of the Baalbek Temple actually are if you are standing in their shadow or beneath their frieze.

When you are in a large famous shrine, like Notre Dame Cathedral in Paris or the Dome of the Rock in Jerusalem, the beauty of the artwork and the sanctity of the magnificent edifice only become clear if you come out of the shadows, enter through the door, and stand beneath the dome alongside a lofty doorpost.

So I entered the historic sacred forest, probing its awesome solemnity, a footstool for the perplexed heart, a sanctum for the humble soul.

I entered the sanctuary, secure and trustful, and walked through arcades paved with black rugs made out of the cedar leaves and soil. I stopped beneath a green dome alongside one of the enormous portals, all the while contemplating the shock that I had felt on arriving and the emotions flooding my mind now that things had become clear to me.

Here now is an immanence embraced by the mountain, its sides perfumed by the Cedars. It is an immanence that wafts beneath the branches. As it brushes against the scattered branches, it creates a sound—not that of the dawn breeze but rather the whisper of the inimitably simple, that discourse to which styles of eloquence and rhetoric genuflect.

In that temple I halted beneath the green dome amid lofty pillars. I bathed the face of doubt in the soil of immanence, brushed the eye of longing with its scent, and at its whisper pricked up the ear of love and forgiveness.

There I heard some ancient tones of love, some strange accents of eloquence, some loving whispers of celebration, all of them falling like cedar needles into the welcoming bosom of immanence, or like April rains on mulberry leaves.

Different kinds of sound: some of them soft and expansive, others loud and harsh, still others like the echoes of evening bells in the mountains, like the cooing of doves in the dawn quietude, like the whisper of trees on the riverbanks, like the lion's roar in the midday heat, like waves crashing on to rocks.

I heard the Phoenician describing the beauties of cedarwood in Egypt so the pharaoh could hear: a solid, polished wood, with lovely colors and veins, and aromatic; an adornment of temples and palaces. Time has no power over it, worms do not go near it. An amazing wood, dry as rock, smooth as glass, lovely as the rose.

I heard the words of that Phoenician repeated at the palace of the kings of Nineveh and Ashur, also of the kings of Persia.

I heard the sound of axes and scythes in the forests and sounds of hammers and saws working in the factories of Tripoli and Byblos.

I heard Ashurbanipal boasting about the tax in cedar trees that he received, while Senacherib would brag about his visit to the Cedars amid the mountain peaks.

After voices of invaders and plunderers I heard others—serious, poetic, holy.

The psalmist shouting the name of the Lebanese cedar trees.

The author of the Song of Songs singing of his dais made of cedarwood and of his bride's fragrance matching that of Lebanon.

I heard Isaiah praising the lofty Cedars of Lebanon, and Amos comparing the tyrannical Amorite with cedars.

I heard the voice of Jesus proclaiming that the beauty of cedars was Lebanon's pride and joy, its peaks garlanded with dense cedar forests; and Ezekiel's voice like the crashing of waves on rocks.

Cedars of Lebanon—gorgeous species, mark of shade, lofty in stature.

Cedars of Lebanon—exalted by waters and raised by floods to the mountain peaks.

Cedars of Lebanon, in whose branches nest all birds of the heavens, beneath whose limbs are born all kinds of animals, in whose shade have dwelt all great peoples.

Splendor in its height, in the extent of its species, in its very creation. Every tree in Eden, God's paradise, has envied it.

I heard the Greek historian supporting the prophet of Israel, I heard the Frankish poets repeating the echoing voices of prophets and historians.

As I listened to the voices of poetry and history, the forest was vanishing bit by bit. At the mountaintop I could see an enormous forest stretching east to west, north to south, with other dense forests beyond it.

In those same forests I heard the sounds of axes and saws, the voices of woodcutters and lumberjacks.

I saw wood from those forests in Egypt, its planks lining the walls of Pharaonic palaces and temples, sprinkling its sawdust over the corpses of embalmed kings, bestowing its scent on the tombs of mummies.

I saw wood from those forests in Ashur's temple and the palaces of Persian kings.

In David's palace, Solomon's Temple, and the shrines of Roman gods in Ephesus and Antioch.

I saw wood from those forests on the high seas with their roaring waves.

Trading vessels, Phoenician, battling the terrors of the ocean at the feet of Hercules, and witnessing the crumbling of limestone rocks on the shores of the British Isles.

Phoenician ships transporting dyes, glass, and textiles from these ancient eastern shores to western and northern shores.

Phoenician ships crossing the Atlantic to the New World and furling their sails by the shores of West Africa at the equator.

I heard the sounds of axes and scythes in those forests.

I heard the sounds of hammers and saws in Byblos's factories.

I saw cedarwood in the war vessels used by the Persians to invade Greece.

In the wood market Alexander the Great wanted the very best in order to construct a causeway at Tyre that would connect the island to the city; he needed some of your cedar so that Tyre could be taught a lesson.

The valleys echo with the sounds of axes, and waves carry the sounds of scythes from Byblos to Tripoli, from Tripoli to Arwad.

King Antiochus ordered the construction of five hundred warships so that he could attack the city that had rebelled against Alexander and use them to sack it—Tyre, a Phoenician bride.

The owners of the forests were Phoenicians, as were the wood merchants and the boatbuilders.

Yes indeed, my child! Those times were not devoid of loyalists devoted to their homeland. Some folk spread rumors about people who put their own interests above those of the homeland. Noisy grumbles and protests could be heard.

And yet, my child, commerce goes on, and in every time and place!

So here we see cedarwood in the fleet of King Antiochus.

And here we see it again, a thousand years later, that same cedarwood in the fleets of the Umayyad caliph Muawiya. Those fleets are of Phoenician manufacture.

We are all for the homeland, all for the flag!

Realities and Details

AT THAT PARTICULAR TIME, the only buildings at the Cedars were a small church and a store. For tourists, there were only old, threadbare tents set up inside the wall. I rented one of them.

"We're staying here for three days," I told Mahboub. "Now you're my guest, and I'm the Lord's guest."

"You usually beat me in everything, sir," he replied. "But, forgive me, I went to the church this morning and heard the priest say Mass. The priest came to see you, sir, and invited you, but you didn't go. So who's the Lord's guest?!"

"On that score you've beaten me, Mahboub!" I said. "Go to Mass tomorrow for both you and me, and give the priest my greetings."

"He told me to give you his greetings," he replied. "The priest is nice and generous. He invited me for breakfast and insisted. So we ate breakfast together, then took a walk in this incredible forest. How many amazing things there are here! The priest showed me the cedar tree in whose root the hermit lived, and another tree with a water basin in it—and it was full and continually refilled. Where does the water come from? One of the Lord's many miracles. The priest told me all about it."

"'He who believes in the stone will find peace.' Didn't our Lord the Messiah say that?"

"Yes, he did, and I'm one of those who believe. I didn't tell you about the gash on my leg. What's the point? I was tired on the way here, but I put up with the pain from the wound and kept walking. All the time you were riding the mule without paying any attention to me."

And I had accused him of being lazy! It was really incredible. Mahboub took off his shoes to show me the wound; it was on his right foot underneath the ankle, and it looked really serious and inflamed. I felt utterly ashamed, humbled, and distressed.

"It was worse than what you can see now," he went on. "But today I've bathed it in water from the cedar tree and—thank God—it's much better."

"We should lance it," I said, "then rub some iodine on it."

I took a razor and bottle out of my bag.

"No, thank you, sir," he said. "The Lord's cure is enough."

More than once I watched him visit the cedar tree with the basin. Once he had bathed the wound with its water, he did the same to his face, as though he were leaving the church.

During those days Mahboub seemed the happiest of men, content and pleasant. All he had to do was eat, chat, visit the tree with the water basin, and . . . sleep. His favorite activity was sleeping after a visit to the tree with the water basin.

Even so, he refused to sleep with me in the tent. Instead, he spread his blanket under the Lord's tent, as he put it, on the soft carpet of cedars.

"I'm sleeping on a blanket and carpet, sir," he told me. "You're sleeping on a blanket and three planks. But don't worry, I'm close by."

"How can anyone be afraid, Mahboub," I asked, "when they're staying beside the Lord's cedars?"

"There's no logic to fear, sir," he replied. "My neighbor, Abu Mikhayil, can grab a raging bull by the horns and pull a snake out of its hole. But when his wife yells, 'Abu Mikhayil!!' he starts running to her like a scared cat. When she swears at him and curses his ancestors, he stands there in front of her shaking like a reed. There's no logic to fear."

"Does that apply to everyone? How about you?"

"I only fear God," he replied, tossing his cigarette away angrily. "But, when I'm with someone like yourself, and mother, brother, aunts, priest, and mayor all start giving me instructions to take care of you, then I get worried. Being responsible for people like you, sir, gets me worried, even if it's only in my imagination. Don't be shocked. When God abandons anyone, there's no difference between his imagination and that of death. Oh Lord, have mercy on us in the hour of abandonment!"

He repeated the phrase as he lit another cigarette. "And don't think," he went on, "that I've mentioned my imaginings in order to belittle that last climb, the one up to the Cedars. By God, I was afraid of my own imagination. The mule was utterly exhausted, and, just like you and me, she was scared of the track we were taking and hating her own life. When she spotted my specter in front of her, she gave a start and freaked out. If I hadn't rushed over and calmed her down, she would have come crashing down and you with her. All of this is part of my imaginings, those of her owner. Will you blame me if I say that you are responsible for the way that I'm scared of my own imagination . . . ?"

"But enough of such talk," he went on. "Please tell me half of what you've learned from books about the Cedars. How old is one of those cedar trees close to the church?"

"One scholar has suggested that the oldest tree is three thousand years old; in other words, it was a tiny plant at the time of Solomon the Wise sitting on his throne in Jerusalem."

"How do scholars come to that conclusion?"

"Trees have rings, which can tell you their age. Can't you tell the age of a pine from its rings?"

"As long as it's still growing and the rings are visible, that's easy. But when it stops growing and it only grows thicker, it's difficult to assess its age."

"It's not the scholars' problem. You can also tell the age from its roots. When they spread, you can see circles in the roots, one after another, running from the core to the outer shell. Like the rings on the trunk, those circles help deciding on the tree's age."

"Have you measured the cedars near the church?"

"Yes, I have, using this rope. Here it is!"

He extended the rope, and we measured it from the top to the place where the knot was tied. It was about twenty arms' lengths; in other words, the diameter of the root of that particular tree was about fourteen meters.

"If we confirm the age of the big tree, can't we also find out the relative age of others as well? Take this high tree, for example: its age is in its height."

"You and I together can wrap our arms around it. So what's its age?"

"It's nearly twenty meters high. I don't think it's more than three hundred years old; actually, that's confirmed by annalistic historians. In the forest today there are about 400 trees of different sizes. According to evidence left to us by Frankish scholars who came to visit, there were more than 25 trees that are three hundred years old. In the eighteenth century, 10 trees were no longer here; in other words, only 15 trees were left, including this big one that we can still see here today. Afterward, the forest began to renew itself, so that in the last century, according to a German scholar who visited at the beginning of the nineteenth century and counted the trees, there were 375. A Swiss scholar also visited and confirmed the counts of previous visitors."

"If there were 375 a hundred years ago and today there are 400, that's only 25 more trees. That's very few."

"If it weren't for the Maronite Patriarchate—something that Al-Duwayhi and other careful documenters tell us—there wouldn't be any increase at all. In fact, there would be a decrease and an imminent danger of them totally disappearing. The patriarchs—God have mercy on them!—started threatening anyone who cut any part of the trees with excommunication."

"May God protect their faith!"

"Unfortunately, Mahboub, excommunication by the patriarchs has no impact on thunder, lightning, rain, and wind, nor on tempests and earthquakes. There have been times in the past when the Lord God has shown His wrath against the Maronites, sending winds and earthquakes against the Cedars as a reminder and punishment. At one point in the Psalms, the Prophet David says: 'The voice of the Lord breaks the cedars; the Lord breaks the cedars of Lebanon.'"

We were soon looking down on the Cedars.

"Your knowledge, sir, is an ocean," he replied, "a veritable ocean. And yet, not all knowledge brings any comfort to people. Excuse me, sir, but I much prefer to stretch out beneath these lofty trees and contemplate something that I don't think you've realized yet—the love that the cedars feel for each other. I always tell Umm Hana that trees are just like men and women—they share love and affection. Just look at that branch extending from this tree to its neighbor, grabbing one of its branches. From the embrace of those two branches a third is born, a son—father, mother, and son—that's a holy family. Then look at that tree with its two trunks. Even though I don't have a great deal of learning, as you point out, sir, I will state that one of them is male and the other female. The Lord of the Cedars has garlanded bride and groom; one has stayed attached to the other until bosom has clung to bosom. Love and affection have endured, and the couple has produced children—those large, lofty branches. This blessed family will now live just as the tree next to the church has lived. It will live for three thousand years, or even more, God willing!"

"God bless you!"

"Write down in that book of yours, sir," he said, "one that people will be reading in a thousand years' time—God willing—just as you have been quoting from the Psalms of David. (I had my doubts about Mahboub's good intentions in making this prayer, but—in any case—I accepted it with all due humility.) Write in your book, sir, that Bou Hanna Mahboub al-Mallah accompanied you to the Cedars, and that I stated that there is more love and affection between its trees than among human beings. The best thing about this forest, apart from the cedar with the water basin in it, is those trees linked together in marriage, each one loving the other."

The Rome Spring

VISITORS TO THE CEDARS in those days had every right to call themselves pilgrims, not merely because of the sanctity of the place but also due to the difficult path to get there, especially the last section of it. It is not surprising that there were very few visitors. While we were staying there, the only people we saw were the priest, the store owner, a few shepherds and woodcutters in the sacred enclosure, and two visitors. No tourists from abroad, or even from Lebanon itself.

I used to watch Mahboub chatting to any shepherd or woodcutter he saw. He wanted to feel more certain about the next phase of our journey, which we had decided on together, as a safety measure for us and the mule as well. We were certainly not going back by the mountain route between Bsharre and the Cedars; we would all be lost, plunging into its abysses.

Even though Mahboub did not know the mountaintop path that we had decided to take back, and even though it required us to climb to the very top of the Cedar Mountain toward Dahr el-Qadeeb, he neither hesitated nor raised the slightest objection.

As we were preparing to leave on the fourth morning, I asked him about his wound. He told me that it was better, but, before he took the nose bag off the mule's neck and tied it behind the saddle ready to leave, I noticed that he went over to his beloved cedar tree, rubbed his foot with water from its roots and then his forehead as well, making the sign of the cross as he did so.

The priest came to say farewell.

"The Cedars' blessings be ever with you!" he said, handing me a sprig of cedar he had brought with him.

His gesture had a very pleasant effect on me, which lasted for a long time. I can still recall it today; thirty years later it still represents all the wonder and gratitude that I felt at the time. Here's the faithful shepherd running after a stray lamb to bring it back to the pen. Jesus told his disciples, "Go look for the lost sheep," and even more than that (as related by Matthew in his Gospel, 18:12).

I bade the reverend priest farewell and entrusted myself to God. Mahboub did likewise, making up for what my prayer lacked by saying, "And to the Lady of the Cedars."

The sun's rays were shining bright, gleaming and glistening on the rim of Dahr el-Qadeeb as we started our ascent of the mountain.

The elevation of mountain heights in Lebanon varies between 1,500 and 1,000 meters. There are some pathways there, only marred by steep inclines leading up to them. The paths themselves are all of only one kind, whether going up or down: open and easygoing, marked by the beauties of the high-level atmosphere.

The Cedars (at 1,925 meters) is reckoned to be in the mountaintops, and from the Cedars still further upward is the skies. No wonder! In those days planes did not belittle the skies as they do today. We consider them part of the earth's soil. But in those days such heights were indeed high, with all the awe, majesty, and esteem associated with them.

Oh then, let us go up above the clouds, to the very peaks, the mountain pinnacles! At the time I think I boasted like Senacherib, king of Ashur, who, when he returned to Nineveh after his raid on Syria, said, "I've visited the Cedars on the Lebanese mountaintops!"

The first hour of our climb was a noble and blessed time, full of an energy and delight that affected the one who decided on this trip, the owner of the mule, and the mule herself. Mahbouba "took off for the hills" (as muleteers say) as though she had drunk water and eaten some barley. Even though she was moving deftly and swiftly, her movements were firm; the echo of her hooves resounded amid the rocks, and sparks and pebbles shot out from beneath her hooves. I did not need to use the halter to stimulate her; nor did I or Mahboub have to yell "dih" to encourage her.

Onward and upward to the heights! At one point Mahbouba stopped for a moment on a bend in the track and turned to look at the western horizon behind her. As it receded, its color looked more and more like the sky. As we headed ever upward, the cedar forest grew smaller and smaller, until eventually it looked just like a pile of twigs in the mountain's shadow.

Onward and upward to the heights! How wonderful the climb was, how fresh the air, and how generous the sun's rays shining in our faces! How generous was the mountain with that warmth, even though the track became narrower and we were more isolated as we approached the very summits of the mountains, with the sky overhead smiling in

Tourists can never truly appreciate the pleasures afforded by mountains—the beauty of them, the deeper significances they possess, and the sources of health and inspiration they offer unless and until they have stood, if only once, on their summit.

We were still on our way up to the summit, to Dahr el-Qadeeb. After the first hour of the climb, Mahbouba's pace began to lag; she was tired and stopped at bends in the track.

Mahboub was the same way, stopping and asking us to pause. He took off his shoe, took a red handkerchief out of his pocket, cut a piece out of it with his knife, and put it on his wound. Then he pushed in the back of his shoe, put it on again, and started walking.

I asked him about the wound. "Much better, thank you, sir," he replied. "It's much better."

Even so, I was aware that behind that response there was a good deal of endurance and silent suffering. I was afraid that the wound might become more inflamed and offered to treat him. He thrust his cane behind his shoulders and shook his head. We continued our ascent, but at a slower pace.

"This is the Baalbek trail," I heard him say. "Only an adventurer would ever risk crossing it!"

We had now reached the summit overlooking Baalbek and its amazing rock. In just a minute you are transferred from west to east as you move upward toward the rock and approach the dividing line. You stand at the central point between two horizons. It is truly amazing. Just a single step toward the east, and you move from the sea climes to the land climes, and from Kadisha Valley to the Baalbek plains, from the Cedars shrine to the Sun Temple.

Before taking the final step and turning your face toward the east, stand on the rim of the western horizon. You now get a view that is unparalleled among the world's mountains. Valleys and ravines separating, then coming together; rivers and streams flowing apart, then meeting again; multicolored ploughed and harvested fields; vales and hills interweaving as they swayed and glistened in a riot of greens and yellows; deep gorges and silent rocks hanging over them. How amazing were the sights of this splendid and unusual view! Beyond it all and at a palpable distance was the blue sea stretching away so as to approach the bright blue sky above. Toward the north on the seaward horizon, when the atmosphere was clear and limpid, you could see a dark spot, which is the Island of Arwad.

As you stood by that rock and walked around it, the seaward view completely disappeared, revealing the eastward view with its plains and villages, its meadows and hillocks, and the colors of its earth and sky.

After spending a while looking at this wonderful scene, we turned toward the south and took the bare, high path, which stretched between the two sides of the mountain and the peaks, so that the two horizons to east and west gradually disappeared.

This path, which begins at Dahr el-Qadeeb, heads downhill, although you neither see it nor feel it; after about fifteen kilometers, it ends up at Aqoura. One of the features of this path is that in the walls to both east and west—which get higher as you head south—there are gaps like windows, which sometimes let you see the horizon to the west, and at others the one to the east. So sometimes you get a glimpse of the sea, and at others of the plains.

Halfway between Dahr el-Qadeeb and al-Aqoura, upward from Tannourine, is the Rome Spring, well-known to shepherds and woodcutters in those regions for its miracle and blessings.

The priest at the Cedars had told us about it and had extolled its beauties, particularly its miracle.

"Drink some of its cold water," he told us. "If there's a shepherd around, you'll see the miracle."

Mahboub's hopes for this well matched those of his earlier belief in the cedar tree with the water basin. He was still putting up with the wound, but was finally let down before he could reach his pilgrimage goal. He had been walking for six hours, and by then his walking was more of a limp.

I dismounted to take a close look at the wound. It had burst open and was oozing pus. I rushed over to the saddlebag and came back with a bottle of antiseptic and cotton dressing. After insisting this time, I bathed the wound. He then asked for a razor, but I refused. I was going to be the surgeon. However, he pulled out a chain with a large Jezzini knife attached to it, and started the operation himself. He cut away the dead oozing skin with vicious strokes that split open the healthy flesh so that blood flowed. All the while his eyes were firmly fixed on the task at hand and his face was completely calm; it was as if he were peeling a cucumber or lemon. Once that was done, he agreed to have it rubbed with iodine paste.

We were still half an hour away from the spring and from noontime. But when I offered him the mule to ride, he refused.

"We're not far from the spring," he said, "and the goats have got there ahead of us."

There indeed was the flock, the goatherd leaning on his rifle, and in the rifle's shadow the spring itself.

The Rome Spring—drink its waters, and watch the miracle!

"What miracle?" I asked the goatherd.

"Follow me," he said.

He went ahead of me down a few steps and stopped at the last one by a small pool, no more than a meter and a half high and three-quarters of a meter wide. It was full, but the only obvious source for the water on any side was under the last step. Between the bottom of the step and the water was an air passage—a gap—about five inches high.

"This spring never fills too much or too little, summer and winter," the goatherd told me. "It can water a hundred head of goats or a thousand without ever going down."

That is what the priest had told us; indeed, in these regions it was generally accepted as true about the Rome Spring.

"Do you want to see?" the goatherd asked. "Stay where you are while I water my goats."

He now started filling bucket after bucket for his goats, pouring the water into a basin alongside the spring.

"It's a blessed spring," he told us, "unchanging, like the Lord's omnipotence!"

Indeed, it did not show any change. The goatherd had filled the basin with water, but the spring showed no sign of a drop in level. The reason why might not make simple folk happy. Using buckets to transfer the water from below the steps to the basin above is a slow operation. Any minimal drop in level soon disappears. If we were able to use a quicker method of raising the water—a pump, for example—then the reason would be obvious and the miracle would be no more.

What is certainly the case is that the pool has a source of water that rarely changes because of its proximity to the permanent icepack on the mountain heights. Underneath the last step there is an outlet through which the water flows into the pool. Both the underground stream and outlet are invisible, so it is not surprising that the goatherd and woodcutter both say that it is a miracle, and the villagers believe them. The miracle is thus more in the minds of people than in the Rome Spring itself or that cedar with the petrified hole in its roots.

I only now need to note that there is no connection between the name of the spring and Rome or the Romans. The phrase is apparently Syriac and means "cold spring."

We sat beside the spring, ate our lunch, and relaxed. We drank some of its cold, pure water, watered the mule, and bathed Mahboub's wound. We then resumed our journey, our hopes buoyed and our energies renewed. We passed white tile quarries that looked just like marble—how many there are in these high locations! Then barns began to tell us that we were approaching farmland and civilization. We reached Aqoura late in the afternoon, and then Majdal and Mghayreh before sunset.

We Were Blessed

AMONG LIFE'S SURPRISES there is one kind where the surprise jolts certainty and alters it, but it rarely upsets or annoys you. However, there is another kind, one that is upsetting and annoying, and yet it rarely affects the absolute conviction and belief in the heart.

Take this first example: I accused Mahboub of being lazy and cowardly. I rushed to judgment, making do with a single indication and piece of evidence. I collected the succession of "truths," and, once I had gathered what I thought was enough, I decided on the accusation and recorded the verdict against the muleteer: he was lazy and cowardly.

Then came the surprise at the Cedars when he showed me his wound. He had been walking with it for fifty kilometers without groaning or saying a single word. He had then walked from the Cedars to Dahr el-Qadeeb and performed the operation on himself on the track high in the mountains. He had done it with a butcher's knife, without a twitch on his face or a single hair on his eyelids. After all that, could I really state that Mahboub was lazy and cowardly?

This then is really the biggest surprise of all. I have had to change my certitude, one that was previously based on trivial "truths," which were not without their own hidden and unrecognized aspects, even though they neither upset nor annoyed me. In fact, truth be told, I relished them.

Take another example: Mahboub firmly believed in the stone, the cedar tree with its basin, and its holy water. He used it to wipe his wound, his face, and his soul, fully expecting a quick cure and seeing—or letting the spring of faith show him—an improvement day-by-day.

But things turned out the opposite of what he wanted. The mountain heights confronted him with a painful reality and caused him enormous pain without ever changing his beliefs or affecting his faith.

I wonder, how many surprises are there that disrupt our certainties, change our beliefs, and put an end to those fixed opinions that we have decided upon in the realms of politics and science? They can upset and aggravate us according to the extent that self-interest and prestige matter to us. However, if we give the truth priority over our own self-interest and prestige, then they can neither upset nor aggravate us.

How many surprises there are that can upset us and cause us harm? Beyond that they lose us money, prestige, and children, or else self-control and efficiency, without changing any deep-rooted attitudes that we have acquired, inherited either from superstition or phony habits and sterile tradition?

This obvious and natural psychological phenomenon is widespread—indeed, almost general. Now I propose to use it to focus on two people who spent a period of time living and working together. You will discover another remarkable psychological phenomenon: anyone who can benefit intellectually—and, indeed, ethically and spiritually—from such surprises and who then prefers the truth to his own self-interest and prestige, will be regarded by people as weak, easily duped, and defeated. By contrast, anyone who suffers pain and adheres ruggedly to what he has inherited and learned from fairy stories and folktales will be considered a tremendous hero by everyone.

That is the way that the two of us, Mahboub and this writer, were regarded by Daoud Malkoun, our host during our second stay in Mghayreh. That night, we were sitting down to a meal and talking about how things stood with us. I made clear what was supremely obvious to me, the humbling reality that conferred all due respect to Mahboub. Daoud praised the muleteer.

"By God," he said enthusiastically, "I'm going to accompany the two of you to Afqa tomorrow. We'll all ride to the grotto. Mahboub deserves the very best donkey. We have a special donkey; you'll like it and feel safe."

That night, instead of drinking some arak, Mahboub used it to wash his wound. In accordance with traditional beliefs, he preferred using it instead of sterilized water (called Sulaymani) and iodine. But the wound kept being more inflamed; before it had been as large as a bean but now it was more like a watch face, and it was oozing pus again. That made me even more worried about Mahboub and put an end to any desire to visit Afqa. I decided that we needed to take the shortest route back to Freike.

There was another factor involved in this radical change of plan that I will not conceal from the reader. I have come to see it as evidence of the general psychological pattern involving the three participants in this tale. That night, I began to shiver and feel a bit feverish. When I got out of bed the next morning, I did not have my usual energy. I checked my tongue in the mirror.

"That's it," I told myself. "There's no more to be said. It's best to go back."

Even so, my two companions in the tale, my fellow traveler and my host, had by now turned into adventurous tourists and were both eager to visit Afqa.

What was truly astonishing amid all these surprises is that my own spirit of adventure had now transferred to Mahboub, while I was now the one with his fears.

"What's the point of having a dangerous military revolver," I asked philosophically, "if Mahboub can't even stand on his feet to defend himself? Have you ever seen a hero riding a donkey or read anywhere other than in romantic stories about Antar on a donkey, like Sancho Panza in *Don Quixote*? Even if we suppose that Sancho Panza's donkey is represented here by Daoud Malkoun's donkey, do you think it'll attack bandits in the Lebanese mountains the same way Panza's attacks windmills on the plains of Spain? However we look at this question, we can see that the donkey, the hero, and the revolver are at odds and don't fit well together—they're completely different."

Thus did I turn away from Afqa, depriving myself of the sight of its grotto and monuments during the course of this trip.

Once we had crossed the vales and hills.

After the discussion that night between the three of us—myself; the valiant Mahboub; and Daoud, the fearless fighter—we all agreed that we would rent a donkey for Mahboub and that the donkeyman should be someone who could travel on foot and knew the mountain tracks well. We also decided that next day we would get up with the morning star, Venus; in other words, before dawn. We would travel fast so as to reach Freike the same day.

That is what happened. The caravan started off with Venus glistening on the eastern horizon. There was an impressive silence, which marked the linkage between night and dawn. At the head of the procession was Mahboub on his donkey; the donkeyman walked alongside, carrying his cane over his shoulders like a rifle. Behind him was Mahbouba, happy and pleasant, as though she too were delighted to see her owner riding.

In God's safe hands we traversed gullies, hills, and springs. Out of the shadows emerged Faytroun. We entered the town and left it while people were either eating lunch or taking a siesta. So we did not see anyone from the Diryan family, who were expecting us to come back and spend at least a week as their guests.

We were getting hungry, and the journey was very tiring. We took off the saddlebags at Al-Kolayat so we could eat lunch and have a rest. Then we went downward to Darya, and from there to the Dog River. The twin mountains kept echoing to the sounds of hooves clopping on the track between the rocks. From there we started climbing up toward Ain el-Kharroubeh, Mayasseh, Wadi Chahine, and Beit Chabab. Just as dusk fell, we made it to the paved road and took it down through the darkness in Chouiyeh to Freike. We entered the village safe and sound just as the moon began to shine down on it from Mount Sannine.

On the third day following our return from the Cedars, Mahboub arrived, limping and leaning on a cane, to visit "his master." "Sir" had been laid up in bed with a skin disease whose microbe had invaded his body on that day when he had been "the Lord's guest" in that ancient tent at the Cedars.

Second Journey

Wherever the Road Wishes

Contents

Brother Hanna

I WOULD REGULARLY TAKE A WALK in the mountains, not merely because I wanted some diversion, but more because I was keen to discover nature's beauty in the scenes and elements that it offered. At first I would take short walks, but, as I grew stronger, I turned into a real hiker, the genuine article, as the saying goes. I used to go down the valley, then start climbing, clambering over rocks and jumping over rubble like the sturdiest village children. In fact, I came to resemble the ones who worked as shepherds and woodcutters, vying with them without the slightest concern. For me, walking now became something to love for itself, like everything else that one is good at and comes to relish. Thus it was that, after my return from my journey to the Cedars, I began to feel a strong desire to take another trip on foot like the muleteers, a long trip that would last for days rather than hours.

I will not conceal from you the fact that my father was one of Lebanon's grandees; even more, he was a Karkhanji, the owner of a silk factory. He used to require of his children that they refrain from any work, however small the task. So it was that, if a water pitcher, for example, was within easy reach of one of us, his children in the house, while he himself sat cross-legged on the couch smoking his nargileh, he would have to clap his hands and issue a command to one of the helpers at home: "You, boy, bring the water pitcher!" If he decided to travel somewhere, it would have to be on a splendid stallion or else a pedigree mule with a saddle blanket and cushions attached to its back. Alongside the animal would walk one or even two of his servants.

For my part, I always recoiled from such customs in every way; pomp never impressed me, nor did its absence bother me—I simply adjusted to the situation. I was now preoccupied by the idea of a walking trip; not only that, but I also decided to do it on my own. In those days I had no problem making up my own mind about things, no matter how difficult they might seem. To which you can add that, like most Lebanese, I come from a stock that is God-fearing, devout, and ascetic. In the past the flower of that same stock had chosen rocks, valleys, and caves as sources of enlightenment. In blunt terms, you can say that their ancestors were ascetic to the point of barbarity—in other words, desolation and hunger; they would shun other people and communal locations and live in imitation of Jesus Christ in word and deed, never carrying gold or silver.

This then explains the major oddity about my forthcoming journey: I had inured myself to emulate my holy ancestors, and, above all, Our Lord Most High. For the journey I would not be bringing any food or money. I would be traveling on my own with God's blessing. However, I was not the only one in the house, nor did I have complete independence when it came to carrying out my decision. When my mother-God bless her soul!—heard about it, she raised her hands in prayer to the heavens and then gave me a look that combined disapproval and anxiety.

"That's impossible" she said, "you must be mad!"

"It's the madness of true faith," I replied. "So what is faith?"

That started a discussion about faith in both theoretical and practical terms. Eventually, we reached an agreement. My mother, who was devout and pure, accepted the idea that I would be traveling like a hermit. I in turn agreed to her demand—namely, that I take a travel companion—I would not travel on my own.

At that time we had a novitiate monk living in our house—in his first year—named Brother Hanna. A young man from the village, he was highly intelligent and had a lot of imagination; he disliked farming and agriculture and despised caring for animals such as cows, sheep, and goats. The idea of walking like muleteers behind a mule did not appeal to him. Brother Hanna often sat in the shade of the ancient olive tree next to the old monastery, dreaming golden dreams of wealth or authority. However, since emigration was not available, it was the idea of authority that had taken wealth's place in his golden dream, the dream of clever, lazy youth . . .

So now I have surprised you with some details about Brother Hanna's inner feelings. He would often say that he longed to serve God; he wanted to be a devout monk. And yet his desires in that direction were tied to worldly ambitions. Yes indeed, Brother Hanna was ambitious, extending his hand to touch the moon. He would see the ladder in front of him like Jacob's ladder, extending from earth to the heavens. He used to repeat to himself and sometimes share with his friends this little ditty about the phases of his upward path: Brother Hanna, Priest Hanna, Director Hanna, Abbot Hanna. Then from among those monks selected by heavenly blessing for the bishopric, who knows, from Abbot Hanna to His Grace Bishop Hanna. And who knows, since the seed of the patriarchate was to be found in every bishop, perhaps that very same seed was to be found inside this son of the village of Freike. With that in mind, attaining the very loftiest rank in the service of Holy God was not an impossibility.

So, through the grace of God, Hanna would be the patriarch of Antioch and the entire Eastern region! That was the golden dream of Hanna al-Mallah as he sat in the shade of the ancient olive tree next to the old monastery. Not only that, but he would say the same thing to some of his friends in Freike. However, once he had run away from home, his father would call him lazy, a coward, always famished. He ran away from work; the kneading machine could relax. And where did he run? To the monastery! As though it were some Barmakid palace! God help him inside there!

It did not take long for Brother Hanna to find out what went on "inside there." In his father's house he would work for two or three hours each day, tending the goats, milking the cow, and lighting the fire for his mother as she baked bread in the baking pan. At the monastery, when he started serving his monastic masters by tilling the fields, it was for twelve hours each day, apart from times set aside for prayers and vigils. In his father's house he used to eat meat two or three times a week, on Sundays and festivals. But then he turned into a model of abstemiousness: only ever eating *makhlouta*, a paste made of lentils and hummus; the only time he would smell meat would be at the abbot's table. In his father's house the bread-baking pan would respond to his touch; he would take out one loaf after another—no objections, no questions. But now, the many loaves and the onions and olives that went with them began to be counted against him. At his parents' home Brother Hanna would hear the usual kind of comments mingled occasionally with complaints about the amounts he was eating and the minimum amount of work he was actually doing. At the monastery complaints and criticisms were the only thing Brother Hanna ever heard, when, for example, he was discovered on one occasion sitting on a rock and relaxing or going into the field with a loaf under his arm. So where now was that ancient olive tree in whose shade he had had his golden dream?

Three whole months of toil, deceit, and hunger—bodily hunger and spiritual hunger. Commands laced with tough language. Three months that he endured and tolerated in honor of Jesus, son of Mary. During that time, whenever he was able to snatch a few minutes for reflection, Brother Hanna could see his golden dream looming before his eyes, getting darker and darker, and then disappearing. Sometimes it looked like a dragon, at others like a snake. He was scared by those visions and their very frequency alarmed him. Then came the day when he was returning from the fields and his own shadow appeared standing right in front of him. He picked up a rock and threw it at his image. One of the monks saw him do it and went rushing to the abbot.

"Brother Hanna's gone mad, Your Grace!" he said. "I've just seen him pelting his own shadow and heard him cursing religion."

The very next day Brother Hanna stood before the abbot and had to listen to words of rebuke and warning. When Brother Hanna spotted the monk who had told the abbot about him, he rounded on the monk, denying the whole thing. Brother Hanna called him a liar and hypocrite. There was a row, during which Brother Hanna threw a rock at the monk and split his head open. With that, Brother Hanna fled the monastery.

Brother Hanna now returned duly penitent to his father's house. However, his father refused to accept his repentance and had to leave his parents' house. The expelled monk now started doing the rounds of the village and its surroundings looking for work, trying to find some kind of livelihood, and—to the extent possible, he being the champion avoider—staving off hunger. His mother took pity on him and gave him work inside our home, her hope being that his heart would regain its sense of well-being and he would go back to the monastery.

As I see it, Brother Hanna enjoyed working in our home for three reasons. All he had to make were coffee and nargilehs to offer to visitors. Then no one supervised him in the kitchen, so he could eat whatever he liked whenever he liked. And he had plenty of spare time, time he managed to fill with reflection and sleep!

Even so, I was fond of would-be monk Hanna; he had little to say and made good coffee. Unlike other monks, he did not spend a lot of time sitting with women and preaching at them. There was another reason too. In spite of my quest for abstinence and moderation, I used to feel a certain pleasure mixed with vanity whenever I had occasion to call on him and say: "Bring some coffee, Brother Hanna," or "Prepare a nargileh, Brother Hanna"!

He would come in, his expression beaming, his face adorned by a youthful round beard. He was tall, and he used to wear a black robe with a cowl. He would have a tray in his hand, raised as high as his beard, as though he had learned how to serve in a Paris hotel or at the Vatican in Rome.

This then was pageantry personified: a monk serving someone who did not particularly care for people wearing robes with cowls. As already noted, I had informed my mother, and she accepted Brother Hanna as a companion for me on this propitious journey.

Praise be to God! Here is the September sun shining from behind Mount Sannine to welcome us.

"Where are we going, Master Ameen?"

"Wherever the road wishes, Brother Hanna," I replied, "and wherever God wills."

We went on our way with God's blessing. Brother Hanna was wearing his black robe with its cowl and had slung his jubbah over his shoulder. I was wearing a European-style suit made of a yellowish (khaki) textile and was carrying an oak cane. What made the attire seem even more peculiar were the cloth gaiters tied military-style around my legs and the wide-brimmed black cap that covered my long hair.

Two people rarely united in a single purpose, the like of whom had rarely been seen on the road.

"I don't think the journey is going to be a long one, Master Ameen."

"That's in our own hands, Brother Hanna," I replied, "and the journey back is in God's hands."

The Mar Girgis Monastery

THIS BOOK is primarily concerned with journeys and panoramas. It is not interested in stories involving individuals or families. Even so, as we gather examples and memories during our travels, we will share them with you and also recount both general and particular historical accounts, be they beneficial or merely amusing.

Take this Mar Girgis monastery, for example. It sits on a rocky hillock between Freike and Chouiyeh; its stonework has been reddened by weather and time—rain, wind, dust, and sun. It is called the Monastery of Mar Girgis Bahirduq (and do not ask me about that particular name—in times ancient and modern there are plenty of such riddles and secret origins for names in this valley).

What I have learned is that in the eighteenth century it was a monastery for monks, then for nuns. It was then converted into a clerical college, then a private home and a press for molasses and wine, then a secular school founded by the late Na'um Makarzil before he emigrated to the United States. The current writer was a student there at the age of ten. Today the monastery is one of those ancient monuments girded in the splendors of antiquity.

The monastery and its many properties are the endowment of "the elders of the Hayek family," at Beit Chabab, "an enduring endowment in return for a blessing they have sought and assistance they have defined." The preserved deed of the property, duly certified by Bishop Basil 'Abd al-Ahad Sa'ada al-Bejjani[1] in 1732, that needy members of

1. Rihani's great-great-great-great grandfather.

the endowers' family retain the right to earn a living from the monastery; the entire family can ask for two Masses to be celebrated each year as acts of mercy and blessing. In other words, the pine forest that covers the hill, the oak and *mallul* (Valonia oak) below it, and the broad swath of land with its flatlands and valleys sown with grapes, mulberries, and olives—all of it belongs to the monastery in return for two Masses to be celebrated by the abbot or one of his deputies, an act of redemption for the souls of the endowers!

After a good deal of time, the monks were replaced by nuns, who, it seems, were far from submissive in the monastery. Among the stories told about them is that at the end of the nineteenth century they ruffled the feathers of the diocesan, Bishop Yusuf Ja'ja', who lost his temper with them. This preeminent cleric was renowned for his sense of justice, his belief in democracy, and his physical strength. He would regularly join his workmen in plowing the fields. His axe blows were powerful, and his hammer strikes would crush rocks. His judgments were just like his hammer blows; the impact was notable, and there was no room for compromise or leniency when it came to justice.

When dissension flared up inside the monastery and sparks of hatred and desire began to shoot out of the church's brazier, the bishop first gave the nuns a warning, then expelled them altogether. He closed the monastery, and it was left empty, with no worshippers male or female.

In a letter written by Bishop Ja'ja' to the Council of the Holy See in Rome—to be forwarded to His Holiness the Pope, he said that was determined to reform the monastery "once he had separated the different factions among the nuns . . . all in the cause of their own peace of mind and comfort." He asked for permission to turn the monastery into a clerical college. The pope gave his permission, but that same clerical college and the Mukarzil secular school that took its place did not last for very long.

Na'um's school may have been short-lived, but it moved around a lot. He founded it in Ain Aar, then moved it one year later to the Mar Girgis monastery. After just six months, it was moved again to

Freike, and just a few months after that it was transferred to the mercy of God . . .

I can recall a notable day when the school was at Ain Aar. The French consul was passing through the town on his way from Beirut to his summer residence in Bikfaya. All the students at the school came out in their festive clothes and lined up in splendid style behind their teacher, Na'um. They all greeted His Excellency the Consul in the town square between the spring's water spout and the silk factory's chimney.

Our teacher—May God forgive him his sins!—had composed a ringing ode in honor of the consul and his country. He chose me as the one to deliver it, and I did so in a tone that the consul liked. He showed his admiration and promised to take me with him when he returned to his country at the end of the summer so that I could become a student in a school there.

This palpable success made me somewhat boastful, and it affected my studies and my behavior. I had been first in the class, but now I was several levels below that. I had been clever, obedient, and respectful, but now I was "a big head," always ill-tempered and argumentative. I can still remember the punishment that our teacher, Na'um, gave me: ten hard strokes with the ruler on my fingernails held together!

I got my revenge on our teacher at the Mar Girgis monastery. One day he called me up to the blackboard. "Take a piece of chalk," he said. I stood in front of the blackboard, chalk in hand, waiting for the dictation. "Write *donkey*," he told me. I wrote it on the board. "Now write *Ameen*," he said. I wrote *Na'um*. All the students burst into laughter. Na'um was furious and told me to stand facing the wall for ten minutes.

We passed by underneath the monastery that had revived these memories from the cycles of the past. Now here we were in front of the ancient church where the small monastery had been before it was transferred to the hilltop and enlarged as a result of the Hayek family's endowment mentioned earlier.

The walls of such a tiny, modest church were lined with creepers and gorse. The dome had no bell, and there was no lock on the door. All around it was the cemetery for the people of Chouiyeh. It consisted for four square rooms topped by a cross and domes. One of the rooms was that of the Al-Rihani family lying in the shadow of three young oak trees beside the road. There were buried my father and mother, my uncle and aunt, my grandfather and grandmother. It is there too, in the same shade of those three oak trees at the top of that hill garlanded with its evergreen pine trees, that I wish to shade my own bones for all eternity.[2] From this point on I intend to bring down God's curse on anyone who cuts down those three holy trees or does them any harm. I ask God Almighty to grant His mercy and blessings to all those who look after them, staving off the ravages of time and decay and pruning them so they can grow in beauty and endure, spreading their shade over the cemetery and church for all passersby in search of relaxation. I now look at those three oaks from the beyond. A thousand years later—and I shall return in a thousand years' time—I shall see them then as I am seeing them now, still standing, with people seeking a blessing from visiting them as they do today in visiting the Cedars.

When I told this to Brother Hanna, he said, "Your words are just like your deeds, Master Ameen. Amazing and weird. Do you really believe that humans return to earth after they have died?"

"Hindus believe in transmigration," I replied. "In other words, the transfer of the rational soul from one body to another. Every human being goes through numerous transformations, which vary according to their good or bad deeds. The ones who do some good deeds go through gradual phases of transmigration, always upward; they return to earth several times until they achieve the level of spiritual perfection. At that point they are absorbed into the eternal emanation, which they term *nirvana*."

Brother Hanna shook his head as he transferred his cloak from one shoulder to the other.

2. That is where he lies.

"That's more than I can comprehend," he said. "If I had the opportunity to return to this earth, I would prefer to take the form of one of those oaks so that I could save them from damage and stay always close to you."

Brother Hanna preserved for all eternity as an oak in the Mar Girgis cemetery. The very concept amazed me, but in his current human form he did not feel secure in the shadow of monasteries.

We passed by the village of Chouiyeh, where my father was born. He asked me about the family. Why had my father decided to move the family home to Freike. It seems that moving house was a necessary feature of life for the Al-Rihani family. More than three hundred years earlier the family elder had moved from Bejjeh in Jbeil to Beit Chabab. A hundred years later the Reverend (then Bishop) Basil 'Abd al-Ahad Sa'ada al-Bejjani[3] moved from Beit Chabab to Chouiyeh. There he built himself a retreat house. The myrtle, which is called Rihan in those parts, used to grow prolifically, so people called it "the myrtle (Rihani) retreat house." Once the name was associated with him, they called it "the Rihani house." Our house below Beit Chabab is still there, but today it is deserted.

The reason why my father moved to Freike was love. My father was a partner with his uncle, Ameen Hashim, in a silk factory in Freike. He had to spend most of his time there. In his uncle's house he used to meet Anisa Jaffal Tu'ma from Qornat al-Hamra, she being in her aunt's house, the wife of my father's uncle. Faris fell in love with Anisa, and she fell in love with him. Love blossomed in their hearts, and the affair was crowned with their marriage. I was their precious firstborn child—may God prolong my life and enhance my circumstances!

Brother Hanna, you will have understood the detailed response that I have provided to your question. Before they were married, Faris and Anisa disagreed about one thing: where they were going to live. Anisa Tu'ma refused to live in Chouiyeh, and Faris al-Rihani refused

3. In those days it was not forbidden for married priests to be appointed bishop.

to move his house to Qornat al-Hamra. But for the sheer power of human love, the disagreement might well have led to real trouble and even estrangement. As it was, that very same love suggested a compromise; for its sake that is what they did. At a family gathering it was agreed that the bridal couple would not live in either Chouiyeh or Qornat al-Hamra, but between the two villages in Freike! And that is what happened.

That is why the people of Chouiyeh are upset with me. The fame that fate has now brought to Freike during my lifetime should really belong to Chouiyeh. Even so, they say that, even if the house is in Freike, the cemetery is here with us. Cemeteries endure, whereas houses do not.

The Day'a and Its Crafts

IT WOULD APPEAR that the people living in Beit Chabab had at some point been enlightened by one of their men of letters or else by the insight of their priests. As a result, they refused to call it by names such as *balda*, *qarya*, and *daskara* (town or village). Instead, they called it *day'a* (also meaning "village"). Not only that, but it was further dignified by the definite article—*the* day'a. All the neighboring villages, from Deek El Mehdi to Chouiyeh, acknowledged the name; people going to or coming from Beit Chabab used to say, "I'm going to the day'a," or "I'm coming from the day'a."

Even so, we are still dealing here with the obscurities of the lexicographer Al-Fairuzabadi and his fellow linguists. The word *day'a*—trust me as we go back to the dictionary—means "fertile land." There is nothing fertile about the land around Beit Chabab. But *day'a* also means "a man's craft and profession." Now here there is a glimmer of light, a measure of truth. Although it was certainly unknown to the people of Beit Chabab, here—for the sake of love and honor—is a manifest reality. Beit Chabab has been renowned for its skills, its many crafts (*day'at*). By all measures, therefore, it genuinely deserves to be called the day'a.

In those days—namely, twenty years ago—the day'a was populous and had flourishing trades and crafts. Bells were forged there, the national cloth (*dima*) was woven there, and pottery was crafted there. Silk cocoons were dissolved in its factories. Its blacksmiths, carpenters, and builders, just like its weavers and potters, were all well-known not only locally but also throughout the Matn and the Lebanese valleys to the north and south.

How beautiful it looks to people approaching from Freike or looking down on it from the western part of Bikfaya! Its houses, orchards, factories, and churches fill the mountainside. It is surrounded by pine forests and garlanded with grape arbors. There are many springs and plenty of water. Smoke rises from the factory chimneys and wafts pleasant scents over its gardens.

A village of outstanding beauty with modest housing developments. It fills the high and lengthy mountain; to the south it connects with Bikfaya Mountain; to the north it adjoins Kesrouan Mountain. The lowest of its houses is at 600 meters above sea level and the highest is at 750. Between the two the houses are clustered on top of each other, spreading out in rows and circles with attractive patterns of white stone and red convex roofs. Spaced between them are mulberry orchards and lofty poplar, walnut, and willow trees.

The marketplace consisted of three squares connected to each other by a cart track with tight bends and steep slopes. However, in the first square you would be welcomed by the Church of the Lady—the Lady of Walnuts—in which case you would pray to her for safe passage (if you were a believer) and then continue in your cart up that spiral path without the slightest worry (God willing).

If, on the other hand, you were not a believer in such female saints and their churches (how many of them there were in the village), then the better plan would be to take the stepped main streets leading to the town center. In that case you would meander your way up to the craft houses and factories.

Brother Hanna and I took those main streets in spite of his hesitation and reluctance; that was because, when it came to walking, he was like running water. He used to take large detours so as to avoid mud and other obstacles. The two of us recklessly climbed one of the streets, and we were not sorry we did so. The first thing to make us stop was a house with a loom; in the pit behind the wooden frame was a lovely young girl using both hands and feet to weave. One hand was on the frame, while the other held on to the shuttle thread. Her bare feet were moving up and down on the two pedals as though she

One hand was on the frame and the other held on to the shuttle thread.

were training them to dance. She then was the constantly moving girl of the constantly moving loom. It was not the loom's noise, like a drum's, that made us stop, but rather the sound of her voice singing the Lebanese *ataaba* (plaint). However, when we both stopped by the open door, she stopped singing and weaving and invited us inside. Another woman was there; she was sitting on a cushion in front of a sewing machine, using her right hand to turn it, while her left hand manipulated the thread around the spindle that the weaving girl was using with her shuttle.

The woman stopped her work, and the young girl came out from behind the loom. They both greeted us. Testing their kindness with a load of questions, we discovered that the girl was a new bride; her husband was director of the silk factory. The woman preparing the spindle for the shuttle was her mother-in-law. We also learned that the town boasted more than a thousand looms to make the national cloth, directed by both men and women. Brothers and sisters, husbands and wives, and occasionally the entire family helped each other in the process.

Here is an example of free noble labor: the loom inside the house is worked whenever they want and however much they want—two, ten, twenty hours per day. Having the loom in the house is a symbol of freedom in labor, but, beyond that, it serves as a bulwark for respectability, a source of revenue, and the major preserver of health and well-being. The hours spent at the loom using both hands and feet are the best kind of sports.

Before the Great War (1914–18), you used to see a loom in every single house in Beit Chabab; in fact, there would often be two or three. The production of national cloth would rival that of silk, at least in quantity if not in price. Merchants used to export it beyond the mountains and outside Syria—to Egypt, Cyprus, and Anatolia.

During and after the Great War, the loom fell out of favor; the weaving craft nearly disappeared as European cloth woven on mechanical looms took over. Emigration took over as well; more than a third of Beit Chabab's inhabitants emigrated. Moral corruption played a role too; women regarded themselves as being above working with looms and relied on their men in Africa for all their needs in clothing and support, in addition to jewels and other frippery.

During the French Mandate, Lebanon suffered a severe economic crisis. People started searching for their ancestors' legacy; in Beit Chabab some people decided to start weaving the national cloth once again and to modernize it and make it more attractive so that people of the time would want to buy it. However, the workers were few in number. Today there are not as many looms in the day'a itself, and even in Bikfaya and its suburbs as there used to be in the day'a alone thirty years ago. But, thank God, the sound of the loom has returned, and the other sound will come back too, that of the young girl at the loom weaving a cloth for her heart out of folk songs!

In spite of emigration, there are other efforts underway to revive the factories that disappeared after the war. However, carpenters, builders, blacksmiths, and potters as a whole (or the majority of them) have become fascinated by Africa, that black sorceress, and have started responding to its call. If there are any carpenters, blacksmiths, or builders in the day'a today, they have no enthusiasm for their job and feel bored because Africa is calling them.

There was no avoiding Africa, even when it came to crafting bells. The Naffa' family had inherited that cryptic secret, passed down from one generation to the next since ancient times. In Lebanon and Syria, when it came to casting bells, who did it as well as the folk in Beit Chabab? Who understands the secret behind that skill? The essence of a bell is in its sound; those same sounds have a magic to which the church bells in Mount Lebanon bear witness. The sounds differ and vary according to the wishes and craft of their maker—from broad, far-echoing tones to sharp, soft, and subtle ones, and between the two extremes exquisite varieties of pitch and reverberation.

At sunset the sound of bells rings from monastery domes on mountaintops, carried on the breeze and magnified by the echoing valleys. It surges and spreads through the air, becoming yet more resonant and moving. It calls to us just as it did to our forebears, sewing humility and devotion in the human soul. Like a poetic ode or song, it reminds us of the past. Sunset bell, prayer bell for those who have gone before us to the haven of eternity—for the sake of the dead. Bell of memories, where sorrow and joy are linked together; bell of hopes, repeated by the ringing tone of iron, perfumed by the valleys with the fragrance of lilies and sweet basil. Every time I hear the evening bell chiming its venerable sound in the monastery dome at the mountaintop in Beit Chabab, I can envisage things made of gold and silk composing mournful chants and smell incense in the air. A vision of Christian art in the heavenly procession, magic in sorrow girded in twilight . . .

So there is Beit Chabab, the day'a of crafts, and yet they are almost disappearing. The bellmaker tells you that demand is limited, profits are small, and life expenses are increasing. It is Africa that keeps calling, always calling, and the Lebanese keep responding. Here I am, you black sorceress, at your service! Life and death are in your hands!

The silk factory. Have you heard about the worm for which mulberry orchards are planted and huts constructed? The precious seed hidden inside is silk thread, a thread of raw silk, a microbe in motion. The worm is ravenous; it eats mulberries leaves night and day for seven days in a row, then fasts for an entire day, and then repeats the process by eating through the layers of green. After several rounds of fasting and eating, it climbs up the wormwood and weaves its cocoon to keep silk protected. Harvest day arrives, and with it hopes for a blessed season. They are transferred to the factories where the worms are to be stifled, a veritable source of prosperity for humans. Those now stifled cocoons are then transferred to the factory ovens filled with hot water. Beside them stand male and female silk winders, who pick up the golden threads with their fingers; the threads are twisted and wound on to spindles. The reels of silk are then packed up in bunches, then bales, and shipped abroad.

Those silk winders, men and women, I heard them chanting prayers at sunset as they busied themselves between the ovens and spindles. A lovely female voice raised her voice to the Virgin: "*Kyrie eleison*, *kyrie eleison*, Lady of Virgins, Lady of Angels." In response, fifty or a hundred voices intoned, "Pray for us!" In this era of industrialization and materialism, troubled and roiled as it is by disputes between workers and their bosses, I wonder if it even occurs to you that there are still human beings who are happy and content in their work and satisfied with their lives; not only that, but they chant while they are working!

This was an amazing phenomenon, and yet in Lebanon there were any number of regular recognized occasions like it. The festival movement arrives—the cocoon festival—and how many thanks for God's blessings come with it! Even the mule caravans used to get the feeling as they transported their precious cargo—sacks of cocoons—from various villages to the factories. They would make their way with their decorations; along with the garlands of seashells would be tiny bells that would proclaim the glad tidings to you: "The cocoons have arrived!" A boon and a delight . . .

But now this same day'a, village of crafts, is a witness to unemployment, laziness, and despair. Closed factories offer condolences along with churches—ten of them in Beit Chabab—and monasteries for monks and nuns. All of its wealth has gone, duly mourned by newspapers (and Beit Chabab has two), as has French clothing—the source of national pride swaggering in natural silk. Now it consumes its bread dipped in African sweat!

Even so, there is a single trade that is still functioning, although production is down. Even potters responded to the call of that black sorceress; from thirty pottery factories there now only remain a few, one of them belonging to my friend and school colleague, Hajj Abou Yasu'. Together we read the alphabet booklet and the first of the Psalms of David. We had to recite both of them to Deacon Matthew under the walnut tree in the lower courtyard. At the time my father was living in Beit Chabab—in the eighth decade of the previous century, when he was director of the one of the silk factories. I think you will remember the well-known adage: "The one who taught me letters, I was one of his slaves." In which case Deacon Matthew—may God have mercy on him!—had a large number of slaves.

I was sympathetic to Deacon Matthew, but Abou Yasu' did not share my opinion. At the time, some students used to comment about their teacher, the Deacon: "The *sabatiya* was wasted on him"; the *sabatiya*—may your days be long!—being loaves of bread that each student used to bring to Teacher Matthew in return for his instruction. Hajj Abou Yasu‘ would still repeat the same phrase, "The *sabatiya* is wasted in him." The reason for that, it would appear, was that the teacher did not manage to light the candle of talent in him as he did with other students—with me, for example. "What's the difference between me and Ameen?" he would often ask. We both learned the letters together in Deacon Matthew's school, beneath the walnut tree in front of the Church of Our Lady of the Walnuts. So where is he today, and where am I? He is a philosopher, but what about me? A potter who keeps toying with dust . . . I think the Deacon gave you the keys of knowledge, Ameen, but left me deprived. So do you still blame me if I say, "The *sabatiya* was wasted on him"?

However, Hajj Abou Yasu‘ was a natural philosopher. He was not enticed by Africa, nor was he taken in by the world. Contentment is an inexhaustible treasure, good health is the greatest boon of all, and a life without need is genuine wealth. He would always repeat those phrases as he listened to the words of the priest on feast days and Sundays. He would commit to memory the ones that matched his own philosophy and discard the rest calmly without either pretense or arrogance. "Man comes from dust, Ameen," he used to say, "and those who work with dust are closer to God than those who work with silk."

This sage potter who plays with clay also believes that God created mankind from the dust of Beit Chabab, that particular clay from which are made flagons and jars. He is one of the subtlest players with clay as well as being the most astute and wise. Even so, like his colleagues and all his cousins, he is still in the same craft and at the same point of advancement. The working hand that turns the clay on the wheel and produces a bowl or flagon is one that still only uses eye and memory to bring us something that for five thousand years has been a perfect example of its art; even five thousand years later it is still part of the same alphabet notebook.

If you want to see the way the potter made oil jars for the Sumerians in ancient times, watch as he smooths the clay and molds it with two hands as soft and smooth as the clay itself, and works the wheel with his bare feet that look like a lump of chalk—"dust to dust, and unto dust shall we return!" then pay a visit to the philosopher potter in the day'a, Beit Chabab.

In the Shadows of Walnut Trees

WE ENTERED BEIT CHABAB and toured its factories and craft houses peacefully and without incident—apart, that is, from a single event, which would not be worth mentioning were it not for the devilish aspects involved. A group of boys surrounded us, and Brother Hanna heard one of them tell his friend, "That's the one who's been excommunicated by the bishop." As Brother Hanna whispered this in my ear, he kept urging me to leave the day'a.

The boys had obviously heard about us; because of that, Brother Hanna was feeling uneasy. He was concerned about my safety, and, indeed, about his own as well. News of his fleeing the monastery had spread and caught people's attention. It was no surprise, therefore, that he had the impression (as he confided to me later) that he had also heard them saying, "He's the one who fled the monastery." Two unbelievers, with the boys ganging up against them. Hurry up, Master Ameen!

At this point I need to acquaint the reader with the details of the excommunication. I have already pointed to the author's unorthodox religious beliefs and the effect they had on the people of Freike. They were at a loss when it came to a heretical notion that was beyond their understanding. However, it was a sign of their good sense that, faced with such perplexity, they chose to remain neutral rather than express their support or opposition.

My book, *The Trilateral Treaty in the Animal Kingdom*, was much talked about at that time; it had its impact in people's hearts, all or most of whom could not read. Rumors multiplied, and they spread beyond the boundaries of Freike. In one of the neighboring villages a religious bigot started firing up his neighbors against "the heretic." The people whom he stirred up formed a committee to defend virtue and belief. They started protesting to the diocesan bishop, asking him to help them uproot the scourge of heresy in their midst. "Excommunication, Your Grace!" they said. "Nothing but excommunication will teach him!" The bishop responded to their demand, issuing a formidable decree of excommunication against Ameen Faris al-Rihani in Freike, diocese of Cyprus,[1] preventing him from receiving the church's secret gifts and from joining or mixing with other believers—to be more precise, having other believers associate with him.

At that time I was assiduously devoted to an ascetic life, preferring complete isolation to mingling with other people. The excommunication order came at exactly the right time. I wrote a letter of thanks to the bishop, and another to the people of Freike in which I urged them to obey their bishop; they should act in accordance with his decree and leave me alone.

This situation lasted for several months, with people split between those who approved the decision and those who did not, those who obeyed the order and others who scoffed at it. Thank God, no one suffered any harm—neither the object of the decree nor his believer neighbors. Even so, for a while the excommunicated one remained a topic of their conversation. He became like the piebald bull, something to point a finger at in the villages neighboring Freike and even in Beit Chabab, as is clear from the incident I have just noted.

So here we were, encircled by a crowd, who proceeded to pelt me with a hail of questions. All of a sudden we heard a voice ringing out like one of the bells of the Naffa' family. It scolded the boys, who all scattered in panic.

"You bring honor to the day'a," said the owner of the voice, apologizing for the boy's meddlesome behavior, "you are very welcome!"

1. In the divisions of the Maronite Church the diocese of Cyprus includes the island of Cyprus itself and the province of Matn in Lebanon. The diocesan seat is in Qornat Chehouane, Matn, Lebanon.

The appearance of Sa'id al-Ha'ik in that place and time had a wonderful effect on both me and my travel companion. We learned that he had spotted us from the balcony of his house and had hurried down to rescue us from the town's boys. He invited us to lunch.

At that time Sa'id was in the vanguard of liberal educated young men. He was the first one to risk his own soul by breeching the bounds of the bishop's decree. He came to visit me in Freike, not to sympathize with my plight but rather to congratulate me. In those days, that was an act of real daring. Not only that, but Sa'id al-Ha'ik in the mountains and Constantin Yanni in Beirut were my very first supporters immediately following my return from America in 1904. I shall always remember their actions and courage.

On our way to Sa'id's house there is no reason why I should not pause and give the reader some details about it, even though he himself never liked increased visibility. Truth itself is no respecter of people's wishes. Sa'id belongs to a noble Lebanese family with great ambitions and a love of adventure. His uncle, Sheikh Abu Iskandar al-Ha'ik—God have mercy on him!—was the first to focus his eyes and heart's desire on the regions to the West beyond the horizon. He traveled first to Egypt, then to England, bringing with him his excellent English for those tourists who needed the information that he could provide.

He was followed by Sa'id's father. Like his brother, he became a travel companion for Brits and Americans who were attracted to our country and would visit as tourists, enjoying themselves and discovering new things. It is thus no surprise that Sa'id decided to emulate his father and uncle, carrying the guide's torch in travel throughout our Arab East. He gained a wide reputation as a guide, and he served as escort for many wealthy, illustrious, and prosperous visitors. He was a benefit to them and benefitted himself as well. Among his own people he became an authority, known for his sound opinions, his daring, and his sense of freedom in both thought and action.

Sa'id traveled twice to the United States of America, where he met my friend—the friend of Arabs and Arabian horses—the famous artist Homer Davenport. While he was there, he heard about me and read my first pamphlet, "Religious Tolerance,"[2] and the second, "The Trilateral Treaty." He came back to Lebanon a year later, bringing both pamphlets with him in his suitcase, along with greetings from liberals across the ocean to the author of these publications.

Not only that, but he also brought back in his knowledge pack some new seeds for people to sow. One of Sa'id's most laudable traits was that he had no desire to be the only one deserving praise for any particular quality or favor. He disliked hearing it said that, apart from him, there were no other liberal young people in Beit Chabab. He possessed some of the personality traits of pure prophets: he would rush to make known the knowledge that he had acquired and never stopped advocating those truths and beliefs about which his convictions were firm.

With all that in mind, Sa'id was inevitably a troublemaker, one of the select few with the necessary fervor and enthusiasm who were unconcerned about the possible distress that might affect them and their friends as a result of that same fervor and enthusiasm. As I have already noted, Sa'id was the very first supporter who visited me in Freike after the clergy had wreaked their anger on its ascetic. Today, thanks to him, there are many Sa'ids, but, in spite of their number, I shall never forget the very first Sa'id. I have started to be concerned about any such increase and the impact it may have on my time alone. The ascetic has begun to ask God's forgiveness for his friend the prophet.

I have now given you information about his most outstanding qualities, but I should not overlook a single one of them. He is a brother in travel, a companion of the great. He is in the very forefront of liberals, and friend of the righteous. You also need to know that he is someone who is fully respected by Arabs; they raise his status to the highest levels—considering him a person of high quality and great

2. A speech that the author delivered in the United States, reprinted in the first part of the *Rihaniyeh.*

generosity. That quality of generosity comes in various categories: gained, inherited, and natural. The person with acquired generosity uses it to gain prestige and dominance. The person who is generous because of inherited wealth is following tradition in order to keep the inheritance, whether laudable or otherwise, within the household. However, the third and last category of generosity—natural generosity—is concerned first and last with generosity, and the person who uses it experiences the greatest pleasure.

Nothing delights Sa'id more than hosting guests; few people know more about it than he, and it may be his profession that gives him that particular quality. The rest comes by virtue of your God, and yet the knowledge alone is enough to amaze you and inspire your admiration. My friend is an authentic Arab when it comes to organizing banquets, and I know of no one more skilled in making the necessary arrangements when the decision to be a host was not planned in advance. If I can use the words, he is the master, the poet, the madman of banquets. I do not believe that any foreigner has passed through Beit Chabab without Sa'id al-Ha'ik hearing about the visitor, stopping him in his tracks, and inviting him to his house as a guest . . .

So we reached the house right in the center of the village on a rise in the mountain and in the shadows of lofty walnut trees. Silvery streams flowed through the property fed by springs from the upper flats. However, the path leading to it, like the one by the front door, had been dug into the mountainside, and only occasionally becomes wider. You enter the house from the east, with the mountain behind you like the Great Wall of China. On the west side a superb, stunning view spread out before you in all directions; from among the villages in the Beit Chabab area, there was Chouiyeh, Qonaytra, and Freike. To the north lay Kesrouan Mountain, with its amazing rocks and steep cliffs, its forests, serene villages, and monasteries duly monopolizing the hills that provide its security. Beyond the monasteries and forests there was a blue line—or, more accurately, a blue wall connected to the sky—the sea as it appeared from high up in the mountains. On the sea were white objects that looked like doves—the sails of vessels that in olden times used to be the mistresses of the Mediterranean.

It was almost noon when we arrived, to be greeted by the distinguished ladies of the house—Sa'id's mother, his wife, and his uncle's wife. They hurried to prepare a "bite to eat" for the guests, but the preliminaries to the "bite" were plentiful. One of the ladies brought us glasses of mulberry juice, then a servant arrived with coffee and nargilehs. Soon after, another servant arrived with a large tray decorated with glass bottles and loaded with hors d'oeuvres.

You might think that, when it comes to Lebanese hospitality, drinks and hors d'oeuvres are a kind of trick being played on the guest, something needed to keep him busy while the meal is being prepared. There is something untoward about that idea. The hors d'oeuvres can amaze you with the sheer number of shapes and colors, simple and complex: cooked greenery, extracted from the sea and beyond, from various orchards and different countries. There is American pork, French pate, Italian sardines, Dutch cheese; pickled eggplant from Damascus, pistachios from Aleppo, edible sea algae from Beirut, raw liver from Beit Chabab, and grilled kidneys. Above all, there are the mixed nuts, the real poem of the hors d'oeuvres. Along with all that, the drinks include arak, beer, whisky, and soda. Our host and friend truly has "the Kurd's saddlebag" from the well-known tale in *A Thousand and One Nights*. "Bring it on, bag servant! Here's to you, bag owner!"

So our host, who has already excelled in matters of taste and hospitality, now proceeds to give you the biggest surprise of all: an invitation to take "a bite" at the table, some hour and a half after your arrival!

Good organization, movement, and elegance—these are the qualities that characterize large houses in cities. Generosity is what marks out the noble Lebanese family, along with speedy preparation which the host regularly achieves as part of his profession: a superb banquet magically brought by the "servant of the Kurdish bag" from the realms of the unseen to the actual world. It begins with European meats mixed with local Lebanese vegetables and finishes with mountain fruits. In between, there are wonderful courses featuring national dishes, *kibbe nayeh* coming first, then grilled chicken and various types of stuffed squash, eggplant, and peppers.

We drank some matured Lebanese wine—better than Spanish sherry, British port, and French Dubonnet—with a superior tang and aroma, and a soft edge and purity of taste to it. We drank to the memory of friends in the West, chief among them Homer Davenport, that American who genuinely loved the people of Syria—may God have mercy on him! We also drank to the memory of friends in our own country, chief among them that man from Beit Chabab, the first one to travel to France, where he became marshal of commerce in Paris, that cultured merchant and authentic Lebanese Arab, 'Abbas al-Bejjani—may God extend the full degree of His mercy on him!

I noticed that Sa'id was paying particular attention to Brother Hanna once he had learned that he had run away from the monastery, that he was about to discard the black robe and leave the mountain, as had his fellow monks before.

Brother Hanna had announced that information after downing two glasses of wine.

"God willing, we'll be going to America," he said in classical Arabic, and then fell silent.

He usually had little say, especially when he was eating. For him, eating and talking did not go together. That said, he was much better at the first than the second. How could it be otherwise when he was launching heroic assaults of the meal in front of him, twirling his bread around the kibbe dish and downing half of it in a trice, grabbing the chicken with both hands and taking both thighs, and devouring the stuffed squash one after the other as though they were olives?!

Sa'id tried to give him a third glass of wine, but I intervened. The echo of my objection struck home, and it was obvious that Brother Hanna had a secret hope: he was obviously thinking that we would be spending a day and night at our host's house, but he was wrong. After such a magnificent banquet, was it reasonable to accept your host's invitation to put you up as well? I decided that it was not, and asked permission to depart.

The expressions of sorrow that followed were genuine, and I will not attempt to describe them here. They involved both the owner of the house and his two generous sisters. They were determined and insistent as they made me promise to come back and spend a few days with them. They reminded me too of all my Kesrouani friends.

Sa'id was not satisfied with a single farewell in his house. He accompanied us to the edge of the village, and we stopped there to say our final farewell.

Mountaintops

MOUNTAINS COME IN VARIOUS TYPES of size and beauty, which cannot be appreciated if you are either on them or close by. They only appear clearly from high vantage points or from viewing locations far enough removed so as not to impede the view while also not enhancing it. Closeness distorts things, while distance misrepresents them. Sometimes they look like ancient ruins, at others like shadows. If you look down on them or can view them from a good vantage point, then you see them as a cluster, fragmented, undulating, interconnected, plunging, towering, welcoming, scowling, comforting, threatening; at one moment mouth wide open beneath your feet, at another spreading their glories before your very eyes, a legitimate path for those with wings and wind.

So here we are at the top of the mountain on which Beit Chabab lies. From the social point of view the villages scattered across its western slopes are tiny and paltry. The inhabitants of the day'a surveying the scene from their heights and slopes are like someone standing on a mountain peak who looks down on someone living on the lower slopes, in a valley, or on one of its hillocks or rises, all of which are insignificant and unpretentious. The inhabitants of these villages are farmers.

Leaving the social aspect aside, the natural vista from the heights of Beit Chabab is superb, varied in its shapes. Its valleys are perched in place and its hills link to each other; it is well protected between its different bluffs, and it teems with little villages and hamlets. How lovely it all looks, the villages bathed in the noontime sun. The red roofs amid the orchards and forests look like coral islands in a sea of emeralds and lapis lazuli.

We bade farewell to the village on its eastern edge, the spot where the morning sun honors it with a smile and a slow-moving pace, and made our way toward the east. There, far above the numerous hills was their mighty lord, Sannine, one of the giants of the Lebanese range. From Freike, I had been used to seeing it at the peak of its glory, in all its splendor. Thus, when I first saw it from a place both higher and closer than Freike, it alarmed me—indeed, it disappointed me.

Can Sannine shine forth in its totality, with its awesome splendor, its radiance, its shadows, its towering heights, its magnetic attraction—head lowered at its feet in foothills and hillocks, valleys and uplands looming below it? Can the mountain shine forth in all its impressive beauty unless it is viewed from a hill to the west toward the sea? If you look at it from Bekaa Plain for example, all you can see is the top half; the bounty afforded by its majestic appearance is totally lost. If you stop by its springhead and look upward, it looks as though it is cut into pieces and mutilated, unsoftened by the sun at dawn, unaffected by sunset.

Sannine! Have you ever seen it bedecked in colors woven for it by the sun on the looms of sea clouds at sunset? Here it is dressed in a silver garment, a purple cloak, a shirt woven in pink and saffron, in a red twilight? Have you seen it at dawn, as the sun appears from behind its throne and spreads its gentle rays across fields and hills and over valleys that slope in front of it, producing impressions from which are drawn the realities of art in life? Sunrise awakens Sannine's desires and slowly clothes her. At that moment, the mountain is a glorious sight. The forests spread out across the hills turn green, and the hills below it are a darker color; the sandy flatlands are yellow, distant valleys are black, and plowed fields are reddish-brown. Between them all lie monasteries, inhabited yet standing alone, their red-colored roofs exposed to the dawn light. Gold gleams in that same light, and they all lift their glass windows to sunset and gleam like diamonds.

In broad daylight the gleam of the sun's vertical rays take away those colors, except for the shafts of light that hit the forests and the red-lined darker rays—the effect of iron oxide—on the stony hills. The coloring is also affected by other weather factors, except at sunrise and sunset. After it has rained, for example, a misty fog will permeate both light and shade. The colors differ one from the other. The effect of iron oxide on rocks turns them even redder, and the green fields turn an even purer color. The edges of hills appear even clearer, and you can easily sense how gorges separate them from each other, albeit obscured by the distance involved.

Now we are walking across the top of Beit Chabab Mountain, which stretches away to the east from Bikfaya to Bteghrine. In height above sea level, the road varies from nine hundred to one thousand meters; in other words, there is a slight incline upward from west to east between Bikfaya and Bteghrine, which does not exceed a hundred meters. On the north side, it breaks up into gorges and valleys, with spurs and smaller hills that slope downward, gradually at times and more precipitously at others—all due to normal factors or earthquakes—until they reach the River Salib.

To the south there are rises whose grades transfer you to another side of the mountain, which is 250 meters above the one we are currently walking along. It goes from the summits of Choueir via Mrouj to Matn. The trail then continues to Aintoura, and above it the freezing heights linked to the loftiest peaks that look down on Bekaa Plain.

In summary, then, the mountain's shape is terraced into various levels, although one part of it is a wide expanse of land and the other is flat and not elevated. Add to that that the different levels crumble and fall apart. Civilization inserts itself into these ravines and clings to their various trails. In humanity's quest for a place to live, the choice is firstly somewhere close to water, and then somewhere with fertile soil and a minimum of rocky terrain. That is the general story.

However, our ancient Lebanese ancestors seem to have preferred rocky terrain remote from generally used pathways. That was not merely to avoid robbers, but to be safe from what was at that time regarded as the evil of all evils, urban slavery and religious persecution.

Bikfaya—"house of rock"—as scholars call it in Syriac. Do any of those people involved in ancient studies and archeology have any idea how Bikfaya was built? Who put down the first rock for the very first of its houses? I can see myself as that Aramean who ran away to escape the enslavement imposed by the king of Jbeil (Byblos) or from the persecution inflicted by the priests of Baal. He built a hut in the shadow of that rock on one of the mountain ledges and called it Bikfaya.

He may well have been a robber or else a criminal on the run, that Dosari man who climbed to the top of the mountain, selected a segment of it, took refuge in a cave, and called it Wadi Chahine, for instance, or else, using his profession, Abou Mizan (scales).

Once we leave Bikfaya, the village, which is a prime summer resort, the mountain slopes down gently. The path gradually widens and passes by fields and hillocks where pastures belonging to Bikfaya rest in peace. They all flourish and bloom, like Wadi Chahine, Ain el-Kharroubeh, Mayasseh, and Hemlaya below Chouiyeh—with Abou Mizan below that. Below Abou Mizan in a hollow in the valley lies Deir Chamra. There too are productive fields that belong to the Mar Antonius monastery (in Beit Chabab). Other lands belong to the Mar Nahra monastery, which lies in a forest situated between Beit Chabab and Bikfaya. All the cultivable lands from the mountaintop down to the river belong to the monasteries!

The monasteries and their properties almost made us forget the road we were taking. To our right, the mountain toward the south was a succession of outcrops. We were passing by the heights of Chouelr, then Mrouj, although they were out of sight. Between the two villages was a wonderful, shady pine forest, which had recently become a travel stop for elegant summer visitors. They started calling it Bois de Boulogne in French, but we are taking revenge on those who call it that by Arabizing and shortening it to Boulan Forest.[1]

On our left now is Chouiyeh, and to our right on a hill sits the twin monastery for pious visitors occupied by both Maronite and Roman Catholic nuns. It is the Orthodox monastery of the Prophet Elias. The two monastic communities are linked together. It was originally

1. It is currently called Boulogna.

the endowment of Bishop Philippos al-Gemayel, whose grandfather had settled in Chouiyeh at the beginning of the eighteenth century. He provoked a dispute between the monks and the bishop as part of which the monks' aspirations—both Aleppan and Lebanese—were involved. The patriarch intervened, and they were able to rescue the monastery from the talons of greed and hatred. The original gift was now consecrated to the Maronite prophet Elias, the exact equivalent of the Orthodox prophet of the same name. Today both monasteries are at peace—thanks be to God! Not only that, but there is also fine aged wine.

An English tourist visiting Lebanon at the beginning of the nineteenth century commented that monasteries welcome and host unexpected visitors, and, with due Eastern hospitality, serve the finest Lebanese vintages. For that very reason he much preferred to stay in monasteries rather than elsewhere. However, unlike the present writer, that Englishman was not excommunicated and deprived of the opportunity to mingle with the believers. I had fully intended to visit the two "Elias monks" and stay overnight, but my colleague Brother Hanna was someone who had run away from monasteries, and so the rules of travel demand that you not subject your travel companion to the evils of fate or the wiles of monks.

So we went on our way and reached Khinshara, which is situated in an area with lots of iron mines. It was exploited in the previous century by Ibrahim Pasha while our country was occupied. That is what the heads of the village told us; they said that the effect of the mines and foundries is still much in evidence. We did not see that effect, but neither did we disbelieve what we were told.

Khinshara also had evidence of some excellent living relics. Undoubtedly, the Lebanese mountain trails owe a debt to this village, and indeed the Lebanese treasure house, with its store of builders and engineers, can claim a prominent place among the renowned family of munificence. That is certainly the case today, while in happier times from the past Khinshara produced a large number of prominent religious figures from the two prominent families, Kfouri and Riashi, who served their Lord, interpreted His will, and comprehended His Godhead. Where are the likes of them among renowned people today?

I almost forgot to mention the members of the Kfouri family in this generation who have followed the lead of their pious ancestors, serving the Lord of Humanity, and providing further service to their fellow human beings in this world before the next. I have no doubt that the spirits of those patriarchs and bishops would cast a favorable glance today on those who are bringing their previous charitable acts to fulfilment, thereby sanctifying their mysteries among their contemporary descendants, in their forefront being the Reverend Paul Kfouri and Professor George Kfouri—may God have mercy on both of them!

Even so, the repute of those two members of the Kfouri family is like a mere seed of grain when compared with the red dome over the repute of that "roaming" Riashi, Professor Alexander, the great teacher of known art, the extoller of passion among people, the kindler of lights for joy in this fleeting existence, and the bringer of knowledge of Jesus to prostitutes and harlots. The late Alexander's reputation was a genuine Dosari one in that it brought together the fame of the pious ancestors of both the Kfouri and Riashi families into a single breath of wind that spread the word in every direction.

We said farewell to Khinshara and its blessed people and continued on our way to Bteghrine, reaching the edge of the village just before sunset.

The Doctor of Bteghrine

"WHICH HOUSE'S DOOR should we knock on here to ask to spend the night?" I asked Brother Hanna before we actually entered the village.

"Don't you know anyone in Bteghrine?" he responded quizzically.

I protested. "Are you assuming," I asked, "that in every single Lebanese village I have a friend who will kindly host us?!"

"Would you stay overnight with a stranger?" he asked disapprovingly.

"Should I worry about being refused," I asked, "when you are with me?"

"Please, Master, don't make fun of me."

"You're afraid we're going to be treated like the two Chaldean vagrants in the Bible. What's the harm with us sleeping out in the open or at the baking oven?"

"I'm used to hardships. It's you I'm concerned about. Your mother entrusted you to my care."

"So, then, answer my original question: which door should we knock on to ask to spend the night?"

"All we can do is to try the village head's house."

"Are you trying to tell me that 'a bird in the hand is worth two in the bush'? You're a fox in monk's clothing. Let's leave Bteghrine and move on to Biskanta."

"Biskanta? Do you want to cross Wadi al-Jamajim at night?"

"What's to stop us?"

"Forgive me, Master, but that's crazy!"

"So you're refusing to be as crazy as me?" I responded somewhat angrily. "Fine, go back to the house. I'm going on to Biskanta by night."

I left him standing where he was, and he hurried to catch up with me, swearing by God and cursing the Devil. He stopped me.

"By God, Master," he panted, "I'm not afraid of sleeping in the open, nor of walking through the night. It's you I'm worried about. Wadi al-Jamajim is really scary."

"Why are you so scared? If there are any wild beasts in that valley, then Saint Francis can be our intercessor. For me, Francis of Assisi is the most virtuous saint; he made pacts of loyalty and fidelity with wolves. If there are any highway robbers in the valley, then they usually steal travelers' property. What can they steal from us? We're not carrying any gold or silver."

"You're absolutely right, Master. But that's not why . . ."

"Tell me what's bothering you!"

"It's not the walking, whether by day or night, that tires me out. But it has a drastic effect on my stomach."

"We had a meal two hours ago, and now you're hungry?!"

"Walking speeds up digestion, Master, and stimulates the appetite."

"So you're thinking about your supper."

"Our supper, Master . . ."

"Tonight you're going to sleep with no supper."

"As you wish, as you wish."

By now we had reached the first house in Bteghrine. I lowered my voice and softened my tone.

"You'll get your wish," I reassured my companion. "Say, 'God willing' . . ."

"God willing!"

"To achieve our hopes we'll make use of God's good will to select a place to stay the night. We'll count twelve houses, and then, counting on God's aid, we'll knock on the door of the thirteenth."

"You choose thirteen as the number? I once heard you say that in America thirteen is bad luck!"

"Are we in America now? Put your trust in God, Brother Hanna."

"I did that when I entered the monastery, Master."

"And He rescued you from it too—may He be exalted and glorified!"

"True enough!"

"Here's the first house in Bteghrine. Now count, and don't make a mistake."

We walked through mulberry orchards, counting houses in a raucous voice that could be heard by people standing in store doorways and boys giggling in the street. It was as though they were saying, "These two strangers must be a bit crazy!"

Finally we reached the thirteenth house facing the roadway, a modest home attached to the wall amid a cluster of chinaberry trees. The door was open, and the owner was standing by it.

"Good evening!" we said in Lebanese dialect.

"And a very good evening to both of you," he replied. "Do come in, please, come in!"

So we did so—or rather, we stood there, feeling relieved and happy. "Please come in," he said for a third time, and went on to say, "It's an honor!"

We entered the house feeling relaxed and found ourselves in a small yard paved with local tiles. On two sides were Arab-style reception rooms with couches, striped Syrian coverlets, and a closet colored a brilliant white.

We sat in the room, following the usual custom in greeting people. The house owner now moved on to the second phase in our conversation, asking us where we had come from.

"From Freike," I replied. "I am Ameen Faris al-Rihani, and my companion is Brother Hanna Jirjis al-Mallah."

I was delighted to see that the two names had the same effect on him and that the renown of the "excommunicated one" had not reached as far as Bteghrine.

He went on to ask us about some people he knew in Freike and its environs. This gave Brother Hanna an opportunity to contribute to the conversation.

He had already indicated to his wife to bring some coffee, and she did so while we were talking. After we had drunk some and expressed our appreciation, the house owner asked us if we had come to consult the doctor.

The doctor! I had already heard about this "doctor of Bteghrine," whose fame was not limited to the Matn region but spread throughout all the regions of Lebanon. People from Kesrouan or Shouf used to say "the doctor of Bteghrine," and that was enough. Some of them knew him by his first name and would call him Habeeb of Bteghrine.

Habeeb was not an official doctor, one of those with fancy degrees printed at that time in Arabic and Turkish, nor was he one of those tricksters—cousins of Gypsies—who could treat every single illness with various herbs and readings from books of magic and astrology.

No, he was a doctor with a minimum of book learning,[1] but a large amount of experiment and experience. He was particularly famous for surgery and orthopedics. People would come to see him from the furthest reaches of the mountains, and he would put them up in his house, which resembled a hospital. He would deal with them kindly, even if the treatment did not always work. One of his finest traits was that he was both generous and modest, never craving money for its own sake.

Yes indeed, he was—God have mercy on him!—one of those blessed people of the old type, a descendant of those charitable people who would do good things for people, even though their knowledge was quite limited. I do not believe that the mistakes that they made in treating people were any worse than the ones committed by official doctors today, or that the victims of their ignorance (or the trickery of a few of them) were any more numerous than the ones in modern hospitals. What is certainly true is that those doctors who were graduated from the school of experience and time were renowned for their kindness. Even the ones who loved money the most would treat sick people free of charge much more than generous and sympathetic medical experts today. Those lofty ethics were indeed blessed, as was the knowledge that refused to corrupt them.

1. There is traditional Arabic saying: "Anyone who gets his grammar from books does not speak properly; anyone who gets his jurisprudence from words makes poor judgments; and anyone who gets his knowledge of medicine from books kills people."

In those days, the time of Habeeb from Bteghrine, along with his righteous predecessors, a member of the sick person's family or one of his friends would come to the doctor's house on his behalf, bringing a mule with an elegant saddle blanket for the doctor to ride. He would get on it, and the mule would set off at an easy pace, with the messenger walking alongside at the same speed. The journey could take a day or two, or even three in some cases. The doctor would arrive at the sick person's house; there he would find him waiting patiently for the blessing of a cure and return to good health. Even if the treatment process required repeat visits, involving long journeys with many difficulties, the sick person never doubted the doctor whether he was cured or died. In either case, there was no hurry.

Today anyone who falls sick in Biskanta, for example, asks for the famous medical expert in Beirut. That doctor will get into his large luxury car, fill it with petrol thanks to American generosity, and reach that village at the foothills of Mount Sannine in an hour and a half. He will find the sick person in a condition that will make him shake his head; he may even have drawn his last breath or almost. He will receive his fee in gold coins and head back to the city as fast as he had come.

In times of old—and indeed, in the times of Habeeb from Bteghrine—the doctor would ride a mule or a female donkey. To the Devil he would say:

> Do not rush me or try to frustrate my hopes. I believe in God and His prophets, in all His saints and forefathers. You are merely the Devil. If you are some kind of evangelist for receiving payment or for "rolling up your sleeves,"[2] then wipe the sweat off your forehead, sit down and rest for a while; and we'll let the mule rest as well. Once we arrive, your effort will fail, God willing, but my hopes will not.

Thus Doctor Habeeb behaved the same way in his house as in his clinic, neither rushing nor being rushed. "Come in!" he told us three

2. "He walks with Azrael behind him Azrael's sleeves rolled up to grab."

times, and then went on to say what an honor it was. He then gave us a Lebanese greeting too. He asked us how we were and about friends in the village and offered us coffee. As we drank it, we had to blow on the surface to cool it down; as Brother Hanna was blowing and drinking, he kept making noises like the nightingale's call. All this happened without any rush, but eventually it was time for business. "Have you come to consult the doctor?" he asked.

As he asked us the question, his tone of voice did not change, nor did his smile disappear.

"We're both fine, thank God!" I replied. "But we're traveling, and we need somewhere to spend the night. And my companion is complaining that he's hungry."

"Of course," he said, "you're very welcome, very welcome!" and repeated himself. He stood up and called his wife.

"I'm sorry, we eat dinner early," he said by way of apology for the apparent oversight. "We've already eaten. But, as the proverb has it, 'The best is always available.'"

After a little while, the lady of the house invited us to the table. In the middle was part of their dinner, potatoes with meat and rice. But in addition—gifts from a generous man—all around it were eggs cooked in oil; large, round white onions; a tomato salad; bowls of cheese and olives; a large tureen of cooked figs; and plenty of thin bread.

Brother Hanna made the sign of the cross over his face and stretched out his hand to grab one of the onions. First he used his teeth to bite off the head, then he put it on the floor and hit it with his hand. We do not think he was content with just eggs and onions. Suffice it to say that, only four hours after the magnificent feast we had enjoyed in Beit Chabab, he managed to demolish the spread on Doctor Habeeb's table. After a sweet course consisting of generous mouthfuls of cooked figs, he smacked his lips gratefully, made the sign of the cross over his face again, and stood up, looking well sated.

He looked satisfied and healthy, clearly wanting the situation to last as long as possible. However, he seems to have been very doubtful about continuing the journey in my company. Before we entered the room where we would be sleeping, I heard him asking the doctor about Wadi al-Jamajim and noticed him shaking his head.

When I woke up the next morning, I called Brother Hanna, but he did not respond.

"Get up, Brother Hanna," I said. "The sun's already up!"

No response, no snoring, no whistling. Maybe he had gone into the house before me. I was wrong about that. Maybe he was waiting outside the house. My hopes were high.

"Where's Brother Hanna?" I asked the doctor, but he did not know, nor did the astrologer.[3] But the doctor's wife said that she had heard the door being opened very early. She looked out of the window and spotted the monk on the path heading for Khinshara as fast as he could!

3. The reader may want to ask what happened to Brother Hanna. The sum total of what I know is that he went back to Freike. Later, he took off his black robe and traveled happily to America.

In those days Doctor Habeeb was the only doctor in Bteghrine. Now he serves as the honored predecessor for a group of official doctors from the Saliba, Murr, and Sawaya families. All of them have gold-embossed certificates to attest to their competence. There is also another group of grandees from those three families bearing the illustrious title of *economos*. Most of them are men of considerable age. Among the most prominent and somewhat younger Bteghrine citizens by origin or birth are the musician Mirti al-Murr, the lawyer Du'aybis al-Murr, and the architect Elias al-Murr. God willing, they can intercede for the betterment of their home village and its doctors.

Wadi al-Jamajim

ON THAT SEPTEMBER DAY the sun was at the starting point of its earthly glory that the dictionary terms *noon*. It was bathing valleys and mountains, villages and vineyards, in its glowing light and warmth. As I stood up to bid farewell to my generous hosts, the doctor and his wife both raised their voices in unison.

"It's not right," they said, "it cannot be!"

They told me that I had to stay for two or three days. I thanked them for their kindness, but insisted that I had to leave. The doctor told me that crossing Wadi al-Jamajim on my own was risky, not without its dangers. Even so, I did not waver in my decision. The lady of the house pointed out that it was a long way; I might not reach Biskanta before sunset. I would be feeling hungry before I even reached the pine forest on the mountain facing Bteghrine. Saying that, she asked me to wait a while. When she came back, she was carrying a small bundle wrapped in newspaper tied with a piece of twine.

"Excuse me," she said. "Look away for a moment."

With that, she attached the small bundle to the bend in my walking stick over my shoulder and added a much larger package—of kindness and generosity—to my heart. As I set off toward Biskanta, I reflected on the innate goodness of the Lebanese people.

"A single generous house liked this one in every Lebanese village," I told myself, "is enough to erase the sins of the entire Lebanese people."

No sooner had I left Bteghrine than I was looking down on the stunning deep valley, Wadi al-Jamajim. The dictionary says that it was called by that name because of a battle that happened in it. The skulls (*jamajim*) of the dead were piled so high that they blocked the flow of the river there.

So here now is the track to the river. It makes its way downward at the top of the valley, then keeps winding round and round. All you can see clearly is just what is in front of you. On the other steep side facing Bteghrine Mountain you can see the entire track as it creeps like a multicolored snake amid the yellow-green thickets and black rocks, rising and twisting from the riverbank to the forest that shades the highest part of the mountain.

Of all the valleys in Lebanon, Wadi al-Jamajim is the wildest and scariest. It is no wonder that Brother Hanna decided to keep his body intact rather than his reputation.

But, in spite of its wildness and scary aspects, the valley also affords natural vistas, replete with all kinds of beautiful and fascinating attractions, and in terms of shape, color, and significance. After going a little way down the winding track we pass through mulberry orchards and vines until we reach rocky clefts covered in gallnut bushes and valonia oak. All around are clumps of gorse, bramble, and laurel. You are greeted by their yellow and violet flowers, their red-and-purple clusters, and their fresh, gentle scents. They welcome you not only by the side of the track but also in the cracks between the rocks and hillocks.

There is an omnipresent perfumer who mixes aromas, blending the dewy scents from the earth with those from the damp trees and fragrant plants. The flowering shrubs left after the dry season (few of whose names are unknown) still manage to exude a lovely, complex, and amazing fragrance, one that botanists and chemists have been unable to analyze.

Here there exists an eternal artist, one who can blend the earth's greenery with the sky's azure blue, the sun's gold, and the clouds' translucent silver. In the realms of color art, he achieves the very limits of impossibility, something that artists aspire to achieve, but in vain.

In various parts of the valley you can see traces of the Great Sculptor. From the rocks He has carved sculptures truly with amazing themes, perplexing mysteries, and stunning shapes. With some of them He has combined art with art, beauty with beauty, and splendor to surpass all splendors. Below the upper part of the mountain is a high wall, a place where the beauties of design and plant life come together. It looks just like the front of a Hindu temple. There is a smooth rock, clearly hewn at a moment of joy and inspiration, that looks just like the Sphinx, with a gorse bush between its paws exuding a lovely springtime scent. It eventually blends into the forest; at every season of the year its mouth releases pure thyme plants to greet the passing traveler.

God salute you, oh Sphinx, speaking with thyme and titmouse. God greet you too, titmouse, your lofty heights for eagles alone and your spiky violet flowers, unrivaled by any other flowers!

Wadi al-Jamajim—may God forgive whoever gave it that name (Skull Valley)! I never came across a skull or any bones from one. I never saw any wild beasts, wolves, hyenas, or anything resembling either of them on the track itself or off it. It may have been the "valley of skulls" in the past, but today it is the valley of wonders. There is a sea of light above a sea of quiet above another sea of safety and serenity. Crickets chant noon and evening melodies, cyclamen and hyacinth chant, and goldfinches sing their songs. From time to time you will also hear the sound of pack animals going up or down its various levels, the echo resounding across the rocks.

Overhanging rocks, and underneath them chasms, deep chasms peopled by eagles' wings, soaring and plunging effortlessly as though made of leather or paper. But then they will spring into life and with a flap of their wings soar high above the mountain.

I walked for an hour without a care in the world, like a promenader entranced or rather a happy worshipper. I forgot all about distances and rocks, abysses and overhangs. Yes indeed, I was totally bewitched by the wonders of creation that I was seeing all around me, by the fragrant scent of flowers and sweet basil that I was smelling, and the sweet melodies of tranquility that I was hearing, all duly embellished by the golden sun.

I only realized how entranced I actually was when the ground gave way under my feet. I started sliding downward, then slithering on my back for a few meters. I was saved by grabbing a myrtle bush. I then crawled my way back up to the track, unharmed—thank God!

This slide reminded me that, during earthquakes, the mountains themselves can break up. A rock may separate from others, or a whole section of the mountain can fall away from the main part and start sliding or rolling down to the lowest point in the valley. Here is a passage that I have read in the history written by Prince Haidar al-Chebabi:

> The lower part of the mountain of the River Safa, which lies below the village of Kfar Nabrakh, was struck by an earthquake. It broke off from the main part of the mountain and tilted the other way below the village of Majd el-Meouch. There it stuck, blocking the flow of the river on either side. As a result, a number of properties were totally destroyed, and the inhabitants of a small village in the valley perished under the rubble. It is said that a man carrying a beehive was walking across the bottom of the mountain. When the earthquake struck and the land tilted, he simply kept walking along with the moving ground beneath him. He was both astonished and terrified as the earth kept moving, but, before he even realized it, he was on the other side below the village of Majd el-Meouch that we have just mentioned. He was completely unharmed, but his mind was adversely affected by the experience he had gone through, with the earth shifting from one side of the valley to the other. This event took place on the eighteenth of December 1767 CE, 1181 AH.

On that September day in 1905, my own mind did not "quake" at what had happened in Wadi al-Jamajim. Actually, I had almost brought my life to an end by standing entranced so close to the edge of the abyss and then sliding part of the way down it on my back. All the while there it was, open-mouthed, ready to pull me down to its eternal tranquility!

This scare that I had had put an end to the sense of pleasure I had been feeling at the beauty and glories of nature. I quickened my pace somewhat; my eyes were like headlamps, glued to the track ahead of me. Eventually I reached the bottom of the valley and sat down on a rock in the shade of an oleander. Looking up at the mountain levels I had just descended, I thanked God that I was safe and sound.

Sitting there at the narrow base of the valley between the two mountains, I felt a bit depressed. All those natural wonders, which just a short while ago had filled my heart with such joy, disappeared from my sensory horizon, but not, of course, from the valley itself, which was still spread out all around me. The sound of water flowing amid the rocks was certainly nicer than the chirping of crickets, and the scent of plants and flowers was stronger in the narrower parts of the mountain than in its open spaces. At the valley's base the peace had more profound significance than at its heights. It was not that the sensory world had changed; none of its beauty and glory had disappeared. It was the human sense that records their very existence that had changed.

The major factor in that change was fear. Had I encountered a highway robber at that moment, I would have forgotten to tell him that I was not carrying any gold or silver. I would have raised my hands in surrender. If I had encountered a wolf, it would not have occurred to me to remind it of the pact between wolves and the most pure Saint Francis of Assisi—God be pleased with him!

So why the fear? Thanks to the myrtle tree, the hand of God saved you from perdition. Should you not be grateful and happy instead? I am indeed both grateful and happy, but the vestige of fear still clings to my heart and lurks there; that vestige is often more powerful that the event that caused it, shifting from heart to imagination. Wadi al-Jamajim now seemed to me like a gigantic, frightening cracked skull, with me a mere insect at its base.

At that point I got to my feet and started singing. However, my voice objected to its own ugliness and took me back to my previous mental state. The same sickly image haunted me: an insect at the base of a skull! That's right, the base of a skull! All of a sudden I came to myself, regained control over my imagination, and banished the nasty image. My mind upbraided the voice that had poked fun at me. I had wanted to sing, but it came out as a whistle. At that moment I realized for sure that the fear that had obsessed me like a nightmare had disappeared, or almost so. The insect at the base of the skull was once again a sentient, thinking human being. It was that person who now stood up with his food bag attached to his cane, and set off up the mountain.

For one or two hours the track that loomed in front of me up the mountain on the other side of the valley looked just like a snake twisting its way endlessly upward with no end in sight. During the prime hours of daylight the September sun put me in mind of August days as I kept walking straight upward without turning to look at anything.

At first I walked fast, but that was a mistake; fairly soon my feet grew tired and my heart felt heavy, as did the cane I was holding.

I felt thirsty . . . and hungry too! I sat down in the shade of a rock to rest for a while and cast an eagle eye over the provisions in front of me. What to do? Could the bread do without any water? Certainly not. So on up the mountain! I started climbing again, with a voice inside me asking, "Where are you, pine forest?" Another hour of exhaustion, thirst, and hunger . . .

Here now is the forest, lavishing its shade on the weary and heavy-laden. God bless the pines and their shade! It grasped my exhaustion and gave me back some strength and hope. With gratitude and thanksgiving I entered the forest and spread myself in the shade of the very first tree.

It was at this point that I realized the mistake I had made, one I did not repeat afterward. Esteemed reader, if you are walking in the mountains and crossing from one mountain to another with a deep valley in front of you, do not pay any attention to the beauties of nature on the way down. Make the descent quickly, without bothering about things around you or in front of you. But then travel upward slowly and enjoy all nature's beauties and wonders. Whenever you are feeling tired, stop for a while and allow your eyes and soul to enjoy your surroundings. While you are fully aware, sniff the pure air, relish the lovely scents, and listen to the crickets chirping and eagles flapping their wings. Then pick some bay and sage leaves and rub your hands and forehead. You will be able to relax and regain some lost energy.

If you do that while you are climbing uphill, you will not feel tired, however rough the terrain.

After a quarter of an hour in the shade of pine trees, I resumed my walk, hoping all the while that I would soon reach a house where I could quench my thirst. No sooner had I left the forest than such a house appeared in front of me, still nestling in the forest's shade. It was an old, square house with a flat clay roof, surrounded by a fig orchard and vines.

Close by, a boy was tending to a cow. I called to him, and he came hurrying over. When I asked him for some water, he rushed into the house and came back with a jug.

By now I had unwrapped the package that the wife of the doctor in Bteghrine had given me: it contained boiled eggs, onions, cheese, olives, and some bread. There was also a separate loaf of bread with a whole pile of figs cooked in carob bean syrup. I spread the newspaper over the soft carpet of dried pine leaves, arranged the food on it, and invited the boy to sit with me and share the food. He thanked me but declined, telling me that he had already had his lunch. But then he agreed to have a piece of the cooked figs. Using half a loaf, I made him a sandwich and handed it to him. He took it and then hurried inside the house.

After a while he came back with grapes in one hand and some green figs in the other. High up in the mountains, both those fruits ripen two or three weeks after they do in Freike and surrounding regions. As we say: "The Lord's Festival Day (August) does the fruits convey (ripened grapes)." Whenever you climb above Freike, the Lord's Festival—or, more precisely, the ripening of fruit—is delayed. While we are busy picking the vines, people in Biskanta are still sifting their clusters.

This young boy brings me the pick of the season, amber-colored grapes and purple figs. Truly he is in the first class of generous Lebanese, one of the old type. When he brought me that jug of water, he reminded me of the Samaritan woman immortalized in the Gospels—as though he hails from her blessed lineage.

I made another sandwich out of the rest of the figs. He took it as he had taken the first, but did not eat it. I asked him why.

"I don't like cooked figs," he told me, "but my little sister inside the house likes them a lot!"

His name is Tannous and he is twelve years old. He has blue eyes and rosy cheeks. His voice has the ring of self-confidence, and his gestures suggest both kindness and energy. He is fond of travelers because he once took "a long trip and met "decent people."

"Where did you go, Tannous?"

"To Faraya, then down to Jounieh. Jounieh's a big city with stores that have everything. We came back home by way of Antelias and Bikfaya. We were away for twelve days, my father and I. We bought this cow and a Cyprus goat. We bought the goat in Faraya and sold it in the Jounieh market; we made two *majeeds* profit."[1]

He told me that he had an elder brother "with a donkey to transport goods" and another sister—not the one who likes cooked figs—who had married "America" the previous year; meaning that a young man from the village had come home from America, married his sister, and taken her back to the place where he had a job.

Blue-eyed Tannous, trader in cows and goats, was intent on traveling to America, where his sister and brother-in-law were living. It is in America that we trade, make a profit, and get rich, God willing!

Before saying farewell to Tannous, I asked him if Biskanta was still a long way.

"Once you get to the first house over there by that rock, it's just a stone's throw away."

1. *Majeed*: the name of a coin used in the Ottoman period.

Sannine

NOWHERE ON EARTH are there mountains more beautiful than those in Lebanon. God guards and protects that beauty in both shape and essence, so in both instances there is no cause for alarm. And yet, who among the Lebanese people, I wonder, is fulfilling the task of protecting their hospitality and generosity? Freedom, there is no doubt about that. The Greek philosopher states that freedom and hospitality are the marks of greatness among peoples. That is absolutely true: free peoples can be welcoming, and the combination of freedom and hospitality endures.

In Lebanon hospitality is still observed as an obligation of human beings, particularly among the middle and lower classes. The upper class, to use civil terminology—meaning the rich—is just like its equivalent in America: they will sometimes offer lavish hospitality in a quest for prestige or to safeguard their reputation, but at other times they will retreat into more Western customs and traditions, using hotels to offer a frigid version of official hospitality. Whenever the number of new hotels in Lebanon increases and the vacation trade spreads, there is a drop in any kind of genuine Arab hospitality, with its wonderful origins and traditions inside Lebanese homes. What is undoubtedly the case is that in the past such hospitality was a general and widespread phenomenon.

Here is what an English tourist visiting the mountains in the previous century has to say:

> The tourist need not worry about the possibility of spending the night in the forest or in a shepherd's hut. One of the nicest things about being a tourist in the Lebanese mountains is that you can

> travel around with the guarantee of finding wonderful hospitality at the day's end. You can always anticipate being able to spend the night as an honored guest in someone's house.

Even a century later you can still find locations in our mountains—Kesrouan for example, parts of the north, and sections of Matn as well (such as the ones that I have just traversed) where that statement still applies. Hospitality is still readily available, an object of Lebanese Arab pride.

These thoughts occurred to me after I had bid Tannous farewell. I was thinking about his natural goodness—his kindness, his politeness, his generosity—all embedded in his farewell words: "We'll travel to America, trade, make a profit, and get rich." Such thoughts and realities kept pulling at me: my mind was overcome, and sentiment took over. Can you possibly deny the powerful truth almost encapsulated today in the combination of emigration, commerce, and money? There is no way of denying it, and no strategy available to avoid the trouble and pain that it brings with it.

That same night my own heart was not without its own sense of trouble as I chatted to the woman whom the fates decreed should be my hostess. I had spotted her as soon as I entered the town; I bade her "good evening," and she responded likewise, although she kept giving me quizzical, inquiring looks. I did not hesitate to start a conversation, which led to some introductions. She asked me if I had been in America, and was clearly delighted by my reply. When she learned that I knew one of her relatives in New York, she was excited to hear me mention his name, although her reaction was a mixture of warm memories and sadness.

She was in her forties and still pretty. After her relative had emigrated, she had had three children, and was now a widow who was good at keeping her personal feelings to herself.

With her three boys—Elias, Boutros, and Paulus—we sat down by a silver platter raised from the ground by a small, low table. On it was today's meal, *mujaddara*, to which had been added an omelet and yogurt in the guest's honor.

Umm Elias offered me a cushion to sit on, noting that in my European clothes I could not sit cross-legged like them. Before dinner she had already posed a whole series of questions and extracted from my soul some of its constituents. Calling me by my first name, she proceeded to ask a series of irksome questions.

"So, Mr. Ameen, are you married?"

"No, Sitt Umm Elias, I'm not."

"Were you successful in America?"

"Thanks be to God!"

"Did you come back to your homeland to look for a wife?"

I did not reply. She re-asked the question a different way.

"I've never known anyone who's come back for another purpose. It's as though there aren't any girls in America. But my nephew did the opposite: he emigrated and got married in America."

She paused for a moment.

"What's your view on marriage?" she asked.

"Marriage, Sitt Umm Elias, has obvious and hidden aspects to it," I said. "God alone knows the hidden ones. The obvious ones are just like the Ottoman sultan's fancy signature. Everyone knows, but no one understands it."

"Complicated and confusing, but pleasant even so. I think that's what you mean. I don't think you would deny that, for young folk like you and my son Elias, marriage is a necessity."

"What does Elias have to say?"

"He's engaged, but reluctant . . ."

"That's harmful. It should be either marriage or canceling the agreement . . ."

"You're right. I've told Elias that many times."

Now Elias spoke angrily. "What's the point of this talk? Let the man eat!"

"You're right," his mother said. "We've been talking too much. You haven't touched the omelet, Mr. Ameen. You seem to be as fond of *mujaddara* as my son Paulus."

Paulus was the second of her boys, still sixteen years old. He was studying in the elementary school in the town.

"I like other things too," he explained. "Men don't prefer one dish over another."

Boutros was the third; he was the cleverest of the three. He leaned toward me with a mischievous glint in his eyes.

"Ask him if he likes pistachio pastry," he said.

"You, sir, light of my eyes," Paulus said, "don't you like it too?"

"Yes I do, yes I do," replied Boutros. "I'm not ashamed, and I won't tell a lie."

"Shame on you!" their mother yelled, "show some tact and shut up! The very mention of pistachio pastry is embarrassing. There a story behind this, Mr. Ameen. We have relatives in Zahle who promised to pay us a visit. I sent Boutros to Beirut to buy some things for the house to offer guests, including a box of pistachio pastries. But then our guests wrote to apologize—they couldn't come on the day they had said—instead, they would visit us on the following Sunday. Sunday came, but none of them came. The box of pastries stayed waiting for them inside the larder. The boys all made a big fuss. The larder was opened, and they all raided it at the same time. Two days later, when the guest arrived, the box was empty! I'll tell you, sir, what I told our guests: 'Don't blame me! As long as there are three boys in the house, sweetmeats don't last very long!'"

I wished her sons health, happiness, and long life, and wished her all blessings and prosperity. I got to my feet, rubbing my forehead and dragging my feet. She was smart enough to understand that I needed to sleep.

"Crossing Wadi al-Jamajim is backbreaking," she jibed. "The best cure for exhaustion is sleep."

It was as though this woman had learned the protocols of hospitality at the house of some generous Arab prince. The house was a large square with a mat on the floor and another smaller one alongside it. There she laid a clean, soft mattress on the floor for me. That night I slept like a log, even though my bed was on the bare, dry floor.

The next day I woke up early, intending to continue walking to the Sannine spring. Through her many questions, Umm Elias had learned some of the reasons for my trip, and she forbade me to leave early. She told me that her brother had a store by the spring, and her son Elias carried goods for him.

"He'll be leaving in an hour," she told me, "and you can go with him. "It's better for you to have someone with you who knows the way."

That is what happened. At noontime Elias and I walked behind a mule loaded with oil, butter, and soap to his uncle's store by the spring. The track from Biskanta was rough and rocky, with a number of short defiles between the long stretches of track across the mountainside. All of them, or at least the vast majority, lay between vines and plowed fields. It all involved two hours of easy walking and a climb of 1,500 feet. In other words, the Sannine spring is as high above Biskanta as Freike is above Antelias (Biskanta is 1,250 meters above sea level, and the spring is at 1,850 meters).

Elias and I followed this track, accompanied by a third person—namely, silence. That companion never left us, except on one occasion, when Elias asked me about his mother's cousin in America. Was the cousin successful, he asked, in business and marriage? I told him what I knew, which was not much. With that the silence resumed. My attention was drawn to the way the mountains and hills piled up, looming, then disappearing, amid the valleys and flatlands to the west of Sannine.

During this period of silence and tranquility, I kept reflecting on the mental and spiritual confrontations involved in their contrasting fertility and barrenness, heat and cold, encounters and embraces, turmoil and tranquility. In spite of everything, how amazing it all was! When I had seen Umm Elias on the track and had followed her to her house, I sensed that she had an alert, fiery, and troubled temperament, someone with firm and decisive nerves. I also felt that behind that temperament lay a spirit that was eager to connect with other spirits. For her a policy of give and take worked well, along with a consideration of the possibilities of happiness and misery in this life. This was the mentality of a literary thinker housed in the body of a mountain peasant woman, the spirituality of a noble princess in a simple, gentle personality. It is thus no surprise that I took a liking to her and joined her in hurrying to the market of thought and spirit. I felt happy and reassured, as though I had known her since childhood. I gave and I took; I spent a lot and I sought answers. Both of us gained and were content.

The boy Elias had not been endowed by God with any of his mother's qualities. I was unable to penetrate any part of his arid, introverted mentality; I had not a single glimpse of his small, concealed spirituality. We traveled together, but we never actually met. For two hours we walked in a tangible separation, if that expression fits, each of us far removed from the other.

Now that I am walking to the spring with Elias, I am staring from the peak of this era into the future. With the transcendent eye I can see on this track a scene spreading bit by bit and all together, which seems to have been created twenty years before its actual existence.

From 1906 we take a leap forward and stop at 1927, between summer and fall, at the base of Mount Sannine outside Biskanta. We are getting ready to walk.

"Bring a cushion for madam, and a carpet for the professor. This mule is stubborn and won't do what it's told. This female mule is for Miss Salma, this one's for Madame Najlaa, and that one for her sister Adele. Hey you! Get all the saddles and bridles ready. You'll be riding with suns and moons. Can you even imagine what would happen if the sun fell off the back of a mule? Saddles and bridles, we're not leaving without them!"

This caravan makes its way to the Sannine spring. The spring sun is actually the author Salma Sayegh, and the summer sun is the intellectual writer Najlaa al-Kfouri. Between those two suns are some bright stars glittering beside them; sometimes in front, at other times behind is another writer, Salma's daughter, 'A'ida, the wife of the poet Salah Labaki.

Amid all the horsemen is the veritable moon of secularism in education, George Kfouri, and alongside him is the mule carrying another moon, this time involving both Parliament and lavish literature, Khalil Takieddine. On his other side is a star that fell before its time, having for the first time opened up Arabic literature's horizons to symbolist poetry, Adeeb Mazhar—God have mercy on his soul! Behind all these people and goading his Cyprus donkey is another moon, the scholar of two faiths, Christian and Muslim, Takieddine Solh, and riding with him is the moon of printing houses in both Lebanon and Syria and publisher of their celebrities in the fields of law and literature—namely, Yousuf Sader. As part of this spectacular procession you could see Ameen the guide, sometimes in the front, at others in the back, praising suns and moons . . . the fount of virtue in literature being honesty.

The caravan that appeared before me in 1906 moved on its way; I can still envision it today if I look back. In both cases it is a caravan of both light and guidance, one that moved one day through the chilly world of Sannine, still one of my most pleasant memories.

In that chilly environment there was a hut in a rock called Shakroub, which throughout the ages had remained a nonentity, just like the farmers and shepherds who regularly took refuge inside it. That is the way it remained until, thirty years after the journey just described, the light of ideas and literature shone on it. I do not know where Mikhail Naimy was at the time, honing his intellect, studying science of various kinds, and acquiring literary talent. However, as I look into the future with a keen and accurate eye, I can see Mikhail adopting Shakroub in the third decade of the twentieth century as a personal refuge, a place where he would cook Sufi dishes and create literary spices and sauces, which he would then distribute to the public in his books and articles. Greetings to our ancestors, hermits of old, devout mystics! Greetings also to Mikhail, who in the twentieth century came back to them by way of America, then Sannine, and immersed himself in their pure community.

Today in New York a voice calls out in longing for Sannine, the sound of the flute in the forest from which it is cut off. That voice belongs to one of Sannine's dearest sons—a voice whose love, longing, and nostalgia have only been amplified by emigration. The song of the nightingale that hid amid his ribs on the day he left Biskanta in the final decade of the nineteenth century has never been silenced. No, that same nightingale stayed, hidden and silent, for a quarter century.

Then came the day when the voice's owner saw snow piling up in the New York markets. He heard the cheeping of a solitary bird hovering over a chimney as it searched for some warmth on a rooftop. It gave him a jolt, but the muse of poetry heard him and led him toward sweet, languishing rhymes.

It was on that day a quarter century ago, in the New York snow and in the shadow of that very chimney, that Sannine's poet was born, some seven thousand miles from Sannine itself. That same day Rachid Ayyoub, the dervish poet, surveyed that passing scene. His body was still fettered by American chains as he wandered to and fro through New York's markets and bookstores. It was as though he were sleep-walking, his sandals gnawed by civilization's gloom, his very ribs pierced to the marrow.

I send you, dervish poet, in Sannine's name, the pure essence of its terebinth, gorse, and broom. I consign it to the winds to carry it to your body's location in New York, where it may anoint your breaths and your rhymes.

With the Muleteers

UMM ELIAS had charged her son with delivering me to her brother Boutros, the owner of the store in the Sannine spring, and that is what he did. Boutros welcomed me and housed me in a wormwood tent on the roof. On the floor was a rug with a folded mattress on it.

"You'll spend the night with us—a blessing indeed!" he said. "Tomorrow morning you can continue to Zahle with the muleteers."

At this period the only signs of habitation at the spring were this store and a house nearby belonging to a farmer.

When we arrived, the owner of the store and his neighbor were having an argument. I discovered that the local shepherd boy used to doze off; meanwhile, the cows would seize the opportunity while he was asleep and start grazing in Boutros's field. The argument resumed in the late afternoon; the exchange of curses might well have led to a bloody confrontation if it were not for the muleteers. The cow herder went home full of resentment—as medieval tales have it, pursued by a veritable hail of foul oaths from Boutros, who from time to time stood there, repeating them two or three times in a row and in a bitter tone of voice:

Boutros: "You're a liar, a hypocrite, a thief!"

Cow herder: "It's you who's the liar! You liar! You're the hypocrite and thief!"

How incredible human beings can be, created by God in His form and likeness. In spite of that they are incapable of living with their neighbors in peace and happiness, even here, at the mountaintops, in the very cradle of tranquility and light! His own ambitions have lifted him some five thousand feet above the phrenetic, conflicting patterns of social life, and yet he has brought with him to the mountain heights the germs of malice and hatred—and all that because a cow has grazed in a field that it likes. Have you ever in your entire life seen cows fighting and scrapping with each other over their pastures? There is plenty of grass in the field to satisfy all of them. But, in spite of its length and breadth, the earth is too small for humanity!

I spent that night in the rooftop tent without praying for the good of anyone. When I woke up early next day, my negative feelings were at their height. I heard the cow owner calling from the roof of his house to the store owner. I watched as Boutros rushed out of the house, assuming that something needed his attention.

"Who called?" I heard him ask.

"You're the hypocrite, you're the liar!" was the response.

And this was happening at dawn before the sun even rose, and at a height of five thousand meters above the depths of human existence. Do you still wish to tell me that the frosty mountain heights are a good place for contemplation and prayer, filling the heart with human love?

I put on my clothes as quickly as possible. The muleteers had already strapped on the saddles, so we set off on foot while, as the poet puts it, "The birds were still in their nests." We came out from the poplar and sycamore trees and passed by the spring, which was bursting out from the rocks. Walking along a rocky track we veered toward an outcrop, which at this point was the horizon itself. From there we looked out on yet another horizon, terrain whose shape looked like a swing between two horizons.

At this point, one of my traveling companions spoke to me.

"In the store we heard that you're an architect," he said.

"By the spring," said another, "we heard you were a schoolteacher."

"People said you're a Protestant priest," said a third. "Which of them is right?"

"They're all right," I replied. "I've worked in all those professions."

"What's your profession today?" the first one asked.

"Preacher of the Gospel," I replied.

"In that case," the second of them told me with a laugh, "you need to listen to this story. A preacher like yourself was passing by a church in the mountain as people were at prayer. He spoke to one of the people standing by the door. With the Bible in one of his back pockets, he cuffed the man on his neck.

"'It's here that the path to Heaven starts,' he said, pointing to his pocket. 'From here!'"

The muleteer's tongue is fertile ground for curses and jokes, colorful and spiky. Generally speaking, he is smart and alert, well taught by open spaces and trained by adversity. In olden times he would sing as he strutted behind his mule with the valleys echoing his voice. He would be patient with everyone except his mule, only addressing it with curses and stones. Even so, he would smile and laugh, as though to say: "What's the harm of such foul language when we're in the open? The mountain sun can purify everything, and the air cleanses it all."

For the reader I now offer this portrait of the muleteers, my travel companions:

Abou Abaa'a wore linen trousers dyed indigo, held up by a leather belt. Attached to the belt by a yellow chain was a long, dagger-like knife. His coat was short and striped, and for headwear he had a long, brown felt cap like the ones worn by Mevlevi dervishes. Around it he wrapped a kaffiyeh, with a forelock dangling over his ear. He spent a lot of time cracking crude jokes about women. His moods were a blend of golden sand and manure. He was the one who told the story about the Bible preacher that we mentioned earlier.

Then there was Abou Kabran, whose actual coat (*kabran*) was made of wool woven out of Bedouin tents. His trousers were tight at the ankles and legs but wider at the crotch. For footwear he wore shoes with heavily nailed soles. He only laughed once a year, and that when he was at confession and receiving Holy Communion. At least, that is what Abou Abaa'a claimed, and Abou Kabran would neither confirm nor deny it.

There was also a city type, dressed to the nines from head to toe—long shoes with untied laces, trousers of dyed linen, above them a vest with only one button done up, and over that a loose-fitting French-style jacket with elbow patches. On his head he wore an old-style red tarboosh. He was totally self-centered and cared about no one else.

Then there was a Bedouin in a crude, striped cloak. Around his neck he was wearing a kaffiyeh with no headband. His boots reached to just below his knees and had ample room for his feet. He kept staring derisively at the city type, assuming that he himself was superior to everyone else. After he had heard the story about the Gospel preacher, he spoke to me:

"That's wonderful, what you said about the pathway to Heaven! Lead us there, we beg you by your parents' lives!"

Abou Abaa'a replied: "Zein, the gentleman is on his way to Zahle to lead the people there. But, by God Almighty, if you preach about the Messiah in Zahle, the Catholics will come after you and beat you up. What's the point of preaching? It should be worth more than profits for priests; what you're doing is important, but it's also risky."

Abou Kabran commented: "The clerical profession—whether Catholics or Protestants—is both profitable and easy. But it is God Almighty who distributes professions among people. For example, both the bishop and I read together from a single book under the oak trees. I was brighter than him; I used to help him and correct his reading mistakes. So where am I today, and where is he? God be praised!"

"We've heard that you don't like money," the Bedouin said, changing the subject. "You're not carrying a single cent in your baggage."

"That's right," I replied.

At that point I look out my watch to check on the time. When the Bedouin saw it, he chuckled.

"For a highway robber," he said, "that watch and the fancy clothes you're wearing, Zein—those shoes and European suit—would be enough. Aren't you scared of highway robbers?"

"Should I be scared," I asked, "when you're my travel companions?"

Abou Tarboosh pointed at the Bedouin. "He's one of them! Thief, thief!"

"Damn you and your parents!" the Bedouin roared at him. "By God, even if you were made of gold, I'd still spit on you!"

And he spat as he was speaking.

"The spit and spitter are both under my feet!" Abou Tarboosh replied.

The Bedouin was about to hit him, but Abou Kabran intervened.

"The likes of you two aren't fit to ride with decent people," Abou Abaa'a told them. "Shut your mouths and act sensibly, or else . . ."

He took a knife out of his belt and gestured with it.

The Bedouin and Abou Tarboosh kept quiet and moved away from each other.

For a while now silence prevailed over the caravan, as we proceeded through regions with many horizons. I had never encountered a mountain path like this one from Sannine to Zahle, not in its rough and varied terrain. At some points it was fairly easygoing, and yet, with its many strange horizons, it was also exhausting and scary.

Picture for yourself a lump of clay in which lowlands cling to mountain spurs; amid those ravines and spurs is a track being followed by a column of ants—our caravan. From the very first spur it plunges into a ravine and then crosses to the next spur, then the third, fourth, fifth, and sixth. None of the ravines was more than a single kilometer wide.

Those low, narrow horizons were enough to give you heart failure. Their sheer numbers manage to obliterate all hope in the traveler's heart; standing between two of them, he has no idea where the chain will end. Where is Zahle? Every time we moved from one horizon and looked over another, I told myself that Zahle had to be over the next horizon. I counted off ten of them, and could only recall the words of the Italian poet Dante, which I had read in his immortal tale, *The Divine Comedy*, in which he gives a wonderful description of the various layers of Hell.

While we were traversing one of these horizons, the track narrowed. We had to move in single file: Abou Tarboosh was first, followed by Abou Kabran, the Bedouin, and Abou Abaa'a. Last was this traveler, who had only one question to ask: "Where's Zahleh?!"

This time I asked the same question in a loud, agonized tone. Soothing balm came in the form of Abou Tarboosh's answer as he was standing at a turn in the track. "Here's the plain," he said, "and, when I say 'plain,' I mean Zahle."

How happy I was as I stood there, looking down on the lush green Bekaa Plain, with its gentle light interspersed with clouds. After a descent, which was neither long nor short, we reached Ain Hazir. We stopped in front of a store, and Abou Kabran called the store's owner by name. A woman emerged, greeting us all cheerfully. She brought us a jug of water, and the four of them had a drink, then said farewell. I was one of those who bade them farewell.

I preferred to rest for a while in Ain Hazir rather than arrive in Zahle feeling weak and exhausted. I was feeling hungry and remembered the provisions that the owner of the store in Sannine had given me, the brother of the Good Samaritan woman in Biskanta. I had given it to Abou Abaa'a, and he had put it in his mule's saddlebag at the back. I was about to ask him for it, but he was already bringing it back.

"So," the rogue said with a wink as he handed it to me, "Masihiyya has made you forget all about your food!"

Her body jiggled a lot, and she walked clumsily. She wore too much kohl and makeup, and it was hard to guess how old she was. Even so, she was used to dealing with large numbers of muleteers and travelers, so it was easy to get her to talk and turn the conversation the way she wanted.

"You're from America!" she surprised me by saying.

"I'm Lebanese," I replied, "but I was in America."

"That's what I meant," she said to confirm the information that she had. "I was in America too, in New York."

She switched to English and asked me if I spoke it. My positive reply delighted her. Offering me a chair, she invited me to sit down, then sat on another one facing me. She started talking about New York and the Syrian street there, and asked me about people she knew. All the while she was chattering as fast as she could and with great delight. I responded in the language she loved, even though her accent was terrible and her pronunciation was atrocious.

"I layik Nayourk, y'know!" she said.

"I like it too," I replied. That phrase *y'know* was a secret password between the two of us. She offered me a glass of arak, but I refused with thanks.

"Would you allow me to open my food parcel in your store?" I asked.

"Shame on you!" she yelled. "You're our guest now. My husband'll be back from the vineyards soon, and you'll have lunch with us. You'll try some of our grapes."

I did my best to dissuade her, but without success. Indeed, she insisted in English that I join her for lunch. She went into a room behind the store, then came back. She went in again, and came back again. These suggestions and revelations continued, as, with each return, she kept asking me questions to remind me about the things she liked about "Nayourk."

On the fourth or fifth time, she returned from the room of secrets at the back, carrying a brass tray with two cups on it.

"Coffee?" she asked. "Do you like coffee? Please have some!"

While we were drinking coffee, her husband came home bearing a basket of grapes. She introduced me to him in English: "He's from America!"

The news did not have much impact on her husband; it was as if she had said I was from Beirut or Zahle. He told me that he had lived in New York for three years, although it felt like thirty. He did not like living abroad. For him, our homeland was the most beautiful of God's countries.

"Don't believe him!" Masihiyya said. "If we had been successful, we would not have come back. How many times have I told you, Hanna, always to tell the truth? Take the cups out, wash them, and put them back in the cupboard.

He did as she asked, while she went ahead preparing the food for lunch. She covered the small table with a cloth of waxen fabric and entered the room to complete her task. Hanna was her lowly and obedient servant; he brought in a platter of boiled eggs, another with spiced eggplant, then yogurt, bread, and grapes.

I ask her permission to add the food I had with me to these dishes. When I opened the parcel, there were three boiled eggs, two onions, and three chunks of fresh cheese wrapped in loaves of bread.

After lunch, I took a nap in a room alongside the store.

Which, besides cooking utensils, contained a couch and a bed. I went to sleep on the couch, but Masihiyya urged me to sleep on the bed.

"You're very welcome!" she said with genuine pleasure.

When I said farewell, she insisted that I spend the day with them.

I thanked her in both Arabic and English, duly recording her name, along with Umm Elias in Biskanta, in the record of unforgettable women.

The Lovely Bride

IN WRITING my account of this journey, I see myself doing something that my predecessors could not do, something that my successors—whether today or in the future—will only be able to do if they follow my lead. If we survey the facts of history and organize them with the skill of a craftsman or artist, a combination of opposites is not impossible, and resurrection from the dead is not unknown. No wonder then if past, present, and future are all present in a single time and place. (Did time have a past and future before the eye of mankind saw it as night and day?) So stand where I am standing at the moment, somewhat removed from the meter of time, and you will witness the miracle—nothing peculiar about it. The tourist in 1906, the orator in 1908, and the author in 1938—they are all combined in a single person, in a single moment, the moment where I find myself. How can it be otherwise, when I now find myself in the company of muleteers speeding to Zahle, as the orator addressed a political meeting in Zahle in the first days of the constitutional period, and as the author recording the two stories and combining the twin opposites? He cites things that are to come with things past, and combines someone who has never known existence with somebody who has traversed multiple horizons in order to understand the refined manners of sublime love.

In memory of the beloved we have quaffed a wine,
a wine whereby we became drunk before the vine was ever created.[1]

1. Translator's note: the first line of the *khamriyya* (wine poem) by the renowned Sufi poet Ibn al-Farid (d. 1234).

Oh Zahle, mistress of the valley, lover of hearts, grant me an increase of love, of light, of pure affection, of sincerity, of loyalty to eloquence. Within your boundaries are liberals and bishops, poets and heroes. With you beauty overflows. On the banks of the Birdawni River there reside in plenty varieties of revelry and ailments of time.

Dear Zahle, mistress of vine and wine steward, lover of lute and flute, melody's daughter declared her love to you, riders sang in your valleys, and princes of poetry and eloquence extolled you. Is it not daily that you are told pure, tough words, devoid of everything but truth and love? So listen carefully to them and commit them to memory.

I visited the valley in its heyday, pure as the mountains' glory. I was bowled over by all its natural beauties, its open spaces bathed in sunshine, its shady locales exuding the scent of sweet basil. Willow trees flaunted themselves on the river's banks, and poplars raised their standards over the rocks. The air, which has been purified by the passes and peaks of Sannine, is inhaled by the birds and sweetens the tone of their songs. Spaced apart amid so much beauty are a few discreet cafes that manage to extract a sense of friendliness and joy from the fenced pastures. The stroller's view is not blocked, nor is the sweet sound of birdsong muted. To the contrary, one can let his thoughts take wing freely and listen as their floating wings beat in the tree branches and valley bends.

Oh valley of vine bowers, bowers of love and beauty, of serenity and majesty, wonder, pleasure, and imagination! Oh Birdawni River, playground of boys and girls, locale of the pure and intelligent, pilgrimage site for hearts that are pious, gracious, obedient, and content, throne of the mistress of rhymes and melodies, howdah for the lovely bride! On those days you belonged to nature and its adoring children, who were living in its pure environment.

On that day I sat beneath the bowers with their silken flowers and greeted their owners with love and respect. I greeted a day that for me will always be a festival and carried away the very fondest and sweetest of memories, lifting the bowers inside my heart to greet them and coddling them with the twin hands of joy and rapture and visits that were "blazes on Sannine's brow."

But then the passage of time decreed that I should be away for a long time, during which things changed, as did the mentality of men and women. Commerce and social matters were all consigned to drums and oboes, to advertising that lures people and spreads banners of glory and profit to the four corners of the earth. Zahle was no exception. Guides started praising the valley, and preachers began spreading the word about its attractions in every town and region: Gorgeous tents! Auberges! Summer vacation! Summer vacation!

People now started coming from everywhere to spend the summer, and merchants and profiteers followed them. Open spaces turned into narrow enclaves, and those enclaves became kitchens and private spots. The scent of sweet basil was replaced by the smell of cooking and smoking nargilehs, the whole scene being permeated by the breaths of revelers and onlookers. The two riverbanks were crammed with cafes. Once birds heard the sound of pounding mortars, they quit the tree branches.

Gorgeous tents! Auberges! Promenaders and summer visitors. I came for a visit one summer evening after it had become even more famous than Moses's burning bush. I was shocked by what I saw: crowds of people crammed onto small patches of land, sitting at tables that were almost attached to each other. People were sitting there, both men and women, back to back, leg to leg, concentrating on their arak and kibbe—drinking, eating, smoking, and getting stoned.

I must ask you, dear reader, to forgive me for my annoyance due to my utmost love! But for that, I would not have written a solitary word about this repulsive scene. How I wish the cafes were not so close to each other and the tables were not crammed one on top the other. All people could see were other people all around them; the only glimpse they had of the valley were the tree branches over other people's heads and the reflections from electric lights.

The pure valley air coming from the peaks and ravines of Sannine was now laden with cooking fumes and nargileh smoke, not to mention carbonic acid! The valley's scent of flowers and sweet basil has now turned into the stench of frying, tobacco, and arak, which blends with the carbonized breaths of human beings. The bird songs in the valley have now been killed off by the constant pounding of mortars in the kibbe ovens! Here come the waiters, their arms rolled up and trays of food and drink over their heads. They walk between the tables and crowds yelling: "Out of the way! Let me through!"

Zahle is a lovely bride, but now she is adorned by her summer visitors. But where are your genius sons to retrieve the lost beauty of your valley? Where is your "Raa'i"[2] to bemoan the source of inspiration in you? Where now is your "Shoukry"[3] to raise his voice against you, as he did against the tyrants? Where today is your "Shibl,"[4] someone to invoke his eloquence to restore to you the scent of sweet basil and to convince the birds to come back and sing their songs in the branches of your willow and poplar trees? Where too are the two Maaloufs, Fawzi and Shafeek,[5] who could weave garlands of poetry and in celebration of your beauty concealed amid dark rocks and silent bowers?

I go back to those glory days of your beauty, and the very memory saddens me. A comforting thought occurs to me: individuals spoil the beauty of nature through actions that are driven by their material schemes, but others compensate for the deeds of their fellow humans with actions inspired by spiritual motivations. Axes may destroy beauty's structures, which can only be viewed complete with the spirit's eye, but other axes can construct edifices for eternal genius. Destroyer and builder are brothers, squabbling over life's constituents; they are both continuously destroying and building. However, the one guarantor of the greatest compensation—or rather, the preservation of every marvelous relic of human genius—is time itself.

2. A reference to Raaji al-Raa'i (writer and lawyer).

3. A reference to Shoukry Bakhkhash (journalist and founder of the newspaper *Zahle Youth* [1910]).

4. A reference to Shibl Damous (member of Parliament and lawmaker; a writer of the Lebanese constitution).

5. Translator's note: two renowned Lebanese poets and brothers who emigrated to Brazil.

I have just said that beauty's structures can only be viewed complete with the spirit's eye; man the destroyer only destroys the manifest elements of such structures. The beauty of their spiritual aspects is transferred or transformed to the builders' shovel: the artist's easel, the singer's guitar, the poet's garret, the litterateur's originality. Those are the brilliant sources of inspiration to be seen in the ruins of the ancients and those of nature as well. Mankind may have raided them for profit and enrichment, but they are still the eternal heritage of beaux arts.

The valley throne was toppled, and poets inherited its glory. The biggest portion of it was won by one of Zahle's eternal sons, Fawzi Maalouf. He carried this glory over the seas, burdened as he was by genius's heavy load and hobbled by its chains. Once there—in Brazil—he cast off those chains and gave us back the valley's inspiration in an immortal poetic work, "On the Carpet of Wind."

Fawzi (God have mercy on him!), and his brother, Shafeek (may he live long!), were two boys who were playing with marbles and flying paper kites on the day that I paid my very first visit to Zahle. I was a guest in the house of my close friend, Professor Issa Iskandar al-Maalouf, the author of several valuable books on history. In fact, as far as I am aware, Shafeek, the younger of the two boys, was not only the first one to compose poetry but also to have it published it in a small collection, called "Dreams." He gave me a copy to comment on, and I wrote him a letter, in part of which I have the following to say:

> I hereby acknowledge that you are a poet. That said, in "Dreams" you are far removed from the essence of life and its major purposes. The tone that you use—one of misery and sadness—was a popular style among poets in the time of Byron, and de Musset. But among people of the East, and especially us Lebanese, it is a cryptic disease. What is the point of a poet crying and moaning like everyone else?
>
> From the artistic perspective, your collection "Dreams" has a good deal of creative imagery, lovely fantasy, subtle expression, and fine style. But, my friend, it is imitative—not, I would add, imitative of Gibran—who, like you, wallows in tears. What I read is Isaiah

> instead of immersing your spirits in the tears of Jeremiah. If you have to look back, then look at Shakespeare and Goethe rather than burning your fingers and eyelids on the cauldrons of Byron and de Musset.
>
> My friend, a poet is not some lily inside a skull. The very image involves a sickening hyperbole, with no trace of either truth or beauty. It suggests a contempt for humanity, something of which—thank God!—you, I, and Gibran are a part. In existence and life there is a beauty that is loftier, more magnificent, greater, and lovelier than the limited and gentle beauty of the iris. You, I, Gibran, sun, moon, and galaxy, all of us are flashes of that same beauty—thanks be to God!
>
> A poet is one of the people, from the solid core of the people. Anyone who thinks himself superior to people is not even close to the most minor of poets. The genuine poet is a mirror of communities, the lamp of their aspirations in the darkness. In misfortunes he is a helper, in disasters a sword. The genuine poet builds for his people castles of love, wisdom, beauty, and hope. Dry your tears—may God preserve you! For this people, stumbling in the dark, raise up a candle of light and hope, of health and well-being.

If these cruel words had been written to some pretentious person, he would have raised a hue and cry, put forward arguments against me, and attacked me in the press in both prose and verse. Either that, or else he would have fallen silent and stopped writing poetry forever. But Shafeek Maalouf published my letter in a newspaper. He kept on writing poetry and consulting volumes of inspiration while distancing himself from sentimentality. Ten years later he published a book, which can be termed the twin of "On the Carpet of Wind." He was kind enough to send me a copy, and I read it. This poet was not the one who wrote "Dreams." Like his original and creative brother, there was no trace of any poet, whether ancient or modern, in his method, his art, or his spirit; nor was there the slightest trace of tears! In a poem that he recited in a ceremony in his honor organized by the Andalusian Group in Sao Paolo, he had this to say:

I have concealed from life's people their tears
and have poured for them a chilled nectar.

Now back to the journey. I will finish this chapter with the title I have given it: Zahle is a lovely bride; to which I will add: adorned by its famous men.

The Lofty Castle

I SAID FAREWELL to Zahle and my host, the renowned polymath and father of three poets, Professor Issa al-Maalouf. Picking up my walking stick again, I put my trust in God and hoped that the final stage of my journey would work out for the best—or, at least, I would complete it with the same amount of benefit and blessing as I had encountered so far.

After leaving Zahle I headed to the southwest, proceeding on a paved road in the Bekaa Plain. There were agricultural fields and vineyards covering the hills, those lowly vines that grow close to the ground with the actual grapes hidden behind their glorious greenery.

The vines here were the brightest green. They were wonderful to look at, well-tended, and produced the most fruit. Every single vine voiced its thanks to the hands that worked on it, cultivating it, pruning it, and giving it their full attention. Those hands derived their skill from a combination of knowledge and experience and their devotion from love.

Vineyards are the pride and joy of the Bekaa Plain. Amid them all are houses that matched them in taste and perfection and that were unspoiled by phony grandeur. Instead, they are modest and had low roofs, something that tells you about their interior as well and makes you feel both admiration and respect. In the middle of the houses is a modest church and another building with a dome unlike other church domes.

We are in Ksara, Ksara of the Jesuit monks. Here there appears one of life's truths, one that both demands admiration and provokes a sense of gloom and melancholy.

Perfect the things you undertake, secure the bonds of reciprocity and good order, persevere and work hard; do all that and you will gain both this world and the world to come. Within your own self be whatever you wish, believer or agnostic, pure or corrupt, affectionate and sympathetic or aggressively critical. Be obedient, diligent, zealous, and patient; you will then obtain the blessing for your greatest good. Everything else is futile, chaff for the wind. Reverend Father, realize all this and put it into practice, not for your own good, not for the good of people, not for the good of the nation, but rather for the greater good, one that encompasses nation and people together; that greater good that begins with your monastic community and, after your church, finishes also with it.

"My son, give me your heart!" said the Prophet David. As if the great Jesuit elder is telling his brother: "My son, give me your will!" or every Jesuit priest talking to workers or a postulant in his charge: "My son, give me your will, your hand, and your mind. Allow your heart to flatter God Almighty. I will guide you along the path that leads to the desired goal even though the road be dark and tortuous."

Give me will, hand, and mind, and I will give you bread and satisfaction, I will give you balanced wisdom. Everything else is futile, chaff in the wind. The best illustration is in Ksara: vineyards—a delight to the eye, a church—an assured refuge and stainless observatory, and excellent wine sold to believers and nonbelievers alike.

There are indeed things to amaze and annoy. The Jesuits provide the very highest ideal of work. Neighbors in the town see it all with their eyes and hear it with their ears, and yet they do not learn or emulate. If you keep passing by superb flourishing vineyards, then you can tell that they belong to the reverend fathers. When you reach the boundaries of their property, you find the vineyards of the local people, which speak volumes about their owners' laziness, ignorance, and neglect. The difference between the two types of vineyards is the same as that between a fat cow and its skinny sister.

I reached Taalabaya, after turning off to visit the house of a rich man's partner. The rich man's mother had said a special prayer on his behalf, but I do not think that it will do him any good on Judgment

Day. He was a profiteer who regularly conned other profiteers with his sweet voice, charming smile, and subtle approach. In administering his affairs, he was a Jesuit: "My son, give me your will, your hand, and your mind. Open your heart for yourself and for God." This man was to be obeyed, working in a wise and modest fashion. This man always worked with a smile, always offering temptation. He would hold out his hand and take your purse, giving you the impression that he was filling it with money, whereas he was actually taking money out. He may well have learned some of his knowledge about people's morals from his neighbors, the Jesuit monks, while on the other hand such qualities may have been instinctive. In any event, he and his partners lived next to the Jesuits, but the evidence from their land showed that they had acquired neither artistic knowledge nor the more obvious signs of initiative and competent work from their neighbors.

I had a bite to eat in the partner's house and then moved on to Chtoura, which at that time was entirely the property of a single woman, Zanamradah, whose name was carved out of iron like her work. She was also a neighbor of the Jesuit monks, involved in both farming and commerce, and she was as successful—or almost so—as they were. Without a doubt the Chtoura wine was just as well-known as that of Ksara; Zanamradah and the Jesuits were clearly rivals.

In the central square of Chtoura—on the Beirut-Damascus Highway at that time—there was just a single inn, a hotel, and a cafe. Everyone yawned there, and she was yawning too in the shade of the willow trees. No one dreamed then that anyone would come to Chtoura, honor the hotel's name, and turn it into a modern residence. Today Elias al-Masabki—relative of saints, feeder of the poor and hungry, protector of tourists, and holder of banquets for the French—back then did everything for nothing most of the time, for the sake of God alone.

With the mention of banquets we will greet their veritable prince and orator as we pass by his lands and residence. He was the bosom friend of rulers and princes, of men with titles and status, and speaker at official celebrations in both Syria and Lebanon. The greatest of all fawners, the most renowned of all cheerers, Saleem Ayyoub Taabet was bound to be there, whenever a prince, man of fortune, or significant statesman was around.

Here is his mansion in Zabdal. The crossroads to the south stretched away amid lush mulberry orchards with poplars and willows on either side, which shaded and accompanied you to Ain el-Barakah in the noble neighborhood.

The name was appropriate. There was a shallow stream, a fountain ready for drinkers' cups, verdant shades of willows, and a serenity that sweet basil suffused with a scent whispered by tree branches every time the breeze blew and gleefully applauded whenever the winds blew from south and west, causing the goldfinches and nightingales to sing their songs. In Ain el-Barakah you could hear whispers of paradise that would make you forget all ties to time and place. If you were alone, then it was an opportunity for dreams; if you were with your beloved, then greetings to the goldfinch and nightingale!

I continued my walk to Mourayjaat, birthplace of three Faaris brothers, Emile, Philip, and Felix, sons of the lawyer Habeeb Faaris—God have mercy on him!—and his French wife, who was a Swedenborgian, a minority community in the country.

At the time I was not acquainted with any of them, so I passed by this haven of intelligence and literary eminence like a stranger. Later I was to compensate for this act of ignorance by forming with them a friendship founded on love and admiration that still exists. I must ask both Philip and Emile to forgive me if I choose to make special use of memory's broom to focus on Felix, who certainly deserves it because he was a Lebanese with a profound love of aromatic mountain plants, both flowering and thorny; it might well be that the thorny varieties had a sweeter scent than the smoother ones.

Felix Faaris—dear brother, dispirited colleague, instiller of his own mother's mystical beliefs in his children—was someone who raised the standard of free thought and free humanistic ideas in his homeland, in speeches and writing, in prose and in verse. He was someone who would pitch the tents of his imagination in the realms of the infinite and steer the caravans of his eloquence through that transient domain. He lavished incredible amounts of the goods he had either been given or had acquired on occupying foreigners—Turks and French, something that he bitterly regretted later on.

Felix Faaris, gesturing to the Gemini from below, casting a sympathetic and kindly look on human quagmires from above, was the eloquent speaker, tormented poet, stunning author, Felix the victim—victim of both literature and politics. Had he chosen to restrict his powers and gifts to literature alone, he would have been one of the greatest litterateurs. Had he instead focused solely on politics, his ideas, actions, integrity, and ability would all have made him a formidable politician. However, in dealing with its geniuses, fate has its own supply of joys and agonies, its shouts and laments.

From Mouravjaat I started climbing up a mountain much like the mountain of life that Felix Faaris had climbed. I felt as dispirited as he had been at what loomed ahead of me: barren landscapes and arid hills twisted and turned all around me. This was the desolate mountain range, the eastern part of which overlooked the Bekaa Plain. The western part facing the Mediterranean was full of villages and orchards, although even the eastern part had its share of open areas mitigated by vineyards and green slopes where herds of goats grazed, their bodies dotting and decorating the dark rocks. It all looked like a picture painted by an artist's brush. These were mountain heights at their driest, especially by Dahr el-Baidar, the highest peak on the mountain (at 1,500 meters), almost as high as the spring at the base of Sannine.

At Dahr el-Baidar we took a gentle downward slope, which kept bending so as sometimes to obscure the valley where the railway ran, while at others it directly overlooked it. We reached Mudeyrej, and from there to the ultimate destination, the summer resort of Beirut's elite, Saoufar, haughty and splendid with its lofty castles, and the major center for summer vacations and gambling in Lebanon.

When I left the house in Freike, I had in mind two principal destinations for this trip: Zahle and Saoufar. The first was because of the love for Zahle's sons that had developed while I was in New York; the second was out of sheer curiosity, to get a glimpse of Beirut's elite at play and the "casino," their pride and joy. For the first time—and for the sake of knowledge rather than ignorance—I could watch the roulette wheel spinning. At that time the Saoufar casino was the only one in Lebanon, and no other vacation spot had the fancy hotels like those in Saoufar. My curiosity then could be excused.

So here I am at the lofty castle, God be praised. Forgive me, dear reader, I have brought the blessing too far forward. I am actually still in the flowering meadow, in the middle of which sits the castle. I am sitting on one of the benches scattered among its soaring trees. I am taking a rest and preparing myself for the great blessing, but I have just caught a glimpse of who and what is all around me. There are eyes, the eyes of men and women, seated at circular tables in the trees, drinking coffee and tea. Darts of curiosity and amazement are being aimed in my direction, and their perpetrators, male and female, keep on whispering and shouting. About what? My clothes? My appearance? I will not deny that, in both aspects, I am a bit unusual. But decent and civilized men and women are not supposed to regard someone as being so strange; either that, or, as a matter of courtesy, they look the other way.

To escape their nasty looks I entered the hotel and made my way through a part that was packed full of people—some entering, others leaving—through the same door. I followed a group on its way inside and found myself in a huge hall full of blue tables at which male and female player were busy playing poker and dice. They were all silent, staid, and something between the two that I cannot name. Was it fatigue? Disgust? Despair still clutching at a ray of hope? Spiritual fossilization? Or a blend of all those things numbing both nerves and minds?

To me they looked like worshippers praying, people smoking hashish in a den, or politicians coming up with conspiracies. I pictured the women with their hands in men's pockets, and the men with their hands in women's handbags. Over them all hovered the spirit of luck, with its two sides—black and white. So let them gamble, feel disgusted, despair, and bury their dead!

Here now was roulette, with its long green table marked with numbers and squares in green and red, adorned with an amazing circle in the middle of which was an even more amazing wheel. Standing behind it was the venerable croupier, with a small white ivory ball in his hand. Next to him was a device with a long pole that he used to take in and push out the money. People standing by the table were placing their money on the numbers or on one of the green and red squares. Play the game, play!

Once the bidding operation was over, the croupier announced solemnly in French: "Rien ne va plus!" The wheel started spinning, with an ivory ball in the middle of the circle. The whole thing spun so fast you could not make anything out. Gradually, it started to slow down, and the ball could be seen as it went round, moving from one slot to another, from one number and color to another. Everyone's eyes were riveted on its movement, their hearts pounding fearfully. Once the wheel stopped spinning, the ball landed in a slot—which meant good fortune for some people, and hell for everyone else. The croupier now handed the winnings to the lucky winners and pulled all the rest of the earnings on the table toward himself. Play the game, play!

I will not conceal from you that I was really fascinated by this first glimpse at this amazing invention. I considered myself fortunate to have achieved a wish that I had long had—namely, to watch a game of roulette. However, while I was savoring this moment of happiness, one of the players who had lost stared hard at me, and seemed to me to be annoyed. The croupier now gestured to the doorman, who came over. He was a giant of a man, wearing traditional Arab garb—broadcloth trousers, embroidered coat, and silk belt. I was still enjoying the moment, but he laid a large, heavy hand on my shoulder.

"You were watching?" he asked.

"Yes, I was."

"Come with me," he said.

"To watch another game?"

"Come with me," he repeated, going in front of me.

I stopped him and demanded an explanation.

Without altering his tone of voice, he simply said the same thing again, his hand still on my shoulder as he opened the door.

"What's the meaning of this?" I asked angrily. "Are you throwing me out?"

This time he added another phrase to the one he had been using. "People who aren't hotel guests are not allowed in!" he said.

I was well aware that the casino was open for both people staying at the hotel and those who were not. But I did not call him a liar. Instead, I thought about my clothes and general appearance.

"I'm going to stay in the hotel," I said.

"Come with me, he said, "and I'll show you the office where you can register your name."

The manager had a softer tone of voice than the doorman, and a sweeter temperament.

"The hotel's full, monsieur," he told me.

"There's not even an empty bed in a small room?"

"Not a single bed, monsieur."

"I can sleep on the couch in the hall."

"That's impossible, monsieur, quite impossible!"

I fully understood what lay behind this phony courtesy. It was all about guests—you have to look after your guests, and particularly what they see.

I walked back toward the door. Passing by a wall mirror, I stopped for a moment.

"Yes," I thought to myself, "you really look disgusting!"

Even so I made up my mind to stay in the hotel that night; I was not going to be defeated . . .

As I left the garden, a new ray of hope occurred to me. The train from Beirut to Saoufar arrives at sunset, transporting vacationers every day to and from their work. There was bound to be someone on the train who knew me, could help me with these ultra-civilized people, and save me from the sheer shame of failure. I sat on a seat in the garden and waited. The train was due fairly soon.

I had been thrown out of the hotel, true enough. By the next day the news had spread to the Beirut press; they published it with a certain amount of exaggeration. Afterward it passed to other newspapers both in Lebanon and America; they amplified it still further so as to attract readers: now I had hit the doorman and cut his head open!

In those days I was thin; the poet al-Mutanabbi's phrase suited me perfectly: "Had I not spoken to you, you would never have seen me." I did not consider myself as being like Samson, with all my strength in my hair. I mentioned above that the doorman was a giant of a man, but I forgot to add that his twin moustaches were huge, thick, long, and tightly twisted. Their proud owner would strike out with the sword to defend their very greatness. Would it make any sense for me to risk my own safety?

I sat there in the garden waiting for release from the unseen world. I was not bothered by the increasing number of people who were staring intently at me now that information about me had made its way inside the hotel. To the contrary, I closed my eyes, consoling myself with a little philosophizing and a reserve of patience. While I was sitting there in such a state, I felt a hand shaking me gently. When I opened my eyes, it was to see my happy release. The train had arrived from Beirut, and the hand belonged to my dear friend Jurji Dimitri Sursok, in his time the restorer of nobility's missteps.

"Is that you, Ameen?" he asked. "When did you arrive? What are you doing here? Let's go inside the hotel."

When I told him my story, he laughed as he surveyed my appearance from head to toe. Then he looked furious. He took my hand, and we both went into the hotel. In the manager's office, my friend vented his anger.

"Do you even know whom you have insulted?" he raged. "This is so-and-so, and he is so-and-so. Where's Merii? Come over here, Merii, and apologize. (The doorman now came over and apologized to both Jurji Bey and myself.)

He now turned back to the manager. "Give him the best room you have!"

Soon afterward the servant arrived with a brush and comb from my friend, and he gestured to the shoeshine. I wiped the dust off my clothes, had a wash, and combed my hair. Once my shoes had been properly shined, I went downstairs, where Jurji Bey was waiting to take me to dinner.

We entered the long dining room. Most of the hotel's guests were already seated at the numerous tables. We walked side by side to the small table reserved for my friend. I was still amazed at the daringly courteous way he had embraced me in spite of my scruffy appearance and introduced me to the traditions of the upper classes. Some of life's delights now returned, and I looked around at the guests to see where were those eyes that had assaulted me in the garden, forcing me to avoid them. Where were they? Now those same eyes were narrowed and turned away, the eyes of the nobility, noble people through power. I was amazed at this social system, one that humiliates and is humiliated, conditioned as it is by ignorance and arrogance, servility and submission.

"Jurji Sursok, the man's friend . . ."

"Shut up, woman!"

"*Mon cher*, he's one of Jurji Dimitri's friends. Look away . . ."

A dance was being held in the hotel that night. My friend and I sat in the hall watching the male dancers, most of whom were wearing dinner dress, and the females, who were dressed in Parisian fashions and décolleté gowns. In those days, those dresses were regarded as somewhat risqué. I spoke to my friend with a totally fake naivete:

"How can I put up with a scene like this without some nice company?"

I pointed to a blonde woman in a violet dress. He called her by name, and she came over, babbling in French. Jurji introduced me to her:

"This is so-and-so, the famous poet and author."

"You're joking!" she cackled, turning her back on us.

"Do you want to meet someone else?" my friend asked me with a laugh.

"Thanks," I replied. "That's enough."

The next morning I called the servant and asked him if the hotel had hot water for a bath.

"Certainly, sir," he replied. "I'll light the fire in the boiler, and in fifteen minutes you can take a bath."

I waited a quarter of an hour and two quarters after that, then went to take a bath. Opening the door, I was dumbstruck; the entire room was filled with smoke as though it were the mouth of an exploding volcano. The fire raged on and filled the hall. Servants came rushing. "Fire, fire!" they yelled.

Fire! Guests heard the word and rushed out of their rooms, men and women—some of them in nightclothes. Everyone was in a panic; they were cramming the staircase and jumping to the ground floor.

What had happened? The servant had lit the fire in the furnace of the water heater and then gone about his other chores. The heater's pipe was cracked, and so the entire room was filled with smoke. Another servant realized what had happened and stood by the door, shaking his head.

I pushed him inside the room.

"Use your hands," I yelled at him. "Open the window!"

After a while, he came over to me. "The smoke's all gone. It went out the window. Please go inside!"

I went inside the room again. By this time the hot water in the water heater was cold again.

"Why don't you repair the pipe?" I asked him.

"If it were just the pipe," he replied, shaking his head, "it would all be simple."

"But don't guests take baths?" I asked.

"Once in a while," he replied, "a guest like you will ask for a bath. We can repair the pipe today, and, God willing, tomorrow you can have your bath."

"Thank you!" I replied. I had had enough . . .

Yes indeed, I had had my fill of life's delights in this posh hotel, this lofty castle.

I had it in mind to finish this trip by walking back to Freike via Hammana, Salima, then Baabdaat, Bikfaya, and Beit Chabab. But my friend Jurji Dimitri Sursok nixed the idea.

"Haven't you had enough," he scolded me, "with six days of walking?!"

"Yes, I have," I replied, "if you so wish!"

Bowing to his wishes, I accompanied him back to Beirut by train.

Third Journey

Jbeil Country (Byblos)

Contents

The Partner[1]

PEOPLE WHO ARE KNOWLEDGEABLE about the history of Lebanese families—prime amongst them being my friend Professor Issa Iskandar Maalouf, state that the majority of families in central and southern Lebanon emigrated from the north and especially Jbeil (Byblos). Whenever I have asked a Lebanese person or a Beiruti of mountainous origins where his ancestors hail from, the only answer that I have received is, "From Byblos." If you ask anyone with a knowledge of Phoenician history or people enthusiastic about everything Phoenician (whether authentic and reasonable or otherwise) where they are from, the response is instantaneous: "We're all from Byblos."

So blessings on Byblos and on the fruit—or rather, the fruits—of its womb! It seems to be the cradle of the Lebanese. Tomorrow, when archeologists are busy digging under the virgin soil, the glorious shores, and the immortal rocks, they may well unearth things that will prove that Byblos is indeed the cradle of humanity. All of the world's civilizations branched out from it and spread to the East and West. I wish them every success and cheer myself with the great news.

For the present, however, it is enough for me to know that Byblos is the fount of joy for my contemporary brothers. Like them, I hail from Byblos. A hundred years ago my ancestors emigrated from the heart of this country, Bejjeh, and settled in Beit Chabab and its surrounding pastures, part of which lay on the shoulder of the valley that

1. In Lebanese parlance, *partner* is someone entrusted with property. In return for his supervision, he is entitled to a specific share of the profits.

came to be called Freike Valley. My grandfather on my father's side—God have mercy on his soul!—always had a soft spot for this particular area and traveled to it a lot. Even after all the rigors of travel, he used to kiss the soil and return to his family with loads of its best produce—its famous tobacco, dried figs, and even some flocks of animals.

So my grandfather was a merchant, but I am not sure that what he brought to Byblos was money. Did he carry a sword and go on raids in the land of his ancestors, returning victorious with his spoils—not silk, but instead a herd of cows and loads of tobacco and figs?

In my youth it never occurred to me to investigate this question, but I realize that my grandfather's business was just like everyone else's in commerce, a source of profit but also subject to losses. There was profit and debt, and, it would appear, penury among certain people in Byblos. My grandfather added land to his profitability, and, like his ancestors, returned to Byblos as a landowner.

My father inherited some of that property, and it weighed him down. He could not sell it at anything close to the base value of the debt; he could not invest it through partners who were lacking in expertise; and he could not transfer them to Freike. So they stayed with him, an ongoing burden for the rest of his days. Then it was my fate—my burden—to assume responsibility for it all and profit from it.

Like my grandfather and father, I too traveled to Byblos once to check on the estate. I arrived at the Ibrahim River (previously the Adonis River) in an ancient cart, splendid in its very antiquity, pulled by two thin, hungry, and pathetic thoroughbred horses. There we stopped, and this was in that happy era before the advent of petrol and iron. In this particular part of the mountain there was no track, even for carts like this one. There was not a single horse or mule near the Ibrahim River, so I hired the only thing available—a donkey. Since its owner did not know the directions, I hired a guide as well.

We climbed up the Ibrahim River Valley, the Valley of Adonis, in a Phoenician village procession—the donkey rider in the middle, the guide in front, and the donkeyman carrying a willow cane bringing up the rear.

The donkeyman was proud of his voice and started singing plaintive love songs, but that annoyed the guide, who told him to stop. But then it occurred to the guide to fulfil his role by entertaining me with some of his own singing. His voice was much worse than the donkeyman's, so I told him to stop as well. We now continued to climb in silence until we eventually reached the spot overlooking the valley where the family treasure was buried.

I can no longer remember that place, but I do recall its name: Bir el-Hait, on the road to Qartaba. I also recall that there was a monastery there. When the abbot spotted our procession—a gentleman mounted on a donkey and two other men in front of and behind him—he thought it was the deputy governor and invited us to relax for a while. I was not all that keen to accept his invitation because I had spotted a priest inside the monastery whom I had previously known in New York and had no positive thoughts about him. So I did not prolong our visit—nor did the abbot, once he knew who I was, insist on offering us a cup of coffee. Instead, we made do with some water from his pitcher and bid him a thankful farewell.

We now descended the slope from Bir el-Hait on foot, pushing the donkey ahead of us, until we finally reached the valley floor. I now reformed our procession, out of respect for the villagers, and especially the "partner," who used to brag to them about his "bosses." Yes indeed, I remounted the donkey, positioned the guide in front and the donkeyman behind, and we then proceeded in such splendor to the village of Hsoun, where the great treasure was to be found.

We looked in on the "partner," who welcomed us with minimal pleasure. However, "the partneress," his wife, sacrificed a Phoenician-era chicken for us and made it the basis of a banquet, which started with olives from our land and finished with cheese from our cows' udders. Now the villagers arrived with the priest at their head and gave us a hearty welcome as they stood watching. They started talking to me, and, as the author, Ibn Zayzafoon puts it, the talk was heavy laden. In fact, to cite the author of the *maqaamat*, they bombarded me with questions about their relatives in America, the silk cocoons in our region, the prices of wheat and barley, about soap, oil, olives, cows and their market, and goats and their pastures.

The partner's clever wife could read in my eyes what my ultimate goal was. On the roof under a wormwood tent that was still damp with the scent of sweet basil, she put down two mattresses—may God honor her!—one on top of the other. For all the kindness and affection in her heart, she could not manage to do anything about their stuffing. Even so, I was grateful for the wormwood scent; I started inhaling like someone intent on getting intoxicated with it and then falling sound asleep on the stone floor.

However, the stars intervened to spoil the effects of the wormwood scent. The night was crystal clear, and the stars were at their very brightest and purest. I started shepherding the stars, as one poet puts it, and adjusting the information that I had about astronomy during the clear nights of Lebanon.

As I lay there, visually measuring the distance between the Pleiades and Libra, or between Ursa Major and Minor, I kept telling myself that I could cross such a distance on a donkey in an hour or two. Deeply inhaling the scent of wormwood, I would say, "Father, I commend to you my spirit," as God—may He be praised and exalted!—was extending His hand to take it.

After that, what could be of any help but dreams and composing some poetry? I think I wrote a couple of verses in English to send to my friend in New York in which I gave him some details about this incredible trip I had taken, the one on a donkey from the Pleiades to Libra! Following every single fantasy of the imagination and every whiff of sage and lupine, I would return to my golden dream and tell my sleepless self by way of reassurance that the partner was bound to pay me his arrears tomorrow, our own share of the land for a period of ten years. Then I can go back to Freike as my ancestors did, successful and wealthier.

Morning arrived with a smile to put an end to dreams. The partner came to see me with news that started and finished with tales of woe and disaster. He told me, his dear master, that his hardships stemmed from time, the government, profiteers, nasty neighbors, and total chaos. Before he even explained things, I deduced that the treasure had vanished; there was no point in even asking about shares or accounts. At this point imagination deserted me, refusing to take me to the ultimate limits of calamity.

We drank some coffee and ate grapes and figs. His wife brought a nargileh that she had borrowed from the house of the village priest. The partner now revealed his situation to me. I discovered that the house was mortgaged and the entire property was deep in debt.

"Fate, dear master," he told me, "is a curse."

Was I now supposed to imitate my own father and my even more generous grandfather—God have mercy on them both!—by removing the debtor's hand from the house and rescuing the property from the ravenous claws of profiteers?

The partner now swore to me by God, the Virgin Mary, and all the saints that he would repay me the money within two years and restore the land to its previous fertility and profitability. Once that happened, we would each get our share every season.

"I swear to God, master, and by all the saints . . ."

I got on my donkey and steered it as fast as possible toward the mountain pass, with the guide and donkeyman hurrying to catch up behind me.

"Sing some folk songs!" I yelled, and they both raised their voices in unison. At that moment I relished the sound and joined them in song.

The Priest's Cairn

EVEN THOUGH MY FIRST VENTURE to Byblos had been a failure, it was still very much on my mind; I never allowed myself to neglect it or lose interest. One day I paid a visit to the famous city on the ancient shore. I was a guest in the house of the director of the castle (at the time I had a number of friends in governmental positions). We spent the evening talking about renowned ancestors who had tamed the waves and fish for their far-reaching goals. That night I dreamed that I was a fleet commander besieging the Welsh on orders from King Azi-Baal.

A few days later I decided to take a trip into the mountains, still singing the praises of the towns that "flowed with milk and honey," towns that my father and grandfather talked about, towns relatively recent in historical terms. I reached Amcheet; there I resided in the shadow of virtue and generosity. I now learned that the forebears of those who my heart adores knew and loved my grandfather, uncle, and father, and, in their honor, gave a warm welcome to guests who came from the Dog River Valley, the twin of the Ibrahim River Valley.

But Amcheet was merely the gateway to Byblos country, and I am not someone who is ever satisfied with stopping at gateways. Where were Bejjeh and Maad, the other third of the country?[1]

Days and nights passed, interspersed with trips to East and West, with me beset by a host of thoughts and emotions.

1. People in the Byblos region say that Bejjeh and Maad are two-thirds of the country.

"What about Byblos?" I would say to myself once in a while. "When are we going to visit that honorable lady?"

So one day we set out on a trip in the modern mode. Our car covered miles in minutes, passing the coast on the way to the mountains at a speed that made snakes dance and froze the very blood in camel's necks—hey, devil's daughter, let the old guy drive the camel litter! We shot past Byblos like an arrow, then entered and left Amcheet like a shell fired from a gigantic cannon. Praise be to God, we started climbing slowly through the beloved territory, through hills and flatlands that were adorned with wormwood and gorse but devoid of humans and jinn. When we reached the valley above Hbaleen, we spotted three ladies on the road that encircled the village. They were wearing European clothes from head to toe, thus canceling the feeling of desolation in that valley and filled the human heart with joy.

We stopped the car and greeted them, and they reciprocated warmly, inviting us to their homes. In their generosity and politeness, they were true daughters of the blessed mountain. Authentic in their ways, the European clothes they were wearing did nothing to alter their innate simplicity of spirit and gentle demeanor. The crimson color on their lips had no corrupting effect on their statements, and the canes they leaned on could not belie the feelings in their hearts.

We bade farewell to the birds that were chirping their welcome to us on the fig-tree branches and to the three ladies who had so enchanted us and drove through Hbaleen, which would have seemed almost empty had we not spotted the ladies—but then, as the old saying has it, there can be no absence with lovely ladies' presence! We kept climbing up to the neighboring village, then turned off to Chamate and paid a visit to its upper house, where a priest, bishop, and Lebanese girls were living. Lebanese girls and women have only ever encountered the beauties of civilization, so may God bless you all, you mountain girls of Lebanon!

Even though faith was a stranger to me, I was still familiar with priests' homes. My grandfather's grandfather on my father's side was a bishop, and people say that he was a pious scholar and intellectual luminary. A family elder once told me that a sheikh of the Khazen family was keen to test my grandfather, Bishop Basil Abdul-Ahad's, knowledge. One day, he had a question for the bishop:

"Everything that God has created brings its own benefits, sir. The exception is these rocks. Of what use are they?"

"Those rocks, my son," the bishop replied immediately, "are the earth's bones."

In this upper house in Chamate, there was a priest. He who had sparred with rocks and beat them. He provided practical proof of what my grandfather the bishop had said. He had clothed "the earth's bones" in "flesh" consisting of soil, which he had carried there. He had then planted bushes and vines, which had flourished and borne fruit, and the shade they provided covered the ground in gentle affection.

This powerful priest in Chamate had had another effect in the way he had overpowered the rocks, something unusual and peculiar. It took the visible form of a huge circular wall running from the mountain's base through its middle to the top. It was eye-catching and aroused both amazement and a certain confusion. What were those mounds, one wondered, and what lay behind them? I had never seen an oven that huge, and there was not enough water on the mountain to justify a dam. Was it some Phoenician castle or a Roman or Crusader site? Once we had arrived, we could not resist asking the question.

"That's the priest's cairn."

We walked over to it with the priest. We found ourselves at the top of a graveyard shaped like a crescent and about fifteen meters from one side to the other. It was about as high as the wall that we had seen from the road.

"It's graveyard," I said.

"It's a cairn," he replied.

Could it be that I knew more about his inner thoughts and noble projects than he did? I would answer, "Yes." This was indeed a graveyard because this reverend and powerful priest had buried in it all the rocks around his house! So, instead of having his workers remove the rocks from his land and toss them down the mountain, where they would end up on the road and block it, he had constructed this lofty wall as a formidable barrage and filled the ditch created behind it with rocks.

So this was indeed a graveyard containing "the earth's bones." One of the priest's ideas as part of the construction process was that, while they were digging, they would construct small squares, meter by meter. When we saw them, they looked like pits on the surface; about a meter deep, they would be filled with soil and planted with shade-giving trees. Thereafter, the priest was going to sit under those trees, on top of "the earth's bones"—he, his family, and friends. They would have a table laid with small bowls and in the middle a bottle of arak! That is what the priest told us—God grant him a long life!

After all this, who can claim that our ancestors were giants and we are pygmies?

It may well be that you will not find the like of this cairn in the Lebanese mountains. However, if you branch off from civilization's highway and delve into village life, you will find peasant colleagues of the priest, in their resolve, ambition, and energy.

In fact, this priest was the father of Bishop Boutros Akl. In that bishop—God grant him a long life and steer us and himself on the right path!—within him were some of those rocks and fruits of Lebanon's soil.

In that house I had the impression that I was in my own home, for reasons that I have partially explained. Here I will simply add that his family are Lebanese from Byblos, as am I. It does not matter whether the clothes are black or purple, they cannot hide the contents of the heart!

If this were simply a cairn, it would suffice as a symbol of love and admiration. However, there are others things beside the cairn and Bishop Boutros. There are also those generous, cultured women who stand in all their courtesy between freedom and tradition. The mind may be free, but behavior was bound to Lebanese tradition, which served as the bastion of morality. One of them talked to us about Gibran, as both an admirer and critic. She went on to say that she also read Rihani and agreed with many of his opinions on national and social issues.

"What about religion?"

"God be praised! If you build cairns between people's minds and raise walls at the boundaries of faith, you can never erect a boundary or obstacle among the pure of heart!"

We returned from Hbaleen and Chamate with sweet memories, only sorry that the day was too short to allow us to do as we really wished—namely, to continue our travels into the heart of the country and to savor the sweet scent of friendly souls and pure hearts.

As we traveled swiftly back, covering the mountains and shore at a speed that surprised the dusk and aggravated the slowly advancing night, I kept thinking about those cultured Lebanese women who were still far removed from the unfulfilled spark of civilization as they huddled in remote villages. I thought as well about young men in the cities who were eager to get married—clever men, even though there may have been few of them in those times. By God, I was thinking about those men and the noble women as well. I will now repeat what I kept telling myself then:

"Look in the mountains, and you'll find. Look more closely, and you'll find and be happy."

Fourth Journey

The Cedars of Jaj

Contents

On the Road

AS THE DAYS ROLLED BY, I never forgot that I had started with a short trip in Lebanon, one that I had never finished. I constantly recalled that the valley I entered and whose natural and human beauties I had experienced led to Jaj, and that Jaj was the gateway to a mountain with a treasure trove of cedars, known only to people who lived close by. The only people who visited the spot may have been hunters, goatherds, and peasants who were still attached to their beloved land.

How to get to Jaj? All I knew about it was the name; I remembered it along with other names of Lebanese pasturelands ever since my youth when I was in New York. Are you surprised that I heard about Byblos when I grew up in New York but hailed originally from Matn? My father—God have mercy on him!—was a merchant in New York, and I was a writer in his store before I became a writer in the store of life. A group of people who worked with my father in commerce migrated from the Byblos region, so as a boy I learned how to pronounce the villages' names—Haqel, Lehfed, Meshmesh, Bejjeh, Maad, and Hbaleen—names that were stored deep in the mind, entered the heart, and willingly stayed there. I have always kept them in my memory; whenever I have visited the villages, I have felt the sheer pleasure of someone returning devotedly to an earlier love.

To all that I will add a page from the book of modern life. In those valleys and flatlands there are litterateurs, lawyers, and doctors, people living according to the religion of their forebears, loving the soil and their fluid property. They were not content with anything other than the rocks in whose shadows they were born and the clefts where they used to play. It was under those oaks and olive trees that they learned their alphabet, may they be blessed! They still live there in mansions that they have built, unbothered by the fact that they are an hour or two from the cart track.

Among these dear friends is an Arab Maronite priest teaching rhetoric in a theological school, but he did other work as well for charity. He was both a scholar and a farmer. On the soil of Saint Augustine and among the wilting sweet basils of Saint Thomas Aquinas he planted Lebanese cedars, myrtle from Syria, palm trees from Iraq, and acacia and oxeye from the Nejd.

Another was a professor teaching higher-level rhetoric at two schools—one national, the other civil. In the small garden of truth he would sow the seeds of the much greater truth and irrigate its flowers with waters drawn from the springs of that great truth. May God greet Mohammed's father, Maroun Abboud, who in summertime would go into retreat in Ain Kfaa.

On both my first and second trips I inquired after Ain Kfaa, my intention being to explore it and surprise my friend who lived there. However, it lay in a secluded mountain valley, and the road there was remote. I envied Mohammed's father, and considered him to be my superior and instructor in matters of wisdom. For his personal retreat he had chosen that location, situated amid the mountain slopes of Lebanon. When it came to isolation, where was Freike in comparison with Ain Kfaa? Up there Mohammed's father was in an impenetrable fortress, near Bejjeh, yet far enough away. He was very far—and I am going to leave a phrase such as *far away indeed* for innovating writers!—from the major highway. In Freike, underneath that road, I was at the mercy of callers and vagrants. I am envious of you, Maroun, and greetings!

Had I sent you a telegram asking you to go to Jaj with us and to make the pilgrimage to the Cedars, you would certainly have done it! Such a pilgrimage would been your very best act of piety toward God; among the pilgrims you would have been especially honored. How could it be otherwise, when the wife of our host was one of those highly educated women who prefer to read refined literature in both prose and verse? The host was one of those worthy doctors who went abroad and experienced times of war in their French, Turkish, and Arab contexts; the bitter and sweet encounters that they had to endure were either concealed or unknown. The two of them honored their being part of Arab culture, loved Lebanon, and cherished their roots all the way back to Adnan of earliest times.

It is not surprising to discover excellent traces and fond memories of Adnan in Byblos. Both Phoenicians and Arabs stem from the same Semitic source and from a single country—that of the Arabs.[1] In La'lou' (Laqlouq) there are ancient Arab trees with deep roots and plentiful shade. Over time the winds have scattered its spirit throughout those valleys and plateaus and amid those soaring high rocks.

Here is the Arab essence of Lebanon. The lady had perfumed the road with her mention of that essence and celebration of its qualities. Here was Lebanon as part of Arab culture. The doctor too was of that same bent. He had made us forget all about the desolate valleys and bare hills beyond as depicted by the popular Lebanese poet Rachid Nakhleh.

I have just talked of "bare hills," and I was not exaggerating. Once we have gone through Hbaleen, the Byblos region is bone dry and desolate, particularly at the end of summer. It was as though this ancient land had tired of civilization. The heart of those mountains and plains had faded away; their very face had turned black. No wonder then that village springs had little water and the soil was unproductive. However, as we climbed up higher from Chamate to Haqel, the air brought some compensation; as we continued upward, the views varied and broadened. There stood Bejjeh on its hill behind Chamate; beyond it on the horizon at the mountaintop were some black shadows amid translucent clouds, which was Maad.

At river mouths, the Lebanon mountain chain has a geological shape that is almost a constant. Those river flows that had carved

1. See my book *The Arab Kings*, part 2, section 4: "The Khalifa family—rulers of Bahrain."

out—mostly to the west—courses to the sea were the valleys, which narrow and widen in accordance with the flat or sloping terrain and the force of the downflow. Those same valleys serve as linking devices in the mountain chain. On their sides and shoulders, on their flatlands, in their clefts, and at their tops villages and farms have been established and terraces have been constructed to keep the soil in place and to allow trees to be planted.

Every one of these valleys has a gateway to the coastal region, which is usually alongside the river. A road—for pack animals in the old days, for carts and cars now—ends up at the furthest and highest village: for example, from Antelias it goes all the way up to Biskanta; from Jounieh to Faraya; from the Ibrahim River to Aqoura; and from Byblos to Jaj.

However, the valley and river do not always run alongside each other; in fact, they may disappear most of the time, as does the Jaj Valley and its river, which is completely dry in summertime. Once we have crossed the bridge (called the Chicken Bridge) near Byblos, the river disappears once we start the climb to Amcheet. We only set eyes on it again after we have climbed up to Hbaleen, then again between Haqel and Lehfed which is almost one thousand meters above sea level. It is hardly surprising, then, that Lehfed is a summer resort for families living in Byblos and Amcheet.

Alongside the road is a stream that flows into a stone drainpipe; in front of it is a cafe set up beneath a tent, a sign of the fact that Lehfed is indeed the summer resort for the Byblos region. For the summer visitor, the pure air and flowing water are only enhanced by this café, roofed in wormwood, providing the visitor with both nargilehs and backgammon. But there are other causes for delight as well: arak, for example, and kibbe are always available. For those hunting in the mountain heights, there is plenty of partridge. With all this available, what need does the summer visitor have for dancing, singing, and beauty queens?

If the reader can put up with the travails of the journey (and talk about it) and will continue to accompany us, he will get to enjoy—God willing!—every heart's delight among the beauties of summertime.

In this particular region of the mountain those same beauties have a pure simplicity, and, to the extent possible, are clearly evident. Most of them are of Phoenician origin, duly softened by the course of time. Or say that it is Arab, with an additional touch of Phoenician pride.

We have already mentioned the road. Before we get to the end of it, we must say something about it. It is still made up of soil and gravel; there is none of that smooth surface that the coastal roads enjoy. From the coast to Lehfed it is a cart track, not a car road—especially at its many narrow bends. The road from Lehfed to Jaj, the roadworks directorate does not even bother with it; it is not their concern. There are no ditches and no paving at all. The capital city is apparently well aware of everything that has been said.

"We've sent protests," the doctor tells me, "we've formed delegations, and we've wasted ink, paper, and shoes with our requests and pleas. The government has neither listened nor responded. But the road from Lehfed to Jaj is only five kilometers. Our men, young and old, felt a spirit of pride, so they got a project organized and dug and paved the road without bothering to ask for assistance from anyone except the people of Jaj."

Lebanese Hospitality

THERE ARE STILL MEN in the Byblos region, and their sisters as well, who, whether in good times or bad, practice the traditional Lebanese custom of hospitality—one that is marked by generosity and graced by kindness and simplicity. The same trait is also to be found in other regions of Lebanon, far removed from the din and glitter of summer resorts.

In Jaj the haven of hospitality is a well-sheltered house with plentiful shade, just like the oak tree by the church there. That particular oak—may God bless both it and you!—had a widespread Byblos reputation, offering shade to conferences of politicians and pupils in alphabet school.

We settled into the house, which overlooks the pine tree and is closely linked to what lies over the horizon to the northeast—namely, Tannourine. You may be unaware of what lies behind this geographical description, so you should realize that between Jaj and Tannourine there are mountains and rocks, partridges' and eagles' nests, and forests of cedar trees safeguarded by the ages. In spite of that, the doctor had invaded the region and taken one of its daughters as a prize. He had thus become Younus al-Mighwar, a relative of Farhat al-Jabbar, thus creating a pact of loyalty and neighborliness between the two villages.

Farhat's daughter was Doctor Yousuf's sister, and Younus's daughter was the doctor's wife. That night, there were two bright stars, the very fulcrum of life, inside the house. The two of them kindled the fires of hospitality and lit the glowing lamps of joy and companionship.

The young folks of the village came to the house, bringing the skills they were born with and those that they had learned through education. There was a reciter, a dancer, and a pan piper. Local village girls, with their gentle beauty, came to help the lady of the house. One of them offered drinks, and another coffee. A third was bringing spring water to the kitchen, and a fourth brought out the nargilehs. They all looked happy and content as they worked, as though they were part of a brother's wedding celebrations. This then was the sense of honor whose very milk nourished the young boys and girls in the village.

It actually felt as though we were at a wedding. When we sat at the table, the master of the house decided that the dinner should be accompanied by music and singing, as though we were in some Parisian hotel. His sister proceeded to sing a verse from a traditional Lebanese *ataaba* in her pleasant voice, accompanied by the pan piper. One of the young men matched her, picking up where she left off without even straying from the melody and theme.

I personally am someone who loves this traditional Arab Bedouin, someone whose love emotions and intense passions are so pure. I also adore the sound of the panpipe, broad and shrill, reflecting the harshness of the desert, its solitary tone a reflection of isolation, ruggedness, and hope. The famous Bedouin dance known as the *dabke* belongs to the higher realms of art in that its very steps involve the whispers of women and the tones of men. Its serene, repetitive movements are linked and interrupted by threatening, commanding gestures: "Hey gorgeous! I swear by the beauty of your figure!"

The gorgeous lady in questions bends her body and shimmies with her legs. The young man then strikes the ground with his foot and completes the verse. "What we're after is a kiss from your cheek so fair!"

That night a chain of young men and women was formed, with the lady of the house at the front waving a handkerchief. The piper started playing, and one of his brothers started shouting, "Clap, young men!" The sheer joy of the moment now took over, and heads and hands grew light. Everyone was bound to the solo melody and amazing verse—one profound melody from the pipe, the other sound from the precise movement of feet. The piper himself, who was standing in the middle of the circular chain would bend his head, then raise it again, melting away in sheer passion and intensifying the dabke's own fire:

> Hey gorgeous! What a figure you've got there!
> What we're after is a kiss from your cheek so fair!
> Hey ho, hey ho!

The dabke over, the central space was cleared for one of the girls who was good at dancing solo. The piper changed his melody. This slender, lovely girl now lowered her eyes, tilted her head to her shoulder, and raised her arms in the air. She started putting her right leg in front and dragging the top of her left foot behind her. She extended her steps and made a circular motion as though she were writing love letters with her feet. Bending her arm, she gave a slight shrug with her shoulder so that her neck grew jealous of the sways to either side; now it too bent and swayed, using forward thrusts to send passionate messages to the heart. With that, ecstasy burst out of the twin doves of the bosom as they bounced and jiggled. The village beauty stood there for a moment, arms spread, her expression showing no trace or realization of the temptations that her gyrations had aroused.

A single moment in that climactic expression of art in all its simplicity, and then she gradually lowered her hand to her waist and held the other one in front of it. Swaying in both directions, she began using her feet again to write love letters, sometimes moving rapidly, at others more slowly. Then she stopped suddenly and gave a final bow, like a school student who has played her role properly.

The only thing wrong with her dance routine was the abrupt way she finished it. Once she had started slowing the pace of her dance, if she had kept on gradually slowing down as she moved out of the center of the space, she could have vanished like a sprite and crowned her artistic performance with a melting moment. That would have been the opposite of how the European-style dancer finishes her routine with a provocative abruptness. In my view, it is the first possibility that is closer to the truth and has a far greater impact on cultured souls.

The night's entertainment was not limited to the singing and dancing that have just been described. The floor was now empty. The

We were all bound to the solo melody and amazing verse.

twin stars of the house—the doctor's wife and sister—had both disappeared. The house was quiet, and silence prevailed. It was the normal interval between two acts in a play performance. For that reason we were a little befuddled, expecting something else to happen.

What did actually happen next—and when it appeared, it caused the entire house to erupt in applause and laughter—was *karakoz*, the clown figure, something moving inside a black bag tied in the middle, swaying slowly to right and left. From inside the bag his hands kept reaching out and gesturing. It was exciting and hilarious; it looked just like scarecrows planted amid vines. This object started to dance, shaking his enormous head, which was half the size of his body, gesturing with his tiny hands, and spinning like a Chinese top.

"That boy's really good!" I told my neighbor.

I had assumed that they had mounted a cage on his head to make it larger.

"He's a boy who's good at dancing," he replied, correcting my mistake. "A round tray is placed on his head, and he wears that loose dress, which is tied over his head and covers everything down to his feet. The two hands that you see are actually sticks attached under the dress in the middle. The sleeves hang down from their exposed edges and shake every time he does a twist.

He was indeed a very strange clown; more than that, a remarkable innovation in satire. I had never seen anything like it before, but, as I was told, it is a well-known and recognized part of Lebanese nightlife. It also had its own dramatic value, the essence of everything satirical and hideous. I think that the only other places where you would find its like is with Japanese deities and Chinese skits.

So *karakoz* the clown performed his routine and left. Now it was the turn of this author, who is regularly oppressed by literature and politics even on vacation. While the clown had been performing, all the village's writers had arrived at the house, eager to offer their greetings and get to know and talk to the great writer, etc. In fact, they had come to fatigue him with questions and discussions—about literature, society, politics, and religion. One was studying law, another medicine, and a third theology—complete with his black robe. A fourth was a graduate of a college, and another was correspondent for one of the major newspapers in the capital city. They all loved literature and poetry and were authorities on politics. Among them were lovers, admirers, discussants, observers, give us your views, philosopher!

A night of enjoyable entertainment soon turned into one of torment. Emulating soothsayers of old, I gave terse responses to questions, and conceded on discussion points simply to be rid of them. I kept consoling myself with the hope that the piper would come back and the lady of the house would recite some more popular poetry. If only . . . ! The clown had brought the night to end with laughter, and the literary types finished it off with a dispute.

> Good and evil are a blend, never separating;
> Every drop of honey has a touch of bitterness.

The Goat Trail and the Jinn Trail

TO THE CEDARS, the Cedars of Jaj, the Cedars of the Lord!

The next morning, we got up early. Our host, Doctor Farhat, and his family were making preparations to travel. There were people in Jaj, who, like us, had no idea what lay beyond those lofty, dark horizons. They were making ready for the first part of the journey.

"It's an hour's walk," they kept saying to urge each other on and encourage us as well, "and less than that for riders."

"Here's your donkey, sir," they told me. "Forgive us, but there's nothing like donkeys for such a tough road."

"Isn't there something wrong," I asked myself, "about hiring a donkey for just one hour in the mountains? Even if it were two hours, would anyone ride a donkey who had previously mounted a horse in the Nejd or a camel in Oman?"

As I thought to myself, my sense of pride and challenge took over. And yet, I really like walking and am always eager to do it, especially high up in the mountains, where the air is dry, the atmosphere is pure, and the warmth of the sun is gentle. I decided to walk, and Doctor Farhat's brother wanted to go with me. Like his father and brother, he was a giant. That morning they were both waiting for me; one of them had a hunting rifle on his shoulder.

We let people get ready, as the muleteers loaded up the food and water. It was just before dawn when we left Jaj. We were supposed to be at the Cedars by then, but I was not the only one in the party; I was simply one of the guests. The others included some women, who never left their boudoirs without rouging their cheeks and putting lipstick on their lips.

We were still in mountain passes where the rocks were fairly small and the stones under our feet were stable. These were amiable passes, their sides softened by oaks, thyme, and ever-present sweet-scented undergrowth. At their bends they overlooked plains with brown soil before plowing and yellow after harvest. You could rest and relax in the shade that they offered.

My two literary companions now started a poetry contest, the aim being, as they both told me, to help me forget the rigors of the trip. They both had an extensive repertoire and ready wits. I was duly amazed by their competence in this particular realm.

"In these far-off mountain villages," Samarani said, "the major task of the litterateur is to recite and memorize poetry." The contest took the form where one of the two would recite a verse, and the other had to come up with another verse that begins with the rhyming letter of the previous verse. To begin with, there was a verse by al-Mutanabbi from one of his poems rhyming on the letter *L*. The response was immediate:

> Let no one purchase a slave unless he comes with a cane;
> Slaves are filthy and troublesome.

What amazed me was that they could continue to conduct this contest for several hours without either of them winning or losing. They would even resume the same contest the next day. When it came to certain rhymes, even the greatest bards would have trouble. The best part of it would be when the verses were by a single poet, and even more miraculous, when the follow-up verse was from the same poem. It was as though one would begin with:

> Your foe is at fault on every tongue
> Even if among your foes were sun and moon

To which the second person would respond:

> Must he gainsay the impact of spear tip on spear
> Never fearing the impact of star and Aldebaran.

As we were climbing with the contest in full swing, the reciter, who was the hunter, spotted a flock of partridge or heard the flapping of their wings. He forgot all about poetry and poets, and started leaping from rock to rock, then sped up, crossed the trail, and disappeared. We did not hear any shots fired, nor see any further sign of the partridge.

My colleague Farhat and I continued walking in silence; we had taken a shortcut above the road. From there we saw our fellow travelers lagging behind in the bend below, all of them, both men and women, riding donkeys—except, that is, for the muleteers and servants. Forgive me, dear reader! I've just realized that I'm afflicted by the cravings of modernist authors by choosing a weird form of the plural of *donkey*—only once, never again. So pardon me, you donkey riders!

Now here is Doctor Farhat shouting at us, his sister telling us to stop, and his wife waving a handkerchief at us. "Stop, stop!" The entire caravan now emerges in single file on the narrow road. We duly stopped to wait for the sixth or seventh member—namely, the doctor's own donkey. When he drew close to us, he dismounted and invited me to get on the donkey. I declined his invitation with thanks. His wife then dismounted as well. Again and with due thanks, I asked her to excuse me.

"I have sworn a pledge, madam," I told her. "I have to go to the Cedars on foot."

"A pledge well received, God willing!" she responded with a laugh.

We then asked where our fellow hunter was.

"He's over there," a servant replied.

"Where?"

Raising his head, he pointed in the distance to a massive crag atop a cluster of shady rocks. Below them and beneath the white cloud, our fellow traveler was standing on a dark rock that looked like the mainstay in nature's own temple. Lowering his rifle, he shouted to us; the sound kept resounding as the echo picked it up.

"By God," Farhat yelled, "he's reciting poetry. I heard the line and its rhyme. It's on the letter *B*. Good for you, Samarani, good for you!

> The whites of our deeds, the blacks of our battles, the greens of
> our meadows,
> and the reds of our cutting blades.

So, Farhat, where are those green meadows now? By now we had reached the summit of the second mountain and followed the track across to the base of the mountain in front of us. There was no trace of greenery protected by shade or any yellowed by the sun. It was all gray interspersed with dark lines and spots, which were shadows created by crags and crevices in the rocks. Between the rock formations were dry streams and defiles covered in stones. Our giant travel companion pointed to the track around the mountain.

"The best idea is for us to 'shortcut' it" (in other words, to take the shortcut).

We had already veered off the pack-animal trail, and then the goat trail. Now here we were leaving both behind and climbing up to places where there was not even a trace of hoofed animals. This was the jinn trail—and what a trail it was, with almost vertical slopes and rocks of various shapes and sizes—limestone and granite, rough and smooth, pointed and round. At times they made your foot slip, at others they would scratch you so that you felt as if they had made a hole in your sandals. The sun was high in the sky, and it was very hot. The sweat was pouring off us, and our throats were parched.

"This huge rock's blocking our way. Give me your hand, sir."

"I'll sit in its shade for a while," I told my giant travel companion. "Then I'll go around it."

As I sat there, I thought back to all the experiences I had had: rocky trails in mountains and deserts, both riding and on foot. Of all the hardships of travel I had been through, this trip was by far the toughest and nastiest. We were walking along edges—like sword blades—clambering upward using our hands.

Should the warriors avoid being taken by sword blades, we have achieved it with our hands.

I thought too about what I had said just half an hour earlier and the vow I had made. I envisioned myself climbing barefoot on the jinn trail, with Saints Anthony and Francis holding my hand.

While we were going through this trial, my companion asked me for my opinion about modernist writers. Good God, what heroism can achieve! Had I felt like responding to his question at that particular moment, I would have said:

"In a situation like this a modernist writer would say, 'I'm breathless' (in other words, my breathing is cut off and I'm exhausted), or else he'll use another weird derivative of the same verb and say, 'I'm out of breath' (in other words, I've burned up because of the glittering heat of the day)."

As it was, I did not respond to his question. Instead, I asked him one:

"Where are the Cedars, my brother? Are they over the top of this mountain?"

He indicated to me that he did not know. He had visited the Cedars once as a boy, and this was his second visit twenty years later.

Even so, he reassured me. Once we reached the summit, he pointed joyfully at the mountain opposite.

"There's the gateway of the rocks," he yelled. "If you look carefully, you can see part of the caravan crossing it. The Cedars are behind it."

Passing through the gorse—God be praised!—we started climbing again and reached the gateway, a narrow defile between the rocks. We went in and emerged to find ourselves in the shadow of yet another enormous, towering, gray-colored mountain!

"Where are the Cedars, my brother?"

"Certainly behind this mountain."

By now, all the trails—the animal trail, the goat trail, and the jinn trail—had become a single track, a veritable cascade of rocks! There was no choice involved, and no point.

Putting our trust in God, we tackled the wasteland. Out of breath and knees twitching, we clambered up the rocks.

"Oh, my knees!" I said, knowing that my companion had told me that he too was exhausted. As we traversed the fifth or sixth mountain, we did not see a solitary branch of a cedar tree. God the Almighty the Great alone has the power and might!

It was at this point that my dear travel companion asked me yet another question.

"What do you think, sir, about . . ." I heard him ask.

"Please," I interrupted him, "postpone your questions until we get to the site of our pilgrimage."

We reached the summit of the sixth mountain and were overlooking the valley of the seventh. God be praised, there were the Cedars!

It seemed that there was only a short gap between us and the Cedars, no more than two hundred meters. We were halfway there when we found ourselves confronted with a horrendous, deep chasm!

Dear literate reader, if you have ever read one of the famous epics—Homer's *Iliad*, for example, or Vergil's *Aeneid*—you will, no doubt, recall the hardships and dangers created by the poet as part of his plans for some higher purpose. This particular trail, which we had managed to traverse safe and sound, was nature's own epic with its higher purpose—the Cedars.

But we were still not there. The Cedars were there right in front of us, and yet the abyss between us and them enveloped them like a halo to the southwest. It served as the swing of their sword, the zone of its sanctum, and the moat of its castle.

We had no choice but to make our way round to them, which was by no means easy—but then nothing is easy in the mountain heights. We circled the halo, where the ground was as rough going up or down as any we had encountered and endured before.

However, as we were making this circuit, poking our way among the rocks, we passed by a natural rocky basin about twenty-five meters deep. In it the sky stored its snow from one winter to the next.

Here then was eternal snow in the Holy Vicinity, eternal purity in the shades of the Cedars!

The Cedars

I PICKED UP A STONE from the track and kissed it three times in piety, praise, and hope before entering the sacred shades.

I begged the Cedars' forgiveness for infringing its solitary sanctuary—that exceptional isolation at the mountaintops, above eagles' nests and the veils of the horizon.

I begged forgiveness because I had come to tear the shroud of their Kaaba, to uncover the essence of their secret.

• • •

Hail, lady of the trees, mistress of the all-powerful mountain!

You raise your green standard over these dark rocks.

Daughter of day and night, sister of sun and moon, talk to me!

Talk to me, teach me, raise me up to the heights of your faith.

I have come to you in quest of knowledge and elevation; to draw from your lofty spring both power and wisdom.

• • •

Speak to me about the winds of the north.

They come to me moaning and wailing, so I stop them so they can rest. They are transformed into perfumed breaths.

Speak to me about pouring rain.

It dances on the rocks all around me and cackles with laughter. It plucks the strings of my lyre, bringing with it the sounds of nightingales and waves.

Speak to me about storms.

They rise from the valleys in fury and descend to reverberate on the horizons. All around me they beat their drums. I open my heart to them, and they enter it in a rage. But then, within my arms, their sounds are turned into those of trumpets, flutes, and panpipes. And then they fall silent and fall asleep beneath the wings of peace.

Speak to me about clouds.

They are my veil, my jellaba, the incense of my sanctum.

Speak to me about snow.

In winter it is my fortress; in spring my shield. It saps the storm's strength and renders gentle the heat of love and beauty. In summer it is the mother of my roots, nursing them beneath the ground and between the bases of rocks. It thrills my heart and lifts up my head in praise and thanksgiving.

Speak to me about floods.

Inside my house they frolic and cause chaos. They strip me of my roots, and so I spread my feathers over them in summer and winter. Time may come to my aid, bringing me soil on the wings of the wind. Then I can clothe my roots in a fresh garment.

Winter is my night companion, spring is my ambassador, summer is my dewy curator, and fall is the priest in my temple.

Speak to me about rocks.

They are what happens both before and after me. My own dust comes from them, and to them is my ultimate return. In life they are the apple of my eye and the ornament of my soul. Indeed, they are my eternal temple, populated by me today but asking about me on the morrow.

Speak to me about day and night.

Daytime is my conversation partner, nighttime my bed. Both play a role in my progress and my fate.

About the sun and moon:

The sun organizes my rationales, the moon stands watch at my door. The sun feeds my greenery and the moon keeps my secrets.

About the stars:

They are the hands of God—pink, silver, golden, violet. They give without being asked and dispense without demanding any return. They are the hands of God, bringing me all the beauty, contentment, serenity, and guidance that is within Him. They are the hands of

God, mistresses of poetry, of art, of pure imagination, and of frenzied rapture.

The stars are the beauties who chant in the shadows of my retreat, the virgins who dance in my temple.

They are the loyal and pure maidens, far and near, who can put an end to my troubles and salve my wounds. They teach me how to smile and weave dreams.

• • •

The Cedars of my mountains, the Cedars of my ancestors.

Your nights are my nights; your stars are also mine.

The Cedars of the Lord

BETWEEN JAJ AND THE CEDARS, the distance comes in different versions. For people walking, it is short. Sturdy farmers and shepherds, for example, can do it in one hour. But people riding animals have to go round, so it takes longer, no less than an hour and a half. And for someone like me who likes to show off, he refuses to ride a donkey, is amazed to find himself clambering up the five mountains in two hours, and then brags about it.

We reached the destination, exhausted and parched. Our companions had arrived ahead of us and had sent some people who could go down into one of the closest snow-filled basins and bring some back. It seems that those who were bringing our water and provisions had been delayed. We could thus observe our companions. Each one had a chunk of ice in his hand, sucking on it to quench his burning thirst.

As for our female companions—cheerful and light in both spirit and foot, we spotted them, by God, at the core of one of the huge cedar trees. They were seated amid its enormous branches, sucking on lumps of ice they were holding and turning their lips bright red. Nothing conceived by the imagination can be more unusual than the truth. So here were the houris of paradise besporting themselves amid the cedar branches and chewing lumps of ice that tasted sweeter than yogurt and honey.

We too sat down under those cedars and raised our faces toward the houris. Opening our mouths, we accepted the ice from their hands; they managed to free and relax our hearts—that is the truth, no mere image. We chuckled like young boys and erased all thoughts of fatigue. Now that a cool breeze had blown, we forgot the sweats of the journey. A cold wind blew all around us, and we were shivering. We longed for sunshine.

We now made our way through the forest, which was situated on a lengthy slope. There were forty or so trees. Five of them were really old and enormous; one of them was about six meters in diameter and about thirty meters tall.

These large cedar trees grew in peculiar shapes, something I had not seen with the Bsharre cedars. When the trunk had risen a meter or two from the ground, it spread out. As a result, a second trunk emerged above the first one, its diameter two or three meters wider than the lower one. The bottom of the tree looked like a table with a circular base; from that table huge branches extended about twenty-five meters high.

In one of the cedars I counted twelve such branches, all of them colossal, strong, and tall. So it would be correct to say that twelve cedars have grown from a single trunk—or, more accurately, from a single table between one and two meters round.

Some of the cedars had double or triple trunks, while others consisted of a single tall, upright trunk, between fifteen and twenty-five meters tall, while the biggest of them are no more than two meters in diameter.

The five largest cedars had been planted in this forest some two or three hundred years ago; the average life of such mother trees was five or six hundred years. During that time period, seeds would fall on soil with little shade or roots, nurtured by the heat of the sun and untrodden by human feet—the way it is today with the cedars in Bsharre. Under the largest trees you can see hundreds of tiny green cedar seedlings shaped like the letter *V*; in other words, with two branches. However, none of them will survive, because the shade is so thick and the ground is full of roots, which suck up all the nutrients; also because the atmosphere is so dry in the summer.

What made me more convinced that the largest cedars were planted in this forest was that there were also some translucent unusual examples, of medium height, scattered across the enclave amid the rocks and on the pebbly slopes. Some of those solitary cedars, isolated in their glory, had a wide, pyramidal shape—in other words, with wide horizontal branches.

We counted these isolated trees, both above and below the main forest to the northwest. There were seventeen, each one a paragon of beauty with its straight growth and its rocky surroundings; such artistic splendor engendered by contrasts—green pyramids amid dark boulders and bare, whitish slopes. When the fog lifts and its edges thin out, each of these lovely, isolated cedars looks like a beautiful woman with a veil, flirting enticingly as she lifts and lowers it; either that, or a dancer in her translucent slacks, showing her gorgeous body, then hiding it again. When the fog finally dissipates, the greenery can now emerge dewy and polished anew, as though at that very moment it had just emerged from God's own dye works.

I said earlier that there were some forty trees in the forest, and a further seventeen scattered around. The warden informed me, and people from Jaj corroborated his information, that in these mountain heights—ranging from the broad horizon, which hid Tannourine from view, and the smaller horizons below it, amid the ravines and valley shoulders—there were seven other cedar forests. The total number of trees in the mountain heights of Jaj was close to four hundred.

These then were the Cedars of Jaj, some two thousand meters above sea level, and no more than about seven hours on foot from Byblos, the ancient Phoenician port. These seven forests were undoubtedly one single enormous forest in ancient times; indeed, the mountains of Jaj were completely covered in cedar trees, called the Cedars of the Lord.

Why were the Cedars of Lebanon so-called? Were they called that in Phoenician times? The answer to the first of those questions is well-known to Christians in the mountains—with not the slightest doubt. The answer to the second is unknown to them and to me also. If anyone can answer it, it will be the expert on Phoenician history, my dear friend Charles Corm. I will therefore hand you over to him and share with you a bit of my own knowledge.

I have opened the encyclopedia and read what it says about cedars. It notes that in the Himalayas, where there are plenty of Buddhist

Have you ever looked at what lies beyond the pillars and walls—at the very spirit of existence and the hand of time.

monasteries, there are cedars like the ones in Lebanon that are called the Cedars of the Lord! Are they so-called because they grow close to the monasteries and temples, or because, of all trees, they are the sturdiest, the most beautifully shaped, and the longest lived? So did this type of cedar—and that was its name in ancient times, even before the Phoenician era—come from the Himalayas? I need to draw the attention of my friend Charles Corm to this matter, he being the expert on Phoenician history.

If we grant that the Cedars of Lebanon are so-called because Solomon, son of David, had some brought to Jerusalem to build the temple—the temple of God, we must also concede that the port where the cedarwood was loaded had to be Byblos. It makes no sense to suggest that King Ahiram of Byblos transported the wood overland to Tyre and then loaded it for transport to Palestine.

The Cedars of Jaj are seven hours from Byblos, and the Bsharre cedars are fifteen hours away.[1] From those two forests the cedarwood was cut and transported by Byblos vessels to Jaffa to build God's temple.

It is my belief that the Byblos wood merchants preferred the forests close by to the ones that were further away because transporting cut wood would be cheaper and easier. That is the plausible explanation that refutes and cancels received wisdom on the subject.

So the Cedars of the Lord are here near Jaj, in the mountains of Tannourine.

1. This is based on horse-riding times.

Rocks

WHAT ABOUT ROCKS?

Have you ever stood among rocks on the mountaintops, contemplating their creation and shapes, the significance of their beauty and splendor?

Have you ever looked through the crumbling natural temples at what lies beyond the pillars and walls, at the very spirit of existence and the hand of time?

In their lofty height is there anything but glory, in their splendor anything but force, in their shock anything but danger, in their rootedness anything but strength, in their hollows anything but weakness, in their rows anything but chaos, and in their angles anything but ignorance and perplexity?

• • •

Rocks lofty, pendant; rocks anchored, leaping, sinking; rocks hindering, sullen, warning; rocks smashing, cleaving; rocks shoulder to shoulder, languishing. Have you ever stopped to contemplate them, trying to enter their heart and the secret elements within?

In their heart is the kernel, which used to sink beneath the waves at the bottom of the seas.

In their heart is the germ of eternal life.

In their heart is the secret atom that lives by splitting, and can thus turn into food and scent for trees and flowers.

In their heart is the prison for egotism and the silence of sadness.

In their heart is the eternal symbol of the power of time.

In their heart is the message of ascent, even amid boulders.

Rocks protecting the gates to the Cedars, and carrying their throne on their shoulders and necks.

From the very seabed to the mountaintops; from the mossy, muddy, germ-filled darkness of the sea base to the very peak of light, crystal, and purity, that is the journey of rocks—indeed, their epic.

In their lofty height is there anything but glory and honor? It holds the shrines of sacrifices and the enigmas of life and death.

In their splendor is there anything but force and splendor? In it lies dark patience, glowering resolution, and never-ending silence.

In their shock is there anything but danger? It contains news of eruptions and infernos, tales of earthquakes and hurricanes.

In their rootedness is there anything but strength? In it there is the eloquence of fate and the chains of night and day.

In their hollows is there anything but evidence of weakness? Within them is evidence of a sympathy that is still lives in their hearts and of a compassion that is still dewy. Those hollows are a home for birds, a refuge for the lizard and panpipes for the winds.

In their rows is there anything but chaos? In them the very priorities of life are represented in liberation and restraint, and the canons of life in variety and unity.

In their angles and interruptions is there anything but ignorance and perplexity? Both of them offer knowledge, guidance, and inspiration to purveyors of art.

• • •

Rocks then are skyscrapers, roadblocks for eagles.

Rocks embrace the plains and stand guard at the wind's narrow passes.

Rocks embellish the mountaintops, raising banners for seclusion.

Rocks perching in silence, mocking thunder and lightning.

Rocks protecting the gates to the Cedars, taking root around them, and carrying their throne on their shoulders and necks.

Beauties beneath the Cedars

WE SAT DOWN in the upper reaches of the forest beneath the largest cedar tree. We were waiting for our other colleagues, who were coming from beyond the southern mountain, from Laqlouq. We had already made a plan with them in Beirut and were sure that they would have gotten here before us.

The group had now arrived, and servants rushed to bring us water from Jaj water that they had chilled with ice from the Cedars. However, once we had quenched our thirst and had a little rest, we felt very hungry. Some of us were a little impatient and started whispering to each other in frustration. Not everyone with us was so fascinated by the cedar trees and rocks. So we had reconcile ourselves to a day of dissatisfaction and started watching the defile between the rocks on the upper horizon—the one that the traveler from Tannourine or Laqlouq has to cross. Our hope was to catch a glimpse of an image that would restore some hope and energy to our souls.

While we were thus occupied, other guests climbing up to the Cedars arrived. Doctor Farhat had invited some of his friends and mine who were spending the summer months in Lehfed. They arrived without our even noticing, but we could hear the sounds of welcome being offered. We went over to join in the welcome and were delighted by the sight of the people who had arrived: among them were three lovely women who could make men forget all about hunger and thirst, particularly in the mountain wastes.

The women were wearing dresses that were simple, yet elegant; they had sandals on their feet and were carrying canes. Their expressions showed no signs of weariness or heat from the sun; instead, their cheeks, rosy and jasmine-colored, were blooming, their lipstick was well placed, and their voices were pure and resonant. It was as though they had only just emerged from their boudoirs.

All that was the initial surprise. After we had all exchanged greetings, there came the questions.

"Did they ride up?"

"We're from this mountain," one of them replied. "This mountain holds no challenges for us."

"So you walked?" I asked, just to make sure.

"Yes, we walked."

"From Jaj?"

"No, from Lehfed."

That was the second surprise, duly tinged with a sense of pride and admiration. Who would not have such feelings when talking about an educated, refined woman who can tackle hardships just as well as men? Not only that, but they can even compete with them, and in terms of resolve and energy, surpass some of them.

Once these new guests had arrived, we all began to feel the refreshing breezes of sociability. Aggravation died down, and conversations took over.

The third surprise was that one of the beauties,[1] "daughters of this mountain," was a literary writer, one of those who love everything Arab and admire Arabic literature. They were all just like Doctor Farhat's wife and sister, good in French but always speaking in Arabic. Dear reader, these women are part of the very heart of Lebanon: they love it as much as the author of *The Inspiring Mountain* (Charles Corm); their feelings about it are as zealous as those of the composer of the country's national anthem; and they are as proud of it as is the writer of these lines. They are indeed noble Lebanese Arab

1. She was Philomene Lahoud. I hesitated to mention her name, but then people told me that it was not a problem. What this writer can remember about her—and she is still alive—is her distinction in two separate beauties: of face and intellect. God is indeed generous and the Great Protector.

women, of whom we can all be proud and to whom we can bow our heads.

Even seated beneath the cedar tree, conversation could be heavy.

"What is beauty?" asked one of the writers present.

Various people took up the question and expressed an opinion.

"Beauty is a matter of taste," one of the women replied, "and tastes differ."

"Real beauty," another woman, even more beautiful than the first, commented, "lies hidden in the visible aspects of beauty."

We all applauded, and the writer cheered, "Joy, joy!"

"If it didn't make the others jealous," he whispered in my ear, "we could elect her queen of beauty!"

At this point my mind was far removed from notions of vacational beauty queens or even summer beauties. In reflecting on Lebanese beauty here at the feet of the Cedars, I was not privileging emotion over mind. Even so, the location had its impact on heads as well as souls. Beneath the Cedars even less beautiful women would still look beautiful; that was undoubtedly true. And there was something else: there was none more beautiful than a beautiful woman at the feet of the Cedars. This is what I told myself when that particular writer surprised me with the idea of electing the queen of beauty.

We now emerged from the shade and started walking among the rocks in broad daylight. I was still thinking about female beauty and using it to furnish a corner of the Lebanese heart. I changed my opinion about the beauty beneath the cedar tree, and now told myself that there was nothing more beautiful than a beautiful woman amid the rocks. I was right on both counts.

The charms of the beautiful woman beneath the cedar tree contrasted with a noble element in the beauties of created beings. And yet, the contrast did not diminish her beauty in any way; indeed, it served to enhance the splendor of those very same human charms. The beauty amid the rocks was the gentlest, loveliest, and softest of God's creations, confronting the roughest, most silent, rugged, and dire of His creations. In the first context she was a fantasy of God's own creativity; in the second, one of His miracles.

There is another difference as well. Certain qualities in a refined woman—bright eyes and a glowing smile, for example, look even lovelier in the shade. But the face as a whole—its complexion, expressions, and light and dark shades—they are all more beautiful amid the rocks in sunlight than they are beneath shady trees.

After such philosophizing, I would say that the nicest thing that a man can do in these mountain heights amid the rocks is to kiss a lovely face in admiration and respect, even if it is his own wife. The memory of that kiss will linger in both hearts, wife and husband, along with memories of the place itself, which will remain as firmly rooted as the rocks themselves and as green as the Cedars. Have any of us men ever done that? At this juncture has the "philosopher" just served as a model for emulation?

Good God, what do esteem and fame bring about?! Dear reader, I was a respected "philosopher" (and may God protect you from philosophy and respect and make all your memories beautiful ones!), I say again, a respected philosopher, but, woe is me, to my regret there was no kiss!

Please forgive me, lovely lady reader! I kiss your hand and place a safflower, the first mountain flower to bloom after the summer, on the tomb of the little hour that we lost . . .

Now, I return to the account of our day. While we were sitting on the rocks, we heard a gunshot. We rushed over to the source of the sound and discovered some hunters having a shooting competition and bragging about it. There was a young man with a cigarette in his hand standing five meters away, while a chaotic shouting match was in progress. We approached the men involved to find out what was going on, and discovered that one was claiming and another boasting that, with a single shot from his revolver, he could split the cigarette in the man's hand in two. The young man was standing there, completely unconcerned and putting on a show of idiotic courage. We put an immediate stop to this would-be heroism.

"Would it diminish the shooter's skill, I wonder," we asked them, "if the cigarette were placed in the rock's hand rather than the young man's? Put it on a rock and prove your point, if you're serious."

Those "heroes" listened and put the cigarette on the rock. The first of them fired his revolver, but the shot went wide. The second fired and hit the rock, but the cigarette stayed where it was. We now congratulated the shooters on their skill, and complimented the courageous but stupid young man on having his hand intact!

Now gunshots started reverberating among the rocks. It seems that the men were tired of waiting; they started shooting for fun. Then we heard them singing, and we watched as, with rifles raised, they started up the track leading to the mountaintop. In the defile, they spotted their friends coming up from Laqlouq. They started singing:

Hey, Master, look and see,
Flags and swords agleam,
Hey, Master, it's been too long

Rifles and revolvers were fired. The curtain was raised on a festive scene, with the women raising their voices in ululations.

Fog had transformed the atmosphere and thickened over the mountains. At this moment it started to dissolve, and the sky started to drizzle on us, creating both a pleasant melody among the cedar branches and a superb scenario with the rain falling on the forest like silver threads.

Just then the prophet of the entire group came up to me. The previous night he had prophesied that today would be rainy. As he approached me, there was the glint of a joke in his eye and a note of triumph at the edge of his mouth. I encouraged him to speak his mind.

"The Lord has not wanted the scenario to be lacking," I said. "He acted it all out in the summertime, now here He is—may He be praised and glorified!—showing us the beauties of winter!"

He nodded his head. "We're very hungry," he said. "Very hungry."

The waiting time was rapidly diminishing. The Laqlouq group appeared, then disappeared again. They were all on foot—God preserve them all, both men and women! The echo of rifle shots and the sound of singing was even more spectacular as they moved further away and disappeared. Inside the house the echo of swords and the jingling of knives and echoes had a much greater effect on people's hearts than proximity and sight would have done.

Who do you think was in the lead? Who was in front? A lovely woman, by God, another beautiful woman, a slender, delicate blonde, who arrived breathing quite calmly, as though she were either coming from or going to church.

We welcomed her and wished her well. Applauding her resolve, we placed her on the seat of honor beneath the largest cedar—with a cloak spread over the rocks. Now the singing continued, more shots were fired, and ululations rang out. From a cluster of rocks close by a group of horsemen emerged, carrying on their shoulders the lord of Laqlouq, a worthy son of the mountains, Asaad Younis.

Him too we welcomed and wished well. Applauding his resolve, we placed him beside the slender blonde on the seat of honor beneath the largest cedar.

Now the rest of the group arrived, with a young boy, Asaad Younis's son, at its head, and another lovely, delicate girl, the blonde's sister.

The gunfire started again, as did the singing. The back of the group now appeared. The "horsemen" were carrying on their shoulders—or rather, over their heads—their leader, the very soul of *The Inspiring Mountain*, the poet of the sun and friend of every gifted and wronged person, Charles Corm.

We welcomed him three times, gave him our warmest greetings, and sat him down on the roughest part of the rock between the two sisters. We needed to put a cloak around him and call the doctor, but the sound of his voice gave denial to his pallor. When he left Laqlouq, he had been feverish, and the fever had worsened on the way. Now, after four solid hours of walking and climbing through the mountains, his temperature was thirty-nine degrees Celsius. Even so, he persevered and bore it all stoically, much to the surprise of his friends and us.

"The amazing views that appeared in front of me, one after the other," Charles Corm told us, "were wonderfully varied in their magnificence and splendor. Thank God, they made me forget about my fever. I can confirm for you that such delight bolsters the knees!"

With that explanation and display of fortitude, we no longer needed to feel sorry for him.

The guns had fallen silent and so had the singing. The panpipe player started blowing into his instrument, and men and women rushed to the central space to form a circle and dance the dabke:

> Sweet gazelle by the stream,
> Take a sip so I can say "cheers"!
> Pity you! If I die,
> Who would you have for lover?

The sound of the pipe grew louder, and everyone clapped their hands, young and old alike. Asaad Younis was at the head of the circle, pounding the soil sometimes like a gazelle, at others like a wolf. His loud Bedouin voice stirred everyone's enthusiasm as it resounded among the cedars and rocks:

"Hey ho, hey ho!"

Then a mat was spread over a large flat space with rocks all around it. One group sat down on it, while the rest formed other circles. The village girls and servants brought out both cooked and raw meats, stuffed vegetables and kebab. Doctor Farhat's sister did the rounds of the guests, carrying glasses, while at her side a young man had a bottle of arak.

> Pour it, ye wine steward
> And say, "Welcome to my beloveds"!

We watched the doctor's wife as she was visible everywhere, manager and servant at the same time. She kept offering food to the different circles of guests and sharing with them the contents of her hand and heart.

The reader will have to accept my apologies for the way I have celebrated these Lebanese women and their like, my sisters in these mountains; sisters who preserve for all of us and the mountains the values of the essential Lebanese heritage—generosity, kindness, chivalry, and humility.

I sat down on the mat between two of them and opposite the two sisters who were always smiling. I was told that they were from Egypt. I was amazed by their beauty, of both figure and character, and also by their resolve and energy. They had both endured the hardships of the trek and surmounted the mountain's obstacles just like men.

Were they from Egypt? No, sir, they were not. Their father was Lebanese, and their mother was a Lebanese woman from Kesrouan. But both parents had emigrated long ago and become Egyptianized—or rather, Europeanized (may God forgive them for doing that!). However, in spite of their becoming Europeanized, the essential seed—their seed—had not lost any of its wonderful Lebanese essence, nor its Lebanese initiative. God bless those two Lebanese sisters! Now that they had made the pilgrimage to the Cedars of Jaj on foot, we could forgive them their French turn of phrase.

The sun started to poke its way gently through the clouds and shed a soft glimmer of light in the distance over the entire spectacle laid out in front of us to the northeast. We could see it lighting up the sea by Ras Shaqaa and shining above the mountains of Koura. Through its translucent veil we could spot Tripoli, and, after a little while, the island of Arwad.

The sun continued to comb the clouds with its golden nails, opening a window for its light to shine over Batroun and a door above Douma. From its gold and the silver of the clouds it began to weave a pattern in our high-up atmosphere, clothing the cedars and rocks in multicolored garments.

Bidding this spectacular, magical scene farewell, we all began the return journey by the shortest route; in other words, using shortcuts with no roads or tracks. We all held each other's hands as we traversed slopes only suitable for rolling or sliding down!

Even so, we still heard the panpipe playing and the singers chanting their songs. Every time we reached a flat spot among the rocks or an extended space at the base of the mountain, the male and female dancers would form some kind of circle and perform the dabke to the very end!

Here is a solitary cedar tree, which stayed with us as we circled around, giving us a kind and generous farewell. Then it left us, shrouded by the towering heights.

The sun set, to the sound of panpipes, bidding it farewell with a melody of parting and rebuke.

We were still only halfway back. We kept jumping over rocks or else walking single file underneath them. It was dusk, and it was running apace, so we had to keep up in order to reach the safety of the main road.

Once there, the sky lit our way with some bright stars and escorted us to Jaj.

Fifth Journey

To Laqlouq

Contents

By the Ibrahim River

WE ARE STILL LIVING in the country from which our ancestors emigrated, in Byblos. Before the caravan sets off—the car caravan, that is—we should introduce our readers to our companions on the journey. There are many of them—and may God grant us safety as we set out on our travels.

I am using the term *many* rather than *a large group* because I abhor this innovation in language use—indeed, this linguistic upheaval—in modern literature. I also abhor those threefold phrases whenever they occur either at the end of a sentence or at a stopping point in the middle. I only ever use words that are inevitable. Silent for the eyes, the heart, and the soul—all dead! Even so, they impinge on the mouth and force it to stop; or, more accurately, it is all frivolous and random. If they occur at the end of the sentence—and how very few writers there are today who can choose good words with which to bring a sentence to a stop, there is no way of avoiding two stops. That involves something worse than death itself—namely, that teeth collide with the tongue since it cannot move quickly enough.

Since I am using *many* here, there is no problem for you; you are in a veritable haven of movement—or indeed, of life.

Perhaps knowledgeable linguists—excuse me, pseudo-knowledgeable linguists—will accept this linguistic abstract from me, as God accepts the Fatiha of the Qur'an from devout believers.[1] Perhaps we will receive from Him that which comes to devout believers, so that

1. The Fatiha is the opening sura of the Qur'an.

the difficult passes in front of us can be easily surmounted, and we only encounter beloved friends in the mountains.

So here we are at the designated time for our meeting, on the Ibrahim River, but not at the usual open place where, at a single glance, we noticed on both sides of the road by the bridge a cafe, women, a tent, and some beds. The women were still there, standing by the doors; their cheeks had the color of pomegranates, their lips wore the smiles of the beloved, and their eyes laden with eye shadow offered greetings of welcome. Byblos, may God bless your Phoenician girls and their ancient Lord who still watches over them and kindles in their hearts some of his temple fire.

We stopped between some of the cafes, but then retraced our steps. We had not lost our way, but the river's songs kept rising and falling. Someone invited us into the portico inside the garden, which lay behind the main road and away from the crowds of people.

Yes indeed, the river had been civilized, whispering, not shouting, and mouthing frank and eloquent remarks about hospitality. How could it be otherwise when the store on the road had turned into the cafe by the defile situated by the inner bank of the river, beneath a curtain of grapevines and Persian cane, shaded by sycamore and willow trees?

On our way there we crossed the old stone bridge, which was still occupied by muleteers and farmers. Between the bridge and the sea alongside the road there was a stretch of high land planted with bananas and lemons, a new crop for this ancient terrain. You barely had time to ask how the terrain was irrigated when the river is so much lower, before someone would tell you: "There's a power station with machinery and pumps to scoop up the river water and lift it forty feet to a point above the orchards' terrain," thus bringing them life and granting them the means for wealth and prosperity.

On the other bank of the river was a mill and an ice factory, both employing men and women. Pack animals kept coming and going, sheep and cows grazed amid the mulberry trees, and flocks of domestic birds enjoyed the refuse—for them the bounty—of the mill.

The cafe was behind the power station and in front of the ice factory. It was modern civilization personified, with all its commercial, agricultural, and industrial aspects. Inside there was another aspect of development: people well trained as waiters with no chatter involved. There was also a row of splendid, lofty sycamores providing shade for a row of tables alongside them, a long line with a concrete railing to separate the two.

The shade that sycamores and willows provided is rarely oppressive or dry. That is because they are continually wafted by the breeze that rarely comes empty-handed. From the sea it brings wafts of its moist, salty wind; from the mountains it passes over orchards, where it could pick up the sweet scents to scatter over the shade of these trees. Alongside the cafe there was a flower garden and below it a vegetable garden; beneath the two was yet another garden of bananas and lemons that disappeared into the valley gorge.

If you spotted some rosy cheeks through one of the windows of the café owner's house—whose broad eaves looked like those of a house in China, I do not think you would prefer that sight to the rose color so close to you here. The very atmosphere of the place lifts you to a higher plane of spiritual pleasure and endows the heart with a joyful feeling purified by a sense of serenity and repose. You are content just to look at the rose, to sit in the willow's shade, to enjoy the scented breeze, and to savor the river's eddies.

You might stand on the riverbank behind the railing, watching those eddies like a traveler on a boat looking at the sea. You give your own dreams free rein, and then the incredible happens, the miracle: while you are staring hard at the flowing water, the scene is reversed, and you imagine yourself on a boat in a river moving in the opposite direction to the flow of the waves, which seem so calm. It is an optical illusion, one that makes you imagine that you are climbing from the river to the mountain!

If this type of promenade game does not appeal to you, and you prefer truth to imagination even in the gardens of the Ibrahim River, then the geese paddling through the river's waves should make you stop and observe. Their haven is close to the mill. Here is a goose floating as it makes its way through the glittering water that soon covers it up to the wings; it spreads them as it rides atop the wave that is carrying it toward the sea. The goose then moves back up the river, swimming with supreme confidence even though she is moving against the flow of the river. The return is neither easy nor short; quite the contrary, she has to keep on swimming hard until she reaches the spot where she entered the river. Once there, she can return to her own games, her pasture, and her haven beneath the mill's willows.

If you are patient enough to watch her for a quarter of an hour, you will be surprised by one aspect of her instinctive intelligence. She can plow through the river waves time after time, riding them down and then swimming against them back up again. Swimming against the current is hard, and she is well aware of the extent of her abilities. So she never goes too far downstream, but only so far and no further. This rarely changes. She swims back upstream to her haven beneath the mill's willows; she is an instinctively intelligent goose. You will seldom encounter a human being who understands and acts on a similar level of wisdom. How many people do not take the process of return into account when they embark on the temptations of desire and pleasure?

Forgive me, dear reader! Perhaps this kind of inquiry does not interest you. Here we are on the riverbank, at a spot where the waves lap gently and linger in the folds of the scented breeze. We sat at tables in the shade of the sycamores. The waiters brought us gaming boards, then nargilehs and coffee, and, after all that, arrack and *mezze*. We then had lunch, including some tasty river fish, of which we ate one after another, along with the heads.

Now we were joined by our travel companion. He rose like the Tammuz sun (meaning both the month of July and the deity) with arms spread and rosy cheeks. He greeted us warmly with tongue, heart, and eyes. Here he is walking between two friends, a man and a woman, from peoples living over the seas—the Mediterranean and the Ocean of Darkness.[2]

2. By which he means the Mediterranean and the Atlantic Ocean.

He is Charles Corm. One day he rose from his bed like Lord Byron, with renown ahead of him bringing him coffee on a silver platter, alongside it a crown of thorns. Or was it laurel? Charles raised it in front of him and gave it a single affectionate glance, no more. Then he stood in front of the mirror and let out a laugh like Rabelais.[3]

"I wish I had died earlier," Fame said, "then I would have been forgotten."

Fame now started following Charles Corm to have her revenge. He ran away and wandered around the valleys—and, as the Qur'an states, poets wander in every valley.[4] Now here he is in the valley of our Phoenician ancestors, the valley of Adonis and Aphrodite, seeking their protection from tyranny.

Here was one of the servants of Fame, that houri of tyranny, coming from America to investigate the reality of this Lebanese, Phoenician, French poet in order to ask him—if he gets hold of him, that is—a human truth that could be touched and seen. I say, "If he gets hold of him" because he might turn out to be a myth from the land of myths, a tangible human, poetic truth. One wonders, why did he laugh that Rabelaisian laugh that wonderful morning?

Is that what garlands are for? Is this how the red lady deals with the houri of tyranny? Even from America, she and her tyranny send you someone who speaks well, bringing with him the cup from which devotees have drunk earlier and wished to be forgotten for all time.

Oh the apathy of memory among people.

Here is a man of words come to spread it!

"You're a poet too? Where did you learn? What's the name of your first collection? How many collections have you written? What's your mother's name? Are you married? Is your wife a poet like you? My

3. A reference to the French writer Francois Rabelais (1483–1553), who was famous for his sarcasm.

4. Translator's note: a reference to a verse in sura 26 (The Poets) of the Qur'an: 26v225.

wife writes as well. Do readers in this country like poetry? What are your favorite foods, drinks, games, colors, etc. . . ."

This man has come from tyranny itself, from the lands beyond the Atlantic. He wanted to collect information for an article or book, like his American colleagues who roam the earth in quest of wonders and curiosities. They enter the city and leave it along with the sun after meeting everyone of any significance. They talk to such people, then write a book about it, although nothing like *The Marvels of Creation*.[5]

This literary writer came with his wife, who was also a writer. She was a young woman with a languid eye and thin lips like a rose petal. He arrived with respects for Charles Corm, who was now accompanying him and his wife by car to the famous Adonis Valley.

Who says that Charles Corm is no good at politics and is a prude? Charles brought this writer to us in order to get rid of him. If we had not had with us some of the genuine masters of conversation, in the forefront our friend Ibrahim Hitti, descendant of the ancient Hittites, we would not have succeeded.

Ibrahim took on this writer and sat him down on the interrogation chair after establishing that he was going to ask the questions. He aimed an entire barrage of questions at both him and his author wife: answer these questions! In this endeavor he was helped by Toufiq Hasan Shartooni, our literary colleague of lofty, shining, and confident brow, with both money and children. If he were not a well-heeled writer or wealthy litterateur, he would be a member of Parliament or government magistrate. In asking his questions, he never went from *A* to *Z* because from *Z* he would always go back and finish with *A*.

His translator was his uncle, Iskandar, always laughing. He was good at English and dealing with money matters. He could be both direct and chatty whether the conversation was nasty or witty.

Among the travel group there were Lebanese women and young girls whose presence enhanced our meetings. Their large, sleepy eyes put those of the blue-eyed American woman to shame.

5. Translator's note: a reference to a work by Al-Qazvini (1203–83).

"Do you speak French well?" we asked her.

"Unfortunately no," she replied and fell silent.

Her forthright husband fell silent too, but only after he had remained stolid—truth be told, memorable but not repeatable—in the face of the onslaught aimed at him by Officer Ibrahim and his two adjutants, Toufiq and Iskandar.

The Lebanese Mandate over Yemen

WE LEFT THE CAFE safe and sound and got in the cars, which took us some fifteen kilometers on the sea road to the suburbs of Byblos, where it turned into a winding road that was newly surfaced with fresh tar. We passed by Blat, the only village between the coast and Tourzaya. In Blat there is an ancient church to which Charles Corm drew our attention.

Whenever Charles Corm draws your attention to an ancient monument in Lebanon, you can say that it is Phoenician or that it contains some Phoenician elements—be it a stone from a temple or a rock from a burial site. It seems that this particular church is constructed from ancient ruins, undoubtedly older than the Greco-Roman period; yes indeed, it is Phoenician.

This road becomes even more developed the further up we go; it is the best road we have encountered that has not yet been covered in tar. From the coast to Tourzaya it is twenty-two kilometers. To the right it overlooks an expansive valley with lots of greenery and farmland. On the slopes facing us there are lots of villages, one of which is Hsoun, the village where the Awdeh[1] is buried. I noticed that it benefited from a gently sloping plain; it was certainly not the way it seemed when we came down to it from Bir el-Hait, and it looked like a deep chasm in the valley. All of which shows that the way things really are is never completely clear if they are only observed from a single viewpoint. Coming from Bir al-Hait, Hsoun seems to be buried in

1. Ancestral treasure.

A peasant's house appeared on one of the mountain peaks. It would be a simple stone hut of the same hue as the rock from which it was made.

the valley; whereas, coming from Tourzaya, it is situated comfortably in the heart of the valley.

Tourzaya, which is 950 meters above sea level, has a gushing spring, a tent, a store, and a kind of hotel with beds gleaming white as they dry in the sunlight. They all—tent, hotel, and store—overlook the valley on whose shoulders Tourzaya rides and shakes her feet. Between those two feet you can see peasant housing and agricultural land, most of which, we were told, is owned by the monks.

We sat in the tent to rest for a while and look out on the valley spread out below us east by west. Below this mountain is buried the *Awdeh* (ancestral treasure), to which I gave one final glance, one of farewell.

Inside the tent we met a member of the Lebanese government under the Dabbas administration, one of its stellar sons who carries a painful memory in his heart and the ribbon of the Legion of Honor in his buttonhole.

The well-paved road continued from Tourzaya to Qartaba, with a side road going up to Ehmej and Laqlouq. That was the one we took, with plenty of curves and steep inclines and poorly surfaced, just the opposite of the carefully paved roads that we had been using.

After climbing about 200 meters we reached Ehmej, the base of the Byblos region's mountain heights from the time of Fakhreddine, through Emir Basheer, to the Ottoman era. The village is 1,300 meters above sea level. Here were its ancient wells, its Phoenician sarcophagi, and its church. Here too were its age-old oaks shading its square, Latin inscriptions, and a road dug by a Roman general to connect Byblos with "the city of the sun" (Baalbek). And here was the home of our friend, also friend of Arabian horses and expert on their particular characteristics and pedigrees; he had published a book on the subject, a service to that "pearl of the desert," the Arabian stallion, which had given birth to noble offspring now scattered across the globe.

Wherever you are in the world—be it Tokyo, London, San Francisco, or Leningrad—when you talk about thoroughbred horses, you mean Arabian. In Lebanon no one knows more about such horses than Najeeb Bey Khoury from Ehmej, who lives in the town and is content with his life's portion in the shade of oak trees and the memory of the heroism of its sons.

We noticed some Public Works laborers, repairing the road. In these mountains there is a splendid, awe-inspiring sight as soon as you leave Ehmej. Greenery is scant, the number of rocks multiplies, and the mountain peaks fuse together. To our right the valley starts to contract, getting narrower and narrower until above Ehmej it turns into a deep, gloomy shadow.

These wonderful vistas reminded me of the mountains in Yemen, especially when a peasant house appeared on one of the mountain peaks. It would be a simple stone hut of the same hue as the rock from which it was made. It is the same in Yemen. They build their towers and fortresses on the mountaintops. Since they all use a single-colored stone from the mountain, the houses all blend together and are not clearly visible to the attacking enemy. Here and there, in both Lebanon and Yemen, people have used a color derived from their environment in order to be invisible, a self-defense mechanism just like birds.

Here laborers and muleteers are still wearing the same short-sleeved, brocade-backed coat, which in the last century was emir's dress but is actually the same Yemeni garment that people still wear there. You might say that mountains are mountains wherever they may be; the two mountains are brothers anywhere—and, if not completely so, then at least partially.

In this context I can now pose a question. These Lebanese people remind me of Yemenis, and on more than one count involving their situation and many of their features and shapes. The elongated skull, for example, the high cheekbones, long nose, cone-shaped face, and wide mouth, all are characteristic of the Himyari people. What, one wonders, is the connection between the Lebanese and those people of South Arabia? Are the Lebanese the ancestors of the Himyari people, or vice versa?

I am inclined to believe that the prehistoric emigration was from north to south, particularly after the last ice age, which covered the entire northern region as far as the Mediterranean some fifty thousand years ago. The inhabitants who survived moved south. Can anyone object to my contention that the prehistoric emigration was from north to south and thus from this blessed location in Lebanon to Khawlan and Hamdan in Yemen?!

Could it be that their forebears were descendants of a people inhabiting these mountains that were later to be called Lebanon? Fleeing the sea of ice, they neither stopped nor felt safe until they reached a mountain range like the one they had left behind. Could it be also that the Yemeni Zaidis today, who decorate their heads with branches of sweet basil, and the Maronites, who still grow sweet basil on the verandas of their mountain homes, are actually cousins, from a single mountain progeny?

Could Zeid ibn Zein al-Abideen be a descendant of Adonis, the ornament of the gods? With all this in mind, do the Lebanese have the right to claim authority over Yemen and to extend their protection to that felicitous country? What would His Beatitude the patriarch have to say about a Lebanese mandate in Sanaa?

The Patriarch's Spring

WE REACHED the head of the valley, which became narrower and less deep as we climbed upward. These geological features high up in the mountains are really eye-catching, especially because they are devoid of anything that might keep them wholly or partially hidden.

After looking down into the valley, we reached its entryway, its head, its narrows, its weakest point, where, in olden times, the rains and winds of hurricanes had cut through. When we say *olden times* here, we mean going back millions of years—between twenty and forty million.

Water had coursed through that passage, those narrows. The plains had dispatched their swollen rivers, which had started digging into the valley to the west; every time the slope increased, so did the force of the water, causing the valley to widen and deepen. Then peasant man arrived after hunter man and built terraces that kept back the soil. They planted wheat and barley. We are the descendants of those peasants, paving roads and traveling in cars to reach the mountain heights whose sides have now bowed to man's powerful arms and whose core has obeyed his voice and the plow.

As we entered the narrows, the road had a peculiar effect on our ribs and stomachs. We felt as though we were traveling as a kind of steam device for crushing rocks, and we were the crushed rocks. I did not feel as sorry for anyone in the group as I did for my friend Charles Corm because I was aware that this road was not hurting him as much as it was affecting his behavior and kindly feelings toward his two American companions. They all got out of the car and started walking to lessen some of the problems caused by the road.

It looked like a pharaoh's obelisk with the house below it like a tomb.

I said earlier that, for people knowledgeable about geology, the high mountains provide the best manifestations of creation and disintegration. The best of such manifestations are their geological surprises. The narrows were actually not all that long; they eventually brought us to lush, open plains, gorgeous green hills, and pearly flowing water.

How lovely are these green fields, lined, colored, and edged with flowers and yellow hues—rows of potatoes like regimented phalanxes; rows of tomatoes like long emerald necklets, fields of wheat and barley, and flatlands where heads of corn swayed, and the sounds of cattle bellowing, donkeys braying, and horses neighing could be heard. To which you can add the gruff, calm voice of human beings, farmers and peasants.

What was that lofty rock behind the house on that hill? It looked like a pharaoh's obelisk with the house below it like a tomb. On a veranda a man and woman were standing; actually, when you came closer, there were three or four men on the veranda and a single woman. They all stood there watching us, expecting that we would stop by the stairs leading up to them.

It was not a tomb. Maybe it was a store on the rock, with an old walnut tree alongside it laden with nuts and offering plentiful shade. The car stopped, and we got out and climbed up to the place, our only motivation being curiosity—for people in quest of knowledge, curiosity is a laudable trait. What we wanted was some information that would benefit readers, now that we had misled them by stating that it was a house on the rock. We were now obliged to tell the truth.

The first thing to correct was that the structure was neither a tomb nor a store. Rather, it was a small house belonging to one of the Ehmej peasants, the owner of the planted fields that we had just passed. He and his wife hastened to greet us and welcome us. The wife brought over some chairs.

"The water jug, please," we asked.

The man had gone away and came back carrying a tray with bottles and glasses on it.

"Have some beer," he said, "then we'll bring some water."

"How can you not stay for some coffee with us?" they insisted.

This kind of hospitality reminded me of Yemen and the sultan, who had sent some of his armed servants to offer us breakfast.

Hospitality never asks questions until its basic functions are completed. While we were drinking coffee, one of the tough local men—and the north regularly produces such people—asked who we distinguished visitors were. One of our group pointed at me and mentioned my name.

The man was astonished and let out a yell. He was someone who reads newspapers and books and was proud of it—I was afraid he might be one of those people who would not be proud.

"The gentleman is Sheikh Boutros Saba Khoury," the wife told us, introducing the person who had asked the question. Sheikh Boutros now proceeded to introduce us to the owner of the house.

"Your hosts are Saba Ibrianos and his *hourma* (wife)."

A very British mode of introduction, as though Ehmej was a town in the Scottish Highlands.

I admired the sheikh for saying *hourma*. For people of taste it is much nicer than saying simply *wife*, *spouse*, *companion*, or *madame*. *Hourma* does not imply any kind of restrictions or fetters as do *the man's consort* and the like. *Hourma* conveys respect, and the word is pure Arabic.

But what about the husband's name: Ibrianos. What is your job, sir, and where do you get that name? That name is enough to kill off any hope of Lebanese-Yemeni unity or of a Lebanese mandate over Yemen. But this man, with the three dreadful names—Boutros, Saba, Ibrianos—was actually the very best of men, honoring his guests, striking with the sword, and building his house (just like his Yemeni colleague in Khawlan) amid the rocks, as did his eagle colleagues.

We asked the lady wife about the walnut tree; how much did it produce?

"Five to six thousand kernels," she replied.

"But your tree, Master," Sheikh Boutros commented, "produces more, and they're nicer and more beneficial."

I choked on my coffee and called Charles Corm over to introduce him to the sheikh.

The way they greeted and honored us before finding out who we were was a splendid example of ancient Lebanese customs, which shine brightly for their hospitality, generosity, and kindness. It is a fine instinct to be found in Lebanese people—one of the qualities that distinguished their ancestors in olden times and continue to be found in these remote locations.

Before saying farewell to this noble and generous man with his awesome name, his lady wife, and the goodly Sheikh Boutros, we did a tour of the house to discover its secret and that of the rock. But there was no secret worth mentioning. There was a tall, obelisk-shaped rock of great age and a hut built alongside it—or, more accurately, in front of it—so that from a distance it looked like a hole at the base of the rock.

A young man came over with the water jug. We had forgotten about it and had drunk instead some stream water as cold as ice. Sheikh Boutros told us some more about the place: the house, rock, walnut tree, and spring were all called the Patriarch's Spring.

"Patriarch's Spring?" we asked in curiosity.

"Even if we clip off two letters from the phrase," the Sheikh commented, "it won't damage either the spring or the patriarch!"

"One day a patriarch passed by here," Toufiq Shartooni told us, "and took a drink from this spring. That's how it got its name."

"I think that's right," Sheikh Boutros responded.

"That's the truth!" Mr. Ibrianos said. "But now we should be calling it Rihani's Spring!"

What can I say about Saba Boutros Ibrianos? Life is never unruffled for anyone. Even if it is pure at its origin, it can still turn murky at the baptismal font.

Laqlouq

THE HIGHEST POINT on the mountain road, one filled with summer resorts, is Dahr el-Baidar (1,550 meters), but it has a rapid downhill slope. In winter the snow melts, and in summer the soil does not produce enough herbage even for goats. You will often see goats there twitching and wagging their tails—no grass and no water.

The extensive plain lying below Dahr el-Baidar is no more than 900 meters above sea level at Chtoura. Because of its central location, its medium altitude, and its plentiful supply of water, it has fertile soil and abundant resources. This is Lebanon, storehouse of varieties of wheat and cereals.

Laqlouq[1] is higher than Dahr el-Baidar (1,750 meters); its soil is rich, and it has plenty of water. That is because it is surrounded by mountains. Out of sheer love, their ice melts, and their streams continually carry downward material to renew its bounty, whether already grown or still buried. Among these mountains—the guardians of Laqlouq's blessings—are peaks over 3,000 meters above sea level.

These fertile levels in the mountain heights were remarkable, lying, as they did, above and below other levels, which were rocky and desolate. It was as though God had decided to dig the mountain or mountains, had thrown a handful of soil into the hole, and then said to man: "Here is your inheritance. If you plow and sow it, you will be successful."

1. Also known as La'lou'.

However, the land around Laqlouq has very few trees. If poplars and prickly willows had been planted at least on the edge of fields to mark properties, then they might have protected the village from the winds, provided it with some shade, and made it a desirable place for nonlocal people to stay. In fact, it would be possible to cultivate the superior American apple in these high locations because of the cold temperature, soil, and water.

It is time to stop talking about agriculture and continue on our way. Leaving the Patriarch's Spring, we pass by Ain Bayyadeh and discover that there are a number of springs in these heights and all share a single name, Laqlouq, which is now opening its arms to welcome us.

The road improves, the horizon expands, and the atmosphere turns into a stage for the rays of the afternoon sun and the gentle breezes of dusk. The ground gives off lovely scents that would flummox the perfumer and even the chemist. Even through analysis they would not be able to identify their complex and mysterious components.

If you happen to be afraid of the cold, I hasten to reassure you that the noonday sun in Laqlouq is hotter than it is on the coast, nor does it take away all its heat at sunset. Some of it is left behind for nighttime, which keeps things warm. In summer you only need one cover at night.

Earlier I used a poetic turn of phrase when talking about digging a hole in the mountain and scattering a handful of soil in it. Now I have to tell you that knowledge and poetry are not all that different on this issue. Some ten or twenty million years ago in the geological history of the earth, this hole, this wide, deep pit was a lake; crocodiles and dolphins swam in it, and it was often visited by goats and deer. Then the waters rose as the result of lengthy storms. Pressure began to build on the mud at the edge of the lake, leading to the collapse of its weakest point. The limestone and sandstone layers in the mountain were pierced to the west, becoming the narrows that we have just passed through. After that, the water started digging into the valley that we overlooked on our way here. It grew wider and deeper, and conducted its business with artistic skill. There were canyons and curves; chasms and plateaus; plains and hills; streams, flatlands; slopes and creeks.

Today that dry lake in which is collected the mountain soil and stream deposits—cracked on its west side and demolished to both east and west, that dry lake is now called Laqlouq.

Where did that name come from? Why was it called that? Since when has it been called by that name? Is it the name of a place, an animal, or a person? As if asking questions had become contagious, I gathered the need to pose this barrage from the American writer, the messenger—or was it the butcher?—of fame to Charles Corm.

Questioning might well be aggravating, and yet ignorance is even more so. Ignorance stands there in amazement—this particular expression occurred to me the following morning, so I must ask you to excuse me for using it here. I stand in amazement before you—in other words, silent, incapable, and also confused, asking questions in the name of and because of this place and yet unable to answer them.

Is it spelled *La'lou'* with the apostrophe or *Laqlouq* with *Q*s? In Ehmej and Tourzaya I heard people saying *Laqlouq*. One of them saw me writing it that way and told me it was wrong; it should be with *Q*s. I also heard other people pronouncing it elegantly as Laqlouq. The villagers in the high mountains are just as baffled and ignorant as I am.

Having admitted that, I think we can indulge in a bit of guesswork and conjecture. Were these springs named Laqlouq from the verb *laqlaqa*, meaning "to make a sound or to chatter"? But none of the many springs there today make any sound worth mentioning. Or is the name of the village derived from the name of the stork (*laqlaaq*)? But no storks are to be found there today, nor is there any trace of them in those mountain heights.

What is undoubtedly true is that Arabs frequented these springs, drank from them, and cleaned their flocks there. They also used to frolic there (a colloquial term meaning "to fool around in the water") and muddy the area around the springs. So they turned the area into marshes and swamps, to which, if possible, the Lebanese colloquial word *laqlouq* (scruffy) applies.

However, educated people in the neighboring villages and those who visit the place during the summer are not happy with this interpretation. They prefer to remove the *Q* sound—in fact, so that some of them can even pronounce it!

One of those people actually surprised me, he being an adherent of the Laqlouq group, by suggesting that the word is actually derived from *lu'lu'* (pearl), a simile for the bubbles that would appear on the water's surface where the spring emerges. That particular interpretation was plausible and indeed eloquent. Even so, I have an interpretation that is better and more logical (and we are now fixing the name as *Laqlouq*): it is derived from the verbal form *la'la'*, meaning "to gleam or shine." When water gushes or flows, it gleams.

We also decided something else. The man who gave it this name was a poet, a leader of the Arab Nouaym tribe. When he first saw the waters in these desolate, lofty heights, he imagined that he had received a blessing from God. In this blissful locale, everything gleamed and glistened. Mouthing poetry, he named it Laqlouq.

Now here we are in the heart of the district, among Arab tents—indeed, among hair tents, with a few stone houses dotted among them. In the square is a stand of poplar, walnut, and willow trees, while in their shade are some insect-infested donkeys and goats. Two little boys in blue shirts are playing, and voices of disapproval could be heard—loud, shrill voices in accents that were neither Bedouin nor those of Aqoura or Ehmej.

Are these voices developing like the people of the district itself? Are these stone houses having an effect on the voices and accents of the people who live there? Between the walls of those houses and beneath the roofs covered in limestone and clay, is the thick tone softening, the loud voice becoming quieter, and the gruff voice becoming smoother? Or is it rather that, whenever a Bedouin looks down at his yellow or shiny black shoes, he feels embarrassed about his thick, coarse tone of voice? He tries to make it sound softer, and those efforts have their own evil effect, corrupting him as they inevitably drag him toward the paradise of civilization.

The Arabs of Laqlouq are from the Noaim tribe, and there are two branches: the Ghashoum and Dowai'ir. Their history in this particular region of Lebanon is as unknown as the name of the place. What is confirmed is that they were here during the era of Emir Basheer, and it is likely that they came here, were moved here, or obtained permission to settle here during the time of Emir Fakhreddeen al-Maany.

Their number stays fairly constant. The elders living in neighboring villages recall and state that there were about eighty homes or about five hundred people, and that is still the case.

When it comes to developments, the best is that people exposed to civilization sent their children to schools, and the worst concerns women—the source of all surprises. We will find out about that at the right time and place.

Emir Basheer

SHEIKH ISKANDAR KHOURY from Ehmej, who was governor of this region during the Ottoman period, tells us:

> In Emir Basheer's times these lands were government property or feudal land. The governor bought them from the people of Ehmej, Tannourine, and Aqoura, and then gave them back in return for 35 piasters that each of the three villages had to pay annually. All the land from Hadeed Spring to Hadath cost 105 piasters. The sale was entirely legal, the deed is recorded, and we have a copy of it.

Sheikh Iskandar records the name Laqlouq that way (without the *q*), "Since neither history nor knowledge can prove otherwise. So we need to go with taste."

Having said that, he hurried to greet the lady of the house.

We were fifty guests, standing in the square in front of the house, each one lost in their own thoughts and hoping to put themselves forward or find an opportunity to mingle with other people, and all out of a desire for cooperation and conversation.

The atmosphere was both pure and transparent. The air felt dry with a chilly nip to it. At first conversation was like the air and atmosphere because the spirit of the city and its civilization was still stiffly ironed into our psyches. Once that stiffness started to dissolve, the sharp, bitter aspects of the soul emerged. Everyone removed their mask, and smiles and accents only proved possible after sunset.

"Is there anywhere in the mountains other than Sofar and Aley to relax in a healthy spot with some fresh air? I've broken my ribs on this trip. When we got out of the car and started walking, I broke the heel of my boot. *Jamais, jamais de la vie . . .*"[1]

The person who said this was a Lebanese French-speaking young woman. Toufiq Shartooni spoke to her in Arabic, Ibrahim Hitti in English, and Iskandar Haddad tried his best at French.

"Dangers are one of the pleasures of travel, miss."

"*Qu'est-ce qu'il dit?*[2] I didn't understand."

"Life's delight takes the form of travel."

People who suck orange juice through a straw in Sofar and Aley think they are badly done by if they are invited to places like this.

"But it's the people who accept the invitation who are to blame."

The young woman took off her red hat in an abrupt, angry way, and used her hand to brush her black hair back violently.

"True enough, true enough!" she commented. "But I was listening to my brother, for the first time and the last."

"She says that every time," her brother replied with a laugh, "but she's always happy and satisfied when she gets back to the house."

While we were in this fix, doing our best to repair this unfortunate young lady's ribs, heart, and bootheel, Charles Corm came hurrying over, a complain in his eyes and an apology on his lips.

"I have to go back to the city now," he said.

We were all astonished and dismayed.

"The American and his wife are my guests. She wants to go back immediately because she's afraid of the road, the heights, and the cold at night. She has no desire to accompany the moon, so I have to go back with them both."

"No, by God," I said. "You don't have to go."

By now anger had taken over from shock.

"I know more than you do about American men and women. I know the language they will understand. You have come with us, and you'll go back with us. Talk to this crazy young woman about Sofar

1. Never, never!

2. What did he say?

and Aley and tell her that Laqlouq does not deserve her anger. I'll rid you now of the American and his wife without damaging your priceless high reputation.

I hurried over to the American professor.

"We have come here, sir, to convene an agricultural conference. It is essential that the poet, whom you have come from America to see in the name of fame, bringing with you a candle of light and a bouquet of flowers, participate in the proceedings. If your wife is afraid of the road and high, dark places and does not wish to stay for the moon to appear, then it would be best for you to hurry back. This driver (and I had made a point of calling Corm's car driver) is an excellent driver with calm nerves. Like his hands, his mind is always on the wheel, and his eyes can see their way through the darkness. Beyond that, he never goes faster than ten miles an hour on curves or downhill. He is at your disposal.

"Take the gentleman and his wife back to their hotel in Beirut," I told the driver. "Then you can go home."

"I'll apologize to the host on behalf of both of you," I told the Americans, "and I'll say farewell to the rest of the party."

It seems that Charles Corm had forgotten all about the Americans in defending his Lebanese sister.

"Shame on you all!" I heard him say as I was making my way back. "If she were not right, would you argue with her? You're arguing with her rather than treating her nicely, asking questions, telling her she is right, and praising her learning, beauty, and patriotism. Did she say she preferred some town in China? No, she kept her preferences within Lebanon. If you feel like arguing, then this lady will do so, and she'll do it in Arabic, just like me."

The lady in question now joined the circle and started defending this pretty and coy black-eyed young woman.

"She's right! There's nothing quite like this desolate land. Young men and women have rocks instead of music, dancing, and fun. Where is the sense of justice in treating them like older folk who have grown tired of the world? I myself loathe rocks whether in the mountains or houses. The young girl is right: there's nothing in Lebanon like Sofar and Aley. There are plenty of outing spots around them as well.

Ibrahim Hitti was standing next to Charles Corm, and I could see him sharpening his knife.

"So, madam," he said, "if you're so convinced that there's nowhere in Lebanon to relax and have fun apart from Sofar and Aley, then why did you put your own comfort at risk by coming to Laqlouq?"

Ibrahim's sharp verbal knife made me feel sorry for the woman. Fortunately, Sheikh Ibrahim Khoury came back, so I grabbed the opportunity to rescue both her and the young woman by asking him a question about Emir Basheer.

"Emir Basheer used to send his horses to spend the spring in Laqlouq," Sheikh Iskandar told us. "Then he would come himself and spend a couple of months by the waters. He adored Laqlouq, professor. Wherever he put up his tent, he would also erect gallows. The spot where the gallows were is well known. So much for Emir Basheer's justice."

Ibrahim Hitti: "And justice included women as well, no doubt about it. But for that, he would not have erected the gallows."

"Women, Brother Ibrahim," Charles Corm said, "are the worst tyrants of all."

"Oh, well said!" Ibrahim replied.

"But men are still the worst criminals," Charles Corm went on. "All the unjust legislation that causes crime and war throughout the world was passed by men."

"True enough," Sheikh Iskandar said. "Women are unlucky. Emir Basheer used to say . . ."

We never got to hear what Emir Basheer used to say because, at that moment, Iskandar Haddad barged in on us.

"Greetings!" he said. "I've come to invite you inside the house in the name of Johnny Walker!"

The Qualities of Lebanese Cuisine

WHO'S JOHNNY WALKER?" asked one of the people standing by the drinks table.

Iskandar Haddad started telling the story of a man who was forever complaining about stomach pains. One doctor suggested taking walks, and another dieting, but the third recommended whisky. The man loved eating and hated walking . . . at this point Iskandar stopped abruptly, looking at the door, then finished off quickly: "His name was Johnny Walker." And with that he greeted Bishop Boutros Akl.

The man of means and the man of religion, each of whom had need of the other.

The man of means cannot do without the divine in order to cover his account in the world to come, and the man of religion needs money to live his life in this world.

However, people said that Bishop Boutros Akl differed in this respect from other wearers of purple. The banker Iskandar may well have been aware of that, because he neither feared the bishop, nor was he bothered by his religion.

Bishop Boutros had another distinguishing characteristic—his flexible social attitudes—he had nothing against sociable meetings, nor did he frown on drinking the odd glass. Furthermore, he had a high level of appreciation for music and singing.

It is thus not at all surprising that Asaad Younis, the master of the house and of Laqlouq, was a close friend of Bishop Boutros. Maronite connections alone would not have been enough to bind the two of them to each other; there was also taste, noble character . . . and wealth. Our host, Asaad Younis, was the chief engineer in Lebanon and an authority on agriculture in the entire Arab East. He was also a friend of writers and artists, a devotee of the famous classical musician Ibrahim al-Mousili,[1] and a lover of both panpipes and flute. He was one of the few people in Lebanon who could perform Bedouin songs well.

During the Great War, Asaad had carried the flute—not a rifle—as a wandering exile in Palestine. Carrying his flute and dressed in dervish garb, he used to move at random from one place to another, singing Bedouin songs. It was this bedraggled look and his songs that enabled him to cross the border and return to his native land.

Today he is able to move a segment of this civilization with all its positives—literature, poetry, art, science, virtue, prestige, and fascinating beauty—to move all of their special qualities from the tablet of civilization in the city to this location, with its rough roads remote and high up, stretching from mountain peaks to overlook other mountains. During the day it seems shod with the sun's own stallion, while at night it carries the moon's saddlebag to this place called Laqlouq.

Gathering them in one place, he offers them the generous hospitality of an authentic Lebanese home.

Many times I have sat at the tables of important people in Europe and America and have tasted the very finest, rarest, and tastiest of foods. I have also dined with emirs and kings in the Arab East, but I have never felt the way I do when I am sitting at a Lebanese table.

Why is that? There is nothing special about the Lebanese table when it comes to arrangement and neatness; the fine, rare dishes; the skill of the chefs; or the courtesy and skill of the servants.

There is undoubtedly something that makes us Lebanese prefer our cuisine to that of others, but that is not what leads me to make an absolute judgment, lifting the tables of mountain people in Lebanon

1. Translator's note: a famous musician and singer from the Abbasid period, who entertained caliphs in Baghdad—including Harun al-Rashid—until his death (742–804 CE).

above those of important people in the West and emirs and kings in the Arab East.

So then, what is it precisely that I prefer? Official dinners are indeed official and stiff, lacking any element to stir your heart.

Behind every official banquet there is a working hand, artistry, and perfection.

Behind every Lebanese banquet—and we cannot say that they are either official, unofficial, or semiofficial without also stating that they are Lebanese—there is artistry, perfection, and heart!

Apart from our mothers, sisters, and wives, who else is as good at cooking popular dishes? Is there any Lebanese dinner party, however many cooks and servants there may be, where the lady of the house is not involved in its preparations? Very often in fact, she is the principal worker involved, helped by other village women. Local girls and boys come to help as well, and all out of love and a sense of honor.

Yes indeed, in this type of Lebanese banquet there is a part of the hostess's heart and those of her helpers, male and female.

What made the party in Laqlouq at the home of Asaad Younis was a speech that Charles Corm gave in Arabic. He is a Lebanese citizen who writes poetry in the language of Racine and Moliere. Paris has sat and listened to him, extolled him and honored him. He is not particularly good at his more recent ancestors—the Arabs, and has no idea of how to say "I love you" in the language of his remote ancestors—the Phoenicians. All that was previously, but now he had shared with us his knowledge, love, and friendship, and stopped us chatting to him in anything but Arabic—the language of speakers of the consonant *daad*.

"It's all a conspiracy on your part," he exclaimed, "but it's a nice one!"

He did not actually use such eloquent terms, but he did say it and helped us understand him.

"You're going to teach me the language of my father and mother," he went on, "and I'll be very grateful."

On that night in Laqlouq, at the dinner table of Asaad Younis, the poet of the sun rose to his feet—the composer of a pearly necklace for its neck, the inspiring poet of the mountains who clothed Lebanon in garments of glory and splendor. Charles Corm rose and spoke in Arabic. He astonished us all and aroused within us both love and admiration.

Are you asking what he said? What does that matter? He spoke in Arabic, and that is enough.

While he was speaking, the *dabke* dance reached a fever pitch in the open space, illuminated by the light of a lamp hanging from a branch of the walnut tree.

This then was the genuine Arab spirit: hospitality, eloquence, generosity, dabke, and panpipe.

Come now and let us watch the dabke, a large, crowded circle. I promised you that I would have something to say about the development of Arab womanhood in Laqlouq. This scene is an example, much better than anything I might write. Those women you can see, with their silk stockings and European-style high-heeled shoes, they are Arabs from Laqlouq!

They may have forgotten all the ancient customs and traditions that they have inherited, but they will never forget the dabke and its accompanying songs.

Horizons

IT IS NOT OUT OF THE QUESTION that in Laqlouq a kind of new agricultural revival occurred, one that included those Noaim Arab Bedouin under its aegis. They and their more settled colleagues jointly participated in sowing and harvesting. It is also not surprising that Arabian horses had some of their former glory restored in these mountains. Farmers would acquire horses, train them, and use them as they did the rounds of these lowlands and areas close by. Not everything that people do in the mountains requires speed, nor does it justify the expense of buying petrol.

It is no surprise that the number of houses built in this plain and the neighboring hills should have increased. It has been turned into a summer resort for people with good taste, intelligence, and prudence, not Westernized types, as is the case in Sofar. I can give additional credence to that because I now see the pioneer of Laqlouq, Asaad Younis, giving up his government post so that he can concentrate on agriculture in the lands of his ancestors. I also hear farmers from Ehmej and Tannourine saying that Laqlouq has a bright future.

That is no false hope or fanciful notion. There is no shortage of feasible factors and reasons. Arabian horses could come back to these regions, and the number of summer residences would increase. People in search of rest and good health would come, as well as the worker looking to calm his nerves in the mountains and escape the responsibilities of life, and the writer desiring horizons of broad inspiration by day and inspiration's dark sky at night with its moon and stars. For any of these wise men, children of simplicity and good taste, it would be possible to go on an excursion every day, riding a fine Arabian stallion through these plains and mountains. As they roamed the heights together, man and horse could proclaim the line of the poet al-Mutanabbi:

> The best place in the world is a swift-moving saddle,
> The best companion for a man is a book.

If you happen to be someone who gets bored by books and reading and does not approve of or enjoy the finch, ibis, hoopoe, and partridge, especially at harvest time, then the partridge, for example, comes to hunt the grasshopper in the crops, and the villagers from Tannourine and Ehmej come out to hunt the partridge.

If you do not find it either relaxing or enjoyable to use a hunting rifle, to read books, or to ride "swift-moving saddles," then you need an hour's walk before sunrise or at sunset, or else a couple of hours in the fresh breeze of dawn and the magical serenity of sunset. Both will enhance or restore the hope in life, the resolve, and the ability to act that you have lost.

The highest point in Laqlouq is the hill on which Assad Younis's house stands (1,853 meters above sea level). From there you can look round in various directions, with wide horizons and mountainous perspectives.

Let us look to the northeast. On the slope of the first mountain is something dark, looking like an ever-present cloud. They are the Hadath cedars; between us and them the village of Tannourine lies hidden about two kilometers away. Beyond that are three peaks, one above the other, the last of which hides the largest cedar forest, the one at Bsharre, which is a two hours' walk or ride from Laqlouq. Between the Hadath mountain and the highest of the three peaks that we have mentioned there is a large gap; when the weather is clear, you can see part of the sea and a section of the city of Tripoli.

Now turn to the northwest. You can see an enormous long, high, dark wall providing shade at the foot of Tannourine in the afternoon hours, while in the morning it spreads its cover over the Cedars of Jaj behind it and the houses of Ehmej on the western side. This is a wall for a fortress in the sky, a rampart for a city in the world of wonders, colored like eagles and lions, with a back like a saw. With its serrated edge, it is at its clearest and brightest between sunset and dusk. At that time it resembles a sharp sword poised to separate Earth from Heaven.

On the highest peak of this mountain range is a flag, which is visible through binoculars. It has been placed there by the Survey Department. Amid the rocks and beneath the flag is a path connecting Laqlouq to the Cedars of Jaj.

If you are unable to walk through rocky terrain and climb up mountains, then beware of this path. A goatherd may tell you that it is walkable; it will only take you two hours to walk from Laqlouq to the Cedars. I am here to tell you that the road is a wreck; if you leave Laqlouq in the morning, you may not get to the Cedars of Jaj before sunset. And that assumes that you will not need either a nurse or doctor once you arrive.

Let us now resume our description of the general view. We are still looking to the northwest. If you turn your attention to the huge wall, you will see at its western end a peak that looks like a pyramid; that is the peak of Mount Hafroun, where there is a ruin that can only be seen from close up on the way back down to Ehmej. It is an ancient site—Phoenician—according to our friend Charles Corm.

To the east the vista reveals beyond the mountains a passable road, as goatherds might claim—an open road between Aqoura and Dahr el-Qadeeb, which we described earlier on our journey to the Cedars.

One more thing: when we look to the south from Laqlouq, if you like watching the moon rise, you can get a view of the full moon that is unparalleled for its size and brilliance, its clear face, visible halo, and apparent proximity to your very footsteps. It rises behind a mountain that rises straight like a wall, with no bends or slopes, and shines its light from the mountaintop in a straight line to the space in front of Asaad Younis's house—the third side of a triangle no more than two kilometers in length.

Two kilometers between you and the moon. These days, a plane can climb up to five kilometers in height, so you say, "So what? What's this about the moon? What about the Laqlouq moon as it weaves a network of rays, which grow longer as the airplane gets closer. Even so, from mountaintop to your own footsteps, it is never longer than two kilometers." But I am not going to get more involved in this topic; I do not want to burden myself and engage the reader by describing realities like illusions. Illusions are indeed like realities.

But let us again go back to what is left of the general scenario. The most important villages to the south of Laqlouq are Qartaba, Aqoura, and Lassa. Among the mountains that seem like clouds on the distant horizon there is one named Mshaa el-Ftooh, beneath which lie the villages of Kesrouan, Mayrouba, Hrajel, and Faraya. However, those villages can only be seen from Laqlouq in the eye of the imagination if such a person can be aware of what lies hidden in those mountains.

Alongside Mount Mshaa el-Ftooh is another mountain, which is both longer and higher. The white patches that glitter in the sunshine are snow in its bends and crevices. They always manage to retain their snow in both summer and winter, lying on the north side of Mount Sannine.

Mount Sannine, may God prolong your life as you gaze down on the village of Freike!

Sixth Journey

Afqa

Contents

Ruins of the Gods

EVERY MOUNTAINOUS REGION in Lebanon has a western boundary—the sea, and an eastern one—the plateaus overlooking Bekaa Plain. The southern and northern borders consist mostly of valleys sloping downward to the west from the peaks and of rivers that flow through them. The Dog River, for example, is the boundary between Matn and Kesrouan; part of the Salib Valley separated Kesrouan from El-Ftooh; and the Ibrahim River flows between the El-Ftooh Mountains and the Byblos region.

Now here we are for the fourth time in the mountains, taking the same track that previously took us to Tourzaya. The Ibrahim River is behind the mountain to the south, and right at its peak lies the village of Bir el-Hait. The river cannot be seen until we reach Mashnaqa, the village known for its ancient ruins.

We keep moving to the east from Tourzaya, overlooking the Farhad Valley to the right. We pass through three villages—Hareek, Souaneh, and Almat—the last of which is the largest and is famous for its tobacco, the kind that my grandfather, uncle, and father flirted with and used in their commercial dealings.

We reached Mashnaqa, some 60 kilometers from Beirut and 1,200 meters above sea level. When we arrived, all we could see was one store beside the road and some muleteers using their animals to transport wood, logs for firewood, and planks and girders for building.

The scene presented a living Phoenician picture, a tableau from the past, authentic in its presentation and significance. Here too were the mountains, at that time decked in forests of cedars and cypress. Woodcutters and merchants accompanied the muleteers . . .

Sow, don't cut! I do not believe that the Phoenicians were friends of trees or that they established some kind of association that established rules regarding the trees' illustrious aspect. Phoenicians simply cut and sold, utterly unconcerned about the future of those forests—pines, cedars, and cypress.

Among the consequences of all the actions of conquering rulers the only positive I can see is the work of the pagan Roman emperor Hadrian, who showed at least half the wisdom of tree lovers today. While he banned cutting, he did not order any planting. As a result, Lebanon did not continue to enjoy the blessing of its forests. Commerce robbed it; valleys, hills, and peaks were stripped of their silken covering. All that was left was what time had managed to preserve or the living seeds that the winds had scattered so that they grew alone or in pairs amid the rocks. In our times, the Association of Friends of Trees has started trying to repair the damage caused by previous generations. Those efforts have been partially successful through both action and counseling, and they would certainly have been more generally effective if the government had given them practical and applicable support. The association has publicized its directives throughout the mountainous region, posted in clear, beautiful script: Sow, don't cut! The director of agriculture has issued his instructions: No cutting without government authorization. But then what? When the government does give permission and fails to provide the required technical supervision for its implementation, the landowner simply does things to satisfy his own motives. His greed and ignorance easily trump both government and association.

We left the woodcutters and muleteers at their work, transporting wood cut from pine, oak, and cypress forests in the mountains above the banks of the Ibrahim River between Mashnaqa and Qartaba. We were walking behind our guide, Professor Yousuf Huwayeck, as fervid a protector of Lebanese monuments as were the Friends of Trees with its trees. We turned off the carriage road, and within minutes we were walking along an ancient path between the rocks until we reached some scattered ruins on the mountain peak.

There were vestiges of a long, square wall enclosing a temple and other buildings attached to it. They were completely ruined, and only the bases of a few temple pillars remained, with thornbushes standing erect beside them.

Inside the wall the children of Almat had planted row upon row of tobacco plants, with no regard to the past. Today the planting process for tobacco is governed by the regulations of the Foreign Monopoly Company.

Here is the tobacco on the ground in this temple, where in the distant past the temple had often been the source of aromas of sacrifice and incense-burning. So light your pipes and open your eyes to your imagination! Yes indeed, Baal Shamin, how many victims had been immolated on your altar? How many of God's servants had come to you in humble plea? How many human hearts had brought you their exposed and beloved burdens? How many faithful hearts lowered their baggage inside your temple and then, between your hands and at your feet, offered all the love, passion, fear, piety, hope, and expectation harbored in their hearts? As with any random fancy and passing whim, they all put up with the hardships of the pilgrimage in order to achieve the one enormous boon—the one enormous, ephemeral boon—a single sacred hour, followed by the hour of license: rapture, pleasure, and divine incarnation.

So light your pipe and open the eyes of your imagination. In these times, burn tobacco in memory of Adonis, young man of young men; Adonis, the supreme deity, god of love, pain, resurrection, and eternity. Can there be any escape or deliverance? Can love ever be without pain? Can pain ever escape death? Does death deprive us of the greatest blessing—resurrection and immortality—whether it be in nature, human life, or the national and social existence of human beings?

If Adonis were with us in body today, standing on this Lebanese mountain, he would notice wild boars in the city and government circles, not in the valleys and forests. He would be slain fighting just like presidents and leaders today. However, the slaying of a deity is different from slaying politicians, be they clerics or tradesmen. No wonder! A slaying that involves the courage of faith and sacrifice bears fruit in the spirit of that same faith and sacrifice in generations of people. On the other hand, a slaying that involves a twisted will with a warped eye, one that finds its perpetrator invited to a feast, offered a bribe, or given a medal, what possible fruit can it bear—God protect you!

So then, light your pipe! Blow your smoke in columns and circles in this space where clusters of priests and worshippers, male and female, have clamored, all of them mourning and weeping over Adonis, weeping courage, heroism, and sacrifice. Today both it and they are a mere memory, memory of a fire that turned into smoke and ashes. The smoke was scattered in the sky above, and the ashes stuck to the rocks and turned them dark and gloomy.

Human beings resorted to these rocks to satisfy a desire for eternal memory and never-ending bliss. They relied on them and trusted in their endurance and fidelity, the stolid fidelity of rocks.

Dig then, digger, and draw a picture of my gods, male and female, beside the beloved's grave. Carve the eternal designs, the immortal word, may you be blessed!

Where is that beloved; where is that gravedigger today? Certainly not in these sarcophagi with the mouths wide open. Peasants have broken their lids in order to make porches for their houses. There is no trace of human bones or bone fragments; they are completely empty, except for the odd spider with its web in a corner, or a worm that has lost its way in its dark, musty spaces. Empty sarcophagi with open mouths day and night, speechless rocks whose carvings have been erased by rains and hurricanes, relics of the past where can be heard the whistle of oblivion.

We stopped between two rocks on the old Qartaba road, a hundred meters from the wall with its empty sarcophagi and outlines carved into the rocks. "The immortal word" and "the eternal designs" on them had been totally erased. My colleague Huwayeck showed me something that looked like the shadow of a person standing there in one of the outlines and a heavily faded design on another. He told me it was a picture of a seated woman keening. Was it Ishtar crying for Adonis? That is what archeologists who have read the inscriptions have claimed.

Forget about the dilapidated ruins and erased monuments, and let us take a look instead from the top of the hill at the sights all around us. To the north is Ehmej, with its church's oak trees looking like a beauty spot on the mountain's cheek. To the west is Tourzaya, perched on the shoulder of the Farhad Valley, with the glass of its coffeehouse gleaming like diamonds in the afternoon sunshine. To the northwest is the steep road up to Almat with its ten bends; we have to cross it to get to Qartaba. To the southeast is the Adonis River Valley, and below it Mount Moses, all decked in its verdant, silky garb. Its various shades of green are brighter in the orchards and darker in the forests. Some grayish spots are also visible—the villages of Chouarna, Ibri, and Frad—each one separated from the others with no visible path or other route between them.

I had seen many things during my trips into the Lebanese mountains, but nothing resembled these three villages in their isolation, loneliness, and difficult access. You had to admire the villagers who would penetrate the dense forests and live in their gloomy depths. They are not jinn, but human beings, ploughmen tilling the land, collecting firewood, eating, and reproducing—as far removed from the world as monks of old. In fact, as I observed their grayish, square roofed houses set amid such serene greenery, I thought of them as being in a kind of spiritual retreat, a place impossible to reach, but ultimately desirable as a destination and place to stay. In this serene spot overlooking the sacred river, the Adonis River, how wonderful to give free rein to the goddesses of remoteness and oblivion. This is a beauty visible to the eye but not appreciated by destructive pleasure, beauty that is beautiful while still remote and intractable.

We went back to the paved road to continue on our way to Qartaba. As we climbed up the eastern part of the mountain, we made our way round the ten bends, one after the other. No sooner had we passed the last of them than the horizon changed. In front of us there unfolded a wonderful new vista, at the bottom of which the river water gleamed. Below Mount Moses a dark, barren summit of the mountain appeared, nestling between the rocks of the Hadeed Spring. There were other peaks visible as well, with bright white patches on their side, one part of Mount Sannine where snow is still visible until the end of summer.

Here now is the Adonis Valley, blessed with verdant scenery and sweet scents. Here too is Adonis's Sufi poem, silken and perfumed, its verses varied in shape, color, and fragrance. Here is a grove of terebinth trees with crimson clusters teasing with their stores of incense; a pine grove with rapture, strength, and immortality all hidden inside its acorns; a forest of cypress, cousin of the cedar and sharer of its glory and splendor; thickets and bushes exuding scents of laurel, thyme, and sage. At the edges and bends in the valley there are swaths of pine trees lending their moist shade to ferns and lilies of the valley. Among the most exotic of notions and secrets there is also a field full of buttercups, which fish love just as much as humans do wine. The fisherman will take it and toss it into the sea; the fish get drunk on it, and the fisherman can catch them intoxicated.

"In memory of the beloved," we ate butternuts.[1] We got drunk and fell into the nets of man—may his mother be bereaved!

There are large expanses of the sacred valley to be crossed. We reach a bend, which hides both the expanses and the bends, but then yet another aspect of this fascinating mountain is revealed. Forests lead to orchards; fields herald golden meadows—orchards and meadows with streams and springs flowing through them, with irrigation canals branching off from them. Orchards and meadows adorned by lofty poplars and sleepy willows. There are flowerbeds and vines; figs, grapes, and ripening fruits; mulberry engaged in its final struggle and ruing the silk season. Plowed fields flaunt a variety of vegetables. Qartaba, named for the great Andalusian city (Cordoba), the Qartaba of the Arabs, 270 kilometers from Beirut and 1,260 meters above sea level. The village's historian and poet is Father Augustin Soukhn, and

1. Translator's note: "In memory of the beloved" is part of the first line of the famous Sufi poem "Al-Khamriyya" by Ibn al-Farid (1181–1234).

he is keen to explain the origin of its name, going back no further than Aramaic. In my view, the majority of names for ancient villages in the mountains are usually derived from either Aramaic or Arabic (the sister language of Phoenician)—and I'll be giving examples of mistaken attributions to Aramaic in many of these names in another chapter, God willing. For now, I am going to challenge Father Soukhn's interpretation with another one:

Qartaba is neither Aramaic nor Arabic—it is Spanish. The Arabs in Spain Arabized it as they did with other names such as Ishbiliya (Seville) and Gharnata (Granada).

When Arab Spain fell and the Arabs were expelled at the end of the fifteenth century, the descendants of Arab conquerors from the Syrian region returned to the lands of their ancestors in the middle of the following century, drawn there by a sense of nostalgia. In my view, some of those who returned to Homs and Hama from Qartaba (Cordoba) entered Lebanon by the easiest and best-known way—Aqoura to Baalbek. Near Aqoura they saw verdant lands full of forests and watercourses, overlooking a stunningly beautiful valley that reminded them of not just Andalusia, but Cordoba, the city they had left behind. They unloaded their baggage, built houses, planted trees and flowers, and called the place Qartaba. The proof of this interpretation lies in the fact that today there are a number of families of Arab origin living in Qartaba. That is according to the village's historian and poet, the Lebanese monk Augustin Soukhn.

The Soukhn family is genuinely Arab: they are related to Kais Tanoukhi, Kaab al-Yamaani, and Saifi bin Sabaa. They are descendants of the ancient Qahtan tribe. In an elegy for one of their notables, their poet once said:

> In Palmyra, Sabaa, and Tihama, our ancestors exude a pure scent.

We stopped in the market to greet people and drank coffee in one of the cafes there. We then continued toward Aqoura, about ten kilometers away. On the road there are some ruins to the side called Dair al-Azrak, the remains of an ancient site, the walls of a temple that had been a Byzantine church. Previously, it had served as both a Roman and Greek temple, and, before that, an altar for sacrifices to one of the Phoenician deities.

Sacrificial altars, temple, ruins, all for the gods, amid these scattered rocks, crumbling pillars, collapsed walls, and open-mouthed doorways, empty in front and behind, paces where time whispers its immortal dictum: "Nothing lasts!"

Today the only things left in these ruins are weeds and oaks offering them shade as they dig their roots between the stones to complete the destruction, roots that look like fossilized snakes under the doorstep, and stones that clung to the roots as though they were begging for life or resorting to them for relief from desolation and evanescence.

For sure these were desolate, harrowing ruins, and their impact stayed with us until we reached Aqoura. We were welcomed by threshing floors basking in the sunshine and peasants doing the threshing, pulling oxen around the blessed circle while, beneath the threshing machine, the wheat was released from its golden fetters, from its ears.

Here is life linked to work. Here is work garlanded with freedom.

Life, work, freedom, one of the manifestations of genuine, eternal holiness.

Aqoura

IT IS GENERALLY ACKNOWLEDGED that the majority of Lebanese families living in the central Lebanese territory hail from the Byblos region. High in the mountains is a village of extreme antiquity with many peoples and migrations—Aqoura. If scholars and archeologists are correct, then humans in the region settled in the high mountains before the plains and seashore. We thus have to transfer the supposed cradle of the Lebanese people from Byblos to the base of the twin mountains, Qurn and Monaitra, the area between those two rocky formations and the springs that flow out of them.

Research on cradle origins—whether human, animal, or vegetable—can only lead us into the arcane regions of early life on this planet of ours; it only makes for further confusion and rarely proves useful. The one glaring reality on the topic is obscurity. For example, if scholars are able to fix the time and place for the birth of the very first grasshopper or cedar plant, then maybe they can also discover the cradle of one of the earth's peoples.

We can now make do with the history at our disposal, written by the revered writer Father Louis Hashem. The first chapter contains useful information, both historical and archeological, and subsequent chapters are a positive ocean of genealogical information that is useful to the people involved, and, surprisingly enough, to other Lebanese as well. The first surprising piece of information is the sheer number of families that migrated to Aqoura in ancient times but left it later on—except for those that stayed. After I had finished reading the first chapter, I thumbed through five hundred subsequent pages until I reached the index. It contains the names of Lebanese families of Aqoura origins, enough to thrill and delight the heart, scattered in every corner of Lebanon, north and south, coast and mountains.

The index contains the names of 250 families. God care for you!—according to the respected historian Father Louis Hashem, we are all from Aqoura; to which I will add, except those from Bejjeh and Maad. The index does not list any name from Bejjeh, but branches of families from there intermarried. Take me, for example. I am from Bejjeh on my father's side, Hashemi, Ghusoubi, and Aqouri from my father's mother, and Ashkari Aqouri from my mother's mother.

Most families from Aqoura, or the most important ones, are of Arab descent. The Hashemis, for example, trace their lineage back to the Prophet's companion, Hashem ibn 'Utba, who later joined Imam 'Ali ibn Abi Taleb's party and resided in Persia. Thereafter, he moved with his children to Lebanon. They converted to Christianity—for their spirits' benefit—the eldest being Sheikh Hashem, the first one to settle in Aqoura. The Noureddine family moved from Damascus to Baalbek, then to Aqoura; there were many branches to the family, among which the Elias branch stands out, well-known today as the Germanus branch. There were also the Kraidi and Harb clans, along with many others, who left Houran and other regions to the south.

However, there is a clear and nasty clash involved in the names of many of these families in Aqoura. Arabic, Persian, Latin, and Aramaic all compete, embrace, and submit to a single, multihued yoke.

As examples, just consider Sakr ibn Qaansooh, Qaansooh ibn Constantin, and his wife, Msihiya. What about Hanna ibn Abi l-Ghaith, a relative of the totally Arab Emad Abi l-Ghaith? Yousuf Arab is fine, but Gregarios Arab is even worse than Rostom ibn Saaseen and Idris ibn Arsenios. May God enhance your refined taste! What about Khaazkiya, a flower among women, from Shiraz in Persia, and her two children, Germanos and Romanos? Or cannot you gauge the heresy in Shidyaaq Sarkees Noureddine and the patriarch Girgis Amyara?

I have no idea why there are so many of these names: Germanos, Romanos, Ibrianos, Finyanos, in this particular part of Lebanon, whereas they are rarely found in other parts.

In the Phoenician era the people of Aqoura were the keenest worshippers of both gods and goddesses and the most devoted to their temples, even in the Greek and Roman periods. In the same way they are, of all Maronites, the most devoted to Saint Maroun, his priests and monks. God, shrine, and temple, religious creed and myth, where did they all come from to permeate the lives of the Aqoura people in former times, from Ishtar to the Virgin Mary and from Baal Shamin to Saint Maroun?

Their revered historian states that Aqoura is a nursery for religious sects, but, thank God, there is only one left in the nursery—or rather, the forest. It is reasonable to suggest that this single community is no different from the earlier ones that preceded it. It is now being replaced by a Lebanese Arab nationalism that, thanks to the forceful role of Aqoura, is in the vanguard of standard-bearers for Arabism!

That Aqoura citizens should be such forceful heroes is hardly a surprise. Both natural and social environments play a major role in the upbringing and character formation of human beings. In mountain heights such as these (1,450–2,300 meters above sea level), people develop big bones, warm blood, and strong nerves.

In Lebanon there are other high-level natural environments like that of Aqoura with similar features—Zahle, Bsharre, and Ehden—for example. But they are not like Aqoura and its neighbors in that they do not have the same destructive natural elements that train people who live in Aqoura to deal with the visible and hidden dangers they face, features that force them to develop special traits needed to defend and protect themselves. They develop a ruggedness, endurance, and defiance that are all basic elements in heroism. However, additional spiritual and moral aspects may develop or not, depending on particular conditions and circumstances.

Throughout the ages hundreds of men of religion have emerged in Aqoura, both pagan and Christian. It contains a large number of churches and the remains of temples. But, as far as we know, there have been no martyrs or saints.

When it comes to defying governors, defending rights—whether justified by oppression or asserted, in civil wars, or what they term *ruckuses*, they are in the very forefront of the Lebanese people. The historian mentioned twenty such incidents, with twenty people dead in twenty years (1905–26); in other words, one person dead per year. He thought the number was too high and apologized. In his view, most of the assaults and feuds resulted from public lands.

There was never a time when the government would resolve a dispute involving people who claimed "a land deed" or move to settle a public land dispute.

All that said, the major factor in this region, and for Aqoura and its inhabitants in general, was Mount Aqoura, facing northeast and extending to the south. It consists of rocky forts and strongholds interspersed with damp-soiled slopes. In spite of all the forts, there will be landsides in springtime once every few years, or more like a dozen. In wintertime there will be dangerous avalanches of snow, and at unpredictable times earthquakes may happen as well to complete the task of the gales and snow.

These then are some of the destructive elements in this natural environment, the factors contributing to the heroic temperament of the people of Aqoura. When disaster strikes the people of a specific town, they all share the burden and overcoming its perils. Their innate strength, resolve, and courage is further enhanced; those traits are passed down to the next generation, and they emerge intrepid and tough.

Landslides, cracks, sinkholes, earthquakes every ten years or so, and yet the people of Aqoura have lived in its shadows since time immemorial, clinging to thunderbolts, fire, rocks, and mire. They never leave and never care. But for their sheer heroism, there would be no Aqoura or its people today.

In 1937 I witnessed the most recent landslide in the history of Aqoura. I had read accounts of the modern landslides and sinkholes that preceded it (1903–29; 1911 in Afqa). On the printed page I only discovered the same things that I had heard from people and observed on the page of life itself. All the modern weapons of war—tanks armed with machine guns, and bomber aircraft—pale into insignificance when compared with hurricanes and earthquakes.

On this northeast mountain there is a pebbly slope, part of which is owned and part of which is public. All of it is grassy and planted; from top to bottom on the riverbanks it is clothed in an emerald garment. On this steep slope there are peasant houses, along with terraces, the walls of which have been built by the owners to keep the soil and plants in place. The mountains stand between two rocky redoubts to north and south. In springtime it is a veritable feast for the eyes, especially if viewed from the southwest entry to Aqoura.

Today (1937) you can see a large space, about forty meters wide and about three hundred meters from top to bottom by the banks of the River Rouwais. It is brown and red, with nothing growing on it, no terraces, and no human construction—a bare, low patch in the middle of the green mountain on either side of it. It is last year's landslide, smaller and less damaging than its predecessors.

Such landslides and sinkholes have four main causes: (1) heavy rainfall; (2) buildups of soil, rubble, and other things on the surface; (3) change in the makeup of the underground soil; (4) collapse of the soil by riverbanks due to floods, causing the land above them to slide. All four factors may come together when there is a landside or slippage.

Landslides occur when earth from higher up tumbles down to areas below. It can start at various points, and rarely keeps to its original path; it continues, splits up, and expands, veering off and moving downward, all during landslide season, which can last for a month or two. Sometimes springs disappear altogether; at others they gush forth. Watercourses get jammed, roads are blocked, and rivers flood; they get clogged and change their courses. When rain mixes with the snow, the risk for people increases, and the damage is more severe.

Sinkholes occur when a patch of land collapses on itself for any number of reasons noted earlier. It shrinks or caves in, taking with it the surface earth and any trees or buildings on it.

> The ice was intense (the cave-in of 1929), and you could see astonishing scenes. The snow rose like huge piles or enormous rocks. In the heavenly heights it looked like tents, grottos, and caves. The

> cavity grew deeper day by day, and the rivers kept tossing rocks around with a thunderous din. The big river joined the small one, then the small one changed course and rejoined the big one by the Abu Mereb expanse. Lakes formed, but, after a few days, they fell apart, and the water drained away and disappeared. The shape of the earth changed.[1]

Valleys turned into hills, and hills into lowlands. Plains became narrows, and narrows were pools of water. The River Dabbagha inundated the Bayada region and destroyed trees—sycamores, willows, and poplars—and took away grapevines and mulberry orchards.

> The Masoud spring was overflowing close to Harf el-Abyad, then it disappeared, and the mills along with it. Cedar trees, with all their straightness, height, thickness, and pure scent all looked peculiar, as did other huge, weighty trees, like ebony.[2]

We asked a peasant working on the threshing floor to describe for us last year's subsidence.

"The ground started cracking and sliding; it was churning with mud. A smoke that smelled like sulfur rose out of the mud."

That is not surprising since, in addition to the things I have already mentioned, Aqoura also has mines, sulfuric springs, and explosives!

Sometimes after a subsidence there is a winter with little cold, rain, or snow. That in turn brings locusts during the following spring from Baalbek to Aqoura and its neighborhood. Then the sliding soil puts paid to the crops.

Landslides and subsidences! The people of Aqoura live on soil that dominates life within its bounds. Yesterday's disaster is forgotten, as the people of Aqoura prepare to welcome the next disaster with a sturdy, calm heart, unruffled, unconcerned. The individual from Aqoura is truly a mighty hero.

1. *History of Aqoura*, 148.
2. *History of Aqoura*, 151.

The Stepped Pyramids[1]

AQOURA HAS NOT BECOME FAMOUS for its ruckuses and landslides alone. Scholars and archeologists have also found there and in its surroundings ancient ruins—temples, shrines, fortresses, and castles dating from various periods—Phoenician, Assyrian, Byzantine, and Crusader.

Conquerors from Babylon and Assyria passed through Aqoura, and at least one Roman ruler visited the town. A group of renowned scholars has also come to Aqoura to study and conduct research, the most famous of them being the Swiss traveler Johann Burckhardt, and the French polymath Ernest Renan. In the town and its environs they discovered ruins, writings, and sarcophagi. The most special of their findings is the ancient road.

The road runs from Byblos to Aqoura, and from there to Lake Yammoune and Baalbek. It is the road taken by conquerors from Babylon and Assyria to the Phoenician coastline and also the trade route from Byblos to the land of the Chaldeans, and from there onward to the Persian Gulf and India.

It is also the Roman military road from Byblos to Baalbek and Palmyra (Tadmur), a road that frequently resounded to heavy loads being transported, gigantic stones and towering Egyptian pillars to build the Temple of the Sun.

Renan maintains that this is the oldest road in the world, since on both sides there are inscriptions in hieroglyphics, Phoenician,

1. Translator's note: I am assuming here that the author is making use of the term *Step(ped) Pyramid*, widely used to refer to the Saqqara Pyramid in Egypt.

cuneiform, Greek, and Latin. "The world's oldest road," that is a major statement made by a meticulous research scholar. It is also possible that the people who planned this were neither Assyrians nor Phoenicians. The person who opened it up may well have been the very first human being, someone who climbed these mountains carrying his pointed flint for hunting. Who knows, perhaps the road is from all the pre-flint ages.

"The world's oldest road," and here I am standing right in the middle, bowing humbly before its renowned French scholar and believing him. That said, I can look to the south from the road and see close by shapes of lofty mountains and towering rocks with their own special magic that no Babylonian goddess possesses and their own antiquity that no human era can match.

True enough, there are natural monuments that can belittle those of nations, hills shaped like pyramids that have witnessed every stage of human and biological development—gelatinous, vertebrate, mammal, bipedal; conquering kings, and the person carrying on his shoulders the head of a leader in knowledge—someone whose brain has the intellectual power to weigh mountains—indeed, to weigh the earth, and to measure the light distance between stars.

These mountains at Aqoura, about which Renan said that they are even more beautiful than the Alps, make you pause, whoever you may be—peasant, scholar, or general. They appeal to you; if you are a writer who is good at combining knowledge and poetry, then they will let your imagination take wing.

You can move from the ancient history of mankind to the ancient history of the universe itself. These amazingly shaped mountain peaks are more deeply based in antiquity and more superb in their shape and message.

If the archeologist says that the road is the world's oldest, and its history goes back beyond that of humanity to the flint era, then it has to be less than twenty thousand years old.

But then, if we are to say that this stepped pyramid at the entrance to Aqoura is the most ancient mountain in Lebanon, then, one wonders, how old can it be? Here we find ourselves in a universe of measurements, akin to and blended with the imaginary world.

How old then is this pyramid, this mountain, this terrain, this entire universe, and how did it begin?

As knowledge progresses and scholars acquire more methods for research and verification, we draw ever closer to the world of poetry and the imagination. The universe seems like a divine poem, with an opening line shrouded in mist and its final strophe today is this writer who stands humbly before it, mouthing a syllable from the words in the very first line.

Scholars used to state that the universe was about 150 fifty million years old, but today, relying on astronomical discoveries made thanks to the world's largest telescope (the Mount Wilson Observatory in the United States), they say that it is more than 50 million years old.

For the history of human beings, ever since we started carving the first words on rocks, we know of nothing older than 7,000 years.

Indeed, these rocks have their own ancient history. In comparison with them, the history of human beings is a grain of mustard seed.

True enough, these rocks have their own phases—from flaming mud, to evaporation, to solidification—but there is no trace of life. In that earliest phase they belong to the same period as gelatinous organisms. They also witnessed phases of freezing cold, associated with fossilized sea creatures. Each of these phases in the life of rocks lasts for a number of years, a fact that gives the inquisitive human mind a severe, indeed stunning, shock.

Previously, we used to compute things this way:[2] the flaming mud era, then the gelatinous organism era, some 44 or 440 million years; from the gelatinous era to sea crabs, between 24 and a 140 million years; from sea crabs to the very first amphibious creature, between 12

2. See the chart and chapter titled "The Record of Rocks," in *The History of the World*, by H.G Wells, 11. The two numbers at each phase combine the differences in scholarly estimates.

and a 120 million years; and, last chart, the era of mammals, grass, and forests, but there are still some 20–100 million years between the era of the first mammals and us.

We used to cite those figures, but today we need to ask Mr. Wells to correct his chart. How can it be otherwise when astronomers have deduced from their research on nebulas that the age of the sun and thus of our universe—one of its planets—is more than a thousand million years?

> When radio-active rocks dissolve, scholars can work out the length of the period since they solidified. They have discovered that the oldest rocks studied this way took solid form 1,750 years ago![3]

So where exactly is the oldest road in the world? You mountains descended from eternity, clothed in immortality, show me! You saw the first fish emerge from the waters to sniff the air and bask in the sunshine. You saw the first crocodile shading itself beneath the palms on those eastern shores. You heard the very first cricket singing its lonely song on summer nights, a place where it was the only singing creature. You saw the first rhinoceros plowing its way through the forest at your feet. So will you not show me the world's oldest road?

You mountains, in front of which the past has paused in all its different roles, you have observed its animals, its peoples, its armies, its kings, its nights; you have heard the howls of foxes, the roar of lions, as well as the groans of human beings. You have also heard their national anthems, their religious chants, and their sighs of longing. You mountains, clothed in immortality, you are greater, lovelier, and finer than the mountains of gods in the capitals of both Greece and Rome.

You stepped pyramids, where whole generations of sea and land creature lie buried, and whose tiered layers, one atop the other, were erected in times when human beings were a secret in the heart of all creatures, your structure speaks of higher art, adorned with caverns

3. *Al-Muqtataf* 93, no. 3 (1938?): 267.

and ledges, its sides perfumed with basil, laurel, terebinth, myrtle, and sage. Standing atop your shoulders are generations of pyramids, one atop the other, built by time itself and stepped by storms and wind. You are indeed mightier, lovelier, holier, and sturdier than all the other pyramids, temples, and towers built by humans, whether in Egypt, India, or China.

That scholar-philosopher poet, who had previously stood on the Acropolis in Athens, extolling the Greek gods with his eloquence steeped in knowledge, philosophy, and poetry, that same scholar had stood in front of you. On that very day he had seen that you were more beautiful than the Alps and had a sweeter perfume.

God forgive Renan, who, at the time, was more interested in the ephemeral relics of mankind rather than the eternal vestiges of nature.

The Anger-Stricken Forest

WE PASSED BY THE SHADOW of the stepped pyramid and crossed a small stone bridge in front of a cave in the mountain between the two levels of the pyramid. We walked toward a fork in the road and turned off in a new direction on a road that workers were still digging.

This road led to the source of the Adonis River and its largest temple—to Afqa. We were thrilled to be able to walk in this location that had been sanctified by the ancients. We approached it as pilgrims, we four believers—Yousuf Huwayeck the artist; two wise men of the world, Yousuf Sader and Ibrahim Hitti; and myself.[1] We were making this pilgrimage on foot in August; it was at a time when the sun opens its doors wide, the universe is bathed in a dazzling light, and fire burns the earth.

How clear is the sky in its shimmering expanse, although it withheld from us any kind of merciful cloud. To a certain extent the mountains compensated for the clear sky's merciless heat by providing us with some cool breezes from high up in the peaks.

We walked for about two kilometers along the road where the workers were digging; there were a lot of rocks, dirt, and dust, but that was not a problem for pilgrims like us. Even so, we turned off the road and followed peasant tracks along the path, which twisted its way

1. Translator's note: Yousuf Huwayeck was a sculptor and pioneer of sculpture in Lebanon and the broader Arab world. Yousuf Sader married Rihani's sister, Adele, and was thus the author's brother-in-law.

between plowed fields and scattered rocks to an ancient cypress forest with lots of obstacles.[2]

In the Lebanese mountains I have never seen trees in such poor condition that your heart sank like the chopped, destroyed, and scattered trees on this road to Afqa. This is the anger-stricken forest, beset by what time and human beings have wreaked on it. There is not a single upright tree there—apart, that is, from a few young ones planted recently—or, to be more accurate, sprouting from mother seeds scattered by the winds. Finding a bit of fertile soil amid the rocks, they have grown here and there into fresh, slender saplings.

The rest of the trees need to have a poet prophet like Jeremiah stop by them. He would mourn their past and elegize their former glory. God protect them from the hand of mankind, eager for a bundle of firewood; from the destroyer of forests, grabbing trunks and branches and opening their hearts to winds and storms. They break apart, and anything still left of their life and beauty withers away.

I can still picture this forest in its glory days on a day when it offers the mountain shade between Aqoura and Afqa. Its greenery rises to the very horizon and covers the road that passes through it on the way to the great temple. I can envision visitors in ancient times—monarchs, generals, and Romans—who made a pilgrimage to this holy place in the name of Venus and Adonis. With them they brought offerings of intercession, as they issued instructions for the preservation of the temple and enhancement of its glory and blessings.

One of those visitors was Hadrian, the peripatetic emperor and devotee of Venus, who built her temples to East and West and banned the chopping of trees—cypress, laurel, and cedar—on Mount Lebanon, particularly on the road to Afqa the revered. I can almost see him, making the pilgrimage along with his royal entourage at the

2. Ancient trees found in the mountains include cedar, cypress, and juniper. The word *araar*, which some writers use to describe the juniper, is actually a Persian word meaning the same thing: juniper. The tree called *sharbeen* in Arabic differs from the juniper in that it has larger leaves and smaller fruit.

beginning of the second century CE, seeing what we have been seeing, the effect of woodcutters' forays, and especially, on the cypress, laurel, and cedar forests. They were already sanctified to the Temple of Venus, and so he ordered that they be preserved and banned cutting them down.

The forest may well have thrived after that and stayed looking glorious until that crucial day for temples, the day when paganism disappeared from Lebanon. After that, the Lebanese went back to the traditions of their ancestors, sending woodcutters with their axes back into the forest to destroy with reckless abandon, not caring in the slightest about the kind of destruction they were wreaking in the valleys and mountains.

That is why only two of the ancient forests are left, in Bsharre and Jaj. This particular one was a kind of pseudo forest, one where the roots and branches let out a scream of protest against the ravages of woodcutters. If you were to see those ancient roots—hollowed out, crunched together, destroyed, and dried out—at dusk or in the moonlight, they would look like deformed creatures or visions embodying people in pain and grief.

Those appalling trunks with their weird shapes had spread their roots over the ground and between the rocks like snakes and serpents. They looked like elephants' heads with their trunks extended, camels' necks with their bodies buried in the sand, goats' horns, and the broken pieces of Laocoon's statue.[3]

They look like hippopotamuses standing on their hind legs with their front legs raised; a genie showing her teeth, her disheveled hair splayed over her shoulders; a trinity of terror—a trunk made up of three hellish curses: your back on your neck, your neck between your legs, God willing! And yet those trunks, split open, crippled, crushed, and destroyed, do not despair of life in spite of their situation. The

3. Laocoon is a statue representing the Trojan priest and his sons, their bodies wrapped in snakes.

new branches that grow on their sides and in their wounds only add to the misery and ugliness of the scene.

Huwayeck the artist did his best to alleviate the impression I had of the scene:

"They're the ghosts of previous visitors, worshippers of Ashtarut!"

"And I've just noticed a huge rock," I said. "Two trunks have grown around it and demolished it. And that hideous crone, clutching a rock to hurl at me, can she be a worshipper of Ashtarut and Adonis as well?"

"Some hideous shapes," the artist replied, "have elements of fine art."

He then reminded me again of that Greek statue—Laocoon, the priest with his two sons, wrestling with the snakes.

How many replicas there were among these tree trunks and roots! Such incredible examples of mutilation and distortion far surpassed any horrors that Homer and Dante could portray.

This then is the anger-stricken forest. I can almost hear it saying, "Sever me from my roots and burn me. Burn my roots, my trunks, my branches. Do not let me remain on the earth's surface as a horrible, terrifying illustration of the vengeance of the gods."

Saint Takla

WE WERE STOPPING in the anger-stricken forest in order to move away and look toward the horizons beyond, however narrow the sides might be. One horizon extended to the southwest, but the others were blocked. Above the Adonis River, Mount Moses connected with Mount Almat. The road kept twisting beyond us, from time to time revealing green fields where rows of maize were raising their flags and potatoes scattered white flowers.

There was a peasant planting seeds for the season. A young man was digging a water channel with his long hoe. As he was digging, he kept singing as a way of relieving the pain of separation and distance buried deep in his heart. He sang *ataaba* in a coarse, deep-toned voice:

> Gone is the boat, its engine unbroken.
> You have forgotten the vow, not as before.
> Now, my dears, I assume you are no more mine.
> Many people have lived without friends.

We kept walking for an hour and a half in the burning sun, although the intense heat was mitigated by the cool breezes from the mountain peaks. The road kept twisting and turning in front of us and then disappearing, without providing us with a single trace or image of our desired goal.

Our companion Huwayeck was an experienced and excellent walker.

"Afqa is an hour from the crossroads," he told us as we continued on our way.

Our other companion, Ibrahim, reminded us of that fact as he tightened the bath towel on his head that he had soaked in the spring.

"No one in the mountains," he said, "is good at being a guide and estimating distances. Here's this art critic, Huwayeck, an expert in arts and sciences and a subtle observer of everything except the trials of human existence; he really doesn't care. Ask him how far it is from one village to another, and he'll give you an answer that is no different from what any goatherd or peasant can tell you. 'Smoking a cigarette!' The cigarette's a whole hour, and that same hour is a goatherd's hour, half a day!"

Our other companion was the oldest among us, the tallest, and the most august. He wore a fez on his head and a traveler's jellaba. In his left hand he carried a rosary, while he kept using his right hand to wipe the sweat off his forehead with a handkerchief. Quiet and patient, he had gone on ahead and was looking down at the cordial pastures down the valley slopes. He greeted his namesake the artist, who returned the greeting and then greeted me too.

"It's from Ibrahim," I said, "and in the name of God, the compassionate, the merciful."

We did not expect to find any sign of human life near Afqa at this time of year. So we were surprised to find a house above the river set on a wide expanse of the mountain. The house was surrounded by orchards and planted fields around the orchards. This was Monaitra, a hermit's farmland—or rather, a paradise set between river and mountain.

We made our way downhill and paused when we were close to the house. We discussed things. I was the one who suggested that we visit the cave and ruins, then go back to Aqoura for lunch. It was almost noon. But then, our very own Nestor, Yousuf Sader, had another thought.[1]

"It would be polite, indeed obligatory," he said, "for us to visit the owner of this house first, and then decide what to do next."

1. In Homer's *Iliad*, Nestor is renowned for his wisdom and sound judgment.

"I don't even know the man," Ibrahim replied with his usual bluntness. "It's not right for us to eat in his house."

"We'll introduce ourselves first," said our resident sage, who knew all about what was right and not right about social conventions, "and, as the old saying has it, we'll be canceling restrictions by accepting collations."[2]

The council thus came to an end. Moving forward, apparently with a single spirit, we made for the house of this owner of paradise. Trusting in God, we entered and found ourselves in a wide-open courtyard sheltered by a huge vine with dangling clusters of grapes. Sadly, they were still green and sour. Beside the house was an uncovered salon with an old man in his nightshirt sitting and smoking a nargileh. Between the salon and the courtyard another man was standing, making a dagger, and still another was sitting by the hearth and making coffee.

The old man greeted Huwayeck but forgot to do the same with us, assuming that he was greeting us—or rather that, by greeting just one of us, he was including everyone else.

I was already familiar with the utensils in the coffeemaker's hands, Bedouin utensils that have often caught my eye and gladdened my heart—coffeepots with long spouts, blue china cups, and the coffee itself.

The servant brought us the coffee with cardamom seed in it. Now I felt as if I were the guest of an Arab sheikh. But, as I was relishing this personal feeling, I heard the old man addressing our companion Huwayeck.

"So where's the picture of Saint Takla?" he asked. "Didn't you promise you'd bring me one next time you visited?"

It was only then that I appreciated the attitude that our companion had adopted in our earlier consultation. Now I understood why he had been so hesitant about agreeing to Yousuf Sader's suggestion. I

2. Translator's note: the original Arabic phrase rhymes.

listened as he mumbled feeble and incoherent words of apology. That only made the old man even angrier. As his protestations grew worse, we decided to intervene out of a desire for a peaceful resolution and the more friendly reception that would follow.

Our colleague welcomed our intervention and prefaced it by introducing us to his host.[3] We then introduced ourselves, but none of the names plucked a single string in the old man's heart.

The salon now turned into a law court. From Sheikh Gabriel Germanus from the Nureddine family, we learned that, in the time of Patriarch Elias Huwayeck, Yousuf's uncle, he had had a meeting one day with Yousuf at the patriarch's residence and had asked him to paint an oil portrait of Saint Takla. He had sent him the cost in advance—five gold Ottoman liras—by way of a bishop. None of it had ever reached Yousuf.

Even so, Yousuf had promised to paint a portrait of the saint's noble countenance for nothing. He had never seen her face, knew nothing about her life, and had never heard anything about the miracles she had performed.

At this point, the wife of Sheikh Germanus asked to speak and said a few relevant words. She sent a servant to the small church close to the house to prove her point. The servant came back with a shiny, colored lithograph made in Germany. The devout lady of the house took it in both hands and kissed it. She then started talking about it and explaining its significance to our artist companion.

"Saint Takla—peace be upon her!—was the daughter of a pagan prince. She converted to Christianity, and that infuriated her father, the king. He ordered that she be thrown to the lions, but, while she was among the beasts, this particular lion (and she pointed to the animal with her finger) kissed her hand, and this other lion kissed her feet. The biggest lion of all stood in front of her like an obedient

3. In the language of the Bedouin, the Arabic word *mu'adhdhib* means "host," and *mu'adhdhab* means "guest."

servant. Here (and she was still pointing with her finger) is the emperor's reception hall, showing him and his entire entourage watching. This is one of Saint Takla's miracles—peace be upon her!"

The artist's eyes lit up.

"Wonderful," he said in a happy, respectful tone. "I will copy this scene exactly as it is, with the lions and monarchs. Sheikh Gabriel, I'll present you with an exact copy in oils."

"Your promise is not enough," the sheikh replied. "You've made that promise many times before and broken it. Can any of your esteemed companions vouch for you this time?"

We all volunteered in unison, our voices emerging from the depths of our being—and from an empty stomach. Sheikh Gabriel Germanus chose Professor Yousuf Sader, both because of his fine reputation and the fact that he owned real estate in Beirut, which underpinned the warranty. If the artist failed to produce this time, then sponsor and property would be in the sheikh's hands.

After the lunch that the sheikh's wife was kind enough to offer us, we learned that Sheikh Gabriel had traveled to America in his youth and settled in San Domingo. Working in commerce, he had grown rich. He had married a noble daughter from the island and brought both her and his wealth back with him to his birthplace, Aqoura. She had died there—God have mercy on her!—and was buried in the Saint Takla church.

We also learned that he had built the tiny church near the house for himself, the peasants who were "his partners," as a permanent memorial to her. In his heart was a place for love, and another for piety.

Sheikh Gabriel Germanus, like his second wife from the Khazen family, was a devotee of Saint Takla—peace be upon her! He had built a church and paid a famous artist to paint her portrait in oils.

The Roman emperor Hadrian was a worshipper of Venus. He built temples to her and brought her sacrifices.

From Hadrian to Germanus; from Venus the goddess to Saint Takla—between them 1,800 years in time, but a mere hair's breadth in faith.

The Mighty Ruins

FROM GERMANUS'S PARADISE in Monaitra to the Afqa grotto, we descended 200 meters on a rough path; in places animal droppings flowed past in the muddy water. On either side prickly gorse and self-planted growth were sprouting, including the elf dock plant, with its seeds as big as myrtles, although they were black and inedible.

While we were on this path, some 1,200 meters above sea level, we came across a small, fossilized oyster, a silent sea creature that speaks! Yes indeed, you daughter of the open sea, you who have carried news of the ages ever since the waves crashed against these boulders and deposited you on the shore beneath these peaks, only to return you to your watery home. In those days you would be stirring inside your moist, transparent shell, but then disaster struck you and your fellow sea creatures. When the waves retreated from these mountains, they left you high and dry. The blue-eyed sea abandoned you to die of thirst amid these rocks, but your tiny size saved you from the destructive disasters. Now here you are, millions of years later, a pebbly shell safe in my hands.

Along these terrifying abysses, another record of time's passage awaited us, a page from geology's textbook. In it we could read the course of creation of limestone layers, stacked one on top of the other. In a semicircular pattern, they started in the north and disappeared to the south. There were towering clefts some five hundred meters above the grotto and valley, their composition made up of different types of soil and rock; some parts were pasturage for sheep and goats; other parts were bare and stony, sloping down steeply and liable to slide during floods.

I told Mayy we'll meet here in Afqa in a thousand years.

This circle of skyscraper walls, adorned with a belt consisting of a pattern of dust-colored rocks, looked like a mountaintop from below and a shelf from above. It formed a slanted composition of limestone layers, with some horizontal layers and others vertical.

This belt was the major feature of the place, a lurking awe, a splendor that both rose high and sloped downward, stretching to the southwest along with the mountain and cut off to the north. About twenty meters' worth of it had broken off in the 1905 landslide that had destroyed the village of Afqa and left no trace. Everywhere layers of limestone were scattered around.

The rock layers had different types of soft and hard textures. Floods and winds were able to do remarkable things with the soft ones, creating caves and peaks or digging deep crevices that caused the area above them to collapse.

In the forest village and all around it, there was evidence of this geological phenomenon, piles of rocks and boulders. They had broken loose from their layer once floods and winds had done their work on the layers below them. It was all evidence of a terrifyingly powerful landslide that had tossed rocks in every direction; you could see them in the plowed fields and on the riverbanks. The forests were perpetually threatened by landslides on the mountain, apparently unconcerned, just like Pompeii in the shadow of Mount Vesuvius.

Before we reached the grotto, we looked to the north and noticed some caves in the initial process of formation. Water was gushing from the rocks, and in two places limestone layers were in the process of becoming caves in a thousand years' time; then water would gush from them as it did now from the main grotto.

I mentioned this to my friend, the author Mayy, who was our neighbor in Freike in the summer of 1938.[1]

1. Translator's note: this is a reference to the renowned author Mayy Ziyadeh (1886–1941). Born and educated in Lebanon, she moved to Egypt in 1908, but returned to her native country in the 1930s. She resided for a period in a house next to that of Rihani, but returned to Egypt, where she died in 1941.

"I'm going to come back here in a thousand years," she said, "and visit this place to check on the accuracy of your prediction!"

"We'll meet here in Afqa in a thousand years!" I agreed.

Mayy may well witness the miracle and be a part of it, sitting here, in the shade of that walnut tree, or even in the shade of the walnut tree that will be there in the future. She will be holding this very book in her hand to read the prediction.

A thousand years earlier, you mighty Roman emperor, were you aware of any of the secrets of the future? I wish I knew whether, on the day that Hadrian made his pilgrimage to this spot, water was gushing from the northern sides of this mountain. I wish I knew whether he had anyone in his entourage who was as interested in scenes of nature as he was in religious rituals. If that were so, then we would know some details about Afqa's natural environment in those times.

The grotto would undoubtedly have been here, with sweet, cool water gushing out as it does today, tumbling like a waterfall below the road. There were two ways to get there, as is the case today: one to the southwest, passing by the Hadeed Spring, the other to the north, which we had taken.

These carved stones scattered over the hilltop and on its sides all the way down to the river, piled up here and there, with chunks of the wall spaced between them, these had all survived the great catastrophe. Abandoned as they are today, in those days they were arranged in an exquisite symmetry, shrines to the loveliest of gods and goddesses, Venus and Adonis.

Temple of Adonis and Venus, of Ashtarte and Tammuz, I can imagine it, standing there on this hill in all its majesty and splendor amid these mountains. It stood in front of these sparkling, foaming waters that gushed out of the grotto, surrounded by a wall, traces of which that can still be seen. It was enclosed by large spaces with tame animals and a holy lake full of fish.

In the open space in front of the temple were two huge statues depicting the male and female reproductive organs.

Temple of Ishtar, temple of Tammuz, holiest shrine in Phoenician lands, it would be teeming with visitors on the annual feast in springtime. Devotees and sufferers would come from every direction—the coast and the interior, Babylon and Assyria. They would come in all humility; they would come as pilgrims bearing their offerings; they would also arrive clamoring and out for gain.

One day, the Temple of Venus, the richest of the Phoenician temples, was visited by the Roman emperor Marcus Crassus, covetous and evil. He had already waged war on the Persians and despoiled Mesopotamia, but now he plundered this temple as well. He spent several days assessing the weight of the gold and silver vessels and other valuables that he stole from the Afqa Temple.

Dear reader, you have already made the pilgrimage with us. Would you like to do it with the Phoenicians? Before you even look down on the temple, you can hear a hue and cry, along with the sound of drums, cymbals, and flutes. There would be the sounds of priests chanting and male and female pilgrims wailing and groaning. The sounds would be filling the space high up in the mountains and would waft down into the valley, where the echoes would resound. Eagles and wolves would be scared.

As you crossed the bend in the road, you could feel the heat of fires and smell the smoke. Then you would look down on the temple in the flat expanse below, situated between the towering mountain peaks.

Here now are the priests and custodians of the temple, three hundred of them, carrying devotional torches as they move in an impressive, awesome procession. What are the torches? Forest trees that have been cut down, with offerings to be burned attached to them.

Here too are the prostitutes, daughters of the temple, performing their dance of reverence and passion. Men beating timbrels too, blowing flutes, banging cymbals and drums, and chanting canticles. Among them would be a circle of dancers, the dervishes of those times, spinning, leaping, swaying chests and hips, and crawling on their bellies.

Then there would be raving people possessed, carrying daggers and bits of pottery with which they were stabbing their chest and slashing their faces and arms. They would sever some of their limbs, while others would castrate themselves and make their organs offerings to the gods and goddesses.

There would be transgender people who had powdered their faces and kept running around the city markets asking for women's clothes, which they put on to replicate their lofty goddess Ashtarut. Then they would take them off and dance naked with the prostitutes, all in honor of licentious intercourse.

What is that they are hurling from the temple roof? Bags with lambs in them? No, do not believe that fable. In those bags are human babies, offered as a sacrifice to the gods . . .

Then came the Greeks, and, after them the Romans. They borrowed many of these myths from their predecessors. They changed and improved them. Ishtar became known as Astarte, then Venus. Rituals and worship were somewhat cleansed of the priests' mumbo jumbo and the worshippers' filth.

Then Christianity arrived, to oppose idols and idol worship altogether. It came to Lebanon at the beginning of the fourth century CE, before Constantine's conversion to Christianity. Immediately after his conversion, Emperor Constantine ordered that all pagan temples be destroyed, in order, as he put it, to smash the very pillars of "that foul idol." The Afqa Temple was demolished in 325 CE, and the town's inhabitants were evacuated to Baalbek.

However, the Lebanese remained devoted to paganism and idols. At the end of the fourth century CE, they rebuilt the Afqa Temple, according to Bishop Yousuf Diryan.[2] Citing Theodoritus, he states that Saint John Chrysostom (345–407), "When he heard that the Phoenicians were still worshipping idols in the south, he gathered a group of monks who were fervent in their beliefs, gave them lofty royal commands, and sent them to destroy the pagan temples and kill the pagan Lebanese."[3]

2. See *Current Proofs Concerning the Marada, Jarajima, and Maronites*, 178.

3. He had written to Rufitus as follows: "I have heard that the flame of Phoenician evil has been rekindled and the pagan's deception has grown stronger.

But it seems that they did not destroy all of them, nor were they able to kill all the pagan worshippers. Small groups of them continued worshipping in the south, and some temples were left standing, including the one at Afqa, until the reign of Justinian (at the end of the sixth century CE). During the reign of that felicitous ruler, earthquakes hit Christianity and its monks (565–27). The great Afqa Temple was dealt a terminal blow, bringing it all crashing to the ground. It became what it still is today, a grim set of desolate ruins, aptly portrayed by Omar Abou Reesha's lines:

> The hand of destruction has grown tired of it,
> Afraid now of the harm of even touching it.
> Here illusion refutes its own ghosts;
> Death itself commits suicide in despair.

How totally appropriate is a poem that describes the illusions and traditions located there, now abandoned by death. In its never-ending renewal, it may well be immortal.

In the remnants of the eastern wall, amid all the foundational fabric on the hillside, has grown a solitary walnut tree and a fig tree.

From that past glory a tradition has been preserved, one that the "lady" of our times has inherited from the goddess of times past. The fig tree is one of a group of holy trees, blessed by the Virgin Mary—to whom be glory!

Indeed, the adherents to Shi'ite beliefs in that region were in the vanguard of those who proclaim "Glory to her!" They come to the fig tree as pilgrims, hang charms on its branches, and make solemn pledges to it. May God bless goddesses in every time!

The Christians attacked them in the name of religion; they were all deceiving themselves."

The Eternal Myth

I NOW TAKE THE READER back to the very first myth and its origins in the Near East. In it there is a glimmer of eternal light, one that flickered for the first time in the heart of a poet or sage who paused to contemplate in amazement some of the wonders of this universe.

It was a myth out of which the priests created an organized religion—one with beliefs, traditions, rituals, and devotions. It was material in both shape and meaning, and yet, in spite of its disavowed material development and its lovely poetic spirit, it remained like its origins, the same in every time and place.

I am taking the reader back to its initial period, to that era that was ancient even in the time of Sanchuniathon, the renowned Phoenician historian, to Ur of the Chaldees, and to the Sumerian city of Lagash.

Back in those early days, the poet saw the grain of wheat buried in the soil and producing twenty or thirty new grains in a single ear. He imagined the secret, the magical force in the dark recesses of the soil.

"There has to be a god tending this force," he told first himself and then his colleagues, "one that renews the phenomenon every year."

Humans had to worship this god so as to guarantee their continuing bounty and satisfaction. That was the basic idea in this primordial myth. In Sumerian that god was called Dumuzi, the son who rises from the lower earth, the prodigal son reborn.

Dumuzi fell in love with his own sister, Inanna, the goddess of earth and heavens. Following his death, she started descending every year to Arali, the lower earth, to bring him back to the earth. Another account states that Dumuzi was god of fields, irrigation, and animals, and served as husband, brother, and lover of the Earth Mother.

Whatever the case, archeology shows that he was the one who ascended from the depths of the earth.

After that, the symbol of life and death was inserted into the myth—wilting plants in summer, turning fresh green in spring. Dumuzi died every summer and was resurrected every spring.

That is why every year in summer, in the month that we know as Tammuz, a funeral ceremony was held for him. In Lagash and Nippur, that month was called "Inanna's departure"; in other words, the month when she disappeared in search of her beloved—Inanna, the goddess of the heavens seeking the god of earth in the depths of the earth.

When the Babylonians adopted this myth from the Sumerians, they called the departure month Tammuz, the month of the god Dumuzi. They called his sister Ishtar "virgin goddess." The connection between Tammuz and Dumuzi is obvious enough, as is the difference between Ishtar and Inanna. The reason for the difference is that the Akkadians called this goddess Ashdad in their local dialect, and the Babylonians adopted it and turned Ashdad into Ishtar. It is also mentioned in the Torah with added *ut*, so that it becomes Ashtarut.

Along with the name changes in the myth, the love theme developed as well, and it did not stay virginal.

In Babylon, Tammuz married Ishtar, and there are several contradictory versions. The goddess wife is mentioned in Babylonian prayers and intercessions as sister sometimes, mother and virgin mother at others, and even as mother wife on occasion. That is in addition to her designation as goddess of fertility and the moon.

This then is the theological dimension that the myth acquired in Babylon at the hands of priests before it spread westward. It is mentioned in Syriac literature and also acted as a religion with the Sabians in Harran, who continued to worship both Ishtar and Tammuz until the Middle Ages. They would exaggerate Tammuz's deeds and miracles—curing diseases, responding to every request, and able to subdue demons—all of them Babylonian vestiges in the myth.

There are other national Babylonian developments as well. At a time when they were fighting the Sumerians and Assyrians to extend their authority over the two countries, they saw it as a good idea to combine Tammuz with their major deity, Marduk; either that, or they took over the original idea of the myth and infused it with Babylonian national identity. They started holding a festival celebration of Marduk in April—in spring, in other words—just like the Sumerian festival.

Here is our great god, imprisoned in the underworld, with our priests mourning him and our women keening by his grave. His wife, Biltis, goes down into the world of darkness to search for him and comes back with him. Marduk rises from his grave, alive, Marduk-Tammuz, the god of life, death, resurrection, and eternity!

From Ur of the Chaldees and Lagash to Babylon and Assyria, and from there to Phoenicia, the eternal myth has traveled and changed somewhat, but without ever losing its significance and purpose.

From Dumuzi to Tammuz, to Adonis, the names may have been many, but the god involved is one. The last name on the list is Adon, meaning "lord."

The name Adon has its own particular Phoenician myth attached to it, a comment on or attachment to the original myth. Adon was the son of Myrrha, the daughter of Cinyras, king of Cyprus. He was born in Arab lands, to which his mother had fled in order to escape her father's cruelty. She then brought him back to Byblos as a young man.

Adon was a paragon of perfect beauty—beauty of both appearance and temperament. Ishtar, goddess of the heavens, heard about him and fell passionately in love with him. She descended from her heavenly heights and lived with him. Adonis loved to hunt. One day, in spite of his beloved's pleas, he went out on his favorite sport. He came across a wild boar and shot an arrow at it. The boar charged at him and killed him.

Another version of the story states that Adonis was the son of his mother, Myrrha, by Theias, the Syrian king. However, Aphrodite, goddess of beauty, seduced the mother through her son. Her love for him was painful, and her husband the king was furious and on the point of killing her. However, Aphrodite inserted some mercy into his heart, and so he turned her into a tree named after her. Ten months later, the tree split open, and Adonis emerged from it. Aphrodite

(Astarte-Ishtar) was enchanted by his beauty and hid him in a box. She handed him over to Persephone, the goddess of darkness, who kept him imprisoned with her and refused to return him to Aphrodite. Aphrodite raised the matter with Zeus, the god of all gods. He ordered that Adonis should spend a third of the year with Persephone, another third with Aphrodite, and the last third free to reside wherever he wished.

In this poetic version of the myth you can see the beauty of truth linked to the beauty of freedom. The god disappears during winter, when he is the husband of Persephone, the goddess of darkness. In springtime he returns to be a husband for Aphrodite, while in the fall he is freed from the scorching heat of summer and the freezing cold of winter. This then is the poetic development of the Sumerian, Babylonian, and Phoenician myth.

The festival in celebration of the myth's god also developed. The Phoenicians used to mourn Adonis and hold wakes every spring. During the Hellenistic period, the festival turned into one of joy and happiness. How could it not be so happy when Adonis had come back to life, resurrected in honor of eternal love, the love of Ishtar, goddess of the moon, of fertility and beauty? She was portrayed as a woman carrying a scepter and mace, with a halo of light around her head and a gold belt at her waist, riding a chariot pulled by a pair of lions.

The glorious Festival of Adonis was celebrated at many locations in the Greek region. In Byblos it dates from the fifth century BCE, and, even before then, there were wakes that involved some obscenities.

Then there is the myth of Attis. He was born to Agdistis, the hermaphrodite of the god Zeus. The mother fell in love with her son, and he ran away. Hiding himself under a pine tree, he died. His mother mourned and cried over him, but violets grew from his blood under the same pine tree (in the Adonis myth, it is the anemone that grew from his blood).

In another version of the story, his mother married her son and wandered aimlessly, mourning her son-husband.

The Roman poet Ovid has another version, which suggests that the mother's love for her son was platonic (from the Sumerian original), so she was a virgin mother. But, in spite of that, she still killed the girl whom Attis loved. That drove him mad, and he inflicted this barbaric crime on himself—the visible aspect, while the more symbolic theological view is the one of Babylonian origin. All women mourned his death and held lamentations every year.

In a third version, the Phoenician and Roman idol worshippers come together. After his disaster, Attis went out hunting. The god Zeus set a wild boar on him. Attis chased it, but it turned on him and killed him. Attis worshippers then introduced to their annual festivals aspects of the devotions to the Greek god of wine, Dionysus (Bacchus to the Romans), in which manifestations of mourning and grief blended with all kinds of debauchery and lewd behavior.

Priest and rulers made full use of these borrowings and interpolations involving deities and worship for their own political and religious purposes. I have already drawn attention to the linkage of Adonis and Marduk in Babylon, later between Adonis and Dionysus, and still later, between the two goddesses Ishtar and Juno, daughter of Jupiter, the god of all gods.

In a similar fashion, the Egyptians incorporated aspects of Markad worship, he being the god of joyous dance, into Bes worship, their god of feasting. There are two stories regarding their borrowings of the myth of eternity and its incorporation into the worship of Isis and Osiris. The first is that Osiris, lord of the underworld, was slain by his brother, Seth. His sister and wife, Isis, managed to get hold of the corpse. She was helped by Apis, god of the underworld, to hold the funeral at which the miracle occurred. So what was that miracle? Here the myth acquires a local Egyptian touch, the priestly magic represented by Isis's love. That magic power restored Osiris's corpse to life, allowing him to walk in triumph to the underworld, where he became its overlord, the god of the dead.

In Isis, Egyptians saw the very highest model for mothers and wives, while Horus, her son, had all the qualities of a loyal son, taking them back to Sumerian origins—the compliant and obedient son.

The second version states that Osiris was the god of agriculture, like Attis emerging from the pine tree and Adonis, from whose blood anemones grew, also like him in his Syrian origins. He entered Egypt along with kings, then changed national identity and joined the goat that was worshipped there. Thereafter his worship became linked with two gods of Memphis, the bull and the raven.

Among the evidence for the fact that Isis came from Syria is that she searched for her dead husband and found him in a cedarwood box in Byblos. To which you can another obvious fact—namely, that the heads of all Egyptian deities are animals, except for Isis and Osiris. They both have human heads, and, among the long-standing traditions within the myth of eternity is that Osiris, like Adonis and Tammuz, is resurrected whenever love thrives—in other words, in springtime.

Just before this particular season, worshippers in all the nations that we have mentioned used to put some seeds in china pots. As they grew, they would symbolize the truth of renewal in eternity. That custom is still followed today, coming to us from the Sumerians, through the route that we have depicted in peoples of the distant past. It is a custom with a history of over six thousand years, one that every community observes to this day. At the end of winter, they put seeds—wheat, lentils, chickpeas—in china pots, and grow until Easter with the Christians and the beginning of spring for Muslims. In both cases the myth is represented in its eternal guise, one that never changes, even if names are different and forms and stories are transformed.

If you have been following the growth of this myth and its transfer from one people to another—from Sumerians to Babylonians, from Assyrians to Phoenicians, and from them to Egyptians, Greeks, and Romans—you will have noticed that Tammuz, Adonis, and Osiris are all connected to the Sumerian Dumuzi, and that Ishtar, Isis, Aphrodite, and Venus are likewise connected with the Sumerian Inanna. You will also have seen that they all have one basic purpose in life: love and pain, death and sacrifice, resurrection and eternity.

However, in all these phases of borrowing, love varies and develops. With the ancients it was platonic, but then it became plain wicked, then theologically wicked, and materially wicked. First there was the beloved, then the wife, the wife mother, the virgin wife mother, the wife sister, and the wife who was both sister and mother to the beloved god. At a certain point in the myth or in the beliefs of some of its adherents, Ishtar and Isis were all three in one. In other phases she was the sister wife. The three became separate, and wicked poetic love was confined to Venus and Aphrodite.

So here is the Sumerian poetic religious myth going back to its origins, duly polished and embellished by the Greeks and Romans and elevated by both peoples to the lofty heights of poetry.

With the Egyptians and Phoenicians, the myth had a theological coloring to it due to the prevalence of the priests in both nations.

It is worth mentioning that these acts of worship to the godly mother and her son—to nature and spring—all these teachings about death, resurrection, and redemption, are the bases of Christianity, which rests on three core beliefs: the heavenly mother, the redeemer God, and resurrection and eternal life.

Festival and Anthem

GREEK AND ROMAN LITERATURE both include tales, in both prose and poetry, describing the Festival of Adonis, held in Byblos and other cities during the Seleucid and Ptolemaic periods. Among the lofty poems composed about this festival is an ode by the Greek poet Theocritus, in which he describes the celebrations of Adonis in Alexandria in splendid oratorical tones that bring that era back to our own times. As you read the poem some two thousand, two hundred years later, you get the feeling that you are actually watching the festivities and listening to the anthems.

Theocritus was born in Syracuse and lived in Sicily in the third century BCE. He made his way to Alexandria in the time of Ptolemy II, whom he eulogized in his poetry. He composed his poem about Adonis while there in 266 BCE.

As part of his wars and conquests, Ptolemy II had already captured Palestine and seized control of Mount Lebanon. He flattered the local peoples' religious beliefs by making their local festival, that of Adonis, into one of the Greek festivals.

The Greeks were superior to all the other civilized peoples in their love of beauty and in their artistic and literary artifacts that extolled beauty in their religion and secular lives. They gave this particular festival a marvelous poetic portrayal. The Ptolemaic rulers gave it particular attention, and the annual celebration in Alexandria was the best Adonisian festival in all the Phoenician and Greek territories.

Theocritus's ode gives a beautiful depiction of the festival; it contains a lively, dynamic, and verbal picture that the poet has adopted from the tablet of existence at that time and dispatched it to future generations through the medium of two women of Alexandria, who watch the festivities and give an authentic and eloquent description of them.

Among the nicest aspects of the ode is the eloquent picture it provides of the women of those times. You notice that, in most of their feminine characteristics and actions, they are no different from the women of today.

So here are Roxana and her companion, Georgia, on their way to the festival hall, along with their maid.

"Hurry up, Georgia! It's almost time for the opening. There may be a crowd, and we won't find a seat."

"God's curse on whoever made these sandals! They're pinching my feet . . ."

"Then take them off! Take them off and carry them with you. You've lovely feet, and there's no harm in leaving them bare. Hurry up; come on, hurry up!"

Now here they are in the crowded hall. Right in the middle, over a brocade couch, was the statue of a Phoenician youth whose beauty had first enchanted the goddess Aphrodite and thereafter every daughter of Eve in the East. They mourned his death and chanted on his festival day in order to resurrect him, the process that would restore to women's hearts that total, comprehensive love—the one single almighty love—a woman's love for her dearly beloved spouse and her beloved son.

No sooner had Roxana spotted the statue and what lay beneath it than she yelled, "There's Adonis on his silver bed. How beautiful he looks, even in death; how beautiful are his features! How lovely too his curly hair next to his mouth!"

Georgia was no less impressed and infatuated than her companion.

"Those lips," she said, "how luscious to pluck the rose from them!"

"Those violet wounds still look as though they were quivering with his breaths of farewell."

"Adon, oh Adon, how beautiful you are, how wonderful even in death!"

As she was shouting these words in a clattering tone of passion, one of the men present yelled at her.

"Enough chatter, woman!" he told her.

The picture portrayed in this ode provides us with a valuable insight into life in the past. The poet titled his work *Adonisasosi*, meaning "women at the Adonis festival." The most important thing for us is that it is a festal anthem recited by a female cantor of the royal temple.

The Anthem

Goddess of Cyprus and beloved of Sicily, return to us![1]

Beloved Aphrodite, abandon the golden shores and hurry back to us. Time has restored your beloved Adonis to us, back from those dark shores where no flowers glowed and no basil blossomed.

Here we are in the month of Tammuz.

Now is the rare, precious hour, bringing us the rarest and most precious of treasures.

With silent steps it approaches; with slow, delicate steps it presents to the world the radiant resurrection.

There is a reason for the slow pace: the immortal memories that it brings to this transient humanity, sweet-scented memories that dress time's wounds and help humans to forget their worries and sorrows.

Daughter of Diana, eternal goddess of beauty and love, with your many secret names, goddess of temples and altars, today your Adonis has returned, so return to him.

The youth of all youths has returned, now of even higher status.

There he sits on his silken couch, adorned with bunches of fruits and flowers.

1. This is translated from the English translation done by my friend Marion Miller, the American poet and expert on Greek literature. His translation of Theocritus's collected poetry has been published in New York.

Their very ripeness and light bring colors of dusk, only enhanced in beauty by a silver table.

They are all enveloped in a transparent covering woven by golden censers in which incense from Syria is burning.

What are those disks? What are those stars? Matchless pieces of halva, made by the hands of beautiful ladies from white flour mixed with crushed thyme and laurel, then kneaded with olive oil and bees' honey. Those same hands have crafted them into fascinating shapes: animals from air, land, and sea, with wings, legs, and claws.

Stop and marvel at these pieces of halva that seem to be running, crawling, and flying.

Beneath an eave made of basil and sweet clover, braided with bay and sage branches, in the dewy house of the sheikh encircled by birds and love and passion, two beds are prepared, covered with lovely brocade and colors.

Indeed, those colors are so attractive that they will even fascinate the inventors of purple.

Those woven patterns are so lovely that they make even shepherds pause.

"Where does wool like that come from?" they ask. "It's like summer clouds."

Twin beds, one for Aphrodite, the other for Adonis, the youth of all time, the groom for every year.

The youth of all lovers! His kiss is like that of light to the morning dew.

Youth of eternity! His mouth is like the rosebud, forever soft and deep red.

Enjoy him, Aphrodite! Spend a lovely evening in your beloved's arms!

Use the night as your coverlet until the morning dew glistens on your bed.

Tomorrow at dawn we will come to greet Adonis and carry his body back to the sea of eternal sorrows.

We will tear our clothes, let down our hair, chant our mourning cries with the waves, and join the winds in lamentations.

Adonis, you are matchless among heroes and unique among demigods.[2]

You are the one unique individual who can return to this earth from the recesses of hell.

Neither the reckless Agamemnon, who wreaked havoc and destruction on the Greeks, nor Pyrrhus and Hector—noble heroes both, nor anyone else who conquered territories and amazed time itself in ancient days and before history itself, none of those heroes and demigods has been blessed in the way that you have. Not one of them has acquired even the slightest portion of the nobility that is yours.

Beloved Adonis, be that noble always!

Envelop us with your noble qualities; detail us for your blessings. Then life will awaken in trees and love will be aroused in human beings.

Fare ye well, Adon, farewell,
For another year—good-bye.
In times of yore, you were a blessing.
You will be so forevermore!

2. Ptolemy honored Adonis like the Phoenicians, but, because of his respect for the gods of his ancestors and his regard for his Greek citizens, he did not allow him to be called a god. He described him as a demigod.

The Adonis River

I PREFER THE ORIGINAL NAME of this river to the one currently used, the origins of which remain unknown. I have been told that Ibrahim was a prince of the Marada, and the river was named after him. To which I say: who are the Marada, and who is their prince, when we were talking about the great god, the most beautiful of the ancient gods, the noblest mythic hero, Adonis?

The river was dedicated to his memory and called by his name in older times. It should be renamed after him out of respect for history and in honor of poetry. In times old and new, Adonis has been the novelty for historians and beloved of poets, from Theocritus and Ovid to Shelley and Shakespeare.

The Adonis River is not one of the world's great rivers; compared with the Nile and Euphrates, it is a mere child; alongside the Ganges and Yangtze, a midget; a mere streamlet alongside the Amazon and Mississippi. In spite of its small size, however, it is long remembered and highly significant, its name often repeated by human beings in their temples, beliefs, poems, and myths.

The river has never known whales and crocodiles, has never heard the lions' roar and the elephants' trumpeting during its Adonisian era. However, it has known incense burning on its banks and listened to anthems chanted in its valley.

No ships have ever sailed on the Adonis River, nor have mariners and soldiers raised their standards over its waters. No towers and castles have been built on its banks. And yet gods have walked on its waves, and night has raised the flag of sorrows over it. Women have knelt in prostration to it, and the heads of monarchs and priests have bowed low.

The Adonis River has no plains swaying with rich greenery, no gleaming cities to rival the stars, and no railroad to carry the invasive train. What it does have is forests producing oils and scents and mountain heights with golden peaks at sunset and swathed in silk in the morning. By the light of night and day there are miracles upon miracles, in valleys and hills.

From the hidden stores of snow on high to the limestone and sandy vaults shrouded in a darkness whose frigid temperatures, like them, are forever there; to the gate guarded by the sun by day and moon and stars by night; to the cave entrance, which today overlooks miserable plains but in olden times looked down on the temple of the goddess of love and beauty. From it, the silvery melt pours in a crystalline cascade, creating an azure lake. From the first waterfall and the first lake it flows into the valley, amid cultivated plains, verdant hills, beneath the doors of people's homes and caves inhabited by bears and wolves, into clefts in the rocks and lakes in the lowlands. It makes its way through gaps, whose sides broaden and narrow, and amid summits that become higher and more daunting every time the gaps get larger. It keeps flowing beneath eagle's perches, sometimes shaded by pine and juniper, at others by sycamores and willows. It reaches the expanse of soft soil near the remains of a Roman canal, and flows onward to orchards of bananas and limes, to the golden shore, to the eternal home, the sea! That is the course of the Adonis River, no more than thirty kilometers from its starting point at a height of two thousand meters—from snow to sand. It is the smallest holy river in the world; in the opinion of many people, the loveliest and most glorious of rivers.

We made a tour of the mountains on either side of its banks, by both its source and its mouth, and looked down into its valley from the ruins at Mashnaqa and on its waters from the meadows of Qartaba. We made a pilgrimage on foot to its source from Aqoura, and then went back to the shore and walked along the left bank toward its sea portico. We climbed the Ftouh Mountain; from one of its outcrops we were able to look down on the canal that, in Roman times, used to carry the waters to Byblos. Today a section of it that still survives stands above the banana and lime orchards. We continued eagerly climbing upward, penetrating deep into the mountain. With that, both river and valley disappeared. We only spotted it again when we were about to reach Yahshoush.[1]

In olden times, Yahshoush had boasted of one of the temples to "the god in pain." We stood on the roof of one of its houses and looked at the river glistening to the west. The mountain sloped gently in that direction, its slopes filled with vines and orchards. We then looked at the river to the east, its waters foaming through the rocks in the valley narrows, all under the watchful eyes of Mount Moses and Mount Mashnaqa.

Adonis, Adonis! Your name still resounds through the mountains and valleys. The memory of you is still freshly perfumed. For your sake, purple anemones still come into bloom every spring, anemones of blood-soaked memory.

Your portrait is drawn in every glorious conflict, between light and darkness, spring and winter, life and death. The wild boar may have killed you, but it failed to destroy you. It severely wounded you, and every single wound pronounced the immortal words: "Life is pain, then death, then resurrection, then immortality."

We left the road in Ghineh and walked through fields planted with mulberry and olive trees, heading toward the rock with an image of Adonis carved on it. It had two panels, one showing the god and wild boar fighting; the other a woman sitting and weeping over the god's mangled corpse.

Under that rock was a sarcophagus with no cover. No doubt, a peasant had broken it to make a doorstep for his house, just as his colleagues had done with the covers of the sarcophagi in Mashnaqa. Today that same sarcophagus is used by this usurper peasant as a water trough to water his fields.

1. *Yahshoush* is a Syriac word meaning "god in pain."

Alongside this same sarcophagus under the ancient rock is yet another act of desecration, one that I would like to serve, as I see it, as a modern footnote to the history of these ancient ruins. Carved into the rock is the following statement in French:

HERE MAURICE BARRES STOPPED TO
LOVE AND UNDERSTAND OUR SOULS.[2]

From that we learn that Maurice Barres, the French writer who went on to reject the social and religious aspects of the community but died in resignation, had visited this place. We also learn that he stood here as a philosopher or a devout poet scholar. He may well have felt baffled and speechless. Either he or one of his admirers may have wanted to join him in eternity with Adonis. He therefore carved the account of his visit into the rock and added to it the phrase, the significance of which I do not believe the scholar-philosopher would have approved.

If the writer had simply said, "Maurice Barres stood here," we could have overlooked this act of desecration. Instead, he had no interest in either archeological investigations or paying his respects to Adonis. He did it, he says, for love and to understand our souls. God bless him!

However, we remain in a quandary regarding the source of conscience in "our souls." Whose souls, vagrant engraver? French souls? Lebanese souls? Phoenician souls, worshippers of Adonis? Or perhaps the souls of colleagues of the person who fought the god and killed him? We find ourselves in a wasteland of semantic pearls, fearing what wild boars may do to him.

Beyond that, illustrious visitor, those words: *love* and *understanding*. What did you bring to this country in your suitcase, being at the time a deputy in the French Parliament?

Here I stand, remembering your visit; but not like you, to understand and love, but rather baffled by, on the one hand, your clever

2. In French: *Ici Maurice Barres s'arreta pour aimer et comprendre nos ames.*

fellow countrymen, who are so driven by glory, and, on the other, my own fellow Lebanese, who are loyal, and whose motivating force is emotion.

Yahshoush

AFQA'S ROAD is different from the one in Byblos that we took previously and described earlier in previous sections of this account. The other road is the Ftouh road (Ftouh in Kesrouan, that is). It starts in Maamaltein, passes through Ghazeer, Aramoun, Kfour, and Ghineh, and finally Yahshoush. Either from there or Ghineh, the traveler stays in the highlands, passing by the Hadeed Spring and continues to the northeast until he reaches Afqa from the south.

Along these two roads there are ruins and remnants of Phoenician and Roman temples and columns. Ghineh was the first, but by no means the last. There are records of an Adonis temple in Yahshoush and remains in the Ftouh heights close by the Roman wall that is the dividing line between Ftouh and Byblos.

Archeologists say that these ancient ruins—temple remains and the like—were stopping points or guesthouses for visitors to the great temple, the Temple of Ishtar and Adonis in Afqa during the Phoenician era, and thereafter the Temple of Venus in Roman times. Visitors during festival seasons, and especially during the annual rite in springtime, would be able to get some rest and hospitality in these locations—according to the archeologists.

However, our colleague Huwayeck, an expert on ancient history and monuments, says that these holy places and religious monuments were actually private acts of piety and devotion erected either to memorialize the dead or out of a desire on the part of some wealthy notables both to perpetuate their memory in this world and guarantee their welfare in the world to come. Proof of that is that beside every temple and column is a cemetery or the sarcophagi that still exist. The notable, priest, or wealthy worshiper would be eager to build a temple or column near his tomb. He would have part of the Adonis myth, his portrait, or a portrait of a keening woman, carved on it, just as Christians do when they have the tombs of their dead decorated with statues or religious symbols.

There is also another similarity in that certain temples and their priests gain a wide reputation for stories of miracles and wonders. Devout believers would arrive with fervent vows, hoping thereby to achieve their desires, and bringing sacrifices to beg for help and seek a cure, just as visitors to Our Lady of Lourdes and Saidnaya do today.

What confirms our colleague Huwayeck's theory is the distances between the temples. The Azrak monastery, for example, is close to the Mashnaqa temple, while between Mashnaqa and the Byblos coast there is no other temple or even a trace of one. It is the same case with Ghineh, which is thirty kilometers from Jounieh; the only trace of another temple is in Yahshoush, which is as close to Ghineh as the Azrak monastery is to Mashnaqa.

The following comment can be added to the previous remarks about the correctness of Huwayeck's opinions: in Yahshoush today there is a church dedicated to Simeon Stylites, founder of the monastery in the mountains honored by his name to the southeast of Aleppo. Can it be right to suggest that all the churches and monasteries constructed in his name from the seashore to Mount Simeon are stopping places or guesthouses for pilgrims coming to the saint's primary headquarters?

Let us now go back to Yahshoush and stand by the mighty oak—oak of the church, of the village, of the village teacher, of the writer from Yahshoush, of eternal Lebanese memories.

This same oak has a value in its own right, extolling its importance and worth. How can it be otherwise, when it is an example of ancient Lebanese oak, surpassing all other examples of this tree that we have seen in the careful attention that it enjoys? As a result, it can outdo all its peers in health, freshness, and growth—its branches and leaves are well balanced, it offers plentiful shade, and has a girth of five meters.

This is the oak of Daoud Barakat—God have mercy on him!—the tree he often sang about and yearned for, adopting it as a symbol for Lebanese nationalism and prestige. It is the tree beneath whose leafy branches he recited the psalms of his namesake, King David, and, after that, the works of Boutros Mouawad the writer, Shoukrallah al-Jorr the poet, and his colleague Khalil Akl, all of them writers from this modest village in the mountains.

Shaded by the tree and by the door of the church is a pond with a curious history recounted to us by one of the old folk of Yahshoush.

Yahshoush, the oldest and largest village in the Ftouh region, was either founded in the sixth century CE, or refounded after existing as a village in Phoenician times. For a long time, most of its inhabitants were Shi'a. In the twelfth century CE, their leader, Ismail Hamadeh, used to sit on his throne, which was placed on a raised site by this pond. He used to pass judgment on his people with a whip in his hand.

The days of Ismail, his throne, and his whip came to an end. Christians started settling in Yahshoush, outnumbering the Shi'a population. The Shi'a were now a minority, and the town became a Christian stronghold, specifically for the Maronites. Their symbols were the oak tree and the Psalms of David. Their patron saint was Saint Simeon Stylites, whose miraculous qualities included killing worms and insects by spreading some of his soil over them.

Saint Simeon's soil—certain death for any creature that coiled and crawled on the earth!

Saint Simeon's soil! How badly Daoud Barakat wanted it for the worms and scorpions of the press, or for anyone carrying a pen, who could only squirm, insult, and cringe.

Daoud Barakat moved from under the oak to a school in Aramoun, then to another in Ghazeer. He enrolled in the Hikma School in Beirut and taught there for a year and for another two years at a school in Bir el-Hait. He then left the mountains and moved to Egypt, gradually rising up the ranks until he became editor-in-chief of the *Al-Ahram* newspaper. He kept the job for thirty-eight years.

Daoud carried his Lebanese identity both in his heart and on his shoulders. He never abandoned it or showed a preference for any other mode of identity. Never once did he say to his identity, "Go away; I'm not going to be a loser!"

With his Lebanese identity, he himself was an oak; to defend it, he used a noble pen, one that spurned slander and insult or anything that provoked intrigues and partisan bickering in people. He never bartered with political principles or Lebanese revivalisms, nor did he exploit ignorance and fanaticism as other pretentious journalists did, either in the lands they migrated to or in their own country.

No one who knew Daoud Barakat, even if they were on opposite sides in Arab-Lebanese politics, would ever be anything but affectionate and respectful.

In his Lebanese identity, he was indeed a supreme model, even though we were and still are sorry that this supreme model should be encapsulated in his oak and church and fenced in by the rocks of tradition.

Such innocent Lebanese nationalism with its limited range is like Yahshoush in the mountains and a village woman among other women. However, modern modes of transport have brought even a village like Yahshoush closer to ports and cities, as has modern education, with the teacher of even village girls in the farthest valleys and peaks of Lebanon. In such a situation, will that Lebanese persona, steeped in village spirit, that village shaded by the church's oak and protected by the lofty mountains, will they emerge unscathed?

The natural horizon of humanity is a factor in their spiritual and intellectual formation. When education is as narrow or broad as that horizon, then the effect on the individual is even stronger and more profound. Once in place, that effect is difficult to counteract, especially if inherited traditions serve to endorse the horizon and education.

So what was the horizon for the young Daoud Barakat? To the north it did not stretch very far, while to the southeast it was like a wall. To the west there was a small gap that gave you a glimpse of the sea on a clear day, while to the northeast the horizon was almost closed off, except perhaps for falcons and eagles.

This then was the horizon of Daoud Barakat as a young man. It was gloomy and desolate, but still offered some splendid views. To the northeast the Yahshoush, Chouiyeh, and Almat Valleys came together. From the three valleys, crumbling, pointed peaks arose, looking like the ones in Switzerland—a rare sight in Lebanon. Above those peaks lay the flatlands of Almat and Mashnaqa, and below them the ten-bend road to Qartaba.

In the Byblos mountain range there were a few villages scattered among the forest and rocks—Fatre, Sannour, and Machchan—and, still higher on the dark horizon, Bir el-Hait.

This then was the flatter part of the Yahshoush horizon. However, the impact of Mount Moses was still very significant, looming over the village like an eternal embodied shadow, offering shade to both the highest house (at 800 meters above sea level) and the lowest (at 550 meters) and offering them a minimum of sunshine.

It looks like night in pursuit of the poet. Even so, springs burst from it, and deep in its valley is a river that joins the Adonis River. On one of its ledges in the middle is a solitary monastery, which may well have been built by Daoud Barakat's ancestors, eagles of Lebanon and faith.

So this is Daoud's Yahshoush—God bless you!—with all your past history. After the oak itself, the most beautiful thing we have seen, there are the vine trellises coiling around the terebinth and oak trees, each trellis with its own throne, proud and independent. In every direction—from the riverbanks to the mountain heights, there are bright thrones, grape trellises, that envelop them, crowning their heads, and penetrating their hearts. From their sides, swaying branches hang down, laden with grapes of many hues—amber, emerald, violet, and turquoise.

These are the palms of Yahshoush, palms of summertime that never breaks its promise, palms for the festival that nature puts on every year, whether the person to be worshipped is Adonis or Simon Stylites.

Seventh Journey

Amcheet

Contents

From Yahshoush to Treguier

THERE IS NOTHING FLIPPANT about this rapid, long-distance shift in our travels. No levity, no confusion, and no mockery. It is carefully planned. We finished the final section of the previous journey with a mention of both Adonis and Saint Simon Stylites. We will begin the first section of this journey by citing two names: Neptune, god of the sea, and Tugdual, a saint of the land.

With the aid of Neptune, the sea-god, and Tugdual, a land saint, we can move from the Phoenician coast to the shores of northern France—namely, Brittany.

But why, one wonders, is there this abrupt move from East to West, from Lebanon to Brittany, from Yahshoush to Treguier? I have mentioned gods and saints, so is there some secret connection to theology?

This discussion brings to mind the conversation between God and the Devil in the Book of Job. God asks the Devil, "Where have you come from?" and the Devil replies, "From traveling the earth."

However, my purpose is not the same as the Devil's, whom God delegated to test Job in his travails. My own goal is far removed from travail and tribulation. It is literary, historical, philosophical, and poetic, and, furthermore, humanistic.

I will clarify for the companion reader even further: our move from Lebanon to Brittany, France, may superficially seem a long one, but its inner significance is close. In fact, Brittany is mountainous like Lebanon, although its mountains are not as high or as splendid as ours in Lebanon. The valleys and flatlands that they encompass are similar, as are the honest men and women, worshippers male and female, who live there. They even have the same kind of rustic simplicity, although it is grim-faced and dry-skinned. They share with the Lebanese a certain simplicity, obstinacy, and tenacity.

There is also a historical linkage between the two regions. In ancient times the Romans occupied Brittany as they did Lebanon, and in both cases it lasted more than five hundred years. Like the Lebanese, the Bretons stuck to their pagan beliefs, and Christianity did not reach them until the fifth century CE. The Bretons fought for their independence just like the Lebanese, and the independence that they won was like shafts of light in darkness, or a kind of violet darkness accompanied by rants and slumber . . .

When they adopted Christianity, churches and monasteries were constructed from the stones of the temples of their idols, as happened in Mount Lebanon. The lives of the Bretons were perfumed with the sweet scent of sanctity exuded by the halos of their national saints, with Saint Malo and Saint Tugdual in their forefront. In the same way, Lebanese lives were perfumed with the scent of pious holy men and saintly ascetics, with Saint Maroun, Saint Simeon, and Saint Qozhaya—peace be on all of them—at their head! Truth be told, both peoples are falcons of faith, with common bases in belief and piety, as well as fantasia in myths and superstitions.

The Bretons were devoted to king and church, while the Lebanese were devoted to church and France. The Bretons rebelled against the revolutionaries in 1792 and against the Jacobites, their religious foes, while, in the first half of the nineteenth century, the Lebanese rebelled against the Ottoman Empire. Wheels turned, and, in the Vendee Mountains of Brittany, the republicans defeated the monarchists. They stripped a thousand soldiers of their weapons and slaughtered them all, just as the Ottomans did to the Maronites as part of our blessed quest for independence.

The Bretons had Bertrand du Guesclin, and the Lebanese Yousuf Bey Karam, two heroes of lost independence.

In Brittany there are many nuns, prayers, and religious festivals as in Lebanon.

When it comes to prominent figures from the two regions, both had their share. From Brittany came a number of politicians and leaders, heroes of both land and sea, including Jacques Cartier—the founder of French Canada, and Robert Surcouf—an important naval commander. In science and literature, Lebanon emerges on top; if, that is, superiority is to be measured in numbers rather than impact. However, if a single one of the unusually gifted people is compared with a hundred more normally talented folk, then the verdict goes to French Brittany, and indeed to a small town there, one with no more than three thousand inhabitants—namely, Treguier, situated on that desolate rocky shore, the Manche (the English Channel).

Treguier has a cathedral with three towers, a monastery dedicated to Saint Tugdual, and a port from which intrepid mariners set sail to fish in distant waters to the north in both new and old worlds, amid ice and snow.

It is in Treguier that Ernest Renan, our next major topic, was born.

It is he that has prompted us to indulge in this abrupt transition and urged us to use the title of this chapter as a means for making such associations and comparisons. Indeed, it is he, but also his sister, Henriette, who is buried in Amcheet—God's mercy on them both!

The Sister Carer

ERNEST RENAN'S FATHER was a Treguier sailor, making his livelihood at sea in commerce and voyages. But on one of those commercial voyages he suffered enormous losses.

At the time, his only daughter, Henriette, was just twelve years old, but mature and composed beyond her age. In 1823, the year of his huge losses, a son was born, whom he named Ernest. The young girl's heart was torn in two by joy and sorrow: joy at the birth of a brother, sorrow at her father's losses.

Henriette may well have sensed what time had in store for her, feeling the troubles that were being tossed on to her shoulders. That is why a sense of foreboding overshadowed even her moments of joy. God may well have kindled in her a sense of affection and solace with the birth of her baby brother, and yet He also decreed that, for the rest of her life, Henriette would have to serve as a caring companion for him, an advisor and aide.

It was not long before Henriette could envision the troubles ahead of her. There was no other hand in the household to whom she could turn for help. Five years after her father's commercial disaster, his ship returned from the sea one day, terrifyingly empty. It entered Treguier port with the sail dangling against the wooden side and no captain. Renan went to sea and never came back. He became one of those unsolved mysteries of the sea; no one came with information about him, and he disappeared without trace. The sea took hold of him and lowered its black veil over his fate.

At the time Henriette was attending a convent school in Treguier, where she was learning the rudiments of science and imbibing the spirit of faith and devotion. She was gradually progressing toward the special blessing, and would have donned the black robe and white cowl of a nun, if it were not for her baby brother, whom she dearly loved, a feeling that only increased as the days went by. Later on, Henriette's brother would express the wish that her desire to become a nun had been fulfilled, because she was the bride of sorrows.

Henriette left the convent, but her heart would still glance at its walls and see the candles always lit on the chapel's altar and the crucified Christ of sorrows.

She was carrying the Psalms of David when she left, that being the biblical book that was the core of her spiritual growth, a process whose development went through some particular phases, which will be explored in the following account of her life.

In those days a number of families from the French nobility, who had left France during the Revolution and Napoleon's era, now returned to Treguier. Among them was a woman who had spent her exile in England and been trained in English cultural traditions. She started teaching in her hometown, and Henriette Renan was one of her pupils. She was to have an enormous influence on Henriette; her morals became more ingrained and exalted, and the scope of her ideas and beliefs widened. Her own Catholic religious values began to waver and gradually collapse.

However, anxieties and sorrows stayed with Henriette. Losses and debts piled up, and the specter of poverty and want loomed large. In every situation she was constantly thinking about her brother's future. One day she noticed him wearing his threadbare clothes and trying to cover up a tear. She burst into tears.

Life confronted Henriette with its very worst. But she decided to work and opened a school in Treguier.

In those days, meaning the Bourbon Restoration,[1] the Brittany département was a center for nobles and royalists returning from exile. Treguier, the lovely small city by the seashore, was like Jounieh in

1. The return of the Bourbon family to the throne of France (1814–30).

Lebanon, attracting many émigrés who settled there and ruined its village atmosphere. People started copying the nobility with all their habits and pretensions, people who had lost all their laudable qualities during political upheavals without acquiring any of the positives in their new existence. Instead, they remained crude illustrations of their former traits—selfish, cruel, obstreperous, petty, and conceited.

However, they were nobles, so how could the villagers not imitate them? How could they not look down their noses at Henriette Renan and her school? Could such grandees send their children to any school apart from one for grandees, a place where they would learn science combined with religion and imbibe the desire to rise in the ranks of society—it being the property of the nobility?

Along with her calm and noble qualities, Henriette did not possess those other traits that can conceal the beauty of a humble, devout soul from the eyes of darkness. She had nothing to help here fight against the bigotry and pretension in people.

It was precisely those noble traits that led to the failure of Henriette's initiative. As Renan himself puts it in his commentary on the apostle Paul, "Our failings fortify us in what we do, and our merits weaken us."

Henriette closed down her school, and went back to her ideas and concerns in order to glean some resolve for defining her eventual goal and the means of achieving it.

I have said that all people saw in her was the schoolteacher. However, a rich and cultured young man saw in her soft hands and gentle gaze—and the purity and nobility of soul that lay behind them—enough to make him declare his love for her. However, Henriette still preferred the hard life she was living to a life of ease in which her brother and mother would have no place.

Henriette remained single, her father's only daughter, drawing her solace from the cup of noble effort and nourishing her love by devoting herself to family duties. When she was offered a post at a girls' school in Paris, she accepted, but she was not happy in her new environment and soon rejected it. This simple provincial girl, daughter of nature and pure of face and spirit, did not glimpse any glimmer of friendship in the City of Light, nor any trace of kindness and affection. How could flowers of the spirit blossom in the big city, where lots of large unruly plants were being destroyed?

In those days that type of boarding school in Paris was a joke, its primary features being ignorance and pretension. That only increased Henriette's distress and hastened the development of her religious views. She realized the illusory nature of some religious convictions and the level of superficiality and hypocrisy in the beliefs of religious bigots. As she navigated the space between pedantry and bigotry and broadened her exposure to the horizons of experience and knowledge, flowers began to bloom in her intellectual garden, and yet in the depths of her soul Henriette retained nature's gift for men and women of discretion, people of faith—namely, the gift of sublime belief unmarred by the vicissitudes of time and unaffected by either science or philosophy.

This was how things were for Henriette in Paris when she invited her brother to join her. He was fifteen years old when he went to the capital city, having acquired the basics of theology at the monastery in Treguier. By that time he had already convinced himself that he would be entering the priesthood, something that did not please Henriette. However, she respected his faith and never uttered a word that might lead him to doubt his views or weaken his resolve.

They lived in Paris for four years. Henriette was teaching at her school and helping to pay for his educational expenses. In 1841, after he had enrolled in the Saint Sulpice Seminary, Henriette traveled to Poland to take the post of teacher for the children of a wealthy family. She was to stay for six years in the mansion of that family, situated on the banks of the Bug River, in a dark, gloomy atmosphere, just like the one in Brittany. If it were not for the kindness and generosity of that family, the mansion would have seemed like a place of exile. As it was, Henriette came to enjoy the pleasure of work for the first time and relished the friendship and comfort that the family showed her.

She took a short trip to Germany and Italy, adding to her knowledge and polishing her acquaintance with literature and art. After the trip, she settled in Berlin.

Henriette was still in touch with her brother, studying theology in Paris; they were constantly corresponding with each other. From his letters Henriette learned that his study of Semitic languages had had a significance impact on the theological knowledge that he had acquired. That delighted her. Since she was gradually rejecting her traditional Catholic beliefs, it helped her eliminate the remaining traces of theology in her brother's soul. Not only that, but Henriette was able to help him solve the problems that were standing in the way of his continuing studies. In addition, she gave him a thousand francs every year so he could complete his studies and included in her letters treasure troves of love, wisdom, and advice.

In every way Henriette was the sister carer, especially during the years when she was living apart from her brother—an ever-ready help with many hands, whether present or absent.

In 1850 Ernest paid her a visit in Berlin and found a distressing, alarming scene. Henriette had struggled and suffered, but had kept things hidden from her beloved brother. Now, was the Henriette that Ernest saw in her forties or fifties?

Time had dealt cruelly with her, falsely adding ten years to her age, something that registered clearly in her wan complexion and wrinkled forehead.

However, she had been victorious in her struggles. She had educated her brother, paid off her father's debts, and removed the mortgage on the inherited estates—which she left unencumbered to her mother.

Between Doubt and Certainty

TREGUIER IS BEAUTIFUL. It has natural vistas and is surrounded by gardens and lush forests. It is equally spectacular for its mansions and towers, its monasteries and churches. What is most accurate is to say that in those days it was still beautiful because the French Revolution had left its natural, historical, religious, and poetic heritage untouched. There were still monasteries and religious schools standing in the shadows of those mansions and castles.

It was in one of those schools that the young Ernest Renan learned the basics of universal science and theology and decided to become a priest. He left the school with prizes, and aspired to high office in the realms of the Catholic Church.

When he joined his sister in Paris, he enrolled in a small theological seminary that did not meet his needs. He moved first to the Issy monastery, then entered the famous seminary of Saint Sulpice in 1841. All this involved his sister's help, although, as we have already noted, she was not happy about his intention and determination to become a priest.

While Renan was at Saint Sulpice, he did not change his intentions. However, he began to have his doubts while at Stavistas College. He had become very proficient in history, linguistics, and religious sciences, and came to realize in the process the dominant role that the church played over intellectual ideas and its total control over their direction.

Renan rejected that domination and refused to submit. These doubts continued to gnaw away at his convictions. Eventually, they nullified most of them and turned him away from his priestly intentions.

He did not conceal from his sister details about the intellectual and spiritual conflict he was going through. She wrote to him from Poland, expressing her happiness at the way his ideas were developing and encouraging his leanings toward free knowledge, stripped of all religious domination, and turning to thought processes released from the chains of particular interests and dominions.

There then followed a series of events that were to bolster the student in his liberal intentions and achieve some of his dreams. In 1836 he made the acquaintance of Berthelot, who later became famous for his chemical research. The two scholars remained friends for the rest of their lives.

The next year Renan won the Volney Prize for his study of the history of Semitic languages.

In 1849 the French government sent him to Italy on a scientific mission. The journey polished his creative and intellectual faculties, in literature, poetry, photography, music, and singing. For a while art and science fought for his attention, and art was the winner, meaning that Renan, the philosopher in quest of the truth, started looking for beauty, whether in history, myth, or religious and secular sciences. While he never saw beauty in reality, he did have the sense that there was an element of truth in every kind of beauty.

Renan came back from Italy, loaded with its poetic and artistic beauties. He visited his sister in Berlin, then set up house with her in Paris. Even after he was married, he never left Henriette; he and his wife lived with her in the house, and his sister continued to help him in his activities and writings.

I mentioned earlier that the Renan family were farmers and sailors, and the way that this struggling class of people managed to produce brilliant children. The sea nourishes simplicity, and the fields whet the intelligence. The sea opens the eyes to the spiritual so they can get used to vast horizons; fields look for energy in thought and launch the imagination in flight.

However, the intellectual heritage will differ in accordance with temperament and character traits. Sometimes it can be bright and flexible, but at others dark and unyielding.

Henriette was her father's daughter: gloomy and cold, shy and withdrawn. She hated all show and glitter. In spite of all that, she was sensitive, emotional, and a profound thinker. She tied her heart to intellectual debates and had a muted love for beauty, one that relished privacy and meditation. She inherited nothing from her mother's soul, which was embodied in her brother. She was her father's daughter; Ernest was his mother's son.

As he grew up, Ernest learned the significance of smiling and sarcasm; or rather, he appreciated them both in literature. Early on, Renan dipped his pen in Voltaire's inkwell, something that did not please Henriette. She was someone who rejected Catholicism and many of its absolutist Christian doctrines, but did not want her brother to imitate Voltaire. He therefore moved away from that style of thinking and writing, but he was stalwart in his continuing adherence to the rights of poetry and the imagination and refused to sacrifice emotions in the cause of the untrammeled intellect. His own style, for which he became famous, was unique, combining simplicity and elegance, smoothness and rigor, compassion and might. Happiness finds its place in his words, whispers, silences, everywhere . . .

The two siblings lived in Paris for eight happy years. Renan had a minor post in the National Library. He used to write articles at night—literary, historical, and critical—for the famous journal *Two Worlds* (*Revue des deux mondes*). His sister used to help him edit and copy them. She would then read the proofs, never missing during the correction process the particular word that was both correct in meaning and at the same time tasteful. Clarity of style was her métier, but it was not tied to her sublime spirit or delicate sensitivity. It therefore comes as no surprise that her brother's literary writings were marked by three superior qualities: clear thought, sparkling style, and perfect diction.

It is worth noting that these twin spirits, united in their free thoughts and agnostic tendencies, always lived in the shadow of monasteries and religious institutions. The house on rue d'Enfer was next to the Carmelite monastery and overlooked its garden. The two of them could look out and enjoy the garden scents.

I wish I knew what effect that had on them both. Did those scents make their way into the philosophy that Renan used to plant in the soil of myths and those other myths that the gates of philosophy used to open? Whatever the case may be, the memory of that house stayed in the hearts of both of them all their lives.

A characteristic feature of the East is that people gifted with a certain amount of divinity can emerge there, and yet all they are endowed with is indolence and laziness. They think, but do not write; indeed, they do not produce any work at all. However, they inspire other people with significant deeds and sayings.

One among such people is Shamsuddeen al-Tabreezi. If it were not for him, Jalaluddeen Rumi would have passed through this world and left it like some empty spiritual vessel.

Shamsuddeen at-Tabreezi was not one to work. He would spend most of his waking hours in a cafe in Damascus, playing chess and sitting with the morning crowd of young men. Once in a while he would gesture to his friend Jalaluddeen and give him a taper of inspiration—a word, a thought, an image.

"Be on your way," he would tell Jalaluddeen, and the man would depart, singing praises to the divinities, "in the state," as they say in Sufi parlance. Meanwhile, Shamsuddeen would return to his morning youth and chessboard.

The ways of the divine are enveloped in riddles and mysteries. I get the impression that Henriette Renan possessed some of those remarkable Eastern qualities, which we can express in non-Sufi terms. Renan himself remarked that his sister was the major factor in his intellectual growth and the calibration of his intentions. She was never lazy and refused to remain in the background. Her greatest pleasure consisted in her isolation and total involvement in her brother's personality. In his life and literary writings, she was the latent, living—actually obvious—factor.

I conceive of this spiritual activity as being a kind of sunbeam reflected on a flowery patch with violets and daisies, set amid branches of a nearby tree swaying in the breeze. The sunbeam seems to be undulating gently amid the flowers, and yet its source remains unseen, untouchable and undefined.

Henriette had grown up in the mode of her own teacher, having imbibed the spirit of that particular English religious sect—the Puritans—pious, devout, and staid. However, her French background meant that she was different. She neither proscribed nor frowned upon human pleasures. In her heart she used to dance; indeed, in her inner spiritual joy, she closely resembled the behavior of Eastern dervishes, even though that feeling of delight was reflected in a philosophical silence that showed on her face and in her eyes. She had inherited simplicity and an acute sensitivity from her father. When it came to work ethic, moral strength, and proper comportment, she had acquired those from fate and that French-English teacher. All those qualities were reinforced by the vicissitudes and sorrows visited upon her by destiny, forces that led her to resist. Such resistance can lead to one of two results: either death or increased power and virtue.

As a young man, Renan studied these morals and behaviors in his sister, and his love and respect for her only increased. Paths of thought and action opened before him, and he started climbing the ladder to success and fame with abundant energy and hope during those years that he lived with his sister on rue d'Enfer—the street of hell.

But, for the first time in his life—in 1859, Renan had a clash with religious authority. Nominated for a chair in Semitic languages at the College de France, he was opposed by the Catholic Party, which launched a fierce attack on him.

"Should this high position dealing with religion," they protested, "be given to this apostate atheist who put on priestly garb only to take it off?"

Empress Eugenie was a supporter of the Catholic Party and men of religion, and so they got what they wanted.

However, their victory over Renan was not complete. Napoleon III had a high opinion of the scholar philosopher, and sent him on a scientific mission to the East.

In fact, he sent him to Syria to study the Phoenician ruins there.

The Historic Mission

AT THAT TIME Renan was studying the life of the Messiah in order to write a book about him. His sister thought that, in order to make his studies complete, he needed to visit the Holy Land. She suggested that he accept the Emperor's mission. He did so.

Emperor Napoleon III was very fond of such plausible missions, and I use the word *plausible* with the various dubious and negative factors in mind. Scholars involved in political methods—and their more cryptic dimensions—view the mission as being closely connected with Napoleon III's Eastern policies, particularly the appalling events that had occurred in Lebanon that year. The Maronites had been slaughtered with the tacit approval of France, supposedly their beloved model. After that disaster, the French fleet had arrived—but why?—for punishment, protection, compensation, or simply a naval cruise? You can consult the history books, but all I need to say at this point is that the French fleet arrived in Beirut, driven by French anger and the politics of their Emperor.

That summer Renan arrived in the bloodied Lebanon to conduct research on Phoenician ruins!

One wonders, was "Sultan" Napoleon III content to get the concession to dig in Byblos and keep the fruits of that project? Was that why the French delegation was so obliging in its negotiations with the government delegate, Fouad Pasha, in the aftermath of the dreadful events of 1860?

Napoleon III had appointed another scholar for yet another scientific project in the East, the Jesuit and former monk William Gifford

Palgrave, who had already traveled to Arabia and explored its regions and deserts, all the way to its core, the Nejd.

At this time, France was competing with England for the affections of the Arabs, desiring to control the Middle East. In fact, England was looking for a shortcut to India, while France kept trying to thwart them or discover such a route first.

Did science and politics come together, did traces of affection commingle, all so as to meet the political goals of the Emperor, first in the Arabian Desert and then here in Lebanon?

In this case I find myself inclining more toward the Renan of *The Life of Jesus* rather than to the explorer of Phoenician ruins. I prefer the scholar who did research in the country that was the stage for the man from Nazareth and the foundation site of Christianity; the one who proclaimed to the envoy of the French emperor the spirit of truth in the firmament of that land with its poetic historical milieu.

Renan arrived in the summer of 1860, accompanied by his sister. He was joined by his wife in January 1861, but she went back to France in August of the same year. A good deal of comment was made about sisterly love and his wife's jealousy, things that at the time only concerned the three of them and their relatives but certainly interest nobody today.

Renan and his sister remained, and Henriette accompanied him on all his travels, from the Jordan depression to the Yarmouk Valley and to the peaks of Lebanon—from the Galilean meadows to the Bekaa Plain and the shores of Phoenicia. She saw, heard, and felt everything that he did. During this Palestine–Syria–Lebanon journey, life appeared to her in all its purity; indeed, it bestowed on her the greatest possible earthly reward.

Henriette's contentment never had any effect on his own happiness or his work. As he himself says, if it were not for her assistance, he would never have managed for a single instant to acquire a knowledge of his subject from numerous perspectives—historical, archeological, social, and poetic.

Henriette used to collect the materials and organize them, making a copy of his writings and studying them carefully. She also kept track of his personal matters and kept a record of his expenses connected with both travel and research. To which we can add the astute opinions that she shared with him about history, archeology, and art, not to mention the pleasant company she provided him everywhere they went.

The two of them set out on their journey, a happy one in both reality and significance. Henriette was the Bedouin Arab in the saddle and on foot, riding and walking beside the men. She went to places that no European women could ever manage to see, desolate and forbidding locations even for the local people. She crossed difficult paths in the folds and narrows of mountains, suspended over abysses and peaks. In a single day she would climb energetically from mountain valley to summit, and then happily go back down from the top to the valley. Neither caves nor plateaus intimidated her.

In Syria fall is the most wonderful season, while spring is the most glorious. The first brings a paradise of amazing, splendid colors, while the second is a paradise of flowers. Both seasons had their universal spiritual secrets, linked to the depths of profound tranquility and the heights of intense creativity. If spring speaks in silver, then fall is quiescent in gold.

The golden fall sunset seems to us to have fascinated both Renan and his sister: the daunting plain with its golden coloring, the holy atmosphere taking hold of their feelings, a holiness to which their prayerful souls could only bow down.

Beside the daunting plain stood mighty peaks and awesome mountain horizons. The sheer contrast between the two vistas offer an eternal splendor, with hills dropping abruptly into the sea and hillocks sloping gently toward the sandy shores. Imagine what inspiration could spring from the twin vistas, especially when dawn drapes them in its pearly light and sunset in its golden glow.

Renan and his sister wandered through the scenarios of this heavenly natural beauty, their very travels a chant sung by hearts overflowing with joy. With such hearts, we now join them as they travel from the sacred house that laughs at the profusion of religious sites within it to Nablus, frowning between two mountains—Curse (Ebal) and

Blessing (Gerizim)—via Mount Carmel and its ocean of flowers, one thousand feet above sea level and Galilee, that paradise leading down to the lake where mourning doves still sing their songs by its gloomy shores, to the Sheikh (Hermon) Mountain, which surveys the Syrian plains and Palestinian caves with loving and angry eyes.

We are on the road, so feuding, contentious faiths are of no interest, nor are monasteries and religious institutions constructed for the god of secular intentions. We do not bother about places sanctified by moths and legends. Our path is one of knowledge, free thought, and spirit only tied to love of God, truth, and the good of humanity. Those were the values proclaimed by Renan and his sister with every feature of history that they saw and every trace of prophecy and poetry that crossed their path. They were always listening to the whisper of time and disregarding the cacophony of days.

They were both very happy, particularly in Lebanon, where they encountered the kind of hospitality that is unrivaled anywhere in the world, one offered by a people where a love and respect for guests is inborn. And that was quite apart from the habits and behavior of the local people that Henriette observed, reminding her of her own country, and especially her own tiny village. She was particularly fond of the Maronites and their religious liturgies. She would join them for prayers at the church just as she had done in Treguier, and her brother—the trinity of her heart, brother, son, beloved—would go with her (taking me back to olden times, to a period when a man would be brother, son, and beloved to a goddess in myth). Now here was Renan going to the Maronite church with his own goddess, holding the hood of her coat over his head to protect him from the rain.

During this short period of time I envision these two souls shielded under the hood of a comprehensive mind, a cosmic consciousness, an immortal composite spiritual force; I envision them both beneath that divine hood, sitting on the roof of the house in Ghazeer, using both eyes and insight to look out on the natural vistas in Kesrouan and the divine atmosphere in Lebanon.

I wish I knew what effect heritage has on the human soul, and what the effects of environment and education are. Can one invoke those two latter factors as a way of overcoming inherited beliefs—beliefs inherited from mother's milk, that luminosity that shows on a mother's face both before and after childbirth; that spiritual glow that is blended with a baby's food and penetrates deep into a human being's basic essence? When that same baby later becomes a philosopher or woodcutter, the traces of that glow, the glow of a mother's heart reflected in her face, are still there, to charm you and win your affection.

I can detect the divine glow reflected in Renan's philosophy in his sister's life. It is not merely the spirit of Christianity but also of those Catholic memories inherited by her from her religious background in their village. It felt as though she were recalling memories of Treguier in Lebanon as she and her brother delved into the core of the universe.

They would sit on that rooftop in Ghazeer on moonlit nights, amid images of doubt and lights of conviction, in an atmosphere sanctified by the secrets and faiths of the ancients. Brother and sister would converse and debate issues of philosophy and religion, with the brother's intellect focusing on analysis and the sister's soul on desert wastes. They were like twin tall palm trees on adjacent islands in a sea of love and tranquility; or two oaks planted next to a church under a solitary star that comprised human thought in all its different dimensions and colors—its depths, its highlands, its horizons—all in one.

Henriette's belief in God was not very common in the era of the French Revolution and its aftermath. Her God was not Voltaire's, nor that of the *Encyclopédie*, a god who had created the world and then left it, abandoning it to its own devices. Nor was He a god who had been created and had created at the same time, His spirit either absent, asleep, or lost. I do not believe that this French lady's beliefs were too far removed from pure Christian faith, stripped of all the distortions of theology.

Her God—yes indeed, Henriette, your own God is our God—hidden, untouchable, invisible, may be permanently so near, yet so far. But in that seclusion is mercy; in that distance is love; in that proximity is serenity and peace of mind.

We are certain that, whether or not you were or were not a believer, in your life here on earth—as now and for evermore—you are one of God's beloveds.

In Lebanon

IN LEBANON, two things kept Renan busy: exploration in Byblos, and writing in Ghazeer and Amcheet. The first required archeological excursions, so he roamed along the shores of ancient Phoenicia and climbed deep into the mountains, reaching Aqoura and Tannourine.

Whether staying somewhere or traveling, Henriette never left her brother in spite of the lack of relaxation and convenience in the mountains when compared with the comforts they could enjoy in the home of their host, Zakhya Mikhael Tobia, in Amcheet. Most of the time, they slept in peasants' houses, which made the hardships of travel that much more trying, since they were deprived of rest day and night.

Those mountain treks came to an end in July 1862 with a trip to Mashnaqa. It was the last one, and was a harbinger of predestined fate. Henriette felt weak; she and her brother moved to a monastery, where she fell ill. What made things that much worse was that they had moved rapidly from the heights of Tannourine to the intense heat of the Toula plains. Even in Hilta, Henriette could not get the rest that she badly needed. The village women all gathered around her, amazed and delighted to see a Frenchwoman for the first time in their lives. They hurried to offer her their services and pestered her with questions and advice. They insisted that she had to stay with them.

The two of them hurried to Amcheet, then moved on to Ghazeer. The sea breeze restored Henriette's health, and the climb from Jounieh to Ghazeer in the moonlight reminded her of the happiness she had felt during the course of her first Lebanese trip.

In his lovely little book *My Sister Henriette*, Renan says that he did not detect in the people of Ghazeer the same decent instinct and winning simplicity that so marked the people of Amcheet. That was because some phony aristocrats lived in Ghazeer, and the local people simply imitated their bad habits and morals rather than their good ones.

Even so, they stayed there happily for the summer and fall because Renan's sister regained her health, and he was enjoying the calm, beautiful surroundings to finish writing his book *The Life of Jesus.* He had just reached the day when Jesus entered Jerusalem.

During this time the pair of them were absolutely delighted with the time spent studying and writing and equally enthralled by the views to both east and west from Ghazeer—villages nestling in the heart of the mountains and resting on their shoulders; plains and highlands sloping down toward the sea. It was all the most beautiful scene they had witnessed in Lebanon. If the Valley of Hammana had been the highlight for Lamartine, then the Ghazeer Bay did the same thing for Renan. There was a natural beauty, one that only poets could capture in full. No wonder then that he could shout, "How wonderful these hours are! Ah me! If only eternity were as lovely!"

He used to work from dawn until evening, his spirit imbibing the glow of sunrise and dipping his quill in the colors of the setting sun. His ideas would come to him decked in the garb of the Lebanese skies—translucent, gleaming bright, and luminescent.

Henriette would copy the pages and edit them, softening some of the harsh logic and reflecting the sunshine on its snowy white pages. The sun's rays at sunrise and sunset were gloriously artistic and amazingly magical. Just as they were able to color the rocks and hills of Lebanon and to enhance their impressive beauty and splendid might, so were they reflected in the hearts of both author and sister and on the pages that his quill adorned and her quill amended. The pages thus glistened with dew from the worshipping heart and a glow from the devoted spirit.

"I shall love this book," Henriette told her brother, "not because we've helped each other write it, but because it gives me great pleasure."

When she used the words *helped each other*, she did not refer to the third partner in the writing process, the Lebanese sun and sky—indeed, Lebanon itself. *The Life of Jesus* is the work of Renan, his sister, and Lebanon.

The two of them used to work during the daytime and spend the evening on the roof in the moonlight. They would chat and discuss, preparing for the things to do on the following day.

If a feeling of happiness lay in the sheer perfection of their work, then it also managed to fill their cups to the brim.

However, there are some people in the East who believe that pessimism lies hidden in a well filled cup—put differently, if the pourer of the drink fills the cup to the brim, he is wishing evil on the drinker. Was fate the drink pourer for Henriette? The sheer pleasure that the two of them felt in their spiritual and intellectual communion, coupled with the sheer purity of their hours at work and the splendor of their times of meditation and conversation, all managed to conceal the black hand that passed over the scenario like a cloud. It may well have been that same delight Henriette felt for her work that made her forget the consequences of her illness.

As brother and sister bade farewell to Ghazeer, they both felt a sense of regret for a blessed period in their lives that was about to come to an end. They returned to Beirut, where they were to spend their last few days.

In Byblos there were still some sarcophagi that needed to be transferred to the destroyer *Caton*, for conveyance to France. Renan did not need to supervise the operation, but it was hard for him and his sister to leave Lebanon before saying farewell to Amcheet and their friends there. So, was this a welcome opportunity, or predestined fate?

They returned by boat to Byblos and went up to their beloved town, where they were warmly welcomed by its people.

They had now returned to their Lebanese paradise, the house where they had lived before, the home of Zakhya, where they thought of themselves as living in their father's house in Treguier.

Once there, facing Byblos, with its golden sands and the lofty mountains with their peaks on the grey, rosy, azure horizons, they both intoxicated themselves on this truly amazing cup. No one even

Henriette's tomb beside the church in the shade of the oak tree.

realized that they were intoxicated, sensed its hidden essence, or felt the slightest bit anxious.

As I pen these words, I have a picture of the spirits of gods and myths that had their bright day on these ancient shores. I envision their spirit dissolving into that cup, intoxicating brother and sister with the purity of days and nights and with the sheer extent of their historical and spiritual memory, that amazing and remote extent . . . where everything incomplete was wanting.

Just ten days before Henriette's death, they started work on *The Life of Jesus* again, totally unaware of the unexpected event heading toward them.

Work on writing and editing soon stopped, halted by the fever that struck the sister before infecting her brother as well.

So what was this malicious fever that caused severe nervous pain? The doctor from the battleship anchored at Byblos was called in. Frowning and shaking his head, he was unable to identify the fever.

Messengers were sent to Beirut; the fleet doctor arrived by sea, and a French doctor who was an expert on local fevers came by land.

The fever hit Renan hard, but he kept trying to write as he sat on a couch close to his beloved sister. But he realized later that the things he had written in those few hours were a confused jumble. The fever kept getting worse for both him and his sister in the adjoining room. Even so, Henriette got up one day at sunrise, went to her brother's room, and stretched out on the couch. She picked up the pages and started turning them over. She tried to do some work, but the fever thwarted her. She looked out of the window at the mountains on the distant horizon, at Mount Moses, where Adonis had died (according to some legends). She looked at Ernest with tears in her eyes, realizing that death was near. She remembered her mother and her little nephew, Ary, and decided to write her will.

"I've always loved you, Ernest," she told him. "Sometimes my love has hurt you because I've shown you a total love that is rare among lovers and even not accepted."

Saying that, Henriette went back to her own room. After that, she never saw him again, nor did he see her. It always grieved him that he was not by her side when she breathed her last. The memory pained him throughout his life.

The captain of the *Caton* sent an ambulance to transfer Henriette to Beirut. The doctors arrived, but it was a sad and troubling hour, their whispers accompanied by shaking heads.

When the news reached Amcheet, the picture was one of gloom. Zakhya's family stood by the door or sat on the steps weeping. The entire village started mourning its princess as she breathed her last.

The doctors held consultations, then the priest who was knowledgeable about popular medicine arrived, planning to offer advice on a phlebotomy. But, like the doctors, he had arrived too late.

"How is she?" the brother asked through a feverish haze.

"There's no hope of recovery," they told him.

Renan fell into a swoon and had a sad dream in which he and Henriette went back to Afqa and sat down, side by side, on the dewy grass beneath the walnut trees. Then they raised a cup of chilled water to their dying lips. Plunging into that water—the very fountain of life—they were weeping and feeling a grievous painful sensation.

When Ernest woke up again, he asked about his sister, only to learn that she had died. She passed away on Tuesday, September 24, 1862.

The priest who had come to cure Henriette by phlebotomy prayed over her while her brother was still in his swoon, having that horrible dream and just a few meters away from her.

Since his own situation had become more serious, he was not allowed to see Henriette. He was transported to the ship in the same ambulance that had transported his sister.

Henriette was transported on a bier to the tomb of Mikhail Tobia, whose son, Zakhya, offered it as a resting place. He requested that, should her body be transported elsewhere thereafter, an inscription over the door should read: "In this tomb lay the body of a Frenchwoman."

May God welcome you, thou noble Lebanese spirit! This exalted Breton spirit is worthy of your respect and grief.

Zakhya's family and the entire population of Amcheet walked in the Maronite funeral procession. Incense was burned, and the sound could be heard of priests intoning funerary chants in that language that Renan knew well and loved so dearly—Syriac.

They laid Henriette in that tomb beside the church in the shade of the oak tree.

Fifty Years Later

THE CAFE was by the sea in Beirut. Small and modest, built out of wood, and roofed with mats, waves played among its supports. It stood beside the huge quadrangle, which in those days was filled with paintings and artifacts. It was in this low corner by the Zaitouna Bay that we used to sit at sunset with glasses of arak and plates of mixed nuts. In the middle would be the glass of Pernod for the sheikh of the circle, Sheikh Iskandar Azar—God have mercy on him!—the leader of the freethinkers at the time.

Among those colleagues were literary friends during the first Hamidian decade of this (twentieth) century who used to rush to this cafe by the sea at sunset, a group of genuine happiness. Among them I can count Beshara Khoury, owner of the *Bark* newspaper; Shibli Mallaat, owner of the *Watan* newspaper; Yousuf Thabet; and Jurji Saad, who was known as "poet of the night" because he often stayed late with the company on a night with a full moon; Pietro Paoli, strongman-author who was to become the writers' bodyguard; Mohyieddine al-Ghazi Khayyat, who would orbit around freedom's borders; Ameen Takieddine, who carried freedom's standard in times of peace; and Jameel Maalouf, who had returned to Lebanon victorious, bringing freedom with him from America.

I cannot recall any one of us beating Jameel when it came time to pay.

One day, in that same cafe, beneath those threadbare mats, facing the setting sun, sometime between summer and fall in 1911, poetry was being scattered all around—some of it hot from the oven, some of it cold and chunky. We were all saved by the circle's sheikh, who had this to say to one of the poets:

"Your poetry is like this mussel—one part of delicious meat in return for 99 percent sharp, black shell. It's only fit for . . ."

With that, he stopped, scooped the meat out of the shell, and ate it. Then he repeated, "It's only fit for . . ." and threw the shell into the sea.

Jameel felt encouraged.

"Literature of the future," he said, "will be in prose, not poetry."

"Some prose is poetry," Mohyieddine commented.

Paoli the strongman now mentioned prose poetry and its writer. I now bashfully withdrew from a subject that was far removed from our prose and poetry.

At the time I was reading Renan's book *The Life of Jesus*, and his little book, *My Sister Henriette*. That led me to mention how much Henriette had contributed to her brother and his writings. I told them that she was buried in Amcheet. Her tomb was a worthy pilgrimage site for devout people.

Mohyieddine took up the topic, moving from pilgrimage to the prophet of Islam, and from him to Khadeeja, his wife. He mentioned the benefits that she had brought to him—prayers and blessings upon him! He then said that he would indeed make the pilgrimage in all humility to the tomb of the French lady in Amcheet.

In fact, the whole group agreed to do the same, and we set a time for the trip. Actually, only three people kept their promise: Petro Paoli, martyr to freedom—God have mercy on him!; Jameel Maalouf, martyr of fate[1]—God provide him with His mercy; and this writer, martyr to nervous pains that he has borne for some thirty-five years, smiling his way through life and never rushing anything.

The three of us rode in a carriage to Byblos in the summer of 1911, fifty years after the death of Henriette Renan.

1. He was hounded by the Turks during the war, which affected his mind.

From there, we set out on foot for Amcheet.

Jameel: "The most beautiful thing Renan ever said was his statement about the highest ideal—namely, that in every era it should be higher than it was in the previous one; freethinkers should be continually striving to achieve that ongoing human progress."

Pietro: "Didn't he also say the freethinkers are few and far between? How ignorant are we about the fate of such thinkers in our own country? By God, my dear Jameel, I would like to impose absolute rule on this country for just one month. Once the gallows had been erected in Bourj Square,[2] the relatively few decent people—namely, the freethinkers—would be spared. Doors would open up for work, Renan's philosophy would then gain support, and his notion of the highest ideal would be achieved."

Jameel: "But in the end, victory belongs to the freethinkers. In every nation, the common people are just that. Tyrannical rulers and profiteering politicians in France and England are no different from the ones in the Ottoman administration."

Pietro: "But there's a difference between their men and our pseudo men . . ."

Jameel interrupted him.

"That's it," he said. "The difference between men and pseudo men. The task for freethinkers in our world is much harder than it is for freethinkers in Europe and America. We are permanently engaged in an ongoing, genuine, determined struggle to find some real men from among the pseudos and freethinkers. We must follow Renan's ideas and keep the fight going."

These words that I am writing now and the contents of previous sections of this journey are the record of my memories from those times. I am also translating from an article I wrote for the New York journal the *Bookman*.[3]

2. Fickle fate willed that, along with his fellow martyrs, he should be a victim of Turkish executions.

3. *Bookman*, February 1912.

On the day we made the pilgrimage, the people of Amcheet were surprised to find some people who had come to their village, asking about the tomb of Henriette Renan, the sister of that "French heretic." One day we met a priest who was living in the house where Renan stayed and his sister died. He had written a section of *The Life of Jesus* there. From the very first moment we told ourselves that this priest had to be a courageous freethinker; either that, or else he did not care about memories.

We learned that he too was a graduate of the famous college where Renan had studied, the Saint Sulpice Seminary in Paris, and that he was a contemporary priest—in other words, well-educated and free in his thinking and conscience—whatever that expression implied in those days.

However, in spite of his claims to be "contemporary," he still called Renan a heretic and made no attempt to conceal his contempt, even from visiting admirers like us. It was as if, in his theological studies, he had specialized in goals and intentions.

The reverend gentleman informed us that a rich Jew had invoked Renan to write his book, which was only approved by Jews and heretics. He went on to say that Renan's sister, who used to wear a nun's habit and visit the church along with the villagers, had helped this person write the book. She and he were both heretics.

However, Tobia, the son of Renan and his sister's host, welcomed us and regaled us with stories about village and mountain affairs so as to divert us from the purpose of our pilgrimage. He invited us to lunch. As he poured some of his delicious vintage wine, he expounded on some of his beliefs as a Lebanese Maronite. Some religious beliefs may be like vintage wine, but they do not make you drunk, and rarely inject a sense of joy into the heart.

We asked Tobia about his father's recollections of Renan. He paused and started stuttering, clearly at a loss as to why we were interested in the topic and worried about our intentions. What was the point in writing about things long forgotten, or about the dead? What good would come from digging up graves and uncovering heresies?

We listened to our host with all necessary discretion and continued our attempts to reassure him, sensing that his resistance was gradually weakening and he was drawing closer to the feelings of our hearts.

His attitude changed even more when Jameel mentioned something that reminded me of an article that he wrote in his book, *The Cedars and Their Superstitions*, where he had used some gentle sarcasm and wit.

"Renan came from a country where people have the same customs and beliefs as the Lebanese," Jameel said, addressing Tobia. "On Epiphany night in Lebanon, bells kneel to the Lord Jesus from trees. In Brittany, where Renan comes from, on the Thursday of Holy Week, the day of washing feet, people gather in the mountains by the ruins of the church of Saint Michael to watch the bells as they make their way to Rome to be blessed by the pope.

"Just as we see the trees kneeling to the Lord Jesus—through the eye of faith, of course, so were the young Renan and his sister watching those bells, draped in baptismal garb, flying to Rome through space in order to acquire the prophetic blessing."

Tobia gave a gentle smile, clothed in all the sweetness of faith.

"God is all powerful," he said as he left the room.

He came back with the papers and a gun. He showed us a photograph of Ernest, which he had presented to his father—"to my old friend, Zakhya," and a letter "to my dear friend" in which Ernest expresses the desire that Zakhya stay with him in his house if he visits Paris. The gun was a present from Renan and his sister in acknowledgment of his kindness to them. Even more significant in Tobia's opinion was a book from the French Foreign Ministry in which the writer states that the Emperor has instructed him to thank Monsieur Zakhya for all the kindness and assistance that he had shown to the Phoenician mission during its work in Syria.

After Tobia had taken these gifts and precious mementos back to their proper place, he took us to the house where Henriette had died, then to the tomb where she had been buried.

She is still there,
She is still with us.

"I hesitate to remove her from these beautiful mountains," Renan said, "where she spent such lovely times with the wonderful people whom she loved. I would have to bury her in one of our gloomy cemeteries which used to scare her."[4]

4. Ernest Renan, *My Sister Henriette*, 91.

Eighth Journey

Gharzouz

Contents

The Boy with the Necklet

IN THE EIGHTH DECADE of the previous century, the silk factory in Freike was functioning at its peak. It had fully a hundred workers, male and female, and its hundred wheels spun glistening with golden threads extracted from cocoons dipped in pools of hot water. Mule caravans loaded with cocoons would amble their way to the factory from all over. Every week they would transport bales of silk to Beirut to be shipped to Lyon, France. The agent of the factory owners in Beirut used to send the price for the silk in Ottoman currency wrapped in sackcloth bags; it would be carried by the same mules returning to Freike.

"Come on, kids, count the money! Count it and put it in the boxes!"

In those happy, silvery days—with caravans carrying silk and coming back from Beirut with loads of Ottoman money, one of the factory owners had a young son in his fourth spring. One day he noticed a mule tied to a mulberry tree in front of the house. Imagining himself a knight, he approached the mule and untied its halter. Climbing up on a ledge, he got on the animal's back. The animal started moving slowly, making sure of what was happening. The little boy now tugged the halter hard, and the mule got the message. It started trotting, then cantering. The little knight panicked and fell to the ground. At that very moment, as the boy was between the mule's back and the ground, one of his neighbors spotted him. He started yelling, beseeching aid from Saint Antony, patron saint of children, and Saint Challita, patron saint of pack animals. He hurried over to the little boy, picked him up, and carried him back to his mother with a bloody head wound.

The wound was not serious and soon started to heal. However, a few days later the boy got an earache, which was very painful and kept oozing. He was taken to see a doctor in Broumana who was very well-known at the time, Doctor Beshara Manassa. He prescribed some medicine and an injection.

The injection upset the boy and did nothing to make the cure any quicker. One day he snatched the needle from the servant as she was giving him the injection. He hit her on the head with it, and it broke.

Two days later, a man from Gharzouz came to Freike to do some bookkeeping. He used to buy cocoons for the factory and stayed with the father of the little boy with the earache. The boy's mother told this man the whole sad story, and he reassured her.

"We have the right medicine, God willing," he told her.

What was this medicine? The devout man from Gharzouz told the boy's devout mother that, in the Batroun region, there was a new saint who had many miracles to his name—the saint of Kfifan. He then described some of the miracles.

"Make a vow to the saint of Kfifan, blessings upon him," the man told her.

The mother duly vowed a pound of candles, an *oka* of incense, and five Ottoman coins.

When the man went back to his home, he sent her a silver necklet for the little boy in Freike, one that he had brought from the Kfifan monastery. The mother put it on the boy and started waiting for the miracle to happen, while still using various medicines to treat his little boy's ear.

The saint did not disappointment, although, as was the case with the medicines and the injection, it only worked slowly. It took two full months for the boy to be completely cured, with him wearing the holy Kfifan necklet around his neck.

Meanwhile, the boy's father received a letter from a friend of his, inviting him and his family to visit Gharzouz. The mother was delighted by the invitation.

"We can visit Gharzouz and the Kfifan monastery," she said.

"As you wish," her loving husband replied.

The happy day arrived, the day when they would be traveling. The "lady" put on a black satin dress and turban of the same material and color. Her watch hung from a gold chain as a pendant on her chest. The "master" wore loose-fitting trousers made of navy-blue serge, tied with a broad striped silk belt. At both back and sides, half of it was hidden beneath a waistcloth with braided edges like trouser pockets. From the front it looked like the imposing seam of a black vest with twenty buttons. It was buttoned from both top and bottom, so as to show the silk shirt beneath it, the yellow color of which matched that of the belt.

The little boy, who was still wearing the Kfifan necklet, was sporting a stripped red-colored coat with long sleeves, tied at the waist with a belt like his father's. On his head he wore a tarboosh topped by a white kaffiyeh. His shoes were black and shiny and had brass buckles. As he walked, he kept looking down at his shoes and admiring them in delight.

"Here's the pound of candles, and here's the oka of incense. George, put them in the saddlebag!"

The servant, George, and the muleteer had both already prepared the male and female mules with stirrups, cushions, and rugs for the comfort and ease of the travelers.

The lady of the house made the sign of the cross on her forehead, then mounted the female mule with George's help. Once she was settled, she sat the little boy with the necklet in front of her. The muleteer, Hanna, walked alongside the male mule that the father was riding, while George walked alongside the mother's mule.

To Gharzouz, to Kfifan!

This then was the journey of the Holy Family—God forbid! It was a family journey accompanied by holiness, with that holiness encircling its young boy's neck.

That little boy is the writer of these lines, and that journey was the very first in his life on this earth.

The Holy Necklet

HOLINESS IS THE MOTHER OF FAITH, and faith is the proof of holiness linked to miracles and wonders. If you number among doubters, then there can be no cure for your eyes or your heart.

If you are biased in favor of your religion, your sect, or subtleties of your beliefs, then purity can cure you of that bias, if only for a while, just as saints can cure you of illness.

"Come unto me, ye pure of heart! Come unto me with hearts like those of children!"

Yes indeed, holiness combined with wonders and miracles transcends the bounds of religions and confessions, drawing to itself the hearts of believers, be they Christian, Muslim, or worshippers of trees and idols.

In particular, if the holy person were Lebanese, then God would acknowledge his prayers and permit miracles to occur through his hands. The mention of his name would rush through mountain villages like a flash of lightning, carried on wings of faith and tongues of purity. People with chronic diseases and ailments, men and women, would come to him from every quarter, begging for help and a cure. Druze would come before Maronite, Shiʿi before Druze, and conservative Orthodox before everyone else.

It is no surprise then that Azar, the Orthodox man from Gharzouz, was one of the people who heard about the saint of Kfifan, believed in him, and started spreading the news about his miracles. As a close friend of the boy's father, he rushed to save his friend's son from imminent deafness by sending him the holy necklet with all its blessings and curative qualities.

So, here now is the little boy, wearing his necklet, with his father in Gharzouz. They have arrived safe and sound and are staying as honored guests with Mr. Azar—indeed, honored and welcomed by his entire family and all the inhabitants of Gharzouz.

"We were there for ten days," my mother used to say as she recalled the visit, "and we received an invitation every single day."

Those ten days were ten festivals. Sheep were slaughtered, and the seals on vintage wine bottles were uncorked—the kind of Lebanese hospitality that I have already described in earlier chapters. I saw it for the very first time when I was four years old and my memory was still young, only absorbing a small portion of the fabulous or scary things I was seeing and feeling.

What I am saying now and have been saying in previous chapters represents the things that my mother told us in times filled with joy. But there are four things that I can remember and portray as they were, or as they happened fifty-five years ago. The first is the mule that threw me to the ground, almost breaking my head open; the second is the syringe that I broke on the head of our servant, Maniyeh (and I can still remember her name—Maniyeh—as we used to call her).

About the journey to Gharzouz, I can clearly remember riding on the mule in front of my mother and the way she wrapped her arms around me when we were going uphill or down. I have never forgotten how happy I was with the silver necklet and the shiny, long, glossy black shoes with their brass buckles. Everything else resides in the memory of my mother, Umm Ameen.

She told me that all these invitations almost prevented her from carrying out her major purpose in coming, the visit to the Kfifan monastery and her fulfilment of the vow she had made to its saint. But her boldness, something that stemmed from her resolve and deep faith, ruled otherwise. In Azar's house she encountered a partner with a similar resolve and boldness—namely, the wife of our generous host. The two women decided to leave early—before dawn—when the men were all still asleep. We told the muleteers to get some food ready and saddle the mules.

My mother's companion wanted the young boy with the necklet, whom she loved dearly, to ride with her on her mule.

"Did the boy agree to leave his mother?" I asked my mother.

"He forgot all about her," she replied.

"Was your companion as beautiful as you are?" I asked her.

"Oh dear," my mother replied smiling. "Am I beautiful?" she asked in a tone of sweet regret. "The wife of our friend in Gharzouz, my son, was a real beauty."

That lovely lady put her foot in the stirrup, grabbed the reins from the muleteer in her right hand, and leaned over with her left hand to clutch me to her chest.

Venus, the morning star, bade us farewell and wished us a safe and prosperous journey. From Gharzouz we traveled northwest through the mountains on "the easy track," as the Bedouin Arabs call it. We passed two villages, Maad and Sofar, and the monastery of Saint Joseph in Jrabta. Halfway there, we stopped to rest for a while, then resumed our journey and arrived at the Kfifan monastery before sunset.

We visited the church and stood by the tomb of the saint, whose body was completely displayed without any sign of decay. We then visited the abbot, and my mother presented him with the object of her vow—a bundle of candles, an oka of incense, and five Ottoman coins. He accepted them in the saint's name, raised his hand over my head in the sign of the cross as a blessing, and then invited the two ladies to dinner. He ordered the servant-monk to prepare a bedroom for the two ladies, but, since they both were eager for the full blessing of the saint, they preferred the church rather than the bedroom. Bedding was laid out for them there.

The little boy slept, like an angel as they say, between his mother and her beautiful companion. It seems that he had a nightmare about the corpse he had seen in the tomb and woke up in a panic. As he was crying, he heard a soft voice calling him by name.

"Don't be scared, little boy, don't be scared."

He assumed the voice belonged either to his mother or the woman in whose arms he was sleeping. He went back to them feeling calmer and more relaxed. But his mother, who had woken up when he had cried out, said that she had heard the voice too. It was the voice of the saint of Kfifan, peace be upon him!

The next morning, when she mentioned this miraculous occurrence, her companion did not deny it for a reason that I did not appreciate at the time, and still do not venture to say that I can appreciate today, some fifty-five years later. With her silence was she respecting my mother's feelings or someone else's? I do not know.

However, I would regularly discuss the subject with my mother whenever this visit came up. The discussion would finish with me stating that the voice I had heard was a woman's voice, while she would insist that it was the saint's, the saint of Kfifan, peace be on him!

Could it be that the saint's necklet had so affected my hearing that I actually thought his voice was a woman's, or had he cured my illness so well that I could easily distinguish a woman's voice from a man's? In the first instance, he was to blame for my mistake; in the second, he deserved praise and gratitude.

With a soul in a red-hot cauldron of perplexity, I ask myself where today is that holiness that used to enfold me in those days, the holiness of that Kfifan necklet, of that beautiful lady from Gharzouz who wrapped me in her arms in the saint's church? Was she still sleeping there in front of that tomb, with its pure corpse shrouded inside, or had she too been shrouded in the tomb of time amid the candles of years long since past?

Dear God, and what of these times, lighting candles of certainty within the soul, only to blow them out; teaching, but then leaving a heritage of woe and grief; giving us a modicum of knowledge, then depriving us of an abundance of purity and bliss; opening the mind, then inflating the head; opening our hearts, only to empty them?

And, after that inflation and emptiness, death, death—unless, that is, we rush to that great doctor, to the hospital of the soul.

There, in that hospital, in that cosmic church, you sleep for a single night, with the holy necklet around your neck and in the arms of God. The next morning, you get up early to wash your heart and mind in the sunlight.

Then you can return to life, empowered by both knowledge and blessing.

The Rouais Rock

NEAR GHARZOUZ, about a quarter of an hour to the southwest, is a high, overhanging rock that looms over land and sea below it. Local people go there for walks, so they call it "the park," or "Rouais Park."

A park, in Gharzouz, the font of poetry, literature, and linguistics? That is incredible, and what is even more so is that poets, writers, and professors in Gharzouz are either ignorant or claim to be ignorant of innovations in language. The discipline was nourished and planted in its modern Egyptian garden, which drew to itself moisture from the university and fertilizer from the Azhar mosque-university in Cairo. The phrase *quite good* was encouraged, for example, and the concept of "excellence" developed and flourished. The phrase *and only that* was also used; the language garden then burst into bloom, embellished with boxthorn and weeds. Every gardener had to plant *and only that* in their patch, or else risk expulsion from the Arab Agricultural Organization.

They cut down all but a single branch of the older civilization's tree, and injected the spirit of modernity into it. The new branch shot up amazingly, and planters from all regions rushed in, asking for these new grafts.

So here now is a single branch, one that is rarely found, even in the likes of "the perfumed garden."[1] It is a modern derivation of the

1. Translator's note: this is the title of the English translation, by Sir Richard Burton, of the renowned erotic work of Sheikh Nafzawi (fifteenth century CE), the Arabic title of which is *Al-Rawd al-'atir fi nuzhat al-khatir*.

material that has been under assault from modernist writers. Now it is "an excursion for the mind," whereas previously it was a source of purity and protection for the heart.

I have no idea what these linguist celebrities have in mind.[2] The dictionary tells us that the word *nazzaha* in Arabic, when applied to camels, means "to take them away from water." The verbal derivative *tanazzuh* means "removal from water or countryside." So did they derive the word *muntazah* (meaning "a park") from *tanazzuh*—in other words, completely reversing the original meaning and applying it to every place where human beings can look for an antidote to boredom, anger, and anxiety? Is it rather that they mean *muntazah* (park) to imply a removal from evil and a separation from squalor?

The dictionary also informs us, based on the work of Ibn al-Sikkeet,[3] in his chapter on inappropriate usages by the common people, that they would say "we're going out *natanazzah*," when they were going to visit gardens. As already noted, the verb implies a distance from countryside and water.

Is it either permissible or appropriate for owners of the linguistic garden—as they adopt new plants from the university and fertilize their growth with offerings from Al-Azhar—to plant colloquial usages and give them a contemporary pollination? May God preserve your own good taste! Can you see any kind of joy, ease, or leisure in the idea of *tanazzuh* as "a stroll," something only accepted by ultramodernists?

2. Translator's note: I feel the need here to apologize to the English reader for the linguistic complications of the section that follows, as Rihani expresses his frustrations with the processes of linguistic change through reference to the morphology and semantics of Arabic. However, on balance I think that this passage (which I have endeavored to make as comprehensible as possible) provides a useful illustration of Rihani's intense interest in, and concern for, the Arabic language, which is such a central part of his heritage.

3. Translator's note: Ibn al-Sikkeet (802–58) was a major Shi'i lexicographer and the author of an early work on word structure in Arabic, *Islah al-mantiq*.

I am not rejecting the contents of dictionaries, nor do I want to take this any further. However, as I relax in the shade of the tree of good taste in the Al-Azhar garden, I have this question to ask:

If derivations of the verb *nazaha* are set apart from *intazaha*, and the meaning of *tanazzuh* is the complete opposite to what is needed and intended, then does analogy and listening allow for *intazaha* and the noun of place form derived from it, something that by now has become well-known and understood, in addition to its being light and gentle with no trace of pedantry?

You owners of linguistic purity, everything that you say and adjudicate is noble and noteworthy, all of it an exquisite blend of the waters of Paradise, save for pedantry, obscurity, and bad taste.

You upholders of modernist bombast, the doubling of consonants in *mutanazzah* is different from the ones in *munazzah* and *munazzih.* The difference between the two of them is just like that between swelling on a camel's back and its hump. Do you make no distinction between health and sickness or between fat and swelling?

They have adjudicated taste, but have not completely overlooked its intent. In the doubling of the consonant *z* in *mutanazzah*, there are three mistakes: firstly, the eye dismisses the form of it; second, the ear finds it too heavy; and thirdly, the tongue rejects the juxtaposition of *m* and *t* in *mutanazzah* as death of the soul and seeping wounds. By contrast, the word *muntazah* has its own grace; the three syllables after it flow smoothly and gently—bringing a tranquility to those in search of leisure.

So it is that, when we are in need of leisure, we can find it in the word *muntazah.* We neither seek nor find it in *mutanazzah.* For that very reason I congratulated the people of Gharzouz on their good taste and also for the stroll (*muntazah*), which we took with a group of young boys and girls.

Among the girls was one with whom literature had been toying. She was beautiful and eloquent, with soft hands and piercing looks. In her eyes I observed an ancient spark, one that reminded me of the lovely woman from Gharzouz who had held on to me on the back of the mule on our way to Kfifan, clutching me to her chest on the night when we slept in the church.

Indeed, I imagined that that woman had come back to life, embodied in this young eloquent interlocutor with the sharp, piercing glances. What was there to justify such an idea or justify such a memory, once the elixir that transforms the human kiss into a royal kiss has been forever lost? I wanted to hug this eloquent beauty to my chest in honor of that lovely lady, daughter of her own village, who had hugged me to her chest those fifty-five years ago. I imagined myself back in that church, performing my religious obligations in front of that holy image of the saint.

But no, my friend, you are bound by ties crafted by time and humanity. If the elixir of purity were to empower the loves of your heart, then what would you do about the poison of human society? If nature was to tell you that you have an authentic model with the birds, or if the church said that "blessed are the pure in heart," what would the civilized mind or restless nerves have to say?

That beautiful, eloquent girl told me that she fully respected the memory that had led me to revisit Gharzouz. During my commemorative visit she stuck to me like a shadow, albeit a gentle one. She took on herself the obligation of making me feel welcome and opened doors that created a heart-stopping impression with their revival of old memories clustered beneath a canopy of nostalgia and grief.

As part of her fulsome welcome she readily answered every single question that I asked, while at the same time asking me dozens of questions of her own.

"What is innovation in literature? Who are the best Lebanese poets? Do you prefer prose poetry to rhyming verse? What do journalists mean when they talk about occasional poets?

One question after another, while I was doing my best to take in some portion of the scene all around me. But her glances and her tuneful voice made that impossible.

She stopped me to ask this question.

"What about weeping poetry, as you call it, poetry of broken hearts (actually, she laughed as she used a different word from Lebanese colloquial). Don't you see any beauty in it? Are sorrows and agonies of heart to be deprived of poetry's ability to offer consolation?"

Other people were moving ahead of us. As I looked with a stumbling heart, I felt as though I were on the edge of an abyss. Truth is no less risky than imagination. Here we were, in a defile between two rocks. There was a high step, so I took her hand to help her up, and my arm happened to touch her buxom chest as I hurried her out of the narrow passage.

"It seems to me," I told her as we reached safer ground, "that you're angry at me for my criticisms of weeping poetry."

"Dear me, no!" she replied. "But I do like Beshara Khoury's poetry. I love Gibran, and everything Professor Rihani writes."

"Everything?" I asked. "You're flattering me. Hurry up, the others are ahead of us."

Ibrahim Hitti and Gabriel Gharzouzy had stayed back to wait for us. Gabriel gave me a dirty look, and Ibrahim gave me a knowing smile. The girl let out a laugh that banished their nasty thoughts.

"Professor Rihani only visits Gharzouz once every fifty years," she said. "I'm very fond of his writings and want to get all I can out of his visit."

"But loving women is always one and the same," Ibrahim said with his habitual bluntness, "no matter how many names and reasons for it there may be."

The girl blushed in embarrassment and turned for refuge to my other friend, Gabriel Gharzouzy.

In his one person Gabriel combined four different experts: tailor, clockmaker, poet, and owner of a famous house in the region.

Gharzouz, Gharzouz, Gharzouz,
In your gaze are . . . and symbols.

That said, he was also the senior professor on celibacy. He neither hated nor loved women. I do not believe that any of his friends knew whether, in the space between love and hatred, there was something of a more practical nature.

"The man who knows what's in a woman's heart," he said as she looked in his direction, "has yet to be born. Men who excoriate them are little different from those who extol them. The truth, young lady, lies with God."

"Gabriel," she retorted in opposition to both men, "you're a devil in human form." Then, pointing at Ibrahim, "He's a human in devil's form."

By now we had reached the rock. The other girls called out to our companion, and some of them hurried over to her. They whispered things in her ear and then laughed. They started chanting in unison: "To me comes the sweet gazelle of intimacy."

At that moment, the distinguished author Adeeb Gharzouzy—supporter of the master of Ras el-Matn, Doctor Oliver, in the magazine he was editing for him—was standing by the rock, waiting to act as our guide.

So here was Rouais Park, the haven of poets and lovers, with the vista spread out before them, from Amcheet to Byblos, the Ibrahim River, and Beirut.

This vista stretched away into the distance, beginning with a flat area that sloped gently toward the sea, finishing at a stretch of sea that extended as far as the Lebanese capital. It is adorned with four peaks, each of which is about ten kilometers from the others. The first and lowest is by the Ibrahim River; the second is by Jounieh; the third is by the Dog River; and fourth and last, the highest of them all, bears the city of Beirut.

To the southwest, on a hill called Manzala, there was an ancient monastery dating back to the seventh century CE. Today it is known as the Monastery of the Forty Martyrs.

There too was ancient Gharzouz, in times when there was plenty of water. People left the site when all the springs dried up, and, according to popular belief, founded the new Gharzouz where it is located today.

The small valley below Manzala is called Zeer al-Ghazala. I note that here in order to record the Lebanese expression used to describe types and shapes of terrain. The gorge that intersects a valley or at the foot of a mountain alongside a rivulet or brook is called a *zira* in these parts (with the plural form *ziyar*).

We all sat down to chat. The conversation was varied and diverse, just like the terrain all around us. The author fired one shot, and the literate girl retorted with questions of her own for me. I answered some of them with as much patience as possible, but turned some of the others into topics for discussion. The boys and girls started discussing and even arguing, at which point I would insist on the truce that I really wanted.

I would advise any author who visits a town where he is very well-known to be prepared to respond to any and all intellectual and existential contingencies.

The first item in his store of provisions should be poetry. He will need to be supplied with a generous amount of it, especially love poems. He should also read some pages from the theology of Saint Thomas and refer to books on agriculture that discuss principles of tree grafting and planting. Then he should demonstrate an interest in international and national politics and a familiarity with literature and the sciences. People from the village—poets, priests, peasants, politicians, linguists, and scholars—will need to be involved in the examination process in order to confirm (and be convinced) that their honored visitor is indeed a leader among writers, prince of poets, or renowned scholar philosopher. When he goes home, he can say to his wife, "How wonderful knowledge is, my dear wife, and how honored and respected is the one who possesses it!"

Alternatively, he might say, "How dishonest those newspapers and magazines are that trumpet the repute of that 'great professor' or 'that renowned philosopher.' All the while, my dear, he has no clue where half the earth is to be found or where the worm comes from that chew on the grapevines. He has no idea about the number of Christ's wounds, and so on and so on . . ."

So, the famous author should make very sure that he is ready to encounter the probing questions of the village professors—if, that is, he wishes to return from his trip with their testimonies in hand.

Village Encyclopedia

GHARZOUZ IS SITUATED on the Byblos arm between two valleys, Al-Uqaiba and Houran. The terrain is flat with no clusters of mountains. To the west it is fairly barren, but in other directions it is fertile. The people of Gharzouz say that the climate is "rocky," by which they mean that it is dry and refreshing and keeps away illness and disease from the village—in fact, from the entire region.

That region of the country is known as the Byblos segment, and it consists of seven ancient villages: Rihaniyeh, Jeddayel, Chikhane, Mounsef, Bekhaaz, Berbara, and Gharzouz. It is known as the Byzantine segment, that (Orthodox) church being the upholder of religious and secular values since time immemorial. The community is still crammed into the area, one that is under the jurisdiction of the Maronite community of Kesrouan, although that has not led to any deviation from their principles or beliefs.

However, in more recent times (in other words, at the end of the nineteenth century), Protestant missionaries invaded Gharzouz, a time when the bread that the missionaries offered was smooth and soft. Some upholders of Orthodox opinion fell into their nets. The Evangelicals duly founded in Gharzouz a school for children who had "seen the light," the American school, which still exists.

In this blessed segment with its seven villages, there is a group of outstanding poets, authors, and journalists, in a profusion that brings glory to their communion as a whole. Among poets, I will mention Saleem Azaar, who carried the burden of his genius to the United States at the dawn of this generation, then came back to Egypt. It was there that God granted him his rest while still in the prime of his youth. He can now sing in the cage of paradise.

Another poet is Nehmeh al-Hajj, who, from time to time, still sings her songs in the hours of twilight as she moves between two patches of gorse—her home and her store.

Still another is the renowned village poet Rasheed Khoury, born in the Lebanese village of Berbara and now living in Berbarya Village in Brazil. There he sings like a lark, night and day, celebrating his twin homelands—Arab and poetry. He never tires, nor do his listeners ever get bored.

There are countless authors and journalists. Some of them undertook exhausting journeys in the realms of the pen. God dealt kindly with them, or else they dealt kindly with themselves. In quest of safety, they left the field and abandoned the search for fame and glory. Others are still in the combat zone, challenging fate and renewing their quest for excellence.

Among such people I will mention Yousuf Chehab from Gharzouz, author of the book *What is Existence*? In the book, Professor Yousuf responds to the question that has left all biologist, geologists, and mythologists baffled. Not only that, but he also composes poetry, thereby bringing to mind the conversation one day between the ant and the cricket.

"So where were you on harvest day?" the ant asked.

"I was chanting poetry," the cricket replied.

Professor Yousuf, who had rejected his ancestors' title, belonged to the Chehab family, who came to the Byblos region in the last century to escape from the Damascus governor's revenge on them.

As is only appropriate for an encyclopedia, I will now state that, in 1860, a dispute arose between the Chehab family and the governor of Damascus. Prince Mansour and the brothers of Prince Ali rebelled against the governor and killed him. When the news reached Mohammed Kabarli, the Ottoman grand vizier at the time, he was furious and decided to act. He sent his son, Ali, to Damascus as governor, and took the sword to the Chehab family. The new governor came to the region to carry out the bloody instructions of the grand vizier. Some of them managed to escape to Byblos, among them Prince Mansour, who settled in Gharzouz. His offspring have thrived in the region ever since, and Professor Yousuf is one of them.

An author from Gharzouz who keeps practicing this rigorous profession is someone whom I mentioned in passing in the previous chapter. He now deserves an affectionate acknowledgment for the kind speech he gave on the day of our visit to Gharzouz.

"Greetings to our honored guest," Adeeb Gharzouzy said, "and congratulations! He has managed to avoid the kind of persecution that prophets and messengers have suffered in days gone by. He should thank God because he is still alive, having avoided the cross or hellfire in this world."

And what of the next world? We praise God and ask Him not to change His customs after He calls us back to Him.

If we were concerned about what the morrow might bring, we were thrilled by the new style of praise and compliments that we encountered again in Gharzouz. From the wonderful examples in both prose and verse that we heard as we gathered around a table in the highest house in the village and also in the circle that was formed in its very finest homes, it became clear how rich Gharzouz is in literature. In the village's most elaborate house they held a feast in our honor. We devoured the kibbe and grilled meat in Elias Rahbani's house. In the home of Azaar's in-laws we behaved like Europeans, although not in either spirit or language.

Naseeb is three persons combined in a single human being: as an author from Gharzouz; as its banker; and as a credit to its young people. To his published books you can add the gospel of this particular era, *Golden Rules Concerning Finance.* His reputation was linked to both literature and good works and disavowed any linkage to the wealthy.

While in Gharzouz, there was one single widespread and general complaint—one that brought together peasant and merchants, rich and poor, people in this region, but also throughout Lebanon and Syria—namely, the oppressive policies of the monopoly tobacco company, one that imposed its iron will on people in both Lebanon and Syria.

This land may be your land, but you have no right to plant tobacco on it, except for a small sliver defined by the company. This tobacco is yours, but you have no right to sell it without the company and at prices that they set. If you fail to abide by those regulations, you are liable to a fine, and any extra tobacco will be either impounded or burned. This land may be yours, but I am the only entity with the discretion on how to exploit it, the entity whose volition the government implements since I am in charge of the concession and the accompanying daylight robbery.

This foreign company is one of the largest in the country, one that we register for tomorrow's children. They will be talking about their forefathers' situation just as we do now when talking about our ancestors in times of Ottoman tyranny and outrage.

The poet from Gharzouz uses the popular form of *zajal* to describe the peasants' situation in those days:

> Woe for your effect, ye peasant!
> All your time is spent without rest.
> Silkworms and tobacco, they are dead.
> The gate to success has not returned.

Even so, the threshing floors in Gharzouz still respond to the peasant's call and preserve for him a modicum of hope. They are a unique geological and agricultural novelty in Lebanon.

Now here is the enormous rock, prominent in the village center. Forming a square with ten threshing floors, each of them has a natural edge that keeps it separate from the others.

In summertime, that rock, along with its threshing floors, was a tremendous spectacle for the farmers of the village. In the daytime they would be at the threshing floors, threshing and sorting the seeds; in the evening they would relax in the moonlight and chat.

In the village and close to it, the rocks are different from the flat ground by the threshing floors, and that makes the atmosphere "rocky" and dry, as I have already noted. But the terrain is dry and thirsty as well. There is little water, and no sign of any springs, all the more remarkable in view of the large number of small villages in the region. The villages stretching from the coast to Gharzouz all use rainwater for drinking. Fortunately, the chalky soil is suitable for water filtration, so you will see people spreading the soil on their roofs and filling their cisterns with the water they collect.

Why do people settle on terrain with no water? What led the first Orthodox person to settle down in Chikhane or Gharzouz? Did some of his community colleagues seek refuge in this barren mountainous region as a means of escaping persecution and exploitation, and indeed because it was so barren, meaning that other people would have no interest in it?

I recall that each of these villages had one or two churches, one or two patron saints. Whether those saints were strict Orthodox or held deviant views, they all had miracles associated with them in both life and death. Some of them were connected to springs and water supply; they would bring staffs like the one that Moses carried, and the rocks would suddenly gush with springs of water.

The Orthodox lady in Gharzouz, just like her Maronite sisters in Lebanon, looks out from the gleaming tower of her church on her pious children as they cover their roofs in chalky soil to purify the water rains, but she never shows any of them where water might be located or any underground source nearby.

We paid a visit to the church of this Gharzouz lady saint that was built in a grim year replete with disasters. The governor of Syria in that particular year was Kanj Yousuf Pasha, who was crazy and issued all sorts of amazing and weird decrees, among them that no man was allowed to use a razor; any man who shaved his beard was to be killed. Another disaster was a plague that struck Aleppo, leading to hundreds of funeral processions leaving the city each day. The Yazbeks, enemies of Emir Basheer, attacked Byblos and sacked it. The emir had Girgis Baz assassinated, for which he was congratulated by the scholar Elias Eddeh, in a poem that begins:

Oh man, did you miss a single fleeting moment;
Make sure you remain vigilant and awake!

At that time—the year 1807, with the plague, the governor's madness, and his willingness to kill beardless men—the people in Gharzouz felt safe and secure, directing their hearts toward the lady saint as they constructed this church for her.

As we made our way back from the church, we passed by a house that was completely derelict apart from three arches that remained standing amid the ruins. One's heart paused in all humility before those arches, recalling, as they did, long-forgotten memories of the beautiful lady, my mother's friend, on our much earlier trip to Gharzouz.

I had actually forgotten to mention that while we were on our way to Rouais Park, but I should not be blamed bearing in mind the beautiful girl walking beside me. I forgot to mention that, close to Rouais, was a place called Asr, an old usage passed down through the generations. Its meaning has been lost, but the general view is that in Asr there was a *qasr* (castle) belonging to the daughter of one of the Phoenician kings.

Yes indeed, there was the king's daughter's castle, and here too was the castle of first love. Beneath these very arches was the birth of one whose heart was opened alongside them, opened into a garden of paradise, between night and day, a time when she would close her eyes and raise their veil. It was in those blissful hours that I sat beside her, silent and meek, listening to her and proffering her my heart in a censer between her hands.

Both of us were young—a miserable, jovial age—orbiting around that eternal entity called love, but without knowing where it was and never daring, even if it claimed to know, to approach the throne.

We used to play in front of that throne without seeing it or else in the castle's court, without either of us mentioning his companion's name—his exalted majesty, love.

She used to talk fast, and occasionally I would do my best to keep up with her without really saying anything. Eventually, I would catch up with her with a laugh, while she remained silent with her eyes closed.

This happened in New York, at a time when I had almost completely forgotten my Arabic. She had learned some English at the American School in Gharzouz. There were three things about her that fascinated me: her tongue, her mouth, and her eyes. When she talked, I felt the sheer pleasure of listening to song, the pleasure of confinement when she said nothing, and the pleasure of misery when she opened and closed her eyes.

Ah God, the fates! So, the very first knot in my heart was when I leaned on the breast of a woman from Gharzouz when I was five years old; the second when I sat beside the gorgeous woman from Gharzouz in New York; and the third was the beautiful woman who accompanied me to Rouais Park. She had reminded me painfully of those past days without even realizing it.

There remain two knots in one of the recesses of my heart: the first was tied in Gharzouz fifty-five years ago, the other in New York ten years later.[1] Both of them are still as the fingernails of their original tier intended—firm, fresh, soft, and fragrant, stamped with the seal of eternal love.

Can anyone tell me what will be the fate of those twin knots after death? Can anyone contradict me when I declare that I will roam the seven heavens with lovely memories in my suitcase, memories of those two knots dedicated to eternal love?

And may God have mercy on everyone who ties an eternal knot in the human heart!

1. She traveled to Brazil and drowned in the Amazon River. See "Al-Zanbaqa al-dhawiya" in the poetry collection *Hitaf al-awdiya*.

From the Roof of Saint Charbel's Monastery

I ASKED MY FRIENDS in Gharzouz whether there was either in the region or nearby a Maronite location that would have the patronage of the major saints of these mountains. They replied in the affirmative and mentioned Maad. God bless Maad! As the Lebanese proverb has it, Maad and Bejjeh constitute two-thirds of the country. It is half an hour from Gharzouz, and no more than a hundred meters higher up.

We climbed up toward Maad, taking the road from which we could see to the northwest the village of Bekhaaz and, below it, Berbara. The road actually climbs up to the highest village in this part of the mountains, Sulayyib Ghalboun, then goes downhill to Bejjeh, Gharzouz's equally famous sister, and Subayyel. From there, one branch leads to Lehfed, and the second to Mayfouk, then Jaj.

The horizon expands in all four directions, and Maad forms the central point of the circle. Here is the monastery of Saint Abda—peace be upon him! We had now returned to the true faith in Christianity. One of the monastery's monks welcomed us and opened all the gates of holiness. One of them took us up to the wide roof where the year's wheat yield was laid out.

All the products from the peasants' fields—pulses, figs, beans, olives, and tobacco—lay in the sun on rooftops, if they were covered in soil, not with pyramids of tiles; the crops would be exposed to the sun to dry so that they would not be spoiled by moisture once they were stored. Everyone in Lebanon stores food supplies for winter, and indeed for every season. The enemies of such storage are worms and mold, and the sustenance of both comes from the moisture stored inside the grains. That is why they are laid out in the sun for several days.

Once the tobacco has been laid out in the sun, it is placed in waterless wells—and, as far as I can tell, for both technical and nontechnical reasons. I learned about the monopoly tobacco company and its operating methods. With that in mind, who could blame the peasant for hiding a portion of his crop?

According to the people of Maad, the tobacco grown there is the best in the Lebanese mountains. It has excellent qualities, and everything planted grows in profusion in the warm red soil, something confirmed for us by the monastery monk who also served as schoolteacher and village shopkeeper. We had previously heard similar claims being made about Almat Valley's tobacco and the Asmar crop from Byblos. In other words, everyone extols the creed of their own tobacco!

However, the priest who welcomed us to the village modified this kind of praise, pointing out that the Asmar tobacco in Byblos was like Maad's tobacco, and, in some respects, might even be better. This reverend priest was director of French studies at the Sagesse College in Beirut. So it was no surprise that he should be a precise arbiter in his verdict. It was he who told us Maad's height above sea level—560 meters in the village square, and 580 in the church square—no more, no less.

One of the great virtues of the people in Maad—as we saw for ourselves—is that they take great care of the oak tree by the church. They want it to be seen as the oldest, biggest, and loveliest oak in Lebanon, so they have constructed a three-meter-high wall for it and filled the enclosure with soil. The roots were thus all underground, and two branches started to appear, each one about two meters in diameter, raising their fresh, leafy branches high into the air.

The church is much older than the oak. People say that it is the oldest Maronite church in the mountains. Its architecture is a mix of old and new, complex in its structure, and supported by columns with Greek coronets.

In the church there is a painting by an Italian artist, the colors and style of which show how ancient it is. One of the art agents told us that it dated back to the ninth or tenth centuries CE. However, the great scholar Ernest Renan stumbled across some Greek script in the church, taking it back to the pre-Christian era.

The major evidence of the church's great age was the room behind the altar, with pictures of both Saint Yuhanna Maroun and Saint Ibrianos (Cyprian) on the wall. There was also another room behind the church. Its eastern wall was in ruins, but on two of the other three walls there were pictures of the prophets and the Marys mourning Jesus, all in a specific Byzantine style. However, the sun was shining down on all these images in order to copy them; in just a few years, that copying process—their complete erasure—would be complete.

This church, whose architecture and decorations were the product of various eras and confessions, is today the house of Saint Charbel—not the Lebanese Charbel, but the Roman Charbelius, who converted to Christianity at the hands of the archbishop of Zaha during the reign of Emperor Trajan.

The most beautiful things for us to see were from the rooftop of Saint Charbel's, not the church itself. Let us climb up to the roof, then, and see a stunning view of the Lebanese horizons, overlooking spaces near and far in the twin regions of Byblos and Batroun.

To the southwest is Chamate, the village of Archbishop Boutros Akl and his retreat house in the troubled Bkerke times. Below it is Ghalboun.

On a mountain spur to the southwest lies Bejjeh, half of it on the top, the rest in the middle, with a lush forest between the two.

Right in front of us were two villages on opposite hills, just like two children of paradise: one is Hbaleen; the other Ain Kfaa. The two hills are in a kind of bowl created by the mountains all around them. On the valley floor to the north there is a river branch called Madfoon (buried). On the way to Batroun you would cross a bridge over it.

Up to that river we are in the Byblos district, and to the north it extends to Batroun. The first of its villages is Sofar, which we mentioned during our trip to Kfifan. To the northeast lie Jrabta, Abdelli, and Toula, then the monastery where my noble saint lies buried. Below it is Jran, the birthplace and burial site of Khairallah Khairallah—both of them well worth the pilgrimage.

Now I ask that you stop at the very core of this vista before us, at Ain Kfaa.

As I am standing on the rooftop of Saint Charbel's monastery in Maad, I feel tempted to rhapsodize about Ain Kfaa and its acerbic author, Maroun Abou Muhammad Abboud—and I use the word *acerbic* to describe the match in his writings between word and meaning. Those who experienced the barbs of Maroun's pen were many.

According to our author, Ain Kfaa is Aramaic; in Arabic it would be *ain makhfiya* (hidden spring). But that is the way it remains, in spite of Maroun's magic lamp.

It is not correct that the town and its author are just like that "hidden spring." That is what led Maroun to copy Abou Nuwaas, who says:

> I have sought refuge from my fate in the shadow of its wing;
> Thus I can see my fate, but it cannot see me.

How could such emulation and copying be correct when Maroun, like Lebanon itself, is the very eye of time? All humility is lost, and the Marouni voice is a martyr.

In my rhapsody to Ain Kfaa from afar, I invoke Maroun himself, the ever generous helper.

In olden times this lovely village was a transit point for caravans coming from Byblos, Jounieh, Beirut, Sidon, and Damascus. They would be laden with goods for the northern regions: Douma, Bsharre, Ehden, and other Lebanese hamlets. The road was always alive with sound, never lacking men, hooves, bells on mules, camels and donkeys always jingling and clanging, muleteers singing *ataaba*, chanting prayers, and, in spite of that, cursing religion.

But today, the road is silent. Sounds of humans, jinn, or animals are only rarely heard, except when Ain Kfaa's writer is either leaving or returning to his Khawarnak fortress,[1] riding his donkey, which was as humble as himself. "In their twin hearts, the donkey's and her master's, there were echoes of the disdained civilization, or voices of writers who groaned at the whip-lashes from Maroun's criticisms."

From the rooftop of the Maad church, Ain Kfaa looks like a desolate island perched on a cone-shaped hillock, 250 meters above the valleys that encircle it, those valleys themselves being 200 meters above sea level. They have a number of deep gorges, like the one in the Freike Valley. Maroun as a boy was just like me in my beautiful valley: he would roll stones to the edge and then listen to their sound and echo as they plunged downward and were smashed on the rocks, before landing up in the plowed fields below. They used to chip off bits of rock and destroy trees. Young Maroun was like young Ameen, utterly delighted by such willful destruction—hey, hey! Watch out, pine! Too bad, locust!

A few days later, the director's duty officer would come to complain on behalf of the affected landowner. I used to pay the fine (but I do not know what Maroun used to do in similar circumstances), and then go straight back, along with a group of village boys, to rolling the rocks. We would choose the very biggest, help each other roll it, and then—hey, hey! Watch out, locust!

Ain Kfaa has its own saint, Rouhana. Like Saint Charbel, he performed a number of miracles that Maroun mentioned in a way that made him choke on his faith. He could not have a conversation with the saint, nor convince him that today the village really needed another miracle.

"Just one miracle, Saint Rouhana! Then we can arouse Ain Kfaa and revive it!"

"Shut up, Maroun, and be content! Anyone who deserves a miracle gets to see it. Or aren't you from and in Ain Kfaa?"

1. Translator's note: Al-Khawarnak is the name of one of two proverbial fortresses in Iraq often mentioned in pre-Islamic poetry, the other being Sadir.

Even so, Maroun mentions other miracles performed by the saint. One day he managed to rescue two young boys from an attacking lion. Saint Rouhana stopped the lion and prevented the attack. How? With a sword? No, by God. Rouhana was not like Saint George, who killed the dragon with a lengthy lance. Saint Rouhana preached peace and love. He saved the two boys by putting a river between the boys and the lion. "Stay right where you are, lion!" Poor lion, standing on the riverbank, totally flummoxed! I used the word *standing*, but Maroun was more precise than me. He said that the lion squatted on the ground and started howling like a rabid dog.

"Where's that river, Saint Rouhana?" he asked, banging his forehead with his fist. "Is there nothing left—no stream, watercourse, culvert, fountain, springlet, nothing?"

"Ain Kfaa bows down in worship to you, but has no spring. It's thirsty, oh blessed one, it's thirsty. Since time immemorial they have been searching for that hidden spring, and they still are. Is it covered in seven layers, as the myth has it? Where are those layers? Maroun is a noble scout, Saint Rouhana, so show him where it is so that he can uncover it—uncover it and worry no more!"

The day will come when Ain Kfaa is happy, happy with its spring, its Maroun, and its road. That same road will brings new chatter, not the old noise of animals and muleteers, but instead of iron, petrol, and car horns.

Giants

FROM GHARZOUZ we made our way back to Seif al-Bahr, passing through Chikhane, Jeddayel, and Rihaniyeh, three villages of the district whose names—except one—mock people's ignorance and preserve their obscure origins since ancient times and until God knows when. What does *Jeddayel* mean—"professor"? God alone knows. What is the connection between this Chikhane and the Yazidi Chikhane near Mosul? God knows! Is there some trace of King Taus in this Chikhane or of the mighty Yazidi Satan? I hereby seek refuge from Satan the accursed. Does anyone really care? No.

That is why, after expressing my reliance on God and even though King Taus may get angry, I will state here that it makes no sense that some citizens of our Chikhane, with their straightforward beliefs, left for Mosul, settled in Yazidi country close by, and adopted their satanic beliefs, calling the place where they settled by the same name as the Lebanese village they had left.

On the other hand, it is possible that some Yazidis left Mosul for Lebanon, founded this village in the Byblos sector, and named it after their original village. They rejected Satan and his worship—at least superficially, initially so as to protect themselves against the hostility of the Orthodox believers in the region, and eventually joined them in their Orthodox faith.

People in Chikhane say that their town has ancient ruins, some buried, others in the open. It is not out of the question that, after due exploration and study, one may come across some relics associated with King Taus or information about Mount Sinjar that would confirm statements about the satanic origins of this village.

Today, however, the village has a lively church, and its female saint—on her be peace!—keeps Satan out of Chikhane.

However, in Jeddayel, there is a clearly visible ruin that points to their existence there and their work. It stops you on your way to the church. God forbid, it is not in the church itself but rather in its enormous oak tree—and that in spite of its age and poor condition. The satans, enemies of all trees, have cut off five huge branches and bored a hole through it from east to west. After hollowing it out, they filled it with stones. Is there any denying the presence of Satan in such a place?

We hurried away from Jeddayel, regretting the fate of its oak tree and invoking curses on its devil. We reached Rihaniyeh, but its name is the only good thing about it. It is the first village on the road from the coast to Gharzouz and is four hundred feet above sea level. Its houses, trees, and hills are covered in a thick layer of dust stirred up by caravans and winds from its limestone terrain.

People who choose to live in this terrain are giants indeed. Even in our own times, some of the people in these villages deserve to be considered as descendants of conquerors, people who subdued the land to their will. Even though the terrain is so arid, it can still nurture giants.

The tailor who is also a poet, Professor Jabra'eel, said that Nawfal Gharzouzy was a giant. One day he received a severe stab wound in the stomach during a battle, and his guts spilled out. He started carrying them home, but an intestine got stuck in a gorse bush. He tugged it out and put it back in the pile of intestines he was carrying. He kept moving, and, when he reached the house, he collected all the intestines and put them back in his abdomen. He then asked for a needle and some twine. There was no doctor, no surgical instruments, and no sterilization. Nawfal stitched his abdomen with the muleteers' needle. Three days later, he was completely cured and went back to work, carrying ropes and long ladders for construction.

Professor Jabra'eel was not one to exaggerate in telling a story or to ramble as he talked. He stopped us by a wall at a Gharzouz house and showed us fully three meters of rope, which Nawfal used to carry on his back, take to the building site, and then climb up two or three levels by the wall in order to put them in their proper place by the tiles.

One of the professor's relatives turned to look at us from his place beside the driver.

"Nawfal could take a coin in his fingers," he told us to confirm what had already been said, "bend it in two and place an egg on top of it."

"Every giant figure is known for that," I replied. "I can remember a man in Freike who could carry enormous packages, as though they were simply a hay sack or a load of wood. I watched him grab a coin between his thumb and forefinger and bend it as though it were a piece of tin.

In the history of Aqoura, we find the following: Emad ibn Abdallah al-Hashem was a giant figure. With a single blow of his sword he cut through a roll of blanket wrapped seven times with an iron rod inside it.

I do not want to challenge your belief by recounting stories from books, heard at threshing floors, or beneath the porches of village stores. I will return to the kind of people whom I have known, people in whom I have observed signs of ability and courage.

During my account of our trip to Byblos, I mentioned our brother, Zakhia, himself a giant in both his abilities and his faith. One day I heard him talking to my mother.

"Through the power of the Virgin Mary," he told her, "I will rip out this tree (a large mulberry tree) by hand. Through that same power, I will jump off this roof and make my way to work safe and sound."

He made the sign of the cross on his forehead and was about to jump—from a height of fifteen meters. My mother stopped him, in spite of her fervent belief in the power of the Virgin Mary.

Zakhia was well-known in Kesrouan, Byblos, and Batroun. People would talk about his deeds and faith as they did about miracles of saints. Nawfal from Gharzouz knew him and acknowledged that he was a friend. He is supposed to have said that Zakhia al-Hsouni used to carry a marble threshold as though it were a mulberry branch.

As far as giant figures like these were concerned, this was all easy and normal. However, Zakhia had an exceptional model in everything involving ability and courtesy—namely, his beloved, spoiled female donkey.

This particular donkey only used to work for one or two days a week. Even then, she was never overburdened at work. Zakhia used to walk either behind or alongside her on the road from Hsoun to the coast and back again. He always talked to her in tones of a spoiled beloved, as though she were a much loved daughter of Eve.

Now you need to gather your beliefs and listen to me. Zakhia and his donkey were on their way back from Jounieh. He had loaded her with "flour for the house," as mountain folk say, implying a sack of flour weighing no more than sixty pounds.

As usual, Zakhia was walking alongside his beloved donkey, with a mulberry stick in his hand that he was using to tickle her neck from time to time. She stopped right in the middle of the road by a very steep path, as though she recognized it. Having stopped, she apparently intended to stay there the whole day or until God fulfilled her desires.

Zakhia spoke to her, cajoled her, and tickled her neck. He then gave her a light tap with the stick, but she moved neither her tail nor her ears.

"Let's go, blessed one! Move it, beloved!"

But the beloved, spoiled donkey neither heard nor responded.

She stood there like a rock. Zakhia stood in front of her, face-to-face, and spoke to her:

"You always do this, you pest. Every time you get to this spot, you think of your master, Zakhia's, back. Do you want to bury your master, who taught you how to be so spoiled?!"

Having said that, Zakhia knelt in front of his donkey with his back toward her. Taking her two front legs in his hands, he lifted them on to his shoulders and carried her and her load on his back. He then started climbing up the pass.

"You've got used to being carried, you pest!" he said.

So, now once again you need to gather your beliefs and listen to me. The things I am telling you are things that I have witnessed myself, not what I have heard or read about in books. I had a friend, very dear, loyal friend, in Qornat al-Hamra, a village next to Freike, who once told, after he had heard me giving a speech, that he wanted me to deliver the eulogy at his funeral. I promised him that I would.

However, on the day that he died, I was up in the mountains, which only doubled my sense of grief. May God have mercy on Abdallah Nasr—teacher Abdallah! That is a title that he thoroughly deserved because, even though he himself was illiterate, he was able to do many good things. His particular profession was carpentry but also anything connected with building and with mountain life. His eye could spot the minutest things, his brain could understand the hardest matters, and his heart has always ahead of his hand when it came to serving people.

Teacher Abdallah was one of those Lebanese who will always respond to requests, whatever the case involved—public or private.

"The water pipe in the village is cracked. Call Abdallah."

"There's a blockage in the ducts to the cistern. Call Abdallah."

"The church altar needs repairing. Call master craftsman Abdallah."

"Someone's bull (very fierce and aggressive) has managed to get out of its enclosure. You need Abdallah."

"The house pump is out of order. Get Abdallah fast!"

In addition to all that, he was the local dentist. To pull teeth, he used the pliers he had for carpentry.

Abdallah had no desire for this world's vanities. In fact, in his later years, he would do things for people and the village without charge—all in God's cause.

In our household Abdallah was the helper about everything—adviser, friend, overseer, accountant, and investigator of everything.

This is just part of what I need to say about him in fulfilment of my promise to him. It falls into its appropriate place, in that the topic we are discussing here is giants.

Abdallah was indeed a giant of a man, skillful in everything. His courage was exactly like his other qualities of courtesy and kindness.

You have just heard the story about the operation that Nawfal from Gharzouz performed on his own abdomen. Abdallah did a similar operation on one of his hands when he was shot.

One day, he confronted a raging bull in the town square. He grabbed the animal by one of its horns and its tail. The bull leapt up, trying to get away. It started kicking with its feet and spinning in fury. Abdallah was still clutching its horn and tail and hung on, spinning and leaping with the animal from time to time and crawling so as to avoid its attacks. It was as if he were a Spanish (bullfighter). Neither of the two combatants slowed down or gave way, but eventually the horn broke off in the giant's hand. That drove the bull to a new level of fury, and it managed to escape his enemy's grip like a stone from a catapult. Abdallah was thrown to the ground with the horn still in his hand.

An example of his courage and courtesy involved the cross on the church dome. Qornat el-Hamra has a huge, superb church, twenty meters high. The dome over it is almost another twenty meters. It is shaped like a pyramid, and you can climb up to it using a ladder on the church roof. People wanted to put a cross on the top, and so the young men of the village were summoned. Yet no one stepped forward to do it.

Abdallah happened to be there; at the time he was seventy-seven years old. He took off his shoes, grabbed the huge cross in his shriveled hand, climbed up to the church roof, and then started up the wooden ladder, which kept twisting and shaking beneath his feet. Having reached the top of the dome, he inserted the cross and made it secure. All the while, the people and youths of the village were watching silently below while, inside the church, the women were praying for him.

Abdallah came down that rickety ladder from the top of the dome as though he were coming down a staircase in his own home. He put his shoes back on, tied his waistband, brushed the dirt off his coat, then hurried home to milk his goat.

Book of Saints

OUR OWN TIME is not one for sainthood and heroism. If there is a mere glimmer of them both that is not accompanied by drums and whistles, it will remain remote from people. Whoever that person may be, he will be neither heard, nor seen, nor heeded. He can live and die, like worms in a field or lilies in the valley.

The ignoramus will say in his heart, as will the scholar in his book, that there is no God. Thus, in this world of ours—a world of oil, steel, and electricity—there can be no prophets or saints.

If we choose to disavow such statements and say that prophets and saints do still exist in our midst—showing themselves today as they did in the past, without any fuss and in all due humility and modesty—then doubters will ask where such people are. If we take such doubters to see one of them and remove the cap of deceit from their heads, then they go on to demand a miracle if we are being truthful.

Esteemed skeptics, let me take you to visit a Lebanese saint in these mountains, a saint today as in the past, someone who escapes from cities unless the times demand sacrifice, and who prefers hunger amid the rocks to satiation in palaces.

We are heading for Kfifan. As we approach Batroun, we climb our way up a mountain that retreats gently in front of us. It does not tower above us like the Kesrouan range that overshadows Jounieh or the Mseilha range that leaps from the sea in a single bound.

In these modest mountains where we are heading—from Byblos to Laqlouq or to Amcheet and Jaj, from Bechta to Gharzouz, Batroun to Kfifan, or Chekka to Amioun—in the mountains the terrain is white and fallow, meaning that it is desolate, arid, pebbly limestone. Villages are few and far between.

Between Batroun and the Kfifan monastery, for example, you pass through a tiny village called Makmal. After it comes Eddeh, some five hundred meters higher up. The road slopes down a bit toward Jran, then up again to the monastery, the goal of our pilgrimage. From Seif al-Bahr we will have covered about thirty kilometers, and the only villages are the ones that I have mentioned. Between them is nothing but dust and rocks, with a few locust and oak trees here and there.

So I will now tell you about saints so you can forget all about the journey there and get you ready for the blessings and well-being that you will get from this visit.

The name, Nimat Allah Hardini—derived from Hardine, his birthplace—is known as the saint of Kfifan and the most renowned Lebanese saint. In life and death he performed miracles, as confirmed by many villagers. You are going to see the greatest of those miracles when you stand in front of his tomb. There he lies under the glass covering, a complete human being, his body intact. It is as though he were in a saintly slumber, one that has lasted now for eighty years.

Among Nimat Allah's remarkable gifts was the ability to sense certain events before they actually happened. He enjoyed the capability—or the blessing—of clairvoyance. For example, one day he looked out of his window in the monastery and noticed that the cattle shed was in a very poor condition—one that worried him. He immediately summoned a servant and told him to get the cattle out of the shed at once. No sooner had the servant done that than the whole shed collapsed, roof and walls all at once.

Among Nimat Allah's miracles that remind you of some Muslim saintly figures is that one day he went into the church to celebrate Mass, but he could not find the server. When he asked where the boy was, they told him that he was sick. He rushed to the boy's house and found him lying in bed with a fever. He placed his hand on the boy's head.

"With God's sanction you are cured," Nimat Allah told the boy. "Now get up and come with me."

The boy duly got out of bed, full of resolve, his fever and weakness having totally disappeared. He went to the church with Nimat Allah and served Mass with him. Once Mass was over, the boy offered up some supplementary prayers, thanking God for his cure.

Neither of these events qualify as miracles according to psychologists. The first is a matter of clairvoyance, the second of suggestion. We believe what the psychologists are saying. In the third instance, can their science uncover the secret or disprove the miracle, which is no different from other miracles performed by well-known saints?

Supplies were running low in the monastery. The chief priest therefore asked Nimat Allah to investigate and tell him what was in short supply so he could get what was needed. Nimat Allah went to the storehouse and asked the agent there to bring him a ewer of water. The man brought the water, and Nimat Allah prayed over it and splashed some around the room. He then went back to the chief priest and told him that there were enough supplies; thank God, there was no need for any more. The chief priest went down himself to check and discovered that there was a plentiful supply of everything. Where had it all come from? The water? Or from Heaven?

Now gird your faith again and follow me. The saint died, and four years later his body was transferred safely to the church. His fame spread throughout Lebanon, and, as we mentioned earlier, that boy, the one with the holy necklet around his neck, was one of the people carried there to be cured.

Some of the people who came there were undoubtedly very sick: crippled, epileptic, and paralyzed. Here was a man from Upper Matn, crippled for thirty years, who passed through Bikfaya on the back of a mule. The doctor, Sheikh Abou Ali al-Jumayyel, spotted him and asked him where he was going.

"To Kfifan," the crippled man replied, "to visit the saint."

"It's easier for the saint to make a new man," Sheikh Jumayyel told him, "than to make you better and cure you!"

Once the visit was over, the man came back the same way. He halted his mule in front of Sheikh al-Jumayyel's house. When the sheikh saw him, he repeated what he had said earlier. The man leapt to the ground from his mule and started running. The sheikh could not believe what he had just seen.

Next there was an epileptic monk from Jaj who came to the Kfifan monastery, spent the night sleeping by the saint's tomb, and emerged the next morning completely cured. He was to live thirty more years in complete health and well-being.

At that time a barren Druze woman arrived from Broumana to ask for the saint's aid. The next year she gave birth to a son. She asked her husband for permission to pay another visit to the saint in order to fulfill her vow. Her husband not only allowed her, but accompanied her on the journey. When they reached Asmar Jbeil, the baby died in his mother's arms. She was afraid of her husband's wrath, so she kept the whole thing secret. When she reached the monastery, she placed the dead baby by the saint's body and left the church, keeping her feelings to herself and hoping dearly that the saint would respond to her pleas. Her husband was waiting for her outside the church. When he saw that she was by herself, he asked her about the baby. She could not come up with an answer and could not help bursting into tears. Her husband yelled at her and was about to hit her, when at that very moment a monk appeared.

"Come and get your baby," he told the mother. "He's filling the church with his screams."

At this point skeptical believers might ask: "Is it certain that the baby was really dead when the mother placed it by the saint's tomb? Isn't it more likely that the baby suffered some kind of seizure in Asmar Jbeil, and it went away at the monastery soon after?"

We were in sacred space, traversing a rich pine forest, not a suitable location for questions from sceptics. Now here was the monastery, situated atop a lovely hill and surrounded by olive groves. The horizon stretched away into the distance. Mountains to the north softened the bitter chill of winter, and those to the east cooled the hot winds in spring and summer.

Here was the abbot, someone we had already met during one of our trips. The surprise here bore with it the same reverence and delight as we had encountered at the Roumiyeh monastery in Qlay-aat. The countenance of the Reverend Antonius possessed that same essence of tranquility, veneration, and amity that characterized saints, while his heart gave us a welcome that resembled the very horizon within which the monastery stood.

When we told him about our purpose in visiting the monastery, he accompanied us to the rock containing the saint's tomb. We entered in awe and looked all around us, unabashed. However, when we stood in front of the tomb itself, we felt sad and apologetic.

Where now was the saint whom my youthful eyes had seen in his tomb fifty-five years earlier? Where was the church that was honored by his holy corpse, the same church where I had slept with my mother and the beautiful woman from Gharzouz?

Was he now enclosed underneath this splendid piece of marble? What lay hidden beneath that rock, that silly piece of marble—with all its pride and arrogance? This was no saint's tomb; it was more like one for a president or other notable figure.

These reactions and impressions were all buzzing around inside my head as I stood in front of the tomb reading the inscription on it:

> FATHER NIMAT ALLAH HARDINI
> BORN 1808
> BECAME A MONK AT QIZHAYYA MONASTERY IN 1830
> ORDAINED PRIEST IN 1833
> TRANSFERRED FROM HIS GRAVE (TO THE CHURCH) BY ORDER OF THE SUPERIORS IN 1862

(And Ameen Rihani paid him a visit, along with his mother and the beautiful leady from Gharzouz in 1881. But, after that, what . . . ?)

From the church he was moved to this rock and placed under this heavy weight of marble in 1926, but by whose order? From Rome, the head of the Vatican himself.

And why is that? Because Rome will never acknowledge the sainthood of Lebanese nationals until many, many years have gone by. Why such hesitation and dilatory behavior? I have no idea, but then nor do the astrologer bosses.

They say that there is a papal commission, known as the Commission to Investigate Candidates for Sainthood, a group that conducts its business with all necessary precision and accuracy, but slowly, oh how slowly.

The entire process involves major expenditures. So, good news, you busybodies and sceptics! We have now discovered the holy secret—money! There can be no beatification without money.[1] Any saint, whose family is not rich or who has no sect, group, or monastic order to take up the case, will die and be buried just like any other monk, bishop, or patriarch from among the heads and senior figures of the would-be Roman Catholic Maronite communion. He will never be beatified, nor will his name be allowed mention among the saints.

The saint of Kfifan is not the only captive to the golden will of Rome. There is also the Lebanese Saint Charbel, Charbel ibn Makhlouf from Bekaa Kafra. He lived, became a monk, turned abstemious and ascetic, and performed miracles. God called him back on the very same day that Patriarch Yuhanna al-Hajj died.

This scholar on Lebanese saints and their miracles told me that locusts had devastated the mountain region and reached as far as the lands of Saint Maroun at Annaya. The monastery abbot gave orders that water should be taken to "the recluse" Charbel. Charbel prayed over the water, which was then sprinkled over the monastery's lands. The locusts withdrew and retired, hungry and defeated. Do any European saints have miracles more amazing than that?

Here is yet another example. A man from the Lahoud family in Amcheet had a sick son who was close to death. He sent word to the Saint Maroun monastery to summon the recluse monk. The monastery abbot told him to go with the messenger, but without telling him where he was going. When they were halfway to the house, the monk told the messenger that he did not need to go any further with him.

1. Beatification for Catholics involves a declaration that the dead person is beatified, as a prelude to being declared a saint at a later stage.

"Why?" the messenger asked.

"Because the boy's dead," the monk replied.

That said, the monk returned to his cell. The abbot sent a monk to Amcheet to check on the story. It was true. The boy had died at the exact moment when the monk had stopped on the road and then returned to the monastery. So, is this account any less remarkable than miracles performed by European saints?

Is there a difference between the tombs of devout people in Europe and those in Lebanon? When the recluse monk Charbel died, light would shine forth from his tomb time after time. A few years later, the tomb was opened. The corpse was found to be completely intact, with no sign of either decay or putrefaction. Indeed, what was even more remarkable was that, when his body was transferred from the tomb to the church, his body perspired as though he were alive; if he had been wounded, blood would have flowed from the wound.

How is it possible for the papal investigative commission to dismiss these accounts as being invalid when Italian churches contain portraits of male and female saints sweating and oozing blood for believers to observe? In 1926 this commission visited Lebanon and observed this devout Lebanese man in his holy slumber. They heard about all his miracles, then issued instructions that he was to be kept hidden until the time came for his beatification.

The Maronites are still building churches dedicated to the Roman Saint Charbel, "Charbelios," Ruhaawii. They seldom bother about Saint Charbel ibn Makhlouf, the Lebanese man from Bekaa Kafra, with his fresh, bleeding wounds. Where then is the true devotion, where is the self-respect? Where, indeed, is the sense of fairness?

Esteemed members of this august commission, here is Father Daniel, a rural monk from Hadath el-Jebbeh. His outward appearance never revealed his inner self. He used to ride horses like a nobleman. Like Moroccans, he could cure people with herbs. He used to work in the monastery, sweeping and cleaning like a servant. People were suspicious of him, and some of them even opposed him. However, there were others who blessed him. Father Daniel died in the Saint Sarkis monastery in Qartaba; at which point, what he had kept hidden was finally revealed—a lengthy garment he could sense—that of blessed hermits.

Shortly after Father Daniel's death, light began to shine forth from his grave. Villagers noticed it and told the monastery monks. Father Daniel was removed from the grave and placed inside the church. The first miracle that God permitted him to perform was to grant a barren woman what she was craving.

"A barren woman becoming pregnant," proclaimed a member of the commission, "is a regular story for candidates for beatification. It's not considered a miracle."

Esteemed sir, your comment carries weight. However, we would like to draw your attention to the statement of the woman in question. She is of poor peasant stock, from the village of Mghayreh near Aqoura. She had an eye disease and headaches. For ten months Doctor Shuqair treated her in Beirut, but then told her that she needed an operation to be fully cured, and the operation was somewhat risky.

"It took ten months of treatment for the doctor to come to that conclusion?" commented the commission's chair. "In any case, what part does the candidate for sainthood play in it?"

"God willing, I propose to lay out the entire case before this august commission. While this poor woman was returning to her home and was passing through Qartaba, she felt inspired to pay a visit to Saint Daniel in the Saint Sarkis monastery."

"Say, 'candidate for sainthood.'"

"Forgive me, esteemed sir, please forgive me! The woman reached the tomb of the 'candidate for sainthood.'"

"I'm poor," she said, praying and weeping. "In both your life and death, you are the physician of poor people. Please cure me, Saint Daniel, please cure me!"

Just three days later this same woman was cured of all her symptoms. When she came to see the monastery abbot, she swore an oath, invoking both God and the Virgin Mary to corroborate her account.

"We need the account of the devil's advocate,"[2] said the commission's chair. "Where is he?""

"In issues involving sainthood in the Maronite church, Your Honor, there is neither devil nor advocate."

"There has to be," replied the commission's chair. "Without his testimony, the investigation is incomplete."

"But Your Honor, that is your system. Here in Lebanon we have no devils and no advocates to poke their noses into our community affairs.

"Remove that from the record," the chair instructed the recorder. He then addressed the lawyer:

"Stop spouting raving nonsense! Do you have any other candidates?"

"Yes, we have a female saint."

"A female candidate for beatification—a female!!"

"Her name's Rafka Rayyis from Himalaya. She joined the Order of the Sacred Heart. When those in charge dissolved the order . . ."

"Why was it dissolved?" the chair asked.

"I'm not representing the order. The people in charge know more about it than I do."

"Were the nuns released from their vows?"

"In this case that was necessary."

"What happened to the candidate after that?"

"She went to Maad to teach children. When she became bored with that, she started praying to God to save her from her plight or else

2. *Advocatus diaboli* is the name given to the official in the Sacred Congregation in Rome who is charged with challenges to candidates for beatification. As an example, the candidate's advocate may state that his candidate was a saint who performed miracles; he will mention some of them and bring in witnesses. The *advocatus diaboli* will then claim that this candidate for sainthood used to steal, commit adultery, and get drunk, or else that he or she put poison in the coffee cup of his or her superior, who then died. He will then bring in as evidence people who knew or colluded with him or her.

to guide her to a monastery where she could escape from the school. God eased her path by providing a man who paid for her admission to the monastery of Saint Simon. There she stayed for several years, serving and living a life of abstinence and prayer. God then tested her with an eye disaster. The Mother Superior gave her permission to go to Beirut in search of a cure. However, in a monks' residence in Byblos she met a doctor and asked his advice. He took an instrument to examine her eyes and managed to knock one of them out. With a howl, Rafka sank to the floor in a faint."

"It seems as though doctors in your country are just like candidates for beatification!" said the chair.

"I'm not advocating for doctors, your honor."

"Lucky you!"

"In defending our national saints, I'm not bothered about luck, good or bad."

"Your candidates, your candidates! Don't force me to correct that mistake again. What happened to candidate Rafka after the doctor knocked her eye out?"

"She forgave him. Yes indeed, she forgave the doctor for his mistake. She had gone to Beirut to seek a cure, but had not succeeded. She was treated at a specialist hospital, and then went back to the monastery with only one eye.

"She returned to the monastery. Just one year later, she lost her sight in the other eye. Now blind, she was transferred to the Saint Joseph monastery in Jrabta in the Batroun district. She started sewing and weaving socks for the nuns. Then God tested her again; she was left completely paralyzed except for her tongue."

With a hand gesture, the chair indicated that we should listen. He paused for a moment to ponder in silence, then indicated to the advocate that he should finish up.

"Rafka now had only her tongue left, and she used it for prayers and intercessions; as she did so, her voice would have the sweetest of tones, praising God for the blessings of life and faith. She lived like that for thirty years, blind and handicapped, offering up her prayers, intercessions, and thanks. It was after her death that she started performing miracles."

"Didn't she perform any miracles when she was alive?" the chair asked.

"I believe that the august commission must surely be above such a display of ignorance. Can't you all see that chanting prayers and intercessions, in spite of blindness and handicaps, is a miracle of all miracles?"

"Stick to the point. Cite one of the candidate's miracles after her death."

"I will cite three. The first . . ."

"Light emanating from her grave?" the chair reacted. "That's an old tune. Wasn't it simply the kind of phosphorescence that emerges from certain graves?"

"If the honorable chair has appointed himself as devil's advocate," the nun's advocate said, "then what's the point of saying anything? Even so, my heart tells me that I must be frank with the august commission. Rafka Rayyis lived and died in poverty. Like her convent and her community, her parents had no money to spend on the beatification process. God willing, the august commission has found itself inspired to do what is good, so beatify Rafka. Should God Almighty not so wish, then there can be no inspiration, no beatification, and no point in any more words from either me or you.

Having said that, the nun's advocate was on the point of leaving, but the chair stopped him.

"It's just as you say," the chair stated. "There's no point in your advocating for your fellow countrymen proposed for beatification. You've been wasting our time, and you have not been polite."

"Before we leave this chamber," the advocate stated angrily, "I want to convey to you some words to take back with you to your country. Every single one of our saints is worth ten or twenty of yours.[3]

3. In early Christian times the word *saint* was used to apply to every Christian believer. In the fourth century CE, the Catholic Church started canonizing martyrs

I'm familiar with all of them. I've perused the *Synaxarion* from cover to cover."

Every member of the august commission now took a long, black cigar out of his pocket and lit it, shaking their heads as they smoked.

---

so as to distinguish them from other believers. In the sixth century CE, it started canonizing ascetics and hermits. Since those times, the number of pious believers has increased in both East and West. In the latter region, they canonize saints, but in our part of the world they hand them over to the devil's advocate.

Jran and Its Owner

FROM THE KFIFAN MONASTERY we made our way back by the same road we had used to get there. Within ten minutes we were looking down on olive and quince orchards on the valley slopes, and then on rocks decorated with oak trees that had grown in their cracks. We were now in Jran, where we dismounted.[1]

I hereby ask God and the reader for forgiveness. This mountainous region of Lebanon has enough names for villages and hamlets to totally aggravate the traveler in search of knowledge. When it comes to offering justifications and explanations for those names, that aggravation may be at its most intense. Experts on the subject are specialists in Aramaic, and they have no hesitation in ascribing the name of every village and region about which we ask for their opinion to the language of the Chaldeans, one to which those who have sought to disparage the Ottomans have applied the same principles.

As if the Chaldeans and Assyrians and all the people who inhabited Mesopotamia were the only ones to inhabit those shores and mountains. They alone named their villages. Were those names all so weird, or were they all Aramaic? Did the Hittites, Amorites, Phoenicians, Persians, Greeks, and Romans not have their own tongues of which they were proud, languages whose words could become embedded amid the rocks of those mountains?

1. Translator's note: Rihani here indulges in a verbal pun: the name of the town is Jran, and the word *jiran*, which he also uses, refers to the neck of a camel, and, in this instance, to adjusting oneself to a situation.

Could it be perhaps that you have never heard of Mudar and Rabia? Or that these Phoenician shores had never heard the Arabic language in times gone by?[2] Here close to Byblos there is a village called Helooueh; another called Ukaibeh; a third called Rihaniyeh (which we passed through on our way to Gharzouz); a fourth called Safra; and a fifth called Albuwar.

Those names all sound like Arabic—not so? Is there any trace of Phoenician or Aramaic in names like Safra, Ukaibeh, or Jran?

At this point, we will pause for a moment and ask the reader's forgiveness for indulging in some linguistic justification for this process, God willing. That same reader may well say, "We know you to be a sage person, but when did you turn into a linguist? Let the reader say what he likes, and let him allow me to say what I like.

The word *jurn* has nothing non-Arabic about it. As is the case with other words, it has a variety of meanings—delicate and frivolous, old and valuable. At this particular moment what interests me are the following:

Jurn. A mortar for pounding seeds.
Ijtarana. To collect seeds in a drying pit.
Ijtarana. Someone who uses a drying pit.
Jurn. In Lebanon today, everyone knows *jurn*, given that we eat kibbe.
Jarn. Pl. *ajraan* and *jiraan*—threshing floor.

All these words are relatively close in their meanings, and they are all in use. The word *jarana* when used for a man means "to be accustomed and inured to something." However, its usage is merely a matter of an undesirable exoticism. Which writer today, however obscurantist and pedantic his wishes, would prefer using *jarana* over the usual Arabic words, *ta'awwada* or *tamarrana*?

Then there is *jarana*, used with reference to shields when they become soft and smooth from excessive wear. Here my initial question involves the shields themselves. In our times of mechanical and

2. Translator's note: Rihani here uses the traditional phrase, "the language of *daad*," that being regarded as a characteristic phoneme of the language.

chemical warfare today, what is the role of shields for Arabs? What is the point of *jaarin* and *jaarina*, meaning "a shield that is clearly worn"? Does anyone relish the idea of invoking the image of the pre-Islamic poet Labeed al-Aamiri, so often cited in dictionaries?

> Bright shields, and every swift steed on which a warrior will battle
> the twin chills of morn and even.

There remains the word *jiraan*, meaning "part of a camel's neck," one that needs to be preserved, if only because of its interesting ancient connections. The story connected with it should really be depicted in song, but I will tell it here because of its unique interest and the allusion derived from it.

Jiraan is the front part of the camel's neck, from the windpipe to the throat. Whips are made from it, they being still used for both decoration and giving warnings. It could be that Germans who read Nietzsche when he talks about whipping women are invoking the image of Aamer ibn al-Harith al-Namari who was nicknamed "camel whip" because he addresses his two wives as follows:

> Take notice, my twin neighbors! I see that the camel whip is almost ready for use.

Al-Harith's two wives were being obstreperous, so he took a camel whip and put it in the sun. He warned them that they would be beaten as soon as it was dry.

When it comes to allusive usages, Arabs have said, "He has accustomed himself" (using the word *jiraan*) and "Islam established itself" in the same way as they have said, "The traveler threw down his cane" when he reached his desired goal.

The word *mijraan* is a threshing floor; as synonyms, it needs no more than *jurn* and *jareen*. With regard to a man who is said to be *mujrin*, meaning "a glutton," it must be one of those semantic leaps that are regularly encountered in dictionaries. Either that, or else it is one of those inane jokes that the lexicographer Al-Fairuzabadi so enjoys. He cites "the *mujrin* man" (i.e., gluttonous) and then links it with *mujarran* (a pliable whip)! So take care, all you gluttons!

So all this is material about *J-R-N*, the verbal root from which the name of the town Jran is derived. That is where Khairallah was born. He is thus Arab, not Aramean.

Khairallah deserves this lexical excursion. God have mercy on him, he remained an Arab during his Lebanese-Parisian life, an Arab with pure intentions and a genuine tongue; he was farsighted in both vision and hope, liberal, ambitious, and honorable.

Khairallah was born in this tiny house, with its lovely porch, courtyard, and upstairs, situated atop the rock enveloped in oaks. As a youngster, he used to wear black clothes and learned some Syriac as a preparation for ordination. However, he changed his mind while in Belgium (where he had been sent by Patriarch Elias Huwayeck in order to complete his theological studies at the University of Louvain). He wrote to the patriarch, saying that the priestly life was not for him. The patriarch respected Khairallah's liberal conscience and continued to admire him for the rest of his life.

In 1910 Khairallah left Belgium and went back to Paris. There he made the acquaintance of Andre Tardieu, who at the time was editor of the newspaper *Le Temps*. Khairallah talked to the editor about French and German politics in the Near East. Tardieu was amazed by what the young man from Lebanon had to say and asked him to write an article about the subject.

Khairallah wrote the article, and that marks the beginning of his career as a political writer; not only that, but the start of his work at a major French newspaper. Later he became editor of its Eastern section, continuing to write about Near Eastern news. For twenty years he composed articles about Arab and Lebanese politics.

Khairallah was an unusual character, a combination of knowledge and vision, of pride and ambition. He loved the truth and was infatuated by the imagination. He would dip his pen in the inkwell of the arid realities of political facts, but would then clothe that same pen in the crimson of respect and dignity. His innate greatness would always be able to transcend his expertise in the minutiae of politics and societal roadblocks. He was well acquainted with the French, along with all their strengths and shortcomings. He used to address them as peers:

"I'm Khairallah; I come from a long line of Lebanese princes. I own a mansion high up in the mountains. Like you, I am free and independent."

He would say such things sitting in his tiny room inside the offices of *Le Temps.* At a modest, empty table, he would regularly be filtering the news from the Near East and edit it all down into a paragraph or two, which he would offer every day as a way of enlightening European minds.

"I could never understand the secret of Khairallah's princely imagination," Mr. Elias Huwayeck told me once. "Like Gibran, he loved the ideas of being a prince with all its prestige and portrayed himself as being part of all that. I only came to understand the secret behind such an engaging illusion when I visited his house in Jran. Standing on the roof by the upstairs section of the house and looking out on the valleys and hills that Khairallah had observed with a child's eyes, I could see that it was all large, grand, and lofty. The young boy who imagined himself a prince in this mansion of his had carried that image with him throughout his life. It turned into a wonderful reality, especially in Paris. What was funny was that, when he used to tell French people about his mansion in Lebanon and his princely heritage, he used to call on me to verify what he was saying."

That same illusion or imaginative trait that was to become a reality in Khairallah's views and sensitivities was undoubtedly responsible for the birth of the pride that helped him remain stalwart. He used to confront French people with a guileless expression, and treated them as equals. What is also undoubtedly the case is that Khairallah lived in Paris as a free and honorable person. He maintained a firm creed and stubborn streak, even though life was tough for him most of the time.

In social terms, Khairallah was mild-tempered and generous, both characteristics enhanced by a comprehensive and radiant cultural outlook. Even though his residence in Paris, in the district known as the Latin Quarter, did not match that of his mansion in Jran—even in its height, He would always welcome his literary colleagues there, people who came to the French capital from America or across the ocean. He would honor them in accordance with his princely imaginings, showing them a kind of pagan Lebanese hospitality, to which would be added the delights of Parisian life. As host, he would often mention Alcibiades, the shameless Greek host, and would point out that comprehensive hospitality demanded the linkage of the very best of both cultures. For drinks, he would only offer arak, symbol of his affection and loyalty to Lebanon.

What happened after those dry journalistic days in the modest editorial corner of *Le Temps*, and those Alcibiadean nights on the fifth floor of number 4, rue Leopold Robert in Montparnasse (meaning "the mountain of Parnassus")? What followed a quarter century of intellectual effort and bohemian fun in the City of Light?

During my trips in Lebanon, I was never overcome by sorrow that would hide all the beautiful aspects of life. I managed to defeat it on the day when I stood in the upstairs room that was opened for me by Khairallah's sister, the sorrowful Rima, who now lived alone in that house in Jran.

Here is where Khairallah's princely imagination had developed. It had transported him to Paris, warming his chilly spirit and stimulating his ambitions and dreams. Along with that imagination he had carried the Lebanese heritage, immortalized in the brilliant minds of this generation, born of wide horizons and towering rocks. With that heritage were two lines of poetry.

The first by Al-Maarri: "On the road to glory, is there not . . . ?"

The second by Al-Mutanabbi: "From my time I desire . . ."

Khairallah engaged in battles in that field teeming with wanderers, male and female. He conducted some raids and scored a victory here and there. Some days and nights he was successful, but then it was time to leave. Fate had issued its decree, and our friend choked on Al-Maarri's line and never completed Al-Mutanabbi's.

Khairallah was transported from Paris in a metal box, and his spoils were sent in a wooden crate.

What spoils?

Books, books, and more books!

An imagination born in this upstairs room, one that then flew into the glowing, agitated air of civilization, to return embodied in two thousand books.

This then is the owner of that imagination and those spoils, now in the village church, buried beneath the earth by the door, trodden every single day by worshippers, male and female.

In Monastery Shadows

THE HERMIT left his cell and encountered the caravan on the highway. He spoke to them:

"The stars fall from the sky, but never reach the earth.

"Poets hover in space, but never reach the heavens.

"Whither, my brothers, whither?

"The abode of the vile is deep; the goal of hoverers is remote. Both of them nighttime without end.

"What is the struggle across oceans in quest of glory or wealth?

"What is the effort in homelands for the sake of freedom and independence?

"In the eye of the sun, in the gaze of nights, what is the Lebanese nation, the Arab nation?

"In Jran you have seen the tragedy of genius. Every Lebanese village has its own tragedy.

"Through the shades of calm and security in the monastery, you have both seen and touched the rays of felicity. On every hill in Lebanon there is a monastery that calls you.

"To the monastery, my brothers, to the monastery!

"He donned a hat and sandals, better than those who donned gauze and bankruptcy. So do not be fooled by the statement of the poet of Maarra:

'On the road to glory, is it not that which I am doing . . . ?'

"He was the one who uncovered all of life's screens. Behind them, all he could see was bankruptcy—bankruptcy of minds, of souls, of ethics, of laws and religions.

"Before him, our wise and pious ancestors had seen the same things. So they constructed monasteries and kindled inside them the paths to a more exalted life and a higher glory.

"If the screen is removed and the doors are opened, what then are politics and dominion, fame and glory, money, prestige, and offspring?

"To the monastery, my brothers, to the monastery!

"Come to the monasteries, you will be relieved of the burdens of life and saved from its tragedies.

"Come to the monasteries, the doors to eternal bliss will be opened to you."

The hermit fell silent. A member of the caravan party challenged him:

"Stars fall from the sky, then disappear into space.

"Poets hover in space so as to reach the stars, rescue them, and use their gleam to light up the world.

"There can be no light without fire, and no life without light.

"Life today is simply an abyss, one into which every coward can sink, while priests hover around like crows, and princes of intellect and masters of time hover above.

"Go back to your cell, hermit. The night, your brother, is summoning you, and the spiders, your daughters, are talking to you. At the door every fantasy will greet you."

The caravan moved on and encountered a peasant in the valley. He addressed them as follows:

"Here is my shovel. It knows the earth's heart and all its secrets.

"Here is my scythe, which can read the plants and everything between its rows.

"But it is a sad and bitter knowledge. There are snakes amid the plants and graves in the earth.

"You're all leaving, emigrating, fleeing.

"I would like to be your companion, but my shovel and scythe are a weight on my neck. Not only that, but there are shovels and scythes in my heart as well.

"You're leaving, but can you remember? Can you think?"

I had thought a good deal, and was about to destroy everything in the heart except rosary and memory.

Our ancestors were pious and devout without entering monasteries, but today our children have to go into monasteries in order to become pious and devout,

Or else, like you, to escape the troubles of life, work, despair, and failure.

I will state, and it is the truth, there is no piety or faith to be found either in monasteries or in fields.

I will state, and it is the truth, that piety and faith are to be found in the obscurities of memory and contentment.

But moderation itself is afraid of hunger and thirsts, while contentment fears poverty and disease.

Fear is to be found everywhere except in monasteries.

Reject what the hermit told you and listen to me instead.

You too are afraid of hunger, poverty, and disease.

In abominations you will never encounter what you can discover in artificial virtues—daughters of the imagination, of hypocrisy, and pretense.

One day you will be as mad as saints. You will leap and dance like dervishes. You will sleep, happy and secure. But then you will wake up in a panic of anxiety.

What will have happened?

In claiming that you are not afraid of hunger or scared of poverty and disease, you have been lying to yourselves.

Let the honest among you go back to the city.

Let the liar enter the monastery.

I will be your guide and accompany you.

Why is it that you remain silent and do not move, either forward or backward?

Do falsehoods change without a return to the city?

Do dreams change without arrival at the monastery?

Your dreams are like your falsehoods. You are cowards. You hover up there in the space of the imagination, but you do not dare enter monasteries.

Are you then scared of isolation? Mountains, with all their towns and villages, are yours.

Are you afraid of the winter cold? Just consider the forests where you cut down as many trees as you wish for warmth.

Are you afraid of that same hunger as I am? Look at the fig and olive orchards, gardens full of peaches, apples, and limes, enough to make you forget all about the hummus and beans in the city.

There are grapevines as well, so you will not lack wine.

There are fields sown with tobacco, so you will not be without cigarettes.

So come on, let us live in the monastery.

The peasant walked ahead of the caravan. One of its members spoke to the peasant as follows:

"You are our brother. We know what is bothering you and arousing your wrath.

"But we have to tell you that slavery has a terminal limit, and poverty likewise has a short term.

"The fruits of the earth belong to those who harvest them; the good things in life belong to those who are aware of the course of that life.

"So bring the glad tidings to your family and neighbors: the morrow is yours, one with great benefits for all peasants and laborers."

The caravan continued on its way. They encountered a literary writer sitting in the porch of the village store. He was holding his stick and a book.

"This is what my father has left me," he told them.

"He enrolled me in school to separate me from spade and plow. He enrolled me so I could become a gentleman. I emerged from it with this stick and book.

"What am I to do with them?

"If I go to the city, it tells me, 'I have no bread for people with sticks and books.'

"If I go back to the fields, they tell me, 'I only have bread for people with spades and plows.'

"Owners of spades and plows go and complain to the authorities. They don't listen. They complain to God, but He does not respond.

"Should the earth respond, then fairness in its produce does not.

"So here I am, between city and fields, but belonging to neither one nor the other.

"I try to hide what lies within in, and yet the monastery can see it.

"I cry to myself, and yet the monastery hears it.

"I wander through the valley, and the monastery calls me.

"Now I will tell you the truth: Lebanon's welfare lies in monasteries. Lebanon's children outside monasteries are deprived, peasants and writers alike.

"We're all deprived.

"You dedicated lovers of the nation, you miserable agitators, you philosophizers about human rights and equality, all you deprived and rejected people, monasteries calling you.

"No good can survive without monasteries.

"No rights persist without monasteries.

"I will tell you the truth: Lebanon's civilization, its glory, its independence, all lie in monasteries.

"The nobility and prestige of all Lebanese lies with the group of generous folk.

"So let us all be part of that blessed community!

"Let us occupy the monasteries, wearing cowls as we do so.

"If they are too small, then we can imitate our ancestors who first built them.

"Let's build as they did, and even more.

"There are lots of sites in the mountains with no monastery.

"Let's crown every mountain peak and hill with a monastery. With all its monasteries, Lebanon will become a wonder of the world—the sole earthly paradise in the world. The Lebanese will all become pious and devout—indeed, saints—people who are never hungry or sad.

"Especially for poets and writers, the monastery will provide everything they need in this lower world of ours: bread, figs, olives, wine, cigarettes, and a comfortable bed.

"There will be lots of time to take siestas, to write, compose poetry, and read.

"Not only that, but there will also be a noble grave, like those of other people, and indeed like those of princes and kings. Here marble encloses the remains of a genius; over there, another marble tomb has been constructed for the bones of a political leader.

"It's part of our good fortune that, after death, tombs inside monasteries started producing miracles. The genius beneath the marble became a prophet, and the journalist in his marble mansion became a saint.

"Are we not, all of us, actors on the road to sainthood?

"I will tell you the truth. If Khairallah were to return to this Lebanese existence and had to choose between a small room in a lowly monastery or a resplendent office in the director's office of *Le Temps* in Paris, he would prefer the former. He would realize that, at least after his death, he would be duly honored. He could rest in a grave untrodden by the feet of mankind."

The writer stood there, shaking his stick and lifting his book. The head of the caravan addressed him as follows:

"The book is a door, but the stick is for clowning. Anyone who rejects the sticks and enters the house through the door realizes all the possible meanings of life as a whole and the best possible actions for the good of himself and all people.

"The spade is a door just like the book.

"Imagination is a road into the very essence of things.

"The peasant with his spade, the writer with his book, the poet with his imagination, they can all instruct the hermit and counsel the generous just as they do with other people.

"People who refuse to learn are miserable, whether they are inside or outside the monastery. Those who do not listen to counsel perish forevermore.

"Brother writer, spread your glory and convey the good news to your brothers and neighbors. There will be no slavery tomorrow, of neither body, mind, nor spirit."

Our Fascinating Sisters

WE ARE STILL in this saintly environment, with Khairallah's upper room behind us and orchards of quince and olives overlooking it. To our right are some hills, one of which is dignified by the tomb of the saint of Kfifan in his monastery. In front of us is the village itself, some four kilometers from the monastery.

Here on these hills and flatlands placed amid mountains ranged on four sides, the sea hides the peaks to the west. A black cloud can been seen on the eastern fringes, the cedar forest. In these dark yellow-green porches, sweet smelling and lit by gentle rays, as calm and unassuming as the people who live there, there is a haven untouched by the good and evil aspects of summer vacation culture.

The spirit of the location enveloped us; we felt like hermits, only sensing the divine bliss. With that, what did it matter whether the road was paved with earth or tar, or whether the drinking water in Kfifan came from roofs or wells?

A few kilometers below Kfifan lay the village of Ibreen, and on the hilltop close by, the convent we were heading toward, one for Lebanese nuns who were known by the name of the village, just as the village was well known by their name—the nuns of Ibreen.

After we reach the hilltop, the road continues through an olive orchard, freshly planted and on the point of producing. It leads to a square in front of a three-story building, the lower part of which is connected, while the upper part is separated in the middle.

In Lebanon it is rare for a monastery to be built according to a plan; the majority of them developed naturally as need required. The managing authority and laboring hands would respond to the call, making use of basic knowledge. Initially, it would be an oblong or square house or a house-like church. Above it, alongside it, or all around it a number of other houses would spring up, each with its own dome, porch, and alcove. The monastery would become a kind of neoclassical hotel, with no clear entrance or exit. The entryway would be an arched vault, which ended in a porch constructed in cement. The visitor could get lost in its intertwining sections and be caught in its architectural chaos.

The Ibreen convent was first designed on paper by architects. The whole thing was sketched by a painter architect and then constructed on this lovely hill according to the plan. It consists of a tall building with a frontage open on two sides; in the middle is a doorway to stairs leading to the convent (for sure). The two wings each have a similar door, one leading to the church, the other to the hospital.

The square building has a large courtyard, surrounded by four arched alcoves. It has a garden of flowers, in the middle of which is a white marble statue of Saint Elias crafted by the famous artist Yousuf Huwayeck. Over the outside door is another of his statues, this one of the Holy Family, after whom the convent is named.

The convent is built exactly to purpose, neatly constructed, with an exterior porch and interior alcoves. The ground level contains the convent's storehouses and a section beneath the church for the tomb of the Patriarch Elias Huwayeck. On the second level are the church and hospital, places for instruction and administration, and a reception hall. On the third level there are other quarters and rooms for the nuns.

In both spirit and architecture, it is in the European style; but those aspects are as far as it goes. In every other way it is entirely Lebanese and Arab—Lebanese at heart, Arab in language—at least, today. Even so, there is also an Arab inclination to extend the purview of the schools that the nuns have founded. Their basic missions is teaching, but, even though it has been limited to Lebanon in principle, it has started to expand beyond those boundaries.

We reached the convent at noon, feeling utterly famished. One of the nuns welcomed us in Lebanese dialect with a nice, warm smile.

We felt that we were in a Lebanese home and shared our impressions with her. The kind sister was delighted by our frankness and hurried away to inform the Mother Superior.

The Mother Superior was no less kind and happy, as she greeted us and made us feel welcome. She gave instructions for food to be prepared.

"Please excuse us," she said, just like any Lebanese woman inside her own home. She made us forget that we were in a convent. If it were not for the black robe and white cowl around her face, we would not have even realized that the woman talking to us was indeed the Mother Superior. To be precise, she was Mother Josephine Huwayeck, superior general for the Maronite Holy Family Association.

The association had been established in 1895 by Patriarch Elias Huwayeck when he was bishop, "In order to teach girls in the national spirit." Three years later, work began on the construction of the monastery, and the work was completed in 1913.

This recently founded association, which only had a single monastery and school at the beginning of this century, is now the largest of its kind in Lebanon, with a number of monasteries, hospitals, and schools.

"Do the nuns pay for the costs of instruction?" I asked the Mother Superior.

She nodded. "Between 40 and 50 percent attend free," she replied with a smile, "and the rest pay different fees according to their family's ability to pay."

Twenty-seven schools, comprising 2,500 girls from these mountains; of those, at least 1,000 are taught for free. The association has not gone bankrupt; in fact, it is still operating successfully.

So are you not as impressed as we are by this national association in Ibreen?

I will now give you more information about the order and its cultured and charity-oriented nuns. Europeans have accused us of an inability to establish and run companies. In this particular charitable and educational company run by women is the conclusive proof of the falsity of that accusation.

As you will have realized, I am not an advocate for nuns and convent education, but, even so, I am bound to respect the truth and show an appreciation for fairness. I am therefore obliged to express my admiration for this national convent that is organized and administered just as effectively as convents run by foreigners.

I will go further, and state that these nuns are our sisters. They are utterly fascinating and delightful—fascinating for their village charm, their Lebanese smiles, and a degree of spiritual purity that keeps them apart from any contrived holiness. It would appear that neither the Holy Spirit nor Father and Son have any desire to change the temperament of these Lebanese women.

We entered the dining room, which had been made ready for guests before we were called to eat. On the table were no more than bread, cheese, and olives, but we wolfed it all down as though it were stuffed lamb. The sister who was looking after us came in and noticed the way we were eating.

"Oh my goodness!" she yelled with a laugh in her village accent, "You really are hungry!"

Then one of the novice nuns came in with the cooked dish, and the routine was repeated, with the nun following her footsteps both in and out. The sweet followed, cooked figs and baklava, fruits, and finally coffee, which was put on a small table in a corner. From there the nun brought it to our table herself.

I was amazed by this protocol, borrowed from grand hotels, hospitality in the most refined style. It represented generosity at its height, and it was being provided in a convent of Lebanese nuns, our fascinating and delightful sisters.

Three of them accompanied us to the lower level to visit the noble tomb, that of the founder of this national order of nuns, Patriarch Elias Huwayeck. We found ourselves in the holiest part of the convent, standing in front of an iron railing that separated it from the rest of the area. In the square separate section was an altar, and over it an oil painting hanging on the wall portraying Jesus's last steps on the road to Golgotha. There were no elaborate holy ornaments on the altar; simply the Gospel and two candlesticks with candles in them.

On the right side of the sanctuary stood the tomb of the patriarch, made in Tripoli of red Lebanese marble, and, alongside it, two similar tombs at ground level—one for Rosalie, the first Mother Superior, and the second for Mother Stephanie, who came after her. In the middle, opposite the marble tomb of the patriarch was a statue of him kneeling in prayer, his hands clasped together. On the marbled-lined walls two lamps of the same stone had been placed over the tombs of the two women, fixed to the walls and always lit.

The statue itself, less than full size, encapsulated all the statues that Yousuf Huwayeck himself had made, works where he was bound by the tastes of the people they represented.

The artist's genius shone forth in this statue, he himself being a liberal thinker and someone of unlimited vision and action. He yielded to art alone; faith in its spirit and creed was his sole compromise.

Here then was the artist, delving into the very core of his subject, in feeling, thought, and artistry. In the patriarch's face and tranquil demeanor he had portrayed piety and righteousness. Total spiritual surrender emerged from his image, right down to his fingernails, which seemed, in their serene, gentle touch, to be repeating what the heart of the supplicant was saying.

You were in touch with the genius of Huwayeck, not just through the statue but also the sanctuary as a whole. He himself had arranged it and supervised every detail. Even the faint glimmer of light from outside made its way into the sanctuary, almost reaching the twin lamps by the tomb—itself a sign of art invoking both humility and admiration.

No wonder! Huwayeck's uncle, the righteous patriarch, was fully worthy of such veneration, just as his own artistic genius deserved such status.

Ninth Journey

In the Recesses of Time

Contents

Stations in the Years

I AM GOING TO TAKE the reader on a long journey back in time through Lebanese history, some four thousand years. As is the case with journeys on earth and in space, we will be making use of both history's lamp, however faint the light may be, and informed and solid imagination. Using them, we will penetrate the obscurities of times past and pass by those stations where history paused for a hundred or hundreds of years, waiting for humans to emerge from the dark recesses of apathy and ignorance and the calamities of war and injustice.

So, dear reader, let us take wing like the light from the stars. Shake off the dust of lethargy and resignation from your wings. Forget the convictions and certainties you have inherited, the knowledge and doubts you have acquired, and the traditions and myths you have so cherished. Come on, let us fly away from the political mire of this age with its social and religious exploitation; let us fly instead through time's own firmament to those major stopping points in the tragedy of civilization, to the dawn of history that concerns us here. Come, let us fly, if only for the sheer pleasure of flight and discovery.

Here we are, at the very first station on our journey, the one closest to our own present. It is the blue-colored station in the modern history of these mountains. It was preceded by human massacres and followed by the major human disaster. A period of bliss, of mini bliss, wedged between two disasters. The time when the Lebanese had forgotten the past and knew nothing of the future. They were far removed from politics and concentrated on fruitful activities—except, that is, for their sheikhs, priests, and consuls of those countries that offered them protection. Those consuls toyed with the mountains' potential and played chess with the dignity of the local leaders. This bliss that the Lebanese were living did not stop them emigrating. Both peasant and writer left the country, and afterward mansions were constructed in the mountains, along with mansions of knowledge and literature in Egypt and America. This then is the blue station, the Mutasarrifate.

Just a short temporal distance away was the gray station, with the word *feudalism* inscribed over the portal. A solitary master to be obeyed, he being the provider of felicity, the guardian of security, and the tyrannical ruler who was fair most of the time. The Lebanese slept soundly during this era, never dreaming of wealth or mansions, nor of liberty and independence, whether total or partial.

The Lebanese people were content in their ignorance, indifference, and obedience. However, its serene gray hue was not entirely clean, since that obedience was fractured by a few sparks from the lamp of knowledge. This was a station based on the confines of terror on the one hand, and hope on the other. It lay between the blue and red stations, like some star whose light twinkled between the winter and spring horizons.

Now here was the red station, bloody red. For fully four hundred years, time was asked to stand still. Days were sown using a single loom, that of rulers trampling on the spirits of slaves and relying on atrocities rarely encountered in the history of peoples. What a period it was, with people going to their graves between the twin shadows of hunger and despair. They would be eating bread dipped in blood and bitter colocynth, although they had to pay their taxes and proclaim the glory of the padishah.

During this period there came a time when, for a while, the fire of rebellion flared in Lebanon. A few Arab lights shone, intent on Lebanese independence; intermittent, to be sure, and soon extinguished, as was the life of their kindlers.

Ignorance was pervasive in every aspect of the region, covering the entire Arab territory, from the Taurus Mountains to those in Yemen, from Kinana territory in the Hejaz to the Mesopotamian river course. Oppression, terror, stupidity, and corruption were all norms of the time, used by people both strong and weak against each other on a duly sanctioned ascending scale of evil.

"Hey you, my foot's on your head, and yours is on someone lower than you."

"Just say 'thanks be to God,' and then pray for the glory and support of the padishah."

It was a ladder involving an equal opportunity for despicable acts, the lowest rung being in people's hearts and the highest in the Yildiz Palace.[1] During the era of the red station, stained as it was with human blood, it was an indelible memory.

But come now, and let us fly again. There is another station in the succession of time's stations, one in which time came to a standstill—at a loss because it did not know which period of history was the very worst: the wars of the conquerors or the Crusades. This one is the black station, lasting two hundred years. Everything sacred linked to the Semitic faiths was lost. Darkness blotted out all heavenly inspiration. Just two stars shone in the sky, each one utterly different: one for the crescent moon, the other for the cross.

Alliances and disagreements caused a good deal of embarrassment. Some kings and princes disavowed their fighting brothers. Christians and Maronites advanced in a peculiar tandem, granting victory to the cross over the crescent. The cross! The crescent! The one who died on the cross, and the one who destroyed the idols in the Kaaba, both asked God to absolve them from their followers and their political and commercial wars.

What then is the Holy Sepulcher, and what is the Holy Land? The Franks returned to their homeland with industrial and artistic knowledge from the East, while the Islamic domains reverted to their former disunity and antagonism. The road now lay open for the Tatars and Turks, who came charging toward them across the breadth of Asia.

Let us now resume our journey in time's firmament.

1. Translator's note: the Yildiz Palace was the Istanbul residence of the Ottoman sultans.

As the black station disappears from view, we enter a region of thick cloud over the Lebanese mountain peaks. Here and there, the clouds thin out, and a few rays of sunshine gleam of the Ghouta section of Damascus.

Now we are at the green station. In a corner are inscribed these words: "Peace for the People of the Book."

Lebanese Christians are indeed People of the Book, and the people in Byblos are the very core of Lebanon.

Even so, there were other people who had goals and requirements with regard to Lebanon. By that, I imply the rulers of Byzantium who refused to relinquish their hold over the Lebanese, and lent support to the Arabs just as the people of Tyre and Tripoli had done with the caliph Muawiya; they built him five hundred boats to attack the Byzantines.

In God's eyes, are believers and atheists equal? Do believers leave the territory of their ruler and religious colleagues to enter Arab territory? Then let the Mardaites save them!

The arrival of these Mardaites (known by the Arabs as Jarajima, a reference to their city, Jurjuma, by Mount Lukkam [in Cilicia]), ruined the peace and amity that the Arabs so desired.

Lahyani Constantine dispatched them to defend Damascus. They then occupied Lebanon and kept fighting the Arabs until the (Umayyad) caliph Abd al-Malik made a treaty with the Byzantine ruler and ordered them to return to their homeland.

Al-Baladhuri notes that Al-Waleed ibn Abd al-Malik sent his brother, Maslama, to Jurjuma.[2] He conquered their city and made a pact with them to settle wherever they wished in the Syrian region. They did not have to renounce Christianity, nor were they required to pay taxes.

2. Translator's note: Al-Baladhuri (d. 892 CE) was a renowned historian whose most famous work is *Futouh al-Buldaan*, which was translated into English by Phillip Hitti and published as *The Origins of the Islamic State* (New York: Columbia University, 1916; reprint New York: Cosimo Classics, 2011). Al-Waleed ibn Abd al-Malik served as Umayyad caliph from 705 to 715 CE.

Yaqout's biographical dictionary states that the caliphs hired some of these Mardaites and used them in their wars.[3] That is hardly surprising when we recall that the Umayyad caliphs were famous for their acumen and far-sightedness. They valued bravery and intelligence alike, and made use of such people in both running and defending the regime.

What is also confirmed is that, once the Mardaite movement fell silent, the majority of Lebanese started paying taxes to the Umayyad caliphs and stayed safe and sound under their wing, a bright period of time that history records as the green station.

By now, a thousand years have passed as part of our journey from the felicitous era of the Lebanese republic to the glorious Arabian era. Before us—or rather, behind us—there is still double that number in years, along with all their gloomy parts, their horizons, and their stations.

As you approach modern Byblos—now named Jbeil after its ancient past, you can hear the clash of spears and groans of people, blending with the noise of the earth as it shakes. The cities on the Phoenician coast will suffer, and those who manage to avoid Persian and Byzantine swords will be eliminated as they fight to occupy the lands of Syria and the Lebanese mountains.

No sooner was war at an end, its eruptions quieted, and people at ease, than the Byzantine ruler started executing the rebels, all in the name of religion.

The Holy Council of Chalcedon (451 CE). Anyone who does not believe in its teaching is to be killed. In fact, the royal Byzantines did kill many Christian "heretics," including 350 Maronite monks at their monastery by the River Al-Asi (Orontes).

Now let us continue our flight to the next station, the tawny one, involving religious heresies. In the view of scholars of the Holy

3. Translator's note: Yaqout al-Hamawi (d. 1229 CE) was a renowned geographer and biographer. His *Irshad al-alibba* (Guide for the Sage) is a major biographical source.

Church, the most nefarious of those heresies, ones that caused much controversy at the Council of Chalcedon, were Arianism (after Arius of Alexandria), which stated that the Messiah possessed humanity but not divinity; the Nestorian doctrine, which assigned to the Messiah two qualities, both divine and human; and Eutychianism, which declared the Messiah to have a single essence and a single nature.

The Eutychian doctrines (named after Eutychus of Constantinople [d. c. 456 CE]) were spread by Yaqoub Baradi'i. The sect was known by his name, the Yaqoubiyye, and its adherents were also called Yaqoubians. Maronites were a part of the same group in their earliest stages.

Then there were the Monothelites, who opposed the view of the Yaqoubians concerning the single nature of the Messiah, but agreed with them in beliefs involving intellect and will, the Messiah's intellect, His nature, His will, His humanity, and His divinity. There was a good deal of talk, but only one religious vision!

Now spread your wings and follow me. Here come the Romans with their helmets and shields, strutting along the city streets.

"I'm a Roman," one of them will say, "and you're all barbarians!"

Here are the castles and forts, the palaces and temples, all belonging to the Romans, as they pray to Jupiter one day and Jesus of Nazareth on another.

Even so, the Romans are both materialistic and arbitrary about everything. With their thick necks and arms, their only interest in religion was how they could maintain control, relax, and make money. The historian Edward Gibbon says, "In Roman dominions there were a number of religions. In the people's opinion, they were all true; in the philosopher's, they were all corrupt; and in the government's, they were all profitable."

The Romans were also famous for their firmly established peace. However, in both its precedents and consequences, its benefits were the result of intense pain. It spread its dark wings over the ruins of cities and among the vestiges of peoples. A Roman peace following the destruction of Basra! Roman pillage, enslavement of conquered peoples—peace, peace!

It is thus no surprise that the philosopher ruler viewed all religions as both false and profitable. Worship whomever and whatever you like. Offer up your children and virgin daughters as sacrificial offerings to the gods. Turn devils into deities. Any of that, provided you pay taxes to Rome and submit to the authority of Roman rulers.

That is the way things were. The flame of paganism, both Greek and Phoenician, remained alight in Lebanon until the beginning of the sixth century CE.

Saint Simeon Stylites did his utmost to guide the pagan Lebanese. He succeeded with many of them, as historians tell us, because of the miracles he was able to perform in front of them, not least among which, needless to say, was the fact that he sat contentedly on top of his pillar for some forty years.

Roman indulgence, Roman peace, Roman slavery!

In Syrian territory and on the Phoenician coast, all this had been preceded by the spread of Greek culture, one grounded in debate and eloquence, one that relished doubt and ridicule, decked as it was in the garb of sloth and luxury. Plato and Epicurus had prepared the ground for Augustus Caesar.

Now here we are at the seventh of the Roman stations, the azure station, with its sad Phoenician chapter. We encounter Hellenized Phoenicians emulating their Seleucid masters, Alexander's successors, in both customs and devotions. They talk and write in their language and forget that it was their ancestors who taught the Greeks their alphabet. The Phoenicians had been lords of the seas and commercial leaders in the cities.

And now for one final flight—one that, in spite of its distance, is a single flight—some 1,500 years from Alexander's conquest to the first Phoenician era, that of Ibishmou Abi and Abishmou in Byblos (Jbeil).

Byblos of the Abishmouites

THERE WERE WAILS of mourning in the kingdom's villages on the banks of the sacred river, the Adon, and also in the mountains beneath the cypress and cedar branches. People were coming to the capital city to take part in the great funeral ceremony, the one for King Abishmou, monarch of Byblos and priest of the god Reshef.

I came with them and attached myself to a group of stragglers, including some mourners, beggars, halva sellers, and people peddling toys and charms. We all walked to the capital together, some sad, others observing, making money, and scrounging. We shortened the journey by telling stories about the late king, mentioning his good and bad points and raising our voices in mourning cries every time we approached a village:

> He was rich, He was pious, powerful among kings;
> Oh, alas, alas!
> Cities and castles weep at his passing!
> Ships and sailors mourn him.
> Oh, alas, alas!
> He was rich, He was pious, powerful among kings.

After walking for a day and half the night, we reached the capital at dawn. Sitting under a palm tree outside the city wall, we waited for the rest of our group to arrive. We all then walked to the landside gate in the wall and entered the city. With two rows of soldiers above us, we proceeded silently behind the forts on both sides of the long passageway between the outer and inner gates.

As we approached the city through the second gate, we all raised our voices in lamentations and weeping, which had a fearful and stunning effect.

> He was wise, he was generous, he was the beloved of all hearts.
> Oh, alas, alas!
> His palace had a hundred doors, with all roads leading to him.
> Oh, alas, alas!

Following this wailing salutation we all made our way down a lengthy staircase to the main square, which was packed with restless crowds. They all started keening for the departed monarch, and so we chimed in to outdo them. We filled the air with our mourning cries, and the square with tears of sorrow.

Next we all left the square and walked through rows of square-built houses, built of white limestone and roofed with cypress wood. Women were standing in the doorways with their hair loosened. They waved their handkerchiefs at us and keened their laments in loud, piercing tones.

We made our way through the city to the great temple, built on a hill near the king's palace. The crowd grew thicker, and the sound of male and female mourners faded as we drew close to the temple. As we trod on the holy ground by the gate, we paused for a moment, as humble as sheep in a pen, and then entered the temple as silent as mountains on a summer night.

> Blessed be the god Reshef
> Blessed be Ishtar, the great goddess!

Some people carried vessels into the temple filled with perfumes. They placed them in the archways of the four alcoves around the great throne, that of Baal, where the priests were standing in front of the sacred idol.

From there now arose the sound of chanting, intoned by the high priest, while the other priests would repeat the incantations whenever his quavering chant came to a pause.

O eternal darkness, we entrust our king to you.
O mighty god, we hand over Abishmou to your care.
And might and long life to his successors.
Felicity and prosperity for Byblos!

As the priest intoned each prayer, the whole assembly repeated them, one after another.

Then one of the temple servants lit the fire in a large brazier in front of the idol. The priest now summoned the owner of the sacrificial victim. The crowd of prayers now made a path for a woman who was carrying a suckling child.

"For Abishmou and Byblos," she said, weeping.

The priest took the baby and presented it to the god. With tears in his eyes, he lifted it up, then turned around and held it up in front of the crowd. As the baby squirmed in the priest's hands, its screams grew louder and louder. The whole temple now resounded with shouts:

For Abishmou,
For his successors,
Glory and honor for Byblos!

The screams of the baby were drowned by the clamor of exuberant paeans of praise. Writhing in total panic, he was seen but not heard. Now the priest's voice rose above the tumult of the crowd. Everyone fell silent in humble submission. The priest now stood in front of the fire and intoned:

O mighty god, accept this sacrifice
For our now departed monarch,
For his long-lived successor,
For Byblos and its people.

The child's mother was standing close to the temple gate, listening and watching. When the priest tossed her child into the fire, she smiled in pleasure and devotion.

Blessed be the god Reshef.
Blessed be the goddess Ishtar.
All glory and honor to Byblos!

We left the temple, our hearts filled with joy and serenity, and headed for the royal palace. Once there, we did several circuits, flaunting our moans and laments.

Along with some other people, I managed to get into the big hall where the king's embalmed corpse lay on his bed. All around him was the equipment for burial and provisions for departure to the next world. I was astonished by what I was seeing and totally fascinated. Lovely cups and vessels filled with food, drink, and scents; the pottery was unrivaled in both shape and sheen, and the colors and designs were unmatched in this world. Superb gold spoons and silver knives; daggers and spears for the king's arms; amulets and charms, all of unrivaled quality. I stood there in all humility in front of his scepter made of the finest brass, decorated with a golden serpent. On it was inscribed: "Abishmou, king of Byblos, priest of the god Reshef."

The priests now said some final prayers over the body of the great king, then some palace men picked up the equipment and provisions, carried the body on their shoulders, and walked in a lengthy solemn procession to its final resting place in the royal graveyard, which stood beyond the wall on a hillside overlooking the sea. They placed it, along with the provisions, amulets, and weapons, in a coffin made of solid stone, closed it up, and fixed the top cover in place. Using thick, tarred ropes, they lowered it into a grave some nine feet deep.

That day, after the burial, rugs were laid out for visitors in the palace and the houses of important figures. They all ate meat, drank wine, and were perfumed with scents, all in memory of the departed monarch. They prayed that his successors would be illustrious and exalted; they also prayed that Byblos and its people would fare well and be successful throughout the ages.

Along with all the visitors from the Byblos region, I noticed a large number of strangers. I was told they had come from neighboring kingdoms: from Arwad and Cyprus, Tyre and Sidon. Others came from regions beyond the Phoenician domains: from Aram, Moab, and Judea. It is no surprise, since King Abishmou was in league with all neighboring monarchs, beloved and honored in every country.

Dear Byblos, may your prestige continue in the era of your successors and indeed in all eras! The king is dead; long live the king! Ibishmou Abi succeeded his father, Abishmou. Byblos celebrated his ascension to the throne. On that day, the young king distributed gold and silver to his people, fed the poor and indigent, and welcomed guests for ten days.

Along with some other people, I stayed for a whole month in the capital city. Every day we would visit the temples, then wander around the city, looking at its crafts and occupying both heart and eye with its stores and factories. We watched people weaving both cotton and silk, and observed fabrics being dyed in bright colors, purple and blue.

We visited a shipbuilder outside the wall, and saw workers laying out and tarring wood and polishing huge, lofty masts cut from cedar trees. I was particularly impressed by the skill and expertise of the peasant workers. The boats we made were undoubtedly the best in the world, the most beautifully shaped, sturdiest in craft, and fullest in sail. Ask the winds, ask the seas, ask the tempests!

The things we were seeing were no more amazing than what we heard. We talked to craftsmen, merchants, and seamen, and their words aroused a passion for travel and commerce. I can repeat some of what they said so they do not lose their value.

"The mountain is sloth," the factory director said, "and the sea is activity."

"Wood is in the mountains," the weavers' union leader told us, "and gold is in the cities."

"Life is commerce," we heard from the owner of the dye factory, "and commerce is the bond tying brotherhood and peace."

Here is another piece of wisdom from one of the jewelers: "Life is just like this mold that I am holding. It's fine if you do the work well, and lousy if you do it badly."

The gods have been gracious to your craftsmen, Byblos, to your seamen and your merchants! In our hearts they have kindled the sparks of labor and adventure and have taught us to enjoy travel and commerce. The gods have also been gracious to your sages, Byblos; from their mouths we have all learned wisdom.

We now entreat the goddess Ishtar to protect your womenfolk, you city of happiness, and give them your blessings so that they may enjoy enhanced health and well-being. We have been happy to bestow our wealth on your markets, temples, and festivities, and felt obliged to express our gratitude and admiration.

Sublime goddess Ishtar! The ladies of Byblos are beautiful, kind, and tender. Not only that, but they are also modest, obedient, and contented. They have given us much for little, and have provided us with wonderful memories. From the sweetness in the mountain retreats they pour their moisture on parched lips and restless hearts.

"From Byblos's workshops and stores we have taken away fabrics, pottery, amulets, and necklaces to give to family and friends in the village."

That is what the Phoenician author Abd Ishmoun ibn Bethaal wrote; it was translated from the original by Heptarchos the Greek, who was born in Samos and lived in Antioch. He witnessed Alexander's conquest and lived into the reign of the second Seleucid king, Antiochus I. An Oxford scholar translated it from Greek, and I have translated it from English into our own noble language, Arabic (1938).

I have sought clarification from a variety of translations so as to avoid the possibility of error and falsehood. Some writers might be tempted to translate this piece of prose into English or other European languages, assuming that it was originally composed in Arabic. But it is enough to know what difficulties it has confronted in its long linguistic journey from Phoenician to Greek, and then, one thousand years later, to English first and then Arabic!

Byblos of the Archeologists

SOME OF US BURY OTHERS; later folk walk on the skulls of their predecessors.

A verse of poetry, partly bland prose, the rest bitter poetry. With a stark profusion of angst and a bitter streak unmitigated by the slightest sympathy, al-Mutanabbi (the great Arab poet) has seen the way that the feet of the living trample on the skulls of the dead. What he says in brief is later elaborated by al- Maarri, who, in talking about the same topic, resorts to a poetry in which a wonderful imagination and sensitivity are combined:

"Lighten your step! I think the earth's surface consists only of dead bodies."

His imagination goes further than that of al-Mutanabbi. In another statement, his eloquence is also finer:

"Many a grave has oft become a tomb for one who scoffs at the cluster of opposites."

When it comes to consistent thought and a sensitivity to the inevitability of man's fate and the thing he builds in this world, Abu al-Ala al-Maarri is superior to al-Mutanabbi:

Every dwelling, built by doves or lords with lofty pillars, all will be destroyed.

According to Shakespeare, all will be destroyed except for graves:

Who is the best builder?

The gravedigger. The grave endures until the Day of Resurrection.

Were the great English poet to look to the day when the archeologist would be standing amid the ruins of Nineveh and Luxor and unearthing the remains of their palaces, the word *gravedigger* in the play *Hamlet* would be more accurate and effective than it actually is.

In life's developments and the coloration of its modern pages, we are agents of destruction, even of what poets have constructed. People who cremate their dead scoff at the words of both al-Mutanabbi and al-Maarri; those who observe the activities of archeological missions today—with scattered graves and empty coffins—negate Shakespeare's eloquent words.

"Every house will be destroyed"—even graves. Every civilization involving peoples from times past is like its people—burying each other and building something new on the remains of the old, each structure constructed with the stones of its obliterated sisters. Earthquakes, storms, and wars may bring them down, but human disasters destroy them as well. They are abandoned, and time shrouds them in a heavy layer of rock, sand, and dust.

Here now is a hill, one rich in content, filled with burials, burials of cities up to the first Christian era. Here too is the evidence and proof of what archeologists tell us, things uncovered by laborers' shovels as they dig into the hill, layer after layer, until they are a few meters below sea level.

Archeologists can use the light of knowledge to illuminate those layers for us. In the first layer, they can show you the ruins of the patriarch's church; in the second, Roman saddles; in the third, Greek coins; in the fourth, smooth Hittite statuary; in the fifth, Palestinian pottery vessels; in the sixth, cylindrical seals with cuneiform inscriptions; below it, statuettes of Hurrian goddesses; in the eighth, metal pots. After those layers—the end of the Iron Age and beginning of the flint age—we reach the third millennium BCE. Archeologists continue their excavations; traces of the very first houses are uncovered, the first constructed by humans, then caves containing remains of porcelain and bones.

Fourteen eras in human history as we descend a kind of stairway three meters below the surface (300–600 CE) to some twelve meters (4500–3800 BCE), and then a further two meters below sea level to soil untrodden by humans, virgin earth. It all covers a span of five thousand years, during which traces of mankind exist in profusion in the north Syrian spot, along with vestiges and traces of peoples all piled one on top of the other.

Buried on top of another, over the length of times and ages.

When it comes to the number of relics and their antiquity, nothing in Byblos can rival the discoveries of the American archeological expedition at Tell Judaidah near Antioch. Even so, Byblos possesses relics of this country's peoples, a country that differs from other Semitic peoples in its preference for peace, its involvement in crafts and commerce, and its daring defiance of the sea's perils. They hoisted their sails over the roaring waves, defying storms and overcoming winds, all of which drove them to islands near and far as they willed; indeed, even further, to the farthest shores of the Mediterranean, the narrows of Hercules—Gibraltar—gateway, to the Sea of Darkness (Atlantic Ocean), and beyond to the British Isles.

Those shores teemed with cities built by this intrepid and courageous people. They flourished, and at the time were regarded as the greatest cities in the world. The people of Arwad, Cyprus, Byblos, Sidon, and Tyre were all pioneers of civilization; they kindled its lights in Asian and European lands in the eras before the golden ages of Greece.

At this point Byblos is our current focus from among all those cities. We have taken the reader back to its earliest period. We have toured the city, looked at its stores and industries, listened to its inhabitants' conversations, and, with them, watched the funeral of King Abishmou. As we stood there by the grave into which the deceased king had been lowered, the only time we observed was his time, and all we sensed was the genuine tragedy of his death. There we stood, secure and safe in our ignorance. We gave no thought to the fact that fate eventually catches up with deceased monarchs—even after thousands of years. In the name of science, human hands will reach out to touch their grave and do their work. The graves will once again be the way they were before they were honored to receive the royal remains—empty and desolate. Nor was any thought given to the fact that Byblos itself, in spite of its lengthy history, would suffer the same fate as other cities that had preceded it in the context of civilization—consigned to the dark shades of oblivion, buried just like its sons and rulers. In the twentieth century, man the explorer arrives, rips its shroud apart in the name of science, and restores its temple to sunlight.

Are we not doing it all in the name of science? But, in place of evidence provided by the imagination, we are substituting flesh and blood proof, involving Prince Maurice Chehab, director of the Lebanese Museum.

One spring day we left Beirut and took a path shaded by cinchona trees amid flourishing orchards of bananas and limes. By the Dog River we came across the sea and remained in sight as we proceeded. This is the nicest seaside path in Lebanon, and we were using it on a lovely day. To our right the sea was calm, while to our left the mountains looked verdant. All around us it was like a joyous festival, with shouts of "Take it easy, don't rush!" Spring is indeed the year's festival, but humans never celebrate with daisies, and cars only respond to fast-burning gas.

Like an arrow, we speed through Jounieh, and in Maamaltein we spot the Roman bridge. At a bend in the road, Prince Maurice shows us a rock containing "the cave of our father, Adam," and "Helena's tower" (is she the blessed lady, King Constantine's mother?). Between road and sea there are enough legends to rival the archeological remains in their quest for eternity, while the remains compete with the legends in their sheer novelty.

Tabarja managed to combine the two elements. It will tell you about Paul the Apostle, and, in its tiny bay and on its banks, it will show you the shipyard. Are the people of Tabarja, with its sailboats, all that is left of Phoenician life on these sleepy shores? Here is what the story has to say about Paul the Apostle: he hired a boat from Tabarja and sailed to Ephesus in it. Some of the storytellers point with awe-filled reverence to a rock on the Tabarja shore, the one from which the apostle jumped into the boat!

Here now is the Ibrahim River (the Adonis River), visible from the sea and greeting us even before we reach it. It is both gentle and generous, the keeper of many natural and divine secrets. The natural ones are neither impossible nor difficult to identify. In this season of the year, the snow is melting up in the mountains, and rivers overflow their banks. When the Adonis River overflows, its downhill slope is so steep that it carries a lot of soil with it, which colors the water. It runs red toward the sea and into it. A mile's distance from the shore, it looks like an island of golden sand or a red river in the blue sea. I have talked about the religious secrets of the river earlier.

We have now arrived at Byblos. The most prominent landmark is the Crusader fortress that served as the headquarters for the directors during the Mutasarrifate period. It is situated between the two Bybloses, one of the living, the other of the dead. The first is southwest of the fortress, the other northeast.

We entered the ancient city, but the hopes we had brought with us led to disappointments. All the building stones used were small and uncarved, whereas the popular notion was that the Phoenicians used to build at least their temples from huge pieces of stone.

The city itself is small, judging by the wall whose foundations had been uncovered, along with a small section of it. In overall size it would have been no larger than one of Beirut's quarters, even though in the past it had been considered one of the largest Phoenician cities.

On the basis of what has been uncovered thus far, it does not have any substantial, tall, and proud monuments. Except for the royal tombs, the relics are all modest and ugly, not at all beautiful. That applies even to artwork on the biggest temple, which is not as large as a church in any Lebanese village.

The temple is a square building with four alcoves. Inside, by a bench in the center, is a statue of the great god Reshef. Inside the alcoves there are statuettes and obelisks like the ones in Egypt, but much smaller. One of them has a hieroglyphic inscription on it and the name of the god, Reshef.

Those statuettes and obelisks are not indicative of a large number of Phoenician deities; there are no more than four or five: Reshef, Ishtar, Adon, and Melqart. They each had "beautiful names" by which the god was called, just as we say, "The compassionate, the merciful, the high, the mighty."[1] The obelisks and statuettes were all people's offerings to the god of the temple. Their sheer variety in size, large and small, polished and unpolished, was evidence enough of the fact that they were offered by people of different life situations.

We walked around one of the few markets in the city (which was founded three thousand years BCE). We looked at the small, square houses, all connected to each other, where time had left three or four bits of wall standing.

We were told that the soil we were walking on was virgin soil, an archeological term referring to land untrodden by humans such as the lands uncovered in Iraq or north Syria; land lying beneath other historical layers. Thus, it was not correct to call the city land, however old it might be, virgin soil.

Byblos had been buried under twelve meters of soil and rock. That establishes the level of the Crusader fortress situated on a hilltop to the north. Archeologists have uncovered the city wall; the remains are between four and five meters high. Like the houses, it was built of small, unhewn stones; the exception was the upper part, which was added in a later period, probably Roman.

Prince Maurice drew our attention to the black color of the stones used for the houses and part of the wall, all of it limestone. They might be either white, or, due to the length of time, grayish, but the blackness was caused by fire. Revolution burst into flame in the second millennium BCE in the wake of a social and economic revolution in Egypt. Following the Egyptian example, the people of Byblos rose up against their rulers and priests.

However, at that time—namely, the beginning of the Twelfth Dynasty—Egypt was safe and secure, enjoying a period of peace, prosperity, and success. The feudal system was predominant, put in place

1. Baal Shamin (Lord of the Heavens), El (the one God), Elion (the highest), etc. The adjective became a name for a new god, and the number of gods proliferated. In our own times there is a similarity in the number of adjectives used by Catholics to describe the Virgin Mary: Lady of the Forest, Lady of the Walnut, Lady of the Immaculate Conception, Lady of the Rosary, etc.

by Pharaoh Amenhotep I. The scholar Aristides had this to say about feudal rulers: "They taught their workers crafts and arts and supervised the labor themselves. The era was one of unprecedented prosperity in the land."

The revolution that Prince Maurice was referring to was, for the most part, that of the Pharaoh Amenhotep IV, otherwise known as Akhenaten, and that is the connection between those events and what happened in Byblos.

During the first imperial era (1730–1580 BCE), the Asian kingdoms, from Jerusalem to Carchemish, from the Phoenician shores to the Euphrates Valley, were under Pharaonic control. Egypt had a representative in every kingdom and princedom, or what today we call a viceroy or high commissioner.

The high commissioner would combine wide authority with political acumen, treating the monarch, prince, or people of the country politely in every aspect that involved their customs and social and religious traditions. He would oversee all matters concerning politics and economy, thereby protecting the interests of His Majesty the Pharaoh. The most important of those interests were the taxes imposed on every king or prince, along with oversight and regulation of his foreign affairs. No negotiations with another monarch were permitted without informing the Pharaoh and getting his permission.

This hegemony reached its acme during the Twelfth Dynasty, in the reign of Thutmose III, and started to decline up until the reign of Akhenaten. During the latter's time it almost disappeared, the reason being that Akhenaten was a mystic, spirit of the god Aten and his high priest. The pharaoh was distracted from foreign affairs by his religious revolution against other gods and priests. Relations between Egypt and monarchs under its suzerainty were disrupted. The first monarch to exploit the opportunity for independence and expansion was Aziro, king of the Hittites, an Amorite lord, who took his armed forces on a victorious raid, marching from the north into Syrian territory, both plain and shore. He moved on to capture the region's cities, including Tyre and Sidon. Their rulers turned their backs on the pharaoh and surrendered to the Hittite ruler.

When he occupied the territory known today as Alawite lands and reached Soumaira, a town on the plain between Tripoli and Tartus, to the north of the Kabir River, Reeb Addi, the ruler of Byblos, was scared about his own authority and wrote to the pharaoh, asking for help. But the pharaoh did not respond. When Soumaira fell into the hands of Aziro and the Egyptian delegate there was killed, Reeb Addi wrote twice, three times, screaming for help, but his screams were lost in the wind. Akhenaten was still involved in his revolution against the ancient gods and their priests, building temples to the new single deity, the sun god Aten, from whose light Akhenaten himself was created.

In spite of this situation, Reeb Addi refused to submit to Aziro, as other rulers of Phoenician cities had done. The Hittite ruler sent tribes from the Bedouin Khobairi tribe to attack him. The people of Byblos opposed the position that their ruler had taken, and so the city was subjected to raids and intrigues. Reeb Addi may have been old and sick, but he never relented or weakened.

Aziro besieged Byblos for three years, but, in spite of the intrigues against him and the effects of age and illness, the Byblos ruler stood his ground. Faced with a similar disaster, would anyone else have been able to resist for more than three years? He kept his resolve and never gave in. Indeed, he went to Beirut, and, for a second or third time, asked the Egyptian monarch for help through his envoy there:[2]

"Help us, help us, monarch of the earth! We stretch our hands to your feet. The Hittites have plundered our land, and the Khobairis are camped beneath our walls."

2. In correspondence between kings of Babylon, Syria, Palestine, and Phoenicia and the ruler of Egypt, written on tablets that were discovered at Tell Amarna in 1883, there are some sixty letters from the unfortunate ruler of Byblos. One of them says: "Previously the monarch used to send money and other necessities to my ancestors. He would also send armies. I have sent my lord the king a messenger requesting assistance from a band of soldiers, but he has not sent me anyone." This shows that some kind of Egyptian rule over Phoenicia predates the era of Prince Ebb Addi.

If it had been Thutmose whom you were calling, Reeb Addi, you would have been heard. But Akhenaten, himself perched over a precipice, neither heard nor responded.

Reeb Addi came back from Beirut bearing the heavy burdens of failure, illness, old age, and loyalty to the pharaoh. When he reached Byblos, he was not allowed to enter the city. Not only that, but he also learned that his brother had taken over as ruler and his sons were hostages in Aziro's hands; it was his traitorous brother who had handed them over.

We have now reached an obscure period in these events, one on which historians have shed no light. Reeb Addi managed to regain control of the kingdom, but histories do not explain how. Even so, he remained loyal to the ruler of Egypt in spite of his wife's and family's insistence that he make peace with the Hittites. It is truly remarkable, remaining loyal to a weak ruler far away while defying a strong sword wielder directly confronting you. There is some kind of secret behind it. Do we see the highest possible model of loyalty and fidelity in this Phoenician ruler's conduct, or are we really dealing with that thing called senility? We are not able to make a decision, but it will have to be enough to finish the tragedy. Soon after Reeb Addi returned to power, Aziro renewed his assault on Byblos, captured it, and put everything and everyone to fire and sword. Reeb Addi and many Byblos citizens were killed.

This disaster occurred at the end of Akhenaten's reign; in other words, some four hundred years after Ishmou Abi's era and about seventy-five years before King Ahiram's reign. During that period (1300 BCE) Pharaoh Ramses II renewed Egyptian connections with Byblos and honored it by supporting the king and treating its people kindly. As examples, he numbered its temples and gave Ahiram precious gifts.

When Ahiram's grave was excavated, they brought out the largest and most exquisite sarcophagus in Byblos. On all four sides, drawings and symbolic and historical writings had been carved. The figure of the lion, which is the focus of the sarcophagus, is Hittite in its art, while the scenes decorating the sides are Egyptian. Here then is the purpose of Byblos's new policy, with the Egyptians and Hittites rivaling each other for control of Phoenician territory. When the two sides fought the Battle of Kadesh, Byblos remained neutral. Even though the Amorites supported Ramses II, it was the Hittites who emerged victorious.

In the royal graveyard beyond the wall archeologists have uncovered a number of sarcophagi, one of them for father and son—Abishmou and Ibishmou Abi. Inside they found silver and brass scepters; gold knives and spoons; statuettes, jewelry, and talismans; and other items, all now on display in three glass cases in the Lebanese Museum.

These then were the tombs of kings, containing everything they believed that they would need for the journey into the eternal darkness. They were found, buried twelve meters under the earth thousands of years ago. Some of the relics were solid stone, while others were made of wood decorated with pieces of colored porcelain.

The graves of the populace consisted of clay pots, big or small, in which the dead person was folded over, just like an unborn child in its mother's womb. In those pots a large number of objects were discovered: porcelain and metal vessels, weapons, bracelets, and gold and silver talismans. The religious conviction was one and the same, enslaving kings and vagabonds alike.

One of the oddest things we saw in the royal graveyard was a tunnel between the graves of the two Shmous, father and son. The father wanted this tunnel to be dug from his own grave to this son's for some reason of his own. Was it spiritual, or somehow connected with more earthly concerns? Unlike the Egyptians, the Phoenicians were not ones to record their intentions and beliefs. Phoenician beliefs were buried with their owners, along with all their symbols and secrets, and sealed in eternal silence.

However, archeologists have their own opinions about such secrets, things odd enough to bear mentioning and recording. One such scholar states that the purpose of digging this tunnel was spiritual, in that it was the father's view that the two spirits would be linked one to the other and could pay each other visits. Another scholar said that the purpose was entirely material. The father was eager to benefit from the sacrifices that his son brought in; he could then share the food, drink, and scents that were brought to his son.

You sons of darkness! What kind of myth is it that you rape, wear, eat, drink, and bed? Even if the prophets who came after you were sighted, what failure will make you suffer its anguish and chew on its sweet and bitter tastes? If only you could watch immortality in nature, renewed by springtime each year; if only you could anoint your spirits with the scent of sweet basil and the flowers that decorate your city, spreading a carpet of love and nostalgia over your graves; then in both life and death you would have dispensed with the humbug of your gods and superstitions of your priests!

If I were asked what the most beautiful thing I had seen in archeological Byblos was, I would reply, "Spring in all its glory." Of those spring offerings the most beautiful would be the flourishing fig tree with which nature has endowed Abishmou's grave. In that spot, where he lies sleeping for eternity in his sarcophagus, the remains of the past live on, and in their brightest and most beautiful hues. To that same grave pit the winds have carried a seed from Byblos's orchards. The sides of the grave have protected it against both cold and heat, and it has been watered by rain-filled clouds. That seed has grown to become a luscious, blossoming fig tree, raising its branches over the grave to soak up the sun's rays, inhale the fresh air in daytime, and, by moonlight, sniff the breeze and scented night.

Immortality in nature! You can see its symbols illuminated in that city in ruins. Among the monarchs' tombs you are greeted by anemones and sweet clover. Wherever you stand, wherever you look, your heart is gladdened by wallflowers and daisies.

Yellow daisies and purple wallflowers are everywhere, found in profusion by the sides of the graves, amid the ruins of houses, by the lintels at the temple entrance, in the shadow of the city wall and on top of it as well—everywhere, and of an indescribable freshness. The daises spread their own gold among the graves of those who were totally enamored of the precious metal.

The wallflowers spread carpets of purple for those spirits that originally discovered the color.

Messenger of the God Amon

THE WALLS OF THE CITY have two gates, each of which has a staircase: one goes down to the sea, the other goes up to the hill where the royal palace is situated. Here the guide stops to tell visitors the story of the messenger who came to Byblos to ask the king for wood for the Egyptian pharaoh. He arrived empty-handed, claiming that he had been robbed on the way, so the king of Byblos refused his request.

"No money," he told the messenger, "no wood."

"I'll write to His Majesty the pharaoh," the messenger replied, "to have him send me some money."

He waited for the king to reply. The king went over to the window and showed him the graveyard.

"Some of your fellow Egyptians have come here asking for wood," the king told him. "Just like you, stranger, they had no money, silver, or gold. They too wrote to Egypt asking for money. They waited and waited for a response, but died while they were still waiting. We've buried them all in this graveyard."

That is the story the guide was telling. It is a good representation of the primary Phoenician trait—their devotion to commercial principles—to be more precise, their love of money. However, in recounting this story as a case of history, there are some things that the guide misses. In his account there is a certain obscurity. Who sent the messenger? Why did he not bring any money with him or goods to exchange, as was the custom in those days? What happened after he wrote to Egypt and waited for ages? Did the money come, so that he could take the wood? Or did he suffer the same fate as his colleagues, buried alongside them in the graveyard? Who were those Egyptians buried in Byblos?

We have looked into the history and learned some details about political and commercial affairs between Egypt and Phoenicia, involving relations, sometimes friendly, and, at others, unfriendly, between the two countries at that time. That might seem to justify the messenger's arrival in Byblos empty-handed in order to request a free supply of cedarwood for the god Amon. It might also explain the commercial attitude of the king of Byblos and his close adherence to Phoenician commercial principles, which brooked no compromise, no matter the will of Amon and the pharaoh. Such a wish would have needed the support of an army and fleet!

So where were the Egyptian army and fleet at the time? The story, it would appear, was not about wood but rather government and colonies. The story also offers some interesting insights into both the political and religious situation in Egypt and Phoenicia, something that brings it all close to the mentalities of our own time—indeed, makes it a worthwhile topic for any and every place and time.

At that particular time the Phoenicians had reestablished good relations with the Egyptian pharaohs. They had also started rebuilding the city, which had been destroyed by the Khobairi tribes and the Hittite Aziro's armies during the reign of King Reeb Addi.

The mighty pharaoh, Ramses II, had made a pact with the princes of Byblos—as they are called in Egyptian histories—that offered protection bolstered by action. New Byblos was calm and welcomed the Egyptian god Amon, for whom the pharaoh built a temple in the city.

Boats from Byblos started plying the seas again, as they had done in the past. Byblos trade recovered its former benefits and success. The prince and his people offered as much praise to the strange god in their city as they did to their own god, Reshef, and his companion goddess, Ishtar. Sailors and merchants carried their portraits on their voyages and offered them all oblations.

All glory and honor to Amon and the pharaoh! Throughout the era of Ramses II, that lengthy and happy period—sixty-seven years and even for a quarter-century afterward, glory and success enfolded the gods and people of Byblos. Then came a chaotic period in Egypt when the nobles and priests took over, parties fought each other, and foreigners gained more influence in the royal court. After a reign that lasted just two years, Pharaoh Seti II fell, and one of the Syrians who had become influential at court became pharaoh. During his reign, which lasted for five years, malice prevailed, and Egypt's power abroad weakened; indeed, had not Ramses III taken over, it would have almost completely disappeared.

This pharaoh managed to repair some of the things that the usurper had undermined. While he tried to reestablish Egyptian authority abroad, he was not entirely successful. "The monarchs of the East," Hittites and Phoenicians reverted to their former ways, pretending to be loyal and compliant; they paid their yearly taxes and kept a close eye on the fortunes of the pharaohs in the Nile Valley.

Those same fortunes headed rapidly downward. Ramses III was succeeded by eight other Ramseses, each one of them inheriting less authority and prestige than his predecessor, until the heritage dwindled to nothing.

It seems that, during this same period, the pharaoh dispatched a delegation to the East on his behalf—a royal mission, no less!—to investigate the affairs of his princes, strengthen ties between them and Egypt, and, in particular, to collect yearly taxes that were still owed.

During the reign of Ramses XII (1147–1123 BCE), we witness a meeting in the royal palace to discuss the delegation about which there had been no news for a while. At the time the delegation was actually in Byblos as guests of its prince and watched over by a platoon of his soldiers! "August delegates, you have honored our country with your visit and brought light to our palaces." However, they were actually housed in one palace with the gates firmly locked; one year went by, then two, then three, with them imprisoned in the palace.

The pharaoh was distracted from their situation by renewed insurrection and destruction in Egypt, something that tore the government apart in the fifth year of Ramses XIII's reign, he being the last one in that dynasty.[1] One of his enemies residing in the north, named Nesubanebded, claimed the monarchy. He soon made himself Pharaoh and set up an independent kingdom in what today is called "the seaside."

The original pharaoh transferred his throne to (Egyptian) Thebes and convened the priests to ask for their advice about the kingdom. They were unanimous in stating that the country's condition stemmed from the situation of its gods—"those gods, O light of the world, are hostile to Egypt."

We see the chief priest of the god Amon complaining of poverty and humiliation. Mighty Amon has no boat worthy of him, but nor does any other god. Other priests repeat the same complaints: How can the gods keep track of their subjects in the Nile Valley? O light of the world, we need cedarwood to build sun boats.

"Send someone to Byblos to get the wood."

"What about the money, O king of kings?"

"Money? The prince of Byblos should remember the traditions of his forefathers. He should recall that he hasn't paid taxes for many years."

Pharaoh delegated to High Priest Hor-hora the task of dispatching a messenger to get the wood.

For the task Hor-hora selected a court official named Wenamun. When Wenamun asked for money, the high priest's response was:

"Our god has a temple in Byblos. The temple's money belongs to its god. That god resides here in Egypt. For many years none of the money from our temple in Byblos has come to Egypt."

"But, O felicitous one," Wenamun replied, "I'm not a temple official, someone who could bring back the money. I'm from the court."

1. Translator's note: I am grateful to my colleague in Egyptology, Professor David Silverman, for the following information: the last pharaoh of this line was actually Ramses XI. According to an extant papyrus, his rival's name was Smendes, but was also known as Nesubanebded. After the death of Ramses XI, Nesubanebded did indeed take over the rule of the whole country. I have, however, left Rihani's text as he wrote it.

"The prince of Byblos owes the pharaoh a large amount of back taxes," Hor-hora told him, "taxes that haven't been paid yet."

"The prince who has not voluntarily paid the taxes he owes," replied Wenamun, "will only do so if you choose to honor him by sending an army battalion."

"Trust Amon, Wenamun," the high priest told him. "Here is a picture of the god, Amon of the way, giver of life and health. Take it to the prince of Byblos, and you will be admitted to his pious and devout heart. He will then recall the traditions of his ancestors and provide you with the wood for Amon's sake—to whom be glory.

The high priest gave the messenger some money for his travel expenses and also gave him a letter addressed to the would-be pharaoh on "the seaside," the one with the long name, so that he would make arrangements for the messenger's journey to Byblos.

The messenger arrived safely at Nesubanebded's headquarters and safely boarded ship. However, he was diverted from his destination when, passing through a village in Palestine, he was attacked by robbers, who took all his money. Continuing his journey with only the picture of the god Amon, he eventually reached Byblos, accompanied by the "god of life and health."

At the time Zakar Baal was ruler of Byblos, king and high priest of the god Reshef. People in Byblos had started shunning the Egyptian god, and so the messenger from Egypt entered the city as an unwelcome stranger. No one welcomed him, and the king did not grant him the honor of an audience.

What an insult to the messenger of Amon! But then, patience is a characteristic of messengers. The god had to work his will with Zakar Baal, then the messenger would be admitted. If things moved slowly, then piety and devoutness would at least get him an audience.

But Zakar Baal was hard-hearted.

"I'll not meet the Egyptian," he said, "I won't do it. He should go back to Egypt."

At that time there was a man in Byblos who was devoted to the worship of the god Amon. He came to see the prince to advise him—or rather, to warn him.

"Receive him," he said, "and treat him properly. Receive him and send him back gently, so you don't bring down on yourself the wrath of the god who is still one of the deities of this city."

That had a soothing effect on Zakar Baal's heart, and he agreed to receive the man.

Wenamun came to the palace. The king was seated on a chair close to a window overlooking the sea. He sat there in a royal pose, his face to the door and his back to the sea.

"I am Zakar Baal," he said, "king of Byblos and high priest of Reshef Baal. Is the pharaoh mightier than the sea? Is the god Baal mightier than the sea?"

The messenger entered, uttering the usual greeting: "All glory and might to Amon!"

The king did not respond to his greeting.

"How long have you been traveling from Egypt?" he asked.

"Five months and a day."

"If you're Amon's messenger, where's his message? Aren't you bringing a message from him?"

"Nesubanebded kept it."

"Do you think so little of Amon's message to us that you give it to someone else?"

"What would you do," he went on angrily, "if the sea turned rough and smashed your ship? Would you ask Amon to come to your aid after you've insulted him so badly? What will Amon do to someone who shows no respect for his message? I don't blame Nesubanebded; relations between him and the pharaoh are no concern of ours. He buys things from us and pays the price. There are twenty ships in the port today carrying commerce between him and us. What is it that you want from us?"

"I've come to ask for wood for the boat of Amon, king of the gods. Your father gave us wood, and you can do the same."

"I can do what my father did, if you can do what the pharaoh's messenger did before you." At that time the pharaoh's messenger arrived with six ships loaded with Egyptian-produced goods. Their treasured goods were first unloaded into our storehouses before the wood was loaded.

Zakar Baal gave instructions to the scribe to bring his account books. When they were brought in, the scribe read out the record of accounts between Zakar Baal's ancestors and the Egyptian pharaohs.

"A thousand pieces of silver," Wenamun heard, "a thousand pieces of copper, five hundred pieces of gold . . ."

The king interrupted the scribe.

"Did my property belong to the ruler of Egypt and were I his servant," he said, "then I would cut the wood for him with my own two hands. Remember, Egyptian messenger, that my father paid no taxes to the pharaoh, nor will I. I'm neither your servant, nor the servant of the one who sent you here. I possess the money. If I call Lebanon, the forest will hear my call, and the wood will come down to the seashore. What have you brought here? Where are your wood-bearing ships? Where are the ropes with which to tie it all down so it won't fall overboard in rough seas? Your journey is indeed ill starred. Have you arrived here empty-handed, bringing only a picture of Amon? We do not deny the might and blessings of the god, but we also state that he is a just god, one who favors behavior based on justice."

"There is not a single vessel on the sea," Wenamun responded, "that is not the god's property. The seas are his, and everything on them. Lebanon is his too, and everything in it. Every single tree in Lebanon belongs to Amon and his sacred boat. That is what the god told my lord Hor-hora, the high priest, and now this is what Hor-hora is saying to you. He is presenting you with the holy picture of Amon. What have you done with it, and indeed with his messenger to you, the one who carried it here? It hasn't bothered you that I've been waiting in your country for twenty days before you agreed to meet me. Now you've started haggling over Lebanon's wood, saying that Lebanon belongs to you and kings of Egypt have sent gold and silver to your ancestors. They were kings' messengers; I am the messenger of the god, king of all gods, the giver of life and health."

The Byblos wall is the only town in Lebanon whose walls are still standing today; from it the road goes north to Tripoli.

"We have believed in Amon, Egyptian messenger, and in Amon of the way, and we constantly praise him for his bounty. But at the same time we say, 'If you believe in him as we do, then do not mock us in his name.' Treat us like our good friend, Nesubanebded. If you would like to write to the one who sent you, then go ahead and write."

It so happened that Wenamun did write to ask for goods and money to be sent to buy wood. Three months later, some ships arrived laden with fabrics, parchment, and buffalo hides, along with gold, silver, and copper coins. Zakar Baal's laborers made use of them and put it all in storehouses. They then handed over the cedarwood to Wenamun.

The day came for Wenamun to ask permission to leave.

"You're luckier than your colleagues before you," Zakar Baal told him (meaning the members of the Egyptian delegation who had been put in prison and died in Byblos). They're all buried in that graveyard" (he pointed to the graves through the window). Would you like to visit their graves?"

Wenamun replied that his visit to the prince was enough.

It so happened that a group of Thekels (Palestinians in the language of that period), the one who had robbed Wenamun of his money, had heard about what had taken place in Byblos regarding his petition. So they kept track of him in eleven boats, and lay in wait for him in the open sea.

On the day when Wenamun set sail from the Byblos port, the Thekel boats surrounded his boat and captured it. He managed to get away and returned to Byblos, where he complained to Zakar Baal. That infuriated the Byblos monarch, and he sent a fleet of his own vessels to combat the pirates. His sense of charity was transcended by his instinct for justice, in that, while Wenamun was in dire straits, he sent him not only food and wine but also a pretty girl from Egypt to alleviate his distress.

Zakar Baal's fleet caught up with the Thekel boats, captured them, and took them to a safe haven. The prince imprisoned the pirates so as to make the sea safe for Wenamun.

However, the sea was not just pirates. When the Phoenician king turned his back on the sea, it launched a gigantic storm without the slightest concern. Once Wenamun had set sail for the second time from the port of Byblos and disappeared from view on the Phoenician shore, the sea launched a terrifying assault on him, and he found himself tossed on the island of Cyprus.

The messenger of the mighty god Amon, lord of the seas! He had managed to escape the tumultuous sea just as he had the pirates and throw his anchor close to the island. However, the wiles of time dogged Wenamun like a shadow. He hardly had time to step foot on Alassa soil (Cyprus) before the populace rose up against him. Wenamun was forced to seek refuge at the palace of Queen Hatiba. They pursued him there, yelling at him and threatening to kill him.

It so happened that the queen was on her way back to the palace. Wenamun asked her for help. She brought in a translator from her retinue and ordered him to unfold this stranger's riddle for her. Wenamun spoke to the translator:

"Tell Her Majesty that her fame has traversed seas and cities and has now reached the sacred seat of the god Amon. We have learned for sure that injustice exists in every country except Cyprus. The queen laughed heartily.

"What are you saying, Egyptian?" she asked. "There are injustices in every country. There's one every single day."

Wenamun tried plucking on a different string.

"The seas have swelled and driven me to your city and to you, O Queen, renowned for both beauty and intelligence, sitting there on the throne of mercy. Is someone who seeks refuge with you to be harmed?"

That struck the queen's female instincts. Comforting the messenger, she sent him and his men under royal guard to the palace guesthouse.

"Thanks be to Amon, Your Majesty! We slept through the night, safe and sound."

Those are the words with which Wenamun concludes his report to High Priest Hor-hora in holy Thebes. We have no idea what happened to him and his wood-laden ships during the time between that night of security and the dark shades of time.

Phoenicia and the Pharaohs

IN THE SECOND HALF of the twenty-first century BCE, Phoenicia was peaceful and secure[1]—putting the best face on it, since we do not really know how things really were. They were surrounded by savage people and two military regimes, Babylon and Egypt. So, while Hammurabi in Babylon (2067–2025 BCE) was conducting raids on Sumer and Elam so as to add them to his territories, his contemporary, Pharaoh Mentuhotep IV, of the Eleventh Dynasty to Nubia to extend Theban control over that area. Meanwhile, the Phoenicians were involved in peaceful activities, crafts and commerce, with their caravans moving east toward the Euphrates, while their ships stopped at islands and ports near and far in the Mediterranean.

With his skill and adventurous spirit, the Phoenician sailor was master of the seas. For his shrewdness and audacity the Phoenician merchant was master of commerce. The Phoenician craftsman was admired for both his skill and taste. On the seashores Phoenician cities were built that valued sea travel and raised commerce and craftsmanship to the very highest levels in life.

The governing authorities and priests by no means disdained the rewards of commerce; in fact, more often than not, they were in charge of it. They were rivals in acquiring wealth and in their ownership of

1. At an Egyptian archeological site, a letter was found in both Hieroglyphic and Greek. In ancient times, Phoenicia was called Kaft, the Phoenician word for palm tree, because palms were found there in plenty. The Egyptians called both Syria and Phoenicia Zahi or Zakhi. The Palestinians were called Thekel—that being the name of a tribe that moved to Palestine from Crete.

property, cattle, and slaves. They all developed an instinct for greed and avarice but also a degree of tolerance. For the sake of gain, they would moderate both temperament and method. Private interest prevailed over public interest. Each one of them strove to be independent of the others so they could have exclusive control of what they had acquired.

It was from these personal qualities that more civic attributes developed. Like individuals, cities were independent of each other; they competed with each other on luxury, prestige, affluence, and comfort. "A people that loves peace, leisure, and comfort," all those factors characteristic of the wealthy. Around those, cities' walls were built to protect them from marauders and raids by savage peoples.

The rulers in those cities were called kings; in addition, they claimed to be kin of the gods. Thus they made gods their associates in governing cities and villages attached to them, and also held celebrations in the gods' honor and made sacrificial offerings to them on their altars. They also involved the priestly class with regard to the money that accrued to the temples. In fact, at some points the king combined in his one person the roles of ruler and high priest. These kingdoms emerged as a result of the instinct toward egotism and local and individual independence—free and independent states in times of peace and security, and failing and parlaying cities in times of danger and war.

These Phoenician kingdoms developed on the shore of the Mediterranean, from Mount Carmel to the Gulf of Iskenderun. In this region, three hundred miles long and ten miles wide, the Phoenicians established six kingdoms and six major cities: Tyre, Sidon, Beirut, Byblos, Arwad, and Soumaira.

They chose shore sites because they were not interested in farming and agriculture. On the shoreline they preferred places suitable for ports and ship factories, for the most part by bays and capes. If their choice in olden times today seems more wrong than right due to the wind gusts we see around cities like Tyre or Byblos, their preference for such locations instead of safer sites—like the Gulf of Iskenderun, for example, or the peaks of Chekka—was correct from their particular point of view. Lebanon's mountains, situated behind the places they had chosen, were forbidding fortresses, protecting the cities from tribal raids and attacks from conquerors like the Hittites, Babylonians, and Assyrians. If any Phoenician city had been founded where Iskenderun is today, for example—it being better situated and more defendable from the seaside than the other cities, it would not have lasted very long because the mountains behind it are split and lie wide open to raiding armies and conquerors. The shortest and easiest route from Carchemish and Babylon to the Mediterranean shore lies through that great bay. Byblos, Sidon, and Tyre all have sturdy fortresses behind them; there is a mountain track between each of them that leads into the interior, thus making things easier for commercial caravans and harder for invading armies.

But, in spite of all this, these cities were not always safe from danger. The rapacious and destructive hands of marauding conquerors managed to get to them. Their known history is silent for a period marked by peace and security, but then it speaks of disaster striking Byblos or Tyre and destroying them. They are then rebuilt, and life and luxury are renewed. Had these Phoenicians kingdoms been united—or, at least, agreed on a mutual defense treaty—then these historic disasters would have been fewer in number. The attackers would have been repulsed from those quiet shores.

The historian George Rawlinson has this to say:[2]

"Not a single treaty was formed between all the Phoenician states, not even a temporary one. The other sister states never offered any help when one of the states was threatened. Introversion, clashing personal interests, and a weak sense of nation, all mitigated against any kind of unified statements or actions during times of danger and hardship. One of the states would fall on its own, and the others would follow, one by one."

2. Translator's note: Rawlinson was a professor of ancient history at Oxford University. His *History of Phoenicia* was published in 1889.

That is exactly true. Those Phoenicians never understood the meaning of cooperation, nor did they feel any inclination toward group solidarity, something that brings with it the benefits of a single sense of nationhood. We have to state that there was no single nation and no national sensitivity; not even a single deity to gather them together and bind them in a single national bond, like the Egyptians, for example, or the Assyrians. Byblos had its king and a portion of the Lebanese forests whose wood he could dispose of as he and his own ambitions and policies saw fit. It had its own gods, who were worshipped and celebrated within the city walls and in its villages. The same was true for Tyre, Sidon, Arwad, and Soumaira.

These cities were walled by religion and politics just as much as by stone. The inhabitants, all descended from a single line of descent, had no notion of national brotherhood, nor did they understand the goals of national life. Beyond that, you can say that they were fighting each other some of the time and indolent all the time.

When Aziro the Hittite invaded the coastal lands, he captured Soumaira and subjugated Arwad. He asked the people of those two kingdoms to help him in his campaign against Reeb Addi, the king of Byblos, and they did so. When Zamreeda, king of Sidon, surrendered to Aziro the Hittite, he helped his conqueror against Abimelech, king of Tyre, so eager was he for booty. When Alexander invaded the Phoenician territories, rulers, priests and notables all came out bearing gifts and welcoming him, all as a release from the Persians who had ruled over the region, all except Tyre, which had rebelled. As a result, Alexander besieged Tyre for seven months. The people of Tyre would have almost succeeded in frustrating Alexander's plans and repelling him from the city's land and sea walls, had it not been for the Phoenician fleet that the kings of Byblos and Cyprus put at Alexander's disposal to help him.

The Semitic people, with their tendency toward independence—or indeed, separation from each other and isolation—something they share with tribes and peoples in their initial phases, craving, in spite of all their differences, the world's material goods and pursuing prestige and luxury, are different from other peoples in the region for their command of industry and commerce. History records the prodigious achievements of the Semitic peoples on the high seas, and the establishment of colonies in distant ports; the culture that they spread—Eastern, Phoenician, Babylonian, and Egyptian—in the lands of Europe and Africa.

In the earliest days of its era, the Semitic people lived alongside the Hittites and Mitannians in Syria, and the Elamites and Hurrians in Mesopotamia. We would not know anything about these minor peoples, both Aryan and Semitic, were it not for the archeological digs that have been undertaken in our current era. Even so, what we have learned about them is not enough to raise them to the level of the Phoenicians, nor does it make them peoples who have borrowed from others in their religion, art, and industry, and have then gone on to embellish and innovate with the things they have borrowed.

The Mitanni kingdom extended between the Euphrates and Khabour Rivers (where Hasja and Qamishli are located today). The Egyptians referred to their kings as "monarchs of the two rivers." They secured independence from Assyria, and among their kings were Artatama, Tourazma (Toushratta), Shouttarna, and Artarouzma (Artashumara)—what wonderful names![3]

Artatama married his daughter legitimately to Pharaoh Thutmose IV, and Shouttarna offered his daughter, Jiloukhiba, as a mistress to Pharaoh Amenhotep III. She was accompanied by a group of women—317 Mitanni women!

The Hittite king Suppiluliuma (1350 BCE) and the Mitanni king Matioutha signed a treaty with the ruler of Assyria. It was written in cuneiform, the state language at that time.

So, what other archeological remains are there of these Mitannis and Hittites? What else contributes to their glory other than records of invasions and royal marriages?

3. Translator's note: the names in parenthesis are as recorded in histories of this people.

Shaushtatar, the Mitanni king, brought back from Assyria silver and gold doors for his palace.

Artatama sent a letter to his son-in-law, the pharaoh, informing him that he was in good health, just like the sun in the sky, and that his army and chariots were all in good condition. He then asks for silver, gold, horses, and chariots. "They tell us," he wrote, "that, for you, gold is like dust on the ground, plentiful." So send gold to your loving father-in-law; send gold and silver.

No, no, by God! Archeologists have not discovered anything worth mentioning when the glories of ancient peoples are the topic. There are just a few ugly stone statues, poorly made, and nasty in both appearance and significance. Just show me a single piece carved by ancient peoples, and I will tell you where that people stand in the history of civilization.

Here is a carved piece of stone, an example of Mitanni art, representing their deity, Enkidu, half bull and half man. However, the human half looks more like an animal than a human being. The god and his equally ugly assistant are twin monstrosities disguised in an Assyrian beard, carrying an umbrella or something like it, over which is the disc of Egypt's winged sun!

They imitated the Egyptians and Assyrians and distorted the things they imitated. The Phoenicians seem to be situated in the forefront of cultured and civilized people at the time. They borrowed from Babylon and Egypt, and did it well, adding some creative touches of their own and marking it with their own particular features. From their artist's hands, objets d'art would emerge as clearly Phoenician in shape and craft, if it was not also Phoenician in spirit and intent.

This intellectual trait is one indication of the fact that Phoenicians were of Arab descent. Among them and those who came after them were those conquerors who borrowed from both Persians and Romans, adding their own touches to those of the other two traditions. Between the two there are ties of kinship and heritage, and similarities in their ability to copy and innovate.

Historians and archeologists are unanimous in stating that, like the Arabs, the Phoenicians are Semites—indeed, that they are of Arab origins. In olden times they moved from the Arab eastern shores of the Persian (Arabian) Gulf, and from Bahrain to the shores of the Mediterranean.[4]

By studying the archeological remains found in an old cemetery in Bahrain, we can deduce that their emigration happened before the Bronze Age, at the end of the flint period, a time when humans could not write since absolutely nothing in written form was discovered in the Phoenician graves in Bahrain.

Historians state that the oldest Asian states were founded at the mouth of the Persian Gulf. Archeologists support that statement through their discoveries at Sumer, confirming that, during their first period (3100 BCE), the Sumerians achieved a high level of civilization.[5] They have also been able to prove that, in ancient times, the mouth of the Persian Gulf was where the city Ur of the Chaldees was discovered, 120 miles north of Basra. If the Phoenicians, one of the Semitic peoples who had settled on the Persian Gulf coast, had moved beyond the era of Sumerian culture, then they would have taken some of it with them to the Mediterranean shore. However, from our knowledge up until now, there is no trace of that culture among the Phoenicians—apart, that is, from what arrived at a later date, blended with Babylonian and Assyrian cultures. All of which means that their emigration must have taken place hundreds or thousands of years before the Sumerian era.

From that emigration until they are first mentioned in historical records, we know absolutely nothing about them. That so-called period of ignorance may have lasted a thousand years before Egyptians hear about them and mention them on their monuments, and also before Syria and its shores are mentioned in a monument to Sargon the Akkadian, who conquered the Sumerian state. King Sargon I (2750 BCE) invaded Syria three times and reached as far as the shore.

4. See this author, *Kings of the Arabs* (1924), part 2.

5. See this author, *The Heart of Iraq* (1935).

However, the first confirmed mention of Phoenicians happened in Egypt in the era of Pharaoh Snefru of the Second (Fourth?) Dynasty (2980–2800 BCE).[6] Snefru dispatched forty ships to the Phoenician shore to collect Lebanese cedar timber. There is no obscurity or ambiguity about this information, recorded in the pharaoh's history. Lebanese cedar had been made famous by Solomon, son of David, in his Psalms, and now here it was again, in the hands of Egyptian craftsmen, some 1,900 years after Solomon's era.

Now here are the Phoenicians in their city, Byblos (Jbeil), established, so the archeologists tell us, early in the thirtieth century BCE, or five thousand years ago.

At that time, Egypt, like Ur of the Chaldees, had achieved a high level of culture. Indeed, it outstripped Sumer in luxury, culture, and art, especially during Snefru's reign, he being the first great pharaoh. So skilled and inventive were shipbuilders in that period that they were able to build him a fleet, one of whose ships was 170 feet long.

Mining flourished in the gold mines of Nubia and the copper mines of Cyprus and the Sinai Peninsula. Industry flourished along with it, and commercial markets and irrigation projects expanded. There was prosperity and good fortune throughout Egypt. It is no wonder then that the prince of Byblos and the wood merchants welcomed these rich Egyptians, and, for a period of about a century, were keen to form friendships and commercial relationships with them.

Then these commercial transactions aroused political ambitions for the Egyptian rulers. In 2750 BCE Pharaoh Sahure of the Fifth Dynasty prepared a fleet that attacked the Phoenician shores. That pharaoh has a monument discovered in his pyramid at Abusir in Egypt: on it is a picture of four ships with their sailors, among them four Phoenician prisoners. This is the oldest picture of its type in the

6. Translator's note: the dynasty number and the dates cited here are at odds with the records of Egyptian history. The dates usually cited for his reign are 2613–2589 BCE.

world—the oldest picture of a ship, and the first image representing those Phoenicians with their typical shape and costume.

Thus, the first information that we have about their history comes from Egyptian archeology, not from the Assyrians, as historians claim. There is no doubt that they were known in the islands and countries lying to the north and west of their shores before the period of Snefru's reign. They were known for commerce and ships, and Lebanon was renowned for its forests. In any case, what is clear is that trade in cedarwood goes back to the third century BCE; in other words, cedar has been cut from Lebanese forests for five thousand years.

It is also clear that the first people to attack the Phoenicians and try to occupy their country because of the cedars were the Egyptians. Given that the Phoenicians were independent in the period before Snefru's reign, it was during that reign (2750 BCE) that the Phoenicians began to experience problems in their foreign contacts.

Unfortunately, concerning those same contacts as they developed from commerce, to politics, and to colonialism, we only know what archeologists have published about the pharaohs in Egypt. Even then, the links are broken, with gaps that sometimes stretch for two or three hundred years.

We have learned that the first person to bring wood from the Phoenician shore was Pharaoh Snefru, and the first one to invade the Phoenicians shores was Pharaoh Sahure. During the reign of Pepi II, who ruled happily for some ninety years (the longest reign in history), commercial relations between Egypt and Phoenicia were fine, with cedarwood being exported from Lebanon.

It is safe to say that, in the period from Snefru to Pepi—more exactly, from their dynasty to the Sixth, some four hundred years—Egypt was Phoenicia's major commercial market, avoiding issues of politics and coercion. That is true, provided that we make exceptions for the sea raids conducted by certain pharaohs, either because they were hot-blooded, or else there was a shortage of funds in the state treasury.

Politics did not enter the picture in any serious fashion until the Twelfth Dynasty (2000–1877 BCE), Egypt's golden age. During that felicitous era, pharaohs started thinking about occupying Asian countries, meaning Palestine, Phoenicia, and Syria. In preparation, they dispatched what we can called "investigative missions." The pharaoh sent his emissaries to Syria and Phoenicia to investigate and collect information. The Egyptian language started to spread through those countries.

Here then is colonial policy, with all its motivations and methods—how very ancient it is! Is it odd that it can lead to another result, besides war? In the first half of the nineteenth century BCE, Syria was invaded by Pharaoh Sesostris (Senusret) III. It was simply a raid, with no occupation to follow.

The flow of information is now interrupted. There is a lengthy gap in Phoenician history, about three hundred years. During that time, the pharaoh's throne fell, and the country was occupied by animal herders, Hyksos. They were then expelled, and the Eighteenth Dynasty was founded, which reestablished Egypt's former glory and gave a boost to the pharaoh's prestige both inside and outside the country.

The first person to conquer Palestine, Syria, and Phoenicia and to extend control over the entire area—from Gaza to Carchemish and the region below the eastern Euphrates—was the head of that dynasty, Pharaoh Thutmose III (1501–1443 BCE), who raided this country seventeen times![7]

Rulers from the coastal regions arrived, bringing taxes and offering their obeisance to the pharaoh.

On a parchment scroll there is a poem to the god Amon, with blessings to the pharaoh included:

> You brought your powerful arm to strike the rulers of Zahi (Syria),
> From the heights of their mountains you cast them under your feet,
> You opened their eyes to look on your light, thou Lord of Light,
> And shone before them, like an image of my glory!

7. Archeologists have different ways of writing the pharaohs' names. Thus, Tuhutmis, Thutmose, and Thotmes; then Amenhotep, Amenotis, and Amnotef.

Seventy years of continuous Egyptian suzerainty, meaning partial independence and taxes. Seventy years of such control, followed by the revolution of the philosopher Sufi Pharaoh, Amenhotep IV—Akhenaten. Egypt's power abroad weakened, and Eastern rulers and kings severed the bonds of such foreign control. Some of them killed the Egyptian envoys in their country and—what was most significant—refused to pay taxes.

Even so, the Egyptian yoke was not really heavy. The pharaoh would send a negotiator or ambassador to act on his behalf. That person would stay in the prince's capital city and conduct an investigation of the financial situation and external politics. He was content to receive the annual tax from the prince, and otherwise gave him complete discretion in his actions—except that he was not to kill the ambassador.

However, those princes and kings would go beyond the pharaoh's requirement when the Egyptian ruler was strong, but much less when he was weak or his kingdom was in turmoil. When they tolerated this relatively light yoke, they were far from proud, and, when they rejected it, they were hardly heroic. They behaved like slaves, lifting their voices to the ill-fated pharaoh and kneeling humbly before the pharaoh's might and power. Here is an example of their letters to the pharaoh, taken from the writings discovered at Tell Amarna:

> To my master, lord, and light, to the sun in the sky and the light of the earth,
>
> I am your servant and the dust under your feet, groom of your horses. Seven times I prostrate myself at my master's feet, seven times I lie down on my chest and back.
>
> I am but a dog to be trodden underfoot by my master.

They would sign their letters with "so and so, your slave" or "so and so, the king's dog."

None of them were ever titled *king* or *prince*. The title they used was *khazano*, meaning "ruler" or "governor."

Here is another letter from the governor of Beirut, named Amounira, a contemporary of the governor of Byblos, Reeb Addi:

> Through the number of prostrations and extensions on front and back, seven times, he says:
>
> When the command of my lord and sun reached me, his slave and dust beneath his feet, it said: "Go to help the supporters of my lord the king." I immediately obeyed his command. Here I am, joining my lord the king's friends with my horses, chariots, and entire wealth.

In another letter he mentions his war chariots and the friendly contacts between himself and Reeb Addi. But it seems that they did not last very long. Once Beirut had surrendered to Aziro the Hittite, they turned against Byblos, which was under siege by Aziro. They launched a raid on its fleet and captured it. Here was one Phoenician group making war on another, and the spoils all went to the foreigner in Egypt.

> All glory and honor to the pharaoh. I bow in prostration at my master's feet. Seven times I lie on my chest and back when the pharaoh is powerful and effective. When internal affairs in Egypt are disrupted and the pillars of monarchy are shaken, the throne and sword of the pharaoh are raised on high. The *khazano* of Kaddas declared himself *pharaoh*, and the *khazano* of Byblos would take over control.
>
> We have recited to you the words of Zakar Baal to the messenger Wenamun: "I am not your servant, nor the servant of the one who sent you. My father never paid taxes to the Lord of Egypt, nor shall I."

I wonder, would he have dared say that if the lord of Egypt had been Thutmose III or Ramses II?

Under the Yokes of East and West

UNTIL THE END of the previous century, historians were citing Herodotus, known as "the father of history," concerning information regarding the ancients and justified his evidence by reference to the Torah. Archeology has supported some of his statements but rejected others.

In Herodotus's historical account of peoples before the Greeks, there are things that modern archeology has not confirmed. For example, how is it possible for the revered "father of history" to know what we have learned today about Egyptian history? Five thousand years later, how are we supposed to know what people five thousand years ago did not know? On the surface it all seems amazing, but actually it is not.

Herodotus visited Egypt in the middle of the fifth century BCE. He stood aghast before the monuments that spoke of the culture, art, science, and civilization that the Egyptians had produced. However, at his time, historical knowledge—duly confirmed and established—was buried alongside the ashes of pharaoh's mummies in tombs like castles and pyramids like fortresses all over the place.

The same applies to accounts of people other than the Egyptians, people who, for the Greeks of that era, were "ancients." Herodotus peered through the gloom that enshrouded them and became aware of some aspects of that ancient past while missing others about which he could not speculate.

Herodotus specified the period during which the Phoenicians moved from the shores of the Persian Gulf—the end of the nineteenth century BCE in our historical reckoning; he was relying on their mention in the Homeric poems. The modern historian, assisted by archeologists, will now say that, in Snefru's reign—the end of the thirtieth century BCE, his fleet came to the Phoenician shores to get cedarwood. In that case, the Phoenicians were settled on those shores, which were called by their name in the thirtieth century BCE and earlier. Herodotus had no way of knowing about the Phoenician burials in Bahrain, some of which were unearthed by an archeologist at the end of the last century.

Archeology thus corrects history. I am not claiming that archeologists do not make mistakes, and yet stones, bricks, and parchment scrolls give us information about the ancients that is more reliable for all ages than orally transmitted material.

Here is a remarkable example of information transmitted orally. Herodotus, writing in the fifth century BCE, talks about the Phoenician emigration. The Roman historian Justinian took the information from him after 700 years, and, 1,600 years later, Rawlinson, Renan, and others followed suit. Other writers copied it too, and still do, basing their use of the information on these rigorous historians and meticulous scholars, etc. It is as though it were all mathematical truth, acknowledging neither doubt nor interpretation.

This writer is not claiming credit for challenging their erroneous transfer of information in the light of his more verifiable citation. The real credit belongs to those scholars and archeologists who, in the last half of the previous century, have made priceless discoveries in Assyria and Egypt.[1]

1. The key to the hieroglyphic language is the Rosetta (Rashid) Stone, discovered in 1799 by the French officer Pierre-Francois Bouchard, a member of Napoleon's army, near the city after which it is named. After the Battle of Alexandria (1801), the British got hold of the stone and took it to the British Museum. On the stone are written three languages: Hieroglyphic, Demotic (colloquial), and Greek. It was that feature that opened for the French scholars Champollion and Mariette the treasures of ancient Egyptian monuments and writings.

The key to the cuneiform language is the Behistun (Bisotun) Stone, still to be found at its site in the Persian mountains. The village of Behistun lies on the slope of Mount Sinjar near Kermanshah. Close to the village is a place that—with its rocks,

The reader has already read about the relations, sometimes friendly, sometimes not, between Phoenicia and Egypt during the reigns of the Pharaohs Snefru, Pepi, Sesostris, Thutmose, Akhenaten, and Ramses, all the way up to the time when the government was divided between Nesubanebded and Hor-hora, the high priest—in other words, until the eleventh century BCE.

Nesubanebded was a contemporary of the Assyrian king Tiglath Pileser, who was keen to conquer and expand his territories. He invaded Syria and reached its shores. Nesubanebded was worried that Tiglath Pileser would continue his march into Egypt, so he sent him some gifts to flatter and assuage him. The Assyrian monarch accepted the gifts and returned to his own country, happy with his victories and spoils.

To the best of our knowledge, Tiglath Pileser abandoned the idea of invasions, and this Assyrian abstinence lasted for a long time. History has clothed it in a garment of silence. We do not know anything about the situation until Shalmaneser II appears on the scene, 150 years after Nesubanebded had made his courteous gesture to Tiglath Pileser.

When Shalmaneser II marched his huge army out of Nineveh and had almost reached the Euphrates River, the rulers of the minor states to the west of the river confronted him—for the first time in their

---

river, and historical remains—resembles the Dog River in Lebanon. Carved into the rocks above the river are Sasanian, Arab, and Ashkani (Parthian) monuments. The most significant of them is one that the ancients, including Herodotus, assumed was of the famous Assyrian queen Semiramis. However, modern archeology has uncovered the truth and solved all its symbols and secrets. It is of King Darius and his conquests in both cuneiform and Persian that, in olden times, was called Ya-zand. The credit for the first study devoted to this monument and the first translations from it is due to the British ambassador to Persia, the renowned scholar Sir Henry Rawlinson, who visited the site and clambered up the rocks to make a copy of the monument. He immediately set about translating it, and published part of it in 1843. The French scholar Doctor Hubert translated the rest with the help of his British colleague's translation. The two translations are the key that unlocked the cuneiform language and provided the basis for the study of Assyrian and Babylonian knowledge.

history. The pharaoh of the time decided to help those states (partly in order to protect his own kingdom) in their alliance against the Assyrian invader. But neither the help nor the alliance were of any use.

The Assyrian returned to his homeland, content, victorious, and loaded with booty. Assyria continued its aspirations toward the kingdoms to the west of the Euphrates and their wealth. Tiglath Pileser III continued the invasions and reached the borders of Egypt.

Egypt had been trying to fortify the minor states against Assyria, but their efforts were only successful in Palestine, where the Hebrews rebelled against Assyrian suzerainty. Sennacherib arrived to punish the rebels, and established his authority over the entire coastal region, except for Tyre. He then marched to Ashkelon, where he encountered a mixed army of Egyptians and Palestinians. Having defeated them, he added Palestine to Syria and Phoenicia, except for Jerusalem. The sheer heroism of the inhabitants of Tyre kept him away from the city, and the plague that afflicted his army was the factor that prevented him from taking Jerusalem.

Meanwhile, Babylon had rebelled against Nineveh, so Sennacherib had to hurry back to his country to quell the revolt. These disturbances in Mesopotamia aroused the residual strength in the Nile Valley. Pharaoh Taharqa undertook to recover a lost period in Egyptian history and a prestige that had disappeared. He joined with the king of Tyre against Esarhaddon, Sennacherib's successor. In his first raid, the Assyrian king retreated in defeat, but he tried again in the following year, 670 BCE.

The Assyrian king's primary goal was Tyre, and this time resistance was useless. The king captured it, and then continued his march into Egypt. At the Battle of the Delta, the Egyptians were defeated, and Taharqa fled to the south. The Assyrian monarch was content with the victory and the spoils he had won. He returned to his homeland, but on the way stopped by the Dog River in order to brag to those who had conquered before him. He recorded his name and exploits on a stone near the monument to Ramses II. So, amid those rocks overlooking that modest river valley, conquerors boast and brag.

It is almost as though Taharqa knew what was carved on that rock—or, from within the realms of the unseen, he had a vision of that Assyrian bragging in front of Ramses II's spirit. He became as angry as a pharaoh could be, decided to reorganize his rebellious forces, and lead them in a second revolt against Assyrian suzerainty. Ashurbanipal, the son of Esarhaddon, arrived to punish the rebellion, and, once again, Taharqa fled the battlefield. They pursued him as far as Thebes, but did not catch him.

Once again, the Assyrian monarch returned to his homeland, victorious and loaded with spoils. The Egyptians rebelled yet again under Taharqa's leadership, along with the crafty Necho, at the time ruler of one of those states. Ashurbanipal launched his final attack on the Egyptians in 661 BCE. He slaughtered them and drove them away, then pursued their stragglers and pharaoh to Thebes. He still did not manage to capture their elusive pharaoh, who sought refuge in the desert and died there.

Ashurbanipal and his rampaging army entered Thebes and put an end to its long, glorious history through pillage, imprisonment, and destruction.

The rulers of the minor states—Phoenicia, Judah, Syria, and others, twenty rulers in all—now came to offer their obeisance to the "conqueror of kingdoms and victor over kings." They offered him obeisance, and all kissed the foot of the Assyrian monarch.

Assyrian control—which was total—lasted for about 150 years (870–727 BCE), a period that was followed by 100 years of disruption and discord.

The Assyrian taxes that were imposed were awful. They came in two parts. The first involved money: gold, silver, and bronze paid annually. The second involved anything sewn, manufactured, or crafted—clothes made of wool, cotton, or silk; weapons, wood, dyes; birds, fish, buffalo hides; precious stones, amulets; and as many Phoenician girls, maids, and concubines as the Assyrian kings wanted. In addition, they had the right to send men to Lebanon to cut as much cedarwood as they wanted.

So, here are the Phoenicians in their festival garb, shouting paeans of praise because barbarian invaders from the north have attacked Assyria with a huge army, roamed the countryside, and rocked the very foundations of the kingdom. Nineveh's power is now weakened, both within and without.

Now the Phoenician cities rebel, throwing off their yoke and proclaiming independence.

This independence lasted for fifty-five years (630–575 BCE), during which Phoenicia regains its liberty, along with some of its florescence and luxury.

What a lousy writer I am! Enthusiasm has sharpened my quill and has made me too hasty in talking about liberty and independence. I need to make some adjustments. In the opinion of historians, that independence was of limited validity, or what today we would call "partial administrative independence."

In those days the Phoenicians would swing between Babylon and Egypt, drawing strength from one of the two until such time as it grew weak, at which point they would transfer their allegiance to the other. Sennacherib once told a delegation, "Anyone who relies on a weak stick will have it break in his hand, and it will pierce his palm."

A brilliant maxim, which they never hesitated about borrowing. They used to swing one way or the other and be pliable according to the balance of power and progress between the Euphrates Valley and the Nile Valley. For Nebuchadnezzar, they were all milk and honey, and for the pharaoh bitter herbs and gall. The next day, the signs would change, in which case they would bring honey to the Egyptian throne and gall to the Babylonian.

Now here is a really serious pharaoh, Necho (609–593 BCE), who set about restoring Egypt's prestige in the Eastern regions. He built a pair of combat stations—one on the Mediterranean coast, the other on the Red Sea. He launched an attack in the name of the Egyptian deities and captured Gaza and Ashkelon—not only that, but Palestine and all the coastal cities (a relic was found in Sidon with a hieroglyphic inscription about Pharaoh Necho's victory).

The power of Assyria had now transferred to Babylon. The king dispatched his son, Nebuchadnezzar, to confront the pharaoh. The two armies met in Syria near Carchemish. The Egyptians were defeated in the battle (605 BCE), but it was not decisive. Nebuchadnezzar heard that his father had died and was forced to return to Babylon to assume the throne.

Phoenicia was now confused and in a real quandary: they did not know to which side to send the honey and to which the gall.

However, Nebuchadnezzar came back to help solve the problem. He returned to complete the task he had started the year before. Entering the region as a conqueror, he marched all the way to Tyre, the defiant city and capital of the rebels! He set about besieging the city, a siege that lasted, so historians tell us, for thirteen years. It came to an end when the bride of Phoenician cites surrendered. With that, Phoenician power waned everywhere, and the partial independence that they had enjoyed was now sealed by the Babylonian yoke. Then Egypt made its move, and Apries (Wahibre Haaibre), Necho's grandson, renewed the attacks on that yoke. His fleet attacked some coastal cities, and his army captured Tyre, which was weakened and in ruins because of the prolonged siege. Other cities also surrendered to him.

Phoenicia lies "between the devil and the deep blue sea," as the English expression has it, or "between two hammers" as the Lebanese put it. Woe on both of you, Egypt and Babylon! What is the winged sun, and the winged lion? Fire for one and den for the other, they are both the same—the prey cannot tell the difference.

So, here we see the roaring lion, pouncing for the third time, with the armies of the winged sun beneath the walls of Jerusalem. And here are the Phoenicians, their vessels of honey and gall smashed to pieces, returning to Melqart, Ishtar, and Tammuz, begging for help and mercy.

Nebuchadnezzar besieged Jerusalem, and the Egyptian armies were not able to break the siege. The prophecy of the young Solomon, who had warned the Hebrews not to weep over Egypt, now came to pass. Jerusalem fell, and the Hebrews were crushed. Nebuchadnezzar now marched on into Egypt and entered it as a conqueror.

The Phoenicians started making flasks again that predicted destiny, filled them with honey, and gave them to the Babylonian monarch, the holder of the new yoke that they tolerated for thirty years.

He who rules by the yoke will in turn be ruled by it, even thirty years later.

Babylon was attacked by an enemy from the East (539 BCE): Cyrus, the Persian king. He massacred the people, humiliated King Nabonidus, and placed the Aryan yoke on the necks of the Semitic Chaldeans.

How did their Semitic brothers in Phoenicia react? Did their necks reject what the Babylonians—with the sturdiest and thickest necks of all—had accepted? For Phoenicia, what was the difference between one yoke and another, since they were by now inured to taking yokes off and putting them on, just as you take off a threadbare coat and put on a new one? Cambyses, Cyrus's successor, reinforced the yoke and made it firm and solid. He also made the people wearing it compliant and eager to work.

Now Egypt is our target, and we need ships.

The Phoenicians built Cambyses a fleet, loaded it with fighting men, and made use of their help to conquer Egypt. Persian rule now expanded to include Egypt (525 BCE).

The entire world was now Persian. If Cambyses was leading the army, then one victory would follow another, and indeed exceed the previous one. Come on now, to the west is a wonderful, rich country called Carthage. Each victory is followed by another, so come on!

O majestic Lord, every operation has its ending. O possessor of power and glory, patience has justifiable limits.

Those Phoenicians are amazing. This time, they were not the most compliant of peoples; they were not compliant at all.

"We do not fight our own people," they told the Persian monarch, "nor do we fight our own brothers here."

History records this display of national pride. Cambyses respected it and praised those who declared it. He changed his plans and returned to his homeland.

It is worth noting at this point that the Persian yoke over the Phoenicians was lighter than the one over the Assyrians and Babylonians. It was attached to Syria under a single governorship and administrative organization. Internal independence was guaranteed, and the taxes levied were halved—175 talents, or about £42,000 sterling.

If we take into consideration the historian Rawlinson's estimate regarding the distribution of those taxes, we can learn the approximate number of inhabitants of Phoenicia at the time. The person being taxed would pay the equivalent of one and a third shillings; every twelve people would pay £1. Thus, the total value, £42,000, would be paid by five hundred thousand taxpayers. Add to that total a factor of three for women and male children who were still minors, and the grand total is two million people.

Phoenicia's partial independence was tied to these conditions: the Phoenician monarchs were not allowed to declare war on any foreign state, nor were they allowed to sign any political agreements with them. In addition to the taxes, they had to offer their share of vessels to the Persian fleet, a share that was bigger than for other states because they were so skilled at building ships.

Within these limits things resembled the kind of modern treaties signed between the governors of the nine protectorates in the Arabian Peninsula and Britain, the one essential difference being that the sultans and sheikhs of those protectorates do not pay taxes; to the contrary, they are entitled to annual contributions in silver and gold from the British government in compensation for an agreement on their part to remain separate and not form alliances against Britain.

At this time in the past, the Persian government was more just and prudent than the British government is today. The Persians did not consider the various Phoenician kingdoms to be separate from each other or alien to each other. They had no right to negotiate or form any kind of political understandings or agreements, as is the case today with the nine protectorates. Indeed, the Persians united the Phoenician kingdoms with Syria. It was a model for unity and solidarity, and so they emulated it.

This narrative is confirmed by the foundation of the Lebanese city of Tripoli. Representatives of the three kingdoms—Tyre, Sidon, and Arwad—met at the spot where the port is today in order to discuss their mutual interests. The representatives of each kingdom stayed in their own place, and the name Tripoli (meaning "three cities") was applied to them.[2]

Tripoli was the capital city of the three kingdoms and seat of their Parliament or of the Phoenician alliance, the first of its kind in Phoenician history. The virtue or primary virtue of the establishment of this institution lies in the complete internal independence enjoyed by the Phoenician kingdoms during the Persian era.

The Persians were followed by Alexander of Macedon, the conquering invader. He arrived, eager to fight the Persians so that he could fulfill a dream that he had, whether awake or drunk: to gain control of the whole world and write the history of nations.

When he reached north Syria, the Phoenicians remained impartial and simply observed. They remained loyal to Persia and did not declare Alexander an enemy. They simply maintained their usual stance in such conflicts, waiting for the result so that they could profit from it and only submitting to more powerful forces.

2. There were three ancient villages, mentioned by the renowned scholar Breasted in his account of the Syrian campaign of Thutmose III in the first half of the fifteenth century BCE. The villages were called Yinwam, Nogus, and Hernekiro. They were not founded in the seventh century BCE, as the *Encyclopaedia Britannica* states, but rather seven or eight centuries later. It is likely that the villages were known by those names when the Phoenicians held their meeting, each group residing in one of the villages. To commemorate the foundation of the threefold alliance, they used a single name: Tripoli.

The reader may ask how it was that a Phoenician town was called by a Greek name. While the histories do not justify any speculation, we can suggest that the name came to be applied during the Seleucid period that followed that of the Persians. It was used by the Greeks or Hellenistic peoples at that time, following the tradition relating to the threefold alliance that was held at the location of the three villages. Mahrifa Durbali may be the ancient name for Tripoli, as mentioned in the correspondence found at Tell Amarna.

After the Battle of Issus and the flight of King Darius, they learned who the strong conqueror was. They also discovered that Alexander did not intend to pursue the defeated Persians and continue his conquests in Asia before he had control of Syria, Egypt, and the Western shores. Alexander sent one of his generals to Damascus to occupy it while he himself marched to Phoenician cities. Arwad was the first to surrender to him, then Byblos, then Sidon.

Like the other cities, Tyre sent messengers to welcome the Macedonian conqueror and present gifts to him. Alexander welcomed them and treated them to a somewhat suspicious hospitality, since he indicated his desire to visit the temple of the god Melqart.

"Was Alexander going to visit the temple on his own?"

"Would the mighty conqueror's stirrups move if not surrounded by his victorious army?"

The people of Tyre were afraid that such piety might demand a martial procession, when they had specifically prevented the Persian soldiers from entering the city. It is thus not surprising that they rejected Alexander's request, nor that he displayed a conqueror's anger. He issued warnings and threats, but Tyre still refused and stood firm. Alexander then besieged the city.

Do people who have eaten colocynth and drunk gall several times fear siege and battle? People who had often resisted invaders, withstood sieges, and, more than once, ennobled the Phoenician name with their resolute struggle . . .

Alexander started filling in the sea between the two cities, the land one and the nearby island, but the people of Tyre defended their city gloriously, duly recorded by history as a splendid and incredible act of defiance.

They would have emerged as victors and humiliators of the Macedonian tyrant, had it not been for the fleet, which, as we have noted earlier, was provided for him by the kings of Cyprus and Byblos.

Tyre fell after a siege lasting seven months. Alexander entered the city after destroying most of it and killing thousands of its people. He entered the city as an avenger, eager to humiliate and destroy. Glory mourned the bride of Phoenician cities, and Ezekiel, the prophet of Israel, elegized it:[3]

> And thou, O son of Adam, lift up an elegy for Tyre.
> City residing by the edge of the sea, merchant to people, your builders perfected your beauty.
> Your boards are fir trees from Senbir.
> Your masts are of Lebanese cedar,
> Your oars from oaks of Bashan.
> Your seats are of boxwood from the isle of Kittim, inlaid with ivory.
> Your sail is made of embroidered linen from Egypt,
> Your cover from azure and purple.
> Your sailors are from Sidon and Arwad,
> Your pilots, O Tyre, are your sages,
> Your caulkers old men from Byblos.
> All the ships of the sea and its sailors were with you, trading in your merchandise.
> Persia, Lydia, and Put were in your army, your men of war . . .
> Heroes were in your towers . . .
> They hung their shields on your walls.
> Merchants from Tarshish supported your markets with silver, iron, tin, and lead.
> The sons of Dedan, Aram, and the islands traded in your markets with dyes, pearls, and emeralds.
> Judah and the people of Israel traded in your market with wheat from Minnith, sweetmeats, honey, oil, and balm. Damascus traded with you, thanks to the abundance of your crafts, wine from Helbon, and white wool.
> Vedan and Javan (Greece) offered yarn in your markets.
> Arabs and rulers of Kedar traded with you in lambs, rams, and equipment.

3. Translator's note: Ezekiel 27:2. While there are a large number of translated versions of Ezekiel's text into English, I have here adhered closely to the extracts from the Arabic translation of the Bible that Al-Rihani has selected.

> Merchants from Sheba, Canneh, Aden, Haran, Chalmad, and Assyria traded with you . . .
>
> Your wealth, your markets, your goods, your sailors, your pilots, your caulkers, your traders, all your warriors, everyone in your community, will fall into the sea on the day when you are overthrown . . .
>
> Merchants among the peoples will belittle you,
> You will be terrified.
> And you will not be distant forever.

During the Hellenistic era, Phoenician cities were easy prey for two Greek states: Syria and Egypt. More than once, they were shifted from Ptolemaic control to Seleucid. Then the kings of Antioch stabilized the situation, and Greek culture spread among the people of the Phoenician cities. That continued until the end of the Seleucid period and the beginnings of the Roman conquest in the first century BCE.

I do not know what Alexander would have done if he had lived long enough to rule these regions for himself. The policy of his successors put an end to the feeling of nationalism among all the peoples they overcame.

"Are you Phoenician?"

"Yes, with the blessing of Melqart and Ishtar, I'm Phoenician."

"Ishtar and Melqart, in the Hellenistic era, were their Phoenician qualities preserved? You Phoenician, aren't your habits, your traditions, and your culture, all Greek?"

Then came the Assyrians from the West—the Romans—and put an end to whatever was left of Phoenicia on those ancient shores.

The historian Rawlinson notes: "Phoenicia was crushed under the iron boots of the Romans. Once again, it was unknown, whether politically or socially. It was simply a geographical location, no more."

Phoenician Literature

ADVOCATES OF PHOENICIA among European scholars state that the Phoenicians had an enjoyable literary tradition, the features of which have been studied; and that alien cultures, prime among them Greek and Roman, overwhelmed it and robbed it of its unique trends. The part that was left was distorted by the translation process.

Lebanese advocates state that the Phoenicians did truly outstanding work in literature, poetry, and natural and religious sciences. Lucian was one of their great authors, Thales a major scientist, and Zeno a philosopher who adorned humanity's way of thinking for all time.

These advocates display a deep-seated fervor and far-reaching imagination. They are not satisfied to focus only on geniuses in literature and the sciences, but extend their fervor to music as well—our Lebanese ancestors, the Phoenicians, they state, deserve the credit for devising the musical alphabet and spreading the first large organs in the West in accordance with technical criteria.

What love can achieve, by God, and what the imagination can create! I have seen Sumerian, Assyrian, Babylonian, and Egyptian musical instruments, but I have never set eyes on a Phoenician instrument or rebec, whether in the Beirut Museum, the British Museum, or the Louvre (in Paris). Even so, I am not going to dispute the statement of the distinguished "Phoenician" musician, whom I have just cited.

To those who sail knowledge's seas, literature scholars who want to snatch Lucian, Thales, and Zeno from their own country, take them in Phoenician ships to Byblos, Beirut and Tyre, and envelop them in a cordon of popular nationalism inside their museums, to such people

I now offer information about them written by European scholars in their respected source works:

Lucian: Born in the capital city of the province of Magog (Samosata) on the western bank of the Euphrates River (195–125 BCE), Lucian practiced law in Antioch, the Seleucid capital, and then started writing. He made his way through Asia Minor, Greece, and Italy, and spent twenty years in Athens. Toward the end of his life, he took a post in the Egyptian government. All his works were written in Greek. In his times, the entire Syrian region was under Seleucid control, and the Greeks formed a large segment of the population. *Larousse* describes Lucian as a Greek writer born in Samosata.

Thales: Born in Miletus on the shore of the Ionian Sea near the island of Kos to two Greek parents, Akramios and Cleopauline. Some people believe that he was of Phoenician origins. The *Encyclopaedia Britannica* chooses to transfer him, stating, "But he is Greek, not Phoenician." Thales visited Egypt and was exposed for the first time to engineering. Hieronymus of Rhodes has this to say: "Thales never studied with any scholars, apart from the things he borrowed from Egyptian priests during his stay there." This scholar composed all his writings in Greek. He was considered one of the seven sages of Greece.[1]

1. In his book *La resurrection d'Homere* (253), Victor Berard notes that Hieronymus says that "Thales, the first Greek philosopher, was descended from a Phoenician family that emigrated to Asia Minor; not only that, but from those Cadmusian families (linked to the name Cadmus) with a lofty reputation among Greeks in Asia."

On page 255, he says, "The Cadmusians boasted about their Phoenician ancestry, indeed their lofty divine ancestry. They claimed to be its descendants and that their language was similarly divine, as the poet asserts."

Larousse and the *Encyclopaedia Britannica* have this to say: Cadmus, son of Agenor, (not Phoenix), king of Phoenicia and brother of Europa. Zeus, the god of all gods, lusted after her; turning himself into a white bull, he carried her off on his back and took her to his own country. Cadmus started searching for her and was advised by a priest in Greece to suspend his search. "On your way you will encounter a cow," he told Cadmus. "Follow it to its sleeping place. Build a city there." He found the cow and followed it. It went to Boethia and lay down to sleep. That is where Cadmus

Zeno: Here is what *Larousse* has to tell us: Born in Citium, he was a Greek philosopher and founder of Stoicism.

European advocates for Phoenicia, who are rigorous scholars—including Berard, Myer, and Rawlinson, do not say that Lucian, Thales, and Zeno were Phoenicians, but they do state that the Phoenicians had a literary influence, most of which has been erased by the ravages of time. They note that one of the cities inhabited by the Phoenicians before the Hebrews came to Palestine was called Sefer Village (*sefer* meaning "book") because people loved knowledge so much, and it produced a large number of authors. The scholars pointed out that many Phoenician merchants were also sages and philosophers, and that the kings of Numidia were steeped in Phoenician culture, acquiring libraries with a large number of Phoenician works in them.

Where is all that written material? None of it has come down to us, and unfortunately only three names of Phoenician authors have reached us from the Greeks: Hipsicratus, Theodotus, and Mochus. A historical work by Mochus on creation was translated into Greek, but time has left no trace of the translation, nor the original. That history, like its author and others, is now merely a memory repeated in marginalia or footnotes.

---

built the city of Thebes. He sent his companions to collect water from a nearby spring. They were attacked and killed by a dragon. Cadmus slew the dragon, and, responding to a sign from the goddess Minerva, planted its teeth in the ground. Rugged warriors emerged, and he plotted to kill them. He did indeed kill all but five of them. Cadmus is credited with the invention of writing and introducing the alphabet to Greece (1600 BCE). He married Hermione, the daughter of the god Ares and the goddess Aphrodite. They had four sons, but their married life was fraught with disasters. Before their deaths, they were transformed into snakes. End of article.

So, if Thales, who lived in the sixth century BCE, was descended from Cadmus, brother (not son) of Phoenix, son of "legends," who lived in the seventeenth century BCE, is it possible for the connection to be one lasting 1,100 years? Which of our illustrious families today—be they nobles or monarchs—can trace their origins back 1,000 years?

The Cadmusians, the gods, the legends—is it even feasible to regard them as "real history" today?

However, there are some fragments, said to be of Phoenician origin, discovered by researchers in Greek writings by Calodius, Dayus, Hieronymus, and others, but scholars disagree about them: a group, including Ewald and Baron Bunsen, say that they are Phoenician in origin, while others, including Dodwell and Van Dael, reject the idea.

There remains the one solitary work of Phoenician literature, which has been mentioned and cited in modern books on history, by which I mean the history of Sanchuniathon. I mentioned earlier Hipsicratus, one of three names that have come down to us without their writings. Some scholars think that he and Sanchuniathon are the same person. Both words—in Greek and Phoenician—are a single epithet to describe this famous author. It means "the sky and its throne." It is as though you were saying, "So-and-so on his lofty throne," or "So-and-so nicknamed the father of nobility."

Before I offer the reader an example of the literature of "the lofty one on his throne"—Hipsicratus Sanchuniathon—I need to point out that, in the Maghreb, there was another author about whom and about whose work there is no doubt. He was a Carthaginian and a famous general, named Mago. His book about agriculture is apparently a major work on the subject in multiple parts.[2] (Cassius) Dionysus translated it into Greek, and (Decimus Junius) Silanus, on orders from the Roman Senate, translated it into Latin.

Also in the Maghreb there was the first explorer-seaman, Hanno (the Navigator) of Carthage. He wrote an account of his ocean journey along the west coast of Africa in a few short pages, some of which you will be able to read in Arabic in another chapter of this book—God willing.

Now I go back to "the lofty one on his throne," Sanchuniathon. I note that the first person to write about him and translate some of his history from Phoenician to Greek was a man who lived in Byblos

2. In the book, including translations from it, (Isaac Preston) Cory's *Ancient Fragments* (1826), it states that the great general Mago composed twenty-eight books on agriculture (books, chapters, notebooks?—God alone knows).

in the first century CE, about one thousand years after Sanchuniathon himself—namely, Philo, the pagan from Byblos. This Greco-Phoenician writer may actually have translated all of Sanchuniathon's history. Most of the translation has been lost, and we only have a small fraction of it.

Part of it was translated into Latin by Eusebius (264–338 CE), the Christian Roman writer known for his learning and his attacks on all kinds of paganism—Latin, Greek, and Phoenician.

Philo may have been committed to the Greek side and Eusebius more to the Christian, but they both translated aspects of pagan Phoenicia that have no literary or historical value. They have provided us with a paltry blend of Greek and Phoenician myths current in the time of Philo, whose life straddled the Greek and Roman eras. Here are some examples taken from the English translation:

> In the beginning there was a dark, blustery wind, its gust blowing everywhere. After a period of time, the wind was enamored of the spirit of life within it, and they were joined in love. From their union there grew a gelatinous substance or a muddy liquid. And from that muddy liquid the germ of life was born. The world was born.

From the outset there was always jealousy in love and misery in marriage. In his Book of Genesis, the Phoenician author says:

> At the time a man was born, named Elion (the lofty)
> And a woman named Ruth. They dwelt together near Mount Jbeil.
> They had a son named Atuktun, later named Uranus (the sky),
> And he had a sister named Gaia (the earth).
> When Uranus inherited his father's kingdom, he married
> His sister, Gaia, and they had four sons:
> Chronos, Petulus, Dagon,[3] and Atlas.[4]
> Uranus had many children by his other wives.
> His wife, Gaia, became very jealous and felt vengeful against him.
> The two quarreled and separated.

3. Dagon (a whale) is a Palestinian god.
4. Atlas is an ancient Greek god.

In spite of that, Uranus would occasionally visit her,
And then leave. He tried to kill the four sons he had had with her,
But he did not succeed. Gaia sought help from her neighbors
Against her tyrannical husband. Chronos placed himself between
them,
Avenging his mother against his father.
A battle occurred between father and son and their adherents.
Chronos the son defeated Uranus the father.
He expelled his father from the kingdom and took over his throne.
Thereafter, Chronos built a wall around his house.
He founded the first Phoenician city, and called it Jbeil (Byblos).

It seems that, from time to time, Uranus would try the same routine against his son who had snatched his kingdom from him. He would be defeated and flee for his life. But, as the saying has it, "The jar does not always stay intact."

In the thirty-second year of Chronos's era,
Uranus launched a savage attack on his son,
But the son set a trap for his father and captured him.
He cut off his organ close to a bubbling river.
The blood flowed out of his reproductive members
Into the river, which turned red.
His soul departed his body there, and the river is sanctified in his
memory.

Chronos became god of the Phoenicians, the one god El. His guise developed in myths that were either created or borrowed. Sanchuniathon, translated by Philo, says:

Chronos had eight eyes, four in front and four behind.
He had four huge wings. He could see while asleep,
And sleep with his eyes open. He flew while seated,
And sat while flying . . .

Just like us today. We sit in an airplane and fly while seated. With regard to eyes, we Lebanese have more of them than did Chronos, god of the Phoenicians. We have imagination, dreams, and fancies—101 eyes. We can see paradise while sleeping; we can be asleep as we walk toward the abyss!

Now it is enough for us to intrude into the table of Philo, the Phoenician! He has the right to speak now. That right resides in cooking. He cooks whatever dish he likes, culled from Greek, Phoenician, Palestinian, and Assyrian myths, and offers them in cool hues in the name of the "the lofty one on his throne," Sanchuniathon the Phoenician:

> At that time two brothers were born, Tikonitus and Genus. They invented brickmaking by mixing chaff with clay. Then they built roofs for houses. Among their progeny were Agros and Agroros. They excelled in inventions and were considered gods. Agroros was the greater of the two gods. The Phoenicians built him a temple, which was carried from place to place by a pair of oxen.
>
> Among the inventions of these two gods was that they gave houses doors with locks and yards in front. Among their progeny are those who till the land, hunt wild dogs, and fish for whales.
>
> From the offspring of farmers and hunters were born Amytus and Mammus, who taught people to raise cattle. Amytus fathered Maysur and Sadek, who both discovered salt. Maysur fathered Thoth, who invented the letters of writing. Among Sadek's descendants are those who invented ships and discovered herbal cures. They taught people the science of spells.

The Phoenicians sanctified the fruits of the earth; they deified them and ate them. One of their sages said, "Life's foundation is the fruits of trees."

In times of war they would raise their hands to the sun, which they had called Baal Shamin (goddess of the sky), and shower her with prayers.

They used to offer child sacrifices to El, the only god, as recorded by both Philo and Eusebius:

Philo says:

> Among the customs of the ancients was that, in times of trouble, they would offer children as sacrifices to the gods, as a way of placating them and begging for mercy. A single disaster does not destroy everybody. King Crotus (Jupiter), who became a god after his death and who descended in a chariot named after him when he was a king on earth, gave birth to a daughter named Anoubarit and a boy named Baoud (the only one). Later he offered the boy as a sacrifice to the gods. When dangers enveloped the country, he used to decorate the temple, dress his son in a king's robes, and offer him as a sacrifice to the gods.

Here now are some details from Eusebius:

> This secret sacrifice, which was common among the Phoenicians, had two conditions: It had to be offered by one of the country's rulers, and the sacrificial victim had to be an only child. From the practice there developed the religious belief in redemption. One of their traditions was that the god El would produce a son named "the only one," born with divine blessings and without stain, to be offered as a sacrifice for his father, as an atonement for the sins of humanity and a protection against injustices and disasters, so that such miseries would not ravage the world, and would not destroy everyone.

Even so, the Phoenician priests would accept the children of ordinary people as sacrifices and compromise on the second condition. The child was not always an only child. What had been a secret ritual was now a public one. This belief in redemption and salvation seems to be Phoenician and Semitic in origin:

> Abraham intended to offer his son, Isaac, as a sacrifice to God.
>
> God sent his only son as a sacrifice and atonement for the world.

Just like the concept of sacrifice is that of resurrection, both spirit and body. The Phoenicians believed in it and made preparations for it. They would provide provisions for that day, the Day of Resurrection, when the kings would rise from their graves in kingly garments—with jewels and weapons, and taking with them the money they needed in silver and gold.

All that would be buried in their carefully guarded tombs. Fearing that those tombs might be opened and their treasures stolen, they inscribed threatening words of warning on their sarcophagi, including the final immortal falsehood: "In my grave is neither money nor treasure."

I will conclude this section with two examples of these inscriptions:

> I am Tabnit, priest of Ashtarut and king of Sidon. I say: "Do not open my tomb and do not disturb me. There is no treasure, gold, or silver inside it. Whoever opens my tomb will never prosper in life, nor find peace in his grave."

Archeologists have opened the tomb three thousand years later. In it they have found lots of gold and silver, trinkets, silver, gold, and bronze jewelry.

After the introduction on the sarcophagus of Eshmounazar, king of the twin cities of Sidon, there is the following:

> I have built this tomb for myself. It contains no treasure, no gold, and no silver. Do not open it, do not move my grave, do not disturb me, and do not bury anyone over me. Anyone who opens the tomb, disturbs me, or moves my grave will have no grave for himself and will remain childless in the lower world . . .
>
> Perhaps in the future, the gods of kings will give us Jaffa and the fertile land on the Plain of Sharon. It will be linked to our lands and remain subject to the twin cities of Sidon forever.

The king of the twin cities of Sidon was ambitious indeed.

Handicrafts and Inventions

IN THIS CHAPTER I will be presenting for you Phoenician works, crafts, and arts, pieces about which there can be no doubt or denial, nor any guesswork and conjecture. "These are our remains, which give evidence of us."

Here then is the Phoenician using his hands in the garden of life, his feet firmly planted in history, and his works revealed in what survives of his monuments. On display are the products of the weaver, the craftsman, the artist, the mason, the maker of trinkets, figurines, and games.

It is a display of art, not the artist. Reality is totally encapsulated in the work itself. You neither see nor know the person who crafted it; there is no personality hidden there, no misleading ego, no one expecting fame, glory, or money. The value of everything is intrinsic to it, stripped of all ephemeral human factors. No worker, craftsman, or artist; they are all indentured servants, exploited by the gods.

This situation demands a certain amount of reflection and thought. Today's artists, eager for fame and asking for money, do injury to genius because of the ephemeral materialistic urges that impact their humanity. They lead us to dislike the arts because their very egotism engenders rivalries and disputes between artists. That is one side of the reality. The other is that the Beaux Arts are not flourishing and expanding at the rate demanded by the spirit of our current era. They have thus been stripped of renowned and well-known human personalities.

Is there a third side to this reality, a front illumined by the other two? Here's to those people who excel in criticism, aesthetics, and good judgment. They can separate the work of art from the artist's personality and look at what has been crafted, rather than the person who crafted it! And here's to the artist who manages to combine modern creativity with that ancient sense of humility!

One source of wonder regarding the anonymous Phoenician artists is their love for perfection on everything they did, a quest for beauty in all its aspects, coupled with a certain impudence in the byways of art and a sarcastic trait in all its heights and depths.

Here I will stop and describe for you artistic statues crafted in stone, pottery, silver, gold, and bronze—most of them small. In my opinion, the most important one are those that depict animals; all the artistic qualities of craft, shape, and meaning are assembled in them. They show a subtlety of vision and craftsmanship and a delicacy of sense and taste in plenty.

You will already be aware that such delicacy of sense and taste cannot happen if the subject is unknown or is treated with indifference. Phoenicians loved animals and knew their characteristics. Whence come these statuettes in their different kinds—lions, tigers, apes, gazelles, horse, oxen, sheep, rabbits, dogs, foxes, snakes, and eagles—all of them works that confirm the Phoenicians' ability to imagine and portray in their carved creations.

Take the example of the seahorse in a variety of forms: standing, walking, lying down; quiet, agitated, screaming, carrying other statues on his back and expressing the artist's skill with his accurate and penetrating looks.

Then stop by the apes, happily laughing with their different shapes, movements, and intentions. Here is a musical ape carrying a guitar and staring off into the world of imagination and beauty.

Here too is the subject of the famous Arabic ode: "Fatima, if only you had espied on the floor of a valley . . ."[1]

1. Translator's note: The opening line of an ode by the *Su'look* (brigand) pre-Islamic poet Bishr ibn Awaana al-Abdi. I thank my colleague Huda Fakhreddine for this reference.

An old, old topic, going back to the Stone Age, when humans were companions and foes of the lion, inhabiting the same forest and chasing the same prey, clashing, fighting, and maiming each other. This particular Phoenician turn at the subject manages to show you the primeval conflict between humans and animals, and the ongoing poetic clash between human beings and lions.

Here now are turtles, frogs, rabbits, and gazelles, with all of which the Phoenicians were devoted companions, observing their movements and feeling great fondness toward them. But for that, they could not have been represented with such amazing accuracy.

The human statuary is less picturesque than that of animals, but still its equal in conception. It seems that Phoenician women, like their Arab counterparts, would hide their bodies in loose-fitting summer clothing. As a result, those Semitic traditions regarding dress prevented the artist from studying the naked body. Thus, statues of naked women are rare among works of art, and the few that exist are ugly, disgusting, and trivial.

However, when it comes to Phoenician ribaldry and sarcasm—especially in men's statuary—we can find some compensation for their lack of art and creativity. They show us how the life of the ancients differed from our own in the topics that manage to provoke a smiling tear or hearty laugh through rare examples of art and wonderful pages from literature.

Here is an example to arrest and inspire ribald folks, be they writers or artists in other high cultures, I mean Abou Kirsh.[2] He is a wit and popular philosopher, good fun, someone portrayed by the Chinese artist as laughing at life and scoffing at the pounds of fat clinging to his bones, which stop him from seeing his own footsteps and shadow.

Here is the Phoenician Abou Kirsh, statues in stone, bronze, and faience, in a variety of guises—eating, drinking, walking, hurrying,

2. Translator's note: the word *kirsh* means "stomach, belly." In Egypt, men with a bulging middle are said to have *kirsh al-bashawaat* (Pasha's belly).

carrying on his shoulders the lamb of life, the burden of life, a year-old sheep, like Atlas carrying the globe.

There is a group of men in weird, funny postures, strutting and fighting. Where, oh where are you, son of Spain, ribald artist, where do you stand, Goya, with regard to this Phoenician artist who preceded you in your portraits of rigid backs and frowning faces?

The major illustration of this combination of art and sarcasm is the naked Phoenician man, with a dagger under his arm, a sword in his right hand, and a spear in his left. And yet, while he still refuses to fight and detests wars, he is armed! He could well be calling for peace in our times.

In our tour we have now reached the jewelry exhibit, with all types of jewels, trinkets, vessels, and amulets crafted from precious metals and valuable stones. They show us what skill and taste those Phoenicians had in making jewelry, engraving, and inlaying, involving metals, stones, and ivory.

These dishes made of alabaster, bronze, gold, and silver, in exquisite shapes with delicate lines and curves and delicate parts neatly fashioned, were for food, wine, and perfumes—the most exquisite things that Phoenicians crafted both inside and outside their own dominions. Archeologists have found some of them in Phoenician settlements over the seas.

Here is a collection of outstanding jewelry: golden necklaces with roaring lions at their edges; other necklaces like snakes, with heads coming together on the women's breasts; onyx and agate chain bracelets, their centerpieces decorated with chrysotile and amethyst pendants in pyramidal and conical shapes; delicately crafted rings inlaid with emeralds and rubies; and earrings reaching to the necks of their wearers and even their shoulders . . . And Phoenician women never forgot to ask their jewelers to make clips for their hair and stick pencils for their eyes.

All these jewels, trinkets, and vessels were discovered in the ruins of Byblos, inside the remains of temples and houses, in the graves of kings and common people, in granite sarcophagi and pottery jars.

Among the loveliest and costliest of the objects was the king's scepter, gold and silver axes with cedar- and cypress-wood grips. The axes were engraved with candle-like cacti and pointed lines as if they were a chain of sevens and eights.[3] It is a kind of filigree known to the Phoenicians and still used by the Arabs in decorating the fronts of shirts and abayas. Prince Maurice Chehab has informed me that the Lebanese Museum has the world's largest collection of gold weapons.

There are archeologists and historians who say that the Phoenicians took their arts and crafts from the Assyrians, Babylonians, and Egyptians.

What is undoubtedly the case is that the native intelligence of the Phoenicians accompanied their astute observations in everything they undertook. They investigated everything they saw, and appreciated exciting ideas and brilliant feats of imagination. Forms that were borrowed adapted to their spirit, and matrices opened up to the symbols of their religion and the traditions of their people.

The majority of those borrowings were connected to symbols and traditions. The gods played a flexible and beneficial role in them. We are with the king in the demands placed on him by the country's politics, especially those abroad, which were subject to continual adjustment and alteration. One day the context would be Egypt, the next day Babylon, and the day after that Assyria and Persia.

"All glory and honor to the pharaoh," the king will say. The god Eshmun says something that gets repeated by the high priest, and the artist decorates the temple of the god and his statue with a disc of the winged sun! "All glory and honor to Egypt." Now here is the goddess of Byblos, superior to the god Eshmun in both fervor and kindness, removing her Phoenician dress and donning the garb of the Egyptian goddess Isis!

3. Translator's note: In Arabic, the numeral *7* is similar in form to the letter *V*, and *8* to an inverted letter *V*.

Phoenicians adopted the calf from the Egyptians and carved Phoenician spells and charms on them. They also adopted the rhinoceros and phoenix as mythical beasts to protect their temples and work alongside their gods. They could then assist them in commerce and provide permanent safety to those traveling.

When it comes to making jewelry and crafting talismans and charm bracelets, they also did their rounds of borrowing. From Egypt they brought parchment and its flowers, and the falcon god Ra, from Assyria the winged lion, and from Babylon some cuneiform designs, which they incorporated in their inventions, thus enhancing the uniqueness of their toys and beauty to their jewelry.

Is there any harm or fault in borrowing, if it is combined with knowledge, taste, and creativity? The great scholar Breasted is totally fair when he says that the Phoenicians were simply imitators who adopted things from foreigners that helped perfect and disseminate their own crafts. Does that apply to the artifacts from Byblos described previously, to the details of architecture, drawing, carving, and coloring with which Hiram of Tyre decorated Solomon's temple? There is another clear piece of evidence as well, that of enemies—duly recorded in the Homeric poems:

> When Achilles stood at the funerary rites of Patroclus, he was presenting the most beautiful cup in the world to the winner in the running race. That cup, he said, was made by the Phoenicians.
>
> When Menelaus offered Telemachus the loveliest and costliest gift he had to offer, a silver cup with a golden top, it was a gift from the king of Tyre.
>
> Queen Hecuba, wife of King Priam, used to flaunt herself in the dresses that Paris brought her from Phoenicia.

Those spectacular, wonderful clothes were reckoned by the Greek hero to be suitable as gifts to bridal ladies. No wonder, they were Phoenician in their coloring, and had been made by the hands of women from Tyre.

Phoenician weaving was renowned in both the East and West, wherever the Phoenicians arrived either in caravans or ships. The fabrics were made of wool, linen, and silk, fascinating and beautiful with their purple designs. Thanks to Phoenician ingenuity, they exuded a beautiful coloring and gentle sheen. They were celebrated in poetry and incorporated into stories for all time, and constituted the primary pillar of Phoenician trade.

I said that they used wool, linen, and silk. The majority of the wool was from the country itself—local. The linen and silk were brought firstly from Egypt, then from Persia. They were woven on Phoenician looms in Sidon, Tyre, and Byblos, and dyed using dyes culled by Phoenicians from the seabed—yes indeed, the seabed, yet another miracle of discovery and inventiveness.

I will tell you the story told by historians and poets. A Phoenician was walking along the seashore between Tyre and Akka at sunset, and spotted a pile of shells from which a red-tinged black liquid was flowing.

The sea throws up these shells at high tide, then leaves them behind for sun and sand when it ebbs. The creatures inside them die of thirst.

That same Phoenician thought about them as their blood stained the dry sand, the gleam of inspiration emanating from them.

He took some of the shells back to his house, while his dream was floating on a sea of sunset hues.

How gorgeous are those colors, on clothes worn by strutting men, and purchased by women at exorbitant prices! This then was the hour of inspiration that preceded the hour of invention.

We do not know what name the Phoenician gave to this creature, but books written by archeologists and historians simply use the Latin name, *Murex trunculus.*

Could this *Murex trunculus* be related to the octopus, from whose ink we extract the brown color that sepia is made for artistic use? No, sir, the octopus is a large, naked, ugly creature, whereas the *Murex trunculus* is tiny and unassuming, hiding inside its shell like snails. Under its head is a gland containing a yellow fluid with a powerful smell like that of garlic. If the fluid is extracted, poured on to a piece of white fabric, and exposed to the sun, it turns, in succession, green, then blue, then red, then purple.

The Phoenicians fished for *Murex trunculus* using nets and baskets, with worms and frogs as bait. They would extract the fluid with the creature still alive, because the color would deteriorate as soon as they were dead.

The gland would then be boiled with a bit of salt in a lead pot (both iron and copper dilute the purple color) until the dye liquid congeals.

This group of shelled creatures included some categories where the dye material differs somewhat, and the Phoenicians took that into account in their chemical laboratories as they blended them together in a succession of experiments until Phoenician dyes became famous in the East and West, for ever recorded in history.

The invention of purple dyes and everything connected with them is undoubtedly Phoenician.

When it comes to the invention of glass, there is some variation. Glass comes into two varieties: granulated and transparent. The first is very old, being discovered in Egypt before the Pharaonic era; the second was invented, so scholars believe, between the fourteenth and fifteenth centuries BCE.

They used to say that the Phoenicians were the first to invent it, but then some of them said that it was not so, and attributed the invention to the Egyptians because of the large amounts of soda in their lakes and of sand in their country.

Phoenician advocates set about providing one proof after another that the Syrian shores were rich in pure sand, with no iron, and suitable for making glass. In olden times the Phoenicians were well aware of that, and bolstered their hopes. However, they had to import the alkali needed either from Egypt or the Syrian interior.

Each of these two groups adhered to their views until, in 1938, a joint Swedish-Egyptian archeological expedition confirmed the views of the first group; they found transparent glass in their excavations in the Nile Delta and were able to correct our information right up to today. Glass was well-known in Egypt in the twentieth century CE. Thus, it was the Egyptians who invented it, not the Phoenicians.

That then is the final, conclusive word today. Archeologists might come up with other discoveries tomorrow, and with them yet another "conclusive word."

That said, there is no dispute over Phoenician plates: they are the most beautiful of their kind at that time period. We have some exquisitely shaped narrow bottles called tear bottles, their name based on the false assumption (the origin of which is unknown to me) that Phoenicians used to fill them with tears over their dead and then put them in their graves.

However, today archeologists can correct our opinion. Those lovely bottles, decorated in the hues of dawn and sunset, were used in ancient times—as they are by us today—to hold perfumes. They would be offered to the gods along with offerings, or spread over the tomb of the dead person. They would then be added to the personal goods, jewelry, or work equipment buried in the grave.

Among those tools would be a saw and axe for cutting down trees, and implements for carving and crafting objects, which were found in these tombs alongside porcelain talismans and charms, and jars, which contained the bones of the best of people in all times—laborers, craftsmen, and artists.

I return now to the resources used by Phoenicians in their craftsmanship. I noted earlier that they brought silk from Persia and linen from Egypt. They invented the dying process, which was one of their most important products, quite apart from the fact that it opened up markets for their fabrics everywhere and doors for colonial expansion across the seas.

There remained the metals for arts and crafts. Where did they bring them from? They obtained the dyes from the seabed. I have also learned and will recount for you the remarkable truth, that they were able to extract precious metals from the very heart of the earth and its rocks. I will therefore finish this chapter by revealing this second wonder.

In these voyages the Phoenicians reached the British Isles, before they reached the heart of the earth, as I see it. They came back with tin and copper from Cyprus and the Sinai Peninsula. From the two metals they made bronze according to the principle still in use today: nine parts copper to one part tin.

However, apart from their sailing exploits, their major activity was mining. Bousidon, the Greek from Tyre who lived in the first century BCE, says that his travels took him to the West, where he reached southern Spain. There he saw mines that the Phoenicians had opened and that were later exploited by both the Carthaginians and Romans.

This man from Tyre was utterly amazed by the engineering works involved. The Phoenicians had drilled into the earth until they hit solid rock, and then drilled sideways at that depth. The tunnels expanded in every direction where the metal appeared. From there and from some other tunnels, they dug upward to introduce some fresh air. Other trenches were dug in the tunnels to deal with the water during rainfall.

I am inclined to believe that it was their tradition of digging graves—for kings in Byblos and Tyre and similar ones in Bahrain, equipped with side chambers and vaults connecting them—may have inspired them to dig gold and silver mines in the earth. Gravediggers turned into miners!

Once they had extracted the minerals from the earth, they would heat them to the desired temperature, then apply the appropriate level of water pressure so that they could knead it like bread dough, then wash and pan it, so that the metal element was separated from the stone residue in which it was enclosed.

Water pressure came from pools that they had built high in the mountains, with canals that connected the pools to the factories where the grinding and panning took place. In general, the same method is used today, with the exception of power from steam and electricity, which have both spared us the need for human forces and Archimedes's water-raising principle.

The Phoenicians did not attempt to separate the mixture of metals from each other, and so the gold sometimes had some silver mixed in with it, and silver had some remnants of lead.

That said, they were clearly pioneers in mining; not only that but also across the widest range, with the highest level of skill, and showing the most courage, initiative, and endurance. Their remarkable achievements reached Job the Righteous. He mentions them in his cries and bitter words (28:4–10):

> They dig mines far some houses of people,
> With no footsteps for feet . . . dangling,
> Far from people, swinging to and fro.

And Job is clearly referring to the Phoenician mine when he says:

> To the flint he stretches his hand,
> Overturning the mountains from their foundations,
> Carving channels into the rocks,
> As his eye gazes at every precious item.

The Development of the Alphabet

BEFORE WE TELL THE STORY of the development of the alphabet—which made it possible for human beings to record their thoughts and information, their religions and laws, their myths and yarns, on columns and bricks, on bronze and porcelain plates, on papyrus, parchment, and paper—the alphabet that has filled the world with useful, funny, and disturbing books, priceless, rubbish, inane (I wonder to which of those three categories this book belongs?), we need to review the writing systems that preceded it: pictorial, cuneiform, and hieroglyphic.

During the second Stone Age, or about twelve thousand years ago, humans were starting to use polished stones, implements made of flint and other things that were different from what they had in the first Stone Age. They started drawing the things they saw and found interesting on rocks and bones—animals, plants, and abstract objects—as a way of expressing the thoughts they had, and the food, tools, and implements they needed.

This pictorial writing spread and reached perfection in China in ancient times and in Central America during the Mayan period. It was still in use up to the nineteenth century CE in certain Mexican cities and also among North American Native tribes.

One of the old inhabitants of Merida—the capital city of Yucatan, Mexico—told me that, right up to the second half of the nineteenth century CE, the city's streets had animal names and were identified by drawings of them—chicken, bull, cat, dog, etc.—which were hung under the streetlamps or on the walls.

I myself have seen examples of Indian inscriptions in their various shapes and designs: a circle representing a mouth, for example, and a circle with lines pointing outward for a speaking mouth. I have also seen a design for a boat with horizontal lines in the middle to represent the men in it, with an arc alongside it for the sky and dots underneath marking the number of days for the voyage.

This language using images and symbols was used by the ancients in the same way as we today use hands and fingers to communicate with people who are deaf and inarticulate.

However, some ancient peoples did not perfect the use of images and symbols—they were not good at illustration. Those include the Sumerians, for example, in the Euphrates Valley, who used lines with heads and crowns—like nails—to communicate and made use of a variety of structures in order to express their needs. That is why their form of writing is termed *cuneiform.*

In the Nile Valley, the hieroglyphic system grew out of basic images and symbols, implying the illustrative language of the priests—*hiero*, meaning "priest," and *glyph*, meaning "image."

Before humans began to "cuneiformize" their ideas and information in the Euphrates Valley and "hieroglyphize" them in the Nile Valley, their attempts at design and illustration lasted for some five thousand years.

Both cuneiform and hieroglyphic writing systems date back to the fourth or fifth millennium BCE; precise dates can only be set in terms of centuries. We can state, for example, that the Sumerians started writing in cuneiform in the final three or four centuries of the fourth millennium (3900–3600 BCE). Between the Sumerians and Egyptians, which people was the pioneer in writing? In other words, where did civilization first appear: In the Euphrates Valley or the Nile Valley? Archeologists disagree about the answer.

I posed this question to my friend Professor Elihu Grant, who spent a number of years excavating in Iraq. He sent me a letter from which I now quote:

> It is undoubtedly the case that both civilizations borrowed from and exchanged with each other, with reference to the specific civilization in the Euphrates Valley. However, I am inclined—perhaps

> due to the fact that I am a specialist in Iraqi archeology—to believe that the Euphrates civilization is older than the Egyptian. However, my special interest in Egyptian archeology would assure you that Egyptian civilization is the oldest in the world. Both opinions are biased. It is entirely possible that a discovery in the Euphrates Valley tomorrow will invalidate Egyptian claims, or that one in the Nile Valley will force the specialist in Iraqi archeology to withdraw. Today the facts state that both civilizations are equally ancient, and it is a waste of time to support one side over the other.

So then, the cuneiform and hieroglyphic languages emerged at the same time, with no more than one, two, or three hundred years separating them. Both emerged from previous systems using designs, symbols, and word fragments.

Cuneiform developed, changed, and fell into disuse, as it moved from Sumerian to Akkadian, to Babylonian, to Assyrian, and to Iranian. From it there emerged in Iranian civilization the first modes of alphabetical writing, to be followed by further experiments in alphabetical forms.

In the second millennium BCE, Akkadian cuneiform was widespread in the Near East. As letters exchanged between the kings of Assyria and Babylon and the pharaohs make clear, accounts and contracts were written in the language, and international treaties were recorded that way, as, for example, between rulers of Mitanni and Assyria.

Hieroglyphic comes in two categories: Hieratic, the language of priests, and demotic, the people's language. In demotic, there is a certain amount of Akkadian cuneiform mixed in, as is the case with French in Lebanese Arabic and English with Adeni and Basran Arabic today. Asian peoples, from Sumer to Egypt, continued to use cuneiform and its demotic form until the twentieth century BCE. The only changes that occurred were in certain dialects and local terms.

Proof that the people of Byblos, for example, were using this hieroglyphic cuneiform language is in what was discovered by archeologists in the tomb of King Ishmou Abi (1900 BCE); namely, a bronze scepter with the king's name inscribed in hieroglyphic characters.

Even more significant than that is the discovery made by Dunand in Byblos, a page-sized bronze tablet on which is inscribed on both faces writing that is crystal clear. The director of the Archeological Institute has informed me that it is in hieroglyphic cuneiform and contains some letters that are still unknown. The tablet dates back to the end of the third millennium (2900 BCE).

However much time specifics may differ, it is undoubtedly the case that alphabetical writing was not known before the twentieth century BCE. It seems likely that, at the beginning of the twentieth century BCE, pioneering thinkers in every nation started thinking about the construction of a simple mode of writing based on the modes of writing that were current at the time. The need was also stimulated by social and political developments and the expansion of communication networks and commerce. Initiatives in the Sinai Peninsula in the nineteenth century BCE were successful.

That stretch of territory, lying between Syria and Egypt, was the locus of pioneers and experimenters in the world of project and gold! There were mines—the land was rich in copper, gold, and precious stones. Thus, it is no wonder that the Semitic inhabitants of the Sinai Peninsula displayed a significant degree of energy and daring in their industrial, commercial, and intellectual ventures, and that initiatives and experiments with alphabetical forms succeeded there first. Sir Flinders Petrie discovered the secret in 1904 at Mount Sinai close to the Egyptian emerald mines: alphabetical letters, the first of their kind in the history of writing. The people involved in the invention were definitely Semites. Of the symbols they discovered from hieroglyphic they made use of the ones that suited their needs in terms of shape and spelling. They consist of a single syllable suitable for alphabetization. They also borrowed parts from animal images and made do with parts from elsewhere, making up thirty alphabetical letters that they considered sufficient for writing purposes.

This Sinaitic alphabet was the mother source of Nabatean, Hebrew, Aramaic, and Phoenician alphabets, all of which went through transformations and changes in accordance with the modernizing needs of their peoples and their numerous dialects.

All this is what partisan archeologists and scholars working on this alphabet have to say. There are others who disagree—in particular, two French scholars. Dussaud stated that the search for the origins of the Phoenician alphabet should not to be in the Sinai Peninsula, but in the remains of the Phoenicians themselves: specifically the sarcophagus of Ahiram, a contemporary of Pharaoh Ramses II. Added to which is the need felt by Phoenician merchants for a simple language in which to bargain and the need of the priestly school in Byblos for a language suitable for educational purposes.

Dunand discovered something even older than Ahiram's sarcophagus: alphabetical script going back to the fourteenth century BCE, over a hundred years earlier than Ramses II and Ahiram, and five hundred years later than the discovery in the Sinai Peninsula. He states that the hieroglyphic cuneiform tablet he discovered may have been a father of the Phoenician alphabet, but, even though it has yet to be interpreted, it is still far from what this highly respected archeologist is inclined to acknowledge. The outer appearance of the written shapes negates that idea.

The American archeologist Albright states that investigation of the vestiges of Palestinian writing brings us to a bridge extending over the gap between the Sinaitic alphabet and other initiatives and experiments in the anterior periods.

Sir Flinders Petrie is of the opinion that the source of all alphabetical writings lies in the ancient invention of alphabetical letters in the Greek Isles.

At this point, expansion of the topic does not concern us, nor is it useful. What we need to be doing is to lay out the facts for the reader and explain the theories behind them.

What is clearly an established fact is that, in the latter half of the second millennium—between 2000 and 1500 BCE—the Semitic and Aryan people of the Middle East were trying to change and improve the usual cuneiform and hieroglyphic forms of writing and their blended forms, with the goal of getting to a style more suited for writing purposes. This was driven by two factors: the spread of foreign trade between these peoples and their need for a simple writing medium for correspondence and accounting, and the level of progress and the outpouring of pioneering ideas aspiring to discovery and invention.

The most obvious illustration of all that lies in the alphabet movement at that time. Archeologists have discovered other alphabet systems, composed of thirty letters and more, like Phoenician in the absence of weak letters, but dissimilar in their derivation from the cuneiform language.

It is the cuneiform language that was discovered in 1929 at Ras Shamra (near Latakia), dating back to between the seventeenth and fifteenth centuries BCE, or two hundred years later than the Sinaitic alphabet (all that being approximate).

Among other alphabetic discoveries is one made in 1868, a relic of King Mesha, known as the Moab Stone, because that was where it was discovered. It is the oldest archeological discovery of alphabets, even though it is the most modern (950 BCE) and comprises the clearest and most perfect example of alphabetical writing discovered by archeology up to today. It is the kind of alphabetical writing ascribed to the Phoenicians, and the first gift of archeologists in their journey back 1,500 years to the experiments and developments in writing that led to the Sinaitic alphabet.

From that time onward, the Phoenicians and their neighbors in the south continued improving this alphabet until, a thousand years later, it had become suitable for expressions of thoughts and imagination of the first poet, Homer, using the subtlest modes of thought and the furthest reaches of the imagination.

Professor John Flight has this to say: "Today it is probably correct to state that the alphabet is a Semitic invention, and that the Sinaite alphabet is the first of those inventions."[1]

In Syria and Palestine, archeologists have discovered in the last twenty years writings other than the ones I have mentioned here.

1. *Haverford Symposium on Archeology and the Bible* (1938), 118.

Here I will list the most important ones along with their archeological dates:

Sinaitic writing	1900–1800 BCE
Cuneiform alphabet (Ras Shamra)	1600–1400 BCE
Byblos alphabet	1500–1400 BE
Ahiram's sarcophagus	900 BCE
Two monuments to Abibaal and Ibibaal (Byblos)	1000 BCE
Moab Stone (near the Dead Sea)	900 BCE
Letter from Tell Duweir (Palestine)	600 BCE

There are also eighteen letters in ink on bits of porcelain, written by border guards during Chaldean invasions of Palestine in 589 BCE to the garrison commander in Tell Duweir.

This story of the development of the alphabet provides an illustration of growth and sophistication, but not what is normally called discovery or invention. In summary of the preceding section, we can say that, in the reign of King Ishmou Abi (1900 BCE), the Phoenicians were using letters and drawings in writing that were a mixture of hieroglyphic, cuneiform, and other alphabets of neighboring peoples. The Sinaitic alphabet preceded the Phoenician one by about four hundred years; both contained similar letters. The urge to get rid of cuneiform and hieroglyphic languages and dialects and initial experiments with alphabets that accompanied the urge appeared in the latter half of the second millennium BCE among Semitic and Aryan peoples in the south and north of the country.

The statement that the Phoenicians were the inventors of the alphabet is not confirmed by archeological discoveries. Its only advocates are three or four scholars, among them the two French scholars Dussaud and Dunand, who were in charge of the excavations in Byblos. They are both specialists, but you have to remember what Professor Grant had to say in my citation from his book about specialists and the way in which they stick rigidly to their own opinions regarding their area of expertise. Before this divergence of opinion and before the discovery of Sinaitic writing, the historian George Rawlinson, a precise and exacting scholar and great admirer of the Phoenicians, wrote: "It is not certain that the Phoenicians invented the alphabetical writing that is attributed to them. They may have been the inventors, but it is certain that they improved whatever was current in those days."[2]

They undoubtedly improved the Sinaitic alphabet, making it more accessible and easier to use. That was a suitable thing for them to do, since they were renowned merchants in the ancient world, and commerce needs its own modes and accounting procedures, involving not only numbers but writing as well.

Commerce and knowledge go hand in hand. In the glorious Babylonian era, the Babylonians were the chief merchants; they started trading to the West and spread knowledge of cuneiform writing wherever they went.

The Phoenicians did the same. During the heyday of their commerce, they spread the alphabet. Among the first people to adopt it were the Greeks, because it was the only alphabet in existence. The Greeks attributed its use to the Phoenicians because, at the time, they did not know any other merchants from the East.

2. George Rawlinson, *History of Phoenicia* (1889), 329.

Phoenicians and Greeks

WHEN SIR FLINDERS PETRIE discovered the Sinaitic alphabet, he started studying it and doing research, something that involved a certain degree of exploratory fervor and imagination. He then put forward his radical theory—namely, that alphabetical writing as a whole had a single point of conception, the Greek Isles, specifically Crete. Some traces of such a system had been discovered in the ancient city of Knossos, and especially in the famous palace of that name. Those architectural, artistic, and cultural monuments were ancient, contemporary with the earliest Egyptian cultural period, equally as advanced and highly cultured. The great Sir Arthur Evans, pioneer archeologist on the island called it "Minoan civilization," a reference to Minos, god of the island, or to one of its kings who adopted the same name. Myths concerning the invention of the alphabet have been attributed to him.

However, archeologists have continued their research and excavations there, resuming their activities after the Great War (World War I). Their discoveries point to the existence of contacts between Minoan and Egyptian civilizations, involving borrowings and imitations that need to be taken into consideration. Among such things are seals on which hieroglyphic writing has been carved, and a vessel on which a picture of papyrus flowers has been painted. Can we use these relics on their own to state that Minoan civilization is the origin and Egyptian civilization is an offshoot?

The written, artistic, and cultural relics, concerning the definition and interpretation of which archeologists are in agreement, are among a set of facts that are worthy of serious consideration. That said, however, I must caution you against delving too deeply in the topic and accepting particular theories, the reason being, as I have explained earlier, that specialists tend to exaggerate and show a bias toward their specialist topic.

Among such exaggerated views, we have that of Sir Flinders Petrie concerning the origin of alphabetic writings and the claims of certain researchers and explorers on the island of Crete to the effect that Minoan culture is the oldest of all, or that Egyptian and Sumerian cultures are of the same vintage!

I would also caution you with regard to theories based on an inscription on a monument, an image on a work of art, or the shape of a particular vessel. A Phoenician shield was discovered in the palace at Knossos. Can we deduce from that either that the Phoenicians occupied Crete in ancient times, or that they tried to do so?

Some of the relics discovered on Crete include a colored porcelain vase and beautifully colored paintings on the walls. On one such vase there is a painting of the sea creature *Murex trunculus*. Are we then to deduce that the Cretans discovered that creature and extracted purple dye from its gland?!

This is the kind of investigation conducted by Victor Berard, the famous French specialist on the Phoenicians. His goal is to provide support for his theories that match those of Sir Flinders Petrie regarding the origin of alphabetic writing. However, Berard turns things around: "Phoenicia and Egypt are the source of Greek civilization"!

I have read Berard's book, *La Resurrection d'Homere* (1930), which is full of literary interpretations and learned comparisons, which were warmly greeted by advocates of the Phoenicians. They can only be carefully assessed by scholars who know ancient languages—Phoenician, Hebrew, Aramaic, Cuneiform, Hieroglyphic, Greek, and Latin.

Do I need to tell the reader that I am not such a scholar? However, I have paused to consider some of theories of a scholar as famous as Berard, which led him to mention Arabic. I understood, but was nevertheless surprised. Before I move on to that specifically, I will first mention some of the proven information and authenticated ideas and theories in his book:

"Over the past twenty years (1890–1910), it has been customary for scholars to deny anything that the ancients ascribe to the Phoenician people. It is a kind of academic anti-Semitic fanaticism led in France by Salomon Reinach and Isidore Levy. Reinach expelled the civilized Phoenicians from ancient Greece, while, with a stroke of his pen, Levy sank them in the Mediterranean Sea and wiped them off the world's tablet."

As far as I am aware, there is no trace of this kind of fanaticism in modern research on the Phoenicians. The book that I am currently holding contains essays by a number of eminent archeologists, none of whom display any bias.[1] All of them establish the facts with a care founded in science and do not indulge in overinterpretation. They share Berard's opinion regarding the statement of the historian Herodotus concerning the Phoenicians: "Phoenician ships would transport to Greece cargoes of goods, half of which were Egyptian and the other half Assyrian." But what about Phoenician goods, oh father of history?! Herodotus is showing some anti-Phoenician prejudice here, since the Phoenicians taught the Greeks many things, not least seamanship.

Seamanship and many other things as well, as Victor Berard tells us. The Phoenicians preceded all other ancient peoples in discovering and colonizing Greek territories. They were pioneers and colonists. They gave the ports and islands they discovered Phoenician names, and brought those regions their goods, civilization, culture, and myths as narrated by the mariners. The poet Homer provides evidence of this in his eternal verse, and that was what led the famous French scholar (Berard) to write *La Resurrection d'Homere.*

The discipline of seamanship is probably Phoenician in origin. However, what is generally acknowledged as the facts today may be either confirmed or contradicted by what archeologists may discover tomorrow. That would either confirm or contradict what Strabo stated long ago—namely, that the people of Sidon were the first ones to use

1. *The Haverford Symposium on Archaeology and the Bible.*

Ursa Major (the Great Bear) for navigation, and Greece adopted it from them.

However, there are times when Berard goes too far in his advocacy of the Phoenicians, and other times when he bogs them down in corrections. As an example, we can note that, after some calculated generalizations, he says that it was the Phoenicians, Egyptians, and Hittites who taught and civilized the ancient Greeks. The ships that transported Phoenician, Egyptian, and Hittite merchandise to Greek lands also carried the complex cultures of those three peoples.

He also states that, at various time periods, the Mediterranean Sea had particular colonial qualities that were Phoenician, Greek, and Arab (during the Umayyad period in Syria and in Andalus [Spain]), and Italian (Venice and Genoa). Then the Turks gave a Moghul-like tinge to it, followed by the French in our times.

So, the Phoenicians were masters of the island archipelago before the Greeks. Where then were the Egyptians, who had conducted their first invasion of Phoenicia in the twenty-eighth century BCE, who had built fleets of ships in the twenty-ninth century BCE? Were they masters of the islands? That is still uncertain; maybe the facts will be uncovered tomorrow. Then we will know for certain which of the three peoples—Phoenicians, Egyptians, and Knossians from Crete—were the first to traverse the seas.

I noted earlier that Berard goes back to Homer's poetry, and especially the *Odyssey*, in order to prove his theory that many myths in the poem and names of characters are of Phoenician origin. On occasion, he says, "Phoenician Semite" so as to broaden the scope of his interpretation. Thus, the hero Proteus in the *Odyssey*, for example, is Bruti, the name that the Egyptian priests gave to the pharaoh. Egypt is thus a source of inspiration for Homer.

Here is an example of Berard's historical and linguistic interpretations. One of the Greek Isles has now got its ancient names of Semitic derivation. Its name today is Corfu, and there is a funny story about it in the *Odyssey.*

One day when Odysseus was returning to Ithaca, the sea god took vengeance on him by tossing his ship on to a rock by the shore. The island was named after the ship, *Kerkyra*, to commemorate the dreadful event. Berard goes on to note that *kerkyra* means "a fast ship," and the word is of Phoenician-Semitic origin. "Arabs and Hebrews," he says, "call fast ships and camels *kurkar* or *kurkour*."

As I have already said, I am not one who can challenge Berard's linguistic knowledge, but I am a writer who owns a dictionary and does not look down on lexicographers. Here then is Al-Fairuzabadi, in his dictionary (*Lisaan al-Arab*) under first letter *K* and second letter *R*: "*Al-Karkar*: an outgrowth on the breast of camels, goats, and bulls"; also, *karkar*, "boisterous laughter."

Perhaps the renowned French scholar had in mind *qarqar*, not *karkar*. So here is what we find under first letter *Q* and second letter *R*: *qarqar*: "of a camel, to grumble, roar"; *al-qarqara*: "flat, soft ground; smooth floor; women's clothing." So where is the "fast ship" or "the flying camel" in either of these two items?[2]

There is yet another example of words of Phoenician or Semitic origins in the *Odyssey*. The word *zephyr* in both English and French is the Greek word *zephyros*, which in Homeric poetry means "a stormy wind on the sea," whereas in French and English it is "a soft, gentle breeze." In Semitic Arabic, it means "the exhalation of breath and the noise that a donkey makes before braying."

Here now is one of the most curious accounts from the fifth book of the *Odyssey*:

> The rapacious Phoenician sailors reached the Island of Syros. In their black ships they were transporting thousands of valuable pieces and toys. In the house of one of the nobles a young Phoenician girl, svelte and with black eyes, and, beyond that, educated and versatile.

Berard chooses to dwell on this point. "So then," he says, "sons of the island monarchs had Phoenician nannies, just like English women today."

2. Translator's note: here the author appears to overlook the existence, at least in Edward Lane's *Arabic-English Dictionary* (based on multiple Arabic dictionaries), of the Arabic word *qurqur*, meaning "a long ship."

He then resumes the story:

> This cultured Phoenician girl met her fellow Phoenicians. They asked, indeed they insisted, that she return with them to her own country. She accepted. However, before she ran away from her master's house, she grabbed as much gold as she could lay her hands on—that "Phoenician nanny"!

Her master had wanted a blessing, but instead what he received was a black curse. There are also other examples of women with twisted intentions and ill will. I once read in a Lebanese newspaper in French an article about Phoenicians with an introduction in which Berard is quoted as saying: "For Greeks, Phoenician culture is like Greek culture for Europeans. That is because European culture—its literature, art, science, and philosophy—is derived from Greek culture. Is it then correct to say, by way of comparison, that Greek culture—its literature, art, philosophy, and science—is derived from Phoenician culture?"

The history of Europe is witness to glorious periods similar to that of Belkis (queen of Sheba), involving aspects of the arts and sciences. Where then in dealing with Phoenicia is that golden age in which we can rightfully say that it served as the source for the arts and sciences that flourished during the famous Hellenistic period? Where are the Phoenician ancestors of the historian Herodotus, the poet Sophocles, and the artist Pheidias? In the time periods of Phoenician history where are the traces of that spring—or rather, those springs that were to burst forth in a single place in the wide world—namely, the city of Athens? And, not only that, but during a single time period, no longer than fifty years, a period with its stellar figures in literature, poetry, art, philosophy, and politics?

It is one of the most remarkable and spectacular eras, unmatched by any previous civilizations—Sumerian, Babylonian, Assyrian, Phoenician, and Egyptian—whether in its origins or effects. There is nothing that comes even close in terms of cultural sophistication and civilized society.

Civilized humanity had gone through a period of four thousand years, with their minds in a kind of matrix created and dominated by priests. Arts and sciences were restricted to what fit within that matrix and did not go beyond it.

Herodotus came to Egypt in search of knowledge, the keys to which were in the hands of priests. They refused him access and only let him look through tiny peepholes during his three-year stay there. Priestly mentality was inflexible, and their knowledge was utterly sterile.

The public human mind—silent, coerced, and suppressed—remained buried under the soil of these civilizations, growing and feeding on whatever sustenance lay beneath the surface out of the sunlight. In Babylon, Assyria, and Egypt, it kept on growing very slowly, save for occasional leaps—and how far apart those eras were!—involving outsized royal personalities.

From Meskalamdug, the Sumerian, and Snefru, the Egyptian, to the age of Pericles the Greek, that makes 2,500 years. Then the big divide happened: things were taken out of the priests' hands, and their matrices and bonds were severed. Human thought emerged from its position in the shadows, and launched itself into the public firmament on the wings of its children's genius. It could now hover in the sky of free thought—that same human intellect that had lived or lingered underground like a snail for two thousand years. Now, in just half a century, it witnessed an amazing efflorescence, although the light only burned bright in a small area of the world, since Egypt had gone dark, Phoenicia had sickened, and the cypresses of both Babylon and Assyria had ossified.

The Greeks borrowed from the Phoenicians and Egyptians, and, through both of them, from the Babylonians and Assyrians as well. They also borrowed from the Persians, and continued to adopt the basic premises of their culture and science from these sources until the end of the fifth century BCE. The sixth century BCE was one of nourishment and growth, and the fifth that followed it one of efflorescence and expansion. In other words, the Greeks incurred debts, but they invested the resources wisely and were then able to export their profits outside their own country. You can say that, at the end of the fifth century BCE and the beginning of the fourth—the era of Plato and Socrates—the Greeks were repaying their debts. One of the things that came their way were some aspects of the Phoenician religion.

Here is what the renowned scholar William Albright has to say: "In the fourth century Greek art began to spread in Phoenicia. That is clear from the carving in the marble sarcophagus discovered in Sidon. Greek crafts and commerce undoubtedly expanded to the cities on the Phoenician and Palestinian shores at least a century before Alexander's conquest."

This reality of give and take also includes the Sinaitic Phoenician Greek alphabet, which the Greeks took from the Phoenicians with their left hand and passed on to the Europeans with their right. The statement concerning this alphabet that advocates of the Phoenicians have drawn from the researches of the great Berard—namely that, were it not for the Phoenicians, the entire world would have been the loser—has been rejected. If the Phoenicians had not passed it on and had it not been devised on the Sinai Peninsula, in Byblos, or in Moab, some other nation in Asia would have done so. The world would not have lost anything, because the Eastern world had reached such a stage of sophistication that would have required an advanced alphabet system.

That is a law of civilization: when a nation's intellectual level reaches a stage that qualifies it for a particular kind of knowledge (and here you need to ignore the Sufi connotations of "qualifies" and say instead, "Makes it necessary to fulfill its needs or continue its intellectual progress, whether in knowledge or discovery"), then intellectuals interested in that knowledge or process of discovery will emerge, moving boldly ahead in a variety of regions. They will appear at the same time and labor on the same task without even knowing each other.

In our own time there are the examples of electricity, anesthesia, blood circulation, and the invention of wireless and radio.

Before the name Edison became synonymous with electricity, a group of scholars in various countries during the eighteenth and nineteenth centuries had undertaken research on the subject and discovered its secrets, among them Knochenbruch in Germany, Franklin in America, Coulomb in France, Galvani in Italy, and Faraday in England.

Before Doctor Harvey (1578–1657) discovered blood circulation, his own teacher, Hieronymus Fabricius (1537–1619), had been doing research both before and at the same time, as had Michael Servetus (1511–53), Volcher Coiter (1534–76), and Andreas Vesalius (1514–64). In our own times, there are examples of these intellectual trends and competitive investigations in electrical research, such as those involving Guglielmo Marconi and Nicola Tesla.

Do you imagine that America would be an unknown continent but for Columbus?

Do you imagine that we would still be writing in hieroglyphic and cuneiform but for the Sinaitic or Byblos alphabet?

If the Phoenicians had not brought them to Greece, do you think they would have been buried along with Ahiram in his sarcophagus?

Reflect carefully on the laws of civilization, and clarify its primary features.

Commerce

THE PHOENICIANS never bothered about the sciences of the mind, deprived as those pursuits were of any practical and profitable aspects. They had no interest in philosophical theories or in poetic phenomena. Specters of spirit and imagination never tempted them. There was no one passionately devoted to the coverlet of truth, nor anyone "wandering in every valley."[1] God protect you, they were materialist, practical, and calculating—the Americans of their age.

Among the variety of literary texts that have reached us up until now, there is no trace of any social, political, health-related, or philosophical learning. We know nothing about the Phoenicians' interest in jurisprudence, social legislation, or medicine. Our knowledge about things dealing with family life and marriage, for example, is that, before Phoenician girls were married, they practiced prostitution—not, so it seems, for love of money but rather for a desire to be married. Girls would donate a portion of their earnings to the temple in a quest for blessing, and keep the rest to "buy" a husband in accordance with the French practice, which is widespread among Eastern Christians today—namely, a dowry (French *dot*). However, in this case the dowry involved her own money, and not her parents'. The girl would be keen on having a large dowry so that she could attract a man from a good family or a young man from the cream of society.

1. Translator's note: this is a quotation from the text of the Qur'an describing poets: Sura 26:225.

This practice then reflected ambition, not sheer greed, and, as such, it was considered justified.

However, the basic principle was founded on a practical philosophy grounded in mutual benefits. In the context of work and the worlds of industry and commerce, Phoenicians were as distinguished in their time as Americans are today. No other ancient people can surpass them when it comes to building ships, traversing the seas, marine exploration, opening mines, making crafts, and creating colonies and settlements. All those things are pillars of civilization today.

There can be no denying that the Phoenicians were pioneers of civilization in ancient times. With their innate intelligence, daring, and courage, they laid the groundwork for the people who came after them and who were more sophisticated and civilized. The credit here goes to those who came first.

It is worth mentioning that they managed to avoid those aspects of corruption that regularly accompany wealth and luxurious living. They did so by showing unusual worldly wisdom, ambition, and fortitude. Thanks to their hardworking men and practical philosophy, Phoenicia flourished, and, for a long period of time, maintained its status among other nations, large and small.

It had what is usually called a golden age—indeed, ages. Historians tell us that the glorious Phoenician era lasted for nine hundred years; in other words, from the beginning of the thirteenth century BCE until the Hellenistic era. That glorious era is contemporaneous with the glories of Sargon; Sennacherib; Solomon, son of David; and Ramses II.

However, there is another side to the issue. If the people's achievements cannot be detached from its political and national situation—one that, during the so-called golden age, was distressing and humiliating (as is the case today with Lebanon), then the Phoenicians actually only had a period of between fifty and a hundred years that deserve to be considered a golden age.

We do not have enough information to be able to make detailed statements about the state of commerce at different time periods—those of complete independence, partial independence, and of dependence and protectorate. Was commerce adversely affected in a way that undermined the country's independence? Or did it continue to expand and undertake new ventures whatever the political and social situation in the country may have been?

We have no knowledge of the situation of the commercial colonies that were founded in distant lands, or their connections with the homeland. Was there merely a sense of national spirit linking the émigrés and their colleagues who stayed behind? Did those émigrés across the seas send back taxes to the government in their country of origin? It is known and acknowledged that they took their gods with them and built them temples in exile, duly accompanied by priests—priests in those days and for all time! The priest would accompany their flock and stay with them, serving as guardians of their souls and partners in their income wherever they settled.

Those Phoenician émigrés, just like the Lebanese ones today, used to send back to their families in the homeland, to their temples, their priests, their high priest, and their government, a portion of their earnings and objects that they had come to admire as designated gifts for God and homeland!

It is also recognized that the Phoenician spirit used to wane in the shadow of conquests, but would rise and flourish whenever touched by the sunshine of independence. But how rare indeed was that feeling of touch between kingdoms and the sun!

What is amazing is how rarely they struggled for independence. They never forged any general alliances as the Greek cities did during their revival—except, that is, for the disputed Tripoli treaty. Instead, they were all independent of each other, in their own cities called kingdoms, and all subservient most of the time to foreign governments, just like the Arabs today in the nine protectorates.

Phoenician merchants brought their goods to people who were still far from being civilized, to others on the threshold, and to still others who had already achieved high levels of civilization. They awoke people from their slumber, motivated the idle, encouraged those on the upward path, and stimulated those with advanced levels of civilized life to new modes of material existence.

Here we see the Phoenician merchant—gentle, kindhearted, lover of peace and luxury—bringing things to dazzle the eye, delight the heart, and instill in people's minds fresh ideas to sharpen the intellect. You backward peoples in the islands and far distant towns, take this bounty and imitate it! Do not believe what poets tell you, especially their blind leader, Homer, who calls the Phoenicians "commercial wolves."

Here is one such Phoenician, who, on one of the commercial voyages, anchors his "black ship" by the island shore and unloads his goods. He lays it all out in rows on the shore, and local people come in droves—men, women, and children eager to take a look and make purchases. They all wander along the rows looking at the goods, while the Phoenician merchant stands on his ship watching and waiting. One man wants an axe engraved in gold, while a woman is after a mirror of polished brass, and a young man chooses a bottle of perfume. Each purchaser places beside the item that he or she has selected either a gold or silver coin or else something produced or manufactured on the island.[2] They all then step back and stand a bit apart.

Once people have finished making their choices and put down the necessary payment for their selection, the Phoenician disembarks from his ship and looks to see how much has been put down. If the amount is enough, he takes it; if not, he leaves it all in place and goes back onboard his ship. The purchasers, men and women, now have to go back to their selections and bargain. Those whose payments had been accepted were free to take what they wanted; those whose offers had been rejected could decide to pay more if they wanted, back and forth, paying a bit more each time, while the merchant on his ship would come down and go back several times. Some deals were successful; others failed. This would go on all day, and then at sunset the

2. In general, trading involved barter. Gold, silver, or brass coinage did not appear until the seventh century BCE. The *Iliad* has examples of such bartering: the price of two shields, for example, was a head of cattle.

merchant would take back onboard his ship whatever goods had not been sold. He would then set sail for another port of call.

This procedure was called silent trade. That was not because the Phoenicians did not know well the languages of the countries they visited but rather because the primary aim of the procedure was buying and selling. The Phoenician experience in such bargaining was a bitter one. Initial greetings led to conversation, but that led to confrontation and knives! So silence was a better idea; this method of buying and selling was a Phoenician invention.

So where does the "wolf" come in, the Phoenician merchant as the "wolf of commerce"? It is actually a poetic whim; even the master poet Homer could not rise above it and avoid it!

Is it reasonable to suggest that the Phoenician merchant could have been so successful if he were not a paragon of honesty and integrity, and if the excellent quality of his merchandise were not recognized everywhere? Is it surprising that people loved them and admired them, waiting eagerly for their ships to arrive, and flocking to the shores to greet them with all the joy of a festival day. They were eager to taste their delicious cakes and acquire their wonderful toys.

These commercial journeys, which were short at first but gradually became longer until they reached as far as the Narrows of Hercules (Gibraltar) and beyond to what today are known as the British Isles. Great credit is thus due to the Phoenicians for establishing communication between Egyptian, Aegean, and Greek cultures, opening up for the Egyptians the route to the Aegean islands and ports to the north.

The Phoenicians' first journey was to Cyprus, then Rhodes and Kos, then Asian port cities, the Greek Isles, and southern Greece itself. They established Phoenician trade communities and colonies, then traveled west to the French coast, where they established a colony, which today is the largest French port, Marseille.

At the end of the twelfth century BCE, the Phoenicians established colonies in Sicily; Utica, located on the coast of Africa near present-day Tunis; and Cadiz, located on the Spanish shore of Europe to the west of the Guadalquivir River—a city that still bears its original Phoenician name. At the beginning of the ninth century BCE, a group of people from Tyre moved west and established the largest colony of all, one that later became a state much feared by Rome—namely, Carthage.

Once Carthage had become so powerful, the Eastern civilizations had been absorbed into the Greek orbit, and Phoenician commerce had declined and retreated, political power in the West belonged to the Carthaginians, and in the North and East to the Greeks.

In land commerce, the Phoenicians were rivals of both Babylon and Assyria, particularly in the ancient period from the twenty-fifth to the fifteenth centuries BCE.

Babylonian caravans arrived on their way to Egypt, and they were robbed by the king of Akka, who, at the time, was paying taxes to the pharaoh. Burnaburiash, king of Babylon, wrote to the pharaoh demanding compensation and the punishment of the perpetrators so that the commercial caravan routes between Babylon and Egypt could be made safe.

However, in spite of the rivalry between the Phoenicians and both Babylon and Assyria when it came to commercial markets, the Phoenicians grabbed both land and sea routes to the east for themselves. They were the great heroes of these strategies during the reign of King Solomon, son of David, and the Persian era.

One of those trade routes was to Armenia, where they took their crafts and fabrics. They came back with horses, mules, and slaves. One of those routes passed by Tadmur (Palmyra), going north to Nineveh and south to Babylon, the Persian Gulf, and then India. In King Solomon's time they had land and sea routes to India, and another one to Jaffa, Jerusalem, and the coast of Elea (the Gulf of Aqaba today), and from there down the Red Sea to the Arabian Sea to Hormuz on the Persian Gulf and a port city that is now Karachi.

Solomon constructed ships at Ezion Geber next to Elea on the shore of Bahr Souf in the land of Edom. Along with Solomon's slaves, Ahiram dispatched on his own ships his slaves, who knew the sea well. They came to Ophir and seized twenty-four loads of gold, which they took back to King Solomon (the Old Testament).

Phoenician vessels, which had accompanied Solomon's ships, returned to the northwest port city of India (Karachi), loaded with sandalwood and large amounts of gold and precious stones.

Lords of the Sea

EUSEBIUS—may God keep his resting place cool!—said, "In older times there lived a man, an honest scholar, named Ibrahim, superior to all others in his knowledge and wisdom. He invented Astronomy and Babylonian magic. Being close to God, he was inspired to move to Phoenicia, went there from the land of the Chaldeans, lived among them, and taught them astronomy and the rotations of sun and moon. Abimelech, king of Tyre, admired him and kept him as a close associate."

Historians agree that the Phoenicians guided themselves on their sea voyages by using the North Star (Polaris).

The great French scholar Bérard states that the first people to plot their voyages over the Mediterranean, to study atmospheric conditions, to confirm the phenomena of ebb and flow, and establish the principles of navigation, were the Phoenicians, the British of that era . . .

They then taught the Greeks what they had learned from the astronomer magician Ibrahim.

It seems that the Phoenicians had no interest in magic and did not bother with it. Either that, or else they learned it from Ibrahim and immediately transferred it to the Egyptian priests, who proceeded to make use of it in their divine profession.

This is a part of the mythological history that we have concerning the Phoenicians, with their sails and their knowledge of seamanship that was a particular skill of theirs, surpassing that of all other ancient peoples in its applicability to goals of both discovery and colonization.

I have already drawn attention to the kindness of the Phoenicians and their love of the good things in life, one of luxury and ease. Such traits rarely coincided with the requirements for sailors—fortitude, courage, and patience in adversity. Even so, those traits and other contrary features were all united in the Phoenician. He was the luxuriant merchant, the sailor distinguished by both his elegance and coarseness, his pursuit of pleasure, his energy in work—steady and stolid, charming and comfortable, daring and robust. He had a tough and ravenous stomach, coupled with an ascetic's willful patience and endurance.

One of the realities of nature is that the deprived person develops a love for the thing of which he is deprived; he craves it continually. The desert Arabs were thoroughly familiar with the hardships and discomforts of their way of life. But, in cities they indulged in pleasures, only losing their rugged endurance after two or three generations in their new environment, with all its luxury and opulence.

The seagoing Phoenicians are like the desert-dwelling Arabs, although in every era they belonged to both environments—attracted by the sea with all its dangers, and by cities with their luxury and easy lifestyle. That produced in them contradictions, both innate and ethical—merchants living in luxury and gruff sailors seeking adventure.

Do you imagine that every sailor who sailed out of a Phoenician port on voyages of discovery and trade, founding settlements and colonies, would always come back to their families and homeland? Did they return safely and profitably?

Sailors have an ancient history written on waves with blood and tears. How many Phoenician ships were overwhelmed by storms and tossed by waves, hurled on to the uneven shore and smashed on its rocks? How many ships had their sails ripped apart by fierce winds and their masts cracked by tumultuous seas? Grasped by the sea, they were like a mouse in a cat's clutches, something to toy with before death. How many of those intrepid Phoenician sailors spent days and nights onboard their ships, battered and buffeted by the winds; then the fates relented and drove them to the shore of some new island or distant port, so that, once they were saved, they turned into explorers? How many times did they lose their way and were left at the mercy of storms and gales; as their food and water ran out, they succumbed to hunger and thirst? How often were they attacked by pirates—and they too were not lacking in pirates of their own, turning oars into weapons as fires raged in men's hands and the rattle of death was drowned out in the clashing waves and the shouts of heroes? Eventually, all that remained on the sea's surface was the wreckage of burned and smashed ships.

This aspect of the life of Phoenician sailors and opulent merchants was known only to the seas. There were no famous poets among the Phoenicians who would extol the sea and perpetuate its memory. No ancient poet praised the exploits of Phoenician sailors and their amazing achievements—or, at the very least, perfumed his verse with the scent of elegy over those maritime disasters.

Historians and archeologists mention the Phoenicians' voyages, commerce, and colonies in dry, stark terms. With a degree of disapproving skepticism, Herodotus records information about their first voyage of exploration around the African continent, one that has been confirmed by historians and archeologists today.

That is the first voyage of exploration in human history. A Phoenician mission undertook it during the reign of Pharaoh Necho, the last of the great pharaohs (609–593 BCE).

Pharaoh Necho's defeat in the battle against the Babylonians in north Syria does not diminish his greatness. Afterward, he devoted his attention to agricultural, economic, and scientific projects, among them the canal that he envisaged connecting the Red Sea to the Mediterranean. He ordered that the project was to start from the Nile and kept on digging, apparently using several thousand workers in the process.

Herodotus claims that some 120,000 workers died (like Arab historians after him, Herodotus was fascinated by numbers, but did not always verify his counts). When the project was finished, engineers warned the pharaoh that the Red Sea was at a higher elevation than the Nile; opening the canal would cause a flood in the Nile Valley that would ruin the country. Even so, it was one of the most outstanding development projects of its time. I will describe it the same way that Plutarch describes a project of the Greek Parliament, the initiation of which was supervised by the great Pericles, but never competed. "In spite of that," Plutarch says, "I feel obliged to mention it as it demonstrates the preeminent thought and work of Pericles."

Like Pericles who came after him, Pharaoh Necho was enthusiastic about public works, especially naval ones. He was fond of the Phoenicians and admired their sailors. For that reason, he selected a group of them to undertake an exploratory mission around the coast of Africa in order to confirm what was generally believed at the time—namely, that the ocean surrounded Egypt.

The Phoenicians set sail from Suez and made their way down the Red Sea. Once past the Bab al-Mandeb, they traveled southwest, passing Somalia. After crossing the equator, they sailed between the African coast and the island of Madagascar and kept sailing southwest until they reached the southern tip of the continent (now known as the Cape of Good Hope). Now they headed northward, passing the West African coast (which their fellow countryman Hanno was to traverse from north to south). Reaching the Straits of Hercules (Gibraltar), they sailed through and into the Mediterranean, returning safe and sound to Egypt.

This voyage lasted for three years. Among the information that we have, I have mentioned that the Phoenicians used to disembark from their ships at certain ports. People used to grow fond of them because of the goods that they had brought with them. In fact, the Phoenicians would stay in those countries for a while and plant and harvest wheat so that they could replenish their supplies and then set sail again.

Something else that verifies the voyage and gainsays Herodotus's skepticism is that, once they had crossed the equator, the Phoenicians noticed the sun shining to their right, but then, as they started sailing north, they saw it where they had seen it before, overhead. Thus, the sun provides evidence of the circumnavigation of the African continent at the end of the sixth century BCE.

About a century after this first Phoenician voyage of exploration, Hanno the Carthaginian undertook his famous journey (470 BCE). Details of the journey were recorded in an official report hanging in the temple of the god El (Jupiter) in Carthage. It was translated into Greek and then into European languages.

The report opens with a short introduction noting the decision that the Carthaginian Hanno should undertake this journey beyond the Straits of Hercules (Gibraltar) and establish Phoenician Libyan colonies and cities. He set sail from Carthage with a fleet of sixty sailing vessels, each ship equipped with fifty oars. Each one was carrying thirty thousand men and women, along with their food supplies and equipment. Hanno or one of his aides provides the following information about the voyage:

"After passing through the Straits, we sailed south for a day and established the first city that we called Themiaterum.[1] We continued west and reached Soloice, a cape on land covered with trees.[2] There we built a temple to the god Neptune.

"From there we sailed for half a day and reached a lake close to the sea, with many gambling joints and lodgings.[3] Nearby, elephants and other land animals were grazing. After two more days sailing to the south,[4] we established five cities close to the sea.[5]

"We now continued sailing and reached the mighty River Leksos, on whose bank resides a tribe of shepherds.[6] We stayed under their protection for a while.

"Below the country of the Leksos peoples dwell the savage Abyssinians in wild terrain surrounded by mountains from which, we are told, the waters of the River Leksos flow. Near those mountains are caves where different types of people live. The Leksos people regard them as enemies and say that they race horses.

1. Today it is Essaouira, due west of Marrakech.

2. Today it is Cape Bojador.

3. A swamp on the coast of Gambia.

4. Actually southeast.

5. The author has mentioned their names, but today they no longer exist.

6. Rio de Oro—"river of gold"—in the land known by that name. Today it has an Arabic name, Al-Shatt. Rio de Oro, which at that time was called Libya, is now under Spanish control (Spanish Sahara).

"We stopped by some people who could translate the languages of those people and went along with them.

"After three days of sailing close to arid shorelines, we reached a bay with a small island where we established a colony called Kerny.[7]

"We now realized from the distance that we had traveled—the equivalent of the distance between the Straits and Carthage, that in Kerny we were now in a direct line south of Carthage itself.

"From Kerny we traveled along a large river called the Kretes[8] and reached a lake with three islands bigger than Kerny Island. After a further day's sailing on the river we arrived at the other end of the lake, where there were many mountains inhabited by savage peoples wearing animal skins. They pelted us with rocks to stop us disembarking.

"Retracing our steps, we reached another big river, in which crocodiles and hippopotamuses were swimming.[9] From there we returned to Kerny.

"Continuing our journey south, close to the shores inhabited by the Abyssinians. They were alarmed by our arrival and ran away. Neither we nor our Leksosian guides knew their language.

"After twelve days of travel, we approached some high mountains, laden with beautifully shaped, sweet-scented trees. We sailed close to them for two days, and reached a wide inlet with an expansive plain on both sides. At night we saw fires burning at various points on both sides. After taking supplies of water onboard, we continued our journey, sticking close to the shore. Five days later, we arrived at a huge bay, which the translators told us was called the West Cape.[10] There was a large island with a salty lake; in the lake was yet another island. All we could see in daylight were trees.[11]

7. The forested island of Agadir by Cape Blanco, at twenty degrees longitude. There is also Cape Etienne in French West Africa.

8. The San Juan or Saint Louis River.

9. The Senegal River.

10. Sierra Leone, the cape and bay, the site of the city of Freetown.

11. Sherbro Island.

"At night we saw fires burning in several places and heard the sounds of people playing pipes, cymbals, and drums, accompanied by the sound of loud, frenzied voices. We were afraid, and our astrologers told us to leave the island.[12]

"We set sail quickly and passed by territories where fires were burning and scents wafted through the air. We watched as sparks and flames made their way down to the sea, so we hurried away in alarm. Four days later, we arrived at another country where fires were burning; they looked like one gigantic blaze, in the middle of which was a flag, also on fire,[13] with sparks and flame shooting out from it so fast that you would imagine they could reach the very stars above. The next day, we learned that it was a hill named 'chariot of the gods.'[14]

"Three days after leaving that place, we arrived in intense heat at a bay called the South Horn,[15] with its own island like the ones we had passed by. The island had its own lake, with another island in the middle occupied by barbarians, the majority of them females with hair covering their entire body. As proof, they are called 'gorillas.'[16]

"When we went looking for the males, they all ran away. We chased after them and caught one. They kept running between the rocks and leaping over them, pelting us with rocks as they did so.[17]

"We also captured three females, but, using their teeth and hands, they managed to overwhelm their guards as they tried to get away and escape. We killed and skinned them, and took the skins back to Carthage, where we hung them in the Temple of Juno.

"We had run out of supplies, so we went no further."

12. Macauley Island.

13. In those countries where the fires were burning, people regularly burned dried grass at that season of the year.

14. Cape Palmas.

15. Cape Three Points (Ghana).

16. A kind of ape.

17. Just like the group of people, "the winds," whom we encountered in Yemen. See *Kings of the Arabs*, part 1.

From Gibraltar—in modern terms—to Saint Louis and Dakar, Ghana and French Guinea, Conakry and Senegal, Sierra Leone, the Ivory and Gold Coasts, Sekondi and Accra, all these names are known to the Lebanese, sons of both North and South, who traveled to those regions at the beginning of the twentieth century, 2,400 years after the voyage the Carthaginian Hanno. The Carthaginians were explorers, while the Lebanese were profiteers.

After this journey back into the recesses of time and books on history and archeology, we now return to the sunlight, to the one immortal book—and one of its nicest chapters—the one on Lebanon.

Journey's End

SCHOLARS AND HISTORIANS today regularly cite the source works and documents relevant to their specific subjects. Whether it is after, before, or part of the introduction, they will record the titles of the books in various languages that they have consulted before starting to write. That way, they can dispense with any further explanations, and the margins of their works remain clear, neat, and untrammeled.

Quite apart from the artistic aspects of clean margins and the citation of sources in one place, this method also involves psychological factors. Dear sage, you get to see a list, both clear and lengthy and in a variety of languages. In such a case, can mistakes or distortions be tolerated? It represents triumph over doubt, the token of confidence and trust.

I have encountered—and read—one such list devoted to modern Arab history, published by the author over thirty-five pages following the introduction. It includes works in Arabic, Turkish, French, English, and German, totaling exactly 659 sources. Some of them come in two, three, or four volumes.

Were we to assume that this esteemed author knew all those languages well, we would also assume that he had actually read them all; in which case, we would go on to assume that the average source consists of two volumes, then the total number reaches 1,390 volumes. One final assumption would say that, if this author were continually devoted to his task—reading one volume every three days, then the entire project would have taken eleven years and 155 days.

This is a good practice, which scholars and historians have adopted in this economic era, one of speed and concision. It is to their credit, those sage scholars, to resist negative trends and to reject the devious and deceitful modes of wireless and cinema. Instead, they read a thousand books, slowly and carefully, before writing a single work.

As part of this practice, a strong tendency has emerged to imitate and compete. I myself have come to insert myself into the ranks of those scholars who choose to verify, historians who undertake detailed research. Shall I then offer the reader a list of books that I have consulted before writing these chapters on the Phoenicians?

Do I say "list"? Certainly not; it is nothing of the kind. It is without any sense of pride that I now place them at the conclusion of this particular "journey." They may perhaps be of some benefit to readers who want to check on things, or others who have the researcher's finger. Peace be upon all of them, Amen!

And now, after this journey in time, in history books and archeology, we can return to the domains of the sun; to the only eternal book and one of its loveliest chapters—to Lebanon.

Sources Used

George Rawlinson, *Phoenicia: History of a Civilization.*

James Breasted, *A History of Egypt from the Earliest Times to the Persian Conquest.*

The Haverford Symposium on Archaeology and the Bible.

Isaac Preston Corey, *Ancient Fragments.*

C. Leonard Woolley, *The Sumerians.*

C. R. Conder, *The Tell Amarna Tablets.*

Victor Berard, *La Resurrection d'Homere.*

H. Lammens, S. J., *Le Liban.*

Translator's Afterword

I FIRST VISITED LEBANON in the summer of 1962. Arriving in the port of Beirut by Greek tramp steamer from Athens, I made my way by service taxi out of the port, up the mountain road to Aley, and then across to Souk el-Gharb, and finally Shemlan. Having taken eight weeks of beginners' Arabic at Oxford University in the spring of 1962, I was attending classes at the Middle East Centre for Arabic Studies (MECAS), the British Foreign Office's Arabic school in the Lebanese mountains. Without the slightest doubt, it was that immediate encounter with the Arabic language as a living, spoken entity, and the experiences gained by touring Lebanon, Syria, and Jordan that summer that triggered my lifelong interest in Arabic and its modern literature.

Now I must fast-forward several decades, during which I mostly concentrated my literary research and translation projects on the modern literature of Egypt and later Morocco, although my teaching responsibilities did not allow me to neglect the creativity of many Lebanese littérateurs, including, for example, the poet Adunis and the novelist Hanan al-Shaikh.[1] The particular occasion that triggered a renewed interest in Lebanon and its writers occurred in June 2012 when George Zaidan organized a conference at the Library of Congress in Washington, DC, devoted to his illustrious ancestor

1. I have translated one of Hanan al-Shaikh's novels into English: *Hikayati sharhun yatul*; English translation, *The Locust and the Bird* (London: Bloomsbury, 2009).

Jurji Zaidan (1861–1914).[2] It was there that I first met May Rihani, Ameen Rihani's niece and director of the Gibran Center at the University of Maryland. I had already contributed an article to a volume devoted to her uncle's role in the Mahjar school and its place in the development of modern Arabic literature,[3] but now a much closer link to the Rihani family was established. Thus, when May invited me to contribute to a conference in honor of Gibran to be held in Beirut in January 2018, I was delighted to be able to accept her invitation.[4] As it turned out, an even closer link to the Rihani family in Lebanon was established during that visit, since, following the conference, May and our local host, Henri Zghaib, arranged for us to visit not only Gibran's hometown and shrine at Bsharre but also the Rihani house in Freike, the very place from which Rihani commences his many excursions into the Lebanese mountains in *The Heart of Lebanon*. Thus, when May suggested to me that I might enjoy reading *The Heart of Lebanon* and translating it into English, I found myself following Rihani's trails from the very house in Freike where we had enjoyed a wholesome breakfast and toured the Ameen Rihani Museum that is housed there.

In 1888 an impressionable, twelve-year-old Ameen Rihani was sent by his father, a silk merchant, to the United States in the company of his uncle. His father joined them a year later. Settling in New York City, they would have been welcomed into a thriving community of

2. The conference proceedings were published as *Jurji Zaidan: Contributions to Modern Arab Thought and Literature*, ed. George C. Zaidan and Thomas Philipp (Washington, DC: Zaidan Foundation, 2013).

3. Roger Allen, "The Nahdah and Its Problematics: Ameen F. Rihani and the Mahjar," in *Ameen Rihani's Arab-American Legacy: From Romanticism to Post-Modernism*, ed. Naji B. Oueijan (Louaize, Lebanon: Notre Dame Univ. Press, 2012, 17–33).

4. My contribution, "Khalil Gibran and the Beginnings of the Arabic Short Story," was published in *Gibran in the 21st Century: Lebanon's Message to the World* (Beirut: Center for Lebanese Heritage Publications at the Lebanese-American University, 2018), 25–43.

émigrés who were clustered together in a multi-block section of southern Manhattan that was known as Little Syria.[5] In the United States, Rihani attended schools, participated in acting troupes, studied the law, and steeped himself in the literary traditions of Europe and the United States. In the course of a remarkable career spent researching a wide variety of topics (including religion, philosophy, and politics), travel to multiple countries (including Saudi Arabia in the 1920s), and writing in both Arabic and English, Rihani earned a wide reputation as a historian, philosopher, and visionary. It was during a return visit to Lebanon that he wrote his English-language novel *The Book of Khalid* (published in 1911, with illustrations by his Mahjar colleague Gibran).[6]

The Heart of Lebanon, published posthumously for the first time in 1947, is thus the work of a renowned returnee to Lebanon from the United States (as Rihani notes in the text): an erudite, much-traveled scholar, philosopher, and littérateur. From the very beginning of the work, Rihani's ability to organize and plan is on full display. Each excursion from Freike is carefully thought out, with sites to be visited and overnight stopping places duly identified. With that in mind, it is not a little sad to note that he had also mapped out a further series of excursions, now included in the text as journeys 10–15 and "miscellaneous" (*mutafarriqat*)—all of them with titles, and some with jottings and even paragraphs for further elaboration once he had completed the journey—excursions that Rihani did not manage to complete before his death in 1940.

The accumulated journeys included in complete form in *The Heart of Lebanon* span a period of several years. Thus, when Rihani finally sat down to bring all his notes, impressions, and memories together,

5. Whatever structures that remained from the early twentieth century were demolished as part of the construction of the World Trade Center complex in the 1970s. However, a single historically landmarked set of buildings still survives on Washington Street, including a Melkite church of St. George.

6. Ameen Rihani, *The Book of Khalid* (New York: Dodd, Mead and Company, 1911).

there were inevitably variations in emphasis and detail as the work proceeded.

In the very first journey, "To the Cedars," Rihani, now returned from the United States to his village of Freike, decides to undertake an excursion to the site that is symbolic of Lebanon and considers the mode of transport that he will need to use. He is directed to Mahboub, the muleteer, and hires him along with his long-suffering and reliable mule, Mahbouba. Together, the two men and the now heavily laden mule leave Freike on this and subsequent journeys, and head into the mountains, following tracks and trails up mountainsides, across ridges, and through river valleys. Rihani provides beautiful descriptions of the vistas that are laid out before him. He gives telling accounts of the difficulties involved in taking some of the more risky routes and of the discussions and arguments with Mahboub as to the advisability of taking them. All the while, the two men engage in frequent exchanges of repartee, with the loyal muleteer on foot, walking behind Rihani, who sits on the mule's back. They pass by mountain dwellers plying their various professions in agriculture, woodcutting, and other trades. They visit towns and villages, where they enjoy traditional Lebanese hospitality, and spend time admiring the beauty of well-known locations and landmarks—the Cedars in both Bsharre and Jaj, for example, the spring in Aqoura, the vistas from the heights of Mount Sannine, and, once over the mountains, the Bekaa Valley with the towns of Zahle and Baalbek. In addition to these sites, Rihani and his travel companion pay visits to a number of churches and monasteries in the mountains, some of them pilgrimage shrines dedicated to Christian figures beatified by the Catholic Church. On the later journeys, however, there is, more often than not, a resort to travel by car, thus along paved roads and more passable tracks, as in the visit to the coastal town of Byblos (Jbeil), the Phoenician port dating back thousands of years, and to a closer focus on encounters and travels with colleagues who are scholars and literary figures. The seventh journey is entirely devoted to an account of the renowned French philosopher Ernest Renan, whose writings had a major influence on

Rihani's own ideas, and who spent many years, along with his beloved sister, Henriette, in Lebanon, where wrote his wrote his *Life of Jesus.* And while the eighth journey brings us closer to Freike and the narrative of a journey to Gharzouz and its monastery, the ninth journey is entirely devoted to a detailed history of the Phoenician peoples, thus reflecting the lifelong interests of Rihani's close friend, the historian Charles Corm (the dedicatee of *The Heart of Lebanon*, whose knowledge and opinions are cited as authoritative throughout the text).

The Heart of Lebanon is thus an accurate reflection of the life, career, and interests of its author: a life that straddles the different cultures, languages, and customs of Lebanon and the United States and their peoples. Against a backdrop of travel, readers encounter depictions of nature in all its beauty, of mountain-dwelling people and their way of life, of local customs and religious beliefs, of monuments, and of varieties of history, from the most ancient to the relatively recent. It is indeed a rich and variegated excursion into "the heart of Lebanon."

I conclude this translator's afterword by expressing my heartfelt thanks to two colleagues and friends who have accompanied this project from its very beginnings. May Rihani, the author's niece and former director of the Khalil Gibran Center at the University of Maryland, first drew my attention to *The Heart of Lebanon* and suggested that I might enjoy translating it into English. She has gone through the translation in its various phases, made any number of suggestions (and corrections) that have been invaluable in producing the text in its current form, and composed a foreword for her uncle's text. In Lebanon, Henri Zghaib has similarly read through the translation and made useful comments. To both these colleagues I express my gratitude. I also acknowledge with thanks the permission of the Ameen Rihani Organization to use the photographs and editorial introduction that are included in this volume. I must also express my debt to the two anonymous reviewers who evaluated the translation for Syracuse University Press. They too had numerous suggestions and editorial comments to make, almost all of which have made their way into the translated text. Finally, I must thank the editorial staff at

Syracuse University Press, and especially Jessica LeTourneur Bax, who have been extremely helpful in bringing this project to a successful conclusion.

Roger Allen
October 2020

Index of People and Places

Ameen Rihani (Amin al-Rihani, 1876–1940) was a pioneer figure in the formation of the émigré Lebanese literary community in the Americas. Sent to New York City by his father in 1888, he pursued his interests in literature and especially poetry—in both English and Arabic—and was a central figure in the cultural activities of the Mahjar community in New York. He returned to Lebanon in 1905. Bridging the two cultural worlds with which he was familiar, Rihani traveled extensively and published a wide variety of books on literature, politics, philosophy, and religion. He died in his native village of Freike, now the site of a museum dedicated to his life and works.

Ameen Albert Rihani is a professor of Arab American literature and twentieth-century Arab thought at Notre Dame University in Lebanon. Professor Rihani also heads the newly established Institute of Lebanese Thought at the university. His academic interests focus on the unpublished works, papers, and letters, written in English, by the founding fathers of Arab American literature during the first half of the twentieth century. Professor Rihani is the author of seventeen books and numerous articles published in coauthored books, refereed journals, and conference proceedings. He is a member of several international associations, such as the Association of College Administration Professionals (ACAP) and the Association for the Advancement of International Education (AAIE). He also administers the Ameen Rihani Museum in Freike, Lebanon.

Roger Allen served as a professor of Arabic and Comparative Literature at the University of Pennsylvania from 1968 until 2011. He is the author of *The Arabic Novel: An Historical and Critical Introduction* (1982, 1995) and *The Arabic Literary Heritage* (1998; in paperback, *Introduction to Arabic Literature*, 2000). He has translated a number of fictional works by modern Arab writers, including the Egyptian Nobel Laureate Naguib Mahfouz, Jabra Ibrahim Jabra, Yusuf Idris, Abdul Rahman Munif, May Telmissany, Bensalem Himmich, Ahmad al-Tawfiq, and Hanan al-Shaykh.

Select Titles in Middle East Literature in Translation

The Book of Disappearance: A Novel
Ibtisam Azem; Sinan Antoon, trans.

A Cloudy Day on the Western Shore
Mohamed Mansi Qandil; Barbara Romaine, trans.

Gaia, Queen of Ants
Hamid Ismailov; Shelley Fairweather-Vega, trans.

In the Alley of the Friend: On the Poetry of Hafez
Shahrokh Meskoob; M. R. Ghanoonparvar, trans.

Jerusalem Stands Alone
Mahmoud Shukair; Nicole Fares, trans.

The Slave Yards: A Novel
Najwa Bin Shatwan; Nancy Roberts, trans.

Tenants and Cobwebs
Samir Naqqash; Sadok Masliyah, trans.

Turkey, Egypt, and Syria: A Travelogue
Shiblī Nu'mānī; Gregory Maxwell Bruce, trans.

For a full list of titles in this series, visit https://press.syr.edu/supressbook-series/middle-east-literature-in-translation/.